RECORD
OF AMERICA

Above Modern ungraded elementary school with several classes at work in adjoining areas. *Courtesy,* Monkmeyer Press Photo Service (Zimbel)
Opposite page Street wear, 1919. *Courtesy,* Abraham & Straus, Brooklyn, N.Y.

SAUL M. FRIEDMAN
The City College of New York
School of Education
EDITORIAL CONSULTANT

EDITORIAL STAFF

J. G. E. HOPKINS, *EDITOR*
MARGARET DODD, *DESIGNER*
MARY McCARTHY, *PICTURE RESEARCHER*
NORMA LOONAN, *EDITORIAL ASSISTANT*

RECORD OF AMERICA

A Reference History of the United States

JOSEPH F. X. McCARTHY

Fordham University
School of Education

VOLUME 10
RESOURCE
UNITS 5-8

CHARLES SCRIBNER'S SONS
NEW YORK

Printed in the United States of America
Library of Congress Catalog Card Number 74-3740

ISBN-0-684-13915-4 VOLUME 1
ISBN-0-684-13916-2 VOLUME 2
ISBN-0-684-13917-0 VOLUME 3
ISBN-0-684-13918-9 VOLUME 4
ISBN-0-684-13919-7 VOLUME 5
ISBN-0-684-13920-0 VOLUME 6
ISBN-0-684-13921-9 VOLUME 7
ISBN-0-684-13922-7 VOLUME 8
ISBN-0-684-13932-4 VOLUME 9
ISBN-0-684-13933-2 VOLUME 10
ISBN-0-684-13862-x COMPLETE SET

Cover photograph by John Veltri

LIST OF DOCUMENTS

THE CIVIL WAR: 1861-1865

UP TO NOW: 1933-1974

RESOURCE UNIT 5

The Civil War: 1861-1865

THE CIVIL WAR

During the winter season of 1860-1861 and the early spring of 1861, Secession was soon followed by armed conflict. The United States engaged in the bloodiest war of the 19th century after years of debate, border skirmishes and ruthless reprisals. Some historians, as they have studied the disputes over abolition and slavery, tariffs and Nullification, and the proper powers of the Federal and State governments, have concluded that the war was indeed an "irrepressible conflict" that had to be fought. Other scholars have concluded on the same evidence that war might have been averted, even as late as the first weeks of 1861. The Civil War has been called "the American "Iliad" because it left behind it, along with much bitterness, an heroic tradition in North and South alike. For all these reasons, students of history continue to ponder over its many phases.

PROBLEMS: *How and why did a shooting war develop from the 1860-1861 efforts of some States to secede from the United States? What was life in the military services really like during the Civil War? How did United States policy toward slavery and the Territories change during the Civil War? What was the apparent state of mind of leaders on both sides as the Civil War drew to a close?*

THE COMING OF WAR

1. Many Southerners—and other Americans as well—learned to know Abraham Lincoln during his debates with Stephen A. Douglas in 1858 during the campaign for a seat in the United States Senate. Southerners were unhappy about Douglas, the Democratic candidate, because he seemed too soft in his efforts to protect slaveowners in the Territories of the United States. Lincoln, who was far firmer than Douglas in opposing slavery in the Territories, became a symbol of what extreme Southerners feared most. Lincoln's first nationally known speech was delivered on June 17, 1858, at the close of the Republican Party Convention in Springfield, Illinois. The Convention had just agreed on Lincoln as its candidate for the Senate. The following sections from his "House Divided" speech can be viewed both as campaign oratory, and as statements of policy for the future. Some in both North and South regarded the speech as a pledge that Lincoln would work for abolition of slavery in the nation.

If we could first know where we are, and whither we are tending, we could better judge what to do, and how to do it. We are now far into the fifth year since a policy was initiated with the avowed object and confident

3

promise of putting an end to slavery agitation. Under the operation of that policy, that agitation has not only not ceased, but has constantly augmented. In my opinion, it will not cease until a crisis shall have been reached and passed. "A house divided against itself cannot stand." I believe this government cannot endure permanently half slave and half free. I do not expect the Union to be dissolved; I do not expect the house to fall; but I do expect it will cease to be divided. It will become all one thing, or all the other. Either the opponents of slavery will arrest the further spread of it, and place it where the public mind shall rest in the belief that it is in the course of ultimate extinction, or its advocates will push it forward till it shall become alike lawful in all the States, old as well as new, North as well as South.

Have we no tendency to the latter condition?

Let any one who doubts, carefully contemplate that now almost complete legal combination—piece of machinery, so to speak—compounded of the Nebraska doctrine and the Dred Scott decision. Let him consider, not only what work the machinery is adapted to do, and how well adapted, but also let him study the history of its construction, and trace, if he can, or rather fail, if he can, to trace the evidences of design, and concert of action, among its chief architects, from the beginning.

The new year of 1854 found slavery excluded from more than half the States by State Constitutions, and from most of the National territory by Congressional prohibition. Four days later, commenced the struggle which ended in repealing that Congressional prohibition. This opened all the National territory to slavery. . . .

The several points of the Dred Scott decision, in connection with Senator Douglas's "care not" policy, constitute the piece of machinery, in its present state of advancement. . . . The working points of that machinery are:

Firstly, That no negro slave, imported as such from Africa, and no descendant of such slave, can ever be a citizen of any State, in the sense of that term as used in the Constitution of the United States. This point is made in order to deprive the negro, in every possible event, of the benefit of that provision of the United States Constitution which declares that "The citizens of each State shall be entitled to all privileges and immunities of citizens in the several States."

Secondly, That, "subject to the Constitution of the United States," neither Congress nor a Territorial Legislature can exclude slavery from any United States Territory. This point is made in order that individual men may fill up the Territories with slaves, without danger of losing them as property, and thus to enhance the chances of permanency to the institution through all the future.

Thirdly, That whether the holding a negro in actual slavery in a free State makes him free, as against the holder, the United States courts will not decide, but will leave to be decided by the courts of any slave State the negro may be forced into by the master. This point is made, not to be pressed immediately; but, if acquiesced in for a while, and apparently indorsed by the people at an election, then to sustain the logical conclusion that what Dred Scott's master might lawfully do with Dred Scott in the free State of Illinois, every other master may lawfully do with any other one, or one thousand slaves, in Illinois, or in any other free State.

2. During the presidential campaign of 1860, Lincoln won without any electoral votes from southern States. During the campaign, several leading "fire-eaters" among the Southerners indicated that they would secede from the Union rather than have as President the man who had delivered the "House Divided" speech. South Carolina led the protesters, and, once Lincoln's election was certain, South Carolina led the States in passing Secession resolutions. A special State Convention passed an Ordinance of Secession and a Declaration of Causes of Secession. Taken together, these might be considered a sort of "Declaration of Independence" by the South.

An Ordinance to dissolve the Union between the State of South Carolina and Other States United with her under the Compact entitled "The Constitution of the United States of America"

We, the People of the State of South Carolina in convention assembled, do declare and ordain, and it is hereby declared and ordained, that the ordinance adopted by us in convention, on the twenty-third day of May, in the year of our Lord one thousand seven hundred and eighty-eight, whereby the Constitution of the United States of America was ratified, and also all acts and parts of acts of the general assembly of this State ratifying amendments of the said Constitution, are hereby repealed; and that the union now subsisting between South Carolina and other States under the name of the "United States of America," is hereby dissolved.

From the Declaration of the Causes of Secession (December 1860)

. . . And now the State of South Carolina having resumed her separate and equal place among nations, deems it due to herself, to the remaining United States of America, and to the nations of the world, that she should declare the immediate causes which have led to this act.

In the year 1765, that portion of the British Empire embracing Great Britain undertook to make laws for the Government of that portion composed of the thirteen American Colonies. A struggle for the right of self-government ensued, which resulted, on the 4th of July, 1776, in a Declaration, by the Colonies, "that they are, and of right ought to be, free and independent states; and that, as free and independent States, they have full power to levy war, conclude peace, contract alliances, establish commerce, and to do all other acts and things which independent States may of right do."

They further solemnly declared that whenever any "form of goverment becomes destructive of the ends for which it was established, it is the right of the people to alter or abolish it, and to institute a new government." Deeming the Government of Great Britain to have become destructive of these ends, they declared that the Colonies "are absolved from all allegiance to the British Crown, and that all political connection between them and the State of Great Britain is, and ought to be, totally dissolved." . . .

Thus were established the two great principles asserted by the Colonies, namely, the right of a State to govern itself; and the right of a people to abolish a Government when it becomes destructive of the ends for which it was instituted. And concurrent with the establishment of these principles, was the fact, that each Colony became and was recognized by the mother country as a free, sovereign and independent state.

In 1787, Deputies were appointed by the States to revise the articles of Confederation; and on 17th September, 1787, these Deputies recommended, for the adoption of the States, the Articles of Union, known as the Constitution of the United States. . . .

Thus was established, by compact between the States, a Government with defined objects and powers, limited to the express words of the grant. This limitation left the whole remaining mass of power subject to the clause reserving it to the States or the people, and rendered unnecessary any specification of reserved rights. We hold that the Government thus established is subject to the two great principles asserted in the Declaration of Independence; and we hold further, that the mode of its formation subjects it to a third fundamental principle, namely, the law of compact. We maintain that in every compact between two or more parties, the obligation is mutual; that the failure of one of the contracting parties to perform a material part of the agreement, entirely releases the obligation of the other; and that, where no arbiter is provided, each party is remitted to his own judgment to determine the fact of failure, with all its consequences.

In the present case, the fact is established with certainty. We assert that fourteen of the States have deliberately refused for years past to fulfil their constitutional obligations, and we refer to their own statutes for the proof.

The Constitution of the United States, in its fourth Article, provides as follows: "No person held to service or labor in one State under the laws thereof, escaping into another, shall, in consequence of any law or regulation therein, be discharged from such service or labor, but shall be delivered up, on claim of the party to whom such service or labor may be due."

This stipulation was so material to the compact that without it that compact would not have been made. The greater number of the contracting parties held slaves, and they had previously evinced their estimate of the value of such a stipulation by making it a condition in the Ordinance for the government of the territory ceded by Virginia, which obligations, and the laws of the General Government, have ceased to effect the objects of the Constitution. The States of Maine, New Hampshire, Vermont, Massachusetts, Connecticut, Rhode Island, New York, Pennsylvania, Illinois, Indiana, Michigan, Wisconsin, and Iowa, have enacted laws which either nullify the acts of Congress, or render useless any attempts to execute them. . . . Thus the constitutional compact has been deliberately broken and disregarded by the non-slaveholding States; and the consequence follows that South Carolina is released from her obligation.

The ends for which this Constitution was framed are declared by itself to be "to form a more perfect union, establish justice, insure domestic tranquility, provide for the common defence, promote the general welfare, and secure the blessings of liberty to ourselves and our posterity."

These ends it endeavored to accomplish by a Federal Government, in which each State was recognized as an equal, and had separate control over its own institutions. The right of property in slaves was recognized by giving to free persons distinct political rights; by giving them the right to represent, and burdening them with direct taxes for, three-fifths of their slaves; by authorizing the importation of slaves for twenty years; and by stipulating for the rendition of fugitives from labor.

We affirm that these ends for which this Government was instituted have been defeated, and the Government itself has been destructive of them by the action of the non-slaveholding States. Those States have assumed the right of deciding upon the propriety of our domestic institutions; and have denied the rights of property established in fifteen of the States and recognized by the Constitution; they have denounced as sinful the institution of Slavery; they have permitted the open establishment among them of societies, whose avowed object is to disturb the peace of and eloin the property of the citizens of other States. They have encouraged and assisted thousands of our slaves to leave their homes; and those who remain, have been incited by emissaries, books, and pictures, to servile insurrection.

For twenty-five years this agitation has been steadily increasing, until it has now secured to its aid the power of the common Government. Observing the *forms* of the Constitution, a sectional party has found within that article establishing the Executive Department, the means of subverting the Constitution itself. A geographical line has been drawn across the Union, and all the States north of that line have united in the election of a man to the high office of President of the United States whose opinions and purposes are hostile to Slavery. He is to be intrusted with the administration of the common Government, because he has declared that that "Government cannot endure permanently half slave, half free," and that the public mind must rest in the belief that Slavery is in the course of ultimate extinction. . . .

On the 4th of March next this party will take possession of the Government. It has announced that the South shall be excluded from the common territory, that the Judicial tribunal shall be made sectional, and that a war must be waged against Slavery until it shall cease throughout the United States.

The guarantees of the Constitution will then no longer exist; the equal rights of the States will be lost. The Slaveholding States will no longer have the power of self-government, or self-protection, and the Federal Government will have become their enemy.

Sectional interest and animosity will deepen the irritation; and all hope of remedy is rendered vain, by the fact that the public opinion at the North has invested a great political error with the sanctions of a more erroneous religious belief.

We, therefore, the people of South Carolina, by our delegates in Convention assembled, appealing to the Supreme Judge of the world for the rectitude of our intentions, have solemnly declared that the Union heretofore existing between this State and the other States of North America is dissolved, and that the State of South Carolina has resumed her position among the nations of the world, as separate and independent state, with full power to levy war, conclude peace, contract alliances, establish commerce, and to do all other acts and things which independent States may of right do.

3. In spite of Secession declarations, no actual full-scale fighting broke out between State forces and United States units until April 1861. Lincoln, as President-elect, made no public statements indicating his policy toward seceding States. Some believed that he might make no effort to prevent Secession, expecting it to blow over without a fight; some believed that a settlement would be reached without bloodshed, as had happened in 1832 and 1833 over South Carolina's Nullification Ordinance. On March 4, 1861, Abraham Lincoln was sworn in as President and delivered his First Inaugural Address (below). This policy statement by the President ended all doubts about how he was planning to act to preserve the Union. Southerners who believed in Secession viewed this speech as a declaration of war.

FELLOW-CITIZENS OF THE UNITED STATES:

In compliance with a custom as old as the government itself, I appear before you to address you briefly, and to take, in your presence, the oath prescribed by the Constitution of the United States to be taken by the President before he enters on the execution of his office.

I do not consider it necessary, at present, for me to discuss those matters of administration about which there is no special anxiety or excitement. Apprehension seems to exist among the people of the southern states, that, by the accession of a republican administration, their property and their peace and personal security are to be endangered. There has never been any reasonable cause for such apprehension. Indeed, the most ample evidence to the contrary has all the while existed and been open to their inspection. It is found in nearly all the published speeches of him who now addresses you. I do but quote from one of those speeches, when I declare that "I have no purpose, directly or indirectly, to interfere with the institution of slavery in the states where it exists." I believe I have no lawful right to do so; and I have no inclination to do so. Those who nominated and elected me did so with the full knowledge that I had made this, and made many similar declarations, and had never recanted them. And, more than this, they placed in the platform, for my acceptance, and as a law to themselves and to me, the clear and emphatic resolution which I now read:

"*Resolved*, That the maintenance inviolate of the rights of the states, and especially the right of each state to order and control its own domestic institutions according to its own judgment exclusively, is essential to that balance of power on which the perfection and endurance of our political fabric depend; and we denounce the lawless invasion by armed force of the soil of any state or territory, no matter under what pretext, as among the gravest of crimes."

I now reiterate these sentiments; and in doing so I only press upon the public attention the most conclusive evidence of which the case is susceptible, that the property, peace, and security of no section are to be in anywise endangered by the now incoming administration.

I add, too, that all the protection which, consistently with the Constitution and the laws, can be given, will be cheerfully given to all the states when lawfully demanded, for whatever cause, as cheerfully to one section as to another.

There is much controversy about the delivering up of fugitives from service or labor. The clause I now read is as plainly written in the Constitution as any other of its provisions:

"No person held to service or labor in one state under the laws thereof, escaping into another, shall, in consequence of any law or regulation therein, be discharged from such service or labor, but shall be delivered up on claim of the party to whom such service or labor may be due."

It is scarcely questioned that this provision was intended by those who made it for the reclaiming of what we call fugitive slaves; and the intention of the law-giver is the law.

All members of Congress swear their support to the whole Constitution—to this provision as well as any other. To the proposition, then, that slaves whose cases come within the terms of this clause "shall be delivered up," their oaths are unanimous. Now, if they would make the effort in good temper, could they not, with nearly equal unanimity, frame and pass a law by means of which to keep good that unanimous oath?

There is some difference of opinion whether this clause should be enforced by national or by state authority; but surely that difference is not a very material one. If the slave is to be surrendered, it can be of little consequence to him or to others by which authority it is done; and should any one, in any case, be content that this oath shall go unkept on a merely unsubstantial controversy as to how it shall be kept?

Again, in any law upon this subject, ought not all the safeguards of liberty known in civilized and humane jurisprudence to be introduced, so that a free man be not, in any case, surrendered as a slave? And might it not be well at the same time to provide by law for the enforcement of that clause in the Constitution which guarantees that "the citizens of each state shall be entitled to all the privileges and immunities of citizens in the several states?"

I take the official oath today with no mental reservations, and with no purpose to construe the Constitution or laws by any hypercritical rules; and while I do not choose now to specify particular acts of Congress as proper to be enforced, I do suggest that it will be much safer for all, both in official and private stations, to conform to and abide by all those acts which stand unrepealed, than to violate any of them, trusting to find impunity in having them held to be unconstitutional.

It is seventy-two years since the first inauguration of a President under our National Constitution. During that period, fifteen different and very distinguished citizens have in succession administered the executive branch of the Government. They have conducted it through many perils, and generally with great success. Yet, with all this scope for precedent, I now enter upon the same task, for the brief constitutional term of four years, under great and peculiar difficulties.

A disruption of the Federal Union, heretofore only menaced, is now formidably attempted. I hold that in the contemplation of universal law and of the Constitution, the union of these states is perpetual. Perpetuity is implied, if not expressed, in the fundamental law of all national governments. It is safe to assert that no government proper ever had a provision in its organic law for its own termination. Continue to execute all the express provisions of our National Constitution, and the Union will endure forever, it being impossible to destroy it except by some action not provided for in the instrument itself.

Again, if the United States be not a government proper, but an association of states in the nature of a contract merely, can it, as a contract, be peaceably unmade by less than all the parties who made it? One party to a contract may violate it—break it, so to speak; but does it not require all to lawfully rescind it? Descending from these general principles, we find the proposition that in legal contemplation the Union is perpetual, confirmed by the history of the Union itself.

The Union is much older than the Constitution. It was formed, in fact, by the Articles of Association in 1774. It was matured and continued in the Declaration of Independence in 1776. It was further matured, and the faith of all the then thirteen states expressly plighted and engaged that it should be perpetual, by the Articles of the Confederation, in 1778; and finally, in 1787, one of the declared objects for ordaining and establishing the Constitution was to form a more perfect Union. But if the destruction of the Union by one or by a part only of the states be lawfully possible, the Union is less perfect than before, the Constitution having lost the vital element of perpetuity.

It follows from these views that no state, upon its own mere motion, can lawfully get out of the Union; that resolves and ordinances to that effect are legally void; and that acts of violence within any state or states against the authority of the United States are insurrectionary or revolutionary, according to circumstances.

I therefore consider that, in view of the Constitution and the laws, the Union is unbroken, and to the extent of my ability, I shall take care, as the Constitution itself expressly enjoins upon me, that the laws of the Union shall be faithfully executed in all the states. Doing this, which I deem to be only a simple duty on my part, I shall perfectly perform it, so far as is practicable, unless my rightful masters, the American people, shall withhold the requisition, or in some authoritative manner direct the contrary.

I trust this will not be regarded as a menace, but only as the declared purpose of the Union that it will constitutionally defend and maintain itself.

In doing this there need be no bloodshed or violence, and there shall be none unless it is forced upon the national authority.

The power confided to me *will be used to hold, occupy, and possess the property and places belonging to the Government*, and collect the duties and imposts; but beyond what may be necessary for these objects there will be no invasion, no using of force against or among the people anywhere.

Where hostility to the United States shall be so great and so universal as to prevent competent resident citizens from holding federal offices, there will be no attempt to force obnoxious strangers among the people that object. While strict legal right may exist of the Government to enforce the exercise of these offices, the attempt to do so would be so irritating, and so nearly impracticable withal, that I deem it best to forego, for the time, the uses of such offices.

The mails, unless repelled, will continue to be furnished in all parts of the Union.

So far as possible, the people everywhere shall have that sense of perfect security which is most favorable to calm thought and reflection.

The course here indicated will be followed, unless current events and experience shall show a modification or change to be proper; and in every case and exigency my best discretion will be exercised according to the circumstances actually existing, and with a view and hope of a peaceful solution of the national troubles, and the restoration of fraternal sympathies and affections.

That there are persons, in one section or another, who seek to destroy the Union at all events, and are glad of any pretext to do it, I will neither affirm nor deny. But if there be such, I need address no word to them.

To those, however, who really love the Union, may I not speak, before entering upon so grave a matter as the destruction of our national fabric, with all its benefits, its memories, and its hopes? Would it not be well to ascertain why we do it? Will you hazard so desperate a step, while any portion of the ills you fly from have no real existence? Will you, while the certain ills you fly to are greater than all the real ones you fly from? Will you risk the commission of so fearful a mistake? All

profess to be content in the Union if all constitutional rights can be maintained. Is it true, then, that any right, plainly written in the Constitution, has been denied? I think not. Happily the human mind is so constituted that no party can reach to the audacity of doing this.

Think, if you can, of a single instance in which a plainly-written provision of the Constitution has ever been denied. If, by the mere force of numbers, a majority should deprive a minority of any clearly-written constitutional right, it might, in a moral point of view, justify revolution; it certainly would if such right were a vital one. But such is not our case.

All the vital rights of minorities and of individuals are so plainly assured to them by affirmations and negations, guarantees and prohibitions in the Constitution, that controversies never arise concerning them. But no organic law can ever be framed with a provision specifically applicable to every question which may occur in practical administration. No foresight can anticipate, nor any document of reasonable length contain, express provisions for all possible questions. Shall fugitives from labor be surrendered by national or by state authorities? The Constitution does not expressly say. Must Congress protect slavery in the Territories? The Constitution does not expressly say. From questions of this class spring all our constitutional controversies, and we divide upon them into majorities and minorities.

If the minority will not acquiesce, the majority must, or the Government must cease. There is no alternative for continuing the Government but acquiescence on the one side or the other. If a minority in such a case will secede rather than acquiesce, they make a precedent which, in turn, will ruin and divide them, for a minority of their own will secede from them whenever a majority refuses to be controlled by such a minority. For instance, why not any portion of a new Confederacy, a year or two hence, arbitrarily secede again, precisely as portions of the present Union now claim to secede from it? All who cherish disunion sentiments are now being educated to the exact temper of doing this. Is there such perfect identity of interests among the states to compose a new Union as to produce harmony only, and prevent renewed secession? Plainly, the central idea of secession is the essence of anarchy.

A majority held in restraint by constitutional check and limitation, and always changing easily with deliberate changes of popular opinions and sentiments, is the only true sovereign of a free people. Whoever rejects it, does, of necessity, fly to anarchy or to despotism. Unanimity is impossible; the rule of a minority, as a permanent arrangement, is wholly inadmissible. So that, rejecting the majority principle, anarchy or despotism, in some form, is all that is left.

I do not forget the position assumed by some that constitutional questions are to be decided by the Supreme Court, nor do I deny that such decisions must be binding in any case upon the parties to a suit, as to the object of that suit, while they are also entitled to a very high respect and consideration in all parallel cases by all other departments of the Government; and while it is obviously possible that such decision may be erroneous in any given case, still the evil following it, being limited to that particular case, with the chance that it may be overrruled and never become a precedent for other cases, can better be borne than could the evils of a different practice.

At the same time the candid citizen must confess that if the policy of the Government upon the vital question affecting the whole people is to be irrevocably fixed by the decisions of the Supreme Court, the instant they are made, as in ordinary litigation between parties in personal actions, the people will have ceased to be their own masters, unless having to that extent practically resigned their Government into the hands of that eminent tribunal.

Nor is there in this view any assault upon the Court or the Judges. It is their duty from which they may not shrink, to decide cases properly brought before them; and it is no fault of theirs if others seek to turn their decisions to political purposes. One section of our country believes slavery is right and ought to be extended, while the other believes it is wrong and ought not to be extended; and this is the only substantial dispute; and the fugitive slave clause of the Constitution, and the law for the suppression of the foreign slave-trade, are each as well enforced, perhaps, as any law can ever be in a community where the moral sense of the people imperfectly supports the law itself. The great body of the people abide by the dry legal obligation in both cases, and a few break over in each. This, I think, cannot be perfectly cured, and it would be worse in both cases after the separation of the sections than before. The foreign slave-trade, now imperfectly suppressed, would be ultimately revived, without restriction, in one section; while fugitive slaves, now only partially surrendered, would not be surrendered at all by the other.

Physically speaking, we cannot separate; we cannot remove our respective sections from each other, nor build an impassable wall between them. A husband and wife may be divorced, and go out of the presence and beyond the reach of each other, but the different parts of our country cannot do this. They cannot but remain face to face; and intercourse, either amicable or hostile, must continue between them. Is it possible, then, to make that intercourse more advantageous or more satisfactory after separation than before? Can aliens make treaties easier than friends can make laws? Can treaties be more faithfully enforced between aliens than laws can among friends? Suppose you go to war, you cannot fight always; and when, after much loss on both sides and no gain on either, you cease fighting, the identical questions as to terms of intercourse are again upon you.

This country, with its institutions, belongs to the people who inhabit it: Whenever they shall grow weary of the existing government, they can exercise their constitutional right of amending, or their revolutionary right to dismember or overthrow it. I cannot be ignorant of the fact that many worthy and patriotic citizens are desirous of having the National Constitution amended. While I make no recommendation of amendment, I fully recognize the full authority of the people over the whole subject, to be exercised in either of the modes prescribed in the instrument itself, and I should, under existing circumstances, favor, rather than oppose, a fair opportunity being afforded the people to act upon it.

I will venture to add that to me the convention mode seems preferable, in that it allows amendments to originate with the people themselves, instead of only permitting them to take or reject propositions originated by others not especially chosen for the purpose, and which might not be precisely such as they would wish either to accept or refuse. I understand that a proposed amendment to the Constitution (which amendment, however, I have not seen) has passed Congress, to the effect that the Federal Government shall never interfere with the domestic institutions of states, including that of persons held to service. To avoid misconstruction of what I have said, I depart from my purpose not to speak of particular amendments, so far as to say that, holding such a provision to now be implied constitutional law, I have no objection to its being made express and irrevocable.

The Chief Magistrate derives all his authority from the people, and they have conferred none upon him to fix the terms for the separation of the states. The people themselves, also, can do this if they choose, but the Executive, as such, has nothing to do with it. His duty is to administer the present government as it came to his hands, and to transmit it unimpaired by him to his successor. Why should there not be a patient confidence in the ultimate justice of the people? Is there any better or equal hope in the world? In our present differences is either party without faith of being in the right? If the Almighty Ruler of nations, with his eternal truth and justice, be on your side of the North, or on yours of the South, that truth and that justice will surely prevail by the judgment of this great tribunal, the American people. By the frame of the Government under which we live, this same people have wisely given their public servants but little power for mischief, and have with equal wisdom provided for the return of that little to their own hands at very short intervals. While the people retain their virtue and vigilance, no administration, by any extreme wickedness or folly, can very seriously injure the Government in the short space of four years.

My countrymen, one and all, think calmly and well upon this whole subject. Nothing valuable can be lost by taking time.

If there be an object to hurry any of you, in hot haste, to a step which you would never take deliberately, that object will be frustrated by taking time; but no good object can be frustrated by it.

Such of you as are now dissatisfied still have the old Constitution unimpaired, and on the sensitive point, the laws of your own framing under it; while the new administration will have no immediate power, if it would, to change either.

If it were admitted that you who are dissatisfied hold the right side in the dispute, there is still no single reason for precipitate action. Intelligence, patriotism, Christianity, and a firm reliance on Him who has never yet forsaken this favored land, are still competent to adjust, in the best way, all our present difficulties.

In your hands, my dissatisfied fellow-countrymen, and not in mine, is the momentous issue of civil war. The Government will not assail you.

You can have no conflict without being yourselves the aggressors. You have no oath registered in heaven to destroy the Government, while I shall have the most solemn one to "preserve, protect, and defend" it.

I am loth to close. We are not enemies, but friends. We must not be enemies. Though passion may have strained, it must not break, our bonds of affection.

The mystic cords of memory, stretching from every battlefield and patriot grave to every living heart and hearthstone all over this broad land, will yet swell the chorus of the Union, when again touched, as surely they will be, by the better angels of our nature.

4. A few days after Lincoln was sworn in as President, delegates from seven southern States agreed on a new Constitution of the Confederate States of America. It provided Southerners with a means of uniting and coordinating any military or diplomatic activities they might undertake. Many features of this Constitution are similar to those of the United States Constitution, which southern leaders had helped form and develop. The text, however, includes several provisions that responded to specific southern complaints against United States law during the decades preceding 1860.

CONSTITUTION
OF THE
CONFEDERATE STATES OF
AMERICA.

We, the people of the Confederate States, each State acting in its sovereign and independent character, in order to form a permanent federal government, establish justice, insure domestic tranquility, and secure the blessings of liberty to ourselves and our posterity—invoking the favor and guidance of Almighty God—do ordain and establish this Constitution for the Confederate States of America.

ARTICLE I.

SECTION 1.

All legislative powers herein delegated shall be vested in a Congress of the Confederate States, which shall consist of a Senate and House of Representatives.

SECTION 2.

1. The House of Representatives shall be composed of members chosen every second year by the people of the several States; and the electors in each State shall be citizens of the Confederate States, and have the qualifications requisite for electors of the most numerous branch of the State Legislature; *but no person of foreign birth, not a citizen of the Confederate States, shall be allowed to vote for any officer, civil or political, State or Federal.*

2. No person shall be a Representative who shall not have attained the age of twenty-five years, and be a citizen of the Confederate States, and who shall not, when elected, be an inhabitant of that State in which he shall be chosen.

3. Representatives and direct taxes shall be apportioned among the several States, which may be included within this Confederacy, according to their separate numbers, which shall be determined, by adding to the whole number of free persons, including those bound to service for a term of years, and excluding Indians not taxed, three-fifths of all slaves. The actual enumeration shall be made within three years after the first meeting of the Congress of the Confederate States, and within every subsequent term of ten years, in such manner as they shall by law direct. The number of Representatives shall not exceed one for every fifty thousand, but each State shall have at least one Representative, and until such enumeration shall be made, the State of South Carolina shall be entitled to choose six; the State of Georgia ten; the State of Alabama nine; the State of Florida two; the State of Mississippi seven; the State of Louisiana six; and the State of Texas six.

4. When vacancies happen in the representation from any State, the Executive authority thereof shall issue writs of election to fill such vacancies.

5. The House of Representatives shall choose their Speaker and other officers, and shall have the sole power of impeachment; except that any judicial or other Federal officer, resident and acting solely within the limits of any State, may be impeached by a vote of two-thirds of both branches of the Legislature thereof.

SECTION 3.

1. The Senate of the Confederate States shall be composed of two Senators from each State, chosen for six years by the Legislature thereof, at the regular session next immediately preceding the commencement of the term of service; and each Senator shall have one vote.

2. Immediately after they shall be assembled, in consequence of the first election, they shall be divided as equally as may be into three classes. The seats of the Senators of the first class shall be vacated at the expiration of the second year; of the second class at the expiration of the fourth year; and of the third class at the expiration of the sixth year; so that one-third may be chosen every second year; and if vacancies happen by resignation, or otherwise, during the recess of the Legislature of any State, the Executive thereof may make temporary appointments until the next meeting of the Legislature which shall then fill such vacancies.

3. No person shall be a Senator who shall not have attained the age of thirty years, and be a citizen of the Confederate States; and who shall not, when elected, be an inhabitant of the State for which he shall be chosen.

4. The Vice President of the Confederate States shall be President of the Senate, but shall have no vote unless they be equally divided.

5. The Senate shall choose their other officers; and also a President *pro tempore* in the absence of the Vice President, or when he shall exercise the office of President of the Confederate States.

6. The Senate shall have the sole power to try all impeachments. When sitting for that purpose, they shall be on oath or affirmation. When the President of the Confederate States is tried, the Chief Justice shall preside; and no person shall be convicted without the concurrence of two-thirds of the members present.

7. Judgment is cases of impeachment shall not extend further than to removal from office, and disqualification to hold and enjoy any office of honor, trust or profit, under the Confederate States; but the party convicted shall, nevertheless, be liable and subject to indictment, trial, judgment and punishment according to law.

SECTION 4.

1. The times, places and manner of holding elections for Senators and Representatives, shall be prescribed in each State by the Legislature thereof, subject to the provisions of this Constitution; but the Congress may, at any time, by law, make or alter such regulations, except as to the times and places of choosing Senators.

2. The Congress shall assemble at least once in every year; and such meeting shall be on the first Monday in December, unless they shall, by law, appoint a different day.

SECTION 5.

1. Each House shall be the judge of the elections, returns, and qualifications of its own members, and a majority of each shall constitute a quorum to do business; but a smaller number may adjourn from day to day, and may be authorized to compel the attendance of absent members, in such manner and under such penalties as each House may provide.

2. Each House may determine the rules of its proceedings, punish its members for disorderly behavior, and with the concurrence of two-thirds of the whole number expel a member.

3. Each House shall keep a journal of its proceedings, and from time to time publish the same, excepting such parts as may in their judgment require secrecy; and the yeas and nays of the members of either House, on any question, shall, at the desire of one-fifth of those present, be entered on the journal.

4. Neither House, during the session of Congress, shall, without the consent of the other, adjourn for more than three days, nor to any other place than that in which the two Houses shall be sitting.

SECTION 6.

1. The Senators and Representatives shall receive a compensation for their services, to be ascertained by law, and paid out of the treasury of the Confederate States. They shall, in all cases, except treason, felony, and breach of the peace, be privileged from arrest, during their attendance at the session of their respective Houses, and in going to and returning from the same; and for any speech or debate in either House, they shall not be questioned in any other place.

2. No Senator or Representative shall, during the time for which he was elected, be appointed to any civil office under the authority of the Confederate States, which shall have been created, or the emoluments whereof shall have been increased during such time; and no person holding any office under the Confederate States shall be a member of either House during his continuance in office. But Congress may, by law, grant

to the principal officer in each of the Executive Departments a seat upon the floor of either House, with the privilege of discussing any measures appertaining to his department.

SECTION 7.

1. All bills for raising revenue shall originate in the House of Representatives; but the Senate may propose or concur with amendments, as on other bills.

2. Every bill which shall have passed both Houses, shall, before it becomes a law, be presented to the President of the Confederate States; if he approve, he shall sign it; but if not, he shall return it, with his objections, to that House in which it shall have originated, who shall enter the objections at large on their journal, and proceed to reconsider it. If, after such reconsideration, two-thirds of that House shall agree to pass the bill, it shall be sent, together with the objections, to the other House, by which it shall likewise be reconsidered, and if approved by two-thirds of that House, it shall become a law. But in all such cases, the votes of both Houses shall be determined by yeas and nays, and the names of the persons voting for and against the bill shall be entered on the journal of each House respectively. If any bill shall not be returned by the President within ten days (Sundays excepted) after it shall have been presented to him, the same shall be a law, in like manner as if he had signed it, unless the Congress, by their adjournment, prevent its return; in which case it shall not be a law. The President may approve any appropriation and disapprove any other appropriation in the same bill. In such case he shall, in signing the bill, designate the appropriations disapproved; and shall return a copy of such appropriations, with his objections, to the House in which the bill shall have originated; and the same proceedings shall then be had as in case of other bills disapproved by the President.

3. Every order, resolution or vote, to which the concurrence of both Houses may be necessary, (except on a question of adjournment.) shall be presented to the President of the Confederate States; and before the same shall take effect, shall be approved by him; or being disapproved by him, shall be re-passed by two thirds of both Houses, according to the rules and limitations prescribed in case of a bill.

SECTION 8.

The Congress shall have power—

1. To lay and collect taxes, duties, imposts, and excises, for revenue necessary to pay all debts, provide for the common defence, and carry on the government of the Confederate States; but no bounties shall be granted from the treasury; nor shall any duties or taxes on importations from foreign nations be laid to promote or foster any branch of industry; and all duties, imposts, and excises shall be uniform throughout the Confederate States:

2. To borrow money on the credit of the Confederate States:

3. To regulate commerce with foreign nations, and among the several States, and with the Indian tribes; but neither this, nor any other clause contained in the constitution, shall ever be construed to delegate the power to Congress to appropriate money for any internal improvement intended to facilitate commerce; except for the purpose of furnishing lights, beacons, and buoys, and other aids to navigation upon the coasts, and the improvement of harbors and the removing of obstructions in river navigation, in all which cases, such duties shall be laid on the navigation facilitated thereby, as may be necessary to pay the costs and expenses thereof:

4. To establish uniform laws of naturalization, and uniform laws on the subject of bankruptcies, throughout the Confederate States; but no law of Congress shall discharge any debt contracted before the passage of the same:

5. To coin money, regulate the value thereof and of foreign coin, and fix the standard of weights and measures:

6. To provide for the punishment of counterfeiting the securities and current coin of the Confederate States:

7. To establish post-offices and post-routes; but the expenses of the Post-office Department, after the first day of March in the year of our Lord eighteen hundred and sixty-three, shall be paid out of its own revenues:

8. To promote the progress of science and useful arts, by securing for limited times to authors and inventors the exclusive right to their respective writings and discoveries:

9. To constitute tribunals inferior to the Supreme Court:

10. To define and punish piracies and felonies committed on the high seas, and offences against the law of nations:

11. To declare war, grant letters of marque and reprisal, and make rules concerning captures on land and water:

12. To raise and support armies; but no appropriation of money to that use shall be for a longer term than two years:

13. To provide and maintain a navy:

14. To make rules for the government and regulation of the land and naval forces:

15. To provide for calling forth the militia to execute the laws of the Confederate States, suppress insurrections, and repel invasions:

16. To provide for organizing, arming, and disciplin-

ing the militia, and for governing such part of them as may be employed in the service of the Confederate States; reserving to the States, respectively, the appointment of the officers, and the authority of training the militia according to the discipline prescribed by Congress:

17. To exercise exclusive legislation, in all cases whatsoever, over such district (not exceeding ten miles square) as may, by cession of one or more States and the acceptance of Congress, become the seat of the government of the Confederate States: and to exercise like authority over all places purchased by the consent of the legislature of the State in which the same shall be, for the erection of forts, magazines, arsenals, dockyards, and other needful buildings: and

18. To make all laws which shall be necessary and proper for carrying into execution the foregoing powers, and all other powers vested by this Constitution in the government of the Confederate States, or in any department or officer thereof.

SECTION 9.

1. The importation of negroes of the African race, from any foreign country other than the slaveholding States or Territories of the United States of America, is hereby forbidden; and Congress is required to pass such laws as shall effectually prevent the same.

2. Congress shall also have power to prohibit the introduction of slaves from any State not a member of, or Territory not belonging to, this Confederacy.

3. The privilege of the writ of *habeas corpus* shall not be suspended, unless when in cases of rebellion or invasion the public safety may require it.

4. No bill of attainder, *ex post facto* law, or law denying or impairing the right of property in negro slaves shall be passed.

5. No capitation or other direct tax shall be laid, unless in proportion to the census or enumeration hereinbefore directed to be taken.

6. No tax or duty shall be laid on articles exported from any State, except by a vote of two-thirds of both Houses.

7. No preference shall be given by any regulation of commerce or revenue to the ports of one State over those of another.

8. No money shall be drawn from the treasury, but in consequence of appropriations made by law; and a regular statement and account of the receipts and expenditures of all public money shall be published from time to time.

9. Congress shall appropriate no money from the treasury except by a vote of two-thirds of both Houses, taken by yeas and nays, unless it be asked and estimated for by some one of the heads of departments, and submitted to Congress by the President; or for the purpose of paying its own expenses and contingencies; or for the payment of claims against the Confederate States, the justice of which shall have been judicially declared by a tribunal for the investigation of claims against the government, which it is hereby made the duty of Congress to establish.

10. All bills appropriating money shall specify in federal currency the exact amount of each appropriation and the purposes for which it is made; and Congress shall grant no extra compensation to any public contractor, officer, agent or servant, after such contract shall have been made or such service rendered.

11. No title of nobility shall be granted by the Confederate States; and no person holding any office of profit or trust under them, shall, without the consent of the Congress, accept of any present, emolument, office or title of any kind whatever, from any king, prince, or foreign state.

12. Congress shall make no law respecting an establishment of religion, or prohibiting the free exercise thereof; or abridging the freedom of speech, or of the press; or the right of the people peaceably to assemble and petition the government for a redress of grievances.

13. A well-regulated militia being necessary to the security of a free state, the right of the people to keep and bear arms shall not be infringed.

14. No soldier shall, in time of peace, be quartered in any house, without the consent of the owner; nor in time of war, but in a manner to be prescribed by law.

15. The right of the people to be secure in their persons, houses, papers, and effects, against unreasonable searches and seizures, shall not be violated; and no warrants shall issue but upon probable cause, supported by oath or affirmation, and particularly describing the place to be searched, and the person or things to be seized.

16. No person shall be held to answer for a capital or otherwise infamous crime, unless on a presentment or indictment of a grand jury, except in cases arising in the land or naval forces, or in the militia, when in actual service in time of war or public danger; nor shall any person be subject for the same offence to be twice put in jeopardy of life or limb; nor be compelled, in any criminal case, to be a witness against himself; nor be deprived of life, liberty, or property without the process of law; nor shall private property be taken for public use, without just compensation.

17. In all criminal prosecutions, the accused shall enjoy the right to a speedy and public trial, by an impartial jury of the State and district wherein the crime shall have been committed, which district shall have

been previously ascertained by law, and to be informed of the nature and cause of the accusation; to be confronted with the witnesses against him; to have compulsory process for obtaining witnesses in his favor; and to have the assistance of counsel for his defence.

18. In suits at common law, where the value in controversy shall exceed twenty dollars, the right of trial by jury shall be preserved; and no fact so tried by a jury shall be otherwise re-examined in any court of the Confederacy, than according to the rules of common law.

19. Excessive bail shall not be required, nor excessive fines imposed, nor cruel and unusual punishments inflicted.

20. Every law, or resolution having the force of law, shall relate to but one subject, and that shall be expressed in the title.

SECTION 10.

1. No State shall enter into any treaty, alliance, or confederation; grant letters of marque and reprisal; coin money; make any thing but gold and silver coin a tender in payment of debts; pass any bill of attainder, or *ex post facto* law, or law impairing the obligation of contracts: or grant any title of nobility.

2. No State shall, without the consent of the Congress, by any imposts or duties on imports or exports, except what may be absolutely necessary for executing its inspection laws; and the net produce of all duties and imposts, laid by any State on imports or exports, shall be for the use of the Treasury of the Confederate States; and all such laws shall be subject to the revision and control of Congress.

3. No State shall, without the consent of Congress, lay any duty on tonnage, except on sea-going vessels, for the improvement of its rivers and harbors navigated by the said vessels; but such duties shall not conflict with any treaties of the Confederate States with foreign nations; and any surplus revenue, thus derived, shall, after making such improvement, be paid into the common treasury. Nor shall any State keep troops or ships-of-war in time of peace, enter into any agreement or compact with another State, or with a foreign power, or engage in war, unless actually invaded, or in such imminent danger as will not admit of delay. But when any river divides or flows through two or more States, they may enter into compacts with each other to improve the navigation thereof.

ARTICLE II.

SECTION I.

1. The executive power shall be vested in a President of the Confederate States of America. He and the Vice President shall hold their offices for the term of six years, but the President shall not be re-eligible. The President and Vice President shall be elected as follows:

2. Each State shall appoint, in such manner as the legislature thereof may direct, a number of electors equal to the whole number of Senators and Representatives to which the State may be entitled in the Congress; but no Senator or Representative or person holding an office of trust or profit under the Confederate States, shall be appointed an elector.

3. The electors shall meet in their respective States and vote by ballot for President and Vice President, one of whom, at least, shall not be an inhabitant of the same State with themselves; they shall name in their ballots the person voted for as President, and in distinct ballots the person voted for as Vice President, and they shall make distinct lists of all persons voted for as President, and of all persons voted for as Vice President, and of the number of votes for each, which lists they shall sign and certify, and transmit, sealed, to the seat of the government of the Confederate States, directed to the President of the Senate; the President of the Senate shall, in the presence of the Senate and House of Representatives, open all the certificates, and the votes shall then be counted; the person having the greatest of votes for President shall be the President, if such number be a majority of the whole number of electors appointed; and if no person have such majority, then, from the persons having the highest numbers, not exceeding three, on the list of those voted for as President, the House of Representatives shall choose immediately, by ballot, the President. But in choosing the President, the votes shall be taken by States—the representation from each State having one vote; a quorum for this purpose shall consist of a member or members from two-thirds of the States, and a majority of all the States shall be necessary to a choice. And if the House of Representatives shall not choose a President, whenever the right of choice shall devolve upon them, before the fourth day of March next following, then the Vice President shall act as President, as in case of the death, or other constitutional disability of the President.

4. The person having the greatest number of votes as Vice President, shall be the Vice President, if such number be a majority of the whole number of electors appointed; and if no person have a majority, then, from the two highest numbers on the list, the Senate shall choose the Vice President; a quorum for the purpose shall consist of two-thirds of the whole number of Senators, and a majority of the whole number shall be necessary to a choice.

5. But no person constitutionally ineligible to the office of President shall be eligible to that of Vice President of the Confederate States.

6. The Congress may determine the time of choosing the electors, and the day on which they shall give their votes; which day shall be the same throughout the Confederate States.

7. No person except a natural born citizen of the Confederate States, or a citizen thereof at the time of the adoption of this Constitution, or a citizen thereof born in the United States prior to the 20th of December, 1860, shall be eligible to the office of President; neither shall any person be eligible to that office who shall not have attained the age of thirty-five years, and been fourteen years a resident within the limits of the Confederate States, as they may exist at the time of his election.

8. In case of the removal of the President from office, or of his death, resignation, or inability to discharge the powers and duties of the said office, the same shall devolve on the Vice President; and the Congress may, by law, provide for the case of removal, death, resignation, or inability, both of the President and Vice President, declaring what officer shall then act as President; and such officer shall act accordingly, until the disability be removed or a President shall be elected.

9. The President shall, at stated times, receive for his services a compensation, which shall neither be increased nor diminished during the period for which he shall have been elected; and he shall not receive within that period any other emolument from the Confederate States, or any of them.

10. Before he enters on the execution of his office, he shall take the following oath or affirmation:

"I do solemnly swear (or affirm) that I will faithfully execute the office of President of the Confederate States, and will, to the best of my ability, preserve, protect, and defend the Constitution thereof."

SECTION 2.

1. The President shall be commander-in-chief of the army and navy of the Confederate States, and of the militia of the several States, when called into the actual service of the Confederate States; he may require the opinion, in writing, of the principal officer in each of the executive departments, upon any subject relating to the duties of their respective offices; and he shall have power to grant reprieves and pardons for offences against the Confederate States, except in cases of impeachment.

2. He shall have power, by and with the advice and consent of the Senate, to make treaties; provided two-thirds of the Senators present concur; and he shall nominate, and by and with the advice and consent of the Senate, shall appoint ambassadors, other public ministers and consuls, judges of the Supreme Court, and all

other officers of the Confederate States whose appointments are not herein otherwise provided for, and which shall be established by law; but the Congress may; by law, vest the appointment of such inferior officers, as they think proper, in the President alone, in the courts of law, or in the heads of departments.

3. The principal officer in each of the executive departments, and all persons connected with the diplomatic service, may be removed from office at the pleasure of the President. All other civil officers of the executive departments may be removed at any time by the President, or other appointing power, when their services are unnecessary, or for dishonesty, incapacity, inefficiency, misconduct, or neglect of duty; and when so removed, the removal shall be reported to the Senate, together with the reasons therefor.

4. The President shall have power to fill all vacancies that may happen during the recess of the Senate, by granting commissions which shall expire at the end of their next session; but no person rejected by the Senate shall be re-appointed to the same office during their ensuing recess.

SECTION 3.

1. The President shall, from time to time, give to the Congress information of the state of the Confederacy, and recommend to their consideration such measures as he shall judge necessary and expedient; he may, on extraordinary occasions, convene both Houses, or either of them; and in case of disagreement between them, with respect to the time of adjournment, he may adjourn them to such time as he shall think proper; he shall receive ambassadors and other public ministers; he shall take care that the laws be faithfully executed, and shall commission all the officers of the Confederate States.

SECTION 4.

1. The President, Vice President, and all civil officers of the Confederate States, shall be removed from office on impeachment, for and conviction of, treason, bribery, or other high crimes and misdemeanors.

ARTICLE III.

SECTION 1.

1. The judicial power of the Confederate States shall be vested in one Supreme Court, and in such inferior courts as the Congress may, from time to time, obtain and establish. The judges, both of the Supreme and inferior courts, shall hold their offices during good behavior, and shall, at stated times, receive for their services a compensation which shall not be diminished during their continuance in office.

SECTION 2.

1. The judicial power shall extend to all cases arising under this Constitution, the laws of the Confederate States, and treaties made, or which shall be made, under their authority; to all cases affecting ambassadors, other public ministers and consuls; to all cases of admiralty and maritime jurisdiction; to controversies to which the Confederate States shall be a party; to controversies between two or more States; between a State and citizens of another State, where the State is plaintiff; between citizens claiming lands under grants of different States; and between a State or the citizens thereof, and foreign states, citizens or subjects; but no State shall be sued by a citizen or subject of any foreign state.

2. In all cases affecting ambassadors, other public ministers and consuls, and those in which a State shall be a party, the Supreme Court shall have original jurisdiction. In all the other cases before mentioned, the Supreme Court shall have appellate jurisdiction both as to law and fact, with such exceptions and under such regulations as the Congress shall make.

3. The trial of all crimes, except in cases of impeachment, shall be by jury, and such trial shall be held in the State where the said crimes shall have been committed; but when not committed within any State, the trial shall be at such place or places as the Congress may by law have directed.

SECTION 3.

1. Treason against the Confederate States shall consist only in levying war against them, or in adhering to their enemies, giving them aid and comfort. No person shall be convicted of treason unless on the testimony of two witnesses to the same overt act, or on confession in open court.

2. The Congress shall have power to declare the punishment of treason; but no attainder of treason shall work corruption of blood, or forfeiture, except during the life of the person attainted.

ARTICLE IV.

SECTION I.

1. Full faith and credit shall be given in each State to the public acts, records, and judicial proceedings of every other State. And the Congress may, by general laws, prescribe the manner in which such acts, records, and proceedings shall be proved, and the effect thereof.

SECTION 2.

1. The citizens of each State shall be entitled to all the privileges and immunities of citizens in the several States; and shall have the right of transit and sojourn in any State of this Confederacy, with their slaves and other property; and the right of property in said slaves shall not be thereby impaired.

2. A person charged in any State with treason, felony, or other crime against the laws of such State, who shall flee from justice, and be found in another State, shall, on demand of the executive authority of the State from which he fled, be delivered up, to be removed to the State having jurisdiction of the crime.

3. No slave or other person held to service or labor in any State or Territory of the Confederate States, under the laws thereof, escaping or lawfully carried into another shall, in consequence of any law or regulation therein, be discharged from such service or labor: but shall be delivered up on claim of the party to whom such slave belongs, or to whom such service or labor may be due.

SECTION 3.

1. Other States may be admitted into this Confederacy by a vote of two-thirds of the whole House of Representatives and two-thirds of the Senate, the Senate voting by States; but no new State shall be formed or erected within the jurisdiction of any other State; nor any State be formed by the junction of two or more States, or parts of States, without the consent of the legislatures of the States concerned, as well as of the Congress.

2. The Congress shall have power to dispose of and make all needful rules and regulations concerning the property of the Confederate States, including the lands thereof.

3. The Confederate States may acquire new territory; and Congress shall have power to legislate and provide governments for the inhabitants of all territory belonging to the Confederate States, lying without the limits of the several States; and may permit them, at such times, and in such manner as it may by law provide, to form States to be admitted into the Confederacy. In all such territory, the institution of negro slavery, as it now exists in the Confederate States, shall be recognized and protected by Congress and by the territorial government: and the inhabitants of the several Confederate States and Territories shall have the right to take to such territory any slaves lawfully held by them in any of the States or Territories of the Confederate States.

4. The Confederate States shall guarantee to every State that now is, or hereafter may become, a member of this Confederacy, a republican form of government; and shall protect each of them against invasion; and on application of the legislature, (or of the executive, when the legislature is not in session,) against domestic violence.

ARTICLE V.

SECTION 1.

1. Upon the demand of any three States, legally assembled in their several conventions, the Congress shall summon a convention of all the States, to take into consideration such amendments to the Constitution as the said States shall concur in suggesting at the time when the said demand is made; and should any of the proposed amendments to the Constitution be agreed on by the said convention—voting by States—and the same be ratified by the legislature of two-thirds of the several States, or by conventions in two-thirds thereof—as the one or the other mode of ratification may be proposed by the general convention—they shall thenceforward form a part of this Constitution. But no State shall, without its consent, be deprived of its equal representation in the Senate.

ARTICLE VI.

1. The Government established by this Constitution is the successor of the Provisional Government of the Confederate States of America, and all the laws passed by the latter shall continue in force until the same shall be repealed or modified: and all the officers appointed by the same shall remain in office until their successors are appointed and qualified, or the offices abolished.

2. All debts contracted and engagements entered into before the adoption of this Constitution shall be as valid against the Confederate States under this Constitution, as under the Provisional Government.

3. This Constitution, and the laws of the Confederate States made in pursuance thereof, and all treaties made, or which shall be made, under the authority of the Confederate States, shall be the supreme law of the land; and the judges in every State shall be bound thereby, anything in the constitution or laws of any State to the contrary notwithstanding.

4. The Senators and Representatives before mentioned, and the members of the several State legislatures, and all executive and judicial officers, both of the Confederate States and of the several States, shall be bound by oath or affirmation to support this Constitution; but no religious test shall ever be required as a qualification to any office or public trust under the Confederate States.

5. The enumeration, in the Constitution, of certain rights, shall not be construed to deny or disparage others retained by the people of the several States.

6. The powers not delegated to the Confederate States by the Constitution, nor prohibited by it to the States, are reserved to the States, respectively, or to the people thereof.

ARTICLE VII.

1. The ratification of the conventions of five States shall be sufficient for the establishment of this Constitution between the States so ratifying the same.

2. When the five States shall have ratified this Constitution, in the manner before specified, the Congress under the Provisional Constitution shall prescribe the time for holding the election of President and Vice President; and for the meeting of the Electoral College; and for counting the votes, and inaugurating the President. They shall, also, prescribe the time for holding the first election of members of Congress under this Constitution, and the time for assembling the same. Until the assembling of such Congress, the Congress under the Provisional Constitution shall continue to exercise the legislative powers granted them; not extending beyond the time limited by the Constitution of the Provisional Government.

Adopted unanimously by the Congress of the Confederate States of South Carolina, Georgia, Florida, Alabama, Mississippi, Louisiana and Texas, sitting in Convention at the capitol, in the city of Montgomery, Alabama, on the Eleventh day of March, in the year Eighteen Hundred and Sixty-One.

HOWELL COBB,
President of the Congress.

5. *If ever there were a "man in the middle" of a crisis it was John J. Crittenden of Kentucky. Crittenden had been a U.S. Senator and Attorney-General of the United States. In 1860 he was elected to Congress as a Representative from Kentucky. He had been a follower of Henry Clay (the Great Compromiser), and he tried at the last minute to hammer out a compromise that would prevent a civil war from spreading. His own family was splitting over the Secession question. Two of his sons would fight as generals: one for the Union, one for the Confederacy. His compromise Resolution, for which he got the approval of the House of Representatives in 1861, was intended to provide a basis for an early settlement of the war. (Quoted from* House Journal, *37th Congress, 1st Session.)*

Resolved, by the House of Representatives of the Congress of the United States,

That the present deplorable civil war has been forced upon the country by the disunionists of the Southern states, now in arms against the constitutional government, and in arms around the capital;

that in this national emergency Congress, banishing

all feelings of mere passion or resentment, will recollect only its duty to the whole country;

that this war is not waged on their part in any spirit of oppression, or for any purpose of conquest or subjugation, or purpose of overthrowing or interfering with the rights of established institutions of those states, but to defend and maintain the supremacy of the Constitution and to preserve the Union with all the dignity, equality, and rights of the several states unimpaired;

and that as soon as these objects are accomplished the war ought to cease.

6.   *Although no actual declaration of war was issued by the United States government, the following two Proclamations by President Lincoln were looked on by Confederates as though they were such a declaration. The first called for volunteers from all the States to put down the "combinations" that were blocking the operation of United States laws. This Proclamation led almost at once to the secession of Virginia, North Carolina, Tennessee and Arkansas. These States of the Upper South had originally remained "in the Union", but objected to the use of force to preserve the Union.*

The second Proclamation by the President directed the U.S. Navy to establish a blockade of southern ports.

Proclamation of April 15, 1861

WHEREAS the laws of the United States have been, for some time past, and now are opposed, and the execution thereof obstructed, in the States of South Carolina, Georgia, Alabama, Florida, Mississippi, Louisana, and Texas, by combinations too powerful to be suppressed by the ordinary course of judicial proceedings, or by the powers vested in the marshals by law:

Now, therefore, I, ABRAHAM LINCOLN, President of the United States, in virtue of the power in me vested by the Constitution and the laws, have thought fit to call forth, and hereby do call forth, the militia of the several States of the Union, to the aggregate number of seventy-five thousand, in order to suppress said combinations, and to cause the laws to be duly executed.

The details for this object will be immediately communicated to the State authorities through the War Department.

I appeal to all loyal citizens to favor, facilitate, and aid this effort to maintain the honor, the integrity, and the existence of our National Union, and the perpetuity of popular government; and to redress wrongs already long enough endured.

I deem it proper to say that the first service assigned to the forces hereby called forth will probably be to repossess the forts, places, and property which have been seized from the Union; and in every event, the utmost care will be observed, consistently with the objects aforesaid, to avoid any devastation, any destruction of, or interference with, property, or any disturbances of peaceful citizens in any part of the country.

And I hereby command the persons composing the combinations aforesaid to disperse, and retire peaceably to their respective abodes within twenty days from this date.

Deeming that the present condition of public affairs presents an extraordinary occasion, I do hereby, in virtue of the power in me vested by the Constitution, convene both Houses of Congress. Senators and Representatives are therefore summoned to assemble at their respective chambers, at twelve o'clock, noon, on Thursday, the fourth day of July next, then and there to consider and determine such measures as, in their wisdom, the public safety and interest may seem to demand.

Proclamation of April 19, 1861

WHEREAS an insurrection against the Government of the United States has broken out in the States of South Carolina, Georgia, Alabama, Florida, Mississippi, Louisiana, and Texas, and the laws of the United States for the collection of the revenue cannot be effectually executed therein conformably to that provision of the Constitution which requires duties to be uniform throughout the United States:

And whereas a combination of persons, engaged in such insurrection, have threatened to grant pretended letters of marque to authorize the bearers thereof to commit assaults on the lives, vessels, and property of good citizens of the country lawfully engaged in commerce on the high seas, and in waters of the United States:

And whereas an Executive Proclamation has been already issued, requiring the persons engaged in these disorderly proceedings to desist therefrom, calling out a militia force for the purpose of repressing the same, and convening Congress in extraordinary session to deliberate and determine thereon:

Now, therefore, I, ABRAHAM LINCOLN, President of the United States, with a view to the same purposes before mentioned, and to the protection of the public peace, and the lives and property of quiet and orderly citizens pursuing their lawful occupations, until Congress shall have assembled and deliberated on the said unlawful proceedings, or until the same shall have ceased, have further deemed it advisable to set on foot a blockade of the ports within the States aforesaid, in pursuance of the laws of the United States and of the law of nations in such case provided. For this purpose a competent force will be posted so as to prevent entrance and exit of vessels from the ports aforesaid. If, therefore, with a view to violate such blockade, a vessel shall approach, or shall attempt to leave either of the said ports, she will be duly warned by the commander of one of the blockading vessels, who will indorse on her register the fact and date of such warning, and if the same vessel shall again attempt to enter or leave the blockaded port, she will be captured and sent to the nearest convenient port, for such proceedings against her and her cargo as prize, as may be deemed advisable.

And I hereby proclaim and declare that if any person, under the pretended authority of the said States, or under any other pretence, shall molest a vessel of the United States, or the persons or cargo on board of her, such person will be held amenable to the laws of the United States for the prevention and punishment of piracy.

7. Many of Lincoln's critics, both North and South, charged that he had delayed too long in making his position clear before the inauguration, and that his call for volunteers had driven several States into the Confederacy. Some argued that he had acted on his own, without Congressional approval; others answered that he had simply moved to protect the Union. The leader of the Confederacy was President Jefferson Davis of Mississippi. He began his presidency by issuing policy orders to General P. G. T. Beauregard and others, and by inviting shipowners to apply for "letters of marque and reprisal" so that they could operate privateers against United States shipping. Davis called the Confederate Congress into special session, and requested that it declare war to establish southern independence. His message, delivered April 29, contained a summary history of southern complaints against Federal policies.

Message of Jefferson Davis

The declaration of war made against this Confederacy by Abraham Lincoln, the President of the United States, in his proclamation issued on the 15th day of the present month, rendered it necessary, in my judgment, that you should convene at the earliest practicable moment to devise the measures necessary for the defense of the country. The occasion is indeed an extraordinary one. It justifies me in a brief review of the relations heretofore existing between us and the States which now unite in warfare against us and in a succinct statement of the events which have resulted in this warfare, to the end that mankind may pass intelligent and impartial judgment on its motives and objects. During the war waged against Great Britain by her colonies on this continent a common danger impelled them to a close alliance and to the formation of a Confederation, by the terms of which the colonies, styling themselves States, entered 'severally into a firm league of friendship with each other for their common defense, the security of their liberties, and their mutual and general welfare, binding themselves to assist each other against all force offered to or attacks made upon them, or any of them, on account of religion, sovereignty, trade, or any other pretense whatever'. In order to guard against any misconstruction of their compact, the several States made explicit declaration in a distinct article—that 'each State *retains its* sovereignty, freedom, and independence, and every power, jurisdiction, and right which is not by this Confederation *expressly delegated* to the United States in Congress assembled'.

Under this contract of alliance, the war of the Revolution was successfully waged, and resulted in the treaty of peace with Great Britain in 1783, by the terms of which the several States were *each by name* recognized to be independent. The Articles of Confederation contained a clause whereby all alterations were prohibited unless confirmed by the Legislatures of *every* State after being agreed to by the Congress; and in obedience to this provision, under the resolution of Congress on the 21st of February 1787, the several States appointed delegates who attended a convention 'for the *sole and express purpose* of revising the Articles of Confederation and reporting to Congress and the several Legislatures such alterations and provisions therein as shall, when agreed to in Congress *and confirmed by the States,* render the Federal Constitution adequate to the exigencies of Government and the preservation of the Union'. It was by the delegates chosen by the *several States* under the resolution just quoted that the Constitution of the United States was framed in 1787 and submitted to the *several States* for ratification, as shown by the seventh article, which is in these words: 'The ratification of the *conventions of nine States* shall be sufficient for the establishment of this Constitution *between the States* so ratifying the same.' . . . The Constitution of 1787, having, however, omitted the clause already recited from the Articles of Confederation, which provided in explicit terms that each State *retained* its sovereignty and independence, some alarm was felt in the States, when invited to ratify the Constitution, lest this omission should be construed into an abandonment of their cherished principle, and they refused to be satisfied until amendments were added to the Constitution placing beyond any pretense of doubt the reservation by the States of all their sovereign rights and powers not expressly delegated to the United States by the Constitution.

Strange, indeed, must it appear to the impartial observer, but it is none the less true that all these carefully worded clauses proved unavailing to prevent the rise and growth in the Northern States of a political school which has persistently claimed that the government thus formed was not a compact *between* States, but was in effect a national government, set up *above* and *over* the States. An organization created by the States to secure the blessings of liberty and independence against *foreign* aggression has been gradually perverted into a machine for their control in their *domestic* affairs. The *creature* has been exalted above its *creators*; the *principals* have been made subordinate to the *agent* appointed by themselves. The people of the Southern States, whose almost exclusive occupation was agriculture, early perceived a tendency in the Northern States to render the common government subservient to their own purposes by imposing burdens on commerce as a protection to their manufacturing and shipping interests. . . .

By degrees, as the Northern States gained preponderance in the National Congress, self-interest taught their people to yield ready assent to any plausible advocacy of their right as a majority to govern the minorities without control. They learned to listen with impatience to the suggestion of any constitutional impediment to the exercise of their will, and so utterly have the principles of the Constitution been corrupted in the Northern mind that, in the Inaugural Address delivered by President Lincoln in March last, he asserts as an axiom, which he plainly deems to be undeniable, that the theory of the Constitution requires that in all cases the majority shall govern. . . .

In addition to the long-continued and deep-seated resentment felt by the Southern States at the persistent abuse of the powers they had delegated to the Congress, for the purpose of enriching the manufacturing and shipping classes of the North at the expense of the South, there has existed for nearly half a century another subject of discord, involving interests of such transcendent magnitude as at all times to create the apprehension in the minds of many devoted lovers of the Union that its permanence was impossible. When the several States delegated certain powers to the United States Congress, a large portion of the laboring population consisted of African slaves imported into the colonies by the mother country. In twelve out of the thirteen States negro slavery existed, and the right of prop-

erty in slaves was protected by law. This property was recognized in the Constitution, and provision was made against its loss by the escape of the slave. The increase in the number of slaves by further importation from Africa was also secured by a clause forbidding Congress to prohibit the slave trade anterior to a certain date, and in no clause can there be found any delegation of power to the Congress authorizing it in any manner to legislate to the prejudice, detriment, or discouragement of the owners of that species of property, or excluding it from the protection of the Government.

The climate and soil of the Northern States soon proved unpropitious to the continuance of slave labor, whilst the converse was the case at the South. Under the unrestricted free intercourse between the two sections, the Northern States consulted their own interests by selling their slaves to the South and prohibiting slavery within their limits. The South were willing purchasers of property suitable to their wants, and paid the price of the acquisition without harboring a suspicion that their quiet possession was to be disturbed by those who were inhibited not only by want of constitutional authority, but by good faith as vendors, from disquieting a title emanating from themselves. As soon, however, as the Northern States that prohibited African slavery within their limits had reached a number sufficient to give their representation a controlling voice in the Congress, a persistent and organized system of hostile measures against the rights of the owners of slaves in the Southern States was inaugurated and gradually extended. . . . Senators and Representatives were sent to the common councils of the nation whose chief title to this distinction consisted in the display of a spirit of ultra-fanaticism, and whose business was not 'to promote the general welfare or insure domestic tranquillity', but to awaken the bitterest hatred against the citizens of sister States by violent denunciation of their institutions; the transaction of public affairs was impeded by repeated efforts to usurp powers not delegated by the Constitution, for the purpose of impairing the security of property in slaves, and reducing those States which held slaves to a condition of inferiority. Finally a great party was organized for the purpose of obtaining the administration of the Government, with the avowed object of using its power for the total exclusion of the slave States from all participation in the benefits of the public domain acquired by all the States in common, whether by conquest or purchase; of surrounding them entirely by States in which slavery should be prohibited; of thus rendering the property in slaves so insecure as to be comparatively worthless, and thereby annihilating in effect property worth thousands of millions of dollars. This party, thus organized, succeeded in the month of

November last in the election of its candidate for the Presidency of the United States.

In the meantime, the African slaves had augmented in number from about 600,000, at the date of the adoption of the constitutional compact, to upward of 4,000,000. In moral and social condition they had been elevated from brutal savages into docile, intelligent, and civilized agricultural laborers, and supplied not only with bodily comforts but with careful religious instruction. Under the supervision of a superior race their labor had been so directed as not only to allow a gradual and marked amelioration of their own condition, but to convert hundreds of thousands of square miles of the wilderness into cultivated lands covered with a prosperous people; towns and cities had sprung into existence, and had rapidly increased in wealth and population under the social system of the South; the white population of the Southern slaveholding States had augmented from about 1,250,000 at the date of the adoption of the Constitution to more than 8,500,000 in 1860; and the productions in the South of cotton, rice, sugar, and tobacco, for the full development and continuance of which the labor of African slaves was and is indispensable, had swollen to an amount which formed nearly three-fourths of the exports of the whole United States and had become absolutely necessary to the wants of civilized man. With interests of such overwhelming magnitude imperilled, the people of the Southern States were driven by the conduct of the North to the adoption of some course of action to avert the danger with which they were openly menaced. With this view the Legislatures of the several States invited the people to select delegates to conventions to be held for the purpose of determining for themselves what measures were best. . . .

BLUE AND GRAY

1. The Civil War is probably the most widely reported of American wars. Soldiers and sailors, officers and civilian leaders on both sides reported their experiences and told about them—often in print— many times after the war. Several hundred eyewitness reports have been published recording battle experiences or camp experiences of troops on both sides. The following passages are excerpts from Hardtack and Coffee, *a book written long after the War. John D. Billings, the author, served with a Massachusetts artillery unit in the Army of the Potomac. His descriptions of everyday Army life in the Union forces represent service in the best supplied and outfitted units of the Army. Conditions in western Union armies, and in the Confederate forces,*

were seldom as comfortable as those Billings describes.

Drilling the Awkward Squad

Hancock told me that the Twentieth Massachusetts Regiment had received an accession of about two hundred German recruits only two or three days before the battle, not one of whom could understand the orders of their commanding officers. It can be easily imagined how much time and patience would be required to mould such subjects as those into intelligent, reliable soldiery.

But outside of this class there were scores of men that spoke English who were incorrigible in almost every military respect. Whenever they were out with a squad—usually the "awkward squad"—for drill, they made business lively enough for the sergeant in charge. When they stood in the rear rank their loftiest ambition seemed to be to walk up the backs of their file-leaders, and then they would insist that it was the file-leaders who were out of step. Members of the much abused front rank often had occasion to wish that the regulation thirteen inches from breast to back might be extended to as many feet; but when the march was backward in line, these front rank men would get square with their persecutors in the rear.

To see such men attempt to change step while marching was no mean show. I can think of nothing more apt to compare it with than the game of Hop Scotch, in which the player hops first on one foot, then on both; or to the blue jay, which, in uttering one of its notes, jumps up and down on the limb; and if such a squad under full headway were surprised with a sudden command to halt, they went all to pieces. It was no easy task to align them, for each man had a line of his own, and they would crane their heads out to see the buttons on the breast of the second man, to such an extent that the sergeant, might have exclaimed, with the Irish sergeant under like circumstances, "O be-gorra, what a bint row! Come out here, lads, and take a look at yoursels!"

The awkward squad excelled equally in the infantry manual-of-arms. Indeed, they displayed more real individuality here, I think, than in the marchings, probably because it was the more noticeable. At a "shoulder" their muskets pointed at all angles, from forty-five degrees to a vertical. In the attempt to change to a "carry," a part of them would drop their muskets. At an "order," no two of the butts reached the ground together, and if a man could not always drop his musket on his *own* toe he was a pretty correct shot with it on the toe of his neighbor. But, with all their awkwardness and slowness at becoming acquainted with a soldier's duties, the recruits of the earlier years in time of need behaved manfully. They made a poor exhibition on dress parade, but could generally be counted on when more serious work was in hand. Sometimes, when they made an unusually poor display on drill or parade, they were punished—unjustly it may have been, for what they could not help—by being subjected to the knapsack drill, of which I have already spoken.

It was a prudential circumstance that the war came to an end when it did, for the quality of the material that was sent to the army in 1864 and 1865 was for the most part of no credit or value to any arm of the service. The period of enlistments from promptings of patriotism had gone by, and the man who entered the army solely from mercenary motives was of little or no assistance to that army when it was in need of valiant men, so that the chief burden and responsibility of the closing wrestle for the mastery necessarily fell largely on the shoulders of the men who bared their breasts for the first time in 1861, '62, and '63.

I have thus far spoken of a recruit in the usual sense of a man enlisted to fill a vacancy in an organization already in the field. But this seems the proper connection in which to say something of the experiences of men who enlisted with original regiments, and went out with the same in '61 and '62. In many respects, their education was obtained under as great adversity as fell to the lot of recruits. In *some* respects, I think their lot was harder. They knew absolutely nothing of war. They were stirred by patriotic impulse to enlist and crush out treason, and hurl back at once in the teeth of the enemy the charge of cowardice and accept their challenge to the arbitrament of war. These patriots planned just two moves for the execution of this desire: first, to enlist—to join some company or regiment; second, to have that regiment transferred at once to the immediate front of the Rebels, where they could fight it out and settle the troubles without delay. Their intense fervor *to do something right away* to humble the haughty enemy, made them utterly unmindful that they must first go to school and learn the art of war from its very beginnings, and right at that point their sorrows began.

I think the greatest cross they bore consisted in being compelled to settle down in home camp, as some regiments did for months, waiting to be sent off. Here they were in sight of home in many cases, yet outside of its comforts to a large extent; soldiers, yet out of danger; bidding their friends a tender adieu to-day, because they are to leave them—perhaps forever—to-morrow. But the morrow comes, and finds them still in camp.

Army Rations

Here is just what a single ration comprised, that is,

what a soldier was entitled to have in one day. He should have had twelve ounces of pork or bacon, *or* one pound four ounces of salt or fresh beef; one pound six ounces of soft bread or flour, *or* one pound of hard bread, *or* one pound four ounces of corn meal. With every hundred such rations there should have been distributed one peck of beans or peas; ten pounds of rice or hominy; ten pounds of green coffee, *or* eight pounds of roasted and ground, *or* one pound eight ounces of tea; fifteen pounds of sugar; one pound four ounces of candles; four pounds of soap; two quarts of salt; four quarts of vinegar; four ounces of pepper; a half bushel of potatoes when practicable, and one quart of molasses. Desiccated potatoes or desiccated compressed vegetables might be substituted for the beans, peas, rice, hominy, or fresh potatoes. Vegetables, the dried fruits, pickles, and pickled cabbage were occasionally issued to prevent scurvy, but in small quantities.

But the ration thus indicated was a camp ration. Here is the *marching* ration; one pound of hard bread; three-fourths of a pound of salt pork, or one and one-fourth pounds of fresh meat; sugar, coffee, and salt. The beans, rice, soap, candles, etc., were not issued to the soldier when on the march, as he could not carry them; but, singularly enough, as it seems to me, unless the troops went into camp before the end of the month, where a regular depot of supplies might be established from which the other parts of the rations could be issued, they were *forfeited*, and *reverted to the government*—an injustice to the rank and file, who, through no fault of their own, were thus cut off from a part of their allowance at the time when they were giving most liberally of their strength and perhaps of their very heart's blood. It was possible for company commanders, and *for no one else* to receive the equivalent of these missing parts of the ration *in cash* from the brigade commissary, with the expectation that when thus received it would be distributed among the rank and file to whom it belonged. Many officers did not care to trouble themselves with it, but many others did, and—forgot to pay it out afterwards. I have yet to learn of the first company whose members ever received any revenue from such a source, although the name of *Company Fund* is a familiar one to every veteran.

The commissioned officers fared better in camp than the enlisted men. Instead of drawing rations after the manner of the latter, they had a certain cash allowance, according to rank, with which to purchase supplies from the Brigade Commissary, an official whose province was to keep stores on sale for their convenience. The monthly allowance of officers in infantry, including servants, was as follows: Colonel, six rations worth $56, and two servants; Lieutenant-Colonel, five rations worth $45, and two servants; Major, four rations worth $36, and two servants; Captain, four rations worth $36, and one servant; First and Second Lieutenants, jointly, the same as Captains. In addition to the above, the field officers had an allowance of horses and forage proportioned to their rank.

I will speak of the rations more in detail, beginning with the hard bread, or, to use the name by which it was known in the Army of the Potomac, *Hardtack*. What was hardtack? It was a plain flour-and-water biscuit. Two which I have in my possession as mementos measure three and one-eighth by two and seven-eighths inches, and are nearly half an inch thick. Although these biscuits were furnished to organizations by weight, they were dealt out to the men by number, nine constituting a ration in some regiments, and ten in others; but there were usually enough for those who wanted more, as some men would not draw them. While hardtack was nutritious, yet a hungry man could eat his ten in a short time and still be hungry. When they were poor and fit objects for the soldiers' wrath, it was due to one of three conditions: First, they may have been so hard that they could not be bitten; it then required a very strong blow of the fist to break them. The cause of this hardness it would be difficult for one not an expert to determine. This variety certainly well deserved their name. They could not be *soaked* soft. . . .

The second condition was when they were mouldy or wet, as sometimes happened, and should not have been given to the soldiers. I think this condition was often due to their having been boxed up too soon after baking. It certainly was frequently due to exposure to the weather. It was no uncommon sight to see thousands of boxes of hard bread piled up at some railway station or other place used as a base of supplies, where they were only imperfectly sheltered from the weather, and too often not sheltered at all. The failure of inspectors to do their full duty was one reason that so many of this sort reached the rank and file of the service.

The third condition was when from storage they had become infested with maggots and weevils. These weevils were, in my experience, more abundant than the maggots. They were a little, slim, brown bug an eighth of an inch in length, and were great *bores* on a small scale, having the ability to completely riddle the hardtack. I believe they never interfered with the hardest variety.

When the bread was mouldy or moist, it was thrown away and made good at the next drawing, so that the men were not the losers; but in the case of its being infested with the weevils, they had to stand it as a rule. . . .

Whenever the army made a move its supply of fresh meat went along too. Who had charge of it? Men were detailed for the business from the various regiments, who acted both as butchers and drovers, and were ex-

cused from all other duty. When a halt was made for the night, some of the steers would be slaughtered, and the meat furnished to the troops upon presentation of the proper requisitions by quartermasters. The butcher killed his victims with a rifle. The killing was not always done at night. It often took place in the morning or forenoon, and the men received their rations in time to cook for dinner.

The manner in which these cattle were taken along was rather interesting. One might very naturally suppose that they would be driven along the road just as they are driven in any neighborhood; but such was not exactly the case. The troops and trains must use the roads, and so the cattle must needs travel elsewhere, which they did. Every herd had a steer that was used both as a pack animal and a leader. As a pack animal he bore the equipments and cooking utensils of the drovers. He was as docile as an old cow or horse, and could be led or called fully as readily. By day he was preceded in his lead by the herdsman in charge, on horseback, while other herdsmen brought up the rear. It was necessary to keep the herd along with the troops for two reasons—safety and convenience; and, as they could not use the road, they skirted the fields and woods, only a short remove from the highways, and picked their way as best they could.

By night one of the herdsmen went ahead of the herd on foot, making a gentle hallooing sound which the sagacious steer on lead steadily followed, and was in turn faithfully followed by the rest of the herd. The herdsman's course lay sometimes through the open, but often through the woods, which made the hallooing sound necessary as a guide to keep the herd from straying. They kept nearer the road at night than in the day, partly for safety's sake, and partly to take advantage of the light from huge camp-fires which detachments of cavalry, that preceded the army, kindled at intervals to light the way, making them nearer together in woods and swamps than elsewhere. Even then these drovers often had a thorny and difficult path to travel in picking their way through underbrush and brambles.

Such a herd got its living off the country in the summer, but not in the winter. It was a sad sight to see these animals, which followed the army so patiently, sacrificed one after the other until but a half-dozen were left. When the number had been reduced to this extent, they seemed to realize the fate in store for them, and it often took the butcher some time before he could succeed in facing one long enough to shoot him. His aim was at the curl of the hair between the eyes, and they would avert their lowered heads whenever he raised his rifle, until, at last, his quick eye brought them to the ground.

From the manner in which I have spoken of these herds, it may be inferred that there was a common herd for the whole army; but such was not the case. The same system prevailed here as elsewhere. For example, when the army entered the Wilderness with three days' rations of meat in their haversacks, the fresh meat to accompany the other three days' rations, which they had stowed in their knapsacks, was driven along in division herds. The remainder of the meat ration which they required to last them for the sixteen days during which it was expected the army would be away from a base of supplies was driven as corps herds. In addition to these there was a general or army herd to fall back upon when necessary to supply the corps herds, but this was always at the base of supplies. Probably from eight to ten thousand head of cattle accompanied the army across the Rapidan, when it entered upon the Wilderness Campaign.

2. Hardtack and Coffee *is a primary source, since it was written by a person who actually took part in the events he recorded. But as we have noted, Billings wrote it a long time after the events, and historians are inclined to regard such later testimony as less reliable than a diary or journal, kept day by day as the events happened. Letters written soon after an event by people who had taken part in it are also good primary sources. The following letter was written by James Potts—a 19-year-old private of the 2nd Pennsylvania—during a lull in the fighting near Richmond, Virginia, in 1862. It was the last letter he ever wrote, for he was killed two days later during the battle of White Oak Swamp.*

The letter was preserved in a family collection of papers and pictures, and we are permitted to print it for the first time by its present possessor, Mr. Harry Gill. The original spelling and sentence structure have been kept but paragraphs have been introduced. Uncertain readings have been indicated by brackets around words.

June 28, 1862
Camp before Richmond

Dear Brothers & Sisters

I am happy to be able to write to you that though having been in the thickest of the fight I am alive and well. On Tuesday we went on Picket and came off on Thursday Morning at twelve o'clock. We were in line and started off about twelve miles towards Hanover Court House, skirmishing all the way. We then fell back to Mechanicsville. We took up our position in a field on the verge of a woods to support a battery which was on our left.

Then the fight commenced and the balls to fly around us. It grew hotter and hotter until an aid came to let us know that three Regiments of Rebels were coming through the Woods to take the battery. Just then a rather unearthly yell came on us. We waited till they were nearer to see them and then we cheered and gave them a volley and received one in return which laid two of our company low, one of them just on my left. Then we had it hot and heavy.

They charged on us and planted their flag just out of the wood. We drove them back and charged through the wood where we received the fire of our own battery. We fought from three o'clock till Sundown, maintaining our ground and saved the battery. We received the cheers and thanks of the battery and the praise of our General.

I can only give you a few outlines of the engagement for we are only resting a little, for there's fightin in our front. We are the color company, and the colors are on the left. I am little and of course am on the left, right underneath the colors. After it was over there was 17 bullet holes in the flag. I don't see how I escaped. The bullets took wind out of my ear, whizzing past front and rear, for some of them were [illegible] in my rear and did not care how they fired.

We slept on the battlefield, listening to the groans of the wounded in the early part of the fight. I stepped into the woods to take aim, and sees a big devil [shrubbing] behind a tree. I put my piece to his ear and made him drop his and then grabs him by the collar hauls him out and took him to the Captain, who took out his Pistol and was going to shoot him, when I gave him a shove back and asked him if he would kill a prisoner. This sobered him and he ordered a man to take him to the rear.

At daybreak the ball opened again but not near us. The whole of our troops evacuated the place and fell back to this place. Here we rested till afternoon when the fight became general. All I can tell you of this fight is we went into the woods with a cheer and took the place of a regiment that were fighting the enemy in the woods opposite. We fought about an hour with our own men firing upon us on our left before we went in. It was nothing but mob fighting, the enemy being demoralized by bad generalship. I look around and but about fifty of our regiment left, the Colonel and staff gone, but the Colors were there and we stuck to them till the [Goslines] Zouaves came and relieved us.

We fell in line again and sat down, when our own men firing upon each other raised a panic, and there worse than a Bull Run ensued. The men got mixed up and rushed pell mell by thousands down the road. We stuck together with a few others and a few reinforcements came and regained our lost ground. By this time it was dark and of course it stopped. This morning we crossed the Chickahominy and are now waiting for another fight. I keep up my spirits and appetite.

JAMES POTTS

3. Officers and enlisted men often had different views of military affairs, with the higher ranking officers usually better informed about where the troops were going and what their tasks were supposed to be. Even high-ranking officers sometimes engaged in practical jokes on each other, as reported in the first of these two passages from Carl Schurz's Autobiography. (*Like many other German-American immigrants, Schurz joined the Union Army. He became a Major General. His* Autobiography *includes many details of his military career, and of his later distinguished career as a U.S. Senator and Secretary of the Interior.*)

A "General's-eye" view of the hardships and sufferings of men on the march then follows. Schurz is describing part of the campaign in eastern Tennessee during the winter of 1863-1864, at a time when Union equipment, supplies, and communications were far superior to those of the Confederate forces, which must have suffered even more in the winter maneuvering.

I noticed a rather decent-looking house by the roadside, from the chimney of which a blue cloud of smoke curled up. In the front yard two orderlies were holding saddled horses. I concluded that there must be general officers inside, and, possibly, something to eat. Seduced by this thought, I dismounted, and found within, toasting their feet by a crackling wood fire, General Sherman and General Jefferson C. Davis, who commanded a division in the Fourteenth Corps attached to Sherman's command— the same General Jeff. C. Davis, who, at the beginning of the war, had attracted much attention by the killing of General Nelson in the Galt House at Louisville. General Sherman kindly invited me to sit with them, and I did so. A few minutes later General Howard entered. He enjoyed the reputation of great piety, and went by the name of "the Christian soldier." General Sherman greeted him in his brusque way, exclaiming: "Glad to see you, Howard! Sit down by the fire! Damned cold this morning!" Howard, who especially abhorred the use of "swear words," answered demurely: "Yes, General, it is *quite* cold this morning." Sherman may have noticed a slight touch of reproof in this answer. At any rate, I observed a wink he gave

General Davis with his left eye, while a sarcastic smile flitted across his features. It became at once clear what it meant, for Davis instantly, while talking about some indifferent subject, began to intersperse his speech with such a profusion of "damns" and the like, when there was not the slightest occasion for it, that one might have supposed him to be laboring under the intensest excitement, while really he was in perfectly cold blood. In fact, as I afterward learned, General Davis was noted for having mastered the vocabulary of the "Army in Flanders" more completely than any other man of his rank. Howard made several feeble attempts to give a different turn to the conversation, but in vain. Encouraged by repeated winks and also a few sympathetic remarks from Sherman, Davis inexorably continued the lurid flow of his infernalisms, until finally Howard, with distress painted all over his face, got up and left; whereupon Sherman and Davis broke out in a peal of laughter. And when I ventured upon a remark about Howard's sufferings, Sherman said: "Well, that Christian soldier business is all right in its place. But he needn't put on airs when we are among ourselves."

A few weeks later, when the Knoxville campaign was over, Sherman addressed a letter to Howard thanking him, most deservedly, for the excellent services rendered by him on that expedition, and praising him as "one who mingled so gracefully and perfectly the polished Christian gentleman and the prompt, zealous, and gallant soldier."

On December 5th, not many miles from Knoxville, we were informed that Longstreet had not waited for the arrival of our forces of relief, but effected his retreat toward Virginia. Thus our expedition had accomplished its purpose. It was a victory achieved by the soldiers' legs. We were allowed a day's rest, and then started on our way back, the same 120 miles and a little more, to our old camp in Lookout Valley. We could march more leisurely, but the return seemed harder than the advance had been. There was not the same spirit in it. Our regular food supplies were entirely exhausted. We had "to live upon the country." We impressed what live stock we could, which was by no means always sufficient. The surrounding population, Union people, were friendly, but poor. Roasted wheat and corn had to serve for coffee, molasses found on the farms, for sugar. But far worse than this, the clothing of the men was in tatters, the shoes worn and full of holes. Perhaps one-fourth of the men had none at all. They protected their feet by winding rags around them. Their miseries were increased by occurrences like this: One day our march was unusually difficult. We passed through a hilly country. The roads were in many places like dry, washed-out beds of mountain torrents, full of boulders, large and small. The artillery horses could not possibly pull their pieces and caissons over these obstacles. They had to be unhitched, and infantry detachments were called upon to help the artillerymen lift their guns and appurtenances over the rocks. This operation had to be repeated several times during the day. Thus the marching column was stopped time and again without affording the soldiers any real rest. On the contrary, such irregular stoppages for an uncertain length of time are apt to annoy and fatigue the marching men all the more. At last, toward dusk of the evening, I struck on our route a large meadow-ground through which a clear stream of water flowed. There was plenty of wood for fires near by. The spot seemed to be made for camping. My orders as to how far I was to march, were not quite definite. I was to receive further instructions on the way. My troops having been on their feet from early morning and having marched under the difficulties described, were tired beyond measure. They just dragged themselves painfully along. I resolved to rest them on this favored spot if permitted, and despatched a staff officer to corps-headquarters, two or three miles ahead, to obtain that permission. Meanwhile, waiting for an answer which I did not doubt would be favorable, camping places were assigned to the different brigades.

After the lapse of about an hour, when a large part of my command had come in and were beginning to build fires and to prepare such food as they had, my officer returned from corps-headquarters, with the positive order that I must, without loss of time, continue my march and proceed about three miles farther, where a camping place would be assigned to me. I thought there must be some mistake, as, according to reports, there was no enemy within many miles, and I despatched a second staff officer to represent to corps headquarters that to start my men again would be downright cruelty to them, and I begged that they be allowed to stay for the night where they were, unless there were real necessity for their marching on. In due time the answer came that there was such necessity. Now nothing was to be done but to obey instantly. My division bugler sounded the signal. There arose something like a sullen groan from the bivouac, but the men emptied the water, which was just beginning to boil in their kettles, upon the ground, and promptly fell into line. We had hardly been on the way half an hour when a fearful thunderstorm broke upon us. The rain came down in sheets like a cloudburst, driving right into our faces. In a few minutes we were all drenched to the skin. I wore a stout cavalry overcoat with cape, well lined with flannel, over my uniform. In an incredibly short time I felt the cold water trickle down my body.

My riding boots were soon full to overflowing. One may imagine the sorry plight of the poor fellows in rags. They had to suffer, too, not only from the water coming down from above, but also from water coming from below. We were again passing through a hilly district. The road ran along the bottom of a deep valley with high ridges on both sides. From these the rain-water rushed down in streams, transforming the road into a swelling torrent, the water reaching up to the knees of the men, and higher. Meanwhile the thunder was rolling, the lightning flashing, and the poor sufferers stumbling over unseen boulders under the water, and venting their choler in wild imprecations.

At last, after having struggled on in this way for about two hours, we emerged from the wooded hills into a more open country—at least I judged so, as the darkness seemed to be a little relieved. The storm had ceased. Riding at the head of my column, I ran against a horseman standing in the middle of the road. "What troops are these?" he asked. "Third Division, Eleventh Corps." He made himself known as an officer of the corps staff. My advance patrol had somehow missed him and gone astray. He brought me an order to put my command into camp "right here on both sides of the road." I asked him what it was that made my march in this dreadful night necessary, but he did not know. It was so dark that I could not distinguish anything beyond half a dozen feet. I did discover, however, that on "both sides of the road" there were plowed fields. There was water from the rain standing in the furrows and the ridges were softened into a thick mire. And there my men were to camp. My staff officers scattered themselves to find a more convenient, or less dismal, location for the men, but they soon returned, having, in the gloom, run into camps occupied by other troops. Nothing remained but to stay where we were. The regiments were distributed as well as possible in the darkness. The men could not stretch themselves out on the ground because the ground was covered or soaked with water. They had to sit down on their knapsacks, if they had any, or on their heels, and try to catch some sleep in that position. About midnight the wind shifted suddenly and blew bitterly cold from the north, so bitterly, indeed, that after a while our outer garments began to freeze stiff on our bodies. I thought I could hear the men's teeth chatter. I am sure mine did. There we sat, now and then dropping into a troubled doze, waiting for day to dawn. As soon as the first gray of the morning streaked the horizon, there was a general stir. The men rose and tossed and swung their limbs to get their blood into circulation. The feet of not a few were frozen fast in the soil, and when they pulled them up, they left the soles of such shoes as they had, sticking in the hardened mud. The pools of water left by the rain were covered with solid crusts of ice, and the cold north wind was still blowing. I started my command as soon as possible in order to get the men into motion, intending to have them prepare their breakfast further on in some more congenial spot. The ranks were considerably thinned, a large number of the men having strayed away from the column and trudged on in the darkness of the night. As we proceeded we saw them crawl out from houses or barns or sheds or heaps of cornstraw or whatever protection from the weather they had been able to find. The hard-frozen and stony road was marked with streaks of blood from the feet of the poor fellows who limped painfully along.

And finally it turned out that all this had been for nothing. Headquarters had been disturbed by a rumor that the enemy was attempting a cavalry raid in our direction, which might have made a drawing together of our forces necessary. But the rumor proved quite unfounded. I have told the story of that dismal night so elaborately to show my reader that even in an ordinary campaign, not to be compared with the retreat of Napoleon's army from the Russian snow-fields, soldiers are sometimes exposed to hardships not always necessary, which in their effects are now and then no less destructive than powder and lead.

4. At sea, the war involved far-flung blockade duty for Union naval vessels, and much attempted blockade-running by ships in the service of the Confederacy. The best known Confederate warship was C.S.S. Alabama. *She was a commerce-raiding cruiser, built in England, and designed to capture and destroy Yankee merchant shipping. During her entire Confederate career, she was commanded by Captain Raphael Semmes. The following extracts from his book* Service Afloat *are, first, a description of* Alabama's *appearance and virtues; second, the commander's report to Flag-Officer (Admiral) Samuel Barron of the final engagement of* Alabama *with U.S.S. Kearsarge.*

I departed on the 13th of August, 1862, in the steamer *Bahama* to join the *Alabama.* Captain James D. Bulloch of the Confederate States Navy, a Georgian who had been bred in the old service but who had retired from it some years before the war to engage in the steam-packet service, accompanied me. Bulloch had contracted for and superintended the building of the *Alabama,* and was now going with me, to be present at the christening of his bantling. I am indebted to him, as

well as the Messrs. Laird (*the British shipbuilding firm*) for a very perfect ship of her class.

She was of about 900 tons burden, 230 feet in length, 32 feet in breadth, 20 feet in depth, and drew, when provisioned and coaled for a cruise, 15 feet of water. Her model was of the most perfect symmetry, and she sat upon the water with the lightness and grace of a swan. She was barkentine rigged with long lower masts which enabled her to carry large fore-and-aft sails, as jibs and try-sails, which are of so much importance to a steamer, in so many emergencies. Her sticks were of the best yellow pine, that would bend in a gale like a willow wand, without breaking, and her rigging was of the best of Swedish iron wire. The scantling of the vessel was light compared with vessels of her class in the Federal Navy, but this was scarcely a disadvantage, as she was designed as a scourge of the enemy's commerce, rather than for battle. She was simply to defend herself if defence should become necessary.

Her engine was of three-hundred horsepower, and she had attached an apparatus for condensing from the vapor of sea water, all the fresh water that her crew might require. She was a perfect steamer and a perfect sailing ship at the same time, neither of her two modes of locomotion being at all dependent upon the other. . . . The *Alabama* was so constructed, that in fifteen minutes her propeller could be detached from the shaft, and lifted in a well contrived for the purpose, sufficiently high out of the water not to be an impediment to her speed. When this was done, and her sails spread, she was to all intents and purposes a sailing ship.

My official report of the engagement, addressed to Flag-Officer Barron, in Paris, . . . was written at Southampton, England, two days after the battle.

SOUTHAMPTON, June 21, 1864

SIR: I have the honor to inform you that in accordance with my intention as previously announced to you, I steamed out of the harbor of Cherbourg between nine and ten o'clock on the morning of the 19th of June for the purpose of engaging the enemy's steamer *Kearsarge,* which had been lying off and on the port for several days previously. After clearing the harbor, we descried the enemy with his head off shore at the distance of about seven miles. We were three quarters of an hour in coming up with him. I had previously pivoted my guns to starboard and made all preparations for engaging the enemy on that side. When within about a mile and a quarter of the enemy, he suddenly wheeled and, bringing his head in shore, presented his starboard battery to me. By this time we were distant about one mile from each other, when I opened on him with solid shot to which he replied in a few minutes and the action became active on both sides. The enemy now pressed his ship under a full head of steam, and to prevent our passing each other too speedily, and to keep our respective broadsides bearing, it became necessary to fight in a circle; the two ships steaming around a common center and preserving a distance from each other of from three quarters to half a mile. When we got within good shell range we opened upon him with shell. Some ten or fifteen minutes after the commencement of the action, our spanker-gaff was shot away and our ensign came down by the run. This was immediately replaced by another at the mizzen-masthead. The firing now became very hot, and the enemy's shot and shell soon began to tell upon our hull, knocking down, killing, and disabling a number of men, at the same time, in different parts of the ship. Perceiving that our shell, though apparently exploding against the enemy's sides, were doing him but little damage, I returned to solid-shot firing, and from that time onward alternated with shot and shell.

After the lapse of about one hour and ten minutes, our ship was ascertained to be in a sinking condition, the enemy's shell having exploded in our side and between decks, opening large apertures through which the water rushed with great rapidity. For some few minutes I had hopes of being able to reach the French coast, for which purpose I gave the ship all steam and set such of the fore-and-aft sails as were available. The ship filled so rapidly, however, that before we had made much progress, the fires were extinguished in the furnaces, and we were evidently on the point of sinking. I now hauled down my colors to prevent the further destruction of life and dispatched a boat to inform the enemy of our condition. Although we were now but 400 yards from each other, the enemy fired upon me five times after my colors had been struck. It is charitable to suppose that a ship of war of a Christian nation could not have done this intentionally. We now directed all our exertions toward saving the wounded and such of the boys of the ship as were unable to swim. These were dispatched in my quarter-boats, the only boats remaining to me; the waist-boats having been torn to pieces. Some twenty minutes after my furnace fires had been extinguished, and when the ship was on the point of settling, every man, in obedience to a previous order which had been given the crew, jumped overboard and endeavored to save himself. There was no appearance of any boat coming to me from the enemy until after my ship went down. Fortunately, however, the steam-yacht _Deerhound_ owned by a gentleman of Lancashire, England— Mr. John Lancaster—who was himself on board,

steamed up in the midst of my drowning men and rescued a number of both officers and men from the water. I was fortunate enough myself thus to escape to the shelter of the neutral flag together with about forty others all told. About this time the _Kearsarge_ sent one, and then, tardily, another boat.

Accompanying, you will find lists of the killed and wounded, and of those who were picked up by the _Deerhound_; the remainder, there is reason to hope, were picked up by the enemy and by a couple of French pilot boats which were also fortunately near the scene of action. At the end of the engagement it was discovered by those of our officers who went alongside of the enemy's ship with the wounded that her midship section on both sides was thoroughly iron-coated; this having been done with chains constructed for the purpose, placed perpendicularly from the rail to the water's edge, the whole covered over by a thin outer planking which gave no indication of the armour beneath. This planking had been ripped off in every direction by our shot and shell, the chain broken and indented in many places and forced partly into the ship's side. She was effectually guarded, however, in this section, from penetration. The enemy was much damaged in other parts, but to what extent it is now impossible to say. It is believed he is badly crippled.

My officers and men behaved steadily and gallantly, and though they have lost their ship, they have not lost honor. Where all behaved so well, it would be invidious to particularize, but I cannot deny myself the pleasure of saying that Mr. Kell, my first lieutenant, deserves great credit for the fine condition in which the ship went into action with regard to her battery, magazine and shell rooms, and that he rendered me great assistance, by his coolness and judgment as the fight proceeded. The enemy was heavier than myself, both in ship, battery, and crew; but I did not know until the action was over that she was also ironclad. Our total loss in killed and wounded is 30, to wit: 9 killed and 21 wounded.

5. _Probably the most famous land campaign of the Civil War was the famous "March to the Sea" by Union forces under General William Tecumseh Sherman. Sherman's army first captured Atlanta, Georgia. Cutting himself off from regular lines of supplies, Sherman then led his army across Georgia to Savannah on the Atlantic Ocean. A wide path was devastated across Georgia, in which railroads, bridges, livestock and other property were all destroyed. Jefferson Davis, President of the Confederacy, was bitterly criticized because of defense plans that went wrong and seemed to open a gap_

for Sherman. Sherman himself was also bitterly criti-
cized for the burning and destruction of property
across Georgia. Both men wrote about the march
after the war. Both accounts would be classified as
primary sources of history, but historians might won-
der how much to rely on either. The authors had
reason to put forward the best possible interpreta-
tion of their own activities.

President Davis's account is from his book The
Rise of the Confederate Government, *published in*
1881; General Sherman's narrative is from the sec-
ond edition of his Memoirs.

Davis Describes the Campaign to Stop Sherman

It was not to be expected that General Sherman
would remain long inactive. The rapidity with which he
was collecting recruits and supplies at Atlanta indicated
that he contemplated a movement farther south, making
Atlanta a secondary base. To rescue Georgia, save the
Gulf states, and retain possession of the lines of communication upon which we depended for the supplies
of our armies in the field, an effort to arrest the further
progress of the enemy was necessary; to this end the
railroads in his rear must be effectually torn up, the
great railroad bridge over the Tennessee River at
Bridgeport destroyed, and the communication between
Atlanta, Chattanooga, and Nashville completely cut off.
If this could be accomplished, all the fruits of Sherman's successful campaign in Georgia would be
blighted, his capture of Atlanta would become a barren
victory, and he would probably be compelled to make
a retreat toward Tennessee, at every mile of which he
might be harassed by our army. Or, should he, relying
on Atlanta as a base, push forward through Georgia
to the Atlantic coast, our army, having cut his communications north of Atlanta, could fall upon his rear,
and, with the advantages of a better knowledge of the
country, of the surrounding devoted population, of the
auxiliary force to be expected under the circumstances,
and our superiority in cavalry, it was not unreasonable
to hope that retributive justice might overtake the ruthless invader.

My first object was to fill up the depleted ranks of
the army, to bring the absentees and deserters back to
the ranks, and to induce the governor and state officials
to cooperate heartily and earnestly with the Confederate
government in all measures that might be found necessary to give the proposed movement a reasonable prospect of success.

The avowed objection of the governor of Georgia to
the acts of Congress providing for raising troops by
conscription, and his persistent opposition to the authority of the Confederate executive to appoint the generals
and staff officers of the volunteer organizations received
from the states to form the provisional army of the
Confederacy, caused him frequently to obstruct the government officials in the discharge of their duty, to withhold the assistance which he might be justly expected
to render, and, in the contemplation of his own views
of the duties and obligations of the executive and legislative departments of the general government, to lose
sight of those important objects, the attainment of which
an exalted patriotism might have told him depended on
the cooperation of the state and Confederate governments. The inordinate exemption from military service
as state officials of men between the ages of eighteen
and forty-five (it was estimated that the number of ex-
empts in November, 1864, amounted to fifteen thousand) was an abuse which I endeavored in vain to
correct. . . .

On November 16th Sherman left his entrenchments
around Atlanta and, dividing his army into two bodies,
each from twenty-five to thirty thousand strong, the
one followed the Georgia Railroad in the direction of
Augusta and the other took the line of the Macon and
Western Railroad to Jonesboro. Avoiding Macon and
Augusta, they passed through central Georgia, taking
Milledgeville on the way, marching in compact column
and advancing with extreme caution, although opposed
only by detachments of Wheeler's cavalry and a few
hastily formed regiments of raw militia. Partial efforts
were made to obstruct and destroy the roads in the front
and on the flanks of the invading army, and patriotic
appeals by prominent citizens were made to the people
to remove all provisions from its path, but no formidable opposition was made, except at the railroad bridge
over the Oconee, where Wheeler, with a portion of his
command and few militia, held the enemy in check for
two or three days. With his small force, General
Wheeler daringly and persistently harassed, and, when
practicable, delayed the enemy's advance, attacking and
defeating exposed detachments, deterring his foragers
from venturing far from the main body, defending all
cities and towns along the railroad lines and affording
protection to depots of supplies, arsenals, and other
important government works. The report of his operations from November 14th to December 20th displays
a dash, activity, vigilance, and consummate skill which
justly entitle him to a prominent place on the roll of
great cavalry leaders. By his indomitable energy, operating on all sides of Sherman's columns, he was enabled
to keep the government and commanders of our troops
advised of the enemy's movement, and, by preventing
foraging parties from leaving the main body, he saved
from spoilation all but a narrow tract of country, and

from the torch millions worth of property which would otherwise certainly have been consumed.

It soon became manifest that Savannah was General Sherman's objective point. That city was occupied by General W. J. Hardee with about eighteen thousand men, a considerable portion of which was composed as militia, local troops, reserves, and hastily organized regiments and battalions made up of convalescents from the hospitals and artisans from the government shops. On December 10th the enemy's columns reached the immediate vicinity of Savannah, and on the 12th they occupied a semicircular line extending from the Savannah River to the Savannah and Gulf Railroad. The defences of the city were strong, the earthworks and other fortifications were flanked by inundated rice swamps extending across the peninsula formed by the Savannah and Ogeechee rivers, and the causeways leading through them were well fortified by works mounting heavy guns. With a sufficient force to occupy his long lines of defense, General Hardee could have sustained a protracted siege. The city was amply supplied, and its lines of communication were still open. Although Sherman had reached Savannah, he had not yet opened communication with the Federal fleet. Fort McAllister, situated on the right bank of the Ogeechee, about six miles from Ossabaw Sound, was a serious obstacle in his way, as it was a work of considerable strength, mounting twenty-one heavy guns, a deep and wide ditch extending along its front, with every avenue of approach swept by the guns mounted upon its bastions. The fort was held by a garrison of two hundred fifty men under the command of experienced officers. The work was attacked on the evening of the 13th, and carried by assault after a short and feeble resistance. In consequence of the loss of this fort, Sherman speedily opened communication with the fleet, and became perfectly secure against any future want of supplies. This also enabled him to obtain heavy ordnance for use against the city. He proceeded immediately to take measures to invest Savannah, and in a few days had succeeded in doing so on every side of the city except that fronting the river. While Hardee's troops had not yielded a single position or lost a foot of ground, with the exception of Fort McAllister, when, on December 20th, he discovered that Sherman had put heavy siege guns in position near enough to bombard the city, and that the enemy was threatening Union Causeway, which extends across the large swamps that lie between Savannah and Charleston, and offered the only practicable line of retreat, he determined to evacuate the place rather than expose the city and its inhabitants to bombardment. He also thought holding it had ceased to be of any special importance, and that troops could do more valuable service in the field. Accordingly, on the night of December 20th, having destroyed the navy yard, the ironclads, and other government property, and razed the fortifications below the city, he withdrew his army and reached Hardeeville on the evening of the 22d, without hindrance or molestation on the part of the enemy.

Sherman Describes the Start of his March to the Sea.

The two general orders made for this march appear to me, even at this late day, so clear, emphatic, and well-digested, that no account of that historic event is perfect without them, and I give them entire, even at the seeming appearance of repetition; and, though they called for great sacrifice and labor on the part of the officers and men, I insist that these orders were obeyed as well as any similar orders ever were, by an army operating wholly in an enemy's country, and dispersed, as we necessarily were, during the subsequent period of nearly six months.

[Special Field Orders, No. 119].
Headquarters Military Division of the Mississippi,
   in the Field, Kingston, Georgia, *November* 8, 1864.
The general commanding deems it proper at this time to inform the officers and men of the Fourteenth, Fifteenth, Seventeenth, and Twentieth Corps, that he has organized them into an army for a special purpose, well known to the War Department and to General Grant. It is sufficient for you to know that it involves a departure from our present base, and a long and difficult march to a new one. All the chances of war have been considered and provided for, as far as human sagacity can. All he asks of you is to maintain that discipline, patience, and courage, which have characterized you in the past; and he hopes, through you, to strike a blow at our enemy that will have a material effect in producing what we all so much desire, his complete overthrow. Of all things, the most important is, that the men, during marches and in camp, keep their places and do not scatter about as stragglers or foragers, to be picked up by a hostile people in detail. It is also of the utmost importance that our wagons should not be loaded with any thing but provisions and ammunition. All surplus servants, non-combatants, and refugees, should now go to the rear, and none should be encouraged to encumber us on the march. At some future time we will be able to provide for the poor whites and blacks who seek to escape the bondage under which they are now suffering. With these few simple, cautions, he hopes to lead you to achievements equal in importance to those of the past.

   By order of Major-General W. T. Sherman,
      L. M. DAYTON, *Aide-de-Camp.*

[Special Field Orders, No. 120.]

Headquarters Military Division of the Mississippi,
in the Field, Kingston, Georgia, *November 9,* 1864.

1. For the purpose of military operations, this army is divided into two wings viz.:

The right wing, Major-General O. O. Howard commanding, composed of the Fifteenth and Seventeenth Corps; the left wing, Major-General H. W. Slocum commanding, composed of the Fourteenth and Twentieth Corps.

2. The habitual order of march will be, wherever practicable, by four roads, as nearly parallel as possible. and converging at points hereafter to be indicated in orders. The cavalry, Brigadier-General Kilpatrick commanding, will receive special orders from the commander-in-chief.

3. There will be no general train of supplies, but each corps will have its ammunition-train and provision-train, distributed habitually as follows: Behind each regiment should follow one wagon and one ambulance; behind each brigade should follow a due proportion of ammunition-wagons, provision-wagons, and ambulances. In case of danger, each corps commander should change this order of march, by having his advance and rear brigades unencumbered by wheels. The separate columns will start habitually at 7 A.M., and make about fifteen miles per day, unless otherwise fixed in orders.

4. The army will forage liberally in the country during the march. To this end, each brigade commander will organize a good and sufficient foraging party, under the command of one or more discreet officers, who will gather, near the route traveled, corn or forage of any kind, meat of any kind, vegetables, corn-meal, or whatever is needed by the command, aiming at all times to keep in the wagons at least ten days' provisions for his command, and three days' forage. Soldiers must not enter the dwellings of the inhabitants, or commit any trespass; but, during a halt or camp, they may be permitted to gather turnips, potatoes, and other vegetables, and to drive in stock in sight of their camp. To regular foraging-parties must be intrusted the gathering of provisions and forage, at any distance from the road traveled.

5. To corps commanders alone is intrusted the power to destroy mills, houses, cotton-gins, etc.; and for them this general principle is laid down: In districts and neighborhoods where the army is unmolested, no destruction of such property should be permitted; but should guerrillas or bushwhackers molest our march, or should the inhabitants burn bridges, obstruct roads, or otherwise manifest local hostility, then army commanders should order and enforce a devastation more or less relentless, according to the measure of such hostility.

6. As for horses, mules, wagons, etc., belonging to the inhabitants, the cavalry and artillery may appropriate freely and without limit; discriminating, however, between the rich, who are usually hostile, and the poor and industrious, usually neutral or friendly. Foraging-parties may also take mules or horses, to replace the jaded animals of their trains, or to serve as pack-mules for the regiments or brigades. In all foraging, of whatever kind, the parties engaged will refrain from abusive or threatening language, and may, where the officer in command thinks proper, give written certificates of the facts, but no receipts; and they will endeavor to leave with each family a reasonable portion for their maintenance.

7. Negroes who are able-bodied and can be of service to the several columns may be taken along; but each army commander will bear in mind that the question of supplies is a very important one, and that his first duty is to see to those who bear arms.

8. The organization, at once, of a good pioneer battalion for each army corps, composed if possible of negroes, should be attended to. This battalion should follow the advance-guard, repair roads and double them if possible, so that the columns will not be delayed after reaching bad places. Also, army commanders should practise the habit of giving the artillery and wagons the road, marching their troops on one side, and instruct their troops to assist wagons at steep hills or bad crossings of streams.

9. Captain O. M. Poe, chief-engineer, will assign to each wing of the army a pontoon-train, fully equipped and organized; and the commanders thereof will see to their being properly protected at all times.

By order of Major-General W. T. Sherman,
L. M. DAYTON, *Aide-de-Camp.*

The greatest possible attention had been given to the artillery and wagon trains. The number of guns had been reduced to sixty-five, or about one gun to each thousand men, and these were generally in batteries of four guns each.

Each gun, caisson, and forge, was drawn by four teams of horses. We had in all about twenty-five hundred wagons, with teams of six mules to each, and six hundred ambulances, with two horses to each. The loads were made comparatively light, about twenty-five hundred pounds net; each wagon carrying in addition the forage needed by its own team. Each soldier carried on his person forty rounds of ammunition, and in the wagons were enough cartridges to make up about two hundred rounds per man, and in like manner two hundred rounds of assorted ammunition were carried for each gun.

The wagon-trains were divided equally between the four corps, so that each had about eight hundred wagons, and these usually on the march occupied five miles or more of road. Each corps commander managed his own train; and habitually the artillery and wagons had the road, while the men, with the exception of the advance and rear guards, pursued paths improvised by the side of the wagons, unless they were forced to use a bridge or causeway in common.

I reached Atlanta during the afternoon of the 14th, and found that all preparations had been made—Colonel Beckwith, chief commissary, reporting one million two hundred thousand rations in possession of the troops, which was about twenty days' supply, and he had on hand a good supply of beef-cattle to be driven along on the hoof. Of forage, the supply was limited, being of oats and corn enough for five days, but I knew that within that time we would reach a country well stocked with corn, which had been gathered and stored in cribs seemingly for our use, by Governor Brown's militia.

Colonel Poe, United States Engineers, of my staff, had been busy in his special task of destruction. He had a large force at work, had leveled the great depot, round-house, and the machine-shops of the Georgia Railroad, and had applied fire to the wreck. One of these machine-shops had been used by the rebels as an arsenal, and in it were stored piles of shot and shell some of which proved to be loaded, and that night was made hideous by the bursting of shells, whose fragments came uncomfortably near Judge Lyon's house, in which I was quartered. The fire also reached the block of stores near the depot, and the heart of the city was in flames all night, but the fire did not reach the parts of Atlanta where the court-house was, or the great mass of dwelling-houses.

The march from Atlanta began on the morning of November 15th, the right wing and cavalry following the railroad southeast toward 'Jonesboro', and General Slocum with the Twentieth Corps leading off to the east by Decatur and Stone Mountain, toward Madison. These were divergent lines, designed to threaten both Macon and Augusta at the same time so as to prevent a concentration at our intended distinction or "objective," Milledgeville, the captial of Georgia, distant southeast about one hundred miles. The time allowed each column for reaching Milledgeville was seven days. I remained in Atlanta during the 15th with the Fourteenth Corps, and the rear-guard of the right wing, to complete the loading of the trains and the destruction of the buildings of Atlanta which could be converted to hostile uses, and on the morning of the 16th started with my personal staff, a company of Alabama cavalry, commanded by Lieutenant Snelling, and an infantry company, commanded by Lieutenant McCrory, which guarded our small train of wagons. . . .

About 7 A.M. of November 16th we rode out of Atlanta by the Decatur road, filled by the marching troops and wagons of the Fourteenth Corps; and reaching the hill, just outside of the old rebel works, we naturally paused to look back upon the scenes of our past battles. We stood upon the very ground whereon was fought the bloody battle of July 22d, and could see the copse of wood where McPherson fell. Behind us lay Atlanta, smouldering and in ruins, the black smoke rising high in air, and hanging like a pall over the ruined city. Away off in the distance, on the McDonough road, was the rear of Howard's column, the gun-barrels glistening in the sun, the white-topped wagons stretching away to the south; and right before us the Fourteenth Corps, marching steadily and rapidly, with a cheery look and swinging pace, that made light of the thousand miles that lay between us and Richmond. Some band, by accident, struck up the anthem of "John Brown's soul goes marching on;" the men caught up the strain, and never before or since have I heard the chorus of "Glory, glory, hallelujah!" done with more spirit, or in better harmony of time and place.

Then we turned our horses' heads to the east; Atlanta was soon lost behind the screen of trees, and became a thing of the past. Around it clings many a thought of desperate battle, of hope and fear, that now seem like the memory of a dream; and I have never seen the place since. The day was extremely beautiful, clear sunlight, with bracing air, and an unusual feeling of exhilaration seemed to pervade all minds—a feeling of something to come, vague and undefined, still full of venture and intense interest. Even the common soldiers caught the inspiration, and many a group called out to me as I worked my way past them, "Uncle Billy, I guess Grant is waiting for us at Richmond!" Indeed, the general sentiment was that we were marching for Richmond, and that there we should end the war, but how and when they seemed to care not; nor did they measure the distance, or count the cost in life, or bother their brains about the great rivers to be crossed, and the food required for man and beast, that had to be gathered by the way. There was a "devil-may-care" feeling pervading officers and men, that made me feel the full load of responsibility, for success would be accepted as a matter of course, whereas, should we fail, this "march" would be adjudged the wild adventure of a crazy fool. I had no purpose to march direct for Richmond by way of Augusta and Charlotte, but always designed to reach the sea-coast first at Savannah or Port Royal, South Carolina, and even kept in mind the alternative of Pensacola.

The first night out we camped by the road-side near Lithonia. Stone Mountain, a mass of granite, was in plain view, cut out in clear outline against the blue sky;

the whole horizon was lurid with the bonfires of rail-ties, and groups of men all night were carrying the heated rails to the nearest trees, and bending them around the trunks. Colonel Poe had provided tools for ripping up the rails and twisting them when hot; but the best and easiest way is the one I have described, of heating the middle of the iron-rails on bonfires made of the cross-ties, and then winding them around a telegraph-pole or the trunk of some convenient sapling. I attached much importance to this destruction of the railroad, gave it my own personal attention, and made reiterated orders to others on the subject.

The next day we passed through the handsome town of Covington, the soldiers closing up their ranks, the color-bearers unfurling their flags, and the bands striking up patriotic airs. The white people came out of their houses to behold the sight, spite of their deep hatred of the invaders, and the negroes were simply frantic with joy. Whenever they heard my name, they clustered about my horse, shouted and prayed in their peculiar style, which had a natural eloquence that would have moved a stone. I have witnessed hundreds, if not thousands, of such scenes; and can now see a poor girl, in the very ecstasy of the Methodist "shout," hugging the banner of one of the regiments, and jumping up to the "feet of Jesus."

I remember, when riding around by a by-street in Covington, to avoid the crowd that followed the marching column, that some one brought me an invitation to dine with a sister of Sam. Anderson, who was a cadet at West Point with me; but the messenger reached me after we had passed the main part of the town. I asked to be excused, and rode on to a place designated for camp, at the crossing of the Ulcofauhachee River, about four miles to the east of the town. Here we made our bivouac, and I walked up to a plantation-house close by, where were assembled many negroes, among them an old, gray-haired man, of as fine a head as I ever saw. I asked him if he understood about the war and its progress. He said he did; that he had been looking for the "angel of the Lord" ever since he was knee-high, and, though we professed to be fighting for the Union, he supposed that slavery was the cause, and that our success was to be his freedom. I asked him if all the negro slaves comprehended this fact, and he said they surely did. I then explained to him that we wanted the slaves to remain where they were, and not to load us down with useless mouths, which would eat up the food needed for our fighting-men; that our success was their assured freedom; that we could receive a few of their young, hearty men as pioneers; but that, if they followed us in swarms of old and young, feeble and helpless, it would simply load us down and cripple us in our great task. I think Major Henry Hitchcock was with me on

that occasion, and made a note of the conversation, and I believe that old man spread this message to the slaves, which was carried from mouth to mouth, to the very end of our journey, and that it in part saved us from the great danger we incurred of swelling our numbers so that famine would have attended our progress. It was at this very plantation that a soldier passed me with a ham on his musket, a jug of sorghum-molasses under his arm, and a big piece of honey in his hand, from which he was eating, and, catching my eye, he remarked *sotto voce* and carelessly to a comrade, "Forage liberally on the country," quoting from my general orders. On this occasion, as on many others that fell under my personal observation, I reproved the man, explained that foraging must be limited to the regular parties properly detailed, and that all provisions thus obtained must be delivered to the regular commissaries, to be fairly distributed to the men who kept their ranks.

6. *Women played an important part in the Civil War. Sick and wounded soldiers in both armies required nursing and hospital services; men far from home were grateful for "food packages", gifts of tobacco, and extra articles of clothing. Two volunteer organizations, the U.S. Sanitary Commission and the U.S. Christian Commission, were set up to handle war relief work. Prominent in the Chicago branch of the Sanitary Commission was Mrs. Mary Livermore who worked tirelessly in, and for, the Union Army hospitals. The three selections which follow are from her remarkable autobiography entitled* My Story of the War, A Woman's Narrative of Four Years' Personal Experience. *It was published in 1889 at Hartford, Connecticut.*

Activities at the Start of the War

The transition of the country from peace to the tumult and waste of war, was appalling and swift—but the regeneration of its women kept pace with it. They lopped off superfluities, retrenched in expenditures, became deaf to the calls of pleasure, and heeded not the mandates of fashion. The incoming patriotism of the hour swept them to the loftiest height of devotion, and they were eager to do, to bear, or to suffer, for the beloved country. The fetters of caste and conventionalism dropped at their feet, and they sat together, patrician and plebeian, Protestant and Catholic, and scraped lint, and rolled bandages, or made garments for the poorly clad soldiery.

An order was sent to Boston for five thousand shirts for the Massachusetts troops at the South. Every church in the city sent a delegation of needle-women to "Union

Hall," heretofore used as a ballroom. The Catholic priests detailed five hundred sewing-girls to the pious work. Suburban towns rang the bells of the town hall to muster the seamstresses. The plebeian Irish Catholic of South Boston ran the sewing-machine, while the patrician Protestant of Beacon Street basted,—and the shirts were made at the rate of a thousand a day. On Thursday, Dorothea Dix sent an order for five hundred shirts for her hospital in Washington. On Friday, they were cut, made, and packed—and were sent on their way that night. Similar events were of constant occurrence in every other city. The zeal and devotion of women no more flagged through the war than did that of the army in the field. They rose to the height of every emergency, and through all discouragements and reverses maintained a sympathetic unity between the soldiers themselves . . .

At a meeting in Washington during the war, called in the interest of the Sanitary Commission, President Lincoln said: "I am not accustomed to use the language of eulogy. I have never studied the art of paying compliments to women. But I must say that if all that has been said by orators and poets since the creation of the world in praise of women, was applied to the women of America, it would not do them justice for their conduct during this war. I will close by saying, God bless the women of America!"

Entirely unacquainted with the requirements of war and the needs of soldiers, it was inevitable that the first movements of women for army relief should be misdirected. They could not manifest more ignorance, however, nor blunder more absurdly, than did the government in its early attempts to build up an effective and disciplined arm. Both learned by blundering.

It was summer; and the army was to move southward, to be exposed to the torrid heats of the season and climate. A newspaper reminiscence of the good service rendered British troops in India by General Havelock set the ball in motion. He had devised a white linen head-dress to be worn over the caps of his men, which defended them from sunstroke, and in his honor it was named the "Havelock." Our men must, of course, be equipped with this protection, and forthwith inexperienced women, and equally inexperienced men in the army, gave orders for the manufacture of Havelocks. What a furor there was over them! Women who could not attend the "sewing-meeting" where the "Havelocks" were being manufactured, ordered the work sent to their homes, and ran the sewing-machines day and night till the nondescript head-gear was completed. "Havelocks" were turned out by thousands, of all patterns and sizes, and of every conceivable material.

In the early inexperience of that time, whenever regiments were in camp, awaiting marching orders, it was the custom of many women to pay them visits, laden with indigestible dainties. These they furnished in such profusion, that the "boys" were rarely without the means of obtaining a "permit" to the hospital until they broke up camp. While the Havelock fever was at its height, the Nineteenth Illinois, commanded by Colonel Turchin, was mustered in, and was ordered to rendezvous at Camp Douglas. A detachment of the "cake and pie brigade," as the rollicking fellows called them, paid the regiment an early visit, and were received by the men who were not under drill, *en Havelock*. As the sturdy fellows emerged from their tents, all wearing "the white nightcaps," as they had irreverently christened the ugly head-dress, their appearance was so ludicrous that a shout went up from officers, soldiers, and lady visitors. They were worn in every imaginable fashion,—as nightcaps, turbans, sunbonnets, bandages, sunshades,—and the fate of the "Havelock" was sealed. No more time nor money was wasted in their useless manufacture.

Hospitals in Southern Illinois

Go where I would, this was "the order of exercises." I went down a flight of crazy stairs, across a bit of plank walk, around a slough of unknown depth, behind somebody's barn, across somebody's back yard, over an extempore bridge of scantling that bent with my weight, then into mud, at the risk of losing rubbers, boots, and I sometimes feared for my feet, and, at last, ferried over a miniature lake in a skiff, I reached my destination. "Living in Cairo converts us soldiers into sailors," said the soldier who rowed me from the "Brick Hospital." "Yes," said another, "the children born in this town are web-footed." They certainly ought to be.

My object in visiting Cairo was to see the hospitals— not the town. I first visited the regimental hospitals, never very attractive institutions. There were some half-dozen of them, established in small dwelling-houses, carriage-houses, sheds, or other accessible places. Were I to describe them, as I saw them, the account would be discredited. Compressed within their narrow limits were more filth and discomfort, neglect and suffering, than would have sufficed to defile and demoralize ten times as much space. The fetid odor of typhoid fever, erysipelas, dysentery, measles, and healing wounds, was rendered more nauseating by unclean beds and unwashed bodies; while from the kitchen, which opened into the hospital wards, came the smell of boiling meat and coffee, befouling still more the air of the unventilated apartments.

The nurses were convalescent soldiers, wan, thin, weak, and requiring nursing themselves; and, though they were kind to their comrades, they were wholly worthless as nurses. I saw no signs of a surgeon in these poor hospitals, although the patients told me a doctor had visited them one, two, or three days before, the statements varying in the different hospitals. Nor were there any signs of woman's presence, save in one instance, where a poor fellow, with mingled tears and laughter, told me that "his wife had come that morning, and now he believed he *should* get well, although the night before he had utterly given up hope."

And, to be sure, I soon met his wife—a cheery, active little woman, under whose vigorous sweeping, and scrubbing, and purifying, a dingy corner chamber was growing sweet and clean. And when she opened her trunk for my inspection, and showed the coarse, but clean sheets, shirts, drawers, and socks, she had brought, with "a new horse blanket for a rug, when *he* put his feet on the floor," I could easily believe her assurance that, "with the cleanliness, and the sun shining through the clear window-panes, and her to make his tea and gruel, he'd a'most think himself at home in a day or two."

It gave me the heartache to see the patient sufferers in those hospitals, for they seemed left to their fate. They were very young, homesick, and ready to break down into a flood of weeping at the first word of sympathy. The sick men were always more despondent than those who were wounded. For under the wasting of camp diseases they became mentally as weak as children; while the men wounded in battle were heroes, and were toned up to fortitude. One fine fellow, not yet twenty, was raving in the delirium of brain fever. He fancied himself at home with his mother, to whom he incessantly appealed for "a drink of water right from the spring at the back of the house, the coldest and clearest in all Illinois."

He was sponged with tepid water, his tangled hair smoothed, his burning head bathed, and his stiff filthy clothing changed for clean garments from the depot of the Chicago Sanitary Commission located in the town. He dropped off into a quiet sleep immediately, which lasted for several hours. Similar beneficial results followed similar small ministrations in all these wretched hospitals. Residents of Cairo were so tortured with the neglect and suffering of these hospitals that they were finally broken up, at their instance, and the patients transferred to the excellent "General Hospitals." The men always rebelled at being sent away from their regiments, and preferred to risk the chances of suffering and neglect with their comrades to any promise of better care, and wiser nursing, separated from them.

There was one General Hospital in Cairo, called by the people the "Brick Hospital." Here the "Sisters of the Holy Cross" were employed as nurses, one or more to each ward. Here were order, comfort, cleanliness, and good nursing. The food was cooked in a kitchen outside the hospital. Surgeons were detailed to every ward, who visited their patients twice daily, and more frequently if necessary. The apothecary's room was supplied with an ample store of medicines and surgical appliances, and the store-room possessed an abundance of clothing and delicacies for the sick.

It was a sad sight to pass through the wards and see row after row of narrow beds, with white, worn, still faces pressed against the white pillows. And it gave one a heartache to take each man by the hand, and listen to his simple story, and to hear his anxieties for wife and children, of whom he received no tidings, or for the dear mother, whom he could hardly name without tears.

Hazards along the Mississippi River

The grand passion of the West during the first half of the war was to re-open the Mississippi, which had been closed by the enemy. This great water highway had been wrested from the possession of the rebels as far south as Vicksburg, which frowned down from its unique eyrie, bristling with batteries, and hurling shot and shell at our brave men encamped at Young's Point, opposite. It seemed, from its position, to be thundering forth the mandate, "Hitherto shalt thou come, but no farther."

General Sherman's attempt to take the fortifications and batteries which defended Vicksburg on the north had failed, and, after a triumphant and conquering expedition up the White River into Arkansas, the whole Western army had been moved down the Mississippi in transports. At that time the men were living in boats, or were vainly seeking dry land for their encampments, amid the swamps, lagoons, bayous, and sloughs of the abominable portion of that country, known as the "river-bottoms." The levees of the river had been cut in many places, as a "military necessity," or from sheer wantonness on the part of the "boys," who gloried in any mischief that brought trouble to the "secesh."

But cutting the levees in this case proved a two-edged sword, not only injuring the enemy but drowning out our own men. Those who could, took to the crowded river-boats. The rest remained in their wet encampments in the pestilential swamps and bottom lands, drenched with the protracted spring rains, almost buried in the unfathomable mud, and drinking death from the crystal waters of the Yazoo. Soon sickness and suffering stalked in among them. . . .

Immense shipments of supplies were sent down on the sanitary boats, with men and women of executive ability, who attended to their safe transmission and equitable distribution. Accompanying these were special corps of relief accustomed to the work in hospitals, and possessed of physical endurance, able to encounter any horror of army life without blenching.

It was with one of these shipments of sanitary stores, and as one of the relief corps, that I went down the Mississippi in March, 1863. Quartermasters, State Surgeon-Generals, members of the Legislature, representatives of the Chicago Chamber of Commerce, a company of nurses whom I was to locate in hospitals, and some two or three women who had been active in working for our invalid soldiers from the very first, made up the delegation. Two of us only—Mrs. Colt, of Milwaukee, and myself—were connected with the Sanitary Commission. Mrs. Colt was the executive woman at the head of the sanitary work in Wisconsin, whose enthusiasm infected the whole state with patriotism and generosity. The sanitary supplies, about thirty-five hundred boxes and packages in all, were sent by the Commission and Chicago Board of Trade.

The programme marked out for us was this. We were to visit every hospital from Cairo to Young's Point, opposite Vicksburg; relieve such needs as were pressing; make ourselves useful in any way among the sick and wounded, co-operating harmoniously as far as possible with medical and military authorities. From every point we were to report our movements, the result of our observations, what we had accomplished, and what we found needing attention, employing the Chicago Press and the bulletins of the Sanitary Commission as our mediums of communication.

Our assortment of stores comprised almost everything necessary in hospital relief; potatoes, onions, sauer-kraut, and vegetables—chiefly for the scorbutic patients, who constituted a majority of the sick—farina, corn starch, lemons, oranges, pearl-barley, tea, sugar, condensed milk, ale, canned fruits, condensed extract of beef, codfish, jellies, a small quantity of the best of brandy, with hospital shirts, drawers, sheets, socks, slippers, bandages, lint, rubber rings, and whatever else might be needed for wounded and sick men. We also took down about five hundred "private boxes," forwarded by private parties for particular companies, or squads, or individuals, and committed to our care for safe transmission and delivery. My own personal outfit consisted of a long pair of rubber boots, reaching to the knee, a teapot, a spirit-lamp to boil it, with a large quantity of Japan tea, condensed milk, sugar and crackers.

Through the daily papers, we volunteered to take letters, messages, or small packages, to parties on our route connected with the army, and to deliver them whenever it was possible. For a week before we started, my time was consumed by people who came to the rooms of the Sanitary Commission on these errands.

I made memoranda of the verbal messages and inquiries, which were many and mostly from the poor and humble. My memorandum book lies before me. Here are samples of these messages:—

"Mercantile Battery, Milliken's Bend, George W——. His mother called. She is well; is not worrying about her son; has gained thirteen pounds since the cold weather. Am to make particular inquiries about her son's habits; does he drink, swear, or smoke? Tell him his mother would rather he would be sent home dead, than that he should return alive and dissipated."

"Young's Point, One Hundred and Thirteenth Illinois, Peter R——. Wife called. She and the six children are well; gets plenty of work, good pay, and the country allowance of three dollars weekly. He is not to worry about them at all—*at all. Must never think of deserting.* Stand it like a man! All the family pray daily to the Virgin for him."

"Lake Providence, Eighteenth Wisconsin, John K——. Father and mother called. Brought four letters for him. Tell him to take care of his health, avoid liquor, *never be attempted to desert.* Brother William, in Second Wisconsin, has got well of his wound, and gone back to the Army of the Potomac."

"Try to learn something concerning Herbert B——, of Fifteenth Wisconsin. Has not been heard from since battle of Stone River." (He was never heard from until the lists of the Andersonville dead were published.)

"Try to get permission for James R—— to go to Helena for his brother's dead body, and take it to Chicago."

"Try to get discharge for Richard R——, dying in Overton Hospital, Memphis, of consumption, and bring him home to his parents."

Scores of pages were filled with similar memoranda.

Our stores, with ourselves, were passed over the Illinois Central Railroad to Cairo, where we found sanitary goods,—mostly for the relief of scorbutic and fever patients,—pouring into the town from every point, all clamoring for immediate shipment. Government had impressed all the boats on the river into its service, and, as there were no troops to be hurried forward, these generous consignments were transhipped as rapidly as possible from the cars to the boats. The boat to which we were assigned was a little, rickety, wheezy, crowded, unsafe craft, which poked along down the river at about one-half the usual rate of speed. It towed along three or four barges of hay, which kept us in constant alarm, as they easily took fire from the sparks of the chimney.

One got loose and drifted away, nobody knew where and nobody seemed to care, since it belonged to "Uncle Sam." We had no doubt it was purposely detached in the night, at a point agreed upon beforehand, where it could easily be secured by the rebels. The officers, like those of almost all the boats at that time, were secretly in sympathy with the rebellion; though, for the sake of the "greenbacks" of the government, they made a show of loyalty to it. They bore themselves very cavalierly towards us, treating us with scant politeness when they noticed us at all, and ignoring us altogether when it was possible to do so.

7. Men on both sides who were prisoners of war were confined either in regular prison-houses or lodged in prison camps. In many cases, and for varying reasons, prisoners of war were badly treated and subjected to unnecessary suffering. This was true of Union prisons as well as Confederate, but the selection from a prisoner's diary which follows tells of life in the great Confederate camp at Andersonville, Georgia. It is quoted from John C. Ransom's Andersonville Diary, *published at Auburn, N.Y. in 1881. The entries are for April and May, 1864.*

They have rigged up an excuse for a hospital on the outside, where the sick are taken. Admit none though who can walk or help themselves in any way. Some of our men are detailed to help as nurses, but in a majority of cases those who go out on parole of honor are cut-throats and robbers, who abuse a sick prisoner. Still, there are exceptions to this rule. We hear stories of Captain Wirtz's cruelty in punishing the men, but I hardly credit all the stories. More prisoners to-day. Some captured near Petersburg. Don't know anything about exchange. Scurvy and dropsy taking hold of the men. Many are blind as soon as it becomes night, and it is called moon blind. Caused, I suppose, by sleeping with the moon shining in the face. Talked with Michael Hoare, an old school-fellow of mine. Mike was captured while we were in Pemberton Building, and was one of Dahlgreen's men. Was taken right in the suburbs of Richmond. Has told me all the news of their failure on account of Kilpatrick failing to make a junction at some point. Mike is a great tall, slim fellow, and a good one. Said he heard my name called out in Richmond, as having a box of eatables from the North. He also saw a man named Strong claim the box with a written order from me. Strong was one of our mess on Belle Isle. He was sent to Richmond while sick, from the Island, knew of my expecting the box, and forged an order to get it. Well, that was rough, still I probably wouldn't have got it anyway. Better him than some Rebel.

Mike gave me a lot of black pepper, which we put into our soup, which is a luxury. He has no end of talk at his tongue's end, and it is good to hear. Recounts how once, when I was about eight or ten years old, and he some older, I threw a base ball club, and hit him on the shins, then ran, and he couldn't catch me. It was when we were both going to school to A. A. Henderson, in Jackson, Michigan. Think I remember the incident, and am strongly under the impression, that he caught me. It is thus that old friends meet after many years. John McGuire is also here, another Jackson man. He has a family at home, and is worried. Says he used to frequently see my brother George at Hilton Head, before being captured.

APRIL 10.—Getting warmer and warmer. Can see the trees swaying back and forth on the outside, but inside not a breath of fresh air. Our wood is all gone, and we are now digging up stumps and roots for fuel to cook with. Some of the first prisoners here have passable huts made of logs, sticks, pieces of blankets, &c. Room about all taken up in here now. Rations not so large. Talk that they intend to make the meal into bread before sending it inside, which will be an improvement. Rations have settled down to less than a pint of meal per day, with occasionly a few peas, or an apology for a piece of bacon, for each man. Should judge that they have hounds on the outside to catch runaways, from the noise. Wirtz don't come in as much as formerly. The men make it uncomfortable for him. As Jimmy Devers says, "He is a terror." I have omitted to mention Jimmy's name of late, although he is with us all the time—not in our mess, but close by. He has an old pack of cards with which we play to pass away the time. Many of the men have Testaments and "House-wives," which they have brought with them from home, and it is pitiful to see them look at these things while thinking of their loved ones at home.

APRIL 11.—Doctor Lewis is very bad off with the scurvy and diarrhœa. We don't think he can stand it much longer, but make out to him he stick it through. Our Government must hear of our condition here, and get us away before long. If they don't, its a poor Government to tie to. Hendryx and myself are poor, as also are all the mess. Still in good health compared with the generality of the prisoners. Jimmy Devers has evidently sort of dried up, and it don't seem to make any difference whether he gets anything to eat or not. He has now been a prisoner of war nearly a year, and is in good health, and very hopeful of getting away in time. Sticks up for our Government, and says there is some good reason for our continued imprisonment. I can see none.

As many as 12,000 men here now, and crowded for room. Death rate is in the neighborhood of eighty per day. Hendryx prowls around all over the prison, bringing us what good news he can, which is not much. A very heavy dew nights, which is almost a rain. Rebels very domineering. Many are tunneling to get out. Our tunnel has been abandoned, as the location was not practicable. Yank shot to-day near our quarters. Approached too near the dead line. Many of the men have dug down through the sand and reached water, but it is poor; no better than out of the creek.

APRIL 12.—Another beautiful, but warm day, with no news. Insects of all descriptions making their appearance, such as lizards, a worm four or five inches long, flea, maggots, &c. There is so much filth about the camp, that it is terrible trying, to live here. New prisoners are made sick the first hours of their arrival by the stench which pervades the prison. Old prisoners do not mind it so much, having become used to it. No visitors come near us any more. Everybody sick, almost, with scurvy—an awful disease. New cases every day. I am afraid some contagious disease will get among us, and if so, every man will die. My blanket a perfect God-send. Is large and furnishes shelter, from the burning sun. Hendryx has a very sore arm which troubles him much. Even he begins to look, and feel bad. James Gordan, or Gordenian (I don't know which), was killed to-day, by the guard. In crossing the creek on a small board crossway, men are often shot. It runs very near the dead line, guards take the occasion to shoot parties who put their hands on the dead line, in going across. Some also reach up under the dead line to get purer water, and are shot. Men seemingly reckless of their lives. New prisoners coming in and are shocked, at the sights.

APRIL 13.—Jack Shannon, from Ann Arbor, died this morning. The raiders are the stronger party now, and do as they please; and we are in nearly as much danger now from our own men as from the Rebels. Captain Moseby, of my own hundred, figures conspicuously among the robberies, and is a terrible villain. During the night some one stole my jacket. Have traded off all superfluous clothes, and with the loss of jacket have only pants, shirt, shoes (no stockings), and hat; yet I am well dressed in comparison with some others. Many have nothing but an old pair of pants, which reach, perhaps to the knees, and perhaps not. Hendryx has two shirts, and should be mobbed. I do quite a business trading rations, making soup for the sick ones, taking in payment their raw food, which they cannot eat. Get many a little snack by so doing.

APRIL 14.—At least twenty fights among our own men this forenoon. It beats all what a snarling crowd we are getting to be. The men are perfectly reckless, and had just as soon have their necks broken by fighting as anything else. New onions in camp. Very small, and sell for $2 a bunch of four or five. Van Tassel, a Pennsyl-

vanian, is about to die. Many give me parting injunctions relative to their families, in case I should live through. Have half a dozen photographs of dead men's wives, with addresses on the back of them. Seems to be pretty generally conceded that if any get through, I will. Not a man here now is in good health. An utter impossibility to remain well. Signs of scurvy about my person. Still adhere to our sanitary rules. Lewis anxious to get to the hospital. Will die anyway shortly, whether there or here. Jimmy Devers, the old prisoner, coming down. Those who have stood it bravely begin to weaken.

APRIL 15.—The hospital is a tough place to be in, from all accounts. The detailed Yankees, as soon as they get a little authority, are certain to use it for all its worth. In some cases before a man is fairly dead, he is stripped of everything, coat, pants, shirt, finger rings (if he has any), and everything of value taken away. These the nurses trade to the guards. Does not seem possible, but such is the case, sad to relate. Not very pleasant for a man, just breathing his last, and perhaps thinking of loved ones at home, who are all so unconscious of the condition of their soldier father, or brother, to be suddenly jerked about, and fought over, with the cursing and blaspheming he is apt to hear. The sick now, or a portion of them, are huddled up in one corner of the prison, to get as bad as they can before being admitted to the outside hospital. Every day I visit it, and come away sick at heart that human beings should be thus treated.

APRIL 26.—Ten days since I wrote in my diary, and in those ten days was too much occupied in trying to dig a tunnel to escape out of, to write any. On the 21st the tunnel was opened, and two fellows belonging to a Massachusetts regiment escaped to the outside. Hendryx and myself next went out. The night was very dark. Came up out of the ground away on the outside of the guard. We crawled along to gain the woods, and get by some pickets, and when forty or fifty rods from the stockade, a shot was fired at some one coming out of the hole. We immediately jumped up and ran for dear life, seemingly making more noise than a troop of cavalry. It was almost daylight, and away we went. Found I could not hurry and slowed up, knowing we would be caught, but hoping to get to some house and get something to eat first. Found I was all broke up for any exertion. In an hour we had traveled perhaps three miles, were all covered with mud, and scratched up. I had fell, too, in getting over some logs, and it seemed to me broken all the ribs in my body.

Just as it was coming light in the east we heard dogs after us. We expected it, and so armed ourselves with clubs, and sat down on a log. In a few moments the hounds came up with us and began smelling of us.

Pretty soon five mounted Rebels arrived on the scene of action. They laughed to think we expected to get away. Started us back towards our charnel pen. Dogs did not offer to bite us, but guards told us that if we had offered resistance or started to run, they would have torn us. Arrived at the prison, and after waiting an hour, Captain Wirtz interviewed us. After cussing us a few minutes, we were put in the chain gang, where we remained two days. This was not very fine, but contrary to expectation, not so bad after all. We had more to eat than when inside, and had shade to lay in, and although my ankles were made very sore, do not regret my escapade. Am not permanently hurt. . . . .

APRIL 28.—Doctor Lewis is still getting worse with scurvy and dropsy combined. Limbs swollen to double their usual size—just like puff-balls. Raiders do about as they please, and their crimes would fill more paper than I have at my disposal.

APRIL 30.—Very small rations given to us now. Not more than one quarter what we want to eat, and that of the poorest quality. The Flying Dutchman (*Wirtz*) offers to give any two at a time, twelve hours the start, and if caught to take the punishment he has for runaways. The offer is made to intimidate those thinking to escape. Half the men would take the consequences, with two hours start.

MAY 1.—Warm. Samuel Hutton, of the 9th Michigan Cavalry, died last night; also Peter Christiancy and Joseph Sargent, of Company D, 9th Michigan, have died within a few weeks. Last evening 700 of the 85th New York arrived here. They were taken at Plymouth, N. C., with 1,400 others, making 2,100 in all. The balance are on the road to this place. Wrote a letter home to-day. Have not heard from the North for nearly six months. Dying off very fast.

MAY 2.—A crazy man was shot dead by the guard an hour ago. The guard dropped a piece of bread on the inside of the stockade, and the fellow went inside the dead line to get it, and was killed. The bread wagon was raided upon as soon as it drove inside to-day and all the bread stolen, for which offense no more will be issued today. . . .

SLAVE AND FREE

1. Many of the angry disputes between the sections of the nation had arisen out of difference over the proper use of the Territories in the West. Holders of slaves wanted to expand that system of labor into the new Territories. On the other hand, many leaders in the South were reluctant to en-courage the general movement of large numbers of people into the Territories for fear that they might become new antislavery States. There had been a long history of opposition to the government granting free land in the Territories, therefore, and laws which offered government land for the asking had been blocked in Congress by Senators and Representatives from the South.

After Secession, Congressmen from the South were no longer present and several important laws affecting the Territories were passed. Two of these laws are quoted below. The first is the Homestead Act, passed in 1862. The second is the law passed (also in 1862) which opened up the Territories by projecting a railroad to the Pacific Coast. For years, a dispute had raged over the route which should be adopted. Southern opinion favored a route which reached California from the south by way of Texas. Now, the central route, favored by the North, was officially approved. The railroad would drive westward from Nebraska.

An Act to secure Homesteads to Actual Settlers on the Public Domain.

Be it enacted, That any person who is the head of a family, or who has arrived at the age of twenty-one years, and is a citizen of the United States, or who shall have filed his declaration of intention to become such, as required by the naturalization laws of the United States, and who has never borne arms against the United States Government or given aid and comfort to its enemies, shall, from and after the first of January, eighteen hundred and sixty-three, be entitled to enter one quarter-section or a less quantity of unappropriated public lands, upon which said person may have filed a pre-emption claim, or which may, at the time the application is made, be subject to pre-emption at one dollar and twenty-five cents, or less, per acre; or eighty acres or less of such unappropriated lands at two dollars and fifty cents per acre, to be located in a body, in conformity to the legal subdivisions of the public lands, and after the same shall have been surveyed: *Provided,* That any person owning or residing on land may, under the provisions of this Act, enter other land lying contiguous to his or her said land, which shall not, with the land so already owned and occupied, exceed in the aggregate one hundred and sixty acres.

SEC. 2. That the person applying for the benefit of this Act shall, upon application to the register of the land office in which he or she is about to make such entry, make affidavit before the said register or receiver that he or she is the head of a family, or is twenty-one or more years of age, or shall have performed service in the Army or Navy of the United States, and that he has never borne arms against the Government of the United States or given aid and comfort to its enemies, and that such application is made for his or her exclusive use and benefit, and that said entry is made for the purpose of actual settlement and cultivation, and not, either directly or indirectly, for the use or benefit of any other person or persons whomsoever; and upon filing the said affidavit with the register or receiver, and on payment of ten dollars, he or she shall thereupon be permitted to enter the quantity of land specified: *Provided however*, That no certificate shall be given or patent issued therefor until the expiration of five years. from the date of such entry; and if, at the expiration of such time, or at any time within two years thereafter, the person making such entry—or if he be dead, his widow; or in case of her death, his heirs or devisee; or in case of a widow making such entry, her heirs or devisee, in case of her death—shall prove by two credible witnesses that he, she, or they have resided upon or cultivated the same for the term of five years immediately succeeding the time of filing the affidavit aforesaid, and shall make affidavits that no part of said land has been alienated, and that he has borne true allegiance to the Government of the United States; then, in such case, he, she, or they, if at that time a citizen of the United States, shall be entitled to a patent, as in other cases provided for by law: *And provided further*, That in case of the death of both father and mother, leaving an infant child or children under twenty-one years of age, the right and fee shall inure to the benefit of said infant child or children; and the executor, administrator, or guardian may, at any time within two years after the death of the surviving parent, and in accordance with the laws of the State in which such children for the time being have their domicile, sell said land for the benefit of said infants, but for no other purpose; and the purchaser shall acquire the absolute title by the purchase, and be entitled to a patent from the United States, on payment of the office fees and sum of money herein specified. . . .

An Act to aid in the Construction of a Railroad and Telegraph Line from the Missouri River to the Pacific Ocean. . . .

Be it enacted, That The Union Pacific Railroad Company . . . is hereby authorized and empowered to lay out, locate, construct, furnish, maintain and enjoy a continuous railroad and telegraph . . . from a point on the one hundredth meridian of longitude west from Greenwich, between the south margin of the valley of the Republican River and the north margin of the valley of the Platte River, to the western boundary of Nevada Territory, upon the route and terms hereinafter provided. . . .

Sec. 2. That the right of way through the public lands be . . . granted to said company for the construction of said railroad and telegraph line; and the right . . . is hereby given to said company to take from the public lands adjacent to the line of said road, earth, stone, timber, and other materials for the construction thereof; said right of way is granted to said railroad to the extent of two hundred feet in width on each side of said railroad when it may pass over the public lands, including all necessary grounds for stations, buildings, workshops, and depots, machine shops, switches, side tracks, turn tables, and water stations. The United States shall extinguish as rapidly as may be the Indian titles to all lands falling under the operation of this Act. . . .

Sec. 3. That there be . . . granted to the said company, for the purpose of aiding in the construction of said railroad and telegraph line, and to secure the safe and speedy transportation of mails, troops, munitions of war, and public stores thereon, every alternate section of public land, designated by odd numbers, to the amount of five alternate sections per mile on each side of said railroad, on the line thereof, and within the limits of ten miles on each side of said road. . . . *Provided* That all mineral lands shall be exempted from the operation of this Act; but where the same shall contain timber, the timber thereon is hereby granted to said company. . . .

Sec. 5. That for the purposes herein mentioned the Secretary of the Treasury shall . . . in accordance with the provisions of this Act, issue to said company bonds of the United States of one thousand dollars each, payable in thirty years after date, paying six per centum per annum interest . . . to the amount of sixteen of said bonds per mile for each section of forty miles; and to secure the repayment to the United States . . . of the amount of said bonds . . . the issue of said bonds . . . shall *ipso facto* constitute a first mortgage on the whole line of the railroad and telegraph. . . .

Sec. 9. That the Leavenworth, Pawnee and Western Railroad Company of Kansas are hereby authorized to construct a railroad and telegraph line . . . upon the same terms and conditions in all respects as are provided (*for construction of the Union Pacific Railroad*). . . . The Central Pacific Railroad Company of California are hereby authorized to construct a railroad and telegraph line from the Pacific coast . . . to the eastern boundaries of California upon the same terms and conditions in all respects (*as are provided for the Union Pacific Railroad*).

Sec. 10. . . . And the Central Pacific Railroad Company of California, after completing its road across said State, is authorized to continue the construction of said railroad and telegraph through the Territories of the United States to the Missouri River . . . upon the terms and conditions provided in this Act in relation to the Union Pacific Railroad Company, until said roads shall meet and connect. . . .

Sec. 11. That for three hundred miles of said road most mountainous and difficult of construction, to wit: one hundred and fifty miles westerly from the eastern base of the Rocky Mountains, and one hundred and fifty miles eastwardly from the western base of the Sierra Nevada mountains . . . the bonds to be issued to aid in the construction thereof shall be treble the number per mile hereinbefore provided . . .; and between the sections last named of one hundred and fifty miles each, the bonds to be issued to aid in the construction thereof shall be double the number per mile first mentioned. . . .

2. *Slavery, of course, was a central issue in the Civil War period. Many abolitionists objected to President Lincoln's policies, for Lincoln refused at first to act forcefully against slavery in the United States. He was attempting as President to maintain the unity of the country, although his own words indicated that he expected slavery to disappear with time. Several abolitionist writers (who were also influential Republicans) attacked his policies. Among them was Horace Greeley, editor and publisher of a widely read newspaper, the New York* Tribune. *After one of Greeley's attacks, Abraham Lincoln responded with the following letter, clearly stating that his first war aim was to preserve the Union.*

EXECUTIVE MANSION,
WASHINGTON, 22 *August* 1862.
Hon. Horace Greeley:

DEAR SIR: I have just read yours of the nineteenth, addressed to myself through the New-York *Tribune.* If there be in it any statements or assumptions of fact which I may know to be erroneous, I do not now and here controvert them. If there be in it any inferences which I may believe to be falsely drawn, I do not now and here argue against them. If there be perceptible in it an impatient and dictatorial tone, I waive it in deference to an old friend, whose heart I have always supposed to be right.

As to the policy I "seem to be pursuing," as you say, I have not meant to leave any one in doubt.

I would save the Union. I would save it the shortest way under the Constitution. The sooner the national authority can be restored, the nearer the Union will be "the Union as it was." If there be those who would not save the Union unless they could at the same time *save* Slavery, I do not agree with them. If there be those who would not save the Union unless they could at the same time *destroy* Slavery, I do not agree with them. My paramount object in this struggle *is* to save the Union, and is *not* either to save or destroy Slavery. If I could save the Union without freeing *any* slave, I would do it; and if I could save it by freeing *all* the slaves, I would do it; and if I could do it by freeing some and leaving others alone, I would also do that. What I do about Slavery and the colored race, I do because I believe it helps to save this Union; and what I forbear, I forbear because I do *not* believe it would help save the Union. I shall do *less* whenever I shall believe what I am doing hurts the cause, and I shall do *more* whenever I shall believe doing more will help the cause. I shall try to correct errors when shown to be errors; and I shall adopt new views so fast as they shall appear to be true views. I have here stated my purpose according to my view of *official* duty, and I intend no modification of my oft-expressed *personal* wish that all men, everywhere, could be free.—Yours,

A. LINCOLN.

3. *Congress moved against slavery in two areas— the District of Columbia and the Territories. Two laws in 1862 ended legal slavery in these areas. Both were signed by President Lincoln. Neither one satisfied the extreme abolitionists. Slavery was still legal in those "slave States" that were still within the Union, and no slaveholder was penalized by these laws. The key passage in the law abolishing slavery in the Territories follows:*

An Act to secure Freedom to all Persons within the Territories of the United States.

Be it enacted . . . , That from and after the passage of this act there shall be neither slavery nor involuntary servitude in any of the Territories of the United States now existing, or which may at any time hereafter be formed or acquired by the United States, otherwise than in punishment of crimes whereof the party shall have been duly convicted.

4. *President Lincoln finally issued his Emancipation Proclamation to take effect on January 1, 1863, only within those areas of the United States still controlled by Confederate forces. He was troubled by constitutional doubts which were not finally solved during his lifetime. The 13th Amendment,*

ending slavery in the United States, was not officially ratified until December 18, 1865.

There follow the texts of the preliminary Proclamation (issued on September 22, 1862) and of the definitive Proclamation of January 1, 1863.

Preliminary Proclamation of Emancipation.

I, ABRAHAM LINCOLN, President of the United States of America, and Commander-in-Chief of the army and navy thereof, do hereby proclaim and declare that hereafter, as heretofore, the war will be prosecuted for the object of practically restoring the constitutional relation between the United States and each of the states, and the people thereof, in which states that relation is or may be suspended or disturbed.

That it is my purpose, upon the next meeting of Congress, to again recommend the adoption of a practical measure tendering pecuniary aid to the free acceptance or rejection of all slave states so called, the people whereof may not then be in rebellion against the United States, and which states may then have voluntarily adopted, or thereafter may voluntarily adopt, immediate or gradual abolishment of slavery within their respective limits; and that the effort to colonize persons of African descent, with their consent, upon this continent or elsewhere, with the previously obtained consent of the governments existing there, will be continued.

That on the first day of January, in the year of our Lord one thousand eight hundred and sixty-three, all persons held as slaves within any state, or designated part of a state, the people whereof shall then be in rebellion against the United States, shall be then, thenceforward, and forever free; and the Executive Government of the United States, including the military and naval authority thereof, will recognize and maintain the freedom of such persons, and will do no act or acts to repress such persons, or any of them, in any efforts they may make for their actual freedom.

That the Executive will, on the first day of January aforesaid, by proclamation, designate the states and parts of states, if any, in which the people thereof respectively shall then be in rebellion against the United States; and the fact that any state, or the people thereof, shall on that day be in good faith represented in the Congress of the United States, by members chosen thereto at elections wherein a majority of the qualified voters of such state shall have participated, shall, in the absence of strong countervailing testimony, be deemed conclusive evidence that such state, and the people thereof, are not then in rebellion against the United States.

That attention is hereby called to an act of Congress entitled "An Act to make an additional Article of War," approved March 13th, 1862, and which act is in the words and figures following:

"Be it enacted by the Senate and House of Representatives of the United States of America in Congress assembled, That hereafter the following shall be promulgated as an additional article of war for the government of the army of the United States, and shall be obeyed and observed at such:

"ARTICLE—. All officers or persons in the military or naval service of the United States are prohibited from employing any of the forces under their respective commands for the purpose of returning fugitives from service or labor who may have escaped from any persons to whom such service or labor is claimed to be due; and any officer who shall be found guilty by a court-martial of violating this article shall be dismissed from the service."

"SECTION 2. *And be it further enacted,* That this act shall take effect from and after its passage."

Also, to the ninth and tenth sections of an act entitled "An Act to suppress Insurrection, to punish Treason and Rebellion, to seize and confiscate Property of Rebels, and for other purposes," approved July 17, 1862, and which sections are in the words and figures following:

"SEC. 9. *And be it further enacted,* That all slaves of persons who shall hereafter be engaged in rebellion against the government of the United States, or who shall in any way give aid or comfort thereto, escaping from such persons and taking refuge within the lines of the army; and all slaves captured from such persons, or deserted by them, and coming under the control of the government of the United States; and all slaves of such persons found *on*, or being within any place occupied by rebel forces and afterwards occupied by forces of the United States, shall be deemed captives of war, and shall be forever free of their servitude, and not again held as slaves.

"SEC. 10. *And be it further enacted,* That no slave escaping into any state, territory, or the District of Columbia, from any other state, shall be delivered up, or in any way impeded or hindered of his liberty, except for crime or some offense against the laws, unless the person claiming said fugitive shall first make oath that the person to whom the labor or service of such fugitive is alleged to be due is his lawful owner, and has not borne arms against the United States in the present rebellion, nor in any way given aid and comfort thereto; and no person engaged in the military or naval service of the United States shall, under any pretense whatever, assume to decide on the validity of the claim of any person to the service or labor of any other person, or surrender up any such person to the claimant, on pain of being dismissed from the service."

And I do hereby enjoin upon and order all persons engaged in the military and naval service of the United States to observe, obey, and enforce, within their respective spheres of service, the act and sections above recited.

And the Executive will in due time recommend that all citizens of the United States who shall have remained loyal thereto throughout the rebellion shall (upon the restoration of the constitutional relation between the United States and their respective states, and people, if that relation shall have been suspended or disturbed) be compensated for all losses by acts of the United States, including the loss of slaves.

In witness whereof, I have hereunto set my hand, and caused the seal of the United States to be affixed.

Done at the city of Washington, this twenty-second day of September, in the year of our Lord one thousand eight hundred and sixty-two, and of the Independence of the United States the eighty-seventh.

ABRAHAM LINCOLN.

By the President:
WM. H. SEWARD, *Secretary of State.*

Proclamation of Emancipation.

Whereas, on the twenty-second day of September, in the year of our Lord one thousand eight hundred and sixty-two, a proclamation was issued by the President of the United States, containing, among other things, the following, to wit:

"That on the first day of January, in the year of our Lord one thousand eight hundred and sixty-three, all persons held as slaves within any state or designated part of a state, the people whereof shall then be in rebellion against the United States, shall be then, thenceforward, and forever free; and the Executive Government of the United States, including the military and naval authority thereof, will recognize and maintain the freedom of such persons, and will do no act or acts to repress such persons or any of them, in any efforts they may make for their actual freedom.

"That the Executive will, on the first day of January aforesaid, by proclamation, designate the states and parts of states, if any, in which the people thereof respectively shall then be in rebellion against the United States; and the fact that any state, or the people thereof, shall on that day be in good faith represented in the Congress of the United States, by members chosen thereto at elections wherein a majority of the qualified voters of such state shall have participated, shall, in the absence of strong countervailing testimony, be deemed conclusive evidence that such state, and the people

thereof, are not then in rebellion against the United States."

Now, therefore, I, ABRAHAM LINCOLN, President of the United States, by virtue of the power in me vested as Commander-in-Chief of the army and navy of the United States in time of actual armed rebellion against the authority and government of the United States, and as a fit and necessary war measure for suppressing said rebellion, do, on this first day of January, in the year of our Lord one thousand eight hundred and sixty-three, and in accordance with my purpose so to do, publicly proclaimed for the full period of one hundred days from the day first above mentioned, order and designate, as the states and parts of states wherein the people thereof respectively are this day in rebellion against the United States, the following, to wit:

Arkansas, Texas, Louisiana (except the parishes of St. Bernard, Plaquemines, Jefferson, St. John, St. Charles, St. James, Ascension, Assumption, Terre Bonne, Lafourche, Ste. Marie, St. Martin, and Orleans, including the city of New Orleans), Mississippi, Alabama, Florida, Georgia, South Carolina, North Carolina, and Virginia (except the forty-eight counties designated as West Virginia, and also the counties of Berkeley, Accomac, Northampton, Elizabeth City, York, Princess Anne, and Norfolk, including the cities of Norfolk and Portsmouth), and which excepted parts are for the present left precisely as if this proclamation were not issued.

And, by virtue of the power and for the purpose aforesaid, I do order and declare that all persons held as slaves within said designated states and parts of states are and henceforth shall be free; and that the Executive Government of the United States, including the military and naval authorities thereof, will recognize and maintain the freedom of said persons.

And I hereby enjoin upon the people so declared to be free, to abstain from all violence, unless in necessary self-defense; and I recommend to them that in all cases, when allowed, they labor faithfully for reasonable wages.

And I further declare and make known that such persons of suitable condition will be received into the armed service of the United States, to garrison forts, positions, stations, and other places, and to man vessels of all sorts in said service.

And upon this act, sincerely believed to be an act of justice, warranted by the Constitution, upon military necessity, I invoke the considerate judgment of mankind and the gracious favor of Almighty God.

In testimony whereof, I have hereunto set my name, and caused the seal of the United States to be affixed.

Done at the city of Washington, this first day of January, in the year of our Lord one thousand eight hundred and sixty-three, and of the Independence of the United States the eighty-seventh.

ABRAHAM LINCOLN.

By the President:

WM. H. SEWARD, *Secretary of State.*

AT THE WAR'S END

1. In November, 1864, President Lincoln was reelected. His Second Inaugural Address, delivered a few weeks before he was murdered, expressed in its final paragraph the President's high hopes and indicated what his future course would be.

FELLOW-COUNTRYMEN: At this second appearing to take the oath of the Presidential office there is less occasion for an extended address than there was at the first. Then a statement somewhat in detail of a course to be pursued seemed fitting and proper. Now, at the expiration of four years, during which public declarations have been constantly called forth on every point and phase of the great contest which still absorbs the attention and engrosses the energies of the nation, little that is new could be presented. The progress of our arms, upon which all else chiefly depends, is as well known to the public as to myself, and it is, I trust, reasonably satisfactory and encouraging to all. With high hope for the future, no prediction in regard to it is ventured.

On the occasion corresponding to this four years ago all thoughts were anxiously directed to an impending civil war. All dreaded it; all sought to avert it. While the inaugural address was being delivered from this place, devoted altogether to *saving* the Union without war, insurgent agents were in the city seeking to *destroy* it without war—seeking to dissolve the Union and divide effects by negotiation. Both parties deprecated war, but one of them would *make* war rather than let the nation survive, and the other would *accept* war rather than let it perish, and the war came.

One-eighth of the whole population were colored slaves, not distributed generally over the Union, but localized in the southern part of it. These slaves constituted a peculiar and powerful interest. All knew that this interest was somehow the cause of the war. To strengthen, perpetuate, and extend this interest was the object for which the insurgents would rend the Union even by war, while the Government claimed no right to do more than to restrict the territorial enlargement of it. Neither party expected for the war the magnitude or the duration which it has already attained. Neither anticipated that the *cause* of the conflict might cease with or even before the conflict itself should cease. Each looked for an easier triumph, and a result less fundamental and astounding. Both read the same Bible and pray to the same God, and each invokes His aid against the other. It may seem strange that any men should dare to ask a just God's assistance in wringing their bread from the sweat of other men's faces, but let us judge not, that we be not judged. The prayers of both could not be answered. That of neither has been answered fully. The Almighty has His own purposes. "Woe unto the world because of offenses; for it must needs be that offenses come, but woe to that man by whom the offense cometh." If we shall suppose that American slavery is one of those offenses which, in the providence of God, must needs come, but which, having continued through His appointed time, He now wills to remove, and that He gives to both North and South this terrible war as the woe due to those by whom the offense came, shall we discern therein any departure from those divine attributes which the believers in a living God always ascribe to Him? Fondly do we hope, fervently do we pray, that this mighty scourge of war may speedily pass away. Yet, if God wills that it continue until all the wealth piled by the bondsman's two hundred and fifty years of unrequited toil shall be sunk, and until every drop of blood drawn with the lash shall be paid by another drawn with the sword, as was said three thousand years ago, so still it must be said "the judgments of the Lord are true and righteous altogether."

With malice toward none, with charity for all, with firmness in the right as God gives us to see the right, let us strive on to finish the work we are in, to bind up the nation's wounds, to care for him who shall have borne the battle and for his widow and his orphan, to do all which may achieve and cherish a just and lasting peace among ourselves and with all nations.

2. Several of the Confederate armies were still in the field, but General Robert E. Lee's Army of Northern Virginia held the principal place in the minds of the people of the North. On April 2 and 3, 1865, a few weeks after Lincoln's Second Inauguration, Lee gave up the defense of Petersburg and Richmond and headed for Danville, hopeful of joining with General J. E. Johnston's force in North Carolina. Assailed on all sides, without food or other supplies, what was left of the Army of Northern Virginia was surrendered by General Lee at Appomattox on April 9, 1865.

In his book Four Years with General Lee, *Colonel Walter Taylor, one of Lee's aides, told the story as he recalled it in 1878.*

After a gallant resistance our forces were retired to the second or inner line of defense around the city of Petersburg, and there maintained their ground till nightfall. By the dawn of day next morning the lines had been evacuated, and the gallant but sadly-reduced Army of Northern Virginia had made good way in its retreat westwardly toward Amelia Court-House. The intention was to take the direction of Danville, and turn to our advantage the good line for resistance offered by the Dan and Staunton Rivers. The activity of the Federal cavalry and the want of supplies compelled a different course, and the retreat was continued up the South Side Railroad toward Lynchburg.

Despite the great numerical superiority of the Federals and their immense resources, General Lee managed to check their pursuit from time to time, and to continue his retreat for seven days, until, on the morning of the 9th of April, our advance under General Gordon was confronted by the enemy in the neighborhood of Appomattox Court-House. The returns from the various commands made that morning showed an aggregate of eight thousand muskets in line of battle.

On the previous evening I became separated from General Lee in the execution of his orders in regard to the parking of our trains in places of safety, and did not rejoin him until the morning of the 9th. After making my report the general said to me, "Well, colonel, what are we to do?"

In reply, a fear was expressed that it would be necessary to abandon the trains, which had already occasioned us such great embarrassment; and the hope was indulged that, relieved of this burden, the army could make good its escape.

"Yes," said the general, "perhaps we could; but I have had a conference with these gentlemen around me, and they agree that the time has come for capitulation."

"Well, sir," I said, "I can only speak for myself; to me any other fate is preferable—"

"Such is my individual way of thinking," interrupted the general.

"But," I immediately added, "of course, general, it is different with you. You have to think of these brave men and decide not only for yourself, but for them."

"Yes," he replied; "it would be useless and therefore cruel to provoke the further effusion of blood, and I have arranged to meet General Grant with a view to surrender, and wish you to accompany me."

Shortly after this the general, accompanied by Colonel Marshall and myself, started back in the direction from which we had come, to meet General Grant as had been arranged.

We continued some distance without meeting any one after passing our lines; but finally came upon a staff-officer sent by General Grant's order to say to General Lee that he had been prevented from meeting him at that point, and to request that he would meet him upon the other road. General Lee then retraced his steps, and, proceeding toward our front in the direction of Appomattox Court-House, dismounted at a convenient place to await General Grant's communication. Very soon a Federal officer, accompanied by one of General Gordon's staff, rode up to where General Lee was seated in a small orchard on the road-side. This proved to be General Forsythe, of General Sheridan's staff, who was sent by General Sheridan to say that, as he had doubt as to his authority to recognize the informal truce which had been agreed upon between General Gordon and himself, he desired to communicate with General Meade on the subject, and wished permission to pass through our lines as the shortest route. I was assigned to the duty of escorting General Forsythe through our lines and back. This was scarcely accomplished, when General Babcock rode up and announced to General Lee that General Grant was prepared to meet him at the front.

I shrank from this interview, and while I could not then, and cannot now, justify my conduct, I availed myself of the excuse of having taken the two rides through the extent of our lines and to those of the enemy, already mentioned, and did not accompany my chief in this trying ordeal.

The scene witnessed upon the return of General Lee was one certain to impress itself indelibly upon the memory; it can be vividly recalled now, after the lapse of many years, but no description can do it justice. The men crowded around him, eager to shake him by the hand; eyes that had been so often illumined with the fire of patriotism and true courage, that had so often glared with defiance in the heat and fury of battle, and so often kindled with enthusiasm and pride in the hour of success, moistened now; cheeks bronzed by exposure in many campaigns, and withal begrimed with powder and dust, now blanched from deep emotion and suffered the silent tear; tongues that had so often carried dismay to the hearts of the enemy in that indescribable cheer which accompanied "the charge," or that had so often made the air to resound with the paean of victory, refused utterance now; brave hearts failed that had never quailed in the presence of an enemy; but the firm and silent pressure of the hand told most eloquently of souls filled with admiration, love, and tender sympathy, for their beloved chief. He essayed to thank them, but too full a heart paralyzed his speech; he soon sought a short respite from these trying scenes and retired to his private quarters, that he might, in solitude and quiet, commune with his own brave heart and be still. Thus terminated the career of the Army of Northern Virginia—an army that was never vanquished; but that, in obedience to the orders of its trusted commander, who was himself yielding obedience to the dictates of a pure and lofty sense of duty to his men and those dependent on them, laid down its arms, and furled the standards never lowered in defeat.

The work of paroling the army was now proceeded with, and was completed on the 10th of April. On the same day General Meade called to pay his respects to General Lee. The latter reported to his staff, after the visit, that the conversation had naturally turned upon recent events, and that General Meade had asked him how many men he had at Petersburg at the time of General Grant's final assault. He told him in reply that by the last returns he had thirty-three thousand muskets. (In his recital of the matter he appealed to me to know if his memory was correct, and was answered in the affirmative.) General Meade then said, "You mean that you had thirty-three thousand men in the lines immediately around Petersburg?" to which General Lee replied "No," that he had but that number from his left on the Chickahominy River to his right at Dinwiddie Court-House. At this General Meade expressed great surprise, and stated that he then had with him, in the one wing of the Federal army which he commanded, over fifty thousand men.

The number of men and officers paroled, including the stragglers who had caught up with the army, and all the extra-duty or detailed men of every description, was in round numbers between twenty-six and twenty-seven thousand.

3. The victorious General Ulysses S. Grant, who received General Lee's surrender, recalled the incident in his own Personal Memoirs *(published many years later, in 1886).*

I rode in to Farmville on the 7th, arriving there early in the day. Sheridan and Ord were pushing through, away to the south. Meade was back towards the High Bridge, and Humphreys confronting Lee as before stated. After having gone into bivouac at Prince Edward's Court House, Sheridan learned that seven trains of provisions and forage were at Appomattox, and determined to start at once and capture them; and a forced march was necessary in order to get there before Lee's army could secure them. He wrote me a note telling me

this. This fact, together with the incident related the night before by Dr. Smith, gave me the idea of opening correspondence with General Lee on the subject of the surrender of his army. I therefore wrote to him on this day, as follows:

> Headquarters Armies of the U. S.,
> April 7, 1865, 5 P.M.
>
> GENERAL R. E. LEE,
> Commanding C. S. A.
> The results of the last week must convince you of the hopelessness of further resistance on the part of the Army of Northern Virginia in this struggle. I feel that it is so, and regard it as my duty to shift from myself the responsibility of any further effusion of blood, by asking of you the surrender of that portion of the Confederate States army known as the Army of Northern Virginia.
>
> U. S. GRANT,
> Lieut.-General

Lee replied on the evening of the same day as follows:

> April 7, 1865
>
> LIEUT.-GENERAL U. S. GRANT,
> Commanding Armies of the U. S.
> GENERAL:—I have received your note of this day. Though not entertaining the opinion you express on the hopelessness of further resistance on the part of the Army of Northern Virginia, I reciprocate your desire to avoid useless effusion of blood, and therefore before considering your proposition, ask the terms you will offer on condition of its surrender.
>
> R. E. LEE,
> General

This was not satisfactory, but I regarded it as deserving another letter and wrote him as follows:

> April 8, 1865
>
> GENERAL R. E. LEE,
> Commanding C. S. A.
> Your note of last evening in reply to mine of same date, asking the condition on which I will accept the surrender of the Army of Northern Virginia is just received. In reply I would say that, peace being my great desire, there is but one condition I would insist upon, namely: that the men and officers surrendered shall be disqualified for taking up arms again against the Government of the United States until properly exchanged. I will meet you, or will designate officers to meet any officers you may name for the same purpose, at any point agreeable to you, for the purpose of arranging definitely the terms upon which the surrender of the Army of Northern Virginia will be received.
>
> U. S. GRANT,
> Lieut.-General

Lee's army was rapidly crumbling. Many of his soldiers had enlisted from that part of the State where they now were, and were continually dropping out of the ranks and going to their homes. I know that I occupied a hotel almost destitute of furniture at Farmville, which had probably been used as a Confederate hospital. The next morning when I came out I found a

Confederate colonel there, who reported to me and said that he was the proprietor of that house, and that he was a colonel of a regiment that had been raised in that neighborhood. He said that when he came along past home, he found that he was the only man of the regiment remaining with Lee's army, so he just dropped out, and now wanted to surrender himself. I told him to stay there and he would not be molested. That was one regiment which had been eliminated from Lee's force by this crumbling process.

Although Sheridan had been marching all day, his troops moved with alacrity and without any straggling. They began to see the end of what they had been fighting four years for. Nothing seemed to fatigue them. They were ready to move without rations and travel without rest until the end. Straggling had entirely ceased, and every man was now a rival for the front. The infantry marched about as rapidly as the cavalry could.

Sheridan sent Custer with his division to move south of Appomattox Station, which is about five miles southwest of the Court House, to get west of the trains and destroy the roads to the rear. They got there the night of the 8th, and succeeded partially; but some of the train men had just discovered the movement of our troops and succeeded in running off three of the trains. The other four were held by Custer.

The head of Lee's column came marching up there on the morning of the 9th, not dreaming, I suppose, that there were any Union soldiers near. The Confederates were surprised to find our cavalry had possession of the trains. However, they were desperate and at once assaulted, hoping to recover them. In the melée that ensued they succeeded in burning one of the trains, but not in getting anything from it. Custer then ordered the other trains run back on the road towards Farmville, and the fight continued.

So far, only cavalry and the advance of Lee's army were engaged. Soon, however, Lee's men were brought up from the rear, no doubt expecting they had nothing to meet but our cavalry. But our infantry had pushed forward so rapidly that by the time the enemy got up they found Griffin's corps and the Army of the James confronting them. A sharp engagement ensued, but Lee quickly set up a white flag.

On the 8th I had followed the Army of the Potomac in rear of Lee. I was suffering very severely with a sick headache, and stopped at a farmhouse on the road some distance in rear of the main body of the army. I spent the night in bathing my feet in hot water and mustard, and putting plasters on my wrists and the back part of my neck, hoping to be cured by morning. During the night I received Lee's answer to my letter of the 8th,

inviting an interview between the lines on the following morning. But it was for a different purpose from that of surrendering his army, and I answered him as follows:

Headquarters Armies of the U. S.,
April 9, 1865

General R. E. Lee,
Commanding C. S. A.

Your note of yesterday is received. As I have no authority to treat on the subject of peace, the meeting proposed for ten A.M. to-day could lead to no good. I will state, however, General, that I am equally anxious for peace with yourself, and the whole North entertains the same feeling. The terms upon which peace can be had are well understood. By the South laying down their arms they will hasten that most desirable event, save thousands of human lives, and hundreds of millions of property not yet destroyed. Sincerely hoping that all our difficulties may be settled without the loss of another life, I subscribe myself, etc.,

U. S. Grant,
Lieutenant-General

I proceeded at an early hour in the morning, still suffering with the headache, to get to the head of the column. I was not more than two or three miles from Appomattox Court House at the time, but to go direct I would have to pass through Lee's army, or a portion of it. I had therefore to move south in order to get upon a road coming up from another direction.

When the white flag was put out by Lee, as already described, I was in this way moving towards Appomattox Court House, and consequently could not be communicated with immediately, and be informed of what Lee had done. Lee, therefore, sent a flag to the rear to advise Meade and one to the front to Sheridan, saying that he had sent a message to me for the purpose of having a meeting to consult about the surrender of his army, and asked for a suspension of hostilities until I could be communicated with. As they had heard nothing of this until the fighting had got to be severe and all going against Lee, both of these commanders hesitated very considerably about suspending hostilities at all. They were afraid it was not in good faith, and we had the Army of Northern Virginia where it could not escape except by some deception. They, however, finally consented to a suspension of hostilities for two hours to give an opportunity of communicating with me in that time, if possible. It was found that, from the route I had taken, they would probably not be able to communicate with me and get an answer back within the time fixed unless the messenger should pass through the rebel lines.

Lee, therefore, sent an escort with the officer bearing this message through his lines to me.

April 9, 1865

Lieutenant-General U. S. Grant,
Commanding U. S. Armies.

General:—I received your note of this morning on the

picket-line whither I had come to meet you and ascertain definitely what terms were embraced in your proposal of yesterday with reference to the surrender of this army. I now request an interview in accordance with the offer contained in your letter of yesterday for that purpose.

> R. E. LEE,
> General

When the officer reached me I was still suffering with the sick headache; but the instant I saw the contents of the note I was cured. I wrote the following note in reply and hastened on:

> April 9, 1865

GENERAL R. E. LEE,
Commanding C. S. Armies.

Your note of this date is but this moment (11.50 A.M.) received, in consequence of my having passed from the Richmond and Lynchburg road to the Farmville and Lynchburg road. I am at this writing about four miles west of Walker's Church and will push forward to the front for the purpose of meeting you. Notice sent to me on this road where you wish the interview to take place will meet me.

> U. S. GRANT,
> Lieutenant-General

I was conducted at once to where Sheridan was located with his troops drawn up in line of battle facing the Confederate Army near by. They were very much excited, and expressed their view that this was all a ruse employed to enable the Confederates to get away. They said they believed that Johnston was marching up from North Carolina now, and Lee was moving to join him; and they would whip the rebels where they now were in five minutes if I would only let them go in. But I had no doubt about the good faith of Lee, and pretty soon was conducted to where he was. I found him at the house of a Mr. McLean, at Appomattox Court House, with Colonel Marshall, one of his staff officers, awaiting my arrival. The head of his column was occupying a hill, on a portion of which was an apple orchard, beyond a little valley which separated it from that on the crest of which Sheridan's forces were drawn up in line of battle to the south.

Before stating what took place between General Lee and myself, I will give all there is of the story of the famous apple tree.

Wars produce many stories of fiction, some of which are told until they are believed to be true. The war of the rebellion was no exception to this rule, and the story of the apple tree is one of those fictions based on a slight foundation of fact. As I have said, there was an apple orchard on the side of the hill occupied by the Confederate forces. Running diagonally up the hill was a wagon road, which, at one point, ran very near one of the trees, so that the wheels of vehicles had, on that side, cut off the roots of this tree, leaving a little embankment. General Babcock, of my staff, reported to me

that when he first met General Lee he was sitting upon this embankment with his feet in the road below and his back resting against the tree. The story had no other foundation than that. Like many other stories, it would be very good if it was only true.

I had known General Lee in the old army, and had served with him in the Mexican War; but did not suppose, owing to the difference in our age and rank, that he would remember me; while I would more naturally remember him distinctly, because he was the chief of staff of General Scott in the Mexican War.

When I had left camp that morning I had not expected so soon the result that was then taking place, and consequently was in rough garb. I was without a sword, as I usually was when on horseback in the field, and wore a soldier's blouse for a coat, with the shoulder straps of my rank to indicate to the army who I was. When I went into the house I found General Lee. We greeted each other, and after shaking hands took our seats. I had my staff with me, a good portion of whom were in the room during the whole of the interview.

What General Lee's feelings were I do not know. As he was a man of much dignity, with an impassable face, it was impossible to say whether he felt inwardly glad that the end had finally come, or felt sad over the result, and was too manly to show it. Whatever his feelings, they were entirely concealed from my observation; but my own feelings, which had been quite jubilant on the receipt of his letter, were sad and depressed. I felt like anything rather than rejoicing at the downfall of a foe who had fought so long and valiantly, and had suffered so much for a cause, though that cause was, I believe, one of the worst for which a people ever fought, and one for which there was the least excuse. I do not question, however, the sincerity of the great mass of those who were opposed to us.

General Lee was dressed in a full uniform which was entirely new, and was wearing a sword of considerable value, very likely the sword which had been presented by the State of Virginia; at all events, it was an entirely different sword from the one that would ordinarily be worn in the field. In my rough traveling suit, the uniform of a private with the straps of a lieutenant-general, I must have contrasted very strangely with a man so handsomely dressed, six feet high and of faultless form. But this was not a matter that I thought of until afterwards.

We soon fell into a conversation about old army times. He remarked that he remembered me very well in the old army; and I told him that as a matter of course I remembered him perfectly, but from the difference in our rank and years (there being about sixteen years' difference in our ages), I had thought it very likely that I had not attracted his attention sufficiently to be remembered by him after such a long interval. Our conversation grew so pleasant that I almost forgot the object of our meeting. After the conversation had run on in this style for some time, General Lee called my attention to the object of our meeting, and said that he had asked for this interview for the purpose of getting from me the terms I proposed to give his army. I said that I meant merely that his army should lay down their arms, not to take them up again during the continuance of the war unless duly and properly exchanged. He said that he had so understood my letter.

Then we gradually fell off again into conversation about matters foreign to the subject which had brought us together. This continued for some little time, when General Lee again interrupted the course of the conversation by suggesting that the terms I proposed to give his army ought to be written out. I called to General Parker, secretary on my staff, for writing materials, and commenced writing out the following terms:

> Appomattox C. H., Va.,
> Ap'l 9th, 1865

GEN. R. E. LEE,
Comd'g C. S. A.

GEN.: In accordance with the substance of my letter to you of the 8th inst., I propose to receive the surrender of the Army of N. Va. on the following terms, to wit: Rolls of all the officers and men to be made in duplicate. One copy to be given to an officer designated by me, the other to be retained by such officer or officers as you may designate. The officers to give their individual paroles not to take up arms against the Government of the United States until properly exchanged, and each company or regimental commander sign a like parole for the men of their commands. The arms, artillery and public property to be parked and stacked, and turned over to the officer appointed by me to receive them. This will not embrace the side arms of the officers, nor their private horses or baggage. This done, each officer and man will be allowed to return to their homes, not to be disturbed by United States authority so long as they observe their paroles and the laws in force where they may reside.

> Very respectfully,
> U. S. GRANT,
> Lt.-Gen.

When I put my pen to the paper I did not know the first word that I should make use of in writing the terms. I only knew what was in my mind, and I wished to express it clearly, so that there could be no mistaking it. As I wrote on, the thought occurred to me that the officers had their own private horses and effects, which were important to them, but of no value to us; also that it would be an unnecessary humiliation to call upon them to deliver their side arms.

No conversation, not one word, passed between General Lee and myself, either about private property, side arms, or kindred subjects. He appeared to have no ob-

jections to the terms first proposed; or if he had a point to make against them he wished to wait until they were in writing to make it. When he read over that part of the terms about side arms, horses and private property of the officers, he remarked, with some feeling, I thought, that this would have a happy effect upon his army.

Then, after a little further conversation, General Lee remarked to me again that their army was organized a little differently from the army of the United States (still maintaining by implication that we were two countries); that in their army the cavalrymen and artillerists owned their own horses; and he asked if he was to understand that the men who so owned their horses were to be permitted to retain them. I told him that as the terms were written they would not; that only the officers were permitted to take their private property. He then, after reading over the terms a second time, remarked that that was clear.

I then said to him that I thought this would be about the last battle of the war—I sincerely hoped so; and I said further I took it that most of the men in the ranks were small farmers. The whole country had been so raided by the two armies that it was doubtful whether they would be able to put in a crop to carry themselves and their families through the next winter without the aid of the horses they were then riding. The United States did not want them and I would, therefore, instruct the officers I left behind to receive the paroles of his troops to let every man of the Confederate army who claimed to own a horse or mule take the animal to his home. Lee remarked again that this would have a happy effect.

He then sat down and wrote the following letter:

> Headquarters Army of Northern Virginia,
> April 9, 1865

GENERAL:—I received your letter of this date containing the terms of the surrender of the Army of Northern Virginia as proposed by you. As they are substantially the same as those expressed in your letter of the 8th inst., they are accepted. I will proceed to designate the proper officers to carry the stipulations into effect.

> R. E. LEE,
> General

LIEUT.-GENERAL U. S. GRANT.

While duplicates of the two letters were being made, the Union generals present were severally presented to General Lee.

The much talked of surrendering of Lee's sword and my handing it back, this and much more that has been said about it is the purest romance. The word sword or side arms was not mentioned by either of us until I wrote it in the terms. There was no premeditation, and it did not occur to me until the moment I wrote it down. If I had happened to omit it, and General Lee had called my attention to it, I should have put it in the terms precisely as I acceded to the provision about the soldiers retaining their horses.

General Lee, after all was completed and before taking his leave, remarked that his army was in a very bad condition for want of food, and that they were without forage; that his men had been living for some days on parched corn exclusively, and that he would have to ask me for rations and forage. I told him "certainly," and asked for how many men he wanted rations. His answer was "about twenty-five thousand": and I authorized him to send his own commissary and quartermaster to Appomattox Station, two or three miles away, where he could have, out of the trains we had stopped, all the provisions wanted. As for forage, we had ourselves depended almost entirely upon the country for that.

Generals Gibbon, Griffin and Merritt were designated by me to carry into effect the paroling of Lee's troops before they should start for their homes—General Lee leaving Generals Longstreet, Gordon and Pendleton for them to confer with in order to facilitate this work. Lee and I then separated as cordially as we had met, he returning to his own lines, and all went into bivouac for the night at Appomattox.

Soon after Lee's departure I telegraphed to Washington as follows:

Headquarters Appomattox C. H., Va.,
April 9th, 1865, 4.30 P.M.

HON. E. M. STANTON:
Secretary of War,
Washington.

General Lee surrendered the Army of Northern Virginia this afternoon on terms proposed by myself. The accompanying additional correspondence will show the condition fully.

U. S. GRANT,
Lieut.-General

When news of the surrender first reached our lines our men commenced firing a salute of a hundred guns in honor of the victory, I at once sent word, however, to have it stopped. The Confederates were now our prisoners, and we did not want to exult over their downfall.

CROSS REFERENCES

Refer to the following articles in the text volumes (Volume 1 through Volume 8) for background of RESOURCE UNIT 5.

ABOLITION
AGRICULTURE AND AGRICULTURAL TECHNOLOGY
ALABAMA CLAIMS

ANDERSON, ROBERT
APPOMATTOX COURT HOUSE
BLOCKADE
BOOTH FAMILY
BROWN, JOHN
BUTLER, BENJAMIN F.
CANADA, RELATIONS WITH
CIVIL LIBERTIES AND CIVIL RIGHTS LEGISLATION
CIVIL WAR
CONFEDERATE STATES OF AMERICA
CONTRABAND
CONSTITUTION OF THE UNITED STATES
CONSTITUTIONAL UNION PARTY
DAVIS, JEFFERSON
DEMOCRATIC PARTY
DRED SCOTT DECISION
ELECTIONS, PRESIDENTIAL
ELECTORAL COLLEGE
EMANCIPATION PROCLAMATION
ERICSSON, JOHN
FOREIGN POLICY OF THE UNITED STATES
FORT SUMTER
FRANCE, RELATIONS WITH
FREEDMEN'S BUREAU
FRÉMONT, JOHN C.
GETTYSBURG, BATTLE OF
GRANT, ULYSSES S.
GREAT BRITAIN, RELATIONS WITH
GREELEY, HORACE
HABEAS CORPUS
HOMESTEAD ACT
HOSPITALS
HOUSTON, SAM
INTERNAL SECURITY AND ESPIONAGE
IRON AND STEEL INDUSTRY
JACKSON, THOMAS J.
JOHNSON, ANDREW
JOURNALISM
LABOR ORGANIZATIONS
LAND-GRANT COLLEGE ACT
LEE, ROBERT E.
LINCOLN, ABRAHAM
MARTIAL LAW
MERCHANT MARINE
MEXICO, RELATIONS WITH
MONTGOMERY, ALABAMA
MORRILL, JUSTIN S.
NAVAL VESSELS
NEUTRALITY
NULLIFICATION
PLANTATION
POLICE POWERS OF STATES
PORTER, DAVID DIXON
RACES AND PEOPLES OF THE UNITED STATES
RAILROADS
RECOGNITION, DIPLOMATIC
RELIGION IN AMERICAN LIFE
REPUBLICAN PARTY

RICHMOND, VIRGINIA
RUSSIA, RELATIONS WITH
SCHURZ, CARL
SCOTT, WINFIELD
SECESSION
SELECTIVE SEVICE
SEWARD, WILLIAM H.
SHERIDAN, PHILIP
SHERMAN, WILLIAM T.
SHILOH, BATTLE OF
SLAVERY IN AMERICA
STATE AND LOCAL GOVERNMENT
STEVENS, THADDEUS
SUMNER, CHARLES
SUPREME COURT DECISIONS
TARIFF POLICIES OF THE UNITED STATES
TAXATION IN THE UNITED STATES
TELEPHONE AND TELEGRAPH INDUSTRY
UNITED STATES ARMY
UNITED STATES NAVY
WELLES, GIDEON
WEST VIRGINIA
WHALING INDUSTRY

In addition to the above, each article on an individual State, either of the Confederacy or of the Union, contains information on the part played by that State in the Civil War.

BOOKS FOR FURTHER READING

Collections of Source Materials

U.S. Army, *The War of the Rebelion: Official Records of the Union and Confederate Armies* (130 vols.); U.S. Navy, *War of the Rebellion: Official Records of the Union and Confederate Navies* (30 vols.); R. B. Harwell, ed., *The Confederate Reader* and *The Union Reader*; B. I. Wiley, *The Life of Johnny Reb* and *The Life of Billy Yank*; *American Heritage Picture History of the Civil War*.

General Histories of the Civil War

B. Catton, *Centennial History of the Civil War*; R. U. Johnson and C. C. Buel, *Battles and Leaders of the Civil War* (8 vols.); J. B. Mitchell, *Decisive Battles of the Civil War*; A. Nevins, *Ordeal of the Union*, Vols IV-VIII; F. Pratt, *Ordeal by Fire: An Informal History of the Civil War*; J. G. Randall and D. Donald, *Divided Union*; K. M. Stampp, *The Causes of the Civil War*; K. P.

Williams, *Lincoln Finds a General: A Military History of the Civil War*, (4 vols.).

Special Aspects of the Civil War

R. Carse, *Blockade*; H. A. Gosnell, *Guns on the Western Waters* (the story of the river gunboats in the Civil War); H. T. Kane, *Spies for the Blue and the Grey*; W. F. Keeler, *Aboard the U.S.S. Monitor: 1862*; J. Monaghan, *Civil War on the Western Border*; G. E. Turner, *Victory Rode the Rails*; R. S. West, *Mr. Lincoln's Navy*.

Biographies and Background

B. A. Botkin, *Lay My Burden Down: A Folk History of Slavery*; M. B. Chesnut, *A Diary from Dixie*; B. Davis, *They Called Him Stonewall*; D. Donald, *Charles Sumner and the Coming of the Civil War*; C. Eaton, *A History of the Southern Confederacy*; D. S. Freeman, *Robert E. Lee* and *Lee's Lieutenants—A Study in Command*; J. F. C. Fuller, *Grant and Lee*; B. Hendricks, *Statesmen of the Lost Cause*; M. K. Leech, *Reveille in Washington, 1861–1865*; Lloyd Lewis, *Sherman, Fighting Prophet*; B. Quarles, *The Negro in the Civil War*; J. G. Randall, *Lincoln the President*; C. Sandburg, *Abraham Lincoln, The War Years*; C. Schurz, *Autobiography*; B. P. Thomas, *Abraham Lincoln, a Biography*; B. P. Thomas and H. Hyman, *Stanton: The Life and Times of Lincoln's Secretary of War*; G. Welles, *The Diary of Gideon Welles*.

Novels and Stories of the Civil War

The titles marked "A" are effective stories of military action; those marked "S" are essentially studies of the effect of the Civil War on people and on general society, both North and South.

Hervey Allen, *Action at Aquila*   (A)
W. Churchill, *The Crisis*   (S)
S. Crane, *The Red Badge of Courage*   (A)
J. W. DeForest, *Miss Ravenel's Conversion from Secession to Loyalty*   (A and S)
C. Dowdey, *Bugles Blow No More*   (A)
E. Glasgow, *The Battle-Ground*   (S)
M. Kantor, *Long Remember*   (A)
Margaret Mitchell, *Gone With the Wind*   (S)
S. W. Mitchell, *Roland Blake*   (S)
T. N. Page, *The Burial of the Guns*   (S)
J. W. Thomason, *Lone Star Preacher*   (A)
S. Young, *So Red the Rose*   (S)

5. THE CIVIL WAR: 1861-1865

1

1. Secession meeting in Charleston, South Carolina, December, 1860. From *Frank Leslie's Illustrated Newspaper*.

2

4

3

5

6

2. Old photograph of Montgomery, Alabama, the Capitol of the Confederacy at the time of the inauguration of Jefferson Davis, early 1861. *Courtesy,* Scribner Art Files. 3. Enthusiasm in the North to maintain the Union expressed in songs and military scenes. From *Harper's Weekly,* November, 1861. 4. Many Southerners turned out to watch the attack on Fort Sumter by the Federal ironclads in Charleston harbor, April, 1863. From the *Illustrated London News,* May, 1863. 5. Later, the grim reality of the war came home to Southerners who fled to the woods to escape the fighting near Vicksburg. From the *Illustrated London News,* August, 1863. 6. "Contrabands" fording the Rappahannock River on their way North. *Courtesy,* Scribner Art Files.

7. Romance flourished during the war as seen in this military wedding in a Northern camp. Pencil sketch by A. R. Waud in the J. Pierpont Morgan Collection, Library of Congress. 8. Civilian aid for Union soldiers was the work of the U. S. Sanitary Commission. Here shown is a Lodge for Invalid Soldiers, Washington, D. C., 1863. From Collections of the Library of Congress. 9. Some women brought comfort to wounded men in hospitals. From *Campaign Sketches: The Letter for Home* by Winslow Homer. 10. Others turned the war to gay social occasions often financed by war profits. A ball for Russian officers on a courtesy call in New York City, 1863. From *Harper's Weekly,* November, 1863.

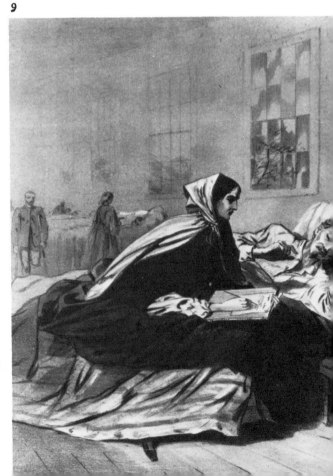

10

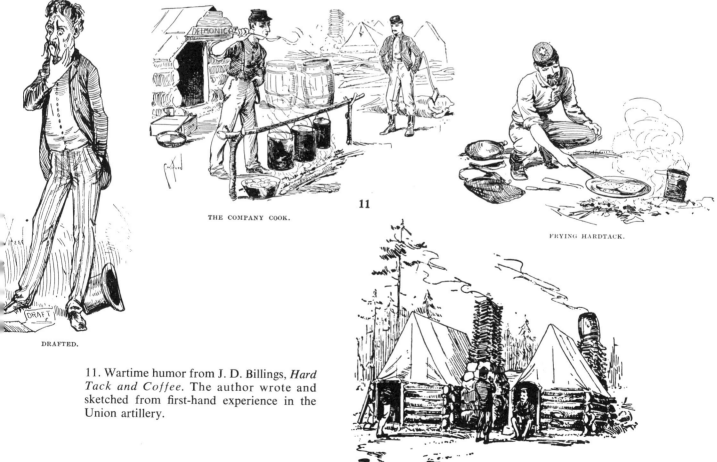

THE COMPANY COOK.

11

FRYING HARDTACK.

DRAFTED.

STOCKADED A TENTS.

11. Wartime humor from J. D. Billings, *Hard Tack and Coffee*. The author wrote and sketched from first-hand experience in the Union artillery.

HARD TACK.

OUR SPECIAL.

HOME ON A FURLOUGH.

GOOD BYE.

THE GIRL HE LEFT BEHIN

EXTRA RATION.

12. Joys and sorrows of a soldier's life drawn by Winslow Homer, later to become a famous American artist. From *Campaign Sketches: Life in Camp,* 1863 and 1864.

RESOURCE UNIT 6

Reconstruction and National Development: 1865-1898

6-A EXPLORATION AND SETTLEMENT

In the years following the Civil War, much work remained to be done by Federal and State surveyors, mapmakers, and geologists, particularly in the new States and Territories west of the Mississippi River. Many mountain and desert areas in the West were still virtually unexplored. And Alaska—the huge, new domain purchased from Russia in 1867—was as yet an unknown quantity and a possible liability.

PROBLEMS: *What natural resources and wonders lay behind western mountain barriers? How would the secrets of the mountains and of Alaska be unlocked? In what ways might these discoveries influence Americans toward wiser use of the land?*

1. Exploration in the years after the Civil War often began with some well known geographic feature. One of these was the Colorado River, known since the days of Coronado's Spanish exploration in the 16th century, but left unexplored along most of its course. No one had yet moved all the way down the Colorado River, at river-level, through the Grand Canyon. John Wesley Powell, a Civil War veteran who had lost an arm in battle, became one of the greatest explorers of the mountain areas of the West. In addition to his own explorations, he helped form public opinion about preserving parts of the unsettled West. The following passage is taken from Powell's own story of his 1869 expedition, entitled Canyons of the Colorado *(1895).*

THE GRAND CANYON

August 13.—We are now ready to start on our way down the Great Unknown. Our boats, tied to a common stake, are chafing each other, as they are tossed by the fretful river. They ride high and buoyant, for their loads are lighter than we could desire. We have but a month's rations remaining. The flour has been resifted through the mosquito net sieve; the spoiled bacon has been dried, and the worst of it boiled; the few pounds of dried apples have been spread in the sun, and re-shrunken to their normal bulk; the sugar has all melted, and gone on its way down the river; but we have a large sack of coffee. The lightening of the boats has this advantage: they will ride the waves better, and we shall have but little to carry when we make a portage.

We are three-quarters of a mile in the depths of the earth, and the great river shrinks into insignificance, as it dashes its angry waves against the walls and cliffs, that rise to the world above; they are but puny ripples, and we but pigmies, running up and down the sands, or lost among the boulders.

We have an unknown distance yet to run; an unknown river yet to explore. What falls there are, we know not; what rocks beset the channel, we know not; what walls rise over the river, we know not. Ah, well! we may conjecture many things. The men talk as cheerfully as ever; jests are bandied about freely this morning; but to me the cheer is somber and the jests are ghastly.

With some eagerness, and some anxiety, and some misgiving, we enter the cañon below, and are carried along by the swift water through walls which rise from its very edge. They have the same structure as we noticed yesterday—tiers of irregular shelves below, and, above these, steep slopes to the foot of marble cliffs. We run six miles in a little more than half an hour, and emerge into a more open portion of the cañon, where high hills and ledges of rock intervene between the river and the distant walls. Just at the head of this open place the river runs across a dike; that is, a fissure in the rocks, open to depths below, has been filled with eruptive matter, and this, on cooling, was harder than the rocks through which the crevice was made, and, when these were washed away, the harder volcanic matter remained as a wall, and the river has cut a gateway through it several hundred feet high, and as many wide. As it crosses the wall, there is a fall below, and a bad rapid, filled with boulders of trap; so we stop to make a portage. Then on we go, gliding by hills and ledges, with distant walls in view; sweeping past sharp angles of rock; stopping at a few points to examine rapids, which we find can be run, until we have made another five miles, when we land for dinner.

Then we let down with lines, over a long rapid, and start again. Once more the walls close in, and we find ourselves in a narrow gorge, the water again filling the channel, and very swift. With great care, and constant watchfulness, we proceed, making about four miles this afternoon, and camp in a cave.

August 14.—At daybreak we walk down the bank of the river, on a little sandy beach, to take a view of a new feature in the cañon. Heretofore, hard rocks, smooth water; and a series of rocks harder than any we have experienced sets in. The river enters the granite!

We can see but a little way into the granite gorge, but it looks threatening.

After breakfast we enter on the waves. At the very introduction, it inspires awe. The cañon is narrower than we have ever before seen it; the water is swifter; there are but few broken rocks in the channel; but the walls are set, on either side, with pinnacles and crags; and sharp, angular buttresses, bristling with wind and wave polished spires, extend far out into the river.

Ledges of rocks jut into the stream, their tops sometimes just below the surface, sometimes rising few or many feet above; and island ledges, and island pinnacles, and island towers break the swift course of the stream into chutes, and eddies, and whirlpools. We soon reach a place where a creek comes in from the left, and just below, the channel is choked with boulders, which have washed down this lateral cañon and formed a dam, over which there is a fall of thirty or forty feet; but on the boulders we can get foothold, and we make a portage.

Three more such dams are found. Over one we make a portage; at the other two we find chutes, through which we can run.

As we proceed, the granite rises higher, until nearly a thousand feet of the lower part of the walls are composed of this rock.

About eleven o'clock we hear a great roar ahead, and approach it very cautiously. The sound grows louder and louder as we run, and at last we find ourselves above a long, broken fall, with ledges and pinnacles of rock obstructing the river. There is a descent of, perhaps, seventy-five or eighty feet in a third of a mile, and the rushing waters break into great waves on the rocks, and lash themselves into a mad, white foam. We can land just above, but there is no foot-hold on either side by which we can make a portage. It is nearly a thousand feet to the top of the granite, so it will be impossible to carry our boats around, though we can climb to the summit up a side gulch, and, passing along a mile or two, can descend to the river. This we find on examination; but such a portage would be impracticable for us, and we must run the rapid, or abandon the river. There is no hesitation. We step into our boats, push off and away we go, first on smooth but swift water, then we strike a glassy wave, and ride to its top, down again into the trough, up again on a higher wave, and down and up on waves higher and still higher, until we strike one just as it curls back, and a breaker rolls over our little boat. Still, on we speed, shooting past projecting rocks, till the little boat is caught in a whirlpool, and spun around several times. At last we pull out again into the stream, and now the other boats have passed us. The open compartment of the *Emma Dean* is filled with water, and every breaker rolls over us. Hurled back from a rock, now on this side, now on that, we are carried into an eddy, in which we struggle for a few minutes, and are then out again, the breakers still rolling over us. Our boat is unmanageable, but she cannot sink, and we drift down another hundred yards, through breakers; how, we scarcely know. We find the other boats have turned into an eddy at the foot of the fall, and are waiting to catch us as we come, for the men have seen that our boat is swamped. They push out as we come near, and pull us in against the wall. We bail our boat, and on we go again.

The walls, now, are more than a mile in height—a vertical distance difficult to appreciate. Stand on the south steps of the Treasury building in Washington, and look down Pennsylvania Avenue to the Capitol Park, and measure this distance overhead, and imagine cliffs to extend to that altitude, and you will understand what I mean; or, stand at Canal Street, in New York, and look up Broadway to Grace Church, and you have about the distance; or, stand at Lake Street bridge, in Chicago, and look down to the Central Depot, and you have it again.

A thousand feet of this is up through granite crags, then steep slopes and perpendicular cliffs rise, one above another, to the summit. The gorge is black and narrow below, red and gray and flaring above, with crags and angular projections on the walls, which, cut in many places by side cañons, seem to be a vast wilderness of rocks. . . .

August 26.—The cañon walls are steadily becoming higher as we advance. They are still bold, and nearly vertical up to the terrace. We still see evidence of the eruption discovered yesterday, but the thickness of the basalt is decreasing, as we go down the stream; yet it has been reinforced at points by streams that have come down from volcanoes standing on the terrace above, but which we cannot see from the river below.

Since we left the Colorado Chiquito, we have seen no evidences that the tribe of Indians inhabiting the plateaus on either side ever come down to the river; but about eleven o'clock to-day we discover an Indian garden, at the foot of the wall on the right, just where a little stream, with a narrow flood plain, comes down through a side cañon. Along the valley, the Indians have planted corn, using the water which burst out in springs at the foot of the cliff, for irrigation. The corn is looking quite well, but is not sufficiently advanced to give us roasting ears; but there are some nice, green squashes. We carry ten or a dozen of these on board our boats, and hurriedly leave, not willing to be caught in the robbery, yet excusing ourselves by pleading our great want. We run down a short distance, to where we feel certain no Indians can follow; and what a kettle of squash sauce we make! True, we have no salt with which to season it, but it makes a fine addition to our unleavened bread and coffee. Never was fruit so sweet as these stolen squashes.

After dinner we push on again, making fine time, finding many rapids, but none so bad that we cannot run them with safety, and when we stop, just at dusk, and foot up our reckoning, we find we have run thirty-five miles again.

What a supper we make; unleavened bread, green squash sauce, and strong coffee. We have been for a few days on half rations, but we have no stint of roast squash.

A few days like this, and we shall be out of prison.

August 27.—This morning the river takes a more southerly direction. The dip of the rocks is to the north, and we are rapidly running into lower formations. Unless our course changes, we shall very soon run again into the granite. This gives us some anxiety. Now and then the river turns to the west, and excites hopes that are soon destroyed by another turn to the south. About nine o'clock we come to the dreaded rock. It is with no little misgiving that we see the river enter these black, hard walls. At its very entrance we have to make a portage; then we have to let down with lines past some ugly rocks. Then we run a mile or two further, and then the rapids below can be seen.

About eleven o'clock we come to a place in the river where it seems much worse than any we have yet met in all its course. A little creek comes down from the left. We land first on the right, and clamber up over the granite pinnacles for a mile or two, but can see no way by which we can let down, and to run it would be sure destruction. After dinner we cross to examine it on the left. High above the river we can walk along on the top of the granite, which is broken off at the edge, and set with crags and pinnacles, so that it is very difficult to get a view of the river at all. In my eagerness to reach a point where I can see the roaring fall below, I go too far on the wall, and can neither advance nor retreat. I stand with one foot on a little projecting rock, and cling with my hand fixed in a little crevice. Finding I am caught here, suspended 400 feet above the river, into which I should fall if my footing fails, I call for help. The men come, and pass me a line, but I cannot let go of the rock long enough to take hold of it. Then they bring two or three of the largest oars. All this takes time which seems very precious to me; but at last they arrive. The blade of one of the oars is pushed into a little crevice in the rock beyond me, in such a manner that they can hold me pressed against the wall. Then another is fixed in such a way that I can step on it, and thus I am extricated.

Still another hour is spent in examining the river from this side, but no good view of it is obtained, so now we return to the side that was first examined, and the afternoon is spent in clambering among the crags and pinnacles, and carefully scanning the river again. We find that the lateral streams have washed boulders into the river, so as to form a dam, over which the water makes a broken fall of eighteen or twenty feet; then there is a rapid, beset with rocks, for two or three hundred yards, while, on the other side, points of the wall project into the river. Then there is a second fall below; how great, we cannot tell. Then there is a rapid, filled with huge rocks, for one or two hundred yards. At the bottom of it, from the right wall, a great rock projects quite half way across the river. It has a sloping surface extending up stream, and the water, coming down with all the momentum gained in the falls and rapids above, rolls up this inclined plane many feet, and tumbles over to the left. I decide that it is possible to let down over the first fall, then run near the right cliff to a point just above the second, where we can pull out into a little chute, and, having run over that in safety, we must pull with all our power across the stream, to avoid the great rock below. On my return to the boat, I announce to the men that we are to run it in the morning. Then we cross the river, and go into camp for the night on some rocks, in the mouth of the little cañon.

After supper Captain Howland asks to have a talk with me. We walk up the little creek a short distance, and I soon find that his object is to remonstrate against my determination to proceed. He thinks that we had better abandon the river here. Talking with him, I learn that his brother, William Dunn, and himself have determined to go no further in the boats. So we return to camp. Nothing is said to the other men.

For the last two days, our course has not been plotted. I sit down and do this now, for the purpose of finding where we are by dead reckoning. It is a clear night, and I take out the sextant to make observation for latitude, and find that the astronomic determination agrees very nearly with that of the plot— quite as closely as might be expected, from a meridian observation on a planet. In a direct line, we must be about forty-five miles from the mouth of the Rio Virgen. If we can reach that point, we know that there are settlements up that river about twenty miles. This forty-five miles, in a direct line, will probably be eighty or ninety in the meandering line of the river. But then we know that there is comparatively open country for many miles above the mouth of the Virgen, which is our point of destination.

As soon as I determine all this, I spread my plot on the sand, and wake Howland, who is sleeping down by the river, and show him where I suppose we are, and where several Mormon settlements are situated.

We have another short talk about the morrow, and he lies down again; but for me there is no sleep. All night long, I pace up and down a little path, on a few yards of sand beach, along by the river. Is it wise to go on? I go to the boats again, to look at our rations. I feel satisfied that we can get over the danger im-

mediately before us; what there may be below I know not. From our outlook yesterday, on the cliffs, the cañon seemed to make another great bend to the south, and this, from our experience heretofore, means more and higher granite walls. I am not sure that we can climb out of the cañon here, and, when at the top of the wall, I know enough of the country to be certain that it is a desert of rock and sand, between this and the nearest Mormon town, which, on the most direct line, must be seventy-five miles away. True, the late rains have been favorable to us, should we go out, for the probabilities are that we shall find water still standing in holes, and, at one time, I almost conclude to leave the river. But for years I have been contemplating this trip. To leave the exploration unfinished, to say that there is a part of the cañon which I cannot explore, having already almost accomplished it, is more than I am willing to acknowledge, and I determine to go on.

2. At almost the same time that Powell was conducting his dangerous voyage through the Grand Canyon, another explorer was at work farther to the north and east. Henry D. Washburn led a small party of men to the headwaters of the Yellowstone River. Their exploration of the Yellowstone Park region was followed by the creation of the country's first National Park. The following passages are taken from a diary of the Washburn Expedition which was conducted from August through September 1870. The author, Nathaniel Pitt Langford, was one of several members of the Washburn group who kept diaries.

Friday, August 26.—For some reason we did not leave camp till 11 o'clock a.m. We forded Gardiner's river with some difficulty, several of our pack animals being nearly carried off their feet by the torrent. We passed over several rocky ridges or points coming down from the mountain, and at one and a half miles came down again into the valley, which one of our party called the "valley of desolation." Taking the trail upon the left, we followed it until it led us to the mouth of a cañon, through which ran an old Indian or game trail, which was hardly discernible, and had evidently been long abandoned. Retracing our steps for a quarter of a mile, and taking a cut-off through the sage brush, we followed another trail upon our right up through a steep, dry coulee. From the head of the coulee we went through fallen timber over a burnt and rocky road, our progress being very slow. A great many of the packs came off our horses or became loosened, necessitating frequent haltings for their readjustment. Upon the summit we found a great many shells.

Descending the divide we found upon the trail the carcass of an antelope which the advance party had killed, and which we packed on our horses and carried to our night camp. In the morning Lieutenant Doane and one of his men, together with Mr. Everts, had started out ahead of the party to search out the best trail. At 3 o'clock p. m. we arrived at Antelope creek, only six miles from our morning camp, where we concluded to halt. On the trail which we were following there were no tracks except those of unshod ponies; and, as our horses were all shod, it was evident that Lieutenant Doane and the advance party had descended the mountain by some other trail than that which we were following. Neither were there any marks of dragging lodge poles. There are seemingly two trails across the mountain,—a circuitous one by as easy a grade as can be found, over which the Indians send their families with their heavily laden pack horses; and a more direct though more difficult, route which the war parties use in making their rapid rides. This last is the one we have taken, and the advance party has doubtless taken the other.

Our camp to-night is on Antelope creek, about five miles from the Yellowstone river. After our arrival in camp, in company with Stickney and Gillette, I made a scout of eight or ten miles through the country east of our trail, and between it and the river, in search of some sign of Lieutenant Doane, but we found no trace of him. Parting from Stickney and Gillette, I followed down the stream through a narrow gorge by a game trail, hoping if I could reach the Yellowstone, to find a good trail along its banks up to the foot of the grand cañon; but I found the route impracticable for the passage of our pack train. After supper Mr. Hauser and I went out in search of our other party, and found the tracks of their horses, which we followed about four miles to the brow of a mountain overlooking the country for miles in advance of us. Here we remained an hour, firing our guns as a signal, and carefully scanning the whole country with our field glasses. We could discern the trail for many miles on its tortuous course, but could see no sign of a camp, or of horses feeding, and we returned to our camp.

Saturday, August 27.—Lieutenant Doane and those who were with him did not return to camp last night. At change of guard Gillette's pack horse became alarmed at something in the bushes bordering upon the creek on the bank of which he was tied, and, breaking loose, dashed through the camp, rousing all of us. Some wild animal—snake, fox or something of the kind—was probably the cause of the alarm. In its flight I became entangled in the lariat and was dragged head first for three or four rods, my head striking a log, which proved to be very rotten, and offered little resistance to a hard head, and did me very little damage.

Towards morning a slight shower of rain fell, continuing at intervals till 8 o'clock. We left camp about 9 o'clock, the pack train following about 11 o'clock, and soon struck the trail of Lieutenant Doane, which proved to be the route traveled by the Indians. The marks of their lodge poles were plainly visible. At about four miles from our morning camp we discovered at some distance ahead of us what first appeared to be a young elk, but which proved to be a colt that had become separated from the camp of Indians to which it belonged. We think the Indians cannot be far from us at this time. Following the trail up the ascent leading from Antelope creek, we entered a deep cut, the sides of which rise at an angle of 45 degrees, and are covered with a luxuriant growth of grass. Through this cut we ascended by a grade entirely practicable for a wagon road to the summit of a divide. From the summit, we descended through a beautiful gorge to a small tributary of the Yellowstone, a distance of two miles, dismounting and leading our horses almost the entire distance, the descent being too precipitous for the rider's comfort or for ease to the horse.

We were now within two miles of the Yellowstone. On the right of the trail, two miles farther on, we found a small hot sulphur spring, the water of which was at a temperature a little below the boiling point, which at this elevation is about 195 degrees. Ascending a high ridge we had a commanding view of a basaltic formation of palisades, about thirty feet in height, on the opposite bank of the Yellowstone, overlooking a stratum of cement and gravel nearly two hundred feet thick, beneath which is another formation of the basaltic rock, and beneath this another body of cement and gravel. We named this formation "Column Rock." The upper formation, from which the rock takes its name, consists of basaltic columns about thirty feet high, closely touching each other, the columns being from three to five feet in diameter. A little farther on we descended the sides of the cañon, through which runs a large creek. We crossed this creek and camped on the south side. Our camp is about four hundred feet in elevation above the Yellowstone, which is not more than two miles distant. The creek is full of granite boulders, varying in size from six inches to ten feet in diameter.

General Washburn was on guard last night, and to-night he seems somewhat fatigued. Mr. Hedges has improvised a writing stool from a sack of flour, and I have appropriated a sack of beans for a like use; and, as we have been writing, there has been a lively game of cards played near my left side, which Hedges, who has just closed his diary, says is a game of poker. I doubt if Deacon Hedges is sufficiently posted in the game to know to a certainty that poker is the game which is being played; but, putting what Hedges tells me with what I see and hear, I find that these infatuated players have put a valuation of five cents per bean, on beans that did not cost more than $1 a quart in Helena, and Jake Smith exhibits a marvelous lack of veneration for his kinswoman, by referring to each bean, as he places it before him upon the table, as his "aunt," or, more flippantly, his "auntie." Walter Trumbull has been styled the "Banker," and he says that at the commencement of the game he sold forty of these beans to each of the players, himself included (200 in all), at five cents each, and that he has already redeemed the entire 200 at that rate; and now Jake Smith has a half-pint cup nearly full of beans, and is demanding of Trumbull that he redeem them also; that is, pay five cents per bean for the contents of the cup. Trumbull objects. Jake persists. Reflecting upon their disagreement I recall that about an hour ago Jake, with an apologetic "Excuse me!" disturbed me while I was writing and untied the bean sack on which I am now sitting, and took from it a double handful of beans.

It seems to me that a game of cards which admits of such latitude as this, with a practically unlimited draft upon outside resources, is hardly fair to all parties, and especially to "The Banker."

Sunday, August 28.—To-day being Sunday, we remained all day in our camp, which Washburn and Everts have named "Camp Comfort," as we have an abundance of venison and trout.

We visited the falls of the creek, the waters of which tumble over the rocks and boulders for the distance of 200 yards from our camp, and then fall a distance of 110 feet, as triangulated by Mr. Hauser. Stickney ventured to the verge of the fall, and, with a stone attached to a strong cord, measured its height, which he gives as 105 feet.

The stream, in its descent to the brink of the fall, is separated into half a dozen distorted channels which have zig-zagged their passage through the cement formation, working it into spires, pinnacles, towers and many other capricious objects. Many of these are of faultless symmetry, resembling the minaret of a mosque; others are so grotesque as to provoke merriment as well as wonder. One of this latter character we named "The Devil's Hoof," from its supposed similarity to the proverbial foot of his Satanic majesty. The height of this rock from its base is about fifty feet. . . .

Wednesday, August 31.—This has been a "red-letter" day with me, and one which I shall not soon forget, for my mind is clogged and my memory confused by what I have to-day seen. General Washburn and Mr. Hedges are sitting near me, writing, and we have an understanding that we will compare our notes when finished. We are all overwhelmed with astonishment and wonder at what we have seen, and we feel that we have been near the very presence of the Almighty. General Washburn has just quoted from the psalm: "When I behold the work of Thy hands, what is man that Thou art mindful of him!"

My own mind is so confused that I hardly know where to commence in making a clear record of what is at this moment floating past my mental vision. I cannot confine myself to a bare description of the falls of the Yellowstone alone, for these two great cataracts are but one feature in a scene composed of so many of the elements of grandeur and sublimity, that I almost despair of giving to those who on our return home will listen to a recital of our adventures, the faintest conception of it.

The immense cañon or gorge of rocks through which the river descends, perhaps more than the falls, is calculated to fill the observer with feelings of mingled awe and terror. This chasm is seemingly about thirty miles in length. Commencing above the upper fall, it attains a depth of two hundred feet where that takes its plunge, and in the distance of half a mile from that point to the verge of the lower fall, it rapidly descends with the river between walls of rock nearly six hundred feet in vertical height, to which three hundred and twenty feet are added by the fall. Below this the wall lines marked by the descent of the river grow in height with incredible distinctness, until they are probably two thousand feet above the water. There is a difference of nearly three thousand feet in altitude between the surface of the river at the upper fall and the foot of the cañon. Opposite Mount Washburn the cañon must be more than half a vertical mile in depth. As it is impossible to explore the entire cañon, we are unable to tell whether the course of the river through it is broken by other and larger cataracts than the two we have seen, or whether its continuous descent alone has produced the enormous depth to which it has attained. Rumors of falls a thousand feet in height have often reached us before we made this visit. At all points where we approached the edge of the cañon the river was descending with fearful momentum through it, and the rapids and foam from the dizzy summit of the rock overhanging the lower fall, and especially from points farther down the cañon, were so terrible to behold, that none of our company could venture the experiment in any other manner than by lying prone upon the rock, to gaze into its awful depths; depths so amazing that the sound of the rapids in their course over immense boulders, and lashing in fury the base of the rocks on which we were lying, could not be heard. The stillness is horrible, and the solemn grandeur of the scene surpasses conception. You feel the absence of sound—the oppression of absolute silence. Down, down, down, you see the river attenuated to a thread. If you could only hear that gurgling river, lashing with puny strength the massive walls that imprison it and hold it in their dismal shadow, if you could but see a living thing in the depth beneath you, if a bird would but fly past you, if the wind would move any object in that awful chasm, to break for a moment the solemn silence which reigns there, it would relieve that tension of the nerves which the scene has excited, and with a grateful heart you would thank God that he permitted you to gaze unharmed upon this majestic display of his handiwork. But as it is, the spirit of man sympathizes with the deep gloom of the scene, and the brain reels as you gaze into this profound and solemn solitude.

The place where I obtained the best and most terrible view of the cañon was a narrow projecting point situated two or three miles below the lower fall. Standing there or rather lying there for greater safety, I thought how utterly impossible it would be to describe to another the sensations inspired by such a presence. As I took in this scene, I realized my own littleness, my helplessness, my dread exposure to destruction, my inability to cope with or even comprehend the mighty architecture of nature. More than all this I felt as never before my entire dependence upon that Almighty Power who had wrought these wonders. A sense of danger, lest the rock should crumble away, almost overpowered me. My knees trembled, and I experienced the terror which causes men to turn pale and their countenances to blanch with fear, and I recoiled from the vision I had seen, glad to feel the solid earth beneath me and to realize the assurance of returning safety.

The scenery surrounding cañon and falls on both banks of the Yellowstone is enlivened by all the hues of abundant vegetation. The foot-hills approach the river, crowned with a vesture of evergreen pines. Meadows verdant with grasses and shrubbery stretch away to the base of the distant mountains, which, rolling into ridges, rising into peaks, and breaking into chains, are defined in the deepest blue upon the horizon. To render the scene still more imposing, remarkable volcanic deposits, wonderful boiling springs, jets of heated vapor, large collections of sulphur, immense rocks and petrifications abound in great profusion in this immediate

vicinity. The river is filled with trout, and bear, elk, deer, mountain lions and lesser game roam the plains, forests and mountain fastnesses.

The two grand falls of the Yellowstone form a fitting completion to this stupendous climax of wonders. They impart life, power, light and majesty to an assemblage of elements, which without them would be the most gloomy and horrible solitude in nature. Their eternal anthem, echoing from cañon, mountain, rock and woodland, thrills you with delight, and you gaze with rapture at the iris-crowned curtains of fleecy foam as they plunge into gulfs enveloped in mist and spray. The stillness which held your senses spellbound, as you peered into the dismal depths of the cañon below, is now broken by the uproar of waters; the terror it inspired is superseded by admiration and astonishment, and the scene, late so painful from its silence and gloom, is now animate with joy and revelry.

The upper fall, as determined by the rude means of measurement at our command, is one hundred and fifteen feet in height. The river approaches it through a passage of rocks which rise one hundred feet on either side above its surface. Until within half a mile of the brink of the fall the river is peaceful and unbroken by a ripple. Suddenly, as if aware of impending danger, it becomes lashed into foam, circled with eddies, and soon leaps into fearful rapids. The rocky jaws confining it gradually converge as it approaches the edge of the fall, bending its course by their projections, and apparently crowding back the water, which struggles and leaps against their bases, warring with its bounds in the impatience of restraint, and madly leaping from its confines, a liquid emerald wreathed with foam, into the abyss beneath. The sentinel rocks, a hundred feet asunder, could easily be spanned by a bridge directly over and in front of the fall, and fancy led me forward to no distant period when such an effort of airy architecture would be crowded with happy gazers from all portions of our country. A quarter of the way between the verge and the base of the fall a rocky table projects from the west bank, in front of and almost within reaching distance of it, furnishing a point of observation where the finest view can be obtained. In order to get a more perfect view of the cataract, Mr. Hedges and I made our way down to this table rock, where we sat for a long time. As from this spot we looked up at the descending waters, we insensibly felt that the slightest protrusion in them would hurl us backwards into the gulf below. A thousand arrows of foam, apparently *aimed at us*, leaped from the verge, and passed rapidly down the sheet. But as the view grew upon us, and we comprehended the power, majesty and beauty of the scene, we became insensible to danger and gave ourselves up to the full enjoyment of it. . . .

3. On March 30, 1867, by the following treaty between the United States and Russia, Alaska became part of the United States. The U.S. Senate consented to the treaty on April 9, and the treaty was ratified and formally proclaimed on June 20. A formal transfer took place at Sitka on October 18, 1867.

THE ALASKA TREATY

The United States of America and his Majesty the Emperor of all the Russians, being desirous of strengthening, if possible, the good understanding which exists between them, have, for that purpose, appointed as their plenipotentaries: the President of the United States, William H. Seward, Secretary of State; and his Majesty the Emperor of all the Russians, the privy counselor Edward de Stoeckl, his envoy extraordinary and minister plenipotentiary to the United States.

And the said plenipotentiaries, having exchanged their full powers, which were found to be in due form, have agreed upon and signed the following articles:—

ARTICLE I.—His Majesty the Emperor of all the Russias agrees to cede to the United States, by this convention, immediately upon the exchange of the ratifications thereof, all the territory and dominion now possessed by his said Majesty on the continent of America and in the adjacent islands, the same being contained within the geographical limits herein set forth, to wit: the eastern limit is the line of demarcation between the Russian and the British possessions in North America, as established by the convention between Russia and Great Britain, of February 28–16, 1825, and described in Articles III, and IV, of said convention, in the following terms:—

"Commencing from the southernmost point of the island called Prince of Wales Island, which point lies in the parallel of 54 degrees 40 minutes north latitude, and between the 131st and 133d degree of west longitude (meridian of Greenwich), the said line shall ascend to the north along the channel called Portland Channel, as far as the point of the continent where it strikes the 56th degree of north latitude; from this last-mentioned point the line of demarcation shall follow the summit of the mountains situated parallel to the coast as far as the point of intersection of the 141st degree of west longitude (of the same meridian); and finally, from the said point of intersection, the said meridian line of the 141st degree, in its prolongation as far as the Frozen Ocean.

"IV. With reference to the line of demarcation laid down in the preceding article, it is understood—

"1st. That the island called Prince of Wales Island shall belong wholly to Russia" (now by this cession to the United States).

"2d. That whenever the summit of the mountains which extend in a direction parallel to the coast from the 56th degree of north latitude to the point of intersection of the 141st degree of west longitude shall prove to be at the distance of more than ten marine leagues from the ocean, the limit between the British possessions and the line of coast which is to belong to Russia as above mentioned (that is to say, the limit to the possessions ceded by this convention) shall be formed by a line parallel to the winding of the coast, and which shall never exceed the distance of ten marine leagues therefrom."

The western limit within which the territories and dominion conveyed are contained passes through a point in Behring's Straits on the parallel of 65 degrees 30 minutes north latitude, at its intersection by the meridian which passes midway between the islands of Krusenstern, or Ignalook, and the island of Ratmanoff, or Noonarbook, and proceeds due north, without limitation, into the same Frozen Ocean. The same western limit, beginning at the same initial point, proceeds thence in a course nearly southwest, through Behring's Straits and Behring's Sea, so as to pass midway between the northwest point of the island of St. Lawrence and the southeast point of Cape Choukotski, to the meridian of 172 west longitude; thence, from the intersection of that meridian, in a southwesterly direction, so as to pass midway between the island of Attou and the Copper Island of the Kormandorski couplet or group in the North Pacific Ocean, to the meridian of 193 degrees west longitude, so as to include in the territory conveyed the whole of the Aleutian Islands east of that meridian.

ARTICLE II.—In the cession of territory and dominion made by the preceding article are included the right of property in all public lots and squares, vacant lands, and all public buildings, fortifications, barracks, and other edifices which are not private individual property. It is, however, understood and agreed that the churches which have been built in the ceded territory by the Russian government shall remain the property of such members of the Greek Oriental Church resident in the territory as may choose to worship therein. Any government archives, papers, and documents relative to the territory and dominion aforesaid, which may be now existing there, will be left in the possession of the agent of the United States; but an authenticated copy of such of them as may be required will be at all times given by the United States to the Russian government, or to such Russian officers or subjects as they may apply for.

ARTICLE III.—The inhabitants of the ceded territory, according to their choice, reserving their natural allegiance, may return to Russia within three years; but, if they should prefer to remain in the ceded territory, they, with the exception of uncivilized native tribes, shall be admitted to the enjoyment of all the rights, advantages, and immunities of citizens of the United States, and shall be maintained and protected in the free enjoyment of their liberty, property, and religion. The uncivilized tribes will be subject to such laws and regulations as the United States may from time to time adopt in regard to aboriginal tribes of that country.

ARTICLE IV.—His Majesty the Emperor of all the Russias shall appoint, with convenient despatch, an agent or agents for the purpose of formally delivering to a similar agent or agents appointed on behalf of the United States the territory, dominion, property, dependencies, and appurtenances which are ceded as above, and for doing any other act which may be necessary to regard therein. But the cession, with the right of immediate possession, is nevertheless to be deemed complete and absolute on the exchange of ratifications, without waiting for such formal delivery.

ARTICLE V.—Immediately after the exchange of the ratifications of this convention, any fortifications or military posts which may be in the ceded territory shall be delivered to the agent of the United States, and any Russian troops which may be in the territory shall be withdrawn as soon as may be reasonably and conveniently practicable.

ARTICLE VI.—In consideration of the cession aforesaid the United States agree to pay at the treasury in Washington, within ten months after the exchange of the ratifications of this convention, to the diplomatic representative or other agent of his Majesty the Emperor of all the Russias, duly authorized to receive the same, seven million two hundred thousand dollars in gold. The cession of territory and dominion herein made is hereby declared to be free and unencumbered by any reservations, privileges, franchises, grants, or possessions, by any associated companies, whether corporate or incorporate, Russian or any other, or by any parties, except merely private individual property-holders; and the cession hereby made conveys all the rights, franchises, and privileges now belonging to Russia in the said territory or dominion, and appurtenances thereto.

ARTICLE VII.—When this convention shall have been duly ratified by the President of the United States, by and with the advice and consent of the Senate, on the one part, and on the other by his Majesty the Emperor of all the Russias, the ratifications shall be exchanged at Washington within three months from the date hereof, or sooner, if possible.

In faith whereof, the respective plenipotentiaries have

signed this convention, and thereto affixed the seals of their arms.

Done at Washington, the 30th day of March, in the year of our Lord one thousand eight hundred and sixty-seven.

                                        WILLIAM H. SEWARD.
                                        EDOUARD DE STOECKL.

4.   William H. Seward, U.S. Secretary of State, became the first American official of cabinet rank to visit Alaska (known to his fellow-Americans as "Seward's Icebox"). He delivered a long and flowery address at Sitka on August 12, 1869. The following passages are quoted from that speech.

Citizens of Alaska, fellow citizens of the United States: . . . It is altogether natural on your part to say, "You have looked upon Alaska: what do you think of it?" Unhappily, I have seen too little of Alaska to answer the question satisfactorily. The entire coast line of the United States, exclusive of Alaska, is 10,000 miles, while the coast line of Alaska alone, including the islands, is 26,000 miles. The portion of the Territory which lies east of the peninsula, including islands, is 120 miles wide. The western portion, including Aleutian Islands expands to a breadth of 2,200 miles. The entire land area, including islands, is 577,390 statute square miles. We should think a foreigner very presumptuous who should presume to give the world an opinion of the whole of the United States of America, after he had merely looked in from his steamer at Plymouth and Boston Harbor, or had run up the Hudson River to the Highlands, or had ascended the Delaware to Trenton, or the James River to Richmond, or the Mississippi no farther than Memphis. My observation thus far has hardly been more comprehensive. I entered the Territory of Alaska at the Portland canal, made my way through the narrow passages of the Prince of Wales Archipelago, thence through Peril and Chatham Straits and Lynn Channel, and up the Chilcat River to the base of Fairweather, from which latter place I have returned through Clarence Straits, to sojourn a few days in your beautiful bay, under the shadows of the Baranoff Hills and Mount Edgecombe. Limited, however, as my opportunities have been, I will, without further apology, give you the impressions I have received. . . .

My visit here happens to fall within the month of August. Not only have the skies been sufficiently bright and serene to give me a perfect view, under the sixtieth parallel, of the total eclipse of the sun, and of the evening star at the time of the sun's obscuration, but I have also enjoyed more clear than there have been cloudy days; and in the early mornings and in the late evenings peculiar to the season I have lost myself in admiration of skies adorned with sapphire and gold as richly as those which are reflected by the Mediterranean. Of all the moonlights in the world, commend me to those which light up the archipelago of the North Pacific Ocean. Fogs have sometimes detained me longer on the Hudson and on Long Island Sound than now on the waters of the North Pacific. In saying this, I do not mean to say that rain and fog are unfrequent here. The Russian pilot, George, whom you all know, expressed my conviction on this matter exactly when he said to me, "Oh, yes, Mr. Seward, we *do* have changeable weather here sometimes, as they do in the other States." I might amend the expression by adding the weather here is only a little more changeable. It must be confessed, at least, that it is an honest climate; for it makes no pretension to constancy. If, however, you have fewer bright sunrises and glowing sunsets than southern latitudes enjoy, you are favored, on the other hand, with more frequent and more magnificent displays of the aurora and the rainbow. The thermometer tells the whole case when it reports that the summer is colder and the winter is warmer in Alaska than in New York and Washington. It results from the nature of such a climate that the earth prefers to support the fir, the spruce, the pine, the hemlock, and other evergreens rather than deciduous trees, and to furnish grasses and esculent roots rather than the cereals of dryer and hotter climates. I have mingled freely with the multifarious population,—the Tongas, the Stickeens, the Cakes, the Hydahs, the Sitkas, the Kootznoos, and the Chilcats, as well as with the traders, the soldiers, the seamen, and the settlers of various nationalities, English, Swedish, Russian, and American,—and I have seen all around me only persons enjoying robust and exuberant health. Manhood of every race and condition everywhere exhibits activity and energy, while infancy seems exempt from disease, and age relieved from pain.

It is next in order to speak of the rivers and seas of Alaska. The rivers are broad, shallow, and rapid, while the seas are deep but tranquil. Mr. Sumner, in his elaborate and magnificent oration, although he spoke only from historical accounts, has not exaggerated—no man can exaggerate—the marine treasures of the Territory. Besides the whale, which everywhere and at all times is seen enjoying his robust exercise, and the sea-otter, the fur-seal, the hair-seal, and the walrus, found in the waters which embosom the western islands, those waters, as well as the seas of the eastern archipelago, are found teeming with the salmon, cod, and other fishes adapted to the support of human and animal life. Indeed, what I have seen here has almost made me a convert to the theory of some naturalists, that the waters of the globe are filled with stores for the sustenance of animal life surpassing the available productions of the land.

It must be remembered that the coast range of mountains, which begins in Mexico, is continued into the Territory, and invades the seas of Alaska. Hence it is that in the islands and on the mainland, so far as I have explored it, we find ourselves everywhere in the immediate presence of black hills, or foot-hills, as they are variously called, and that these foot-hills are overtopped by ridges of snow-capped mountains. These snow-capped mountains are manifestly of volcanic origin; and they have been subjected, through an indefinite period, to atmospheric abrasion and disintegration. Hence they have assumed all conceivable shapes and forms. In some places they are serrated into sharp, angular peaks, and in other places they appear architecturally arranged, so as to present cloud-capped castles, towers, domes, and minarets. The mountain sides are furrowed with deep and straight ravines, down which the thawing fields of ice and snow are precipitated, generally in the month of May, with such a vehemence as to have produced in every valley immense level plains of intervale land. These plains, as well as the sides of the mountains, almost to the summits, are covered with forests so dense and dark as to be impenetrable, except to wild beasts and savage huntsmen. . . . Klakautch, the Chilcat, who is known and feared by the Indians throughout the whole Territory, and who is a very intelligent chief, informs me that beyond the mountain range which intervenes between the Chilcat and the Yukon Rivers you descend into a plain unbroken by hills or mountains, very fertile, in a genial climate, and, as far as he could learn, of boundless extent. We have similar information from those who have traversed the interior from the shore of the Portland canal to the upper branches of the Yukon. We have reason, therefore, to believe that beyond the coast range of mountains in Alaska we shall find an extension of the rich and habitable valley lands of Oregon, Washington Territory, and British Columbia.

After what I have already said, I may excuse myself from expatiating on the animal productions of the forest. The elk and the deer are so plenty as to be undervalued for food or skins, by natives as well as strangers. The bear of many families,—black, grizzly, and cinnamon; the mountain sheep, inestimable for his fleece; the wolf, the fox, the beaver, the otter, the mink, the raccoon, the marten, the ermine; the squirrel,—gray, black, brown, and flying,—are among the land fur-bearing animals. The furs thus found here have been the chief element, for more than a hundred years, of the profitable commerce of the Hudson Bay Company, whose mere possessory privileges seem, even at this late day, too costly to find a ready purchaser. This fur-trade, together with the sea fur-trade within the Territory, were the sole basis alike of Russian commerce and empire on this continent. This commerce was so large and important as to induce the government of Russia and China to build and maintain a town for carrying on its exchanges in Tartary on the border of the two empires. It is well understood that the supply of furs in Alaska has not diminished, while the demand for them in China and elsewhere has immensely increased.

I fear that we must confess to a failure of ice as an element of territorial wealth, at least as far as this immediate region is concerned. I find that the Russian American Company, whose monopoly was abolished by the treaty of acquisition, depended for ice exclusively upon the small lake or natural pond which furnishes the power for your saw-mill in this town, and that this dependence has now failed by reason of the increasing mildness of the winter. The California Ice Company are now trying the small lakes of Kodiac, and certainly I wish them success. I think it is not yet ascertained whether glacier ice is pure and practical for commerce. If it is, the world may be supplied from the glaciers, which, suspended from the region of the clouds, stand forth in the majesty of ever-wasting and ever-renewed translucent mountains upon the banks of the Stickeen and Chilcat Rivers and the shores of Cross Sound.

Alaska has been as yet but imperfectly explored; but enough is known to assure us that it possesses treasures of what are called the baser ores equal to those of any other region of the continent. We have Copper Island and Copper River, so named as the places where the natives, before the period of the Russian discovery, had procured the pure metal from which they fabricated instruments of war and legendary shields. In regard to iron the question seems to lie not where it can be found, but whether there is any place where it does not exist. Mr. Davidson, of the Coast Survey, invited me to go up to him at the station he had taken up the Chilcat River to make his observations of the eclipse, by writing me that he had discovered an iron mountain there. When I came there, I found that, very properly, he had been studying the heavens so busily that he had but cursorily examined the earth under his feet, that it was not a single iron mountain he had discovered, but a range of hills the very dust of which adheres to the magnet, while the range itself, two thousand feet high, extends along the east bank of the river thirty miles. Limestone and marble crop out on the banks of the same river and in many other places. Coal-beds, accessible to navigation, are found at Kootznoo. It is said, however, that the concentrated resin which the mineral contains renders it too inflammable to be safely used by steamers. In any case, it would seem calculated to supply the fuel requisite for the manufacture of iron. What seems to be excellent cannel coal is also found in the Prince of Wales Archipelago. There are also mines at Cook's Inlet. Placer and quartz gold mining is pursued under many social disadvantages upon the Stickeen and elsewhere, with a degree of success which, while it does not warrant us in assigning a superiority in that respect to the Territory, does nevertheless warrant us in regarding gold mining as an established and reliable resource....

6-B THE ARMY BETWEEN WARS

Once the Civil War ended, the vast majority of the troops left the military service and returned to civilian life. The U. S. Army continued through 1876 to police the Reconstruction of the South. Its principal duty as a fighting force, however, was the control and subjugation of the Indians in the West and Southwest.

PROBLEMS: *What part did the military play in American history during the peacetime years following 1865? Was American military strength neglected during these years?*

1. The principal sources of information about the military life of the United States in this period are to be found in the books written by leading officers about their careers and activities. These are often considered as primary sources of history, especially when they contain official military records—copies of orders, or design diagrams for forts or posts. General Philip H. Sheridan, one of the outstanding Civil War cavalry officers, commanded troops in the West after the war. His account of strategy and communications problems in coping with hostile Indians (from his Personal Memoirs, *first published in 1888) now follows.*

At the period of which I write, in 1868, the Plains were covered with vast herds of buffalo—the number has been estimated at 3,000,000 head—and with such means of subsistence as this everywhere at hand, the 6,000 hostiles were wholly unhampered by any problem of food-supply. The savages were rich too according to Indian standards, many a lodge owning from twenty to a hundred ponies; and consciousness of wealth and power, aided by former temporizing, had made them not only confident but defiant. Realizing that their thorough subjugation would be a difficult task, I made up my mind to confine operations during the grazing and hunting season to protecting the people of the new settlements and on the overland routes, and then, when winter came, to fall upon the savages relentlessly, for in that season their ponies would be thin, and weak from lack of food, and in the cold and snow, without strong ponies to transport their villages and plunder, their movements would be so much impeded that the troops could overtake them.

At the outbreak of hostilities I had in all, east of New Mexico, a force of regulars numbering about 2,600 men —1,200 mounted and 1,400 foot troops. The cavalry was composed of the Seventh and Tenth regiments; the infantry, of the Third and Fifth regiments and four companies of the Thirty-Eighth. With these few troops all the posts along the Smoky Hill and Arkansas had to be garrisoned, emigrant trains escorted, and the settlements and routes of travel and the construction parties on the Kansas-Pacific railway protected. Then, too, this same force had to furnish for the field small movable columns, that were always on the go, so it will be rightly inferred that every available man was kept busy from the middle of August till November; especially as during this period the hostiles attacked over forty widely dispersed places, in nearly all cases stealing horses, burning houses, and killing settlers. It was of course impossible to foresee where these descents would be made, but as soon as an attack was heard of assistance was always promptly rendered, and every now and then we succeeded in killing a few savages. As a general thing, though, the raiders escaped before relief arrived, and when they had a few miles the start, all efforts to catch them were futile. I therefore discouraged long pursuits, and, in fact, did not approve of making any at all unless the chances of obtaining paying results were very evident, otherwise the troops would be worn out by the time the hard work of the winter was demanded from them.

To get ready for a winter campaign of six months gave us much to do. The thing most needed was more men, so I asked for additional cavalry, and all that could be spared—seven troops of the Fifth Cavalry—was sent to me. Believing this reinforcement insufficient, to supplement it I applied for a regiment of Kansas volunteers, which request being granted, the organization of the regiment was immediately begun at Topeka. It was necessary also to provide a large amount of transportation and accumulate quantities of stores, since the campaign probably would not end till spring. Another important matter was to secure competent guides for the different columns of troops, for, as I have said, the section of country to be operated in was comparatively unknown.

In those days the railroad town of Hays City was filled with so-called "Indian scouts," whose common boast was of having slain scores of redskins, but the real scout—that is, a guide and trailer knowing the habits of the Indians—was very scarce, and it was hard to find anybody familiar with the country south of the Arkansas, where the campaign was to be made. Still, about Hays City and the various military posts there was some good material to select from, and we managed to employ several men, who, from their experience on the Plains in various capacities, or from natural instinct and aptitude, soon became excellent guides and courageous and valuable scouts, some of them, indeed, gaining much distinction. Mr. William F. Cody ("Buffalo Bill), whose renown has since become world-wide, was one of the men thus selected. He received his sobriquet from his marked success in killing buffaloes for a contractor, to supply fresh meat to the construction parties on the

Kansas-Pacific railway. He had given up this business, however, and was now in the employ of the quartermaster's department of the army, and was first brought to my notice by distinguishing himself in bringing me an important despatch from Fort Larned to Fort Hays, a distance of sixty-five miles, through a section infested with Indians. The despatch informed me that the Indians near Larned were preparing to decamp, and this intelligence required that certain orders should be carried to Fort Dodge, ninety-five miles south of Hays. This too being a particularly dangerous route—several couriers having been killed on it—it was impossible to get one of the various "Petes," "Jacks," or "Jims" hanging around Hays City to take my communication. Cody learning of the strait I was in, manfully came to the rescue, and proposed to make the trip to Dodge, though he had just finished his long and perilous ride from Larned. I gratefully accepted his offer, and after four or five hours' rest he mounted a fresh horse and hastened on his journey, halting but once to rest on the way, and then only for an hour, the stop being made at Coon Creek, where he got another mount, from a troop of cavalry. At Dodge he took six hours' sleep and then continued on to his own post—Fort Larned—with more despatches. After resting twelve hours at Larned, he was again in the saddle with tidings for me at Fort Hays, General Hazen sending him, this time, with word that the villages had fled to the south of the Arkansas. Thus, in all, Cody rode about 350 miles in less than sixty hours, and such an exhibition of endurance and courage was more than enough to convince me that his services would be extremely valuable in the campaign, so I retained him at Fort Hays till the battalion of the Fifth Cavalry arrived, and then made him chief of scouts for that regiment.

2.   Army officers traditionally kept their hands off civilian policy matters. However, many Army leaders complained vigorously that civilian officials of various government agencies provoked the Indians to fight, and then left the Army in a position where it had to carry on a campaign that need not have been fought. Sheridan himself did not live to finish the section of his Personal Memoirs *which dealt with this point, but his brother (also a general) completed the work and included the following passage on Indian relations, in particular with Chief Joseph and the Nez Percés.*

Against tremendous odds Chief Joseph had successfully conducted the flight of a tribe of savages, encumbered by their women and children, for a distance of nearly fifteen hundred miles through a hostile region, crossing great rivers and rugged mountains *en route*—a feat that is perhaps without parallel in Indian warfare.

The outbreak of the Nez Percés, who for many years had been devoting themselves to a pastoral life, the Sioux war, and other recent serious disturbances at widely separated points, led General Sheridan, in his annual report, to bring plainly to the attention of the public his opinion that the discontent of the Indians was no longer due to their restriction to reservations and curtailment of nomadic habits, but was attributable to bad treatment, and that many bloody conflicts might have been, and further general outbreaks would be prevented if their affairs were properly and honestly administered. Admitting that there would perhaps be a continuance of small forays on the part of the savages till their warlike characteristics were worn away by attrition with civilization, he contended that whole tribes at this stage of their environment would not take up arms against the Government if fairly treated; and he pointed out that not only could they no longer depend for subsistence on the buffalo and other game, but that the appropriations of Congress for their maintenance, already meager to the starvation point, were so mismanaged and diverted by corrupt agents, in collusion with equally corrupt traders and contractors, that the Indians were driven to fight in very desperation.

The Secretary of the Interior defended the Indian Service in a letter to the Secretary of War, and demanded the evidence on which Sheridan based his report, protesting that an executive branch of the Government should not be assailed by another with charges of corruption and mismanagement on mere hearsay. In reply the General pointed to the files of the Indian Bureau, already burdened with official and uncontradicted detailed reports of corrupt practices extending over a long period of years. Most of these reports had passed through Sheridan's hands officially, and no one was better aware than he of the facts they disclosed; but the Secretary chose to disregard the records of his own office, and to assume that Sheridan had reported without sufficient data; he therefore again insisted on proof. This time Sheridan fairly overwhelmed him with an army of evidence, which showed with great particularity of time, place, and circumstance so many instances of outrageous imposition and corruption in Indian affairs that the public, hitherto content in the belief that outbreaks were attributable solely to the Indians themselves, changed its opinion with a sudden vehemence that carried it far over to the other side and placed the Indian on a pedestal. The controversy between the army and the Indian Bureau was an unpleasant one to both parties, but in the end beneficial to the Indian; for, though his transfer to the War Department was prevented, the agitation so awakened the interest of Congress that Senator Dawes and other eminent men gave the subject their deep personal attention. Investigations were set on foot, appropriations increased, and projects allotting lands in severalty adopted. So many were the reforms inaugurated that the service of Indian affairs was finally lifted out of the mire of corruption that had long made it a discredit to our civilization.

As if more fully to confirm General Sheridan's views relative to the causes of Indian hostilities, two bloody affairs occurred about this time: one in 1878, with a band of Northern Cheyennes recently deported from Dakota to the Indian Territory; the other in 1879, with a band of Utes in the Uintah Valley, Utah, both of which were due to ill-treatment and mismanagement. The outbreak of the Northern Cheyennes arose from an endeavor to force them to live with the Southern Cheyennes. Although some had friends and kindred in the latter tribe, a great number of the band were intermarried with the Sioux, and were naturally desirous of remaining in Dakota with their relatives. Ignoring these conditions, however, and the strong affection of the Indian for his habitat and kin, the Indian Bureau adhered to and carried out its impracticable idea to the extent of removing the Northern Cheyennes to Fort Reno preparatory to settling them on the Southern Cheyenne reservation. Some were satisfied, but about four hundred would not affiliate with the Southern Cheyennes at all; and these, with characteristic dignity, demanded their return to the land of their birth. All appeals were without effect. Cheyennes in name, Cheyennes they must remain! Throughout the spring and summer ominous mutterings of discontent were heard; but toward autumn, as nothing transpired, hope was entertained that they would finally acquiesce in the situation. It had been reported that they intended to make a dash north, but the report was not credited by those in authority. Nevertheless the Indians made the dash. They stole away in the darkness of the night, leaving their lodges standing as a blind to conceal their departure. Their escape was discovered next morning, and two troops of cavalry from Fort Reno, under Captain Rendlebrock, started immediately in pursuit. They struck them twice, but signally failed to stop their flight, and the Indians crossed the Arkansas without difficulty. Sheridan then directed Colonel Lewis, Nineteenth Infantry, with troops from Fort Dodge and other points along the Arkansas, to take a hand and inflict severe punishment, as by this time the bands had begun to murder settlers. In a few days they were brought to bay in a sharp fight, but again escaped, Colonel Lewis being mortally wounded. The chase that followed was long and tortuous, the troops suffering such terrible hardship from lack of food and water in the sandhills of northern Nebraska that, on emerging, they were unfit to be continued in the field. The Indians now separated into three bands, one remaining in the sandhills, the others continuing north. Though up to this time it had not been possible to compel their surrender, a large number had been killed, and the rest became so exhausted that the band was not long after run down, its capture being effected mostly by the Third Cavalry, operating under Major Carleton. After the capture they were taken to Fort Robinson, not far from their Sioux relatives, where they begged to be allowed to remain; but on being informed that they must return to the Indian Territory, they sternly declared that they would rather die, so strong was their sense of the injustice. In this state of mind they were confined and strongly guarded. Brooding over their troubles in confinement once more made them desperate. Their appeals being unheeded, they made another rush for freedom. Surprising and overwhelming their guards, they escaped from the fort before the garrison could be put under arms; but as they were on foot the cavalry overtook them in a few miles, and was compelled to kill a large number of the warriors before the recapture could be effected. In the end the Northern Cheyennes were permitted to locate near their Sioux relatives.

The outbreak of the Utes referred to above was also occasioned by mismanagement and ignorance of the Indian character. Their agent, a good man but not a practical one, endeavored to put into force by iron-clad methods industrial theories good enough, perhaps, for a partly civilized people, but unsuited to savages who as yet knew nothing but war and the chase. He first tried persuasion. Failing in that, he threatened punishment and withheld food. His undertaking not only proved futile, but had a horrible ending. The Utes at once became sulky and hostile, threatening in turn the agent and his white employees. The agent, becoming alarmed, called for protection, and Sheridan at once sent three troops of cavalry and a company of infantry to White River, under Major Thornburgh, Fourth Infantry; but before they could reach the scene of the trouble the agent and most of his employees were murdered, and the white women about the agency carried off to suffer the indescribable horrors of savage captivity. With appetites whetted by blood, the Indians planned an ambuscade for Thornburgh, and, not far from the agency, caught him almost unawares, attacking him with such overwhelming numbers as to place his little command in a state of siege behind a hastily constructed shelter. Thornburgh and twelve men were killed and three of-

ficers and forty-three men wounded. Colonel Wesley Merritt, Fifth Cavalry, was at once ordered to their aid with additional troops, and this admirable officer, with characteristic ardor and judgment, accomplished the unprecedented march of one hundred and seventy miles in fifty-four and a half hours, raising the siege and relieving his distressed comrades a full day earlier than it was thought possible that his command could be brought to the field.

The Indians fled southward to the mountains, sending runners, however, to the confederated Utes in southern Colorado, and offering them such inducements to join in the outbreak as to make it evident that they too must be reckoned with in subsequent operations. To meet this new phase of the situation, Sheridan held Merritt at White River, and organized a large force to operate from the Uncompaghre, under Colonel R. S. Mackenzie, Fourth Cavalry, intending that the two commands should make a concerted winter campaign. But at this juncture it developed that the Indian Bureau, acting without the knowledge of the military, had induced the Indians to give up their captives by promises of gifts to the chiefs and assurances of immunity from punishment to all. This remarkable adjustment of course put an end to further military operations.

3. Relations between whites and Indians during these years, as in earlier periods of our history, were marked by a series of wars and of broken treaties. Ordinarily, white writers wrote of the "redskins" as "savages" and "treacherous". People generally had no idea of the hardships imposed on Indians by unfair white traders and government officials. Helen Hunt Jackson presented a strong case for the Indian in her widely read book, A Century of Dishonor *(Boston, 1886). After a series of chapters, detailing unfair treatment of Indians in all parts of the country, the author concluded as follows:*

THERE are within the limits of the United States between two hundred and fifty and three hundred thousand Indians, exclusive of those in Alaska. The names of the different tribes and bands, as entered in the statistical tables of the Indian Office Reports, number nearly three hundred. One of the most careful estimates which have been made of their numbers and localities gives them as follows: "In Minnesota and States east of the Mississippi, about 32,500; in Nebraska, Kansas, and the Indian Territory, 70,650; in the Territories of Dakota, Montana, Wyoming, and Idaho, 65,000; in Nevada and the Territories of Colorado, New Mexico, Utah and Arizona, 84,000; and on the Pacific slope, 48,000."

Of these, 130,000 are self-supporting on their own reservations, "receiving nothing from the Government except interest on their own moneys, or annuities granted them in consideration of the cession of their lands to the United States."

This fact alone would seem sufficient to dispose forever of the accusation, so persistently brought against the Indian, that he will not work.

Of the remainder, 84,000 are partially supported by the Government—the interest money due them and their annuities, as provided by treaty, being inadequate to their subsistence on the reservations where they are confined. In many cases, however, these Indians furnish a large part of their support—the White River Utes, for instance, who are reported by the Indian Bureau as getting sixty-six per cent. of their living by "root-digging, limiting, and fishing;" the Squaxin band, in Washington Territory, as earning seventy-five per cent., and the Chippewas of Lake Superior as earning fifty per cent. in the same way. These facts also would seem to dispose of the accusation that the Indian will not work.

There are about 55,000 who never visit an agency, over whom the Government does not pretend to have either control or care. These 55,000 "subsist by hunting, fishing, on roots, nuts, berries, etc., and by begging and stealing;" and this also seems to dispose of the accusation that the Indian will not "work for a living." There remains a small portion, about 31,000, that are entirely subsisted by the Government.

There is not among these three hundred bands of Indians one which has not suffered cruelly at the hands either of the Government or of white settlers. The poorer, the more insignificant, the more helpless the band, the more certain the cruelty and outrage to which they have been subjected. This is especially true of the bands on the Pacific slope. These Indians found themselves of a sudden surrounded by and caught up in the great influx of gold-seeking settlers, as helpless creatures on a shore are caught up in a tidal wave. There was not time for the Government to make treaties; not even time for communities to make laws. The tale of the wrongs, the oppressions, the murders of the Pacific-slope Indians in the last thirty years would be a volume by itself, and is too monstrous to be believed.

It makes little difference, however, where one opens the record of the history of the Indians; every page and every year has its dark stain. The story of one tribe is the story of all, varied only by differences of time and place; but neither time nor place makes any difference in the main facts. Colorado is as greedy and unjust in 1880 as

was Georgia in 1830, and Ohio in 1795; and the United States Government breaks promises now as deftly as then, and with an added ingenuity from long practice.

One of its strongest supports in so doing is the widespread sentiment among the people of dislike to the Indian, of impatience with his presence as a "barrier to civilization," and distrust of it as a possible danger. The old tales of the frontier life, with its horrors of Indian warfare, have gradually, by two or three generations' telling, produced in the average mind something like an hereditary instinct of unquestioning and unreasoning aversion which it is almost impossible to dislodge or soften.

There are hundreds of pages of unimpeachable testimony on the side of the Indian; but it goes for nothing, is set down as sentimentalism or partisanship, tossed aside and forgotten.

President after president has appointed commission after commission to inquire into and report upon Indian affairs, and to make suggestions as to the best methods of managing them. The reports are filled with eloquent statements of wrongs done to the Indians, of perfidies on the part of the Government; they counsel, as earnestly as words can, a trial of the simple and unperplexing expedients of telling truth, keeping promises, making fair bargains, dealing justly in all ways and all things. These reports are bound up with the Government's Annual Reports, and that is the end of them. It would probably be no exaggeration to say that not one American citizen out of ten thousand ever sees them or knows that they exist, and yet any one of them, circulated throughout the country, read by the right-thinking, right-feeling men and women of this land, would be of itself a "campaign document" that would initiate a revolution which would not subside until the Indians' wrongs were, so far as is now left possible, righted.

In 1869 President Grant appointed a commission of nine men, representing the influence and philanthropy of six leading States, to visit the different Indian reservations, and to "examine all matters appertaining to Indian affairs."

In the report of this commission are such paragraphs as the following: "To assert that 'the Indian will not work' is as true as it would be to say that the white man will not work.

"Why should the Indian be expected to plant corn, fence lands, build houses, or do anything but get food from day to day, when experience has taught him that the product of his labor will be seized by the white man to-morrow? The most industrious white man would become a drone under similar circumstances. Nevertheless, many of the Indians" (the commissioners might more forcibly have said 130,000 of the Indians) "are already at work, and furnish ample refutation of the assertion that 'the Indian will not work.' There is no escape from the inexorable logic of facts.

"The history of the Government connections with the Indians is a shameful record of broken treaties and unfulfilled promises. The history of the border white man's connection with the Indians is a sickening record of murder, outrage, robbery, and wrongs committed by the former, as the rule, and occasional savage outbreaks and unspeakably barbarous deeds of retaliation by the latter, as the exception.

"Taught by the Government that they had rights entitled to respect, when those rights have been assailed by the rapacity of the white man, the arm which should have been raised to protect them has ever been ready to sustain the aggressor.

"The testimony of some of the highest military officers of the United States is on record to the effect that, in our Indian wars, almost without exception, the first aggressions have been made by the white man; and the assertion is supported by every civilian of reputation who has studied the subject. In addition to the class of robbers and outlaws who find impunity in their nefarious pursuits on the frontiers, there is a large class of professedly reputable men who use every means in their power to bring on Indian wars for the sake of the profit to be realized from the presence of troops and the expenditure of Government funds in their midst. They proclaim death to the Indians at all times in words and publications, making no distinction between the innocent and the guilty. They irate the lowest class of men to the perpetration of the darkest deeds against their victims, and as judges and jurymen shield them from the justice due to their crimes. Every crime committed by a white man against an Indian is concealed or palliated. Every offence committed by an Indian against a white man is borne on the wings of the post or the telegraph to the remotest corner of the land, clothed with all the horrors which the reality or imagination can throw around it. Against such influences as these the people of the United States need to be warned."

To assume that it would be easy, or by any one sudden stroke of legislative policy possible, to undo the mischief and hurt of the long past, set the Indian policy of the country right for the future, and make the Indians at once safe and happy, is the blunder of a hasty and uninformed judgment. The notion which seems to be growing more prevalent, that simply to make all Indians at once citizens of the United States would be a sovereign and instantaneous panacea for all their ills and all the Government's perplexities, is a very inconsiderate one. To administer complete citizenship of a

sudden, all round, to all Indians, barbarous and civilized alike, would be as grotesque a blunder as to dose them all round with any one medicine, irrespective of the symptoms and needs of their diseases. It would kill more than it would cure. Nevertheless, it is true, as was well stated by one of the superintendents of Indian Affairs in 1857, that, "so long as they are not citizens of the United States, their rights of property must remain insecure against invasion. The doors of the federal tribunals being barred against them while wards and dependents, they can only partially exercise the rights of free government, or give to those who make, execute, and construe the few laws they are allowed to enact, dignity sufficient to make them respectable. While they continue individually to gather the crumbs that fall from the table of the United States, idleness, improvidence, and indebtedness will be the rule, and industry, thrift, and freedom from debt the exception. The utter absence of individual title to particular lands deprives every one among them of the chief incentive to labor and exertion—the very mainspring on which the prosperity of a people depends."

All judicious plans and measures for their safety and salvation must embody provisions for their becoming citizens as fast as they are fit, and must protect them till then in every right and particular in which our laws protect other "persons" who are not citizens.

There is a disposition in a certain class of minds to be impatient with any protestation against wrong which is unaccompanied or unprepared with a quick and exact scheme of remedy. This is illogical. When pioneers in a new country find a tract of poisonous and swampy wilderness to be reclaimed, they do not withhold their hands from fire and axe till they see clearly which way roads should run, where good water will spring, and what crops will best grow on the redeemed land. They first clear the swamp. So with this poisonous and baffling part of the domain of our national affairs—let us first "clear the swamp."

However great perplexity and difficulty may be in the details of any and every plan possible for doing at this late day anything like justice to the Indian, however hard it may be for good statesmen and good men to agree upon the things that ought to be done, there certainly is, or ought to be, no perplexity whatever, no difficulty whatever, in agreeing upon certain things that ought not to be done, and which must cease to be done before the first steps can be taken toward righting the wrongs, curing the ills, and wiping out the disgrace to us of the present condition of our Indians. . . .

4. Peacetime has never been a very healthy period for the American armed forces. In the long period of peace following the Civil War, the Army considered itself practically "starved" for supplies and funds. One especially disturbing concern was the proper defense of American coastlines in the age of the steel-clad warship. An Army officer (Captain F. V. Greene) wrote the following, taken from an article on "Our Defenceless Coasts" in Scribner's Magazine *for 1887.*

The very elements of wealth and population which have made an invasion (*of the United States*) impossible have brought an increase of danger in another direction. They have built up on the shores of the Atlantic and Pacific Oceans and the northern lakes a series of great cities, containing an aggregate population of more than five million souls, and destructible property which is carried on the assessors' books with a valuation of $4,000,000,000 (and has probably an actual value of nearly twice as much), yielding annually a product in manufactured goods alone valued at over one thousand million dollars.

Every man, woman, and child in this great population, every dollar in this vast aggregation of wealth, is to-day in danger of destruction by a hostile fleet; for it is certainly a fact that the shells of an enemy's vessels could, in a few weeks, or even days, after declaration of war reach every portion of it—so utterly defenceless are our harbors against the ships and guns which have been developed in the last twenty years, during which we have done nothing. So that while the idea of invasion and conquest may now be dismissed as visionary, the problem of national defence has simplified itself to merely protecting life and property against a possible enemy in our sea-board and lake-board cities. It is, in brief, a problem of national insurance on life and property, to provide for just those cases of danger which are specially excepted from all ordinary policies—cases which lie beyond the grasp of private enterprise, and not only fall within the legitimate province of general government, but are expressly provided for in the Constitution, which gives power to Congress to provide for the common defence. The usual annual premium on policies of insurance on life or property, with good risks, is from one to one and a half per cent. One per cent. on the $4,000,000,000 of destructible property within reach of hostile shells is $40,000,000. Less than half that amount, viz., $20,000,000, expended annually for six years, would give us a complete system of insurance —i.e., it would give us harbor defences stronger than any ships which could be brought against them. It is probable that so large a sum could not be judiciously expended in one year, and the expenditure would be less, and the number of years greater; but with $10,000,000 a year for six years, fully three-fourths of the lives and property on our coasts could be placed out of danger. This amount is about three per cent. of our annual appropriations for the support of the Government and its obligations. . . .

We are to-day, in the matter of coast defence, just where we were during the civil war; we are a whole generation behind the other nations of the world, and a generation, too, in which more advance has been made in methods of coast attack than in the whole previous method of the world's history. And this in spite of the fact that we alone of all the nations of the world have a series of great cities on our ocean coasts. It is doubtful if all the nations of Europe combined have as many lives and as much property within reach of hostile ironclads as we have, since all their chief cities are inland. Yet we have absolutely no means of defence. There has been no such spectacle in the previous history of the world, as this of a rich and pre-eminently powerful people inviting attack upon life and property—or the payment of enormous ransoms as the price of their safety—by leaving its coasts wholly undefended against the implements of war of the period. Nor can any valid reason be given why we alone of all the world should expect immunity from such attacks.

6-C POLITICAL PROBLEMS

After the shooting stopped, and the Civil War was at an end, the United States faced a serious task of rebuilding. The States of the old Confederacy had been overcome on the battlefield. Much of their manpower and property had been destroyed. Their status within the United States was in doubt. A whole system of human relations had been changed —at least legally—by the defeat of the armies of the South. Rebuilding the warehouses and railroads, the homes and docks, represented a major effort; rebuilding the political and social relationships among the States would require a different kind of effort. The whole prewar system of political parties had been shaken by events of the late 1850's and 1860's. The newly formed Republican party began to dominate the country's politics, and the remnants of the Democratic party searched for some new basis on which it could restore its power.

PROBLEMS: *How would the Southern States be "reconstructed" as members of the Union? How would Southern society be affected, now that the slaves were free men? In what ways would political life in the United States be changed during the 30 years following the Civil War? What part did farmers and laboring men take in these changes?*

1. The Reconstruction of the Southern States became the major activity of the first dozen years after Appomattox. President Lincoln, whose plan for re-union of the States was based on "malice toward none", was shot down before he had a chance to carry out his plans for recognizing new State governments in the South. His successor, Andrew Johnson, ran up against strong Congressional opposition. Congress, in the hands of "Radical Republicans", won its contest with President Johnson. As a result, Congress passed a number of laws, in which the "Congressional" plan for Reconstruction was set down.

Reprinted below are the essential parts of six key laws passed during Reconstruction. These laws supported the powers that Congress exercised during the period, and they spelled out certain protection for the newly freed slaves. Since many of the laws were lengthy, and included details about how the laws were to be carried out, the selections below do not include the entire text of the laws; only sections that express the viewpoint of the Congress on the direction of Reconstruction have been quoted from the U.S. Statutes at Large *(a collection of U.S. laws). The first and last are "Civil Rights" laws; the others are called "Reconstruction Acts."*

An Act to protect all Persons in the United States in their Civil Rights, and furnish the Means of their Vindication (April 9, 1866).

Be it enacted . . ., That all persons born in the United States and not subject to any foreign power, excluding Indians not taxed, are hereby declared to be citizens of the United States; and such citizens of every race and color, without regard to any previous condition of slavery or involuntary servitude, except as a punishment for crime whereof the party shall have been duly convicted, shall have the same right, in every State and Territory in the United States, to make and enforce contracts, to sue, be parties, and give evidence, to inherit, purchase, lease, sell, hold, and convey real and personal property, and to full and equal benefit of all laws and proceedings for the security of person and property, as is enjoyed by white citizens, and shall be subject to like punishment, pains, and penalties, and to none other, any law, statute, ordinance, regulation, or custom, to the contrary notwithstanding.

SEC. 2. *And be it further enacted*, That any person who, under color of any law, statute, ordinance, regulation, or custom, shall subject, or cause to be subjected, any inhabitant of any State or Territory to the deprivation of any right secured or protected by this act, or to different punishment, pains, or penalties on account of such person having at any time been held in a condition of slavery or involuntary servitude, except as a punishment for crime whereof the party shall have been duly convicted, or by reason of his color or race, than is prescribed for the punishment of white persons, shall be deemed guilty of a misdemeanor, and, on conviction, shall be punished by fine not exceeding one thousand dollars, or imprisonment not exceeding one year, or both, in the discretion of the court.

SEC. 3. *And be it further enacted*, That the district courts of the United States, within their respective districts, shall have, exclusively of the courts of the several States, cognizance of all crimes and offences committed against the provisions of this act, and also, concurrently with the circuit courts of the United States, of all causes, civil and criminal, affecting persons who are denied or cannot enforce in the courts or judicial tribunals of the State or locality where they may be any of the rights secured to them by the first section of this act. . . . The jurisdiction in civil and criminal matters hereby conferred on the district and circuit courts of the United States shall be exercised and enforced in conformity with the laws of the United States, so far as such laws are suitable to carry the same into effect; but in all cases where such laws are not adapted to the object, or are deficient in the provisions necessary to furnish suitable remedies and punish offences against law, the common law, as modified and changed by the constitution and statutes of the State wherein the court having jurisdiction of the cause, civil or criminal, is held, so far as the same is not inconsistent with the Constitution and laws of the United States, shall be extended to and govern said courts in the trial and disposition of such cause, and, if of a criminal nature, in the infliction of punishment on the party found guilty.

SEC. 4. *And be it further enacted*, That the district attorneys, marshals, and deputy marshals of the United States, the commissioners appointed by the circuit and territorial courts of the United States, with powers of arresting, imprisoning, or bailing offenders against the laws of the United States, the officers and agents of the Freedmen's Bureau, and every other officer who may be specially empowered by the President of the United States, shall be, and they are hereby, specially authorized and required, at the expense of the United States, to institute proceedings against all and every person who shall violate the provisions of this act, and cause him or them to be arrested and imprisoned, or bailed, as the case may be, for trial before such court of the United States or territorial court as by this act has cognizance of the offence. And with a view to affording reasonable protection to all persons in their constitutional rights of equality before the law, without distinction of race or color, or previous condition of slavery or involuntary servitude, except as a punishment for crime, whereof the party shall have been duly convicted, and to the prompt discharge of the duties of this act, it shall be the duty of the circuit courts of the United States and the superior courts of the Territories of the United States, from time to time, to increase the number of commissioners, so as to afford a speedy and convenient means for the arrest and examination of persons charged with a violation of this act. . .

SEC. 8. *And be it further enacted*, That whenever the President of the United States shall have reason to believe that offences have been or are likely to be committed against the provisions of this act within any judicial district, it shall be lawful for him, in his discretion, to direct the judge, marshal, and district attorney of such district to attend at such place within the district, and for such time as he may designate, for the purpose of the more speedy arrest and trial of persons charged with a violation of this act; and it shall be the duty of every judge or other officer, when any such requisition shall be received by him, to attend at the place and for the time therein designated.

SEC. 9. *And be it further enacted*, That it shall be lawful for the President of the United States, or such person as he may empower for that purpose, to employ such part of the land or naval forces of the United

States, or of the militia, as shall be necessary to prevent the violation and enforce the due execution of this act.

SEC. 10. *And be it further enacted,* That upon all questions of law arising in any cause under the provisions of this act a final appeal may be taken to the Supreme Court of the United States . . .

An Act to provide for the more efficient Government of the Rebel States (March 2, 1867).

WHEREAS no legal State governments or adequate protection for life or property now exists in the rebel States of Virginia, North Carolina, South Carolina, Georgia, Mississippi, Alabama, Louisiana, Florida, Texas, and Arkansas; and whereas it is necessary that peace and good order should be enforced in said States until loyal and republican State governments can be legally established: Therefore,

Be it enacted . . . , That said rebel States shall be divided into military districts and made subject to the military authority of the United States as hereinafter prescribed, and for that purpose Virginia shall constitute the first district; North Carolina and South Carolina the second district; Georgia, Alabama, and Florida the third district; Mississippi and Arkansas the fourth district; and Louisiana and Texas the fifth district.

SEC. 2. *And be it further enacted,* That it shall be the duty of the President to assign to the command of each of said districts an officer of the army, not below the rank of brigadier-general, and to detail a sufficient military force to enable such officer to perform his duties and enforce his authority within the district to which he is assigned.

SEC. 3. *And be it further enacted,* That it shall be the duty of each officer assigned as aforesaid, to protect all persons in their rights of person and property, to suppress insurrection, disorder, and violence, and to punish, or cause to be punished, all disturbers of the public peace and criminals; and to this end he may allow local civil tribunals to take jurisdiction of and to try offenders, or, when in his judgment it may be necessary for the trial of offenders, he shall have power to organize military commissions or tribunals for that purpose, and all interference under color of State authority with the exercise of military authority under this act, shall be null and void.

SEC. 4. *And be it further enacted,* That all persons put under military arrest by virtue of this act shall be tried without unnecessary delay, and no cruel or unusual punishment shall be inflicted, and no sentence of any military commission or tribunal hereby authorized, affecting the life or liberty of any person, shall be executed until it is approved by the officer in command of the district, and the laws and regulations for the government of the army shall not be affected by this act, except in so far as they conflict with its provisions: *Provided,* That no sentence of death under the provisions of this act shall be carried into effect without the approval of the President.

SEC. 5. *And be it further enacted,* That when the people of any one of said rebel States shall have formed a constitution of government in conformity with the Constitution of the United States in all respects, framed by a convention of delegates elected by the male citizens of said State, twenty-one years old and upward, of whatever race, color, or previous condition, who have been resident in said State for one year previous to the day of such election, except such as may be disfranchised for participation in the rebellion or for felony at common law, and when such constitution shall provide that the elective franchise shall be enjoyed by all such persons as have the qualifications herein stated for electors of delegates, and when such constitution shall be ratified by a majority of the persons voting on the question of ratification who are qualified as electors for delegates, and when such constitution shall have been submitted to Congress for examination and approval, and Congress shall have approved the same, and when said State, by a vote of its legislature elected under said constitution, shall have adopted the amendment to the Constitution of the United States, proposed by the Thirty-ninth Congress, and known as article fourteen, and when said article shall have become a part of the Constitution of the United States said State shall be declared entitled to representation in Congress, and senators and representatives shall be admitted therefrom on their taking the oath prescribed by law, and then and thereafter the preceding sections of this act shall be inoperative in said State: *Provided,* That no person excluded from the privilege of holding office by said proposed amendment to the Constitution of the United States, shall be eligible to election as a member of the convention to frame a constitution for any of said rebel States, nor shall any such person vote for members of such convention.

SEC. 6. *And be it further enacted,* That, until the people of said rebel States shall be by law admitted to representation in the Congress of the United States, any civil governments which may exist therein shall be deemed provisional only, and in all respects subject to the paramount authority of the United States at any time to abolish, modify, control, or supersede the same; and in all elections to any office under such provisional governments all persons shall be entitled to vote, and none others, who are entitled to vote, under the provisions of the fifth section of this act; and no persons shall be eligible to any office under such provisional governments who would be disqualified from holding office under the provisions of the third *article* of said constitutional amendment.

An Act supplementary to an Act entitled "An Act to provide for the more efficient Goverment of the Rebel States," . . . and to facilitate Restoration (March 23, 1867).

Be it enacted . . . , That before . . . September 1, 1867 . . . the commanding general in each district defined by . . . the act of March 2, 1867 . . . shall cause a registration to be made of the male citizens of the United States, twenty-one years of age and upwards, resident in each county or parish in the State or States included in his district, which registration shall include only those persons who are qualified to vote for delegates by the act aforesaid, and who shall have taken and subscribed the following oath or affirmation: "I, ―― ――, do solemnly swear (or affirm), in the presence of Almighty God, that I am a citizen of the State of ――; that I have resided in said State for ―― months next preceding this day, and now reside in the county of ――, or the parish of ――, in said State (as the case may be); that I am twenty-one years old; that I have not been disfranchised for participation in any rebellion or civil war against the United States, or for felony committed against the laws of any State or of the United States; that I have never been a member of any State legislature, nor held any executive or judicial office in any State, and afterwards engaged in insurrection or rebellion against the United States, or given aid or comfort to the enemies thereof; that I have never taken an oath as a member of Congress of the United States, or as an officer of the United States, or as a member of any State legislature, or as an executive or judicial officer of any State, to support the Constitution of the United States, and afterwards engaged in insurrection or rebellion against the United States, or given aid or comfort to the enemies thereof; that I will faithfully support the Constitution and obey the laws of the United States, and will, to the best of my ability, encourage others so to do, so help me God." . . .

Sec. 2. *And be it further enacted,* That after the completion of the registration hereby provided for in any State, at such time and places therein as the commanding general shall appoint and direct, of which at least thirty days' public notice shall be given, an election shall be held of delegates to a convention for the purpose of establishing a constitution and civil government for such State loyal to the Union, said convention in each State, except Virginia, to consist of the same number of members as the most numerous branch of the State legisature of such State . . . (*as in 1860*) . . . , to be apportioned among the several districts, counties, or parishes of such State by the commanding general, giving to each representation in the ratio of voters registered as aforesaid as nearly as may be. The convention in Virginia shall consist of the same number of members as represented the territory now constituting Virginia in the most numerous branch of the legislature of said State . . . to be apportioned as aforesaid.

Sec. 3. *And be it further enacted,* That at said election the registered voters of each State shall vote for or against a convention to form a constitution therefor under this act. . . . If a majority of the votes given on that question shall be for a convention, then such convention shall be held as hereinafter provided; but if a majority of said votes shall be against a convention, then no such convention shall be held under this act: *Provided,* That such convention shall not be held unless a majority of all such registered voters shall have voted on the question of holding such convention.

Sec. 4. *And be it further enacted,* That the commanding general of each district shall appoint as many boards of registration as may be necessary, consisting of three loyal officers or persons, to make and complete the registration, superintend the election, and make return to him of the votes, lists of voters, and of the persons elected as delegates by a plurality of the votes cast at said election; and upon receiving said returns he shall open the same, ascertain the persons elected as delegates, according to the returns of the officers who conducted said election, and make proclamation thereof; and if a majority of the votes given on that question shall be for a convention, the commanding general, within sixty days from the date of election, shall notify the delegates to assemble in convention, at a time and place to be mentioned in the notification, and said convention, when organized, shall proceed to frame a constitution and civil government according to the provisions of this act, and the act to which it is supplementary; and when the same shall have been so framed, said constitution shall be submitted by the convention for ratification to the persons registered under the provisions of this act at an election to be conducted by the officers or persons appointed or to be appointed by the commanding general, as hereinbefore provided, and to be held after the expiration of thirty days from the date of notice thereof, to be given by said convention; and the returns thereof shall be made to the commanding general of the district.

Sec. 5. *And be it further enacted,* That if, according to said returns, the constitution shall be ratified by a majority of the votes of the registered electors qualified as herein specified, cast at said election, at least one half of all the registered voters voting upon the question of such ratification, the president of the convention shall transmit a copy of the same, duly certified, to the President of the United States, who shall forthwith transmit the same to Congress . . . ; and if it shall moreover appear to Congress that the election was one at which all the registered and qualified electors in the State had an opportunity to vote freely and without restraint, fear, or the influence of fraud, and if the Congress shall be satisfied that such constitution meets the approval of a majority of all the qualified electors in the State, and if the said constitution shall be declared by Congress to be in conformity with the provisions of the act to which this is supplementary, and the other provisions of said act shall have been complied with, and the said constitution shall be approved by Congress, the State shall be declared entitled to representation, and senators and representatives shall be admitted therefrom as therein provided.

An Act supplementary to an Act entitled "An Act to provide for the more efficient Government of the Rebel States," . . . and the Act supplementary thereto . . . (July 19, 1867).

Be it enacted . . . , That it is hereby declared to have been the true intent and meaning . . . that the governments then existing in the rebel States of Virginia, North Carolina, South Carolina, Georgia, Mississippi, Alabama, Louisiana, Florida, Texas, and Arkansas were not legal State governments; and that thereafter said governments, if continued, were to be continued subject in all respects to the military commanders of the respective districts, and to the paramount authority of Congress.

SEC. 2. *And be it further enacted*, That the commander of any district named in said act shall have power, subject to the disapproval of the General of the army of the United States, and to have effect till disapproved, whenever in the opinion of such commander the proper administration of said act shall require it, to suspend or remove from office, or from the performance of official duties and the exercise of official powers, any officer or person holding or exercising, or professing to hold or exercise, any civil or military office or duty in such district under any power, election, appointment or authority derived from, or granted by, or claimed under, any so-called State or the government thereof, or any municipal or other division thereof, and upon such suspension or removal such commander, subject to the disapproval of the General as aforesaid, shall have power to provide from time to time for the performance of the said duties of such officer or person so suspended or removed, by the detail of some competent officer or soldier of the army, or by the appoint-

ment of some other person, to perform the same, and to fill vacancies occasioned by death, resignation, or otherwise.

SEC. 3. *And be it further enacted*, That the General of the army of the United States shall be invested with all the powers of suspension, removal, appointment, and detail granted in the preceding section to district commanders.

SEC. 4. *And be it further enacted*, That the acts of the officers of the army already done in removing in said districts persons exercising the functions of civil officers, and appointing others in their stead, are hereby confirmed: *Provided*, That any person heretofore or hereafter appointed by any district commander to exercise the functions of any civil office, may be removed either by the military officer in command of the district, or by the General of the army. And it shall be the duty of such commander to remove from office as aforesaid all persons who are disloyal to the government of the United States, or who use their official influence in any manner to hinder, delay, prevent, or obstruct the due and proper administration of this act and the acts to which it is supplementary.

SEC. 5. *And be it further enacted*, That the boards of registration provided for in the act . . . [of March 23, 1867] . . . , shall have power, and it shall be their duty before allowing the registration of any person, to ascertain, upon such facts or information as they can obtain, whether such person is entitled to be registered under said act, and the oath required by said act shall not be conclusive on such question, and no person shall be registered unless such board shall decide that he is entitled thereto; and such board shall also have power to examine, under oath, . . . any one touching the qualification of any person claiming registration; but in every case of refusal by the board to register an applicant, and in every case of striking his name from the list as hereinafter provided, the board shall make a note or memorandum, which shall be returned with the registration list to the commanding general of the district, setting forth the grounds of such refusal or such striking from the list: *Provided*, That no person shall be disqualified as member of any board of registration by reason of race or color.

SEC. 6. *And be it further enacted*, That the true intent and meaning of the oath prescribed in said supplementary act is, (among other things,) that no person who has been a member of the legislature of any State, or who has held any executive or judicial office in any State, whether he has taken an oath to support the Constitution of the United States or not, and whether he was holding such office at the commencement of the rebellion, or had held it before, and who has afterwards engaged in insurrection or rebellion against the United States, or given aid or comfort to the enemies thereof, is entitled to be registered or to vote; and the words "executive or judicial office in any State" in said oath mentioned shall be construed to include all civil offices created by law for the administration of any general law of a State, or for the administration of justice.

SEC. 7. *And be it further enacted*, That the time for completing the original registration provided for in said act may, in the discretion of the commander of any district, be extended to . . . [October 1, 1867] . . . ; and the boards of registration shall have power, and it shall be their duty, commencing fourteen days prior to any election under said act, and upon reasonable public notice of the time and place thereof, to revise, for a period of five days, the registration lists; and upon being satisfied that any person not entitled thereto has been registered, to strike the name of such person from the list, and such person shall not be allowed to vote. And such board shall also, during the same period, add to such registry the names of all persons who at that time possess the qualifications required by said act who have not been already registered; and no person shall, at any time, be entitled to be registered or to vote by reason of any executive pardon or amnesty for any act or thing which, without such pardon or amnesty, would disqualify him from registration or voting.

SEC. 8. *And be it further enacted*, That section four of said last-named act shall be construed to authorize the commanding general named therein, whenever he shall deem it needful, to remove any member of a board of registration and to appoint another in his stead, and to fill any vacancy in such board.

SEC. 9. *And be it further enacted*, That all members of said boards of registration and all persons hereafter elected or appointed to office in said military districts, under any so-called State or municipal authority, or by detail or appointment of the district commanders, shall be required to take and to subscribe the oath of office prescribed by law for officers of the United States.

SEC. 10. *And be it further enacted*, That no district commander or member of the board of registration, or any of the officers or appointees acting under them, shall be bound in his action by any opinion of any civil officer of the United States.

SEC. 11. *And be it further enacted*, That all provisions of this act and of the acts to which this is supplementary shall be construed liberally, to the end that all the intents thereof may be fully and perfectly carried out.

Act of March 11, 1868.

Be it enacted . . . , That hereafter any election author-

ized by the act (*of March 23, 1867*) . . . , shall be decided by a majority of the votes actually cast; and at the election in which the question of the adoption or rejection of any constitution is submitted, any person duly registered in the State may vote in the election district where he offers to vote when he has resided therein for ten days next preceding such election, upon presentation of his certificate of registration, his affidavit, or other satisfactory evidence, under such regulations as the district commanders may prescribe.

SEC. 2. *And be it further enacted*, That the constitutional convention of any of the States mentioned in the acts to which this is amendatory may provide that at the time of voting upon the ratification of the constitution the registered voters may vote also for members of the House of Representatives of the United States, and for all elective officers provided for by the said constitution; and the same election officers who shall make the return of the votes cast on the ratification or rejection of the constitution, shall enumerate and certify the votes cast for members of Congress.

Second Civil Rights Act (March 1, 1875)

Whereas, it is essential to just government we recognize the equality of all men before the law, and hold that it is the duty of government in its dealings with the people to mete out equal and exact justice to all, of whatever nativity, race, color, or persuasion, religious or political; and it being the appropriate object of legislation to enact great fundamental principles into law: Therefore,

Be it enacted . . . , That all persons within the jurisdiction of the United States shall be entitled to the full and equal enjoyment of the accommodations, advantages, facilities, and privileges of inns, public conveyances on land or water, theaters, and other places of public amusement; subject only to the conditions and limitations established by law, and applicable alike to citizens of every race and color, regardless of any previous condition of servitude.

SEC. 2. That any person who shall violate the foregoing section by denying to any citizen, except for reasons by law applicable to citizens of every race and color, and regardless of any previous condition of servitude, the full enjoyment of any of the accommodations, advantages, facilities, or privileges in said section enumerated, or by aiding or inciting such denial, shall, for every such offense, forfeit and pay the sum of five hundred dollars to the person aggrieved thereby, to be recovered in an action of debt, with full costs; and shall also, for every such offense, be deemed guilty of a misdemeanor, and, upon conviction thereof, shall be fined not less than five hundred nor more than one thousand dollars, or shall be imprisoned not less than thirty days nor more than one year . . .

SEC. 3. That the district and circuit courts of the United States shall have, exclusively of the courts of the several States, cognizance of all crimes and offenses against, and violations of, the provisions of this act . . .

SEC. 4. That no citizen possessing all other qualifications which are or may be prescribed by law shall be disqualified for service as grand or petit juror in any court of the United States, or of any State, on account of race, color, or previous condition of servitude; and any officer or other person charged with any duty in the selection or summoning of jurors who shall exclude or fail to summon any citizen for the cause aforesaid shall, on conviction thereof, be deemed guilty of a misdemeanor, and be fined not more than five thousand dollars.

2. *The difference in approach between the Presidents and Congress is obvious from the following two documents issued by Presidents Lincoln and Johnson. In these, the Presidents relied on their own view of their powers to pardon (to extend amnesty) and to proclaim the beginning and ending of certain kinds of military action. On December 8, 1863, Abraham Lincoln made this proclamation:*

Whereas, it is now desired by some persons heretofore engaged in said rebellion to resume their allegiance to the United States, and to reinaugurate loyal state governments within and for their respective states: Therefore—

I, ABRAHAM LINCOLN, President of the United States, do proclaim, declare, and make known to all persons who have, directly or by implication, participated in the existing rebellion, except as hereinafter excepted, that a full pardon is hereby granted to them and each of them, with restoration of all rights of property, except as to slaves, and in property cases where rights of third parties shall have intervened, and upon the condition that every such person shall take and subscribe an oath, and thenceforward keep and maintain said oath inviolate; and which oath shall be registered for permanent preservation, and shall be of the tenor and effect following, to wit:—

"I, —— ——, do solemnly swear, in presence of Almighty God, that I will henceforth faithfully support, protect, and defend the Constitution of the United States and the Union of the States thereunder; and that I will, in like manner, abide by and faithfully support all acts of congress passed during the existing rebellion with reference to slaves, so long and so far as not repealed, modified, or held void by congress, or by decision of the supreme court; and that I will, in like manner, abide by

and faithfully support all proclamations of the President made during the existing rebellion having reference to slaves, so long and so far as not modified or declared void by decision of the supreme court. So help me God."

The persons excepted from the benefits of the foregoing provisions are all who are, or shall have been, civil or diplomatic officers or agents of the so-called Confederate government; all who have left judicial stations under the United States to aid the rebellion; all who are, or shall have been, military or naval officers of said so-called Confederate government above the rank of colonel in the army or of lieutenant in the navy; all who left seats in the United States congress to aid the rebellion; all who resigned commissions in the army or navy of the United States and afterwards aided the rebellion; and all who have engaged in any way in treating colored persons, or white persons in charge of such, otherwise than lawfully as prisoners of war, and which persons may have been found in the United States service as soldiers, seamen, or in any other capacity.

And I do further proclaim, declare, and make known that whenever, in any of the States of Arkansas, Texas, Louisiana, Mississippi, Tennessee, Alabama, Georgia, Florida, South Carolina, and North Carolina, a number of persons, not less than one tenth in number of the votes cast in such state at the presidential election . . . (*of 1860*) . . . , each having taken the oath aforesaid, and not having since violated it, and being a qualified voter by the election law of the state existing immediately before the so-called act of secession, and excluding all others, shall reestablish a state government which shall be republican, and in nowise contravening said oath, such shall be recognized as the true government of the state, and the state shall receive thereunder the benefits of the constitutional provision which declares that "the United States shall guaranty to every state in this Union a republican form of government, and shall protect each of them against invasion; and on application of the legislature, or the executive, (when the legislature cannot be convened,) against domestic violence."

And I do further proclaim, declare, and make known that any provision which may be adopted by such state government in relation to the freed people of such state, which shall recognize and declare their permanent freedom, provide for their education, and which may yet be consistent as a temporary arrangement with their present condition as a laboring, landless, and homeless class, will not be objected to by the National Executive.

And it is suggested as not improper that, in constructing a loyal state government in any state, the name of the state, the boundary, the subdivisions, the constitution, and the general code of laws, as before the rebellion, be maintained, subject only to the modifications made necessary by the conditions hereinbefore stated, and such others, if any, not contravening said conditions, and which may be deemed expedient by those framing the new state government.

To avoid misunderstanding, it may be proper to say that this proclamation, so far as it relates to state governments, has no reference to states wherein loyal state governments have all the while been maintained. And, for the same reason, it may be proper to further say, that whether members sent to congress from any state shall be admitted to seats constitutionally rests exclusively with the respective houses, and not to any extent with the Executive. And still further, that this proclamation is intended to present the people of the states wherein the national authority has been suspended, and loyal state governments have been subverted, a mode in and by which the national authority and loyal state governments may be reestablished within said states, or in any of them; and, while the mode presented is the best the Executive can suggest, with his present impressions, it must not be understood that no other possible mode would be acceptable.

On December 25, 1868, President Andrew Johnson issued the following:

Whereas the President of the United States has heretofore set forth several proclamations, offering amnesty and pardon to persons who had been or were concerned in the late rebellion against the lawful authority of the Government of the United States, which proclamations were severally issued on the 8th day of December 1863, on the 26th day of March 1864, on the 29th day of May 1865, on the 7th day of September 1867, and on the 4th day of July in the present year:

And whereas the authority of the Federal Government having been re-established in all the States and Territories within the judisdiction of the United States, it is believed that such prudential reservations and exceptions as of the dates of said several proclamations were deemed necessary and proper may now be wisely and justly relinquished, and that a universal amnesty and pardon for participation in said rebellion extended to all who have borne any part therein will tend to secure permanent peace, order, and prosperity throughout the land, and to renew and fully restore confidence and fraternal feeling among the whole people, and their respect and attachment to the national government, designed by its patriotic founders for general good:

Now, therefore, be it known that I, ANDREW JOHNSON, President of the United States, by virtue of the power and authority in me vested by the Constitution, and in the name of the sovereign people of the United States, do hereby proclaim and declare unconditionally, and without reservation, to all and to every person who directly or indirectly participated in the late insurrection or rebellion, a full pardon and amnesty for the offence of treason against the United States, or of adhering to their enemies during the late civil war, with restoration of all rights, privileges, and immunities under the Constitution and the laws which have been made in pursuance thereof.

3. Carl Schurz rose to the rank of General in the Union forces. He later served as one of the country's most valuable Secretaries of the Interior. The Civil War had just ended when Schurz toured the South and reported (as below) on events and conditions to the government in Washington. He foresaw many troubles during Reconstruction, especially in the reaction of white people in the South to the new freedmen.

In some places that I visited I found apprehensions entertained by whites of impending negro insurrections. Whenever our military commanders found it expedient to subject the statements made to that effect by whites to close investigation, they uniformly found them unwarranted by fact. In many instances there were just reasons for supposing that such apprehensions were industriously spread for the purpose of serving as an excuse for further persecution. In the papers annexed to this report you will find testimony supporting this statement. The negro is easily led; he is always inclined to follow the advice of those he trusts. I do, therefore, not consider a negro insurrection probable as long as the freedmen are under the direct protection of the government, and may hope to see their grievances redressed without resorting to the extreme means of self-protection. There would, perhaps, be danger of insurrections if the government should withdraw its protection from them, and if, against an attempt on the part of the whites to reduce them to something like their former condition, they should find themselves thrown back upon their own resources. Of this contingency I shall speak below.

Education.—That the negroes should have come out of slavery as an ignorant class is not surprising when we consider that it was a penal offence to teach them while they were in slavery; but their eager desire to learn, and the alacrity and success with which they avail themselves of every facility offered to them in that respect, has become a matter of notoriety. The statistics of the Freedmen's Bureau show to what extent such facilities have been offered and what results have been attained. As far as my information goes, these results are most encouraging for the future.

I stated above that, in my opinion, the solution of the social problem in the south did not depend upon the capacity and conduct of the negro alone, but in the same measure upon the ideas and feelings entertained and acted upon by the whites. What their ideas and feelings were while under my observation, and how they affected the contact of the two races, I have already set forth. The question arises, what policy will be adopted by the "ruling class" when all restraint imposed upon them by the military power of the national government is withdrawn, and they are left free to regulate matters according to their own tastes? It would be presumptuous to speak of the future with absolute certainty; but it may safely be assumed that the same causes will always tend to produce the same effects. As long as a majority of the southern people believe that "the negro will not work without physical compulsion," and that "the blacks at large belong to the whites at large," that belief will tend to produce a system of coercion, the enforcement of which will be aided by the hostile feeling against the negro now prevailing among the whites, and by the general spirit of violence which in the south was fostered by the influence slavery exercised upon the popular character. It is, indeed, not probable that a general attempt will be made to restore slavery in its old form, on account of the barriers which such an attempt would find in its way; but there are systems intermediate between slavery as it formerly existed in the south, and free labor as it exists in the north, but more nearly related to the former than to the latter, *the introduction of which will be attempted*. I have already noticed some movements in that direction, which were made under the very eyes of our military authorities, and of which the Opelousas and St. Landry ordinances were the most significant. Other things of more recent date, such as the new negro code submitted by a committee to the legislature of South Carolina, are before the country. They have all the same tendency, because they all spring from the same cause.

It may be objected that evidence has been given of a contrary spririt by the State conventions which passed ordinances abolishing slavery in their States, and making it obligatory upon the legislatures to enact laws for the protection of the freedmen. While acknowledging the fact, I deem it dangerous to be led by it into any delusions. As to the motives upon which they acted when abolishing slavery, and their understanding of the bearings of such an act, we may safely accept the standard they have set up for themselves. When speaking of popular demonstrations in the south in favor of submission to the government, I stated that the principal and almost the only argument used was, that they found themselves in a situation in which "they could do no

better." It was the same thing with regard to the abolition of slavery; wherever abolition was publicly advocated, whether in popular meetings or in State conventions, it was on the ground of necessity—not unfrequently with the significant addition that, as soon as they had once more control of their own State affairs, they could settle the labor question to suit themselves, whatever they might have to submit to for the present. Not only did I find this to be the common talk among the people, but the same sentiment was openly avowed by public men in speech and print. Some declarations of that kind, made by men of great prominence, have passed into the newspapers and are undoubtedly known to you. I append to this report a specimen, (accompanying document, No. 40,) not as something particularly remarkable, but in order to represent the current sentiment as expressed in the language of a candidate for a seat in the State convention of Mississippi. It is a card addressed to the voters of Wilkinson county, Mississippi, by General W. L. Brandon. The general complains of having been called "an unconditional, immediate emancipationist—an abolitionist." He indignantly repels the charge and avows himself a good pro-slavery man. "But, fellow-citizens," says he, "what I may in common with you have to submit to, is a very different thing. Slavery has been taken from us; the power that has already practically abolished it threatens totally and forever to abolish it. But does it follow that I am in favor of this thing? By no means. My honest conviction is, we must accept the situation as it is, until we can get control once more of our own State affairs. We cannot do otherwise and get our place again in the Union, and occupy a position, exert an influence that will protect us against greater evils which threaten us. I must, as any other man who votes or holds an office, submit for the time to evils I cannot remedy."

General Brandon was elected on that platform, and in the convention voted for the ordinance abolishing slavery, and imposing upon the legislature the duty to pass laws for the protection of the freedmen. And General Brandon is certainly looked upon in Mississippi as an honorable man, and an honest politician. What he will vote for when his people have got once more control of their own State affairs, and his State has regained its position and influence in the Union, it is needless to ask. I repeat, his case is not an isolated one. He has only put in print what, as my observations lead me to believe, a majority of the people say even in more emphatic language; and the deliberations of several legislatures in that part of the country show what it means. I deem it unnecessary to go into further particulars.

It is worthy of note that the convention of Mississippi —and the conventions of other States have followed its example—imposed upon subsequent legislatures the obligation not only to pass laws for the protection of the freedmen in person and property, but also *to guard against the dangers arising from sudden emancipation.* This language is not without significance; not the blessings of a full development of free labor, but only the dangers of emancipation are spoken of. It will be observed that this clause is so vaguely worded as to authorize the legislatures to place any restriction they may see fit upon the emancipated negro, in perfect consistency with the amended State constitutions; for it rests with them to define what the dangers of sudden emancipation consist in, and what measures may be required to guard against them. It is true, the clause does not authorize the legislatures to re-establish slavery in the old form; but they may pass whatever laws they see fit, stopping short only one step of what may strictly be defined as "slavery." Peonage of the Mexican pattern, or serfdom of some European pattern, may under that clause be considered admissible; and looking at the legislative attempts already made, especially the labor code now under consideration in the legislature of South Carolina, it appears not only possible, but eminently probable, that the laws which will be passed to guard against the dangers arising from emancipation will be directed against the spirit of emancipation itself.

A more tangible evidence of good intentions would seem to have been furnished by the admission of negro testimony in the courts of justice, which has been conceded in some of the southern States, at least in point of form. This being a matter of vital interest to the colored man, I inquired into the feelings of people concerning it with particular care. At first I found hardly any southern man that favored it. Even persons of some liberality of mind saw seemingly insurmountable objections. The appearance of a general order issued by General Swayne in Alabama, which made it optional for the civil authorities either to admit negro testimony in the State courts or to have all cases in which colored people were concerned tried by officers of the bureau or military commissions, seemed to be the signal for a change of position on the part of the politicians. A great many of them, seeing a chance for getting rid of the jurisdiction of the Freedmen's Bureau, dropped their opposition somewhat suddenly and endeavored to make the admission of negro testimony in the State courts palatable to the masses by assuring them that at all events it would rest with the judges and juries to determine in each case before them whether the testimony of negro witnesses was worth anything or not. One of the speeches delivered at Vicksburg, already referred to in another connexion, and a card published by a candidate for office, (accompanying document No. 14,) furnish specimens of that line of argument.

In my despatch from Montgomery, Alabama, I suggested to you that instructions be issued making it part of the duty of agents of the Freedmen's Bureau to appear in the State courts as the freedmen's next friend, and to forward reports of the proceedings had in the principal cases to the headquarters of the bureau. In this manner it would have been possible to ascertain to what extent the admission of negro testimony secured to the colored man justice in the State courts. As the plan does not seem to have been adopted, we must form our conclusions from evidence less complete. Among the annexed documents there are several statements concerning its results, made by gentlemen whose business it was to observe. I would invite your attention to the letters of Captain Paillon, agent of the Freedmen's Bureau at Mobile; Major Reynolds, assistant commissioner of the bureau at Natchez; and Colonel Thomas, assistant commissioner for the State of Mississippi. (Accompanying documents Nos. 41 and 27.) The opinions expressed in these papers are uniformly unfavorable. It is to be hoped that at other places better results have been attained. But I may state that even by prominent southern men, who were anxious to have the jurisdiction of the State courts extended over the freedmen, the admission was made to me that the testimony of a negro would have but little weight with a southern jury. I frequently asked the question, "Do you think a jury of your people would be apt to find a planter who has whipped one of his negro laborers guilty of assault and battery?" The answer almost invariably was, "You must make some allowance for the prejudice of our people."

It is probable that the laws excluding negro testimony from the courts will be repealed in all the States lately in rebellion if it is believed that a satisfactory arrangement of this matter may in any way facilitate the "readmission" of the States, but I apprehend such arrangements will hardly be sufficient to secure to the colored man impartial justice as long as the feelings of the whites are against him and they think that his rights are less entitled to respect than their own. More potent certainly than the laws of a country are the opinions of right and wrong entertained by its people. When the spirit of a law is in conflict with such opinions, there is but little prospect of its being faithfully put in execution, especially where those who hold such opinions are the same who have to administer the laws.

The facility with which southern politicians acquiesce in the admission of negro testimony is not surprising when we consider that the practical management of the matter will rest with their own people. I found them less accommodating with regard to "constitutional amendment." Nine-tenths of the intelligent men with whom I had any conversation upon that subject expressed their willingness to ratify the first section, abolishing slavery throughout the United States, but not the second section, empowering Congress "to enforce the foregoing by appropriate legislation." I feel warranted in saying that, while I was in the south, this was the prevailing sentiment. Nevertheless, I deem it probable that the "constitutional amendment" will be ratified by every State legislature, provided the government insists upon such ratification as a *conditio sine qua non* of readmission. It is instructive to observe how powerful and immediate an effect the announcement of such a condition by the government produces in southern conventions and legislatures. It would be idle to assume, however, that a telegraphic despatch, while it may beat down all parliamentary opposition to this or that measure, will at the same time obliterate the prejudices of the people; nor will it prevent those prejudices from making themselves seriously felt in the future. It will require measures of a more practical character to prevent the dangers which, as everybody that reads the signs of the times must see, are now impending.

4. *There was serious question about what to do with some of the former Confederate leaders. Union troops had captured President Jefferson Davis in the closing hours of the war, and many Union men wished to see Davis tried for treason and hanged. Others felt that this would be unwise. While the two groups debated what to do with Davis, the former Confederate President was imprisoned at a military post. His continued imprisonment without trial led to one curious development. Horace Greeley, one of the country's leading abolitionists before the Civil War and an outstanding newspaper publisher, offered bail, so that Davis could be freed pending trial like any other American. Greeley talks about it in his book,* Recollections of a Busy Life.

Mr. George Shea, the attorney of record for the defence in the case of The United States *versus* Jefferson Davis, indicted for treason, is the son of an old friend, and I have known and liked him from infancy. After it had become evident that his client had no immediate prospect of trial, if any prospect at all, Mr. Shea became anxious that said client be liberated on bail. Consulting me as to the feasibility of procuring some names to be proffered as bondsmen of persons who had conspicuously opposed the Rebellion and all the grave errors which incited it, I suggested two eminent Unionists, who, I presumed, would cheerfully consent to stand as security that the accused would not run away to avoid the trial he had long but unsuccessfully invoked. I added, after reflection, "If *my* name should be found necessary, you may use that." He thanked me, and said

he should proffer it only in case the others abundantly at his command would not answer without it. Months passed before I was apprised, by a telegram from Washington, that my name *was* needed; when I went down and proffered it. And when, at length, the prisoner was brought before the United States District Court at Richmond, I was there, by invitation, and signed the bond in due form.

I suppose this would have excited some hubbub at any rate; but the actual tumult was gravely aggravated by gross misstatements. It was widely asserted that the object of giving bail was to screen the accused from trial,—in other words, to enable him to run away,—when nothing like this was ever imagined by those concerned. The prisoner, through his counsel, had assiduously sought a trial, while the prosecution was not ready, because (as Judge Underwood was obliged to testify before a Committee of Congress) no conviction was possible, except by packing a jury. The words "straw bail" were used in this connection; when one of the sureties is worth several millions of dollars, and the poorest of them is abundantly good for the sum of $5,000, in which he is "held and firmly bound" to produce the body of Jefferson Davis whenever the plaintiff shall be ready to try him! If he only *would* run away, I know that very many people would be much obliged to him; but he won't.

It was telegraphed all over the North that I had a very affectionate meeting and greeting with the prisoner when he had been bailed; when in fact I had never before spoken nor written to him any message whatever, and did not know him, even by sight, when he entered the court-room. After the bond was signed, one of his counsel asked me if I had any objection to being introduced to Mr. Davis, and I replied that I had none; whereupon we were introduced, and simply greeted each other. I made, at the request of a friend, a brief call on his wife that evening, as they were leaving for Canada; and there our intercourse ended, probably forever. . . .

5. *The way in which "carpetbag" political leaders from the North tried to insure that black voters would vote Republican may be studied in the following extracts from the "Loyal League Catechism".*

A DIALOGUE BETWEEN A WHITE REPUBLICAN AND A
COLORED CITIZEN, PUBLISHED BY THE UNION
REPUBLICAN CONGRESSIONAL COMMITTEE,
WASHINGTON, D. C.

The following is a dialogue between a newly enfranchised freedman and a sound Radical Republican. The new-made voter is seeking light upon the subject of his political duties and his Radical friend gives him plain facts, and demonstrates clearly with which party he and all like him should act. It would be well for colored voters generally to seek out some tried Radical friend and question him upon all subjects about which they have any doubt. The dialogue is submitted with the hope that the facts set forth therein will remove doubts from the minds of many who have been unable to receive proper information upon the position in which they should stand at this time:

The Dialogue.

QUESTION. With what party should the colored man vote?

ANSWER. The Union Republican party.

Q. Why should the colored man vote with that party?

A. Because that party has made him free and given him the right to vote.

Q. Was Mr. Lincoln a Republican?

A. He was a Republican President.

Q. Are all the Republicans in favor of universal freedom?

A. They are.

Q. What is the difference between Radicals and Republicans?

A. There is none. The word Radical was applied to the Republican party by its enemies, and has been accepted by it.

Q. The Radicals and Republicans are then one and the same party?

A. They are, and they are all in favor of freedom and universal justice.

Q. What is the meaning of the word Radical as applied to political parties and politicians?

A. It means one who is in favor of going to the root of things; who is thoroughly in earnest; who desires that slavery should be *abolished*, that every disability connected therewith should be *obliterated*, not only from the national laws but from those of every State in the Union.

Q. Is Mr. Sumner a Republican?

A. He is, and a Radical, so are Thad. Stevens, Senator Wilson, Judge Kelley, Gen. Butler, Speaker Colfax, Chief Justice Chase, and all other men who favor giving colored men their rights.

Q. To which party do the friends of the colored men in Congress belong?

A. To the Republican Party.

Q. What is a Democrat?

A. A member of that party which before the rebellion sustained every legislative act demanded by the slaveholders such as the Fugitive Slave Law, and the attempt made to force slavery upon the Western Territories.

Q. What was the position of the Democratic Party during the war?

A. It opposed the war; declared Mr. Lincoln's management of it a failure; resisted every measure in Congress looking to emancipation, and denounced the Government for arming colored men as soldiers.

Q. What has that party done since the surrender of the rebels?

A. It has sustained Mr. Johnson in his efforts to restore your old masters to power in the country, and opposed every act for your benefit which the Republican Congress has adopted.

Q. Is it known by any other name?

A. It is known as Conservative, Copperhead and rebel. Under each name it is still the same enemy of freedom and the rights of man.

Q. Would the Democrats make slaves of the colored people again if they could?

A. It is fair to presume they would, for they have opposed their freedom by every means in their power, and have always labored to extend slavery.

Q. Would Democrats allow colored men to vote?

A. No! They have always opposed it in Congress and in the various State Legislatures.

Q. Who abolished slavery in the District of Columbia?

A. A Republican Congress and Abraham Lincoln, a Republican President.

Q. Who freed the slaves of the South?

A. Abraham Lincoln, the Republican President, by proclamation.

Q. Who passed the Freedman's Bureau Bill?

A. A Republican Congress by more than a two-thirds vote over the veto of Andrew Johnson, the leader of the Democratic or conservative party.

Q. Who gave us the Civil Rights Bill?

A. The same Republican Congress.

Q. What party gave us the right to vote?

A. The Republican party.

Q. What has the Democratic, Conservative or Copperhead party ever done for the colored people?

A. It has tried to keep them in slavery, and opposed giving them the benefit of the Freedman's Bureau and Civil Rights Bills, and the right to vote.

Q. Why cannot colored men support the Democratic party?

A. Because that party would disfranchise them, and, if possible, return them to slavery and certainly keep them in an inferior position before the law.

Q. With whom do the disloyal white men of the South desire the colored men to vote?

A. With the Democratic party.

Q. Would not the Democrats take away all the negro's rights?

A. They would.

Q. Then why do they pretend to be the best friends of the colored men?

A. Because they contend that they are fitted only for slavery, or an inferior position, and are happier in either condition.

Q. How would it suit them to be served in the same manner?

A. They would not endure it. They call themselves a superior race of beings, and claim they are born your rulers.

Q. Why do they not do unto others as they would be done by?

A. Because they are devoid of principle, and destitute of all sense of justice where the colored man is concerned.

Q. Do all white people belong to a party which would treat us in that way?

A. They do not. There are many who have stood up nobly for your rights, and who will aid you to the end; indeed, all the Republicans are such.

Q. To what party do the people of the South belong?

A. The larger portion belong to the Democratic party.

Q. Are the slave holders and the leaders of the rebellion members of that party?

A. They are, and would not regard you as having any right if they were in power.

Q. The colored men should then vote with the Republican or Radical Party?

A. They should, and shun the Democratic party as they would the overseer's lash and the auction block.

Q. Has the Republican party ever deceived the colored people?

A. It has not. While the Democratic party has always been opposed to their freedom, their education, and their right to vote, the Republican party has always been their friend.

Q. To what party do the leading colored men belong?

A. Without exception they belong to the Republican party.

Q. What are the most prominent principles advocated by the Republican party?

A. Equal rights before the law and at the ballot box for all men without regard to race or color; that is, that every man shall have the same rights and liberties as any other man.

Q. Does not the Military Reconstruction Act secure to us these rights?

A. Yes, but you may yet be deprived of them if your enemies get into power.

Q. What would the people think if the colored men voted with the Democratic party?

A. The people of the North would think that they did not fully understand their own rights nor the duties devolving on them; and the people of the South would proudly say, "We have always told you that the negro did not wish to be free."

Q. What use has been made of the money which the colored people of the Southern States have paid as taxes?

A. It has been used to establish schools for *white* children; to pay the expenses of making and executing laws in which the colored men have had no voice, and in endeavoring to have the Supreme Court set aside the law which gives you the right to vote.

6. Controversy between the President and the "Radical" Republicans who controlled Congress and wanted Congressional Reconstruction led to the impeachment of Andrew Johnson in the spring of 1868. He was charged with a number of offenses— as follows.

Articles exhibited by the House of Representatives of the United States, in the name of themselves and all of the people of the United States, against Andrew Johnson, President of the United States, in maintenance and support of their impeachment against him for high crimes and misdemeanors in office.

ARTICLE I

That said Andrew Johnson, President of the United States on February 21, 1868, at Washington, in the District of Columbia, unmindful of the high duties of his office, of his oath of office, and of the requirement of the Constitution that he should take care that the laws be faithfully executed, did unlawfully, and in violation of the Constitution and laws of the United States issue an order in writing for the removal of Edwin M. Stanton from the office of Secretary for the Department of War, said Edwin M. Stanton having been theretofore duly appointed and commissioned by and with the advice and consent of the Senate of the United States, as such Secretary, and said Andrew Johnson, President of the United States, on August 12, 1867, and during the recess of said Senate, having suspended by his order Edwin M. Stanton from said office, and within twenty days after the first day of the next meeting of said Senate, that is to say, on the twelfth day of December in the year last aforesaid having reported to said Senate such suspension with the evidence and reasons for his action in the case and the name of the person designed to perform the duties of such office temporarily until the next meeting of the Senate, and said Senate there-afterwards, on January 13, 1868, having duly considered the evidence and reasons reported by said Andrew Johnson for said suspension, and having refused to concur in said suspension, whereby and by force of the provisions of [*the Tenure of Office Act, March 2, 1867*], . . . said Edwin M. Stanton did forthwith resume the functions of his office, whereof the said Andrew Johnson had then and there due notice, and said Edwin M. Stanton, by reason of the premises, on said twenty-first day of February, being lawfully entitled to hold said office of Secretary for the Department of War, which said order for the removal of said Edwin M. Stanton is in substance as follows, that is to say:

"EXECUTIVE MANSION
"Washington, D. C., February 21, 1868.
"SIR: By virtue of the power and authority vested in me as President by the Constitution and laws of the United States you are hereby removed from office as Secretary for the Department of War, and your functions as such will terminate upon the receipt of this communication.

"You will transfer to Brevet Major General Lorenzo Thomas, Adjutant General of the Army, who has this day been authorized and empowered to act as Secretary of War *ad interim*, all records, books, papers, and other public property now in your custody and charge.
"Respectfully yours,
"ANDREW JOHNSON.

"To the Hon. EDWIN M. STANTON,
"Washington, D. C."
Which order was unlawfully issued with intent then and there to violate the act entitled "An act regulating the tenure of certain civil offices," passed March second, eighteen hundred and sixty-seven, and with the further intent, contrary to the provisions of said act, in violation thereof, and contrary to the provisions of the Constitution of the United States, and without the advice and consent of the Senate of the United States, the said Senate then and there being in session, to remove Edwin M. Stanton from the office of Secretary for the Department of War, the said Edwin M. Stanton being then and there Secretary for the Department of War, and being then and there in the due and lawful execution and discharge of the duties of said office, whereby said Andrew Johnson, President of the United States, did then and there commit and was guilty of a high misdemeanor in office.

ARTICLE II

That on February 21, 1868, at Washington, in the District of Columbia, said Andrew Johnson, President of the United States, unmindful of the duties of his office, of his oath of office, and in violation of the Constitution of the United States, and contrary to the provisions of [the Tenure of Office Act], without the advice and consent of the Senate of the United States, said Senate then and there being in session, and without authority of the law, did, with intent to violate the Constitution of the United States, and the act aforesaid, issue and deliver to one Lorenzo Thomas a letter of authority in substance as follows, that is to say:

"EXECUTIVE MANSION
"Washington, D. C., February 21, 1868.
"SIR: The Hon. Edwin M. Stanton having been this day removed from office as Secretary for the Department of War, you are hereby authorized and empowered to act as Secretary of War *ad interim*, and will immediately enter upon the discharge of the duties pertaining to that office.

"Mr. Stanton has been instructed to transfer to you all the records, books, papers, and other public property now in his custody and charge.
"Respectfully yours,
"ANDREW JOHNSON.
"To Brevet Major General LORENZO THOMAS,
"Adjutant General U.S. Army, Washington, D.C."

Then and there being no vacancy in said office of Secretary for the Department of War, whereby said Andrew Johnson, . . . did then and there commit and was guilty of a high misdemeanor in office.

ARTICLE III

That said Andrew Johnson, . . . on [February 21, 1868], at Washington, in the District of Columbia, did commit and was guilty of a high misdemeanor in office in this, that, without authority of law, while the Senate of the United States was then and there in session, he did appoint one Lorenzo Thomas to be Secretary for the Department of War *ad interim*, without the advice and consent of the Senate, and with intent to violate the Constitution of the United States, no vacancy having happened in said office of Secretary for the Department of War during the recess of the Senate, and no vacancy existing in said office at the time, and which said appointment, so made by said Andrew Johnson, of said Lorenzo Thomas, is in substance as follows, that is to say: [*Here follows the same note that is reproduced in Article II.*]

ARTICLE IV

That said Andrew Johnson . . . [on February 21, 1868], at Washington, in the District of Columbia, did unlawfully conspire with one Lorenzo Thomas, and with other persons to the House of Representatives unknown, with intent, by intimidation and threats, unlawfully to hinder and prevent Edwin M. Stanton, then and there the Secretary for the Department of War, duly appointed under the laws of the United States, from holding said office of Secretary for the Department of War, contrary to and in violation of the Constitution of the United States, and of the provisions of an act entitled "An act to define and punish certain conspiracies," approved July thirty-first, eighteen hundred and sixty-one, whereby said Andrew Johnson, President of the United States, did then and there commit and was guilty of a high crime in office.

ARTICLE V

That said Andrew Johnson . . . [on February 21, 1868] and on divers other days and times in said year, before [March 2, 1868], at Washington, in the District of Columbia, did unlawfully conspire with one Lorenzo Thomas, and with other persons to the House of Representatives unknown, to prevent and hinder the execution of [the Tenure of Office Act] . . . and in pursuance of said conspiracy, did unlawfully attempt to prevent Edwin M. Stanton, then and there being Secretary for the Department of War, duly appointed and commissioned under the laws of the United States, from holding said office, whereby the said Andrew Johnson, President of the United States, did then and there commit and was guilty of a high misdemeanor in office.

ARTICLE VI

That said Andrew Johnson, . . [on February 21, 1868], at Washington, in the District of Columbia, did unlawfully conspire with one Lorenzo Thomas by force to seize, take, and possess the property of the United States in the Department of War, and then and there in the custody and charge of Edwin M. Stanton, Secretary for said department, contrary to the provision of [the Conspiracy Act, July 31, 1861] . . and with intent to violate and disregard [the Tenure of Office Act] . . whereby said Andrew Johnson, President of the United States, did then and there commit a high crime in office.

ARTICLE VII

That said Andrew Johnson . . [on February 21, 1868], at Washington, in the District of Columbia, did unlawfully conspire with one Lorenzo Thomas with intent unlawfully to seize, take, and possess the property of the United States, in the Department of War, in the custody and charge of Edwin M. Stanton, Secretary for said department, with intent to violate and disregard [the Tenure of Office Act] . . whereby said Andrew Johnson, President of the United States, did then and there commit a high misdemeanor in office.

ARTICLE VIII

That said Andrew Johnson, . . with intent unlawfully to control the disbursements of the moneys appropriated for the military service and for the Department of War, on [February 21, 1868] . . at Washington, in the District of Columbia, did unlawfully and contrary to the provisions of [the Tenure of Office Act] . . and in violation of the Constitution of the United States, and without the advice and consent of the Senate of the United States, and while the Senate was then and there in session, there being no vacancy in the office of Secretary for the Department of War, and with intent to violate and disregard the act aforesaid, then and there issue and deliver to one Lorenzo Thomas a letter of authority in writing, in substance as follows, that is to say: [Here follows the same note that is reproduced in Article II]. . .

Whereby said Andrew Johnson, President of the United States, did then and there commit and was guilty of a high misdemeanor in office.

ARTICLE IX

That said Andrew Johnson . . [on February 22, 1868] . . at Washington, in the District of Columbia, in disregard of the Constitution and the laws of the United States duly enacted, as commander-in-chief of the army of the United States, did bring before himself then and there William H. Emory, a major general by brevet in the army of the United States, actually in command of the department of Washington and the military forces thereof, and did then and there as such commander-in-chief, declare to and instruct said Emory that part of a law of the United States, passed March second, eighteen hundred and sixty-seven, entitled "An act making appropriations for the support of the army for the year ending June thirtieth, eighteen hundred and sixty-eight, and for other purposes," especially the second section thereof, which provides, among other things, that "all orders and instructions relating to military operations, issued by the President or Secretary of War, shall be issued through the General of the army, and in case of inability, through the next in rank," was unconstitutional, and in contravention of the commission of said Emory, and which said provision of law had been therefore duly and legally promulgated by General Orders for the government and direction of the army of the United States, as the said Andrew Johnson then and there well knew, with intent thereby to induce said Emory, in his official capacity as commander of the department of Washington, to violate the provisions of said act, and to take and receive, act upon, and obey such orders as he, the said Andrew Johnson, might make and give, and which should not be issued through the General of the army of the United States, according to the provisions of said act, and with the further intent thereby to enable him, the said Andrew Johnson, to prevent the execution of the [*Tenure of Office Act*] . . and to unlawfully prevent Edwin M. Stanton, then being Secretary for the Department of War, from holding said office and discharging the duties thereof, whereby said Andrew Johnson, President of the United States, did then and there commit and was guilty of a high misdemeanor in office.

And the house of Representatives, by protestation, saying to themselves the liberty of exhibiting at any time hereafter any further articles, or other accusation or impeachment against the said Andrew Johnson, President of the United States, and also of replying to his answers which he shall make unto the articles herein preferred against him, and of offering proof to the same, and every part thereof, and to every other article, accusation, or impeachment which shall be exhibited by them, as the case shall require, DO DEMAND that the said Andrew Johnson may be put to answer the high crimes and misdemeanors in office herein charged against him, and that such proceedings, examinations, trials, and judgments may be thereupon had and given as may be agreeable to law and justice.

ARTICLE X

That said Andrew Johnson, President of the United States, unmindful of the high duties of his office, and the dignity and properties thereof, and of the harmony and courtesies which ought to exist and be maintained between the executive and legislative branches of the government of the United States, designing and intending to set aside the rightful authority and powers of Congress, did attempt to bring into disgrace, ridicule, hatred, contempt, and reproach the Congress of the United States, and the several branches thereof, to impair and destroy the regard and respect of all the good people of the United States for the Congress and legislative powers thereof, (which all officers of the government ought inviolably to preserve and maintain,) and to excite the odium and resentment of all the good people of the United States against Congress and the laws by it duly and constitutionally enacted; and in pursuance of his said design and intent, openly and publicly, and before

divers assemblages of the citizens of the United States, convened in divers parts thereof to meet and receive said Andrew Johnson as the Chief Magistrate of the United States, did, on August 8, 1866 . . and on divers other days and times, as well before as afterward, make and deliver, with a loud voice, certain intemperate, inflammatory, and scandalous harangues, and did therein utter loud threats and bitter menaces, as well against Congress as the laws of the United States duly enacted thereby, amid the cries, jeers, and laughter of the multitudes then assembled and in hearing, which are set forth in the several specifications hereinafter written, in substance and effect, that is to say:

Specification first.—In this, that at Washington, in the District of Columbia, in the Executive Mansion, to a committee of citizens who called upon the President of the United States, speaking of and concerning the Congress of the United States, said Andrew Johnson, President of the United States, heretofore, to-wit, on . . [August 18, 1866] . . did, in a loud voice, declare, in substance and effect, among other things, that is to say:

"So far as the executive department of the government is concerned, the effort has been made to restore the Union, to heal the breach, to pour oil into the wounds which were consequent upon the struggle, and (to speak in common phrase) to prepare, as the learned and wise physician would, a plaster healing in character and coextensive with the wound. We thought, and we think, that we had partially succeeded; but, as the work progresses, as reconstruction seemed to be taking place, and the country was becoming reunited, we found a disturbing and marring element opposing us. In alluding to that element I shall go no further than your convention, and the distinguished gentleman who has delivered to me the report of its proceedings. I shall make no reference to it that I do not believe the time and occasion justify.

"We have witnessed in one department of the government every endeavor to prevent the restoration of peace, harmony and union. We have seen hanging upon the verge of the government, as it were, a body called, or which assumed to be, the Congress of the United States, while, in fact, it is a Congress of only a part of the States. We have seen the Congress pretend to be for the Union, when its every step and act tended to perpetuate disunion and make a disruption of the States inevitable. . . . We have seen Congress gradually encroach, step by step, upon constitutional rights, and violate day after day and month after month, fundamental principles of the government. We have seen a Congress that seemed to forget that there was a limit to the sphere and scope of legislation. We have seen a Congress in a minority assume to exercise power which, allowed to be consummated, would result in despotism or monarchy itself."

Specification second.—In this, that at Cleveland in the State of Ohio, heretofore, to-wit, on . . [September 3, 1866] . . before a public assemblage of citizens and others, said Andrew Johnson, President of the United States, did, in a loud voice, declare, in substance and effect, among other things, that is to say:

"I will tell you what I did do. I called upon your Congress that is trying to break up the government. . .

"In conclusion, beside that, Congress had taken much pains to poison their constituents against him. But what had Congress done? Have they done anything to restore the union of these States? No; on the contrary, they have done everything to prevent it; and because he stood now where he did when the rebellion commenced, he had been denounced as a traitor. Who had run greater risks or made greater sacrifices than himself? But Congress, factious and domineering, had undertaken to poison the minds of the American people."

Specification third.—In this, that at St. Louis, in the State of Missouri, heretofore, to-wit, on . . [September 8, 1866] . . before a public assemblage of citizens and others, said Andrew Johnson, President of the United States, speaking of and concerning the Congress of the United States, did, in a loud voice, declare in substance and effect, among other things, that is to say:

"Go on. Perhaps if you had a word or two on the subject of New Orleans you might understand more about it than you do. And if you will go back—if you will go back and ascertain the cause of the riot at New Orleans, perhaps you will not be so prompt in calling out 'New Orleans.' If you will take up the riot at New Orleans, and trace it back to its source or its immediate cause, you will find out who is responsible for the blood that was shed there. If you will take up the riot at New Orleans and trace it back to the radical Congress, you will find that the riot at New Orleans was substantially planned. If you will take up the proceedings in their caucusses you will understand that they there knew that a convention was to be called which was extinct by its power having expired; that it was said that the intention was that a new government was to be organized, and on the organization of that government the intention was to enfranchise one portion of the population, called the colored population, who had just been emancipated, and at the same time disfranchise white men. When you design to talk about New Orleans you ought to understand what you are talking about. When you read the speeches that were made, and take up the facts on the Friday and Saturday before the convention sat, you will there find that speeches were made incendiary in their character, exciting that portion of the population, the black popula-

tion, to arm themselves and prepare for the shedding of blood. You will also find that the convention did assemble in violation of law, and the intention of that convention was to supersede the reorganized authorities in the State government of Louisiana, which had been recognized by the government of the United States; and every man engaged in that rebellion in that convention, with the intent of superseding and upturning the civil government which had been recognized by the government of the United States, I say that he was a traitor to the Constitution of the United States, and hence you find that another rebellion was commenced, having its origin in the radical Congress. . .

"So much for the New Orleans riot. And there was the cause and the origin of the blood that was shed, and every drop of blood that was shed is upon their skirts, and they are responsible for it. I could test this thing a little closer, but will not do it here tonight. But when you talk about the causes and consequences that resulted from proceedings of that kind, perhaps, as I have been introduced here, and you have provoked questions of this kind, though it does not provoke me, I will tell you a few wholesome things that have been done by this radical Congress in connection with New Orleans and the extension of the elective franchise.

"I know that I have been traduced and abused. I know it has come in advance of me here as elsewhere, that I have attempted to exercise an arbitrary power in resisting laws that were intended to be forced upon the government; that I had exercised that power; that I had abandoned the party that elected me, and that I was a traitor, because I exercised the veto power in attempting, and did arrest for a time, a bill that was called a 'Freedman's Bureau' bill; yes, that I was a traitor. And I have been traduced, I have been slandered, I have been maligned, I have been called Judas Iscariot, and all that. Now, my countrymen, here to-night, it is very easy to indulge in epithets; it is easy to call a man Judas and cry out traitor; but when he is called upon to give arguments and facts he is very often found wanting. Judas Iscariot—Judas. There was a Judas, and he was one of the twelve apostles. Oh! yes, the twelve apostles had a Christ. The twelve apostles had a Christ, and he never could have had a Judas unless he had had twelve apostles. If I have played the Judas, who has been my Christ that I have played the Judas with? Was it Thad. Stevens? Was it Wendell Phillips? Was it Charles Sumner? These are the men that stop and compare themselves with the Saviour; and everybody that differs with them in opinion, and to try to stay and arrest their diabolical and nefarious policy, is to be denounced as a Judas. . .

"Well, let me say to you, if you will stand by me in

this action, if you will stand by me in trying to give the people a fair chance—soldiers and citizens—to participate in these offices, God being willing, with your help, I will kick them out, I will kick them out just as fast as I can.

"Let me say to you, in concluding that what I have said I intended to say. I was not provoked into this, and I care not for their menaces, the taunts, and the jeers. I care not for threats. I do not intend to be bullied by my enemies nor overawed by my friends. But, God willing, with your help, I will veto their measures when any of them come to me."

Which said utterances, declarations, threats, and harangues, highly censurable in any, are peculiarly indecent and unbecoming in the Chief Magistrate of the United States, by means whereof, said Andrew Johnson has brought the high office of the President of the United States into contempt, ridicule, and disgrace, to the great scandal of all good citizens, whereby said Andrew Johnson, President of the United States, did commit, and was then and there guilty of a high misdemeanor in office.

ARTICLE XI

That said Andrew Johnson, President of the United States, unmindful of the high duties of his office, and of his oath of office, and in disregard of the Constitution and laws of the United States, did, heretofore, to-wit, on the eighteenth day of August, A. D. eighteen hundred and sixty-six, at the city of Washington, in the District of Columbia, by public speech, declare and affirm, in substance, that the thirty-ninth Congress of the United States was not a Congress of the United States authorized by the Constitution to exercise legislative power under the same, but on the contrary, was a Congress of only a part of the United States, thereby denying and intending to deny, the power of the said thirty-ninth Congress to propose amendments to the Constitution of the United States; and in pursuance of said declaration, the said Andrew Johnson, President of the United States, afterwards, to-wit on February 21, 1868 . . at the city of Washington, in the District of Columbia; did unlawfully, and in disregard of the requirements of the Constitution, that he should take care that the laws be faithfully executed, attempt to prevent the execution of [*the Tenure of Office Act*] . . by unlawfully devising and contriving, and attempting to devise and contrive means by which he should prevent Edwin M. Stanton from forthwith resuming the functions of the office of Secretary for the Department of War; and, also, by further unlawfully devising and contriving, and attempting to devise and contrive means, then and there, to pre-

vent the execution of . . the Army Appropriation Act and the Reconstruction Act, both of March 2, 1867 . . whereby the said Andrew Johnson, President of the United States, did, then . . . commit, and was guilty of, a high misdemeanor in office.

SCHUYLER COLFAX.
Speaker of the House of Representatives.
Attest:
EDWARD MCPHERSON,
Clerk of the House of Representatives.

7. In 1877, Rutherford B. Hayes became President after a long and dangerously contested election crisis. Hayes ordered U.S. Army troops withdrawn from duty as virtual governors of the States of the South. In his diary, he noted down his hopes for the nation, following his orders to pull the Army out.

23d March, 1877.—It is not the duty of the President of the United States to use the military power of the Nation to decide contested elections in the States. He will maintain the authority of the U.S. and keep the peace between the contending parties. But local self government means, the determination by each State for itself of all questions as to its own local affairs.

The real thing to be achieved is safety and prosperity for the colored people. Both Houses of Congress and the public opinion of the Country are plainly against the use of the army to uphold either claimant to the State Government in case of contest. The wish is to restore harmony and good feeling between Sections and races. This can only be done by peaceful methods. We wish to adjust the difficulties in La. and S.C. so as to make one government out of two in each State. But if this fails—if no adjustment can be made, we must then adopt the non intervention policy, except so far as may be necessary to keep the peace.

8. During the 1870's and 1880's, labor began to organize and make itself a powerful influence in politics and the national economy. The first document which follows is a part of the report on conditions in the textile factory towns, issued in 1882 by the Bureau of Statistics of Labor of Massachusetts. The second document, from Terence V. Powderly's Thirty Years of Labor, *gives his philosophy of labor organization as expressed in the constitution of the Knights of Labor. The third document is a statement of the contrasting policy of other labor leaders, as contained in the Resolutions by which the American Federation of Labor was established.*

From the Massachusetts Bureau Report

To remove discontent in Fall River, and prevent its growth in Lowell and Lawrence, legislation on some of the points considered may be found necessary; but more can be done by an awakening of honest public sentiment in these cities. Such a sentiment will bring about the education, by all practicable means, of those who have been denied its advantages, or who have been too poor to secure them; will consider it a vital necessity to educate the present generation; will encourage thrift, and the securing of homes by thrifty operatives; will insist upon clean, wholesome, healthy homes for all who are willing to work, and that the occupants shall keep them clean; will discourage the employment of married women and of children in mills, which, while it gives the manufacturer cheaper help, yet works an injustice to the man who should be the mainstay, as to support, of the family; will try to prevent an increase in drunkenness and crime, and work to decrease the disgrace and burden of both; will inculcate an obedience to law and true moral principles by both employers and employés, and thus do away with trustees, assignments (*ways of collecting workers' debts through employers*), cheating, Sunday work, intemperance, and profanity, and many other irritating conditions; will demonstrate the grand work of machinery in elevating the masses, and demand that the operative shall share more and more in the resulting wealth, will increase the number of religious, moral, social, and educational aids to the people, and throw about them in their homes and employments all the safeguards that science and inventive genius can supply; and, finally, bring the question home to the heart of each employer as to whether *he* is doing what he should do as a man of education and wealth for his fellow men. It is this individual work that makes moral revolutions easy. One model boarding house in Lowell should lead manufacturers in Lawrence and Fall River to follow the example. Mill libraries, relief societies, halls for social recreation, and similar aids to a higher and healthier life, should be equal to the demand in every city. As the employer grows towards his employés they will grow towards him. He is the strong man, and should take the initiative, and not wait for the force of law to remedy grievances that he could easily have averted. This may be generalization; but it will require general self-denial and general advancement by all the parties interested to secure the

good results enumerated. If it should be asked, What specific legislation can be instituted to remove any of the causes, either of discontent or unwholesome conditions? we say, emphatically, Give a State Board of Health full power to clean out every tenement "rookery" in the State; especially give it power to enforce all the laws relating to health in our great manufacturing cities. Give it power to close unhealthy and filthy tenements, without waiting for an epidemic. Let the State declare by its Board of Health that families shall not live in filth. If the homes of the operatives were as clean, as well ventilated, and as well conditioned, generally, as the mills, there would be little for health officers to do. If the corporations would place some of their money reserve—which is really undivided profits—in a way to secure a happier condition of their people, they would find, in the long run, an augmented reserve instead of a diminished one. It is an American political idea to have faith in the people,—and they are certainly as worthy of such faith socially and industrially as they are politically. Again, it is the testimony of great and wealthy individual factory proprietors in England that the expenditures for furnishing their operatives with every facility for comfort and health in their mills—such as the supplying of dining-rooms, bath and wash rooms, elevators, etc.—have brought not only happier conditions to their people, but also increased interest on the part of the latter in the mills and their products, and that such outlays have been more than balanced by positive money returns.

From Powderly's Book

The recent alarming development and aggression of aggregated wealth, which, unless checked, will invariably lead to the pauperization and hopeless degradation of the toiling masses, render it imperative, if we desire to enjoy the blessings of life, that a check should be placed upon its power and upon unjust accumulation, and a system adopted which will secure to the laborer the fruits of his toil; and as this much-desired object can only be accomplished by the thorough unification of labor, and the united efforts of those who obey the divine injunction that "In the sweat of thy brow shalt thou eat bread," we have formed the * * * * * with a view of securing the organization and direction, by co-operative effort, of the power of the industrial classes; and we submit to the world the objects sought to be accomplished by our organization, calling upon all who believe in securing "the greatest good to the greatest number" to aid and assist us:—

I. To bring within the folds of organization every department of productive industry, making knowledge a stand-point for action, and industrial and moral worth, not wealth, the true standard of individual and national greatness.

II. To secure to the toilers a proper share of the wealth that they create; more of the leisure that rightfully belongs to them; more societary advantages; more of the benefits, privileges, and emoluments of the world; in a word, all those rights and privileges necessary to make them capable of enjoying, appreciating, defending and perpetuating the blessings of good government.

III. To arrive at the true condition of the producing masses in their educational, moral, and financial condition, by demanding from the various governments the establishment of bureaus of Labor Statistics.

IV. The establishment of co-operative institutions, productive and distributive.

V. The reserving of the public lands—the heritage of the people—for the actual settler;—not another acre for railroads or speculators.

VI. The abrogation of all laws that do not bear equally upon capital and labor, the removal of unjust technicalities, delays, and discriminations in the administration of justice, and the adopting of measures providing for the health and safety of those engaged in mining, manufacturing, or building pursuits.

VII. The enactment of laws to compel chartered corporations to pay their employes weekly, in full, for labor performed during the preceding week, in the lawful money of the country.

VIII. The enactment of laws giving mechanics and laborers a first lien on their work for their full wages.

IX. The abolishment of the contract system on national, State, and municipal work.

X. The substitution of arbitration for strikes, whenever and wherever employers and employes are willing to meet on equitable grounds.

XI. The prohibition of the employment of children in workshops, mines and factories before attaining their fourteenth year.

XII. To abolish the system of letting out by contract the labor of convicts in our prisons and reformatory institutions.

XIII. To secure for both sexes equal pay for equal work.

XIV. The reduction of the hours of labor to eight per day, so that the laborers may have more time for social enjoyment and intellectual improvement, and be enabled to reap the advantages conferred by the labor-saving machinery which their brains have created.

XV. To prevail upon governments to establish a purely national circulating medium, based upon the faith and resources of the nation, and issued directly to the people, without the intervention of any system of banking corporations, which money shall be a legal tender in payment of all debts, public or private. . . .

Resolution of The A. F. of L.

On May 18, 1886, a conference of the chief officers of the various national and international trade unions was held in Philadelphia, Pa., at which twenty national and international unions were represented and twelve more sent letters of sympathy tendering their support to the conference. This made at that time thirty-two national and international trades unions with 367,736 members in good standing.

Since then quite a number of trades union conventions have been held, at all of which the action of the trades union conference has been emphatically and fully endorsed and a desire for a closer federation or alliance of all trades unions has been generally expressed. Not only that but a great impetus has been given to the formation of national trades unions and several new national unions have recently been formed, while all the trades societies with national or international heads have increased in membership and grown stronger in every respect.

The time has now arrived to draw the bonds of unity much closer together between all the trades unions of America. We need an annual Trades Congress that shall have for its object:

1. The formation of trades unions and the encouragement of the trades union movement in America.

2. The organization of trades assemblies, trades councils or central labor unions in every city in America and the further encouragement of such bodies.

3. The founding of state trades assemblies or state labor congresses to influence state legislation in the interest of the working masses.

4. The establishment of national and international trades unions based upon the strict recognition of the autonomy of each trade, and the promotion and advancement of such bodies.

5. An American Federation or Alliance of all national and international trades unions to aid and assist each other and furthermore to secure national legislation in the interest of the working people and influence public opinion by peaceful and legal methods in favor of organized labor.

6. To aid and encourage the labor press of America and to disseminate tracts and literature on the labor movement. . . . Whereas the Knights of Labor have persistently attempted to undermine and disrupt the well-established trades unions, organized and encouraged men who have proven untrue to their trade, false

to the obligation of their union, embezzlers of moneys and expelled by many of the unions and conspiring to pull down the trades unions:

Resolved: That we condemn the acts above recited and call upon all workingmen to join the unions of their respective trades and urge the formation of national and international unions and the centralization of all under one head, the American Federation of Labor.

9. One of the principal complaints of farmers and small businessmen had to do with abuses by the railroads. The following extracts from a U.S. Senate report describe some of the abuses about which Grangers and other Americans were complaining in the 1870's and 1880's.

Discriminating and extortionate charges, however, constitute the chief grounds of complaint. The principal causes which are supposed to produce such charges, and which have aggravated and intensified the public discontent, may be summarized as follows:

1. *"Stock-watering,"* a well-known process by which the capital stock of a company is largely increased, for purely speculative purposes, without any corresponding expenditure on the part of its recipients.

2. *Capitalization of surplus earnings.* By this process the net profits, over and above the amount paid on interest and dividends are supposed to be expended in permanent improvements, and charged up to capital account, for which additional stock is issued, and increased charges rendered necessary to meet the increased dividends required. It is insisted that this is a double form of taxation: first, in the exorbitant charges from which such surplus profits are derived; and, second, in the conversion of such surplus into capital-stock, thereby compelling the business of the country to pay increased charges on all future transactions, in order to provide dividends on capital thus unjustly obtained. It is argued, with great force, that as all the legitimate claims of railroad companies are met by the public, when it has paid a fair and reasonable return for the capital invested and services rendered, any surplus earnings expended in improvements should inure to its benefit, instead of being made the basis for future exactions. In brief, the people believe that by this process they are first robbed, and then compelled to pay interest on their own money.

3. The introduction of intermediate agencies, such as car-companies, fast-freight lines, &c.

4. "Construction rings" and other means by which the managers are supposed to make large profits in the building of railways, which are charged up to the cost of the road.

5. Unfair adjustments of through and local rates, and unjust discriminations against certain localities, whereby one community is compelled to pay unreasonable charges in order that another more favored may pay less than the services are worth. This will be fully considered hereafter, in the discussion of "equal mileage rates."

6. General extravagance and corruption in railway management, whereby favorites are enriched and the public impoverished.

7. Combinations and consolidations of railway companies, by which free competition is destroyed, and the producing and commercial interests of the country handed over to the control of monopolies, who are thereby enabled to enforce upon the public the exorbitant rates rendered necessary by the causes above named.

8. The system of operating fast and slow trains on the same road, whereby the cost of freight movement is believed to be largely increased. This is perhaps the misfortune rather than the fault of railway companies. It is doubtless a necessity, growing out of the conditions under which our railway system has been developed.

10. The Populist Party drew many discontented Americans under its banner. In 1892, this "third" party summed up its points of view in a published platform. The Populist Platform of 1892 (which follows) is an important document, not because the Populists won the election, but because so many of their ideas were taken over by the major parties in later elections.

Our country finds itself confronted by conditions for which there is no precedent in the history of the world; our annual agricultural productions amount to billions of dollars in value, which must, within a few weeks or months, be exchanged for billions of dollars' worth of commodities consumed in their production; the existing currency supply is wholly inadequate to make this exchange; the results are falling prices, the formation of combines and rings, the impoverishment of the producing class. We pledge ourselves that if given power we will labor to correct these evils by wise and reasonable legislation, in accordance with the terms of our platform.

We believe that the power of government—in other words, of the people—should be expanded (as in the case of the postal service) as rapidly and as far as the good sense of an intelligent people and the teachings of experience shall justify, to the end that oppression, injustice, and poverty shall eventually cease in the land.

While our sympathies as a party of reform are naturally upon the side of every proposition which will tend to make men intelligent, virtuous, and temperate, we nevertheless regard those questions, important as they are, as secondary to the great issues now pressing for solution, and upon which not only our individual prosperity but the very existence of free institutions depend; and we ask all men to first help us to determine whether we are to have a republic to administer before we differ as to the conditions upon which it is to be administered, believing that the forces of reform this day organized will never cease to move forward until every wrong is righted and equal rights and equal privileges securely established for all the men and women of this country.

We declare, therefore—

First.—That the union of the labor forces of the United States this day consummated shall be permanent and perpetual; may its spirit enter into all hearts for the salvation of the Republic and the uplifting of mankind.

Second.—Wealth belongs to him who creates it, and every dollar taken from industry without an equivalent is robbery. 'If any will not work, neither shall he eat.' The interests of rural and civil labor are the same; their enemies are identical.

Third.—We believe that the time has come when the railroad corporations will either own the people or the people must own the railroads; and should the government enter upon the work of owning and managing all railroads, we should favor an amendment to the constitution by which all persons engaged in the government service shall be placed under a civil-service regulation of the most rigid character, so as to prevent the increase of the power of the national administration by the use of such additional government employes.

FINANCE.—We demand a national currency, safe, sound, and flexible, issued by the general government only, a full legal tender for all debts, public and private, and that without the use of banking corporations; a just, equitable, and efficient means of distribution direct to the people, at a tax not to exceed 2 per cent. per annum, to be provided as set forth in the sub-treasury plan of the Farmers' Alliance, or a better system; also by payments in discharge of its obligations for public improvements.

1. We demand free and unlimited coinage of silver and gold at the present legal ratio of 16 to 1.

2. We demand that the amount of circulating medium be speedily increased to not less than $50 per capita.

3. We demand a graduated income tax.

4. We believe that the money of the country should be kept as much as possible in the hands of the people, and hence we demand that all State and national revenues shall be limited to the necessary expenses of the government, economically and honestly administered.

5. We demand that postal savings banks be established by the government for the safe deposit of the earnings of the people and to facilitate exchange.

TRANSPORTATION.—Transportation being a means of exchange and a public necessity, the government should own and operate the railroads in the interest of the people. The telegraph and telephone, like the post-office system, being a necessity for the transportation of news, should be owned and operated by the government in the interest of the people.

LAND.—The land, including all the natural sources of wealth, is the heritage of the people, and should not be monopolized for speculative purposes, and alien ownership of land should be prohibited. All land now held by railroads and other corporations in excess of their actual needs, and all lands now owned by aliens, should be reclaimed by the government and held for actual settlers only.

EXPRESSION OF SENTIMENTS

Your Committee on Platform and Resolutions beg leave unanimously to report the following:

Whereas, Other questions have been presented for our consideration, we hereby submit the following, not as a part of the Platform of the People's Party, but as resolutions expressive of the sentiment of this Convention.

1. RESOLVED, That we demand a free ballot and a fair count in all elections, and pledge ourselves to secure it to every legal voter without Federal intervention, through the adoption by the States of the unperverted Australian or secret ballot system.

2. RESOLVED, That the revenue derived from a graduated income tax should be applied to the reduction of the burden of taxation now levied upon the domestic industries of this country.

3. RESOLVED, That we pledge our support to fair and liberal pensions to ex-Union soldiers and sailors.

4. RESOLVED, That we condemn the fallacy of protecting American labor under the present system,

which opens our ports to the pauper and criminal classes of the world and crowds out our wage-earners; and we denounce the present ineffective laws against contract labor, and demand the further restriction of undesirable emigration.

5. RESOLVED, That we cordially sympathize with the efforts of organized workingmen to shorten the hours of labor, and demand a rigid enforcement of the existing eight-hour law on Government work, and ask that a penalty clause be added to the said law.

6. RESOLVED, That we regard the maintenance of a large standing army of mercenaries, known as the Pinkerton system, as a menace to our liberties, and we demand its abolition; and we condemn the recent invasion of the Territory of Wyoming by the hired assassins of plutocracy, assisted by Federal officers.

7. RESOLVED, That we commend to the favorable consideration of the people and the reform press the legislative system known as the initiative and referendum.

8. RESOLVED, That we favor a constitutional provision limiting the office of President and Vice-President to one term, and providing for the election of Senators of the United States by a direct vote of the people.

9. RESOLVED, That we oppose any subsidy or national aid to any private corporation for any purpose.

10. RESOLVED, That this convention sympathizes with the Knights of Labor and their righteous contest with the tyrannical combine of clothing manufacturers of Rochester, and declare it to be a duty of all who hate tyranny and oppression to refuse to purchase the goods made by the said manufacturers, or to patronize any merchants who sell such goods.

11. In 1896, the Democratic National Convention was swept off its feet by a single speech, delivered by William Jennings Bryan. Bryan summed up in this statement many of the complaints of American farmers and laborers. He attracted many of the discontented people in America into the Democratic party and provided the party with a new direction, clearly different from that of the Republicans, and also quite different from its own past philosophy. This famous "Cross of Gold" speech was repeated by Bryan at county fairs, mass meetings, and from the rear platforms of railroad coaches as he challenged William McKinley for the presidency in 1896. Important parts of the speech follow.

I would be presumptuous, indeed, to present myself against the distinguished gentlemen to whom you have listened if this were a mere measuring of abilities; but this is not a contest between persons. The humblest citizen in all the land, when clad in the armor of a righteous cause, is stronger than all the hosts of error. I come to speak to you in defense of a cause as holy as the cause of liberty—the cause of humanity. . . .

When you *(turning to the gold delegates)* come before us and tell us that we are about to disturb your business interests, we reply that you have disturbed our business interests by your course.

We say to you that you have made the definition of business man too limited in its application. The man who is employed for wages is as much a business man as his employer, the attorney in a country town is as much a business man as the corporation counsel in a great metropolis; the merchant at the cross-roads store is as much a business man as the merchant of New York; the farmer who goes forth in the morning and toils all day—who begins in the spring and toils all summer—and who by the application of brain and muscle to the natural resources of the country creates wealth, is as much a business man as the man who goes upon the board of trade and bets upon the price of grain; the miners who go down a thousand feet into the earth, or climb two thousand feet upon the cliffs, and bring forth from their hiding places the precious metals to be poured into the channels of trade are as much business men as the few financial magnates who, in a backroom, corner the money of the world. We come to speak for this broader class of business men.

Ah, my friends, we say not one word against those who live upon the Atlantic coast, but the hardy pioneers who have braved all the dangers of the wilderness, who have made the desert to blossom as the rose—the pioneers away out there (pointing to the West), who rear their children near to Nature's heart, where they can mingle their voices with the voices of the birds—out there where they have erected schoolhouses for the education of their young, churches where they praise their Creator, and cemeteries where rest the ashes of their dead—these people, we say, are as deserving of the consideration of our party as any people in this country. It is for these that we speak. We do not come as aggressors. Our war is not a war of conquest; we are fighting in the defense of our homes, our families, and posterity. We have petitioned, and our petitions have been scorned; we have entreated, and our entreaties have been disregarded; we have begged, and they have mocked when our calamity came. We beg no longer; we entreat no more, we petition no more. We defy them. . . .

They tell us that this platform was made to catch votes. We reply to them that changing conditions make new issues; that the principles upon which Democracy rests are as everlasting as the hills, but that they must be applied to new conditions as they arise. Conditions have arisen, and we are here to meet these conditions. They tell us that the income tax ought not to be brought in here; that it is a new idea. . . . The income tax is just. It simply intends to put the burdens of government justly upon the backs of the people. I am in favor of an income tax. When I find a man who is not willing to bear his share of the burdens of the government which protects him, I find a man who is unworthy to enjoy the blessings of a government like ours.

They say that we are opposing national bank currency; it is true. If you will read what Thomas Benton said, you will find he said that, in searching history, he could find but one parallel to Andrew Jackson; that was Cicero, who destroyed the conspiracy of Cataline and saved Rome. Benton said that Cicero only did for Rome what Jackson did for us when he destroyed the bank conspiracy and saved America. We say in our platform that we believe that the right to coin and issue money is a function of government. We believe it. We believe that it is a part of sovereignty, and can no more with safety be delegated to private individuals than we could afford to delegate to private individuals the power to make penal statutes or levy taxes. . . . Those who are opposed to this proposition tell us that the issue of paper money is a function of the bank, and that the Government ought to go out of the banking business. I stand with Jefferson, rather than with them, and tell them, as he did, that the issue of money is a function of government; and that the banks ought to go out of the governing business. . . .

And now, my friends, let me come to the paramount issue. If they ask us why it is that we say more on the money question than we say upon the tariff question, I reply that, if protection has slain its thousands, the gold standard has slain its tens of thousands. If they ask us why we do not embody in our platform all the things that we believe in, we reply that when we have restored the money of the Constitution all other necessary reforms will be possible; but that until this is done there is no other reform that can be accomplished. . . .

Mr. Carlisle said in 1878 that this was a struggle between "the idle holders of idle capital" and "the struggling masses, who produce the wealth and pay the taxes of the country"; and, my friends, the question we are to

decide is: Upon which side will the Democratic party fight; upon the side of "the idle holders of idle capital" or upon the side of "the struggling masses"? That is the question which the party must answer first, and then it must be answered by each individual hereafter. The sympathies of the Democratic party, as shown by the platform, are on the side of the struggling masses who have ever been the foundation of the Democratic party. There are two ideas of government. There are those who believe that, if you will only legislate to make the well-to-do prosperous, their prosperity will leak through on those below. The Democratic idea, however, has been that if you legislate to make the masses prosperous, their prosperity will find its way up through every class which rests upon them.

You come to us and tell us that the great cities are in favor of the gold standard; we reply that the great cities rest upon our broad and fertile prairies. Burn down your cities and leave our farms, and your cities will spring up again as if by magic; but destroy our farms and the grass will grow in the streets of every city in the country.

My friends, we declare that this nation is able to legislate for its own people on every question, without waiting for the aid or consent of any other nation on earth; and upon that issue we expect to carry every State in the Union. I shall not slander the inhabitants of the fair State of Massachusetts nor the inhabitants of the State of New York by saying that, when they are confronted with the proposition, they will declare that this nation is not able to attend to its own business. It is the issue of 1776 over again. Our ancestors, when but three millions in number, had the courage to declare their political independence of every other nation; shall we, their descendants, when we have grown to seventy millions, declare that we are less independent than our forefathers? No, my friends, that will never be the verdict of our people. Therefore, we care not upon what lines the battle is fought. If they say bimetalism is good, but that we cannot have it until other nations help us, we reply that, instead of having a gold standard because England has, we will restore bimetalism, and then let England have bimetalism because the United States has it. If they dare to come out in the open field and defend the gold standard as a good thing, we will fight them to the uttermost. Having behind us the producing masses of this nation and the world, supported by the commercial interests, the laboring interests, and the toilers everywhere, we will answer their demand for a gold standard by saying to them: You shall not press down upon the brow of labor this crown of thorns, you shall not crucify mankind upon a cross of gold.

6-D SOCIAL DEVELOPMENTS

A number of great changes took place in American life between 1865 and 1898. Railroads were extended and industrial plants grew rapidly. Many American towns became cities, as people moved from the farms to take jobs in factories and swelled the population of the towns. Immigrants swarmed into the United States, many of them settling in towns and cities rather than on the land in farming areas as immigrants had formerly done.

PROBLEMS. *In what ways was American life changed by the industrial and technological developments of this period? Were Americans really "taming the continent", as they developed new systems of agriculture, cattle ranching, and industry?*

1. The people of the United States were concerned with the railroads and their operation for a number of reasons. For one, both citizen and immigrant alike looked on the chugging steam-engine as a kind of magic carpet, capable of taking them to most parts of the country speedily and in some comfort. Robert Louis Stevenson, the Scottish novelist, traveled across the continent on the railroad in the early 1880's. The following sketch of an emigrant train is taken from Stevenson's account of his trip. He published it first in Longman's Magazine *(London), and afterwards included it in his book* Across the Plains.

The benches can be made to face each other in pairs, for the backs are reversible. On the approach of night the boards are laid from bench to bench, making a couch wide enough for two, and long enough for a man of the middle height; and the chums lie down side by side upon the cushions with the head to the conductor's van and the feet to the engine. When the train is full, of course this plan is impossible, for there must not be more than one to every bench, neither can it be carried out unless the chums agree. It was to bring about this last condition that our white-haired official now bestirred himself. He made a most active master of ceremonies, introducing likely couples, and even guaranteeing the amiability and honesty of each. The greater the number of happy couples the better for his pocket, for it was he who sold the raw material of the beds. His price for one board and three straw cushions began with two dollars and a half; but before the train left, and I am sorry to say long after I had purchased mine, it had fallen to one dollar and a half. (I cannot suppose that emigrants are thus befooled and robbed with the connivance of the Company; yet this was the Company's servant. It is never pleasant to bear tales; but this is a system; the emigrants are many of them foreigners and therefore easy to cheat, and they are all so poor that it is unmanly to cheat them; and if the white-haired leach is not contumeliously discharged in this world, I leave him with all confidence to the devil in the next. As for the emigrant, I have better news for him. Let him quietly agree with a chum, but bid the official harpy from his sight; and if he will read a few pages farther, he shall see the profit of his reticence.)

The match-maker had a difficulty with me; perhaps, like some ladies, I showed myself too eager for union at any price; but certainly the first who was picked out to be my bedfellow declined the honour without thanks. He was an old, heavy, slow-spoken man, I think from Yankeeland, looked me all over with great timidity, and didn't know the young man, he said. The young man then began to excuse himself in broken phrases. He might be very honest, but how was he to know that? There was another young man whom he had met already in the train; he guessed *he* was honest, and would prefer to chum with *him* upon the whole. All this without any sort of excuse, as though I had been inanimate or absent. I began to tremble lest every one should refuse my company, and I left rejected. But the next in turn was a tall, strapping, long-limbed, small-headed, curly-haired Pennsylvania Dutchman, with a soldierly smartness in his manner. To be exact, he had acquired it in the navy. But that was all one; he had at least been trained to desperate resolves, so he accepted the match, and the white-haired swindler pronounced the connubial benediction, and pocketed his fees.

The rest of the afternoon was spent in making up the train. I am afraid to say how many baggage-wagons followed the engine—certainly a score; then came the Chinese, then we, then the families, and the rear was brought up by the conductor in what, if I have it rightly, is called his caboose. The class to which I belonged was of course far the largest, and we ran over, so to speak, to both sides; so that there were some Caucasians among the Chinamen and some bachelors among the families. But our own car was pure from admixture, save for one little boy of eight or nine who had the whooping-cough. At last, about six, the long train crawled out of the Transfer Station and across the wide Missouri river to Omaha, westward bound.

It was a troubled, uncomfortable evening in the cars. There was thunder in the air, which helped to keep us restless. A man played many airs upon the cornet, and none of them were much attended to, until he came to "Home, Sweet Home." It was truly strange to note how the talk ceased at that, and the faces began to lengthen. I have no idea whether musically this air is to be considered good or bad; but it belongs to that class of art which may be best described as a brutal assault upon the feelings. Pathos must be relieved by dignity of treatment. If you wallow naked in the pathetic, like the author of "Home, Sweet Home," you make your hearers weep in an unmanly fashion; and even while yet they are moved, they despise themselves and hate the occasion of their weakness. It did not come to tears that night, for the experiment was interrupted. An elderly, hard-looking man, with a goatee beard, and about as much appearance of sentiment as you would expect from a retired slaver, turned with a start and bade the performer stop that "damned thing." "I've heard about enough of that," he added; "give us something about the good country we're going to." A murmur of adhesion ran round the car; the performer took the instrument from his lips, laughed and nodded, and then struck into a dancing measure; and, like a new Timotheus, stilled immediately the emotion he had raised.

The day faded; the lamps were lit; a party of wild young men, who got off next evening at North Platte, stood together on the stern platform, singing "The Sweet By-and-Bye" with very tuneful voices; the chums began to put up their beds; and it seemed as if the business of the day were at an end. But it was not so; for, the train stopping at some station, the cars were instantly thronged with the natives, wives and fathers, young men and maidens, some of them in little more than nightgear, some with stable-lanterns, and all offering beds for sale. Their charge began with twenty-five cents a cushion, but fell, before the train went on again, to fifteen, with the bedboard gratis, or less than one-fifth of what I had paid for mine at the Transfer. This is my contribution to the economy of future emigrants.

A great personage on an American train is the newsboy. He sells books (such books!), papers, fruit, lollipops, and cigars; and on emigrant journeys, soap, towels, tin washing-dishes, tin coffee pitchers, coffee, tea, sugar, and tinned eatables, mostly hash or beans and bacon. Early next morning the newsboy went around the cars, and chumming on a more extended principle became the order of the hour. It requires but a co-partnery of two to manage beds; but washing and eating can be carried on most economically by a syndicate of three. I myself entered a little after sunrise into articles of agreement, and became one of the firm of Pennsylvania, Shakespeare, and Dubuque. Shakespeare was my own nickname on the cars; Pennsylvania that of my bedfellow; and Dubuque, the name of a place in the State of Iowa, that of an amiable young fellow going west to cure an asthma, and retarding his recovery by incessantly chewing or smoking, and sometimes chewing and smoking together. I have never seen tobacco so sillily abused. Shakespeare bought a tin washing-dish, Dubuque a towel, and Pennsylvania a brick of soap. The partners used these instruments, one after another, according to the order of their first awakening; and when the firm had finished there was no want of borrowers. Each filled the tin dish at the water filter opposite the stove, and retired with the whole stock in trade to the platform of the car. There he knelt down, supporting himself by a shoulder against the woodwork, or one elbow crooked about the railing, and made a shift to wash his face and neck and hands,—a cold, an insufficient, and, if the train is moving rapidly, a somewhat dangerous toilet.

On a similar division of expense, the firm of Pennsylvania, Shakespeare, and Dubuque supplied themselves with coffee, sugar, and necessary vessels; and their operations are a type of what went on through all the cars. Before the sun was up the stove would be brightly burning; at the first station the natives would come on board with milk and eggs and coffee cakes; and soon from end to end the car would be filled with little parties breakfasting upon the bed-boards. It was the pleasantest hour of the day.

2. Railroads began to develop special ways of handling freight during this period. Some of them are described in the following extracts from an article in Scribner's Magazine *for 1899.*

In the early period of railways in this country, when they were built chiefly to promote local interests, and the movement of either freight or passengers over long distances was a comparatively small portion of the traffic, it was customary for all roads to do their business in their own cars, transferring any freight destined to a station on a connecting road at the junction or point of interchange of the two roads. While this system had the advantage of keeping at home the equipment of each road, it resulted in a very slow movement of the freight. As the volume of traffic grew, and the interchange of commodities between distant points increased, this slow movement became more and more vexatious. Soon the railway companies found it necessary to allow their cars to run through to the destination of the freight without transfer, or they would be deprived of the business by more enterprising rivals. So that to-day a very large proportion of the freight business of the country is done without transfer; the same car taking the load from the initial point direct to destination. The result of this is, however, that a considerable share of all the business of any railway is done in cars belonging to other companies, for which mileage has to be paid; while, in turn, the cars of any one company may be scattered all over the country from Maine to California, Winnipeg to Mexico.

The problem that constantly confronts the general superintendent of a railway is, how to improve the time of through freight, thereby improving the service and increasing the earnings of the company; and at the same time, how to secure the prompt movement of cars belonging to the company, getting them home from other roads, and reducing as far as possible upon his own line the use of foreign cars, and the consequent payment of mileage therefor.

By common consent the mileage for the use of all eight-wheel freight cars has been fixed at three-quarters of a cent per mile run; four-wheel cars being rated at one-half this amount, or three-eighths of a cent. This amount would at first sight appear to be insignificant, yet in the aggregate it comes to a very considerable sum. In the case of some of the more important roads in the country, even those possessing a large equipment, the balance against them for mileage alone often amounts to nearly half a million annually.

It becomes therefore of the first importance to reduce to a minimum the use of foreign cars, thereby reducing the mileage balance; at the same time avoiding any action that will interfere with or impede in any way the prompt movement of traffic. . . .

The movement of "straight" cars and "solid" trains is comparatively simple. But there is a very large amount of through freight, particularly of merchandise, that cannot be put into a "straight" car. A shipper in New York can depend on his goods going in a straight car to St. Louis, Denver, St. Paul, etc., but he can hardly expect a straight car to any one of hundreds of intermediate cities and towns. Still less is it possible for a road at a small country town, where there are perhaps but one or two factories, to load straight cars to any but a very few places. To overcome this difficulty, transfer freight houses have to be provided. These are usually located at important terminal stations.

To them are billed all mixed cars containing through freight. These cars are unloaded and reloaded, and out of a hundred "mixed" cars will be made probably eighty straight and the balance local. This necessarily causes some delay, but it is practically a gain in time in the end, as otherwise every car would have to be reloaded, and held at every station for which it contained freight.

The variety of articles that are offered to a railway company for transportation is endless. Articles of all sizes and weights are carried, from shoe-pegs by the carload to a single casting that weighs thirty tons. The values also vary as widely. Some cars will carry kindling wood or refuse stone that is worth barely the cost of loading and carrying a few miles, while others will be loaded with teas, silks, or merchandise, where perhaps the value of a single carload will exceed twenty-five or thirty thousand dollars. The great bulk of all freight is carried in the ordinary box cars, coal in cars especially planned for it, and coarse lumber and stone on flat or platform cars. But very many cases arise that require especial provision to be made for each. Chicago dressed beef has made the use of the refrigerator cars well known. These cars are also used for carrying fruit and provisions. They are of many kinds, built under various patents, but all with a common purpose, that is to produce a car wherein the temperature can be maintained uniformly at about 40 degrees. On the other hand potatoes in bulk are brought in great quantities to the Eastern seaboard in box cars, fitted with an additional or false lining of boards, and in the centre an ordinary stove in which fire is kept up during the time the potatoes are in transit.

An improvement on this plan is afforded by the use of cars known as the Eastman Heater Cars. They are provided with an automatic self-feeding oil-stove, so arranged that fire can be kept up under the car for about a fortnight without attention. These are largely used in the fruit trade.

For carrying milk, special cars have to be provided, as particular attention has to be given to the matter of ventilation in connection with a small amount of cooling for the proper carrying of the milk. Not only the cars but the train service has to be especially arranged for in particular cases.

As an instance, the Long Island Railroad Company makes a specialty of transporting farmers' truck wagons to market. For this purpose they have provided long, low, flat cars, each capable of carrying four truck wagons. The horses are carried in box cars, and one farmer or driver is carried with each team, a coach being provided for their use. During the fall of the year, they frequently carry from 45 to 50 wagons on one train, charging a small sum for each wagon, nothing for the horses or men. These trains run three times weekly, and are arranged so as to arrive in the city about midnight, returning the next day at noon. The trains by themselves are not very remunerative, but by furnishing this accommodation, farmers who are thirty or forty miles out on Long Island can have just as good an opportunity for market-gardening as those who live within driving distance of the city. This builds up the country further out on the island, which in turn gives the road other business.

3. Railroading was a major industry and the country's principal means of transportation; therefore, strikes on the railroads were of vital concern to everyone. During one strike, President Hayes ordered the U.S. Army to make sure that the rail lines were protected and that the U.S. mails went through. The President prepared a speech on railroad strikes. His notes in preparation for it are quoted below from his Diary.

Sunday, 5th August, 1877. . . . The strikes have been put down by *force,* but now for the *real* remedy. Cant something be done by education of the strikers, by judicious control of the capitalists, by wise general policy to end or diminish the evil? The R.R. strikers, as a rule are good men sober intelligent and industrious.

The mischiefs are

1. Strikers prevent men willing to work from doing so.
2. They seize and hold the property of their employers.
3. The consequent excitement furnishes opportunity for the dangerous criminal classes to destroy life and property.

Now, "every man has a right if he sees fit to quarrel with his own bread and butter, but he has no right to quarrel with the bread and butter of other people." Every man has a right to determine for himself the value of his own labor, but he has no right to determine for other men the value of their labor. (not good).

Every man has a right to refuse to work if the wages dont suit him, but he has no right to prevent others from working if they are suited with the wages.

Every man has a right to refuse to work, but no man has a right to prevent others from working.

Every man has a right to decide for himself the question of wages, but no man has a right to decide that question for other men.

4. The United States was still basically a farming country in the 1880's, but it was turning—and rapidly—into an industrial country. Farmers struggled with high interest charges on money they borrowed, with high railroad rates, and with great natural plagues. Grasshoppers swept through the Great Plains several times and destroyed crops. The account that follows was written by Stuart Henry, an American writer who was more famous for his books on sophisticated life in Paris.

The Grasshopper Plague

IN 1874 came a gigantic calamity in the form of a raid of grasshoppers which ate up every bit of green vegetation from the Rocky Mountains to and beyond the Missouri River. I recall that when coming home late one afternoon for supper I stepped back surprised to see what became known as Rocky Mountain locusts covering the side of the house. Already inside, they feasted on the curtains. Clouds of them promptly settled down on the whole country—everywhere, unavoidable. People set about killing them to save gardens, but this soon proved ridiculous. Specially contrived machines, pushed by horses, scooped up the hoppers in grain fields by the barrelful to burn them. This, too, was then nonsensical. Vast hordes, myriads. In a week grain fields, gardens, shrubs, vines, had been eaten down to the ground or to the bark. Nothing could be done. You sat by and saw everything go.

When autumn came with the country devastated, the population despaired again when seeing the insects remaining for the winter with the apparent plan of being on hand for the next season. It seemed that they could be counted on as a curse for all time, since the Rocky Mountain locusts, as the name indicates, appeared new to science, to the civilized world. No one, accordingly, knew of their habits. And their ingenuity confounded close observers. As if intending to stay permanently on the plains, they bored holes only in hard ground, in roads and other firm places, for their winter occupancy. Intelligently did they avoid soft ground, since tenancy there would be more easily, more apt to be, disturbed.

To add to the terror of the locust invasion was the general accompaniment of weather tending always to be dry. Kansans—"people of the south wind." This poetic Indian meaning might bear a still more distinctive signification if it ran "people of the hot southwest wind." For continental western Kansas, lying in the exact center of the United States, turned out to be subject in summer to burning south or southwest winds untempered by cooling salt breezes creeping up from the Gulf of Mexico or cooling zephyrs descending from Canada. The middle area often missed the relief that either the southern or northern areas might experience. And a steady hot current of air, though mild in velocity, brought the dreaded dry times.

How one hated to see the heavens seal their cisterns and the plains to be sear! A few showers would dash upon the ground and run to cover in the creek and river beds, not stopping to penetrate to roots. Matters seemed, indeed, to be made worse by these spurts of moisture, the blazing sun promptly coming out afterward, baking the earth harder.

Almost hilarious, many of the old-timers during such months! They underwent the stark privations in very fair style, having been shown to be prophets with honor in their own land.

"Hee-hee! Didn't I tell you so? This ain't no farmin' country. Too droughty. Lucky fer cattle if lucky fer anything. An' these 'ere Easterners ruinin' the buffalo grass by plowin' it up! Spilin' everything. Yaps that want to farm better stay back East where there ain't anything better to do. They have driv' out the Texas cattle trade. What have they got left? Mighty little, by cracky!"

People still often considered the plains fit at best for very light spring crops. If these shrank up just before harvest, there would be left after June nothing to fall back upon during the rest of the year. The small corn areas along the streams then resembled patches of sticks. The local livestock in 1874 had to be disposed of, fodder lacking. Pitiful little vegetable gardens shriveled. The few flower plots planted by housewives were at first bravely watered. Like tiny, ghastly totem poles did the scarred stalks afterward look.

In a hot droughty summer most of the wells and springs gave out early. Water in creeks trickled so shallowly that dogs lay panting in them while hardly able to immerse more than their paws. Then the burning spell! The southwest wind blew at frequent intervals out of its Sahara ovens, sweeping the land with a flinty dust. You thought of it as a finely textured burial shroud. People told the old joke: "We'd have had to soak our pigs overnight so that they could hold swill." The nights proved as debilitating as the days, since humanity couldn't sleep for the heat. This was the worst of it—they couldn't sleep. No part of each twenty-four hours furnished forgetfulness of the nightmare of failure.

In that country of poor farming and upon a population heedless about laying by supplies for a scarce period, the disaster of 1874 doubled its effect. One conceded: Of what use to work? Farmers, of course, stood out of a job. They loafed in town from midsummer on. For many said they could hardly have plowed or broken prairie. The lumps of sod needed to be knocked up by axes. Seven months before there would be a thing to do. Locusts and scanty rainfall together!

One watched the office men in towns lounging day after day at their doors or hanging out of their windows, with nothing on hand. Business collapsed. It looked like an idiotic insult to ask any one for what he owed. Tillers of soil could not be counted on to pay anyhow till after harvest, once a year, and now, in 1874, no harvest. The merchants, townsmen in general, were expected to cash up from month to month. They stared blankly at the streets, trying to figure how they could get through the winter with their money and credit mostly gone up the spout. The sight of farmers dawdling in stores and saloons added to the dismalness. What if *next* year brought a blank? Too awful to contemplate! Meanwhile—it looked like sheer unavoidable starvation.

Moral stamina? One knew how the women slouched around red-hot cookstoves three times a day for the regular if skimpy meals. Some strength *must* be kept up, some flesh *must* be kept on bones. Even wives who had had a little pardonable vanity life quit trying to save their complexions. They let their tresses go dry and stick out any way. Hair got crinkly, few bothering much about brushes and combs. Hollow-eyed, fagged out, the fair sex came to care little how they looked, what they wore. The story was told of seeing on a street a woman in a garment she had sewed together from the halves of different flour sacks without taking the pains to remove their brands, the result being shocking. Men swore and played poker no more. Fathers dreaded to face their children, who grew raggeder. As for their dirtiness, who, you might almost ask, hardly dared spare water to wash them? Husbands hated to go home to meals, for they must meet the appeals of their wives to climb on wagons and strike out for back home.

"Sell for what you can get, John—give it away—leave it—only let's get out. I don't have to ride on a railroad. A schooner headed east looks awful good to me."

Prayer meetings being held, a few of the men who had not gone to church dropped in and sat before pulpits, heads bowed, humbled in respect. They wondered now if there might be some virtue in supplication. At least they risked no money nor chances by attending meeting. Anything, even prayer, to see mud puddles drowning out the hoppers! But the believers in the great god luck—the majority—stood, in the main, by their guns. They didn't think petitions by four-hundred-dollar-a-year ministers had enough breeze behind them to be shot clear up to Heaven so that the yelpings could be heard there. Wouldn't luck bring a favorable year next time, since this one could be called a ripper? Herein lay the dependable thing about luck: It always changes.

5. There are many books available in which men of the Old West tell of their memories of the great days of cowboys, buffalo hunters, and "bad men". In the selection that follows, Theodore Roosevelt sums up his own experiences of the West. It appeared first as part of an article in the Century Magazine *for 1888, and was included later in the book entitled* Ranch Life and the Hunting Trail.

Cattle-ranching can only be carried on in its present form while the population is scanty; and so in stock-raising regions, pure and simple, there are usually few towns, and these are almost always at the shipping-points for cattle. But, on the other hand, wealthy cattle-men, like miners who have done well, always spend their money freely; and accordingly towns like Denver, Cheyenne, and Helena, where these two classes are the most influential in the community, are far pleasanter places of residence than cities of five times their pop-

ulation in the exclusively agricultural States to the eastward.

A true "cow town" is worth seeing—such a one as Miles City, for instance, especially at the time of the annual meeting of the great Montana Stock Raisers' Association. Then the whole place is full to overflowing, the importance of the meeting and the fun of the attendant frolics, especially the horse-races, drawing from the surrounding ranch country many hundreds of men of every degree, from the rich stock-owner worth his millions to the ordinary cowboy who works for forty dollars a month. It would be impossible to imagine a more typically American assemblage, for although there are always a certain number of foreigners, usually English, Irish, or German, yet they have become completely Americanized; and on the whole it would be difficult to gather a finer body of men, in spite of their numerous shortcomings. The ranch-owners differ more from each other than do the cowboys; and the former certainly compare very favorably with similar classes of capitalists in the East. Anything more foolish than the demagogic outcry against "cattle kings" it would be difficult to imagine. Indeed, there are very few businesses so absolutely legitimate as stock-raising and so beneficial to the nation at large; and a successful stock-grower must not only be shrewd, thrifty, patient, and enterprising, but he must also possess qualities of personal bravery, hardihood, and self-reliance to a degree not demanded in the least by any mercantile occupation in a community long settled. Stockmen are in the West the pioneers of civilization, and their daring and adventurousness make the after-settlement of the region possible. The whole country owes them a great debt.

The most successful ranchmen are those, usually Southwesterners, who have been bred to the business and have grown up with it; but many Eastern men, including not a few college graduates, have also done excellently by devoting their whole time and energy to their work—although Easterners who invest their money in cattle without knowing anything of the business or who trust all to their subordinates, are, naturally enough, likely to incur heavy losses. Stockmen are learning more and more to act together; and certainly the meetings of their associations are conducted with a dignity and good sense that would do credit to any parliamentary body.

But the cowboys resemble one another much more and outsiders much less than is the case even with their employers, the ranchmen. A town in the cattle country, when for some cause it is thronged with men from the neighborhood, always presents a picturesque sight. On the wooden sidewalks of the broad, dusty streets the men who ply the various industries known only to frontier existence jostle one another as they saunter to and fro or lounge lazily in front of the straggling, cheap-looking board houses. Hunters come in from the plains and the mountains, clad in buckskin shirts and fur caps, greasy and unkempt, but with resolute faces and sullen, watchful eyes, that are ever on the alert. The teamsters, surly and self-contained, wear slouch-hats and great cowhide boots; while the stage-drivers, their faces seamed by the hardship and exposure of their long drives with every kind of team, through every kind of country, and in every kind of weather, proud of their really wonderful skill as reinsmen and conscious of their high standing in any frontier community, look down on and sneer at the "skin-hunters" and the plodding drivers of the white-topped prairie-schooners. Besides these there are trappers, and wolfers whose business is to poison wolves, with shaggy, knock-kneed ponies to carry their small bales and bundles of furs—beaver, wolf, fox, and occasionally otter; and silent sheep-herders, with cast-down faces, never able to forget the absolute solitude and monotony of their dreary lives, not to rid their minds of the thought of the woolly idiots they pass all their days in tending. Such are the men who have come to town, either on business or else to frequent the flaunting saloons and gaudy hells of all kinds in search of the coarse, vicious excitement that in the minds of many of them does duty as pleasure—the only form of pleasure they have ever had a chance to know. Indians too, wrapped in blankets, with stolid, emotionless faces, stalk silently round among the whites, or join in the gambling and horse-racing. If the town is on the borders of the mountain country, there will also be sinewy lumbermen, rough-looking miners, and pack-ers whose business it is to guide the long mule and pony trains that go where wagons cannot and whose work in packing needs special and peculiar skill; and mingled with and drawn from all these classes are desperadoes of every grade, from the gambler up through the horse-thief to the murderous professional bully, or, as he is locally called, "bad man"—now, however, a much less conspicuous object than formerly.

But everywhere among these plainsmen and moun-tain men, and more important than any are the cowboys —the men who follow the calling that has brought such towns into being. Singly, or in twos or threes, they gal-lop their wiry little horses down the street, their lithe, supple figures erect or swaying slightly as they sit loosely in the saddle; while their stirrups are so long that their knees are hardly bent, the bridles not taut enough to keep the chains from clanking. They are smaller and less muscular than the wielders of axe and pick; but they are as hardy and self-reliant as any men who ever breathed—with bronzed, set faces, and keen eyes that look all the world straight in the face without flinching as they flash out from under the broad-brimmed hats. Peril and hardship, and years of long toil broken by weeks of brutal dissipation, draw haggard lines across their eager faces, but never dim their reckless eyes nor break their bearing of defiant self-confidence. They do not walk well, partly because they so rarely do any work out of the saddle, partly because their *chaparejos* or leather overalls hamper them when on the ground; but their appearance is striking for all that, and picturesque too, with their jingling spurs, the big revolvers stuck in their belts, and bright silk handkerchiefs knotted loosely round their necks over the open collars of the flannel shirts. When drunk on the villainous whiskey of the frontier towns, they cut mad antics, riding their horses into the saloons, firing their pistols right and left, from boisterous light-heartedness rather than from any vi-ciousness, and indulging too often in deadly shooting affrays, brought on either by the accidental contact of the moment or on account of some long-standing grudge, or perhaps because of bad blood between two ranches or localities; but except while on such sprees they are quiet, rather self-contained men, perfectly frank and simple, and on their own ground treat a stranger with the most whole-souled hospitality, doing all in their power for him and scorning to take any reward in return. Al-though prompt to resent an injury, they are not at all apt to be rude to outsiders, treating them with what can almost be called a grave courtesy. They are much better fellows and pleasanter companions than small farmers or agricultural laborers; nor are the mechanics and workmen of a great city to be mentioned in the same breath.

The bulk of the cowboys themselves are South-westerners; but there are also many from the Eastern and the Northern States, who, if they begin young, do quite as well as the Southerners. The best hands are fairly bred to the work and follow it from their youth up. Nothing can be more foolish than for an Easterner to think he can become a cowboy in a few months' time. Many a young fellow comes out hot with enthusiasm for life on the plains, only to learn that his clumsiness is greater than he could have believed possible; that the cowboy business is like any other and has to be learned by serving a painful apprenticeship; and that this ap-prenticeship implies the endurance of rough fare, hard living, dirt, exposure of every kind, no little toil, and month after month of the dullest monotony. For cow-boy work there is need of special traits and special train-ing, and young Easterners should be sure of themselves before trying it: the struggle for existence is very keen in the far West, and it is no place for men who lack the ruder, coarser virtues and physical qualities, no matter how intellectual or how refined and delicate their sensibilities. Such are more likely to fail there than in older communities. Probably during the past few years more than half of the young Easterners who have come West with a little money to learn the cattle business have failed signally and lost what they had in the beginning. The West, especially the far West, needs men who have been bred on the farm or in the workshop far more than it does clerks or college graduates.

Some of the cowboys are Mexicans, who generally do the actual work well enough, but are not trustworthy; moreover, they are always regarded with extreme disfavor by the Texans in an outfit, among whom the intolerant caste spirit is very strong. Southern-born whites will never work under them, and look down upon all colored or half-caste races. One spring I had with my wagon a Pueblo Indian, an excellent rider and roper, but a drunken, worthless, lazy devil; and in the summer of 1866 there were with us a Sioux half-breed, a quiet, hard-working, faithful fellow, and a mulatto, who was one of the best cow-hands in the whole roundup.

Cowboys, like most Westerners, occasionally show remarkable versatility in their tastes and pursuits. One whom I know has abandoned his regular occupation for the past nine months, during which time he has been in succession a bartender, a school-teacher, and a probate judge! Another, whom I once employed for a short while, had passed through even more varied experiences, including those of a barber, a sailor, an apothecary, and a buffalo-hunter.

As a rule the cowboys are known to each other only by their first names, with, perhaps, as a prefix, the title of the brand for which they are working. Thus I remember once overhearing a casual remark to the effect that "Bar Y Harry" had married "the Seven Open A girl," the latter being the daughter of a neighboring ranchman. Often they receive nicknames, as, for instance, Dutch Wannigan, Windy Jack, and Kid Williams, all of whom are on the list of my personal acquaintances.

No man travelling through or living in the country need fear molestation from the cowboys unless he himself accompanies them on their drinking-bouts, or in other ways plays the fool, for they are, with us at any rate, very good fellows, and the most determined and effective foes of real law-breakers, such as horse and cattle thieves, murderers, etc. Few of the outrages quoted in Eastern papers as their handiwork are such in reality, the average Easterner apparently considering every individual who wears a broad hat and carries a six-shooter a cowboy. These outrages are, as a rule, the work of the roughs and criminals who always gather on the outskirts of civilization, and who infest every frontier town until the decent citizens become sufficiently numerous and determined to take the law into their own hands and drive them out. The old buffalo-hunters, who formed a distinct class, became powerful forces for evil once they had destroyed the vast herds of mighty beasts the pursuit of which had been their means of livelihood. They were absolutely shiftless and improvident; they had no settled habits; they were inured to peril and hardship, but entirely unaccustomed to steady work; and so they afforded just the materials from which to make the bolder and more desperate kinds of criminals. When the game was gone they hung round the settlements for some little time, and then many of them naturally took to horse-stealing, cattle-killing, and highway robbery, although others, of course, went into honest pursuits. They were men who died off rapidly, however; for it is curious to see how many of these plainsmen, in spite of their iron nerves and thews, have their constitutions completely undermined, as much by the terrible hardships they have endured as by the fits of prolonged and bestial revelry with which they have varied them.

6. American life was not made up entirely of work or travel. The number of students in colleges was increasing, and student teams began to play against one another in intercollegiate sports. Paul Bourget, a French writer, went to one of the early football games between the University of Pennsylvania and Harvard University. His description below, written for a French audience, reports what happened— with the suggestion that the Americans were still perhaps a little barbaric. The passage is from his book entitled Outre-Mer: Impressions of America *(1895).*

The most vehement of those (*American*) pleasures and the most deeply national are those of sport. Interpret the word in its true sense, and you will find in it nothing of the meaning which we French attach to it, who have softened the term in adopting it, and who make it consist above all of elegance and dexterity. For the American "sport" has ever in it some danger, for it does not exist without the conception of contest and daring.

Among the distractions of sport, none has been more fashionable for several years past than football. I was present last autumn, in the peaceful and quiet city of Cambridge, at a game between the champions of Harvard College—the "team," as they say here—and the champions of the University of Pennsylvania. I must go back in thought to my journey in Spain to recall a popular fever equal to that which throbbed along the road between Boston and the arena where the match was to take place. The electric cars followed one another at intervals of a minute, filled with passengers, who, seated or standing, or hanging on the steps, crowded, pushed, crushed one another. Although the days of November are cruelly cold under a Massachusetts sky, the place of contest, as at Rome for the gladiatorial combats, was in a sort of open-air enclosure. A stone's throw away from Memorial Hall and the other buildings of the university, wooden stands were erected. On these stands were perhaps fifteen thousand spectators, and in the immense quadrilateral hemmed in by the stands were two teams composed of eleven youths each waiting for the signal to begin.

What a tremor in that crowd, composed not of the lower classes, but of well-to-do people, and how the excitement increased as time went on! All held in their hands small red flags and wore tufts of red flowers. Crimson is the color of the Harvard boys. Although a movement of feverish excitement ran through this crowd, it was not enough for the enthusiasts of the game. Propagators of enthusiasm, students with unbearded deeply lined faces, passed between the benches and still further increased the ardor of the public by uttering the war cry of the university, the "Rah! rah! rah!" thrice repeated, which terminates in the frenzied call, "Haaarvard." The partisans of the "Pennsies" replied by a similar cry, and in the distance, above the palings of the enclosure, we could see clusters of other spectators, too poor to pay the entrance fee, who had climbed into the branches of the leafless trees, their faces outlined against the autumn sky with the daintiness of the pale heads in Japanese painted fans.

The signal is given and the play begins. It is a fearful game, which by itself would suffice to indicate the differences between the Anglo-Saxon and the Latin world —a game of young bulldogs brought up to bite, to rush upon the quarry; the game of a race made for wild attack, for violent defense, for implacable conquests and desperate struggles. With their leather vests, with the Harvard sleeves of red cloth, and the Pennsylvania blue-and-white vests and sleeves, so soon to be torn—with the leather gaiters to protect their shins, with their great shoes and their long hair floating around their pale and flushed faces, these scholarly athletes are at once admirable and frightful to see when once the demon of contest has entered into them. At each extremity of the field is a goal, representing, at the right end, one of the teams, at the left the other. The entire object is to throw an enormous leather ball, which the champion of one or the other side holds in turn. It is in waiting for this

throw that all the excitement of this almost ferocious amusement is concentrated. He who holds the ball is there, bent forward, his companions and his adversaries likewise bent down around him in the attitude of beasts of prey about to spring. All of a sudden he runs to throw the ball, or else with a wildly rapid movement he hands it to another, who rushes off with it. All depends on stopping him.

The roughness with which they seize the bearer of the ball is impossible to imagine without having witnessed it. He is grasped by the middle of the body, by the head, by the legs, by the feet. He rolls over and his assailants with him, and as they fight for the ball and the two sides come to the rescue, it becomes a heap of twenty-two bodies tumbling on top of one another, like an inextricable knot of serpents with human heads. This heap writhes on the ground and tugs at itself. One sees faces, hair, backs, or legs appearing in a monstrous and agitated melee. Then this murderous knot unravels itself, and the ball, thrown by the most agile, bounds away and is again followed with the same fury. It continually happens that, after one of those frenzied entanglements, one of the combatants remains on the field motionless, incapable of rising, so much has he been hit, pressed, crushed, thumped.

A doctor whose duty it is to look after the wounded arrives and examines him. You see those skilled hands shaking a foot, a leg, rubbing the sides, washing a face, sponging the blood which streams from the forehead, the eyes, the nose, the mouth. A compassionate comrade assists in the business and takes the head of the fainting champion on his knee. Sometimes the unlucky player must be carried away. More frequently, however, he recovers his senses, stretches himself, rouses up, and ends by scrambling to his feet. He makes a few steps, leaning on the friendly shoulder, and no sooner is he able to walk than the game begins afresh, and he joins in again with a rage doubled by pain and humiliation.

If the roughness of this terrible sport was for the spectators only the occasion of a nervous excitement of a few hours, the young athletes would not give themselves up to it with this enthusiasm which makes them accept the most painful, sometimes the most dangerous of trainings. . . .

No sooner are such matches as these in preparation than the portraits of the various players are in all the papers. The incidents of the game are described in detail with graphic pictures, in order that the comings and goings of the ball may be better followed. Conquerors and conquered are alike interviewed. From a celebrated periodical the other day I cut out an article signed "A Football Scientist," wherein the author sought to show that the right tactics to follow in this game were the same as those used by Napoleon.

CROSS REFERENCES

Refer to the following articles in the text volumes (Volume 1 through Volume 8) for background of RESOURCE UNIT 6.

RESOURCE UNIT 6-A

ALASKA
ALASKA PURCHASE
ARCTIC EXPLORATION
ARIZONA
BOUNDARIES OF THE UNITED STATES
BUFFALO (BISON)
CONTINENTAL DIVIDE
EXPLORATION AND DISCOVERY
NEVADA
NEW MEXICO
NORTH DAKOTA
POWELL, JOHN WESLEY
RUSSIA, RELATIONS WITH
SAMOA
SEWARD, WILLIAM HENRY
SOUTH DAKOTA
WYOMING

RESOURCE UNIT 6-B

CUSTER, GEORGE ARMSTRONG
GATLING GUN
JACKSON, HELEN HUNT
NAVAL VESSELS
RACES AND PEOPLES OF THE UNITED STATES
SHERMAN, WILLIAM TECUMSEH
SHERIDAN, PHILIP
UNITED STATES ARMY
UNITED STATES NAVY

RESOURCE UNIT 6-C

AGRARIAN REVOLT
ALABAMA CLAIMS
ALTGELD, JOHN P.
AMNESTY
ARTHUR, CHESTER A.
ATLANTA, GEORGIA
BLACK CODES
BLAINE, JAMES G.
BLAND-ALLISON ACT
BLOODY SHIRT
BURLINGAME TREATY
CHILE, RELATIONS WITH
CHINA, RELATIONS WITH
CIVIL LIBERTIES AND CIVIL RIGHTS LEGISLATION
CIVIL SERVICE
CLEVELAND, GROVER
CONGRESSIONAL RECONSTRUCTION
CONSTITUTION OF THE UNITED STATES
CREDIT MOBILIER
DEMOCRATIC PARTY
DONNELLY, IGNATIUS
ELECTORAL COMMISSION
FOREIGN POLICY OF THE UNITED STATES
FREEDMEN'S BUREAU
GARFIELD, JAMES ABRAM
GRANGERS
GRANT, ULYSSES S.
GREAT BRITAIN, RELATIONS WITH
GREELEY, HORACE
GREENBACK PARTY
HANCOCK, WINFIELD SCOTT
HANNA, MARCUS A.
HAYES, RUTHERFORD B.
IMPEACHMENT
JOHNSON, ANDREW
MCKINLEY, WILLIAM
PAN-AMERICAN CONFERENCES
PENDLETON ACT
POPULIST PARTY
PRESIDENTIAL ELECTIONS
RECONSTRUCTION
REPUBLICAN PARTY
ROOSEVELT, THEODORE
TARIFF POLICIES OF THE UNITED STATES
TAXATION IN THE UNITED STATES
TILDEN, SAMUEL JONES
UNION LEAGUE
WEAVER, JAMES BAIRD
WHISKEY RING

RESOURCE UNIT 6-D

AGRICULTURE AND AGRICULTURAL TECHNOLOGY
AMERICAN FEDERATION OF LABOR
ANTI-SALOON LEAGUE
BANKS AND BANKING
BARBED WIRE
BARNUM, PHINEAS T.
BLACK FRIDAY
CAPITAL AND CAPITALISM
COOKE, JAY
CORPORATIONS
COXEY'S ARMY
DARWINISM
DEPRESSIONS AND PANICS
EADS, JAMES B.
ELECTRIC POWER AND LIGHT INDUSTRY
FARMERS' ORGANIZATIONS
FINANCE
GOMPERS, SAMUEL
GOULD, JAY
HILL, JAMES J.
HOLMES, OLIVER WENDELL, JR.
HOMESTEAD STRIKE

BOOKS FOR FURTHER READING

Exploration and Settlement

W. Blassingame, *They Rode the Frontier*; T. C. Blegen, *Land of Their Choice: The Immigrants Write Home*; H. Chevigny, *Russian America*; T. D. Clark, *Frontier America: The Story of the Westward Movement*; E. Dick, *The Sod-House Frontier, 1854–1890*; J. F. Dobie, *The Longhorns*; O. Handlin, *The Uprooted: The Epic Story of the Great Migrations That Made the American People*; B. McKelvey, *The Urbanization of America*; T. Penfield, *Western Sheriffs and Marshals*; J. W. Powell, *First Through the Grand Canyon*.

The Army Between Wars

F. Downey, *Indian-Fighting Army*; Dunn, J. P., *Massacres of the Mountains*; H. H. Jackson, *A Century of Dishonor*; S. L. A. Marshall, *Crimsoned Prairie*; R. N. Utley, *Frontier Regulars*

Political Problems

(*Reconstruction*). H. K. Beale, *The Critical Year: A Study of Andrew Johnson and the Reconstruction*; C. Bird, *The Invisible Scar*; C. G. Bowers, *The Tragic Era:*

The Revolution After Lincoln; W. R. Brock, *An American Crisis: Congress and Reconstruction, 1865–1867*; P. H. Buck, *The Road to Reunion: 1865–1900*; W. L. Fleming, ed., *Documentary History of Reconstruction, Political, Military, Social, Religious, and Industrial*; J. H. Franklin, *From Slavery to Freedom: A History of American Negroes*; J. A. Garraty, *The New Commonwealth*, and also his *The Transformation of American Society*; J. G. Randall and D. Donald, *The Civil War and Reconstruction*; J. F. Shenton, *The Reconstruction: A Documentary History, 1865–1877*; K. M. Stampp, *Era of Reconstruction*; C. V. Woodward, *Reunion and Reaction*.

(*After Reconstruction*), C. D. Bowen, *Yankee from Olympus: Justice Holmes and his Family*; J. S. Ezell, *The South Since 1865*; H. U. Faulkner, *Politics, Reform and Expansion: 1890–1900*; R. B. Hayes, *Hayes, The Diary of a President, 1875–1881* (ed., T. H. Williams); J. D. Hicks, *The Populist Revolt*; M. K. Leech, *In the Days of McKinley*; A. Nevins, *Grover Cleveland: A Study in Courage*; K. H. Porter and D. B. Johnson, *National Party Platforms, 1840–1964*.

Social Developments

M. Antin, *The Promised Land*; H. Adams, *The Education of Henry Adams*; G. W. Allen, *William James: A Biography*; E. Bok, *The Americanization of Edward Bok*; A. Carnegie, *The Autobiography of Andrew Carnegie*; T. C. Cochran and W. Miller, *The Age of Enterprise: A Social History of Industrial America*; R. Cromie, *The Great Chicago Fire*; B. De Voto, *Mark Twain's America*; S. Gompers, *Seventy Years of Life and Labor*; R. Hofstadter, *Social Darwinism in American Thought*; R. W. Howard, *The Great Iron Trail: The Story of the First Transcontinental Railroad*; E. C. Kirkland, *Industry Comes of Age: Business, Labor and Public Policy, 1860–1897*; A. Lutz, *Susan B. Anthony*; A. Nevins, *John D. Rockefeller*; J. Riis, *The Making of an American*; F. A. Shannon, *The Farmer's Last Frontier: Agriculture, 1860–1897*; R. L. Taylor, *Vessel of Wrath*; B. T. Washington, *Up From Slavery*; W. P. Webb, *The Great Plains*.

NOVELS AND STORIES

Reconstruction Days to 1900

Mark Twain and C. D. Warner, *The Gilded Age*
    The moral letdown after the Civil War
Mark Twain, *Roughing It*   Nevada and California
    in the 1860's
Joel C. Harris, *Gabriel Tolliver*   The New South
Ellen Glasgow, *The Deliverance*   The New South

C. B. Davis, *Nebraska Coast*   Pioneer life, 1860's

Hamlin Garland, *A Son of the Middle Border*   Pioneer Wisconsin and Dakota. An autobiography.

Willa Cather, *My Antonia*   Nebraska immigrant settlers

Willa Cather, *A Lost Lady*   The decay of the pioneer spirit

Willa Cather, *Death Comes for the Archbishop*   New Mexico

Paul Horgan, *A Distant Trumpet*   Arizona Territory

Conrad Richter, *The Sea of Grass*   Cattlemen versus homesteaders

O. E. Rölvaag, *Giants in the Earth*   Norwegian settlers in Dakota

Walter Van T. Clark, *The Ox-Bow Incident*   Mob law and vigilantes

Owen Wister, *The Virginian*   Classic "cowboy" story

Mari Sandoz, *Miss Morissa*   Nebraska frontier in the 1870's

Glenway Westcott, *The Grandmothers*   A Wisconsin family chronicle

Booth Tarkington, *The Magnificent Ambersons*   Rise and fall of a pioneer family

Edith Wharton, *The Age of Innocence*   New York in the 1870's

Edith Wharton, *The Custom of the Country*   The "new-rich" in the late 19th century

6. RECONSTRUCTION AND NATIONAL DEVELOPMENT: 1865-1898

1. By the 1870's the bustle had replaced the crinoline, giving women more freedom of movement. Drawing by Arthur Lumley. *Courtesy,* Scribner Art File.

CLOTHING, 1865-1898

2. Ladies played croquet in formal street dress in 1866. From Godey's *Lady's Book*. 3. "The Bathers" from *Harper's Weekly*, 1873. 4. By the 1890's sportswear was worn by the woman on the golf course. Drawing by A. B. Frost from *Harper's Bazar*, 1894.

4

5

6

5. Women cyclists appeared in bloomers and above-the-ankle skirts. From *Harper's Bazar,* 1894. 6. Formal occasions, such as attending the opera, called for sweeping skirts. For men, full evening dress including top hats were necessary. From *Harper's Weekly,* April, 1894.

7. This bride and her attendants in the mid-1890's wore gowns lavishly trimmed with beads, sequins, and pearls. From *Harper's Bazar,* 1894. 8. On the campus, college girls wore the fashionable "dog-collar" along with fancy hats. *Courtesy,* Nebraska State Historical Society. 9. Frou-frou, or ruffles a-plenty, and the pompadour hairstyle were popular at the turn of the century. From *Puck,* August, 1900.

7

9

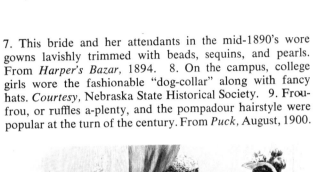

8

INTERIORS AND HOUSE FURNISHINGS, 1865-1898

10. Solid, elaborately carved furniture was typical of the period after the Civil War. A bedroom suite of 1876. *Courtesy,* Grand Rapids Public Museum. 11. Another example is this parlor organ (ca. 1880), made by the Jacob Estey Organ Company of Brattleboro, Vermont. *Courtesy,* Collections of Greenfield Village and the Henry Ford Museum. 12. A millionaire could live in a French chateau on Fifth Avenue, such as this one, (ca. 1881) designed for William K. Vanderbilt by R. M. Hunt. From *Harper's Weekly.*

10

11

12

13

13. Ostentatious splendor marks this drawing room of the Fifth Avenue home of W. C. Whitney. The architect was Stanford White. *Courtesy,* Museum of the City of New York. 14. This entrance hall was more typical of the period's taste. *Courtesy,* Iowa State Department of History and Archives, Des Moines.

15. Indian and frontier motifs adorn this compote made in Philadelphia ca. 1875. *Courtesy,* The Brooklyn Museum. 16. These vases by Louis Tiffany were inspired by the graceful lines of Art Nouveau, ca. 1890-1910. *Courtesy,* The Metropolitan Museum of Art. 17. The "Turkish Den" in the Planters Hotel, St. Louis, — an example of the sham exotic so popular in the 1890's. *Courtesy,* Missouri Historical Society, St. Louis.

15

16

17

18

19

LIFE IN AMERICA

18. The Civil War had left many Southern families in great distress. From *Leslie's Illustrated Newspaper,* February, 1867.   19. To help with Reconstruction, primary schools for freedmen such as this one at Vicksburg, Mississippi were established. From *Harper's Weekly,* 1866.   20. In the West, gold mining towns, like Virginia City, Montana, boomed and "hurdy-gurdy" girls provided company for the lonely miners. From Albert D. Richardson, *Beyond the Mississippi . . .* 1867.

20

21. These "Christmas Belles" in the North enjoyed the popular pastime of sleighing. From *Harper's Weekly,* January, 1867. 22. "Fast Trotters on Harlem Lane," New York, 1870. Lithograph by Currier & Ives. *Courtesy,* The J. Clarence Davies Collection, Museum of the City of New York.

23. In rural communities the general store was a social center and inc the post office. "The Village Post Office" by Thomas Waterman Wood, *Courtesy*, New York State Historical Association, Cooperstown, New 24. Farm reform in musical style. From C.A. Hall, *Songs for the G*, 1873. *Courtesy*, University of Texas Library. 25. Old-time farming oxen and a simple plough was still practiced in some parts of the Sou 1880. *Courtesy*, Scribner Art File.

26

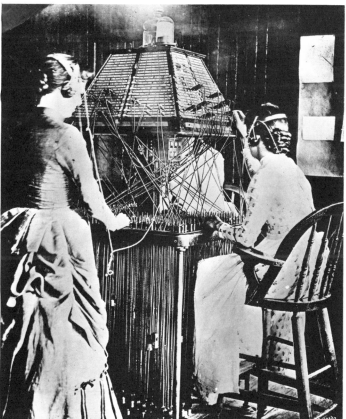

27

28

26. As the railroads pushed West, uniting the nation, they carried immigrant settlers, businessmen and foreign laborers, among others. Here seen is the waiting room of the Union Pacific Depot, Omaha, in 1877. From *Frank Leslie's Illustrated Newspaper*. 27. Jacket of one of the books that started the cowboy legend, 1885. *Courtesy,* University of Illinois Library. 28. By the 1880's the telephone was another connecting link among the States. Here shown is the pyramid switchboard in Richmond, Virginia, 1881. *Courtesy,* American Telephone and Telegraph Company.

THE FRENCH FLAT OF THE VERY NEAR FUTURE
EVERYTHING ON THE PREMISES

F. Opper

IN THE KITCHEN

IN THE PARLOR

29

30

29. In New York City, the apartment house, a new type of dwelling, seemed to promise its residents the last word in living convenience. As a humorous comment, this cartoon from *Puck,* 1883, shows forerunners of the radio, the supermarket, and facsimile newspapers.   30. Country dwellers continued to wrestle with the rigors of nature. "A Winter-Morning: Shovelling Out," drawing by Winslow Homer. From *Every Saturday,* January 14, 1871. 31. Frequent flooding from the Mississippi brought misery to these Arkansas farmers. From *Frank Leslie's Illustrated Newspaper* April, 1882.

31

32. During the latter half of the 19th century European immigrants poured in, attracted by the American need for laborers. *Courtesy*, Scribner Art File.   33. To help people acquire good manners, pictorial etiquette lessons were available. Same source.   34. The "good old summertime" of 1896 brought a new treat, the trolley-car excursion. From *Harper's Weekly*.

33

FIG. 11. BAD MANNERS AT THE TABLE.

No. 1.	Tips back his chair.	
" 2.	Eats with his mouth too full.	
" 3.	Feeds a dog at the table.	
" 4.	Holds his knife improperly.	
" 5.	Engages in violent argument at the meal-time.	
" 6.	Lounges upon the table.	
" 7.	Brings a cross child to the table.	

No. 8. Drinks from the saucer, and laps with his tongue the last drop from the plate.
" 9. Comes to the table in his shirt-sleeves, and puts his feet beside his chair.
" 10. Picks his teeth with his fingers.
" 11. Scratches her head and is frequently unnecessarily getting up from the table.

35. Young women studied along with men in the Botanical Laboratory at the University of Wyoming in Laramie, ca. 1890. *Courtesy, Scribner Art File.* 36. Other young ladies, known as the "Dollar Princesses" were busy abroad seeking titled husbands. Cartoon from *Puck,* 1895.

35

36

37

37. The "Gay Nineties" saw the advent of the moving picture. In this Koster and Bial's Music Hall program, it is listed as Edison's Latest Marvel. *Courtesy,* Museum of the City of New York. 38. An evening at a roof garden offering refreshment and entertainment was a pleasant way to spend a summer night in New York. Here seen is the glass roof of the Olympia. From *Harper's Weekly,* September, 1896. 39. An ice-cream soda at the drug store. Note the derby hat worn by all. *Courtesy,* Ravenswood-Lake View Historical Association and The Chicago Public Library, Illinois.

40. This view of Broadway, north from Cortlandt and Maiden Lane, ca. 1885, remained the same for many years with its bustling activity and tangle of telegraph wires. Courtesy, The New-York Historical Society.

RESOURCE UNIT 7

Early Twentieth Century:
1898-1933

7-A EXPLORATION

By the start of the 20th century, most areas within the United States had been fairly well explored and at least roughly mapped. Parts of the mountain States in the West were still being explored, and much of Alaska was only vaguely known. However, the major exploring work done by Americans was turning outward from the United States toward other areas. As the nation itself began to take a great part in international affairs, American explorers entered the field of international exploration. Much effort went into polar expeditions, which also drew the attention and rivalry of explorers from other nations. Technical developments of the 20th century added new tools for explorers (the gasoline engine and the camera, for example), and the development of the airplane added a whole new field for pioneering—the ocean of air that surrounds the world.

PROBLEMS: *In what ways did 20th century American exploration resemble earlier exploring expeditions? How did technology influence the work of aviation pioneers and polar explorers? To what extent were American explorers working for mankind as well as for their own country's honor?*

1. During the early years of the 20th century, the imagination of the public was stirred by efforts of explorers to reach the North and the South Poles.

Expeditions from the United States (and other countries) had sought to reach the North Pole on several occasions during the 19th century, but without success. Now, two *American exploring teams engaged in a race to be first at the Pole. One, headed by Dr. Frederick Cook, laid claim to the honor; but the other, led by Robert E. Peary (a Navy engineer officer, later made Admiral) produced more solid evidence that it had been first. Peary had made a number of explorations in the Far North before he succeeded in reaching the North Pole on April 6, 1909. In the final stage of the journey, he was accompanied by four Eskimos and by Matthew Henson, a black American mariner, who later wrote an account of his work with Peary (A Negro Explorer at the North Pole). Peary paid a handsome tribute to Henson in a foreword to the book.*

"The example and experience of Matthew Henson, who has been a member of each and all of my Arctic explorations since '91 (my trip in 1886 was taken before I knew Henson) is only another one of

the multiplying illustrations of the fact that race, or color, or bringing-up, or environment, count nothing against a determined heart, if it is backed and aided by inelligence. . . .

"Again, it is an interesting fact that in the final conquest of the prize of the centuries, not alone individuals, but races *were represented. On that bitter brilliant day in April 1909, when the Stars and Stripes floated at the North Pole, Caucasian, Ethiopian, and Mongolian stood side by side at the apex of the earth, in the harmonious companionship resulting from hard work, exposure, danger, and a common object."*

The description of the dash for the Pole which follows is taken from Matthew Henson's book.

Without an instant's hesitation, the order to push on was given, and we started off in the trail made by the Captain to cover the Farthest North he had made and to push on over one hundred and thirty miles to our final destination.

The Captain had had rough going, but, owing to the fact that his trail was our track for a short time, and that we came to good going shortly after leaving his turning point, we made excellent distance without any trouble, and only stopped when we came to a lead barely frozen over, a full twenty-five miles beyond. We camped and waited for the strong southeast wind to force the sides of the lead together. The Esquimos had eaten a meal of stewed dog, cooked over a fire of wood from a discarded sledge, and, owing to their wonderful powers of recuperation, were in good condition; Commander Peary and myself, rested and invigorated by our thirty hours in the last camp, waiting for the return and departure of Captain Bartlett, were also in fine fettle, and accordingly the accomplishment of twenty-five miles of northward progress was not exceptional. With my proven ability in gauging distances, Commander Peary was ready to take the reckoning as I made it and he did not resort to solar observations until we were within a hand's grasp of the Pole.

The memory of those last five marches, from the Farthest North of Captain Bartlett to the arrival of our party at the Pole, is a memory of toil, fatigue, and exhaustion, but we were urged on and encouraged by our relentless commander, who was himself being scourged by the final lashings of the dominating influence that had controlled his life. From the land to 87° 48′ north, Commander Peary had had the best of the going, for he had brought up the rear and had utilized the trail made by the preceding parties, and thus he had kept himself in the best of condition for the time when he made the spurt that brought him to the end of the race. From 87° 48′ north, he kept in the lead and did his work in such a way as to convince me that he was still as good a man as he had ever been. We marched and marched, falling down in our tracks repeatedly, until it was impossible to go on. We were forced to camp, in spite of the impatience of the Commander, who found himself unable to rest, and who only waited long enough for us to relax into sound sleep, when he would wake us up and start us off again. I do not believe that he slept for one hour from April 2 until after he had loaded us up and ordered us to go back over our old trail, and I often think that from the instant when the order to return was given until the land was again sighted, he was in a continual daze.

Onward we forced our weary way. Commander Peary took his sights from the time our chronometer-watches gave, and I, knowing that we had kept on going in practically a straight line, was sure that we had more than covered the necessary distance to insure our arrival at the top of the earth.

It was during the march of the 3d of April that I endured an instant of hideous horror. We were crossing a lane of moving ice. Commander Peary was in the lead setting the pace, and a half hour later the four boys and myself followed in single file. They had all gone before, and I was standing and pushing at the upstanders of my sledge, when the block of ice I was using as a support slipped from underneath my feet, and before I knew it the sledge was out of my grasp, and I was floundering in the water of the lead. I did the best I could. I tore my hood from off my head and struggled frantically. My hands were gloved and I could not take hold of the ice, but before I could give the "Grand Hailing Sigh of Distress," faithful old Ootah had grabbed me by the nape of the neck, the same as he would have grabbed a dog, and with one hand he pulled me out of the water, and with the other hurried the team across.

He had saved my life, but I did not tell him so, for such occurrences are taken as part of the day's work, and the sledge he safeguarded was of much more importance, for it held, as part of its load, the Commander's sextant, the mercury, and the coils of piano-wire that were the essential portion of the scientific part of the expedition. My kamiks (boots of sealskin) were stripped off, and the congealed water was beaten out of my bearskin trousers, and with a dry pair of kamiks, we hurried on to overtake the column. When we caught up, we found the boys gathered around the Commander, doing their best to relieve him of his discomfort, for he had fallen into the water also, and while he was not complaining, I was sure that his bath had not been any more voluntary than mine had been.

When we halted on April 6, 1909, and started to build the igloos, the dogs and sledges having been secured, I noticed Commander Peary at work unloading his sledge and unpacking several bundles of equipment. He pulled out from under his *kooletah* (thick, fur outergarment) a small folded package and unfolded it. I recognized his old silk flag, and realized that this was to be a camp of importance. Our different camps had been known as Camp Number One, Number Two, etc., but after the turning back of Captain Bartlett, the camps had been given names such as Camp Nansen, Camp Cagni, etc., and I asked what the name of this camp was to be—"Camp Peary"? "This, my boy, is to be Camp Morris K. Jesup, the last and most northerly camp on the earth." He fastened the flag to a staff and planted it firmly on the top of his igloo. For a few minutes it hung limp and lifeless in the dead calm of the haze, and then a slight breeze, increasing in strength, caused the folds to straighten out, and soon it was rippling out in sparkling color. The stars and stripes were "nailed to the Pole."

A thrill of patriotism ran through me and I raised my voice to cheer the starry emblem of my native land. The Esquimos gathered around and, taking the time from Commander Peary, three hearty cheers rang out on the still, frosty air, our dumb dogs looking on in puzzled surprise. As prospects for getting a sight of the sun were not good, we turned in and slept, leaving the flag proudly floating above us.

This was a thin silk flag that Commander Peary had carried on all of his Arctic journeys, and he had always flown it at his last camps. It was as glorious and as inspiring a banner as any battle-scarred, blood-stained standard of the world—and this badge of honor and courage was also blood-stained and battle-scarred, for at several places there were blank squares marking the spots where pieces had been cut out at each of the "Farthests" of its brave bearer, and left with the records in the cairns, as mute but eloquent witnesses of his achievements. At the North Pole a diagonal strip running from the upper left to the lower right corner was cut and this precious strip, together with a brief record, was placed in an empty tin, sealed up and buried in the ice, as a record for all time.

Commander Peary also had another American flag, sewn on a white ground, and it was the emblem of the "Daughters of the Revolution Peace Society"; he also had and flew the emblem of the Navy League, and the emblems of a couple of college fraternities of which he was a member.

It was about ten or ten-thirty A. M., on the 7th of April, 1909, that the Commander gave the order to build a snow-shield to protect him from the flying drift of the surface-snow. I knew that he was about to take an observation, and while we worked I was nervously apprehensive, for I felt that the end of our journey had come. When we handed him the pan of mercury the hour was within a very few minutes of noon. Lying flat on his stomach, he took the elevation and made the notes on a piece of tissue-paper at his head. With sunblinded eyes, he snapped shut the *vernier* (a graduated scale that subdivides the smallest divisions on the sector of the circular scale of the sextant) and with the resolute squaring of his jaws, I was sure that he was satisfied, and I was confident that the journey had ended. Feeling that the time had come, I ungloved my right hand and went forward to congratulate him on the success of our eighteen years of effort, but a gust of wind blew something into his eye, or else the burning pain caused by his prolonged look at the reflection of the limb of the sun forced him to turn aside; and with both hands covering his eyes, he gave us orders to not let him sleep for more than four hours, for six hours later he purposed to take another sight about four miles beyond, and that he wanted at least two hours to make the trip and get everything in readiness.

I unloaded a sledge, and reloaded it with a couple of skins, the instruments, and a cooker with enough alcohol and food for one meal for three, and then I turned in to the igloo where my boys were already sound asleep. The thermometer registered 29° below zero. I fell into a dreamless sleep and slept for about a minute, so I thought, when I was awakened by the clatter and noise made by the return of Peary and his boys.

The Commander gave the word, "We will plant the stars and stripes—*at the North Pole!*" and it was done; on the peak of a huge paleocrystic floeberg the glorious banner was unfurled to the breeze, and as it snapped and crackled with the wind, I felt a savage joy and exultation. Another world's accomplishment was done and finished, and as in the past, from the beginning of history, wherever the world's work was done by a white man, he had been accompanied by a colored man. From the building of the pyramids and the journey to the Cross, to the discovery of the new world and the discovery of the North Pole, the Negro had been the faithful and constant companion of the Caucasian, and I felt all that it was possible for me to feel, that it was I, a lowly member of my race, who had been chosen by fate to represent it, at this, almost the last of the world's great *work*.

2. American exploration of the Polar regions continued on and off through the period 1898-1933. Some of the most dramatic and valuable achievements were the work of Commander (later Admiral)

Richard E. Byrd, an officer of the U.S. Navy. Byrd was the first person to reach both Poles—North and South. He describes his work below in a brief and modest summary of the facts which he wrote for the Dictionary of American History *(edited by James Truslow Adams). "Little America" which he mentions was a base camp in Antarctica, from which he and his men conducted their explorations and scientific observations. Byrd employed the most modern equipment available, including aircraft.*

On April 5, 1926, Commander Byrd sailed on the S.S. *Chantier* for Kings Bay, Spitzbergen, which he intended using as the base for a flight to the North Pole. The vessel arrived in the bay on April 29. The only pier in the harbor was occupied by a Norwegian gunboat; therefore, it was necessary to ferry the big tri-motored Fokker airplane, *Josephine Ford*, ashore through the drifting ice, which choked the bay, on a raft constructed from four ship's boats. This operation was successfully accomplished. After being held up by defects in the skis for some days, Byrd and his pilot, Floyd Bennett, eventually took off for the Pole shortly after midnight on May 9. The flight proceeded uneventfully until the airplane was one hour's flight short of the Pole, at which time a leak was discovered in an oil tank. In spite of this they continued onward. At 9:02 A. M., Greenwich Civil Time, the Pole was reached. After circling around it, the course was set for Spitzbergen. The return flight was uneventful, and the motors continued to function in spite of the oil leak.

Early in the Antarctic spring of 1929 Byrd made a flight from his base at Little America to the foot of the Queen Maud Mountains and laid down a gasoline base. On Nov. 29, 1929, at 3:29 P.M., the polar flight party took off in the Ford airplane, *Floyd Bennett*, for the Pole. At 9:15 they started up the Liv Glacier Pass for the Polar Plateau. The plane was so heavily loaded that she could not gain enough altitude to clear the head of the glacier. It was necessary to dump several hundred pounds of emergency food to lighten the plane enough to clear the "Hump." Once over the plateau the plane made good time. At 1:14, Greenwich Civil Time, the Pole was reached. A few minutes later the course was changed to head back to the mountains. This part of the flight developed into a race against clouds moving in from the east. The party just managed to get down Axel Heiberg Glacier before it was enshrouded. After a short flight to the eastward the plane was landed at the fuel base. At six o'clock the return journey to Little America began. Shortly after ten the party landed at the camp.

3. The airplane itself provided a new frontier for men to explore. The years 1898-1933 include the years in which modern aircraft were developed from powered kites to fairly dependable means of transport. Several airplane flights had "hopped" across bays, the English Channel, and over longer and longer stretches of water by the year 1927, so a great contest was set up with a prize for the first non-stop flight from New York across the Atlantic Ocean to Paris. There were no restrictions on how many pilots might fly in the winning plane. Excitement was very high, because of the length and danger of the flight. Several well-known pilots tried and failed, but on May 20-21 an almost unknown American flier, Charles A. Lindbergh, succeeded. His flight was more dramatic than that of any team of fliers, for he flew "solo"—unaided—across the ocean. The following selections have been taken from General Lindbergh's book, The Spirit of St. Louis, *in which he recalled what he had done and how he had felt during his epic sky journey.*

I lean back in the wicker seat, running my eyes once more over the instruments. Nothing wrong there. They all tell the proper story. Even the tachometer needle is in place, with the engine idling. Engine revolutions are like sheep. You can't notice that a few are missing until the entire flock is counted. A faint trace of gasoline mixes with the smell of newly dried dope *(chemical used to tighten the fabric covering)*—probably a few drops spilled out when the tanks were filled. I turn again to the problem of take-off. It will be slow at best. Can the engine stand such a long ground run at wide-open throttle, or will it overheat and start to miss?

Suppose I can hold the runway, suppose I *do* get off the ground—will fog close in and force me back? Suppose the ceiling drops to zero—I can't fly blind with this overload of fuel; but the wheels have doubtful safety factors for a landing. Shall I cut the switch and wait another day for confirmation of good weather? But if I leave now, I'll have a head start on both the Fokker and the Bellanca. Once in the air, I can nurse my engine all the way to Paris—there'll be no need to push it in a race. And the moon's past full—it will be three weeks to the next one; conditions then may be still worse.

Wind, weather, power, load — — — gradually these elements stop churning in my mind. It's less a decision of logic than of feeling, the kind of feeling that comes when you gauge the distance to be jumped between two stones across a brook. Something within you disengages itself from your body and travels ahead with your vision to make the test. You can feel it try the jump as you stand looking. Then uncertainty gives way to the conviction that it *can* or can't be done. Sitting in the cockpit, in seconds, minutes long, the conviction surges through me that the wheels *will* leave the ground, that the wings *will* rise above the wires, that it *is* time to start the flight.

I buckle my safety belt, pull goggles down over my eyes, turn to the men at the blocks, and nod. Frozen figures leap to action. A yank in the ropes—the wheels are free. I brace myself against the left side of the cockpit, sight along the edge of the runway, and ease the throttle wide open. Now, in seconds, we'll have the answer. Action brings confidence and relief. . . .

I'm flying with my head thrown back, looking up through the skylight at the handful of stars above me, glancing down at intervals to make sure my compass heading is correct. When you can see stars close to the horizon it's easy to hold on course. They draw you toward them like a beacon on the earth. But looking straight up for guidance is like dangling at the end of a rope; it's almost impossible to keep from turning slightly.

The stars blink on and off as haze thickens in places and then thins out again. I hold on to them tightly, dreading the blind flying that lies ahead the moment I let them go, hoping I can climb above the haze into the crystal blackness of the higher night—hoping, climbing, and yet sinking deeper with every minute that I fly.

Soon haze becomes so thick that, except for those dim points of light, it might as well be cloud. At any moment those stars may blink their last and die, leaving me stranded thousands of feet below the surface, like a diver whose life line has been cut. I'd thought I could climb above the fog and leave it beneath me, a neat and definite layer. Now, I realize what a formidable enemy it is. Its forces have been in ambush all around me, waiting only for the cool of night to show their form.

Why try to hold on to those stars? Why not start in now on instruments? After all, they were put there so I could fly through fog. This game of hide and seek with a half-dozen stars is child's play. But if I start flying blind, God only knows how many hours of it lie ahead. It might go on through the entire night—the monotony of flying with my eyes always on the instrument board; the strain of flying by intellect alone, forcing the unruly senses of the body to follow the doubted orders of the mind—the endless bringing of one needle after another back to its proper position, and then finding that all except the one my eyes hold tight have strayed off again.

The *Spirit of St. Louis* is too unstable to fly well on instruments. It's fast, and it has a greater range than any plane that flies; but it's high-strung, and balanced on a pin point. If I relax pressure on stick or rudder for an instant, the nose will veer off course.

And there's the question of staying awake. Could I keep sufficiently alert during long, monotonous hours of flying with my eyes glued to the instruments, with nothing more to stimulate my mind than the leaning of a needle? It was difficult enough to stay awake over the ice fields southwest of Newfoundland, when my eyes could travel the whole horizon back and forth, and with the piercing light of day to stir my senses. How would it be with fog and darkness shutting off even the view of my wing tips? . . .

There, on my left, is Plymouth, and the same harbor from which the *Mayflower* once sailed, against weeks of adverse winds and hardships. Yesterday, I flew almost over Plymouth Rock, on the coast of Massachusetts. Today, my course takes me above the mother city in England—a gray city, curving around its ship-filled harbor, smoke from its chimneys drifting leisurely along my line of flight; a low city compared to the steel-skeletoned skyscrapers we build in America. Beyond, the green, indented, rolling coast parallels my course for another thirty miles. . . .

From Start Point of England to Cape de la Hague of France is eighty-five miles. In the past, I would have approached an eighty-five-mile flight over water, in a land plane, with trepidation. It would have appeared a hazardous undertaking. This evening, it's just part of the downhill glide to Paris. Why, I should be able to paddle halfway across the Channel with my hands if I were forced down. What's eighty-five miles in contrast to an ocean—or to that space above the clouds at night? It's not even as long as the little bay of water between Cape Cod and Nova Scotia. It's less than that short hop across the ice fields between Cape Breton Island and Newfoundland. And here the ocean is no wilderness; it's a populated country, filled with ships. Dozens of them ply back and forth along the coast—fishing smacks to ocean liners—dots all over the surface, as far as I can see. Probably some of them have come from New York, too; churning through the water for days to make their crossing.

How safe the people on those ships have been, but how little they know the air and ocean! Security and luxury shield one off from life. You never see the sky until you've looked upward to the stars for safety. You never feel the air until you've been shaken by its storms.

You can never understand the ocean until you've been alone in its solitude. To appreciate fully, you must have intercourse with the elements themselves, know their whims, their beauties, their dangers. Then, every tissue of your being sees and feels, then body, mind, and spirit are as one.

The men who sailed in open boats a thousand years ago—they knew. They were at the mercy of the storm wind. They felt the wet, salty closeness of the ocean. They hadn't bought tickets under colored posters, or been assured return from voyage started. . . .

The *Spirit of St. Louis* is a wonderful plane. It's like a living creature, gliding along smoothly, happily, as though a successful flight means as much to it as to me, as though we shared our experiences together, each feeling beauty, life, and death as keenly, each dependent on the other's loyalty. *We* have made this flight across the ocean, not *I* or *it*.

I throw my flashlight on the engine instruments. Every needle is in place. For almost thirty-three hours, not one of them has varied from its normal reading—except when the nose tank ran dry. For every minute I've flown there have been more than seven thousand explosions in the cylinders, yet not a single one has missed.

I'm leveled off at four thousand feet, watching for the luminosity in the sky ahead that will mark the city of Paris. Within the hour, I'll land. The dot on my map will become Paris itself, with its airport, hangars, and floodlights, and mechanics running out to guide me in. All over the ground below there are clusters of lights. Large clusters are cities; small ones, towns and villages; pin points are buildings on a farm. I can image that I'm looking through the earth to the heavens on the other side. Paris will be a great galaxy lighting up the night.

Within the hour I'll land, and strangely enough I'm in no hurry to have it pass. I haven't the slightest desire to sleep. My eyes are no longer salted stones. There's not an ache in my body. The night is cool and safe. I want to sit quietly in this cockpit and let the realization of my completed flight sink in. Europe is below; Paris, just over the earth's curve in the night ahead—a few minutes more of flight. It's like struggling up a mountain after a rare flower, and then, when you have it within arm's reach, realizing that satisfaction and happiness lie more in the finding than the plucking. Plucking and withering are inseparable. I want to prolong this culminating experience of my flight. I almost wish Paris were a few more hours away. It's a shame to land with the night so clear and so much fuel in my tanks.

I'm still flying at four thousand feet when I see it, that scarcely perceptible glow, as though the moon had rushed ahead of schedule. Paris is rising over the edge of the earth. It's almost thirty-three hours from my take-off on Long Island. As minutes pass, myriad pin points of light emerge, a patch of starlit earth under a starlit sky—the lamps of Paris—straight lines of lights, curving lines of lights, squares of lights, black spaces in between. Gradually avenues, parks, and buildings take outline form; and there, far below, a little offset from the center, is a column of lights pointing upward, changing angles as I fly—the Eiffel Tower. I circle once above it, and turn northeastward toward Le Bourget. . . .

Four fifty-two on the clock. That's 9:52, Paris time. Le Bourget isn't shown on my map. No one I talked to back home had more than a general idea of its location. "It's a big airport," I was told. "You can't miss it. Just fly northeast from the city." So I penciled a circle on my map, about where Le Bourget ought to be; and now the *Spirit of St. Louis* is over the outskirts of Paris, pointed toward the center of that circle. . . .

7-B MILITARY DEVELOPMENTS

There was a marked change in American military thinking during the years from 1898 to 1933. Two major wars were fought, and military strategy was changed by them. Bases were set up in widely scattered parts of the world. It appeared likely that, if war came again, it would involve the United States with other countries as allies. The American people began to wonder about the proper relationship between their armed forces and the rest of American society.

PROBLEMS: *In what ways did American wartime experience change the country's viewpoint toward its armed forces? In what ways did a changing industrial and technological world influence thinking about the armed forces?*

1. One of the world's most influential military thinkers was an American naval officer, Alfred Thayer Mahan. Mahan was best known as a writer and thinker about naval history, and about the place of naval power in national defense forces. Mahan's ideas influenced many Americans and foreigners as well in planning their naval forces. The following extract from his writings was published shortly before the War with Spain.

Indications are not wanting of an approaching change in the thoughts and policy of Americans as to their relations with the world outside their own borders. For the past quarter of a century, the predominant idea, which has asserted itself successfully at the polls and shaped the course of the Government, has been to preserve the home market for the home industries. The employer and the workman alike have been taught to look at the various economical measures proposed from this point of view, to regard with hostility any step favoring the intrusion of the foreign producer upon their own domain, and rather to demand increasingly rigorous measures of exclusion than to acquiesce in any loosening of the chain that binds the consumer to them. The inevitable consequence has followed, as in all cases when the mind or the eye is exclusively fixed in one direction, that the danger of loss or the prospect of advantage in another quarter has been overlooked; and although the abounding resources of the country have maintained the exports at a high figure, this flattering result has been due more to the superabundant bounty of Nature than to the demand of other nations for our protected manufactures.

For nearly the lifetime of a generation, therefore, American industries have been thus protected, until the practice has assumed the force of a tradition, and is clothed in the mail of conservatism. In their mutual relations, these industries resemble the activities of a modern ironclad that has heavy armor, but inferior engines and guns; mighty for defense, weak for offense. Within, the home market is secured; but outside, beyond the broad seas, there are the markets of the world, that can be entered and controlled only by a vigorous contest, to which the habit of trusting to protection by statute does not conduce.

At bottom, however, the temperament of the American people is essentially alien to such a sluggish attitude. Independently of all bias for or against protection, it is safe to predict that, when the opportunities for gain abroad are understood, the course of American enterprise will cleave a channel by which to reach them. . . .

The interesting and significant feature of this changing attitude is the turning of the eyes outward, instead of inward only, to seek the welfare of the country. To affirm the importance of distant markets, and the relation to them of our own immense powers of production, implies logically the recognition of the link that joins the products and the markets—that is, the carrying trade; the three together constituting that chain of maritime power to which Great Britain owes her wealth and greatness. Further, is it too much to say that, as two of these links, the shipping and the markets, are exterior to our own borders, the acknowledgment of them carries with it a view of the relations of the United States to the world radically distinct from the simple idea of self-sufficingness? We shall not follow far this line of thought before there will dawn the realization of America's unique position, facing the older worlds of the East and West, her shores washed by the oceans which touch the one or the other, but which are common to her alone.

Coincident with these signs of change in our own policy there is restlessness in the world at large which is deeply significant, if not ominous. It is beside our purpose to dwell upon the internal state of Europe, whence, if disturbances arise, the effect upon us may be but partial and indirect. But the great seaboard powers there do not stand on guard against their continental rivals only; they cherish also aspirations for commercial extension, for colonies, and for influence in distant regions, which may bring, and, even under our present contracted policy, already have brought them into collision with ourselves. The incident of the Samoa Islands, trivial apparently, was nevertheless eminently suggestive of European ambitions. America then roused from sleep as to interests closely concerning her future. At this moment internal troubles are imminent in the Sandwich Islands, where it shold be our fixed determination to allow no foreign influence to equal our own. All over the world German commercial and colonial push is coming into collision with other nations. . . .

There is no sound reason for believing that the world

has passed into a period of assured peace outside the limits of Europe. Unsettled political conditions, such as exist in Haiti, Central America, and many of the Pacific Islands, especially the Hawaiian group, when combined with great military or commercial importance as is the case with most of these positions, involve, now as always, dangerous germs of quarrel, against which it is prudent at least to be prepared. Undoubtedly, the general temper of nations is more averse from war than it was of old. If no less selfish and grasping than our predecessors, we feel more dislike to the discomforts and sufferings attendant upon a breach of peace; but to retain that highly valued repose and the undisturbed enjoyment of the returns of commerce, it is necessary to argue upon somewhat equal terms of strength with an adversary. It is the preparedness of the enemy, and not acquiescence in the existing state of things, that now holds back the armies of Europe.

On the other hand, neither the sanctions of international law nor the justice of a cause can be depended upon for a fair settlement of differences, when they come into conflict with a strong political necessity on the one side opposed to comparative weakness on the other. In our still pending dispute over the seal-fishing of Bering Sea, whatever may be thought of the strength of our argument in view of generally admitted principles of international law, it is beyond doubt that our contention is reasonable, just, and in the interest of the world at large. But in the attempt to enforce it we have come into collision not only with national susceptibilities as to the honor of the flag, which we ourselves very strongly share, but also with a state governed by a powerful necessity, and exceedingly strong where we are particularly weak and exposed. Not only has Great Britain a mighty navy and we a long defenseless seacoast, but it is a great commercial and political advantage to her that her larger colonies, and above all Canada, should feel that the power of the mother country is something which they need, and upon which they can count. . . . Whatever arrangement of this question is finally reached, the fruit of Lord Salisbury's attitude scarcely can fail to be a strengthening of the sentiments of attachment to, and reliance upon, the mother country, not only in Canada, but in the other great colonies. These feelings of attachment and mutual dependence supply the living spirit, without which the nascent schemes for imperial federation are but dead mechanical contrivances; nor are they without influence upon such generally unsentimental considerations as those of buying and selling, and the course of trade.

This dispute . . . may serve to convince us of many latent and yet unforeseen dangers to the peace of the western hemisphere, attendant upon the opening of a canal through the Central American Isthmus. In a general way, it is evident enough that this canal, by modifying the direction of trade routes, will induce a great increase of commercial activity and carrying trade throughout the Caribbean Sea; and that this now comparatively deserted nook of the ocean will become like the Red Sea, a great thoroughfare of shipping, and will attract, as never before in our day, the interest and ambition of maritime nations. Every position in that sea will have enhanced commercial and military value, and the canal itself will become a strategic centre of the most vital importance. Like the Canadian Pacific Railroad, it will be a link between the two oceans; but, unlike it, the use, unless most carefully guarded by treaties, will belong wholly to the belligerent which controls the sea by its naval power. In case of war, the United States will unquestionably command the Canadian Railroad, despite the deterrent force of operations by the hostile navy upon our seaboard; but no less unquestionably will she be impotent, as against any of the great maritime powers, to control the Central American canal. Militarily speaking, and having reference to European complications only, the piercing of the Isthmus is nothing but a disaster to the United States, in the present state of her military and naval preparation. It is especially dangerous to the Pacific coast; but the increased exposure of one part of our seaboard reacts unfavorably upon the whole military situation.

Despite a certain great original superiority conferred by our geographical nearness and immense resources—due, in other words, to our natural advantages, and not to our intelligent preparations—the United States is woefully unready, not only in fact but in purpose to assert in the Caribbean and Central America a weight of influence proportioned to the extent of her interests. We have not the navy, and, what is worse, we are not willing to have the navy, that will weigh seriously in any disputes with those nations whose interests will conflict there with our own. We have not, and we are not anxious to provide, the defense of the seaboard which will leave the navy free for its work at sea. We have not, but many other powers have, positions, either within or on the borders of the Caribbean which not only possess great natural advantages for the control of that sea, but have received and are receiving that artificial strength of fortification and armament which will make them practically inexpugnable. On the contrary, we have not on the Gulf of Mexico even the beginning of a navy yard which could serve as the base of our operations.

Let me not be misunderstood. I am not regretting that we have not the means to meet on terms of equality the great navies of the Old World. I recognize, what few at least say, that despite its great surplus revenue, this country is poor in proportion to its length of seaboard and its exposed points. That which I deplore, and which is a sober, just, and reasonable cause of deep national concern is that the nation neither has nor cares to have its sea frontier so defended, and its navy of such power, as shall suffice, with the advantages of our position, to weigh seriously when inevitable discussions arise—such as we have recently had about Samoa and Bering Sea, and which may at any moment come up about the Caribbean Sea or the canal. Is the United States, for instance, prepared to allow Germany to acquire the Dutch stronghold of Curaçao, fronting the Atlantic outlet of both the proposed canals of Panama and Nicaragua? Is she prepared to acquiesce in any foreign power purchasing from Haiti a naval station on the Windward Passage, through which pass our steamer routes to the Isthmus? Would she acquiesce in a foreign protectorate over the Sandwich Island, that great central station of the Pacific, equidistant from San Francisco, Samoa, and the Marquesas, and an important post on our line of communication with both Australia and China? Or will it be maintained that any one of these questions, supposing it to arise, is so exclusively one-sided, the arguments of policy and right so exclusively with us, that the other party will at once yield his eager wish, and gracefully withdraw? Was it so at Samoa? Is it so as regards the Bering Sea? The motto on so many ancient cannon, *Ultima ratio regum*, is not without its message to republics.

It is perfectly reasonable and legitimate, in estimating our needs of military preparation, to take into account the remoteness of the chief naval and military nations from our shores, and the consequent difficulty of maintaining operations at such a distance. It is equally proper, in framing our policy, to consider the jealousies of the European family of states, and their consequent unwillingness to incur the enmity of a people so strong as ourselves; their dread of our revenge in the future, as well as their inability to detach more than a certain part of their forces to our shores without losing much of their own weight in the councils of Europe. In truth, a careful determination of the force that Great Britain or France could probably spare for operations against our coasts, if the latter were suitably defended, without weakening their European position or unduly exposing their colonies and commerce, is the starting-point from which to calculate the strength of our own navy. . . .

Though distant, our shores can be reached; being defenseless, they can detain but a short time a force sent against them. With a probability of three months' peace in Europe, no maritime power would fear to support its demands by a number of ships with which it would be loath indeed to part for a year.

Yet, were our sea frontier as strong as it now is weak, passive self-defense, whether in trade or war, would be but a poor policy, so long as this world continues to be one of struggle and vicissitude. All around us now is strife; "the struggle of life," "the race of life," are phrases so familiar that we do not feel their significance till we stop to think about them. Everywhere nation is arrayed against nation; our own no less than others. What is our protective system but an organized warfare? In carrying it on, it is true, we have only to use certain procedures which all states now concede to be a legal exercise of the national power, even though injurious to themselves. It is lawful, they say, to do what we will with our own. Are our people, however, so unaggressive that they are likely not to want their own way in matters where their interests turn on points of disputed right, or so little sensitive as to submit quietly to encroachment by others in quarters where they long have considered their own influence should prevail?

Our self-imposed isolation in the matter of markets, and the decline of our shipping interest in the last thirty years, have coincided singularly with an actual remoteness of this continent from the life of the rest of the world. . . .

When the Isthmus is pierced, this isolation will pass away, and with it the indifference of foreign nations. From wheresoever they come and whithersoever they afterward go, all ships that use the canal will pass through the Caribbean. Whatever the effect produced upon the prosperity of the adjacent continent and islands by the thousand wants attendant upon maritime activity, around such a focus of trade will centre large commercial and political interests. To protect and develop its own, each nation will seek points of support and means of influence in a quarter where the United States always has been jealously sensitive to the intrusion of European powers. The precise value of the Monroe Doctrine is understood very loosely by most Americans, but the effect of the familiar phrase has been to develop a national sensitiveness, which is a more frequent cause of war than material interests; and over disputes caused by such feelings there will preside none of the calming influence due to the moral authority of international law, with its recognized principles, for the points in dispute will be of policy, of interest, not of conceded right. Already France and Great Britain are giving to ports held by them a degree of artificial strength uncalled for by their present importance. They look to the near future. Among the islands and on the mainland there are many positions of great importance, held now by weak or unstable states. Is the United States willing to see them sold to a powerful rival? But what right will she invoke against the transfer? She can allege but

one, that of her reasonable policy supported by her might.

2. During the War with Spain (1898), the Navy played a brilliant part. Naval victories over Spanish fleets in the Philippine Islands and in Cuba made victory in the war certain. Mahan's viewpoint seemed to have been justified.

The victory in the Philippines at Manila Bay was reported by George Dewey, who commanded the squadron there, as follows:

HONGKONG, *May 7, 1898.* (Manila, May 1.) SECRETARY OF THE NAVY, *Washington*:

THE squadron arrived at Manila at daybreak this morning. Immediately engaged enemy and destroyed the following Spanish vessels: *Reina Christina, Castillia, Don Antonio de Ulloa, Don Juan de Austria, Isla de Luzon, Isla de Cuba, General Lezo, Marques del Duero, El Correo, Velasco,* one transport *Isla de Mandano,* water battery at Cavite. I shall destroy Cavite arsenal dispensatory. The squadron is uninjured. Few men were slightly wounded. I request the Department will send immediately from San Francisco fast steamer with ammunition. The only means of telegraphing is to the American consul at Hongkong.

DEWEY.

U.S. NAVAL FORCE ON ASIATIC STATION, *Flagship Olympia, Cavite, Philippine Islands, May 4, 1898.*

SIR: I have the honor to submit the following report of the operations of the squadron under my command:

The squadron left Mirs Bay on April 27, immediately on the arrival of Mr. O. F. Williams, United States consul at Manila, who brought important information and who accompanies the squadron.

Arrived off Bolinao on the morning of April 30 and, finding no vessels there, proceeded down the coast and arrived off the entrance to Manila Bay on the same afternoon. . . .

Entered the Boca Grande, or south channel, at 11.30 p.m., steaming in column at distance at 8 knots. After half the squadron had passed, a battery on the south side of the channel opened fire, none of the shots taking effect. The *Boston* and *McCulloch* returned the fire.

The squadron proceeded across the bay at slow speed, and arrived off Manila at daybreak, and was fired upon at 5.15 a.m. by three batteries at Manila and two at Cavite and by the Spanish fleet anchored in an approximately east and west line across the mouth of Bakor Bay, with their left in shoal water in Canacao Bay.

The squadron then proceeded to the attack, the flagship *Olympia*, under my personal direction, leading, followed at distance by the *Baltimore, Raleigh, Petrel, Concord,* and *Boston,* in the order named, which formation was maintained throughout the action. The squadron opened fire at 5.41 a.m. While advancing to the attack, two mines were exploded ahead of the flagship, too far to be effective.

The squadron maintained a continuous and precise fire at ranges varying from 5,000 to 2,000 yards, countermarching in a line approximately parallel to that of the Spanish fleet. The enemy's fire was vigorous, but generally ineffective.

Early in the engagement two launches put out toward the *Olympia* with the apparent intention of using torpedoes. One was sunk and the other disabled by our fire and beached before an opportunity occurred to fire torpedoes. At 7 a.m. the Spanish flagship *Reina Christina* made a desperate attempt to leave the line and come out to engage at short range, but was received with such galling fire, the entire battery of the *Olympia* being concentrated upon her, that she was barely able to return to the shelter of the point. The fires started in her by our shell at this time were not extinguished until she sank.

At 7.35 a.m., it having been erroneously reported to me that only 15 rounds per gun remained for the 5-inch rapid-fire battery, I ceased firing and withdrew the squadron for consultation and a redistribution of ammunition, if necessary.

The three batteries at Manila had kept up a continuous fire from the beginning of the engagement, which fire was not returned by this squadron. The first of these batteries was situated on the south mole head at the entrance to the Pasig River, the second on the south bastion of the walled city of Manila, and the third at Malate, about one-half mile farther south. At this point I sent a message to the Governor-General to the effect that if the batteries did not cease firing the city would be shelled. This had the effect of silencing them.

At 11.16 a.m., finding that the report of scarcity of ammunition was incorrect, I returned with the squadron to the attack. By this time the flagship and almost the entire Spanish fleet were in flames, and at 12.30 p.m. the squadron ceased firing, the batteries being silenced and the ships sunk, burnt, and deserted.

At 12.40 p.m. the squadron returned and anchored off Manila, the *Petrel* being left behind to complete the destruction of the smaller gunboats, which were behind the point of Cavite. This duty was performed by

Commander E. P. Wood in the most expeditious and complete manner possible.

The Spanish lost the following vessels:

Sunk—*Reina Christina, Castilla, Don Antonio de Ulloa.*

Burnt—*Don Juan de Austria, Isla de Luzon, Isla de Cuba, General Lezo, Marques del Duero, El Correo, Velasco,* and *Isla de Mindanao* (transport).

Captured—*Rapido* and *Hercules* (tugs) and several small launches.

I am unable to obtain complete accounts of the enemy's killed and wounded, but believe their loss to be very heavy. The *Reina Christina* alone had 150 killed, including the captain, and 90 wounded.

I am happy to report that the damage done to the squadron under my command was inconsiderable. There were none killed, and only 7 men in the squadron very slightly wounded. As will be seen by the reports of the commanding officers which are herewith inclosed, several of the vessels were struck and even penetrated, but the damage was of the slightest, and the squadron is in as good condition now as before the battle. . . .

On May 2, the day following the engagement, the squadron again went to Cavite, where it remains. . . . On the 3d the military forces evacuated the Cavite Arsenal, which was taken possession of by a landing party. On the same day the *Raleigh* and *Baltimore* secured the surrender of the batteries on Corregidor Island, paroling the garrison and destroying the guns. . . .

3. The Spanish-American War involved land actions as well as sea battles. Ashore, although American arms were successful, the results were not at all so one-sided as they appeared at first. Many correspondents covered this war for newspapers in the United States and in other countries. Richard Harding Davis, one of America's best known newspapermen, recorded some of his observations in his private letters. Here are two letters to his brother describing conditions in the Army base at Tampa, Florida.

TAMPA—May 14, 1898.

DEAR CHAS.

On reflection I am greatly troubled that I declined the captaincy. It is unfortunate that I had not time to consider it. We shall not have another war and I can always be a war correspondent in other countries but never again have a chance to serve in my own. The people here think it was the right thing to do but the outside people won't. Not that I care about that, but I think I was weak not to chance it.

I don't know exactly what I ought to do. When I see all these kid militia men enlisted it makes me feel like the devil. I've no doubt many of them look upon it as a sort of a holiday and an outing and like it for the excitement, but it would bore me to death. The whole thing would bore me if I thought I had to keep at it for a year or more. That is the fault of my having had too much excitement and freedom. It spoils me to make sacrifices that other men can make. Whichever way it comes out I shall be sorry and feel I did not do the right thing. Lying around this hotel is enough to demoralize anybody. We are much more out of it than you are, and one gets cynical and loses interest. On the other hand I would be miserable to go back and have done nothing. It is a question of character entirely and I don't feel I've played the part at all. It's all very well to say you are doing more by writing, but are you? It's an easy game to look on and pat the other chaps on the back with a few paragraphs, that is cheap patriotism. They're taking chances and you're not and when the war's over they'll be happy and I won't. The man that enlists or volunteers even if he doesn't get further than Chickamauga or Gretna Green and the man who doesn't enlist at all but minds his own business is much better off than I will be writing about what other men do and not doing it myself, especially as I had a chance of a life time, and declined it. I'll always feel I lost in character by not sticking to it whether I had to go to Arizona or Governor's Island. I was unfortunate in having Lee and Remington to advise me. We talked for two hours in Fred's bedroom and they were both dead against it and Lee composed my telegram to the president. Now, I feel sure I did wrong. Shafter did not care and the other officers were delighted and said it was very honorable and manly giving me credit for motives I didn't have. I just didn't think it was good enough although I wanted it too and I missed something I can never get again. I am very sad about it. I know all the argument for not taking it but as a matter of fact I should have done so. I would have made a good aide, and had I got a chance I certainly would have won out and been promoted. That there are fools appointed with me is no answer. I wouldn't have stayed in their class long.

DICK.

TAMPA, May 29, 1898.

DEAR CHAS.:

The cigars came; they are O. K. and a great treat after Tampa products. Captain Lee and I went out to the volunteer camps today: Florida, Alabama, Ohio and Michigan, General Lee's push, and it has depressed me very much. I have been so right about so many things these last five years, and was laughed at for making much of them. Now all I urged is proved to be correct; nothing our men wear is right. The shoes, the hats, the coats, all are dangerous to health and comfort; one-third of the men cannot wear the regulation shoe because it cuts the instep, and buy their own, and the volunteers are like the Cuban army in appearance. The Greek army, at which I made such sport, is a fine organization in comparison as far as outfit goes; of course, there is no comparison in the spirit of the men. One colonel of the Florida regiment told us that one-third of his men had never fired a gun. They live on the ground; there are no rain trenches around the tents, or gutters along the company streets; the latrines are dug to *windward* of the camp, and all the refuse is burned to windward.

Half of the men have no uniforms nor shoes. I pointed out some of the unnecessary discomforts the men were undergoing through ignorance, and one colonel, a Michigan politician, said, "Oh, well, they'll learn. It will be a good lesson for them." Instead of telling them, or telling their captains, he thinks it best that they should find things out by suffering. I cannot decide whether to write anything about it or not. I cannot see where it could do any good, for it is the system that is wrong—the whole volunteer system, I mean. Captain Lee happened to be in Washington when the first Manila outfit was starting from San Francisco, and it was on his representations that they gave the men hammocks, and took a store of Mexican dollars. They did not know that Mexican dollars are the only currency of the East, and were expecting to pay the men in drafts on New York. Isn't that a pitiable situation when a captain of an English company happens to stray into the war office, and happens to have a good heart and busies himself to see that our own men are supplied with hammocks and spending money. None of our officers had ever seen khaki until they saw Lee's, nor a cork helmet until they saw mine and his; now, naturally, they won't have anything else, and there is not another one in the country. The helmets our troops wear would be smashed in one tropical storm, and they are so light that the sun beats through them. They are also a glaring white, and are cheap and nasty and made of pasteboard. The felt hats are just as bad; the brim is not broad enough to protect them from the sun or to keep the rain off their necks, and they are made of such cheap cotton stuff that they grow hard when they are wet and heavy, instead of shedding the rain as good felt would do. They have always urged that our uniforms, though not smart nor "for show," were for use. The truth is, as they all admit, that for the tropics they are worse than useless, and that in any climate they are cheap and poor.

I could go on for pages, but it has to be written later; now they would only think it was an attack on the army. But it is sickening to see men being sacrificed as these men will be. This is the worst season of all in the Philippines. The season of typhoons and rainstorms and hurricanes, and they would have sent the men off without anything to sleep on but the wet ground and a wet blanket. It has been a great lesson for me, and I have rubber tents, rubber blankets, rubber coats and hammocks enough for an army corps. I have written nothing for the paper, because, if I started to tell the truth at all, it would do no good, and it would open up a hell of an outcry from all the families of the boys who have volunteered. Of course, the only answer is a standing army of a hundred thousand, and no more calling on the patriotism of men unfitted and untrained. It is the sacrifice of the innocents. The incompetence and unreadiness of the French in 1870 was no worse than our own is now. It is a terrible and pathetic spectacle, and the readiness of the volunteers to be sacrificed is all the more pathetic. It seems almost providential that we had this false-alarm call with Spain to show the people how utterly helpless they are.

With love,

DICK.

4. *John Black Atkins, a British war correspondent, representing the* Manchester Guardian, *accompanied the American troops in Cuba. In the following passage, he describes part of the attack on Santiago. While his description concentrated on the fighting phase of the Army's activity, his comments about planning and fire control help bear out Davis' criticisms.*

ABOUT five o'clock on the evening of Sunday, July 10, began what is known as the second bombardment. The firing was desultory, and almost entirely on the American side. . . .

When I awoke the next morning the first thing I saw was a new regiment of volunteers just come to the front, with the sunlight aslant on their faces. They all expected to receive their baptism of fire that day; their friends rallied them on the expectation, and they on their side replied facetiously. After the first sunlight came a dullness over the whole sky, so that the day was like night sick—to reverse Shakespere's phrase. A mist still lay over part of Santiago; everything was still, and dead, and wet, and silent; the leaves of the palms seemed as though they must fall for every heaviness. Perhaps the valley was never more strangely rich and beautiful.

A shell came up from the American fleet, fired blindly at a range of over 8,000 yards, and plunged with a shrill cry into the mist; we could not see it burst. The American artillery was now a little stronger than on July 1. To the sixteen guns with which the fighting had begun eight mortars had been added and were now in position. But I heard an officer say that the ammunition for them could be fired away in half an hour with only four mortars in use. The siege guns which came with the first expedition had never been taken off the ships. General Randolph, who had lately arrived with General Miles, brought with him six batteries, and some of these guns were at the front and some were on their way there, but apparently none had yet been put in position. The artillery was of course delayed by the badness of the roads. When I left the front for the last time some of General Randolph's guns were still stuck in a mud pool. The engineers appeared to do little. Where were they? Were they all building permanent forts in the United States? Of the brooks that one crossed on the ordinary route between General Shafter's headquarters and the front not one was bridged over; one would think that with so much timber handy they could have been bridged at about the rate of one an hour. As it was, waggons sometimes overturned in them, and soldiers who had to wade through them were made unnecessarily wet.

The American intention was to surround the city as nearly as possible by extending the right of the line till it reached beyond the end of the harbour. Most of the infantry firing was in that direction, and for this reason General Lawton's division was strengthened by the transference to it of a brigade from General Kent's division. As on the previous evening, the firing was slight; the most active guns of all were those of the Rough Riders. Perhaps there never were volunteers who went about their business with greater zest than these, or who learned more in so short a time. Not content with the amount of ordinary artillery, they carried about with them quick-firing guns as a kind of personal equipment. Someone had presented this Colt to the regiment, someone else that Gatling, others had bought among them the dynamite gun. Sometimes there was a noise exactly like rapping on a door—that was one of the Colts at work; sometimes there was a noise like the grinding of coffee—that was one of the Gatlings.

One of these nights I spent in the Rough Riders' camp. The men in the trenches were like men out for a holiday; their chief characteristic was a habit of cheering on every possible occasion; they used to cheer when they went into the trenches, and cheer when they came out; they used to cheer when there was food, but also when there was no food. The camp used to laugh for hours over some quite silly joke, which seemed at the time to be mightily amusing and witty, and afterwards it would turn out that it was only that the silliness had been opportune. It was vastly amusing, for example, to hear a certain officer, whose name had incessantly to be repeated, spoken of as General Mango, or another officer spoken of as Lieutenant-Colonel Cocoanut. These light-hearted people did as much firing as they were allowed to do with the quick-firing instruments which one had come to look upon almost as their playthings. The dynamite gun was not fired very often, because it used to become jammed, but everybody loved it as a great big expensive toy. The firing string was not very long—not longer than that of an ordinary field-piece—but, as the operator used to explain, if the gun blew up you were no better off fifty yards away than five. When the gun was fired there was very little noise —only the sound of a rocket; but when the shell exploded there was a tremendous detonation. It was said that everything near the explosion was devastated. In one case a Spanish gun and a tree were seen to be hurled bodily into the air. It was my singular misfortune, however, to find no traces of the devastation done by this terrible instrument.

Colonel Roosevelt, the lieutenant-colonel of the Rough Riders, since elected Governor of New York, was a man who impressed one. He is the typical strong man, with the virtues and defects of the strong man; creating opposition and making enemies, but in the end beating down in his own direct, honest, didactic way the opposition which he himself has created, and turning, often, into friends the enemies whom he himself has made. So that in every adventure he almost inevitably—to use the expressive American phrase—'gets there.' The impulse of which he is capable was illustrated by his sudden resignation of his Assistant Secretaryship to the Navy to command this whimsical, gallant regiment. The Rough Riders were the devotees of his person.

All the morning of July 11 the bombardment was a half-hearted affair. Neither side left its trenches. At noon General Toral, who had succeeded General Linares, sent out a flag of truce saying that he would meet General Miles personally in conference the next day. With the flag the firing ceased, and, as all the world knows, never began again.

5. *When the United States entered World War I, one of the major problems was to provide safe passage across the Atlantic to France for the troops who would fight against the Germans. This operation was complicated by the numbers of men and ships needed, and was endangered by submarines. The passage that follows describes the transatlantic movement of the 42nd Division.*

It is from an article by Captain (later Admiral) Yates Sterling, who was in charge of the convoy. The article appeared in the issue of U.S. Naval Institute Proceedings *for September, 1925.*

The embarking of the troops at Hoboken (*aboard the transport vessels*) was a very drab business. The ships were ready but neither the material nor the personnel had been given a trial in feeding and housing such an enormous number of men. In fact, in all of the ships many dock-yard workmen were on board until the last gangway was put ashore. The commissary department, led by the most experienced naval paymasters, but padded out with many raw recruits, could only imagine how it was to be done. Many of the soldiers were to catch sight of the ocean for the first time. German propaganda had insinuated the subconscious belief, not at all borne out by conscious reasoning, that the ocean was as thickly strewn with submarines and mines as Fifth Avenue with automobiles, or Broadway with chorus girls. One could hear the troops talking in low tones at night, fearing to raise their voices above a whisper.

The convoy sailed at night. No white lights of any kind were lighted except in the engine and fire rooms, and below decks where it was sure lights could not be seen from outside. In other localities where it was necessary for some illumination, in order to regulate troop traffic, pale blue lights were used which gave a gruesome and none too cheerful aspect to the moist and hot berthing spaces below decks, crowded to the ceiling with men.

The ships were untried. The personnel were in great part composed of men who knew but little of life at sea. Even the old timers were unfamiliar with the present conditions made necessary by war. It was imperative immediately upon leaving port to form the convoy. Big ships maneuvered at close distance to each other and at almost full speed. The captains and the principal officers engaged in this difficult maneuver for the first time. Captains remained on or near the navigating bridge at all times. The safety of their ships lay heavy on their minds.

Once on the ocean and in the broad white light of day much of the unreasoned fears passed. It was a long way to longitude 20 W, where the submarines began their piratical work and the convoy would require eight days at least to arrive within the danger zone.

There were many things to be done. The organization so carefully worked over by the executive officers for taking care of the troops had to be frequently tested, amended, and again tried until everything was as good as could be made. One important change was made in the abandon ship method. An attempt had been made in the organization to assign specified men to definitely located rafts or boats. This was all thrown out and the troops under their officers were formed instead on the upper open decks in groups of seventy-five or one hundred and merely told when the order to abandon ship was given to use the nearest jacob ladders and life lines plentifully provided and just "step into the water," where life rafts would be plentifully provided. The temperature of the water at that time was about 45° Fahrenheit; however, later, off the coast of France, it was only about 50°.

The navy crews were made as large as berthing facilities allowed, but there was so much work to be done that many additional details were given to the Army; guards at boat drills, magazine guards, and so forth. Of course, all troop spaces were policed and guarded by the Army.

Brigadier General Chas. P. Summerall, commanding the 67th Field Artillery Brigade, was the commanding officer of troops on the *Lincoln* (*the liner President Lincoln*). His one idea seemed to be to help the Navy in their new work. He appreciated the shortage of skilled men and said to the commanding officer, "Captain, in our outfit, we have every known trade; we've even got sailors if you need them." That ship used soldiers freely.

The convoy sailed in line-abreast formation and, at night, with no lights showing. When the moon was obscured the next ship abreast could be seen as a deeper shadow in the gloom unless by chance she edged in too close and then to the captain and officer of the deck she loomed like a mountain too near for comfort. On the other hand, if the end ships were kept too wide they were liable to lose touch entirely during darkness and at daylight be miles ahead or miles astern of the formation. In the beginning careful routing of convoys was difficult, especially as the ocean was fairly full of neutral shipping. Often a tramp steamer would find itself heading through a convoy at night. Its actions would at once reflect the coolness of the man on the tramp's bridge. It might be expected to charge down one way, then change its mind and come charging back another way. It went without saying that troopships took no chances; they discounted brains on the bridge of the tramp and gave him a wide berth. Then there was the danger of running pell-mell into a big merchant convoy on a converging course, especially nearing the coast of France. Then quick action by the convoy commander of the fast troopships was required to avoid a mishap.

Every man of the artillery brigade carried by the *President Lincoln* will doubtlessly not soon forget, even after his hazardous service at the front in France, the two hours that vessel was stopped in the war zone, east of longitude 20°, to repair a disabled air pump. The troops were all at their abandon ship stations with life preservers adjusted. The gun crews were alert, and all lookouts on their toes to discover a periscope. The rest of the convoy swept on and quickly disappeared beyond the horizon. A lone destroyer remained, circling about the huge vessel at high speed. The two hours seemed an eternity to those in authority. Possibly there was not a submarine within a hundred miles, yet one might have been near enough to make an attack and, if so, 6,000-odd men would have been set adrift five hundred miles from land, mostly on life rafts to which they could only cling, and with the water temperature 50°. There were six destroyers altogether guarding the convoy. If all six performed rescue work they could not accommodate with standing room all of the shipwrecked men on this one big ship, and to perform this act of mercy, they must desert the remainder of the convoy they were guarding and seek port at full speed.

Just before this convoy arrived at St. Nazaire, the entrance to the River Loire was mined by an enemy submarine, so the convoy was conducted by a circuitous route, through tortuous channels and between menacing rocks to a point inside of the mined area.

The little French pilot boarded the ship and received a cordial welcome from the happy troops. The atmosphere of constraint suddenly disappeared as the big convoy entered the sheltered waters of Quiberon Bay and they were anxious to let off steam that had been bottled up for two weeks. The regimental bands played with a renewed vigor. Everybody was happy. The submarines had been fooled.

At the entrance to the river a thick blanket of fog was encountered. To the westward was the open sea and only a short distance away the mine field. The pilot said, shrugging expressive shoulders, "I cannot see the buoy, therefore we must stop and anchor." Six loaded transports awaited the finding of that buoy. Meanwhile, worse luck, the guarding destroyers considering their duty completed had all turned northward and had disappeared in the fog. They had other convoys to protect.

It is not a pleasant feeling to poke the big blunt bow of a 20,000-ton liner into a fog to find a tiny buoy surrounded on all sides by treacherous rocks, shoals, and enemy mines, and amidst the strongest known currents; but, on the other hand, there was the necessity to anchor in that dangerous locality six ships carrying 20,000 men. One submarine might, by some evil streak of devil's luck, sink all of them and on the threshold of France.

"There's the buoy!" Everyone seemed to understand the importance of keeping that buoy in sight. Night was fast falling but once within the headlands of the river, the fog melted. Up the river the convoy steamed and the biggest turned in toward the locks in order to enter at the top of the tide. "How long are you?" asked the pilot of the captain of the biggest ship, while that ship was entering the lock. When told, the pilot looked serious for a few minutes, apparently calculating. "It's all right," he finally announced; "there's ten feet to spare." It was the largest ship that had ever entered that locked harbor. The captain was confident all the time that the all-knowing ones at home had made sure of the fit—yet it was none too much to spare.

Sunny France was in tears on the arrival of the convoy but the populace were out in full force to welcome the troops. There was no more soul-stirring sight than those six huge ships loaded down with khaki-clad men, their white faces gleaming in the flood of great cargo and illuminating lights on the docks, passing each other close aboard as one after another was docked into the small harbor and berthed alongside the piers. Bands were playing "Over There," "It's a Long Long Trail," "Keep the Home Fires Burning," and so forth. Each ship, as it entered the harbor, cheered those it passed, until there was a continuous roar of young American voices mingled with stirring music and song. The rain, an insidious French drizzle, could not dampen the soldiers' spirits.

They were "over there"!

6. *After the "Great War" ended in Europe, the armed forces underwent a great contraction. Men left the services for civilian life; military equipment ceased to enjoy a high priority in government budgeting. A disarmament treaty led to the destruction of many warships. One major debate developed among the military leaders of the country: what role should aviation play in the future of the armed forces of the United States? General William Mitchell had once commanded the American Army fliers in France; in peacetime, he became the spokesman for independent air power within the armed forces. When his viewpoint was rejected, Mitchell turned to the public, and published severe criticisms of his military superiors in such statements as the following (part of an article in* Aviation, *September, 1925). These became a basis for a court-martial that forced Mitchell out of the service, but permitted him to carry on his fight as a civilian.*

All aviation policies, schemes, and systems are dictated by the nonflying officers of the Army or Navy, who know practically nothing about it. The lives of the airmen are being used merely as pawns in their hands.

The great Congress of the United States, that makes laws for the organization and use of our air, land, and water forces, is treated by these two departments as if it were an organization created for their benefit, to which evidence of any kind, whether true or not, can be given without restraint. Officers and agents sent by the War and Navy departments to Congress have almost always given incomplete, miserable, or false information about aeronautics, which either they knew to be false when given or was the result of such gross ignorance of the question that they should not be allowed to appear before a legislative body.

The airmen themselves are bluffed and bulldozed so that they dare not tell the truth in the majority of cases, knowing full well that if they do they will be deprived of their future career, sent to the most out-of-the-way places to prevent their telling the truth, and deprived of any chance for advancement unless they subscribe to the dictates of their nonflying, bureaucratic superiors. These either distort facts or openly tell falsehoods about aviation to the people and to the Congress.

Both the War and Navy departments maintain public propaganda agencies which are supposed to publish truthful facts about our national defense to the American people. These departments, remember, are supported by the taxes of the people and were created for the purpose of protecting us from invasion from abroad and from domestic disturbances from within. What has actually happened in these departments is that they have formed a sort of union to perpetuate their own existence, and acting, as we might say about a commercial organization that has entire control of a public necessity, "as an illegal combination in restraint of trade."

The conduct of affairs by these two departments, as far as aviation is concerned, has been so disgusting in the last few years as to make any self-respecting person ashamed of the clothes he wears. Were it not for the patriotism of our air officers and their absolute confidence in the institutions of the United States, knowing that sooner or later existing conditions would be changed, I doubt if one of them would remain with the colors—certainly not if he were a real man. . . .

When I came back from the war in 1919, I attempted to get airships for the purpose of making them into airplane carriers. That is, having airplanes take off from them and land on them, so that they could get out in the middle of the ocean if necessary and attack hostile vessels in case of war. I obtained permission immediately from the then chief of staff, General March, and the then secretary of war, Secretary Baker. I sent Major Hensley to Europe with money to get the ships. We had even gone so far as to order the gasoline to Germany for the voyage of the ships to this country.

Mysteriously, the order was rescinded—all work was stopped—it was said at the time that it was against the provision of the treaty, which I do not believe was the case. Work had already been begun on the frames by the Germans. This was the ZR-2, rechristened the *Los Angeles*, which the Navy obtained recently, six years after I ordered it. What has it been used for? Nothing but parading around the country. It is evident that whenever a warship is developed as an airplane carrier, the necessity for any naval surface airplane carrier may be done away with. Is this the reason the Navy has the *Los Angeles*?

The Germans are the only people who have had real experience with airships. They had many a disaster before they learned how to handle them. I have seen German Zeppelins years ago in terrific storms. A storm has little effect on an airship properly constructed and ably handled. . . .

What is our Navy for? Presumably it is to control lines of sea communication on the high seas. What is it actually? It is entirely and completely outpointed by Great Britain in the Atlantic. When can it do across the Pacific as at present organized? Nothing—against an insular Asiatic power whom you all know.

The Navy has about $1.5 billion invested in navy yards. The upkeep and depreciation of these amount to about $150 million a year. How many of these are useless and how many of them are of any profit? Probably not many. Suppose we took $50 million of this and applied it to the development of aircraft and submarines under competent airmen and submarine men? What could we do with it?

Every time a battleship is built, the ship itself, when it is completed, may cost from $50 million to $75 million. It has to be protected by submarines, destroyers, cruisers, and aircraft, the total cost of which is around or over $100 million, so that every time a battleship is built, the expenditure of $100 million is necessary. I believe a battleship today is a useless element in the national defensive armament. . . .

Now, let us turn to the War Department. The War Department has done nothing this summer to develop air power and has undertaken to prove by tests that antiaircraft guns can protect cities, which is known everywhere to be false. They have fixed up a scheme to give

constructive hits when the guns firing do not hit the targets at all. The firing has been at targets towed at a constant altitude, over courses which have now been flown hundreds of times, at greatly reduced speeds and never in excess of 75 miles an hour. Even this was only because the wind was helping the plane along and under weather conditions that have been ideal. In spite of all this preparation, the results have been laughable.

As an example of one of these performances, the War Department has taken the lid off for publicity in the II Corps area—that means around New York—with the result that the Coast Artillery tells the papers the story in greatly exaggerated terms, whereas the chief of air service has been completely muzzled. An interesting example of some of the antiaircraft target practice was the testing of the listening device for aircraft at Camp Dix, July 27.

The umpire had told Captain Hall, commanding the airplane bombers at Mitchell Field, that in the next antiaircraft test he was at liberty to fly under conditions which would be used in war. Captain Hall informed the umpire ahead of time that he would glide into the target. Before this, the Coast Artillery had all their practice with planes that had flown over at a fairly constant altitude and with their motors open. The night of the test, planes got their proper altitude, played around a little just out of range of the searchlights and just within range of the listening devices on the ground. The artillery thought that this was easy because they picked up the planes far off and plotted their course absolutely, but all of a sudden sounds from the airplanes stopped. Five or ten minutes later, the bombers dropped their bombs directly on the target. All around not a sound had been heard before this.

The fury of the ground officers, artillery officers, and others was tremendous. The air service had not acted fair and had fooled them, all of which a kind enemy, of course, in war would never do. Discussion even went so far that it had to be pointed out that it was provided in our bombardment manual to attack a place in this fashion. This is only one instance of the ridiculous performance.

So far, practically the only bombardment airplanes we have in this country have been used up towing these targets for ground shooting, which other airplanes could just as well have done. The actual cost out of air service funds appropriated will be approximately $200,000 by the time they are completed this fall.

Why are things done this way? The Coast Artillery now has about ninety-two stations. For the ten years prior to 1920, about $2 billion were spent on coast defense—not $2 million, but $2 billion. What good are these coast defenses? None—except those in the immediate vicinity of large cities, where a submarine might emerge at close range and plant a few shells in the city.

What could the saving do on these useless expenditures if used by the troops of the mobile army stationed in Texas and other frontier points, living in shacks, unequipped with modern conveniences, cut down on every activity and rendered almost incapable, in case the Constitution is menaced, of putting down insurrections or executing the laws when all other means fail and patrolling our frontiers and holding our insular possessions—what would only a small part of this tremendous expenditure mean in the development of aircraft?

Not one heavy bomb has been dropped by the air service line units in target practice for two years. Only about four or five modern sights are on hand with the bombing groups, and today I, who know our personnel better than any living man, can only put my hand on two perfectly capable bombardment crews to handle our aircraft in case we are attacked.

The other thing that the War Department has done this summer is to study how the fliers' pay could be reduced or taken away from them. Think of it, the whole effort of the War Department during the summer was to fool the people into thinking that aircraft cannon are a protection and to keep the rightful flying pay away from the pilots.

To make a long story short, we are utterly disgusted with the conduct of our military affairs applying to aviation. Our pilots know they are going to be killed if they stay in the service, on account of the methods employed in the old flying coffins that we are still flying. Those pilots that still remain have held on so long that if they got out they would starve. They don't dare open their mouths and tell the truth because they and their families might be booted out to some obscure place. No finer body ever existed in the makeup of our country than these men. . . .

The Department of Aeronautics should be divided into three principal subdivisions, one charged with the development of civil aviation. This should provide for the airways throughout the country; the aids to air navigation, and provide an efficient weather service and storm warnings; a legal department to make recommendations about all our navigation laws, inspection of pilots and aircraft, so as to be sure the public is safeguarded when traveling or using aircraft. There should

also be formed an aeronautical corporation similar to our Inland Waterways Corporation, which should operate between the great centers of population so as to show what things could be carried safely and at a profit through the air. All figures on this should be made public, so that as soon as possible any civilian company desiring to take it over should be allowed to do so. At the present stage of the development of aeronautics, the government must assist, as all aeronautics is a national asset.

The second division should be a section of fabrication or construction. In this department, special studies should be made of the kind of aircraft that are necessary, of their airworthiness and safety. They should be made in accordance with the desires and wishes of the flying men, by experts, and thoroughly tried out before being issued. No aircraft should be built by the government. All should be built by civilian organizations so as to keep up competition, invention, and initiative by the people.

The third division should be the Air Force, that part specifically charged with the air defense of the whole country. Provision should be made for a suitable number of well-trained flying men and good airplanes to defend this country in case of trouble. Only a small part of the total need be kept constantly under arms; the rest should be working in civil life and the mechanics keeping up their work in the factories and in the industries which go to make up aircraft, being called out for a suitable period of training when necessary.

Practically every civilized country has now adopted this sane, economical, and logical system. With a plan of this kind working, the question of who is to command any undertaking is absolutely fixed—if the predominant is to be a sea force, the Navy ought to have command of the undertaking and the Army and Air Force report to it. If it is going to be a land campaign, the Army should have charge of it and all the elements of the Navy and Air Force report to it. If it is to be an air campaign, the Air Force should have charge and the Army and Navy report to it. The secretary of national defense could determine this.

With an adequate Air Force in this country, it is difficult to see how any hostile host can touch our soil, coming from Europe or from Asia. . . .

7-C PROGRESSIVISM, WAR, AND ISOLATIONISM

During the years from 1898 to 1933, the United States faced a different set of political problems from those met in its earlier history. One theme that became important during this period was the relation between business and government, between the personal interest of individuals and the general welfare of the country. This is related to the great political debates over the system known as "Progressivism".

Another theme emerged with the war in 1898. The role of the United States as a world power began to be of real concern to Americans. Many were surprised to find their country a major world power, and there was a long and bitter debate over how the United States should relate itself to foreign countries.

PROBLEMS: *Should the United States government interfere with the workings of a "free market" by attempting to regulate business? What kinds of government action should be undertaken to control very large banks and banking systems? Should the United States play an active part in running international organizations? What should the United States do to assist or protect other countries with political ideals like those of Americans?*

1. The first President who is usually described as a "Progressive" was Republican Theodore Roose-velt. Roosevelt reached the White House by accident, after President William McKinley was killed. (For what "Progressive" meant, see the article on that subject in the text section of RECORD OF AMERICA.*)*

The passage that follows, from a speech which Theodore Roosevelt delivered at Providence, R.I. in August, 1902 (contained in full in Roosevelt's Collected Works, *National Edition, Volume 16, published in 1925), we find his views on big fortunes, big business, and the common good of the United States.*

Of course a great fortune if used wrongly is a menace to the community. A man of great wealth who does not use that wealth decently is, in a peculiar sense, a menace to the community, and so is the man who does not use his intellect aright. Each talent—the talent for making money, the talent for showing intellect at the bar, or in any other way—if unaccompanied by character, makes the possessor a menace to the community. But such a fact no more warrants us in attacking wealth than it does in attacking intellect. Every man of power, by the very fact of that power, is capable of doing damage to his neighbors; but we cannot afford to discourage the development of such men merely because it is possible they may use their power for wrong ends. If we did so we should leave our history a blank, for we should have no great statesmen, soldiers, merchants, no great men of arts, of letters, of science. Doubtless on the average the most useful citizen to the community as a whole is the man to whom has been granted what the Psalmist asked for—neither poverty nor riches. But the great captain of industry, the man of wealth, who, alone or in combination with his fellows, drives through our great business enterprises, is a factor without whom the civilization that we see roundabout us here could not have been built up. Good, not harm, normally comes from the up-building of such wealth. Probably the greatest harm done by vast wealth is the harm that we of moderate means do ourselves when we let the vices of envy and hatred enter deep into our own natures.

But there is other harm; and it is evident that we should try to do away with that. The great corporations which we have grown to speak of rather loosely as trusts are the creatures of the State, and the State not only has the right to control them, but it is in duty bound to control them wherever the need of such control is shown. There is clearly need of supervision—need to possess the power of regulation of these great corporations through the representatives of the public—wherever, as in our own country at the present time, business corporations become so very powerful alike for beneficent work and for work that is not always beneficent. It is idle to say that there is no need for such supervision. There is, and a sufficient warrant for it is to be found in any one of the admitted evils appertaining to them.

We meet a peculiar difficulty under our system of government, because of the division of governmental power between the nation and the States. When the industrial conditions were simple, very little control was needed, and the difficulties of exercising such control under our Constitution were not evident. Now the conditions are complicated and we find it hard to frame national legislation which shall be adequate; while as a matter of practical experience it has been shown that the States either cannot or will not exercise a sufficient control to meet the needs of the case. Some of our States have excellent laws—laws which it would be well indeed to have enacted by the national legislature. But the wide-spread differences in these laws, even between adjacent States, and the uncertainty of the power of enforcement, result practically in altogether insufficient control. I believe that the nation must assume this power of control by legislation; if necessary by constitutional amendment. The immediate necessity in dealing with trusts is to place them under the real, not the nominal, control of some sovereign to which, as its creatures, the trusts shall owe allegiance, and in whose courts the sovereign's orders may be enforced.

This is not the case with the ordinary so-called "trust" to-day; for the trust nowadays is a large State corporation, which generally does business in other States, often with a tendency toward monopoly. Such a trust is an artificial creature not wholly responsible to or controllable by any legislation, either by State or nation, and not subject to the jurisdiction of any one court. Some governmental sovereign must be given full power over these artificial, and very powerful, corporate beings. In my judgment this sovereign must be the National Government. When it has been given full power, then this full power can be used to control any evil influence, exactly as the government is now using the power conferred upon it by the Sherman antitrust law.

2.   When it came time to elect a President in 1912, Roosevelt entered the campaign against his own hand-picked Republican successor as President, William Howard Taft, and the Democratic candidate, Woodrow Wilson. Although Taft's record as a "trust-buster" was better than Roosevelt's, the ex-President had come to the conclusion that Taft was too conservative—that he was not progressive enough. Failing to block Taft in the regular Republican Convention, Roosevelt ran as a third-party candidate—the candidate of the Progressive Party. The meaning of Progressivism—as Theodore Roosevelt believed it to be—is expressed in the following quotation from one of Roosevelt's campaign speeches of 1912.

We are for liberty. But we are for the liberty of the oppressed, and not for the liberty of the oppressor to oppress the weak and to bind burdens on the shoulders of the heavy-laden. It is idle to ask us not to exercise the power of the government when only by the power of the government can we curb the greed that sits in high places, when only by the exercise of the government can we exalt the lowly and give heart to the humble and the downtrodden.

We care for facts and not for formulas. We care for deeds and not for words. We recognize no sacred right of oppression. We recognize no divine right to work injustice. We stand for the Constitution. We recognize that one of its most useful functions is the protection of property. But we will not consent to make of the Constitution a fetich for the protection of fossilized wrong. We call the attention of those who thus interpret it to the fact that, in that great instrument of justice, life and liberty are put on a full level with property, indeed, are enumerated ahead of it in the order of their importance. We stand for an upright judiciary. But where the judges claim the right to make our laws by finally interpreting them, by finally deciding whether or not we have the power to make them, we claim the right ourselves to exercise that power. We forbid any man, no matter what their official position may be, to usurp the right which is ours, the right which is the people's. We recognize in neither court nor Congress nor President, any divine right to override the will of the people expressed with due deliberation in orderly fashion and through the forms of law.

We Progressives hold that the words of the Declaration of Independence, as given effect to by Washington and as construed and applied by Abraham Lincoln, are to be accepted as real, and not as empty phrases. We believe that in very truth this is a government by the people themselves, that the Constitution is theirs, that the courts are theirs, that all the governmental agents and agencies are theirs. We believe that all true leaders of the people must fearlessly stand for righteousness and honesty, must fearlessly tell the people what justice and honor demand. But we no less strongly insist that it is for the people themselves finally to decide all questions of public policy and to have their decision made effective.

In the platform formulated by the Progressive party we have set forth clearly and specifically our faith on every vital point at issue before this people. We have declared our position on the trusts and on the tariff, on the machinery for securing genuine popular government, on the method of meeting the needs of the farmer, of the business man, and of the man who toils with his hands, in the mine or on the railroad, in the factory or in the shop. There is not a promise we have made which cannot be kept. There is not a promise we have made that will not be kept. Our platform is a covenant with the people of the United States, and if we are given the power we will live up to that covenant in letter and in spirit.

We know that there are in life injustices which we are powerless to remedy. But we know also that there is much injustice which can be remedied, and this injustice we intend to remedy. We know that the long path leading upward toward the light cannot be traversed at once, or in a day, or in a year. But there are certain steps that can be taken at once. These we intend to take. Then, having taken these first steps, we shall see more clearly how to walk still further with a bolder stride. . . .

Our people work hard and faithfully. They do not wish to shirk their work. They must feel pride in the work for the work's sake. But there must be bread for the work. There must be a time for play when the men and women are young. When they grow old there must be the certainty of rest under conditions free from the haunting terror of utter poverty. We believe that no life is worth anything unless it is a life of labor and effort and endeavor. We believe in the joy that comes with work, for he who labors best is really happiest. We must shape conditions so that no one can own the spirit of the man who loves his task and gives the best there is in him to that task, and it matters not whether this man reaps and sows and wrests his livelihood from the rugged reluctance of the soil or whether with hand or brain he plays his part in the tremendous industrial activities of our great cities. We are striving to meet the needs of all these men, and to meet them in such fashion that all alike shall feel bound together in the bond of a common brotherhood, where each works hard for himself and for those dearest to him, and yet feels that he must also think of his brother's rights because he is in very truth that brother's keeper.

3. Woodrow Wilson was elected President in 1912, the only Democrat to occupy the White House in the period 1898 to 1933. His first Inaugural Address follows. In it, he outlined the progressive measures which he intended to take. Note that Wilson's remarks at the outset of his term as President were devoted almost entirely to the internal affairs of the United States.

There has been a change of government. It began two years ago, when the House of Representatives became Democratic by a decisive majority. It has now been completed. The Senate about to assemble will also be Democratic. The offices of President and Vice President have been put into the hands of Democrats. What does the change mean? That is the question I am going to try to answer, in order, if I may, to interpret the occasion.

It means much more than the mere success of a party. The success of a party means little except when the Nation is using that party for a large and definite purpose. No one can mistake the purpose for which the Nation now seeks to use the Democratic Party. It seeks to use it to interpret a change in its own plans and point of view. Some old things with which we had grown familiar, and which had begun to creep into the very habit of our thought and of our lives, have altered their aspect as we have latterly looked critically upon them with fresh, awakened eyes; have dropped their disguise and shown themselves alien and sinister. Some new things, as we look frankly upon them, willing to comprehend their real character, have come to assume the aspect of things long believed in and familiar, stuff of our own convictions. We have been refreshed by a new insight into our own life.

We see that in many things that life is very great. It is incomparably great in its material aspects, in its body of wealth, in the diversity and sweep of its energy, in the industries which have been conceived and built up by the genius of individual men and the limitless enterprise of groups of men. It is great, also, very great, in its moral force. Nowhere else in the world have noble men and women exhibited in more striking forms the beauty and the energy of sympathy and helpfulness and counsel in their efforts to rectify wrong, alleviate suffering, and set the weak in the way of strength and hope. We have built up, moreover, a great system of government, which has stood through a long age as in many respects a model for those who seek to set liberty upon foundations that will endure against fortuitous change, against storm and accident. Our life contains every great thing, and contains it in rich abundance.

But the evil has come with the good, and much fine gold has been corroded. With riches has come inexcusable waste. We have squandered a great part of what we might have used, and have not stopped to conserve the exceeding bounty of nature, without which our genius for enterprise would have been worthless and impotent, scorning to be careful, shamefully prodigal as well as admirably efficient. We have been proud of our industrial achievements, but we have not hitherto stopped thoughtfully enough to count the human cost, the cost of lives snuffed out, of energies overtaxed and broken, the fearfully physical and spiritual cost to the men and women and children upon whom the dead weight and burden of it all has fallen pitilessly the years through. The groans and agony of it all had not yet reached our ears, the solemn, moving undertone of our life, coming up out of the mines and factories and out of every home where the struggle had its intimate and familiar seat. With the great Government went many deep secret things which we too long delayed to look into and scrutinize with candid, fearless eyes. The great Government we loved has too often been made use of for private and selfish purposes, and those who used it had forgotten the people.

At last a vision has been vouchsafed us of our life as a whole. We see the bad with the good, the debased and decadent with the sound and vital. With this vision we approach new affairs. Our duty is to cleanse, to reconsider, to restore, to correct the evil without impairing the good, to purify and humanize every process of our common life without weakening or sentimentalizing it. There has been something crude and heartless and unfeeling in our haste to succeed and be great. Our thought has been "Let every man look out for himself, let every generation look out for itself," while we reared giant machinery which made it impossible that any but those who stood at the levers of control should have a chance to look out for themselves. We had not forgotten our morals. We remembered well enough that

we had set up a policy which was meant to serve the humblest as well as the most powerful, with an eye single to the standards of justice and fair play, and remembered it with pride. But we were very heedless and in a hurry to be great.

We have come now to the somber second thought. The scales of heedlessness have fallen from our eyes. We have made up our minds to square every process of our national life again with the standards we so proudly set up at the beginning and have always carried at our hearts. Our work is a work of restoration.

We have itemized with some degree of particularity the things that ought to be altered, and here are some of the chief items: A tariff which cuts us off from our proper part in the commerce of the world, violates the just principles of taxation, and makes the Government a facile instrument in the hands of private interests; a banking and currency system based upon the necessity of the Government to sell its bonds 50 years ago and perfectly adapted to concentrating cash and restricting credits; an industrial system which, take it on all its sides, financial as well as administrative, holds capital in leading strings, restricts the liberties and limits the opportunities of labor, and exploits without renewing or conserving the natural resources of the country; a body of agricultural activities never yet given the efficiency of great business undertakings or served as it should be through the instrumentality of science taken directly to the farm, or afforded the facilities of credit best suited to its practical needs; watercourses undeveloped, waste places unreclaimed, forests untended, fast disappearing without plan or prospect of renewal, unregarded waste heaps at every mine. We have studied as perhaps no other nation has the most effective means of production, but we have not studied cost or economy as we should either as organizers of industry, as statesmen, or as individuals.

Nor have we studied and perfected the means by which government may be put at the service of humanity, in safeguarding the health of the Nation, the health of its men and its women and its children, as well as their rights in the struggle for existence. This is no sentimental duty. The firm basis of government is justice, not pity. These are matters of justice. There can be no equality or opportunity, the first essential of justice in the body politic, if men and women and children be not shielded in their lives, their very vitality, from the consequences of great industrial and social processes which they can not alter, control, or singly cope with. Society must see to it that it does not itself crush or weaken or damage its own constituent parts. The first duty of law is to keep sound the society it serves. Sanitary laws, pure-food laws, and laws determining conditions of labor which individuals are powerless to determine for themselves are intimate parts of the very business of justice and legal efficiency.

These are some of the things we ought to do, and not leave the others undone, the old-fashioned, never-to-be-neglected, fundamental safeguarding of property and of individual right. This is the high enterprise of the new day: To lift everything that concerns our life as a Nation to the light that shines from the hearthfire of every man's conscience and vision of the right. It is inconceivable that we should do this as partisans; it is inconceivable we should do it in ignorance of the facts as they are or in blind haste. We shall restore, not destroy. We shall deal with our economic system as it is and as it may be modified, not as it might be if we had a clean sheet of paper to write upon; and step by step we shall make it what it should be, in the spirit of those who question their own wisdom and seek counsel and knowledge, not shallow self-satisfaction or the excitement of excursions whither they can not tell. Justice, and only justice, shall always be our motto.

And yet it will be no cool process of mere science. The Nation has been deeply stirred, stirred by a solemn passion, stirred by the knowledge of wrong, of ideals lost, of government too often debauched and made an instrument of evil. The feelings with which we face this new age of right and opportunity sweep across our heartstrings like some air out of God's own presence, where justice and mercy are reconciled and the judge and the brother are one. We know our task to be no mere task of politics, but a task which shall search us through and through, whether we be able to understand our time and the need of our people, whether we be indeed their spokesmen and interpreters, whether we have the pure heart to comprehend and the rectified will to choose our high course of action.

This is not a day of triumph; it is a day of dedication. Here muster, not the forces of party, but the forces of humanity. Men's hearts wait upon us; men's lives hang in the balance; men's hopes call upon us to say what we will do. Who shall live up to the great trust? Who dares fail to try? I summon all honest men, all patriotic, all forward-looking men, to my side. God helping me, I will not fail them, if they will but counsel and sustain me!

4.   Robert M. La Follette of Wisconsin, one of the outstanding Progressive Republican Senators, delivered speeches on many topics during the period we are considering. La Follette himself headed a Progressive Party ticket in 1924, but was soundly defeated. In 1912, LaFollette wrote the following passage about the problems of big banking and big business generally.

THE trust problem has become so interwoven in our legal and industrial system that no single measure or group of measures can reach all of it. It must be picked off at every point where it shows its head.

Every combination of a manufacturing business with the control of transportation, including pipe lines, should be prohibited, in order that competitors may have equal facilities for reaching markets.

The control of limited sources of raw material like coal, iron ore, or timber, by a manufacturing corporation, should be broken up and these resources should be opened to all manufacturers on equal terms.

It is claimed on all sides that competition has failed. I deny it. Fair competition has not failed. It has been suppressed. When competitors are shut out from markets by discrimination, and denied either transportation, raw material or credit on equal terms, we do not have competition. We have the modern form of highway robbery. The great problem of legislation before us is first for the people to resume control of their government, and then to protect themselves against those who are throttling competition by the aid of government.

I do not say that competition does not have its evils. Labor organizations are the struggling protest against cutthroat competition. The anti-trust law was not intended or understood to apply to them. They should be exempt from its operation.

The tariff should be brought down to the difference in labor cost of the more efficient plants and the foreign competitor, and where there is no difference the tariff should be removed. Where the protective tariff is retained its advantages must be passed along to labor, for whose benefit the manufacturer contends it is necessary.

The patent laws should be so amended that the owners of patents will be compelled to develop them fully or permit their use on equal terms by others.

More vital and menacing than any other power that supports trusts is the control of credit through the control of the people's savings and deposits. When the Emergency Currency Bill was before Congress in 1908, Senator Aldrich slipped into the conference report certain provisions which he had withdrawn in the Senate, and withdrew provisions which he had first included. He eliminated protection against promotion schemes, excluded penalties for false reporting, dropped provisions for safeguarding reserves, inserted provisions for accepting railroad bonds as security. Now he comes with another plausible measure to remedy the admitted evils of our inelastic banking system.

When we realize that the control of credit and banking is the greatest power that the trusts possess to keep out competitors, we may well question their sincerity in offering a patriotic measure to dispossess themselves of that power. It is the people's money that is expected to give security to this plan and the people must and shall control it.

The proposed Aldrich Currency Plan is the product of a commission composed of men who are or have been members of the committees of the two houses of Congress, which have controlled all legislation relating to currency and banking. With such a record it behooves the public to examine with the utmost care any plan which they recommend, however plausible it may appear upon its face. A critical study of the scheme of this commission will convince any student of government finance, that under the guise of providing elasticity to our currency system, it is in reality an adroit means of further concentration and control of the money and credits of the United States under a fifty-year franchise, augmenting the power of those who already dominate the banking and insurance resources of the country.

Our National Banking Law is a patchwork of legislation. It should be thoroughly revised. And all authorities agree that a comprehensive plan for an emergency currency is vitally important. When the basic principle of such a plan is once determined, when it is settled that government controlled banks are to be, *in fact*, controlled by the government *in the public interest*, the details can easily be worked out.

An emergency currency circulation should be backed by proper reserves, issued only against commercial paper that represents actual and legitimate business transactions. No plan should be adopted which admits of control by banking interests which, under existing conditions, means, in the end, control by the great speculative banking groups.

In all our plans for progressive legislation, it must not be forgotten that we are only just beginning to get control of the railroads. The present law is an improvement, but the Interstate Commerce Commission requires to be greatly strengthened. It should have a much larger appropriation, enabling it to prosecute investigations in all parts of the country. It should make physical valuations of the railroads, eliminating watered stock, monopoly values and the unwarranted inflation of railway terminals to conceal monopoly values. And the Commerce Court should be abolished as a mere subterfuge interposed to handicap the commission.

As a first necessary step for the regulation of interstate commerce, we *must* ascertain the reasonable value of the physical property of railroads, justly inventoried, upon a sound economic basis, distinguishing *actual* values from *monopoly* values derived from violations of law, and must make such discriminating values the *base line* for determining rates. The country should know how much of the eighteen billions of capitalization was contributed by those who own the railroads, and how much by the people themselves. We should also provide for the extension of the powers and the administrative control of the Interstate Commerce Commission.

I have sketched the growth and power of the great interests that to-day control our property and our governments. I have shown how subtle and elusive, yet relentless, they are. Rising up against them is the confused voice of the people. Their heart is true but their eyes do not yet see all the intricate sources of power. Who shall show them? There are only two agencies that in any way can reach the whole people. These are the press and the platform. But the platform in no way compares with the press in its power of continuous repeated instruction.

One would think that in a democracy like ours, people seeking the truth, able to read and understand, would find the press their eager and willing instructors. Such was the press of Horace Greeley, Henry Raymond, Charles A. Dana, Joseph Medill, and Horace Rublee.

But what do we find has occurred in the past few years since the money power has gained control of our industry and government? It controls the newspaper press. The people know this. Their confidence is weakened and destroyed. No longer are the editorial columns of newspapers a potent force in educating public opinion. The newspapers, of course, are still patronized for news. But even as to news, the public is fast coming to understand that wherever news items bear in any way upon the control of government by business the news is colored; so confidence in the newspaper as a newspaper is being undermined.

Cultured and able men are still to be found upon the editorial staffs of all great dailies, but the public understands them to be hired men who no longer express honest judgments and sincere conviction, who write what they are told to write, and whose judgments are salaried.

To the subserviency of the press to special interests in no small degree is due the power and influence and prosperity of the weekly and monthly magazines. A decade ago young men trained in journalism came to see this control of the newspapers of the country. They saw also an unoccupied field. And they went out and built up great periodicals and magazines. They were free.

Their pages were open to publicists and scholars and liberty, and justice and equal rights found a free press beyond the reach of the corrupt influence of consolidated business and machine politics. We entered upon a new era.

The periodical, reduced in price, attractive and artistic in dress, strode like a young giant into the arena of public service. Filled with this spirit, quickened with human interest, it assailed social and political evils in high places and low. It found the power of the public service corporation and the evil influences of money in the municipal government of every large city. It found franchises worth millions of dollars secured by bribery; police in partnership with thieves and crooks and prostitutes. It found juries "fixed" and an established business plying its trade between litigants and the back door of blinking justice.

It found Philadelphia giving away franchises, franchises not supposedly or estimated to be worth $2,500,-000, but for which she had been openly offered and refused $2,500,000. Milwaukee they found giving franchises worth $8,000,000 against the protests of her indignant citizens. It found Chicago robbed in tax-payments of immense value by corporate owners of property through fraud and forgery on a gigantic scale; it found the aldermen of St. Louis, organized to boodle the city with a criminal compact, on file in the dark corner of a safety deposit vault.

The free and independent periodical turned her searchlight on state legislatures, and made plain as the sun at noonday the absolute control of the corrupt lobby. She opened the closed doors of the secret caucuses, the secret committee, the secret conference, behind which United States Senators and Members of Congress betrayed the public interest into the hands of railroads, the trusts, the tariff mongers, and the centralized banking power of the country. She revealed the same influences back of judicial and other appointments. She took the public through the great steel plants and into the homes of the men who toil twelve hours a day and seven days in the week. And the public heard their cry of despair. She turned her camera into the mills and shops where little children are robbed of every chance of life that nourishes vigorous bodies and sound minds, and the pinched faces and dwarfed figures told their pathetic story on her clean white pages.

The control of the newspaper press is not the simple and expensive one of ownership and investment. There is here and there a "kept sheet" owned by a man of great wealth to further his own interests. But the papers of this class are few. The control comes through that community of interests, that interdependence of investments and credits which ties the publishers up to the banks, the advertisers and the special interests.

We may expect this same kind of control, sooner or later, to reach out for the magazines. But more than this: I warn you of a subtle new peril, the centralization of advertising, that will in time seek to gag you. What has occurred on the small scale in almost every city in the country will extend to the national scale, and will ere long close in on magazines. No men ever faced graver responsibilities. None have ever been called to a more unselfish, patriotic service. I believe that when the final test comes, you will not be found wanting; you will not desert and leave the people to depend upon the public platform alone, but you will hold aloft the lamp of Truth, lighting the way for the preservation of representative government and the liberty of the American people.

5. The Federal Reserve Act, passed in 1913, established an entirely new system of banking for the United States. Its purposes were many, but one was clearly to prevent a handful of banks in one city (New York) from dominating all banking in the United States. In the following selection, an official of the Treasury (the Comptroller of the Currency) reports to Congress in 1915 on the purposes of the system.

Experience had shown that the system of accumulating and impounding reserves for the national banks of the reserve cities, as well as those of the country banks, in the three "central reserve" cities of New York, Chicago, and St. Louis worked badly. The funds of the banks throughout the country were stored up and concentrated in these three cities. The banks in these cities, especially in New York, had become accustomed to lending largely in Wall Street on demand, on bond and stock collateral, the reserve balances which these banks held for other banks, and upon which they usually paid the depositing banks 2 per cent per annum interest. Periodically, or in the crop-moving season, when the country banks had to withdraw their deposits from the centers, the national banks in the large cities would call in these loans on bonds and stocks, money rates would advance, and stocks decline. This process went on from year to year.

When there was sudden strain and need, as in 1893 and 1907, the banks throughout the country having or anticipating a demand from their customers for money would seek to draw in their balances from New York and the other large cities. The New York banks, however, at these times unable to meet the demands upon them, would suspend currency shipments and resort to the usual remedy of issuing clearing-house certificates for protection until normal conditions should be resumed, and the banks in other large cities thereupon generally would be forced to follow the lead set by the New York banks, would hold onto the money of their correspondents, and issue clearing-house certificates, while currency was being bought and sold at a premium of 2 to 5 per cent.

AIMS OF FEDERAL RESERVE SYSTEM

The Federal Reserve System has been designed to correct these and other evil and dangerous conditions and to furnish to the banks and to the people of the country new and additional banking and financial facilities by providing.

First.   A currency or circulating medium which will not only pass without question at its face value in every part of the country, but which will expand when necessary to meet legitimate demands of increasing business, and which will also contract at the proper time when no longer required and when its continuance in circulation would threaten or promote inflation.

Second.   An improved system for the management and handling of the bank reserves, whereby these reserves become readily and easily available to meet demands for increased money and credit and where the proper utilization of that portion of the bank reserves not held in the vaults of the respective individual banks may be made available as a means of relief and to prevent the financial crisis or market panic from which the country has suffered so often when the country banks have tried to bring home their reserves to treat the wants of their customers.

Third.   A clearing or collection system by which the checks on national banks and other banks which are members of the Federal Reserve System drawn on solvent banks by solvent drawers, may be cashed or collected at par in every part of the country, without the burden and expense of the exchange and collection charges which have been a material expense and a serious drawback to business operations.

Fourth.   The Federal reserve banks furnish through their capital, their large deposits, and their note-issuing power the facilities by which all members of the system, in any emergency, may rediscount their eligible paper and obtain funds to meet any sudden or unexpected demands. These reserve banks also provide their member banks in ordinary times with money and credit to enable them to meet the legitimate demands of customers for increased accommodations when the member banks themselves have not the needed funds.

Fifth.   The Federal Reserve System, by providing a source from which all well-managed banks at all times may secure funds to meet any emergency, makes unnecessary the carrying by member banks of the reserves formerly required for national banks. By the reduction in reserve requirements provided by the act the loanable funds of the national banks upon the inauguration

of the Federal Reserve System were increased immediately, through the release of reserves, by an amount figured at considerably more than $400,000,000.

The other direct advantages provided by the Federal reserve act are (a) the opportunity given to national banks under certain conditions to lend money on improved, unincumbered farm property; (b) the power conferred on national banks to establish branches in foreign countries; (c) the establishment and authorization of bank acceptances; (d) the provisions for open-market operations by Federal reserve banks; and, finally (e) the adoption of the new method for the compensation of bank examiners, which insures a more thorough and systematic examination of national banks than was possible under the antiquated fee system.

6.   *"Trust-busting" was one of the activities of the Progressive Era. The Standard Oil Company, one of the largest of the Trusts and clearly the best known, came in for special attention and was prosecuted. A new government office, the U.S. Bureau of Corporations, issued a Report in 1907 charging Standard Oil with a number of serious business offenses. The selection which follows is quoted from that Report.*

The obnoxious character of the Standard's price policy and methods is . . . made clear by the present report. The Standard has repeatedly asserted that combination, as illustrated by its own history, is a great benefit to the public, in reducing costs and consequently prices. It may readily be that in some industries combination has had these beneficial results. It is probable that the Standard, by reason of its undoubtedly great efficiency, could, had it been content with reasonable profits, have made prices to consumers lower than would have been possible for smaller concerns, and thus have maintained its great proportion of the business by wholly fair and legitimate means.

The Standard is, however, a most conspicuous example of precisely the opposite—of a combination which maintains a substantial monopoly, not by superiority of service and by charging reasonable prices, but by unfair methods of destroying competition; a combination which then uses the power thus unfairly gained to oppress the public through highly extortionate prices. It has raised prices instead of lowering them. It has pocketed all the advantages of its economies instead of sharing them with the public, and has added still further monopoly profits by charging more than smaller and less economical concerns could sell for if the Standard allowed them the chance.

Some of the unfair and illegal means by which the

Standard has been able to do this have been proved in the reports already published by this Bureau: namely, railroad discriminations, wide-reaching in extent and enormous in degree; failure to perform the duties of a common carrier in pipe-line transportation, and unjust methods of destroying competition in that business; and price discrimination of the most flagrant character. In the present report the following facts are established: The Standard has not reduced margins during the period in which it has been responsible for the prices of oil. During the last eight years covered by this report (1898 to 1905) it has raised both prices and margins. Its domination has not been acquired or maintained by its superior efficiency, but rather by unfair competition and by methods economically and morally unjustifiable. The Standard has superior efficiency in running its own business; it has an equal efficiency in destroying the business of competitors. It keeps for itself the profits of the first and adds to these the monopoly profits secured by the second. Its profits are far above the highest possible standard of a reasonable commercial return, and have been steadily increasing. Finally, the history of this great industry is a history of the persistent use of the worst industrial methods, the exaction of exorbitant prices from the consumer, and the securing of excessive profits for the small group of men who over a long series of years have thus dominated the business.

Through most of the years between 1898 and 1933, questions of peace and war were urgently debated among the nations. For the United States, the period began with a brief and victorious war against Spain.

7. *On April 11, 1898, President William McKinley sent a message to Congress, requesting a declaration of war against Spain. Congress declared war on April 20.*

A part of the President's message is quoted below. It had several purposes in view, in addition to the obvious one. It was designed to be read and studied by people in other countries as a justification of the fight with Spain. It was also intended to influence the American public to support the war by summing up the "case" against Spain.

EXECUTIVE MANSION,
11 *April* 1898.
To the Congress of the United States:

Obedient to that precept of the Constitution which commands the President to give from time to time to the Congress information of the state of the Union and to recommend to their consideration such measures as he shall judge necessary and expedient, it becomes my duty to now address your body with regard to the grave crisis that has arisen in the relations of the United States to Spain by reason of the warfare that for more than three years has raged in the neighboring island of Cuba. . . .

The present revolution is but the successor of other similar insurrections which have occurred in Cuba against the dominion of Spain, extending over a period of nearly half a century, each of which during its progress has subjected the United States to great effort and expense in enforcing its neutrality laws, caused enormous losses to American trade and commerce, caused irritation, annoyance, and disturbance among our citizens, and, by the exterior of cruel, barbarous, and uncivilized practices of warfare, shocked the sensibilities and offended the human sympathies of our people.

Our trade has suffered, the capital invested by our citizens in Cuba has been largely lost, and the temper and forbearance of our people have been so sorely tried as to beget a perilous unrest among our own citizens, which has inevitably found its expression from time to time in the National Legislature, so that issues wholly external to our own body politic engross attention and stand in the way of that close devotion to domestic advancement that becomes a self-contained commonwealth whose primal maxim has been the avoidance of all foreign entanglements. All this must needs awaken, and has, indeed, aroused, the utmost concern on the part of this Government, as well during my predecessor's term as in my own.

In April 1896, the evils from which our country suffered through the Cuban War became so onerous that my predecessor made an effort to bring about a peace through the mediation of this Government in any way that might tend to an honorable adjustment of the contest between Spain and her revolted colony, on the basis of some effective scheme of self-government for Cuba under the flag and sovereignty of Spain. It failed through the refusal of the Spanish government then in power to consider any form of mediation or, indeed, any plan of settlement which did not begin with the actual submission of the insurgents to the mother country, and then only on such terms as Spain herself might see fit to grant. . . .

The overtures of this Government made through its new envoy, General Woodford, and looking to an immediate and effective amelioration of the condition of the island, although not accepted to the extent of admitted mediation in any shape, were met by assurances that home rule in an advanced phase would be forthwith offered to Cuba, without waiting for the war to end, and that more humane methods should thenceforth prevail in the conduct of hostilities. Coincidentally with those declarations the new government of Spain continued and completed the policy, already begun by its predecessor, of testifying friendly regard for this nation by releasing American citizens held under one charge or another connected with the insurrection, so that by the end of November not a single person entitled in any way to our national protection remained in a Spanish prison. . . .

The war in Cuba is of such a nature that, short of subjugation or extermination, a final military victory for either side seems impracticable. The alternative lies in the physical exhaustion of the one or the other party, or perhaps of both. . . .

Realizing this, it appeared to be my duty, in a spirit of true friendliness, no less to Spain than to the Cubans, who have so much to lose by the prolongation of the struggle, to seek to bring about an immediate termination of the war. To this end I submitted on the 27th ultimo, as a result of much representation and correspondence, through the United States minister at Madrid, propositions to the Spanish Government looking to an armistice until 1 October for the negotiation of peace with the good offices of the President.

In addition I asked the immediate revocation of the order of reconcentration, so as to permit the people to return to their farms and the needy to be relieved with provisions and supplies from the United States, co-operating with the Spanish authorities, so as to afford full relief.

The reply of the Spanish Cabinet was received on the night of the 31st ultimo. It offered, as the means to bring about peace in Cuba, to confide the preparation thereof to the insular parliament, inasmuch as the concurrence of that body would be necessary to reach a final result, it being, however, understood that the powers reserved by the constitution to the central Government are not lessened or diminished. As the Cuban parliament does not meet until the 4th of May next, the Spanish Government would not object for its part to accept at once a suspension of hostilities if asked for by the insurgents from the general in chief, to whom it would pertain in such case to determine the duration and conditions of the armistice. . . .

With this last overture in the direction of immediate peace, and its disappointing reception by Spain, the Executive is brought to the end of his effort.

In my annual message of December last I said:

Of the untried measures there remain only: recognition of the insurgents as belligerents; recognition of the independence of Cuba; neutral intervention to end the war by imposing a rational compromise between the contestants, and intervention in favor of one or the other party. I speak not of forcible annexation, for that can

not be thought of. That, by our code of morality, would be criminal aggression. . . .

There remain the alternative forms of intervention to end the war, either as an impartial neutral, by imposing a rational compromise between the contestants, or as the active ally of the one party or the other.

As to the first, it is not to be forgotten that during the last few months the relation of the United States has virtually been one of friendly intervention in many ways, each not of itself conclusive, but all tending to the pacific result, just and honorable to all interests concerned. The spirit of all our acts hitherto has been an earnest, unselfish desire for peace and prosperity in Cuba, untarnished by differences between us and Spain and unstained by the blood of American citizens.

The forcible intervention of the United States as a neutral to stop the war, according to the large dictates of humanity and following many historical precedents where neighbouring States have interfered to check the hopeless sacrifices of life by internecine conflicts beyond their borders, is justifiable on rational grounds. It involves, however, hostile constraint upon both the parties to the contest, as well to enforce a trace as to guide the eventual settlement.

The grounds for such intervention may be briefly summarized as follows:

First. In the cause of humanity and to put an end to the barbarities, bloodshed, starvation, and horrible miseries now existing there, and which the parties to the conflict are either unable or unwilling to stop or mitigate. It is no answer to say this is all in another country, belonging to another nation, and is therefore none of our business. It is specially our duty, for it is right at our door.

Second. We owe it to our citizens in Cuba to afford them that protection and indemnity for life and property which no government there can or will afford, and to that end to terminate the conditions that deprive them of legal protection.

Third. The right to intervene may be justified by the very serious injury to the commerce, trade, and business of our people and by the wanton destruction of property and devastation of the island.

Fourth, and which is of the utmost importance. The present condition of affairs in Cuba is a constant menace to our peace and entails upon the Government an enormous expense. With such a conflict waged for years in an island so near us and with which our people have such trade and business relations; when the lives and liberty of our citizens are in constant danger and their property destroyed and themselves ruined; where our trading vessels are liable to seizure and are seized at our very door by war ships of a foreign nation; the expeditions of filibustering that we are powerless to prevent altogether, and the irritating questions and entanglements thus arising—all these and others that I need not mention, with the resulting strained relations, are a constant menace to our peace and compel us to keep on a semi-war footing with a nation with which we are at peace.

These elements of danger and disorder already pointed out have been strikingly illustrated by a tragic event which has deeply and justly moved the American people. I have already transmitted to Congress the report of the naval court of inquiry on the destruction of the battleship *Maine* in the harbor of Havana during the night of the 15th of February. The destruction of that noble vessel has filled the national heart with inexpressible horror. Two hundred and fifty-eight brave sailors and marines and two officers of our Navy, reposing in the fancied security of a friendly harbor, have been hurled to death, grief and want brought to their homes, and sorrow to the nation.

The naval court of inquiry, which, it is needless to say, commands the unqualified confidence of the Government, was unanimous in its conclusion that the destruction of the *Maine* was caused by an exterior explosion—that of a submarine mine. It did not assume to place the responsibilty. That remains to be fixed.

In any event, the destruction of the *Maine*, by whatever exterior cause, is a patent and impressive proof of a state of things in Cuba that is intolerable. . . .

The long trial has proved that the object for which Spain has waged the war cannot be attained. The fire of insurrection may flame or may smolder with varying seasons, but it has not been and it is plain that it cannot be extinguished by present methods. The only hope of relief and repose from a condition which can no longer be endured is the enforced pacification of Cuba. In the name of humanity, in the name of civilization, in behalf of endangered American interests which give us the right and the duty to speak and to act, the war in Cuba must stop.

In view of these facts and of these considerations I ask the Congress to authorize and empower the President to take measures to secure a full and final termination of hostilities between the Government of Spain and the people of Cuba, and to secure in the island the establishment of a stable government, capable of maintaining order and observing its international obligations, insuring peace and tranquillity and the security of its citizens as well as our own, and to use the military and naval forces of the United States as may be necessary for these purposes. . . .

8.   A few weeks after the War with Spain began, Congress agreed to annex the Hawaiian Islands to the United States. This annexation was done by

"Joint Resolution" of Congress (quoted below) rather than by formal treaty, to insure that a majority of Congress would agree to the taking over of the islands. It was a similar arrangement to the annexation of Texas in 1845. The once independent Republic of Hawaii, however, did not achieve statehood on annexation.

Joint Resolution: To provide for annexing the Hawaiian Islands to the United States (dated July 7, 1898).

WHEREAS the Government of the Republic of Hawaii having, in due form, signified its consent, in the manner provided by its constitution, to cede absolutely and without reserve to the United States of America all rights of sovereignty of whatsoever kind in and over the Hawaiian Islands and their dependencies, and also to cede and transfer to the United States the absolute fee and ownership of all public, Government, or Crown lands, public buildings or edifices, ports, harbors, military equipment, and all other public property of every kind and description belonging to the Government of the Hawaiian Islands, together with every right and appurtenance thereunto appertaining: Therefore.

Resolved . . . That said cession is accepted, ratified, and confirmed, and that the said Hawaiian Islands and their dependencies be, and they are hereby, annexed as a part of the territory of the United States and are subject to the sovereign dominion thereof, and that all and singular the property and rights hereinbefore mentioned are vested in the United States of America.

The existing laws of the United States relative to public lands shall not apply to such lands in the Hawaiian Islands; but the Congress of the United States shall enact special laws for their management and disposition: *Provided,* That all revenue from or proceeds of the same, except as regards such part thereof as may be used or occupied for the civil, military, or naval purposes of the United States, or may be assigned for the use of the local government, shall be used solely for the benefit of the inhabitants of the Hawaiian Islands for educational and other public purposes.

Until Congress shall provide for the government of such islands all the civil, judicial, and military powers exercised by the officers of the existing government in said islands shall be vested in such person or persons and shall be exercised in such manner as the President of the United States shall direct; and the President shall have power to remove said officers and fill the vacancies so occasioned.

The existing treaties of the Hawaiian Islands with foreign nations shall forthwith cease and determine, being replaced by such treaties as may exist, or as may be hereafter concluded, between the United States and such foreign nations. The municipal legislation of the Hawaiian Islands, not enacted for the fulfillment of the treaties so extinguished, and not inconsistent with this joint resolution nor contrary to the Constitution of the United States nor to any existing treaty of the United shall otherwise determine.

Until legislation shall be enacted extending the United States customs laws and regulations to the Hawaiian Islands the existing customs relations of the Hawaiian Islands with the United States and other countries shall remain unchanged.

9. At the end of the War with Spain, the United States found itself holding a number of islands which it had not previously claimed. The Philippines and Puerto Rico, once Spanish possessions, were under the Stars and Stripes by the end of 1898. The Treaty of Paris, signed in December of that year, brought peace. It also provided the start of an American "empire" over these islands. As an international treaty, it carried serious obligations for the United States. Significant sections of the Treaty are here given.

ARTICLE I.

Spain relinquishes all claim of sovereignty over and title to Cuba.

And as the island is, upon its evacuation by Spain, to be occupied by the United States, the United States will, so long as such occupation shall last, assume and discharge the obligations that may under international law result from the fact of its occupation, for the protection of life and property.

ARTICLE II.

Spain cedes to the United States the island of Porto Rico and other islands now under Spanish sovereignty in the West Indies, and the island of Guam in the Marianas or Ladrones.

ARTICLE III.

Spain cedes to the United States the archipelago known as the Philippine Islands, and comprehending the islands lying within the following line:

A line running from west to east along or near the twentieth parallel of north latitude, and through the middle of the navigable channel of Bachi, from the one hundred and eighteenth (118th) to the one hundred and twenty seventh (127th) degree meridian of longitude east of Greenwich, thence along the one hundred and twenty seventh (127th) degree meridian of longitude east of Greenwich to the parallel of four degrees and forty five minutes (4° 45') north latitude, thence along the parallel of four degrees and forty five minutes (4° 45') north latitude to its intersection with the meridian of longitude one hundred and nineteen degrees and thirty five minutes (119° 35') east of Greenwich, thence along the meridian of longitude one hundred and nineteen degrees and thirty five minutes (119° 35') east of Greenwich to the parallel of latitude seven degrees and forty minutes (7° 40') north, thence along the parallel of latitude seven degrees and forty minutes (7° 40') north to its intersection with the one hundred and sixteenth (116th) degree meridian of longitude east of Greenwich, thence by a direct line to the intersection of the tenth (10th) degree parallel of north latitude with the one hundred and eighteenth (118th) degree meridian of longitude east of Greenwich, and thence along the one hundred and eighteenth (118th) degree meridian of longitude east of Greenwich to the point of beginning.

The United States will pay to Spain the sum of twenty million dollars ($20,000,000) within three months after the exchange of the ratifications of the present treaty.

ARTICLE IV.

The United States will, for the term of ten years from the date of the exchange of the ratifications of the present treaty, admit Spanish ships and merchandise to the ports of the Philippine Islands on the same terms as ships and merchandise of the United States.

ARTICLE V.

The United States will, upon the signature of the present treaty, send back to Spain, at its own cost, the Spanish soldiers taken as prisoners of war on the capture of Manila by the American forces. The arms of the soldiers in question shall be restored to them.

Spain will, upon the exchange of the ratifications of the present treaty, proceed to evacuate the Philippines, as well as the island of Guam, on terms similar to those agreed upon by the Commissioners appointed to arrange for the evacuation of Porto Rico and other islands in the West Indies, under the Protocol of August 12, 1898, which is to continue in force till its provisions are completely executed. . . .

ARTICLE VI.

Spain will, upon the signature of the present treaty, release all prisoners of war, and all persons detained or imprisoned for political offences, in connection with the insurrections in Cuba and the Philippines and the war with the United States.

Reciprocally, the United States will release all persons made prisoners of war by the American forces, and will undertake to obtain the release of all Spanish prisoners in the hands of the insurgents in Cuba and the Philippines.

The Government of the United States will at its own cost return to Spain and the Government of Spain will at its own cost return to the United States, Cuba, Porto Rico, and the Philippines, according to the situation of their respective homes, prisoners released or caused to be released by them, respectively, under this article.

ARTICLE VII.

The United States and Spain mutually relinquish all claims for indemnity, national and individual, of every kind, of either Government, or of its citizens or subjects, against the other Government, that may have arisen since the beginning of the late insurrection in Cuba and prior to the exchange of ratifications of the present treaty, including all claims for indemnity for the cost of the war.

The United States will adjudicate and settle the claims of its citizens against Spain relinquished in this article.

ARTICLE VIII.

In conformity with the provisions of Articles I, II, and III of this treaty, Spain relinquishes in Cuba, and cedes in Porto Rico and other islands in the West Indies, in the island of Guam, and in the Philippine Archipelago, all the buildings, wharves, barracks, forts, structures, public highways and other immovable property which, in conformity with law, belong to the public domain, and as such belong to the Crown of Spain.

And it is hereby declared that the relinquishment or cession, as the case may be, to which the preceding paragraph refers, cannot in any respect impair the property or rights which by law belong to the peaceful possession of property of all kinds, of provinces, municipalities, public or private establishments, ecclesiastical or civic bodies, or any other associations having legal capacity to acquire and possess property in the aforesaid territories renounced or ceded, or of private individuals, of whatsoever nationality such individuals may be.

The aforesaid relinquishment or session, as the case may be, includes all documents exclusively referring to the sovereignty relinquished or ceded that may exist in the archives of the Peninsula. Where any document in such archives only in part relates to said sovereignty, a copy of such part will be furnished wherever it shall be requested. Like rules shall be reciprocally observed in favor of Spain in respect of documents in the archives of the islands above referred to.

In the aforesaid relinquishment or cession, as the case may be, are also included such rights as the Crown of Spain and its authorities possess in respect of the official archives and records, executive as well as judicial, in the islands above referred to, which relate to said islands or the rights and property of their inhabitants. Such archives and records shall be carefully preserved, and private persons shall without distinction have the right to require, in accordance with law, authenticated copies of the contracts, wills and other instruments forming part of notarial protocols or files, or which may be contained in the executive or judicial archives, be the latter in Spain or in the islands aforesaid.

ARTICLE IX.

Spanish subjects, natives of the Peninsula, residing in the territory over which Spain by the present treaty relinquishes or cedes her sovereignty, may remain in such territory or may remove therefrom, retaining in either event all their rights of property, including the right to sell or dispose of such property or of its proceeds; and they shall also have the right to carry on their industry, commerce and professions, being subject in respect thereof to such laws as are applicable to other foreigners. In case they remain in the territory they may preserve their allegiance to the Crown of Spain by making, before a court of record, within a year from the date of the exchange of ratifications of this treaty, a declaration of their decision to preserve such allegiance; in default of which declaration they shall be held to have renounced it and to have adopted the nationality of the territory in which they may reside.

The civil rights and political status of the native inhabitants of the territories hereby ceded to the United States shall be determined by the Congress.

ARTICLE X.

The inhabitants of the territories over which Spain relinquishes or cedes her sovereignty shall be secured in the free exercise of their religion.

ARTICLE XI.

The Spaniards residing in the territories over which Spain by this treaty cedes or relinquishes her sovereignty shall be subject in matters civil as well as criminal to the jurisdiction of the courts of the country wherein they reside, pursuant to the ordinary laws governing the same; and they shall have the right to appear before such courts, and to pursue the same course as citizens of the country to which the courts belong.

ARTICLE XII.

Judicial proceedings pending at the time of the exchange of ratifications of this treaty in the territories over which Spain relinquishes or cedes her sovereignty shall be determined according to the following rules:

1. Judgments rendered either in civil suits between private individuals, or in criminal matters, before the date mentioned, and with respect to which there is no recourse or right of review under the Spanish law, shall be deemed to be final, and shall be executed in the form by competent authority in the territory within which such judgments should be carried out.

2. Civil suits between private individuals which may on the date mentioned be undetermined shall be prosecuted to judgment before the court in which they may then be pending or in the court that may be substituted therefor.

3. Criminal actions pending on the date mentioned before the Supreme Court of Spain against citizens of the territory which by this treaty ceases to be Spanish shall continue under its jurisdiction until final judgment; but, such judgment having been rendered, the execution thereof shall be committed to the competent authority of the place in which the case arose.

ARTICLE XIII.

The rights of property secured by copyrights and patents acquired by Spaniards in the Island of Cuba, and in Porto Rico, the Philippines and other ceded territories, at the time of the exchange of the ratifications of this treaty, shall continue to be respected. Spanish scientific, literary and artistic works, not subversive of public order in the territories in question, shall continue to be admitted free of duty into such territories, for the period of ten years, to be reckoned from the date of the exchange of the ratifications of this treaty.

ARTICLE XIV.

Spain shall have the power to establish consular officers in the ports and places of the territories, the sovereignty over which has been either relinquished or ceded by the present treaty.

ARTICLE XV.

The Government of each country will, for the term of ten years, accord to the merchant vessels of the other country the same treatment in respect of all port charges, including entrance and clearance dues, light dues, and tonnage duties, as it accords to its own merchant vessels, not engaged in the coastwise trade.

This article may at any time be terminated on six months' notice given by either Government to the other.

ARTICLE XVI.

It is understood that any obligations assumed in this treaty by the United States with respect to Cuba are limited to the time of its occupancy thereof; but it will upon the termination of such occupancy advise any Government established in the island to assume the same obligations.

10.   The island of Cuba presented many problems, among them the creation of a modern sanitary system, and finding the money for its independent government. Some Americans wanted the United States to take over Cuba, as the other Spanish dependencies had been taken over by the Treaty. The Teller Amendment, however, made it official U.S. policy to maintain Cuba's independence, and there was strong American opposition to any further intervention by the United States in the affairs of overseas peoples. In 1903, the Platt Amendment (named for its sponsor, Senator O. H. Platt of Connecticut) was tacked on to an appropriations bill, passed by Congress, and established a kind of U.S. protectorate over Cuba.

ART. I. The Government of Cuba shall never enter into any treaty or other compact with any foreign Power or Powers which will impair or tend to impair the independence of Cuba, nor in any manner authorize or permit any foreign Power or Powers to obtain by colonization or for military or naval purposes, or otherwise, lodgement in or control over any portion of said island.

ART. II. The Government of Cuba shall not assume or contract any public debt to pay the interest upon which, and to make reasonable sinking-fund provision for the ultimate discharge of which, the ordinary revenues of the Island of Cuba, after defraying the current expenses of the Government, shall be inadequate.

ART. III. The Government of Cuba consents that the United States may exercise the right to intervene for the preservation of Cuban independence, the maintenance of a Government adequate for the protection of life, property, and individual liberty, and for discharging the obligations with respect to Cuba imposed by the Treaty of Paris on the United States, now to be assumed and undertaken by the Government of Cuba.

ART. IV. All Acts of the United States in Cuba during its military occupancy thereof are ratified and validated, and all lawful rights acquired thereunder shall be maintained and protected.

ART. V. The Government of Cuba will execute, and as far as necessary extend, the plans already devised or other plans to be mutually agreed upon, for the sanitation of the cities of the island, to the end that a recurrence of epidemics and infectious diseases may be prevented, thereby assuring protection to the people and commerce of Cuba, as well as to the commerce of the southern ports of the United States and the people residing therein.

ART. VI. The Isle of Pines shall be omitted from the boundaries of Cuba, specified in the Constitution, the title thereto being left to future adjustment by treaty.

ART. VII. To enable the United States to maintain the independence of Cuba, and to protect the people thereof, as well as for its own defense, the Government of Cuba will sell or lease to the United States lands necessary for coaling or naval stations at certain specified points to be agreed upon with the President of the United States. . . .

11. President Theodore Roosevelt went a much longer way toward setting up an American Empire. His "Roosevelt Corollary" to the Monroe Doctrine remained official United States policy until 1938, when President Franklin D. Roosevelt renounced it. Like Monroe's original Doctrine, the Corollary was announced in a message to Congress, December 6, 1904.

The steady aim of this Nation, as of all enlightened nations, should be to strive to bring ever nearer the day when there shall prevail throughout the world the peace of justice. There are kinds of peace which are highly undesirable, which are in the long run as destructive as any war. Tyrants and oppressors have many times made a wilderness and called it peace. Many times peoples who were slothful or timid or shortsighted, who had been enervated by ease or by luxury, or misled by false teachings, have shrunk in unmanly fashion from doing duty that was stern and that needed self-sacrifice, and have sought to hide from their own minds their shortcomings, their ignoble motives, by calling them love of peace. The peace of tyrannous terror, the peace of craven weakness, the peace of injustice, all these should be shunned as we shun unrighteous war. The goal to set before us as a nation, the goal which should be set before all mankind, is the attainment of the peace of justice, of the peace which comes when each nation is not merely safe-guarded in its own rights, but scrupulously recognizes and performs its duty toward others. Generally peace tells for righteousness; but if there is conflict between the two, then our fealty is due first to the cause of righteousness. Unrighteous wars are common, and unrighteous peace is rare; but both should be shunned. The right of freedom and the responsibility for the exercise of that right can not be divorced. . . .

If these self-evident truths are kept before us, and only if they are so kept before us, we shall have a clear idea of what our foreign policy in its larger aspect should be. It is our duty to remember that a nation has no more right to do injustice to another nation, strong or weak, than an individual has to do injustice to another individual; that the same moral law applies in one case as in the other. But we must also remember that it is as much the duty of the Nation to guard its own rights and its own interests as it is the duty of the individual so to do. Within the Nation the individual has now delegated this right to the State, that is, to the representative of all the individuals, and it is a maxim of the law that for every wrong there is a remedy. But in international law we have not advanced by any means as far as we have advanced in municipal law. There is as yet no judicial way of enforcing a right in international law. When one nation wrongs another or wrongs many others, there is no tribunal before which the wrongdoer can be brought. Either it is necessary supinely to acquiesce in the wrong, and thus put a premium upon brutality and aggression, or else it is necessary for the aggrieved nation valiantly to stand up for its rights.

Until some method is devised by which there shall be a degree of international control over offending nations, it would be a wicked thing for the most civilized powers, for those with most sense of international obligations and with keenest and most generous appreciation of the difference between right and wrong, to disarm. If the great civilized nations of the present day should completely disarm, the result would mean an immediate recrudescence of barbarism in one form or another. Under any circumstances a sufficient armament would have to be kept up to serve the purposes of international police; and until international cohesion and the sense of international duties and rights are far more advanced than at present, a nation desirous both of securing respect for itself and of doing good to others must have a force adequate for the work which it feels is allotted to it as its part of the general world duty. Therefore it follows that a self-respecting, just, and far-seeing nation should on the one hand endeavor by every means to aid in the development of the various movements which tend to provide substitutes for war, which tend to render nations in their actions toward one another, and indeed toward their own peoples, more responsive to the general sentiment of humane and civilized mankind; and on the other hand that it should keep prepared, while scrupulously avoiding wrongdoing itself, to repel any wrong, and in exceptional cases to take action which in a more advanced stage of international relations would come under the head of the international police. . . .

It is not true that the United States feels any land hunger or entertains any projects as regards the other nations of the Western Hemisphere save such as are for their welfare. All that this country desires is to see the neighboring countries stable, orderly, and prosperous. Any country whose people conduct themselves well can count upon our hearty friendship. If a nation shows that it knows how to act with reasonable efficiency and decency in social and political matters, if it keeps order and pays its obligations, it need fear no interference from the United States.

Chronic wrongdoing, or an impotence which results in a general loosening of the ties of civilized society, may in America, as elsewhere, ultimately require intervention by some civilized nation, and in the Western Hemisphere the adherence of the United States to the Monroe Doctrine may force the United States, however reluctantly, in flagrant cases of such wrongdoing or impotence, to the exercise of an international police power. If every country washed by the Caribbean Sea would show the progress in stable and just civilization which with the aid of the Platt amendment Cuba has shown since our troops left the island, and which so many of the republics in both Americas are constantly and brilliantly showing, all question of interference by this Nation with their affairs would be at an end.

Our interests and those of our southern neighbors are in reality identical. They have great natural riches, and if within their borders the reign of law and justice obtains, prosperity is sure to come to them. While they thus obey the primary laws of civilized society they may rest assured that they will be treated by us in a spirit of cordial and helpful sympathy. We would interfere with them only in the last resort, and then only if it became evident that their inability or unwillingness to do justice at home and abroad had violated the rights of the United States or had invited foreign aggression to the detriment of the entire body of American nations. It is a mere truism to say that every nation, whether in America or anywhere else, which desires to maintain its freedom, its independence, must ultimately realize that the right of such independence can not be separated from the responsibility of making good use of it.

In asserting the Monroe Doctrine, in taking such steps as we have taken in regard to Cuba, Venezuela, and Panama, and in endeavoring to circumscribe the theater of war in the Far East, and to secure the open door in China, we have acted in our own interest as well as in the interest of humanity at large. There are, however, cases in which, while our own interests are not greatly involved, strong appeal is made to our sympathies. Ordinarily it is very much wiser and more useful for us to concern ourselves with striving for our own moral and material betterment here at home than to concern ourselves with trying to better the condition of things in other nations. We have plenty of sins of our own to war against, and under ordinary circumstances we can do more for the general uplifting of humanity by striving with heart and soul to put a stop to civic corruption, to brutal lawlessness and violent race prejudices here at home than by passing resolutions about wrongdoing elsewhere. Nevertheless there are occasional crimes committed on so vast a scale and of such peculiar horror as to make us doubt whether it is not our manifest duty to endeavor at least to show our disapproval of the deed and our sympathy with those who have suffered by it. The cases must be extreme in which such a course is justifiable. There must be no effort made to remove the mote from our brother's eye if we refuse to remove the beam from our own. But in extreme cases action may be justifiable and proper. What form the action shall take must depend upon the circumstances of the case; that is, upon the degree of the atrocity and upon our power to remedy it. The cases in which we could interfere by force of arms as we interferred to put a stop to intolerable conditions in Cuba are necessarily very few.

12. Another cornerstone of American foreign policy in the 20th century was established in 1899. John Hay, then U.S. Secretary of State, proclaimed the "Open Door" policy in China. Like several other important pieces of policy, this was set up without the action of Congress. It was simply stated in a circular letter from the Secretary of State.

John Hay's Letter of September 6, 1899

Sir: The Government of Her Britannic Majesty has declared that its policy and its very traditions precluded it from using any privileges which might be granted it in China as a weapon for excluding commercial rivals, and that freedom of trade for Great Britain in that Empire meant freedom of trade for all the world alike. While conceding by formal agreements, first with Germany and then with Russia, the possession of "spheres of influence or interest" in China in which they are to enjoy special rights and privileges, more especially in respect of railroads and mining enterprises, Her Britannic Majesty's Government has therefore sought to maintain at the same time what is called the "open-door" policy, to insure to the commerce of the world in China equality of treatment within said "spheres" for commerce and navigation. This latter policy is alike urgently demanded by the British mercantile communities and by those of the United States, as it is justly held by them to be the only one which will improve existing conditions, enable them to maintain their positions in the markets of China and extend their operations in the future. While the Government of the United States will in no way commit itself to a recognition of exclusive rights of any power within or control over any portion of the Chinese Empire under such agreements as have within the last year been made, it can not conceal its apprehension that under existing conditions there is a possibility, even a probability, of complications arising between the treaty powers which may imperil the rights insured to the United States under our treaties with China.

This Government is animated by a sincere desire that the interests of our citizens may not be prejudiced through excusive treatment by any of the controlling powers within their so-called "spheres of interest" in China, and hopes also to retain there an open market for the commerce of the world, remove dangerous sources of international irritation, and hasten thereby united or concerted action of the powers at Pekin in favor of the administrative reforms so urgently needed for strengthening the Imperial Government and maintaining the integrity of China in which the whole western world is alike concerned. It believes that such a result may be greatly assisted by a declaration by the various powers claiming "spheres of interest" in China of their intentions as regards treatment of foreign trade therein. The present moment seems a particularly opportune one for informing Her Britannic Majesty's Government of the desire of the United States to see it make a formal declaration and to lend its support in obtaining similar declarations from the various powers claiming "spheres of influence" in China, to the effect that each in its respective spheres of interest or influence—

FIRST. Will in no wise interfere with any treaty port or any vested interest within any so-called "sphere of interest" or leased territory it may have in China.

SECOND. That the Chinese treaty tariff of the time being shall apply to all merchandise landed or shipped to all such ports as are within said "sphere of interest" (unless they be "free ports"), no matter to what nationality it may belong, and that duties so leviable shall be collected by the Chinese Government.

THIRD. That it will levy no higher harbor dues on vessels of another nationality frequenting any port in such "sphere" than shall be levied on vessels of its own nationality, and no higher railroad charges over lines built, controlled, or operated within its "sphere" on merchandise belonging to citizens or subjects of other nationalities transported through such "sphere" than

shall be levied on similar merchandise belonging to its own nationals transported over equal distances.

The recent ukase of His Majesty the Emperor of Russia, declaring the port of Ta-lien-wan open to the merchant ships of all nations during the whole of the lease under which it is to be held by Russia, removing as it does all uncertainty as to the liberal and conciliatory policy of that power, together with the assurances given this Government by Russia, justifies the expectation that His Majesty will cooperate in such an understanding as is here proposed, and our ambassador at the court of St. Petersburg has been instructed accordingly to submit the propositions above detailed to His Imperial Majesty, and ask their early consideration. Copy of my instruction to Mr. Tower is herewith inclosed for your confidential information.

The action of Germany in declaring the port of Kiaochao a "'free port," and the aid the Imperial Government has given China in the establishment there of a Chinese custom-house, coupled with the oral assurance conveyed the United States by Germany that our interests within its "sphere" would in no wise be affected by its occupation of this portion of the province of Shang-tung, tend to show that little opposition may be anticipated from that power to the desired declaration.

The interests of Japan, the next most interested power in the trade of China, will be so clearly served by the proposed arrangement, and the declaration of its statesmen within the last year are so entirely in line with the views here expressed, that its hearty cooperation is confidently counted on.

You will, at as early date as practicable, submit the considerations to Her Britannic Majesty's principal secretary of state for foreign affairs and request their immediate consideration. . . .

13. *When the "Great War" broke out in Europe in August, 1914, President Woodrow Wilson proclaimed American neutrality. In the first document that follows, he appealed to the people of the United States to be truly neutral. However, this appeal, and others that the President made to the belligerents, did not halt the war and the President was obliged to ask Congress for a declaration of war against the Central Powers (principally Germany and Austria-Hungary). His reasons will be found in the second document that follows.*

Appeal for Neutrality, August 19, 1914
My Fellow Countrymen:

I suppose that every thoughtful man in America has asked himself, during these last troubled weeks, what influence the European war may exert upon the United States, and I take the liberty of addressing a few words to you in order to point out that it is entirely within our own choice what its effects upon us will be and to urge very earnestly upon you the sort of speech and conduct which will best safeguard the Nation against distress and disaster.

The effect of the war upon the United States will depend upon what American citizens say and do. Every man who really loves America will act and speak in the true spirit of neutrality, which is the spirit of impartiality and fairness and friendliness to all concerned. The spirit of the Nation in this critical matter will be determined largely by what individuals and society and those gathered in public meetings do and say, upon what newspapers and magazines contain, upon what ministers utter in their pulpits, and men proclaim as their opinions on the street.

The people of the United States are drawn from many nations, and chiefly from the nations now at war. It is natural and inevitable that there should be the utmost variety of sympathy and desire among them with regard to the issues and circumstances of the conflict. Some will wish one nation, others another, to succeed in the momentous struggle. It will be easy to excite passion and difficult to allay it. Those responsible for exciting it will assume a heavy responsibility, responsibility for no less a thing than that the people of the United States, whose love of their country and whose loyalty to its Government should unite them as Americans all, bound in honor and affection to think first of her and her interests, may be divided in camps of hostile opinion, hot against each other, involved in the war itself in impulse and opinion if not in action.

Such divisions among us would be fatal to our peace of mind and might seriously stand in the way of the proper performance of our duty as the one great nation at peace, the one people holding itself ready to play a part of impartial mediation and speak to counsels of peace and accommodation, not as a partisan, but as a friend.

I venture, therefore, my fellow countrymen, to speak a solemn word of warning to you against that deepest, most subtle, most essential breach of neutrality which may spring out of partisanship, out of passionately taking sides. The United States must be neutral in fact as well as in name during these days that are to try men's souls. We must be impartial in thought as well as in action, must put a curb upon our sentiments as well as upon every transaction that might be construed as a preference of one party to the struggle before another.

My thought is of America. I am speaking, I feel sure, the earnest wish and purpose of every thoughtful American that this great country of ours, which is, of course, the first in our thoughts and in our hearts, should show herself in this time of peculiar trial a Nation fit beyond others to exhibit the fine poise of undisturbed judgment, the dignity of self-control, the efficiency of dispassionate action; a Nation that neither sits in judgment upon others nor is disturbed in her own counsels and which keeps herself fit and free to do what is honest and disinterested and truly serviceable for the peace of the world.

Shall we not resolve to put upon ourselves the restraints which will bring to our people the happiness and the great and lasting influence for peace we covet for them?

Woodrow Wilson's Message, April 2, 1917

Gentlemen of the Congress: I have called the Congress into extraordinary session because there are serious, very serious, choices of policy to be made, and made immediately, which it was neither right nor constitutionally permissible that I should assume the responsibility of making.

On the 3d of February last I officially laid before you the extraordinary announcement of the Imperial German Government that on and after the 1st day of February it was its purpose to put aside all restraints of law or of humanity and use its submarines to sink every vessel that sought to approach either the ports of Great Britain and Ireland or the western coasts of Europe or any of the ports controlled by the enemies of Germany within the Mediterranean. That had seemed to be the object of the German submarine warfare earlier in the war, but since April of last year the Imperial Government had somewhat restrained the commanders of its undersea craft in conformity with its promise then given to us that passenger boats should not be sunk and that due warning would be given to all other vessels which its submarines might seek to destroy, when no resistance was offered or escape attempted, and care taken that their crews were given at least a fair chance to save their lives in their open boats. The precautions taken were meagre and haphazard enough, as was proved in distressing instance after instance in the progress of the cruel and unmanly business, but a certain degree of restraint was observed. The new policy has swept every restriction aside. Vessels of every kind, whatever their flag, their character, their cargo, their destination, their errand, have been ruthlessly sent to the bottom without warning and without thought of help or mercy for those on board, the vessels of friendly neutrals along with those of belligerents. Even hospital ships and ships carrying relief to the sorely bereaved and stricken people of Belgium, though the latter were provided with safe-conduct through the proscribed areas by the German Government itself and were distinguished by unmistakable marks of identity, have been sunk with the same reckless lack of compassion or of principle.

It is a war against all nations. American ships have been sunk, American lives taken, in ways which it has stirred us very deeply to learn of, but the ships and people of other neutral and friendly nations have been sunk and overwhelmed in the waters in the same way. There has been no discrimination. The challenge is to all mankind. . . .

With a profound sense of the solemn and even tragical character of the step I am taking and of the grave responsibilities which it involves, but in unhesitating obedience to what I deem my constitutional duty, I advise that the Congress declare the recent course of the Imperial German Government to be in fact nothing less than war against the Government and people of the United States; that it formally accept the status of belligerent which has thus been thrust upon it; and that it take immediate steps not only to put the country in a more thorough state of defense but also to exert all its power and employ all its resources to bring the Government of the German Empire to terms and end the war. . . .

While we do these things, these deeply momentous things, let us be very clear, and make very clear to all the world what our motives and our objects are. My own thought has not been driven from its habitual and normal course by the unhappy events of the last two months, and I do not believe that the thought of the nation has been altered or clouded by them. . . . Our object now, as then, is to vindicate the principles of peace and justice in the life of the world as against selfish and autocratic power and to set up amongst the really free and self-governed peoples of the world such a concert of purpose and of action as will henceforth ensure the observance of those principles. Neutrality is no longer feasible or desirable where the peace of the world is involved and the freedom of its peoples, and the menace to that peace and freedom lies in the existence of autocratic governments backed by organized force which is controlled wholly by their will, not by the will of their people. We have seen the last of neutrality in such circumstances. We are at the beginning of an age in which it will be insisted that the same standards of conduct and of responsibility for wrong done shall be observed among nations and their governments that are observed among the individual citizens of civilized states.

We have no quarrel with the German people. We have no feeling towards them but one of sympathy and friendship. It was not upon their impulse that their Government acted in entering this war. It was not with their previous knowledge or approval. It was a war determined upon as wars used to be determined upon in the old, unhappy days when peoples were nowhere consulted by their rulers and wars were provoked and waged in the interest of dynasties or of little groups of ambitious men who were accustomed to use their fellow men as pawns and tools. Self-governed nations do not fill their neighbour states with spies or set the course of intrigue to bring about some critical posture of affairs which will give them an opportunity to strike and make conquest. Such designs can be successfully worked out only under cover and where no one has the right to ask questions. Cunningly contrived plans of deception or aggression, carried, it may be, from generation to generation, can be worked out and kept from the light only within the privacy of courts or behind the carefully guarded confidences of a narrow and privileged class. They are happily impossible where public opinion commands and insists upon full information concerning all the nation's affairs.

A steadfast concert for peace can never be maintained except by a partnership of democratic nations. No autocratic government could be trusted to keep faith within it or observe its covenants. It must be a league of honour, a partnership of opinion. Intrigue would eat its vitals away; the plottings of inner circles who could plan what they would and render account to no one would be a corruption seated at its very heart. Only free peoples can hold their purpose and their honour steady to a common end and prefer the interests of mankind to any narrow interest of their own. . . .

One of the things that has served to convince us that the Prussian autocracy was not and could never be our friend is that from the very outset of the present war it filled our unsuspecting communities and even our offices of government with spies and set criminal intrigues everywhere afoot against our national unity of counsel, our peace within and without, our industries and our commerce. . . .

We are accepting this challenge of hostile purpose because we know that in such a government, following such methods, we can never have a friend; and that in the presence of its organized power, always lying in wait to accomplish we know not what purpose, there can be no assured security for the democratic governments of the world. We are now about to accept gage of battle with this natural foe to liberty and shall, if necessary, spend the whole force of the nation to check and nullify its pretensions and its power. We are glad, now that we see the facts with no veil of false pretence about them, to fight thus for the ultimate peace of the world and for the liberation of its peoples, the German peoples included: for the rights of nations great and small and the privilege of men everywhere to choose their way of life and of obedience. The world must be made safe for democracy. Its peace must be planted upon the tested foundations of political liberty. We have no selfish ends to serve. We desire no conquest, no dominion. We seek no indemnities for ourselves, no material compensation for the sacrifices we shall freely make. We are but one of the champions of the rights of mankind. . . .

It is a distressing and oppressive duty, gentlemen of the Congress, which I have performed in thus addressing you. There are, it may be, many months of fiery trial and sacrifice ahead of us. It is a fearful thing to lead this great peaceful people into war, into the most terrible and disastrous of all wars, civilization itself seeming to be in the balance. But the right is more precious than peace, and we shall fight for the things which we have always carried nearest our hearts—for democracy, for the right of those who submit to authority to have a voice in their own governments for the rights and liberties of small nations, for a universal dominion of right by such a concert of free peoples as shall bring peace and safety to all nations and make the world itself at last free. To such a task we can dedicate our lives and our fortunes, everything that we are and everything that we have, with the pride of those who know that the day has come when America is privileged to spend her blood and her might for the principles that gave her birth and happiness and the peace which she has treasured. God helping her, she can do no other.

14. Even though the war of 1914-1918 was the greatest bloodbath in history until that time, there were serious hopes and plans for peace after the fighting ended. President Wilson seized the imagination of all the countries in the war with his appeal for peace based on "Fourteen Points", which he set forth in a speech to Congress on January 8, 1918. The text of these famous "points"—the President's program for lasting peace—reads as follows.

I. Open covenants of peace, openly arrived at, after which there shall be no private international understandings of any kind but diplomacy shall proceed always frankly and in the public eye.

II. Absolute freedom of navigation upon the seas, outside territorial waters, alike in peace and in war, except as the seas may be closed in whole or in part by international action for the enforcement of international covenants.

III. The removal, so far as possible, of all economic barriers and the establishment of an equality of trade conditions among all the nations consenting to the peace and associating themselves for its maintenance.

IV. Adequate guarantees given and taken that national armaments will be reduced to the lowest point consistent with domestic safety.

V. A free, open-minded, and absolutely impartial adjustment of all colonial claims, based upon a strict observance of the principle that in determining all such questions of sovereignty the interests of the populations concerned must have equal weight with the equitable claims of the government whose title is to be determined.

VI. The evacuation of all Russian territory and such a settlement of all questions affecting Russia as will secure the best and freest coöperation of the other nations of the world in obtaining for her an unhampered and unembarrassed opportunity for the independent determination of her own political development and national policy and assure her of a sincere welcome into the society of free nations under institutions of her own choosing; and, more than a welcome, assistance also of every kind that she may need and may herself desire. The treatment accorded Russia by her sister nations in the months to come will be the acid test of their good will, of their comprehension of her needs as distinguished from their own interests, and of their intelligent and unselfish sympathy.

VII. Belgium, the whole world will agree, must be evacuated and restored, without any attempt to limit the sovereignty which she enjoys in common with all other free nations. No other single act will serve as this will serve to restore confidence among the nations in the laws which they have themselves set and determined for the government of their relations with one another. Without this healing act the whole structure and validity of international law is forever impaired.

VIII. All French territory should be freed and the invaded portions restored, and the wrong done to France by Prussia in 1871 in the matter of Alsace-Lorraine, which has unsettled the peace of the world for nearly fifty years, should be righted, in order that peace may once more be made secure in the interest of all.

IX. A readjustment of the frontiers of Italy should be affected along clearly recognizable lines of nationality.

X. The peoples of Austria-Hungary, whose place among the nations we wish to see safeguarded and assured, should be accorded the freest opportunity of autonomous development.

XI. Rumania, Serbia, and Montenegro should be evacuated; occupied territories restored; Serbia accorded free and secure access to the sea; and the relations of the several Balkan states to one another determined by friendly counsel along historically established lines of allegiance and nationality; and international guarantees of the political and economic independence and territorial integrity of the several Balkan states should be entered into.

XII. The Turkish portions of the present Ottoman Empire should be assured a secure sovereignty, but the other nationalities which are now under Turkish rule should be assured an undoubted security of life and an absolutely unmolested opportunity of autonomous development and the Dardanelles should be permanently opened as a free passage to the ships and commerce of all nations under international guarantees.

XIII. An independent Polish state should be erected which should include the territories inhabited by indisputably Polish populations, which should be assured a free and secure access to the sea, and whose political and economic independence and territorial integrity should be guaranteed by international covenant.

XIV. A general association of nations must be formed under specific covenants for the purpose of affording mutual guarantees of political independence and territorial integrity to great and small states alike.

15. The Versailles Treaty was never approved or accepted by the U.S. Senate. "Isolationist" members and others, led by Senator Henry Cabot Lodge of Massachusetts, objected particularly to the Treaty's provision for a League of Nations and for the obligations of membership as stated in "Article X" of the League's Covenant.

Article X.

The Members of the League undertake to respect and preserve, as against external aggression, the territorial integrity and existing political independence of all Members of the League. In case of any such aggression, or in case of any threat or danger of such aggression, the Council shall advise upon the means by which this obligation shall be fulfilled.

16. The U.S. Senate rejected the Versailles Treaty by a vote of 35 (against) to 49 (in favor). Approval of the Treaty would have required 56 Senators to vote in favor. It seemed as if the general feeling of the United States favored the preservation of peace through retention of the nation's freedom of action, and by encouraging disarmament. One gesture in

this direction was the Kellogg-Briand Pact of 1928. Its preamble and first two articles follow.

Treaty between the United States and other powers providing for the renunciation of war as an instrument of National Policy.

Deeply sensible of their solemn duty to promote the welfare of mankind;

Persuaded that the time has come when a frank renunciation of war as an instrument of national policy should be made to the end that the peaceful and friendly relations now existing between their peoples may be perpetuated;

Convinced that all changes in their relations with one another should be sought only by pacific means and be the result of a peaceful and orderly process, and that any signatory Power which shall hereafter seek to promote its national interests by resort to war should be denied the benfits furnished by this Treaty;

Hopeful that, encouraged by their example, all the other nations of the world will join in this humane endeavor and by adhering to the present Treaty as soon as it comes into force bring their peoples within the scope of its beneficent provisions, thus uniting the civilized nations of the world in a common renunciation of war as an instrument of their national policy. . . .

ARTICLE I. The High Contracting Parties solemnly declare in the names of their respective peoples that they condemn recourse to war for the solution of international controversies, and renounce it as an instrument of national policy in their relations with one another.

ARTICLE II. The High Contracting Parties agree that the settlement or solution of all disputes or conflicts of whatever nature or of whatever origin they may be, which may arise among them, shall never be sought except by pacific means.

17. Three years later, U.S. Secretary of State Henry L. Stimson found it necessary to send a letter to the governments of China and Japan relative to U.S. policy in East Asia. In the selection that follows, the so-called Stimson Doctrine was announced.

With the recent military operations about Chinchow, the last remaining administrative authority of the Government of the Chinese Republic in South Manchuria, as it existed prior to September 18, 1931, has been destroyed. The American Government continues confident that the work of the neutral commission recently authorized by the Council of the League of Nations will facilitate an ultimate solution of the difficulties now existing between China and Japan. But in view of the present situation and of its own rights and obligations therein, the American Government deems it to be its duty to notify both the Governments of the Chinese Republic and the Imperial Japanese Government that it can not admit the legality of any situation *de facto* nor does it intend to recognize any treaty or agreement entered into between those governments, or agents thereof, which may impair the treaty rights of the United States or its citizens in China, including those which relate to the sovereignty, the independence, or the territorial and administrative integrity of the Republic of China, or to the international policy relative to China, commonly known as the open-door policy; and that it does not intend to recognize any situation, treaty, or agreement which may be brought about by means contrary to the covenants and obligations of the pact of Paris of August 27, 1928, to which treaty both China and Japan, as well as the United States, are parties.

7-D SOCIAL ATTITUDES, 1898-1933

During these years, many Americans agreed that "big" was good, and "bigger" was better. This idea applied to the size of buildings, the extent of businesses, the casts in moving pictures, and even the salaries of professional athletes. Self-reliance and "rugged" individualism were greatly valued. At the same time, there were signs of an increasing concern about mistreatment of individuals by others, and there was a widespread worry over the proper way for individuals to relate to their society.

PROBLEMS: *What were some of the reasons for the interest in bigness and in individual prestige or power? What signs could be seen of a movement to curb excessive individualism in the interest of society as a whole?*

1. Andrew Carnegie, one of the best known industrial leaders in our history, was a spokesman for the individual, successful businessman. Carnegie gathered great wealth for himself, but he thought a good deal about the reasons why men should gather great wealth. His viewpoint, which influenced many Americans during the period, was expressed in such words as the following:

To-day the world obtains commodities of excellent quality at prices which even the generation preceding this would have deemed incredible. In the commercial world similar causes have produced similar results, and the race is benefited thereby. The poor enjoy what the rich could not before afford. What were the luxuries have become the necessaries of life. The laborer has now more comforts than the farmer had a few generations ago. The farmer has more luxuries than the landlord had, and is more richly clad and better housed. The landlord has books and pictures rarer, and appointments more artistic, than the King could then obtain.

The price we pay for this salutary change is, no doubt, great. We assemble thousands of operatives in the factory, in the mine, and in the counting-house, of whom the employer can know little or nothing, and to whom the employer is little better than a myth. All intercourse between them is at an end. Rigid Castes are formed, and, as usual, mutual ignorance breeds mutual distrust. Each Caste is without sympathy for the other, and ready to credit anything disparaging in regard to it. Under the law of competition, the employer of thousands is forced into the strictest economies, among which the rates paid to labor figure prominently, and often there is friction between the employer and the employed, between capital and labor, between rich and poor. Human society loses homogeneity.

The price which society pays for the law of competition, like the price it pays for cheap comforts and luxuries, is also great; but the advantages of this law are also greater still, for it is to this law that we owe our wonderful material development, which brings improved conditions in its train. But, whether the law be benign or not, we must say of it, as we say of the change in the conditions of men to which we have referred: It is here; we cannot evade it; no substitutes for it have been found; and while the law may be sometimes hard for the individual, it is best for the race, because it insures the survival of the fittest in every department. We accept and welcome, therefore, as conditions to which we must accommodate ourselves, great inequality of environment, the concentration of business, industrial and commercial, in the hands of a few, and the law of competition between these, as being not only beneficial, but essential for the future progress of the race.

Having accepted these, it follows that there must be great scope for the exercise of special ability in the merchant and in the manufacturer who has to conduct affairs upon a great scale. That this talent for organization and management is rare among men is proved by the fact that it invariably secures for its possessor enormous rewards, no matter where or under what laws or conditions. The experienced in affairs always rate the MAN whose services can be obtained as a partner as not only the first consideration, but such as to render the question of his capital scarcely worth considering, for such men soon create capital: while, without the special talent required, capital soon takes wings. Such men become interested in firms or corporations using millions; and estimating only simple interest to be made upon the capital invested, it is inevitable that their income must exceed their expenditures, and that they must accumulate weath. Nor is there any middle ground which such men can occupy, because the great manufacturing or commercial concern which does not earn at least interest upon its capital soon becomes bankrupt. It must either go forward or fall behind: to stand still is impossible. It is a condition essential for its successful operation that it should be thus far profitable, and even that, in addition to interest on capital, it should make profit. It is a law, as certain as any of the others named, that men possessed of this peculiar talent for affairs, under the free play of economic forces, must, of necessity, soon be in receipt of more revenue than can be judiciously expended upon themselves; and this law is as beneficial for the race as the others.

Objections to the foundations upon which society is based are not in order, because the condition of the race is better with these than it has been with any others which have been tried. Of the effect of any new substitutes proposed we cannot be sure. The Socialist or An-

archist who seeks to overturn present conditions is to be regarded as attacking the foundation upon which civilization itself rests, for civilization took its start from the day that the capable, industrious workman said to his incompetent and lazy fellow, "If thou dost not sow, thou shalt not reap," and thus ended primitive Communism by separating the drones from the bees. One who studies this subject will soon be brought face to face with the conclusion that upon the sacredness of property civilization itself depends—the right of the laborer to his hundred dollars in the savings bank, and equally the legal right of the millionaire to his millions.

To those who propose to substitute Communism for this intense Individualism the answer, therefore, is: The race has tried that. All progress from that barbarous day to the present time has resulted from its displacement. Not evil, but good, has come to the race from the accumulation of wealth by those who have the ability and energy that produce it. But even if we admit for a moment that it might be better for the race to discard its present foundation, Individualism,—that it is a nobler ideal that man should labor, not for himself alone, but in and for a brotherhood of his fellows, and share with them all in common, realizing Swedenborg's idea of Heaven, where, as he says, the angels derive their happiness, not from laboring for self, but for each other,—even admit all this, and a sufficient answer is, This is not evolution, but revolution. It necessitates the changing of human nature itself—a work of aeons, even if it were good to change it, which we cannot know. It is not practicable in our day or in our age. Even if desirable theoretically, it belongs to another and long-succeeding sociological stratum. Our duty is with what is practicable now; with the next step possible in our day and generation. It is criminal to waste our energies in endeavoring to uproot, when all we can profitably or possibly accomplish is to bend the universal tree of humanity a little in the direction most favorable to the production of good fruit under existing circumstances. We might as well urge the destruction of the highest existing type of man because he failed to reach our ideal as to favor the destruction of Individualism, Private Property, the Law of Accumulation of Wealth, and the Law of Competition; for these are the highest results of human experience, the soil in which society so far has produced the best fruit. . . .

This, then, is held to be the duty of the man of Wealth: First, to set an example of modest, unostentatious living, shunning display or extravagance; to provide moderately for the legitimate wants of those dependent upon him; and after doing so to consider all surplus revenues which come to him simply as trust funds, which he is called upon to administer, and strictly bound as a matter of duty to administer in the manner which, in his judgment, is best calculated to produce the most beneficial results for the community—the man of wealth thus becoming the mere agent and trustee for his poorer brethren, bringing to their service his superior wisdom, experience, and ability to administer, doing for them better than they would or could do for themselves.

2. Not all Americans were convinced by Mr. Carnegie's eloquent argument. Many concerned thinkers, observers, and writers brought forth evidence of great unfairness in the system, resulting in overwork for laboring men and women and underpayment. The journalists who exposed bad government, bad housing, bad working conditions, and bad business ethics, were called "muckrakers". Among them were Ida Tarbell (who attacked the Standard Oil trust), Lincoln Steffens (who wrote of "the Shame of the Cities"), and Upton Sinclair, whose indictment of the meat-packing industry in his novel The Jungle *brought about an almost instant public outcry for reform. There follow, first, a quotation from John Spargo's* The Bitter Cry of the Children *(1906) which deals with exploitation of child labor in the coal mines; and second, a part of a U.S. Department of Labor Report of similar practices in 1919.*

Children in the Mines

Work in the coal breakers is exceedingly hard and dangerous. Crouched over the chutes, the boys sit hour after hour, picking out the pieces of slate and other refuse from the coal as it rushes past to the washers. From the cramped position they have to assume, most of them become more or less deformed and bent-backed like old men. When a boy has been working for some time and begins to get round-shouldered, his fellows say that "He's got his boy to carry round wherever he goes."

The coal is hard, and accidents to the hands, such as cut, broken, or crushed fingers, are common among the boys. Sometimes there is a worse accident: a terrified shriek is heard, and a boy is mangled and torn in the machinery, or disappears in the chute to be picked out later smothered and dead. Clouds of dust fill the breakers and are inhaled by the boys, laying the foundations for asthma and miners' consumption.

I once stood in a breaker for half an hour and tried to do the work a twelve-year-old boy was doing day after day, for ten hours at a stretch, for sixty cents a day. The gloom of the breaker appalled me. Outside the sun shone brightly, the air was pellucid, and the birds sang in chorus with the trees and the rivers. Within the breaker there was blackness, clouds of deadly dust enfolded everything, the harsh, grinding roar of the machinery and the ceaseless rushing of coal through the chutes filled the ears. I tried to pick out the pieces of slate from the hurrying stream of coal, often missing them; my hands were bruised and cut in a few minutes; I was covered from head to foot with coal dust, and for many hours afterwards I was expectorating some of the small particles of anthracite I had swallowed.

I could not do that work and live, but there were boys of ten and twelve years of age doing it for fifty and sixty cents a day. Some of them had never been inside of a school; few of them could read a child's primer. True, some of them attended the night schools, but after working ten hours in the breaker the educational results from attending school were practically nil. . . .

As I stood in that breaker I thought of the reply of the small boy to Robert Owen *(British social reformer).* Visiting an English coal mine one day, Owen asked a twelve-year-old lad if he knew God. The boy stared vacantly at his questioner: "God?" he said, "God? No, I don't. He must work in some other mine." It was hard to realize amid the danger and din and blackness of that Pennsylvania breaker that such a thing as belief in a great All-good God existed.

From the breakers the boys graduate to the mine depths, where they become door tenders, switch boys, or mule drivers. Here, far below the surface, work is still more dangerous. At fourteen or fifteen the boys assume the same risks as the men, and are surrounded by the same perils. Nor is it in Pennsylvania only that these conditions exist. In the bituminous mines of West Virginia, boys of nine or ten are frequently employed. I met one little fellow ten years old in Mt. Carbon, W. Va., last year, who was employed as a "trap boy." Think of what it means to be a trap boy at ten years of age. It means to sit alone in a dark mine passage hour after hour, with no human soul near; to see no living creature except the mules as they pass with their loads, or a rat or two seeking to share one's meal; to stand in water or mud that covers the ankles, chilled to the marrow by the cold draughts that rush in when you open the trap door for the mules to pass through; to work for fourteen hours—waiting—opening and shutting a door —then waiting again—for sixty cents; to reach the surface when all is wrapped in the mantle of night, and to fall to the earth exhausted and have to be carried away to the nearest "shack" to be revived before it is possible to walk to the farther shack called "home."

Boys twelve years of age may be legally employed in the mines of West Virginia, by day or by night, and for as many hours as the employers care to make them toil or their bodies will stand the strain. Where the disregard of child life is such that this may be done openly and with legal sanction, it is easy to believe what miners have again and again told me—that there are hundreds of little boys of nine and ten years of age employed in the coal mines of this state.

Report of the Department of Labor

Although unlike in many ways, the mining towns throughout the anthracite region (*of Pennsylvania*) bear the mark of the pit, and their general problems are similar. Everywhere the industry has wrought great changes in the face of the landscape. It is a black country dominated by the great breakers which rise above the towns. The streams are black with soot and there are black piles of refuse and culm, and the men returning from work wear masks of coal dust. Trees have been cut down for mine timber, so that only stumps and scrubby bush, saplings, or misshaped trees are left. The earth mixed with the slate and coal dust is for the most part bare, and the few gardens, which demonstrate that the ground can still be cultivated, emphasize the general desolation. Throughout the region are fissures and cave-ins where the props in the mines have given way.

The district selected by the Children's Bureau in 1919 for a study of the problems of adolescent children lies in the central field in Schuylkill County, where the mountains cut the land into valleys and basins, narrow and irregular in outline. It includes the boroughs of Shenandoah, Gilberton, and Frackville and surrounding patches up to the boundary line of Mahanoy City on the east and Girardville on the west. The characteristics of the anthracite region seem especially prominent here.

Shenandoah, the business and educational center of the district, is a congested town shut in by high hills. In its setting of culm heaps there is no touch of color or beauty, but, from the hills above it, long ranges of mountains may be seen, and in the scrubby brush which covers the hills great masses of wild rhododendron blossom in the spring. The air is usually filled with the sulfurous dust which blows from the culm banks and the coal dust which comes from the breakers and the coal cars. The noise of the coal as it rushes down the breakers and of the chugging of the mine fans and other machinery is almost incessant.

For most of its length, Gilberton Borough is a single row of houses along the trolley. Here, much of the land has been undermined—a model mining town of the district. The patches which are located conveniently along the railroad and trolley lines are set amidst great heaps of culm and refuse, while the isolated ones are surrounded by brush, which is green in summer.

In all these communities the life revolves around the mines. In Shenandoah, at the time the study was made, there were three overall, two cigar, and two shirt factories, and one mining-cap factory. These employed chiefly the wives and daughters of the mine workers. Two packinghouses, with their accompanying slaughterhouses and fertilizer plants, bottling works, and two lumber companies, employed a larger proportion of men. As Shenandoah is the business center of the district, there were also retail stores, bakeries, and banks, as well as freight houses and railroad and building operations, which offered some opportunities for employment.

In Frackville there were a nightdress and pajama factory and an overall factory dependent on the women and girls for a labor supply. In the patches and in Gilberton there was no possibility of employment except in the mines or in a few small retail stores. . . .

The mine workers of the United States, as a rule, have been recruited from recently arrived immigrants; and at every period the nationalities which were coming to the country in the largest numbers have tended to displace the older miners. During this process of displacement the population usually is highly complex, with a concentration of particular nationalities in individual mining towns as there has been in individual industrial towns. Thus, Poles have predominated in one, Lithuanians in another, Italians in a third, Slovaks in a fourth, and so on. . . .

By the time this study was begun, the federal child labor tax law was in effect. This act does not prohibit the employment of children but places a 10 percent tax on the net income of any mill, cannery, workshop, factory, or manufacturing establishment employing children between fourteen and sixteen years of age more than eight hours a day or six days a week, or before 6 A.M. or after 7 P.M., and on any mine or quarry in which children under the age of sixteen years are employed.

Prior to 1909, Pennsylvania had prohibited the employment of children under sixteen years of age in the mines, but the only kind of certificate or work permit required was the parent's affidavit; and experience proved that in Pennsylvania, as in other states, a law of this sort did not keep children under that age out of the mines. In 1909 this law was amended so as to require documentary proof of the child's age, but it is reported that "through an unfortunate error in drafting the bill," the minimum age was reduced to fourteen years for employment inside the anthracite mines. This was amended in 1915, so that at the time the federal law went into effect no minor under sixteen years of age could be legally employed or permitted to work "in any anthracite or bituminous coal mine or in any other mine."

While the Pennsylvania act provided for the enforcement of this and all other sections of the state child labor law by the commissioner of labor and industry, the inspection of the mines, in practice, was left to the Department of Mines. The breaker boys in the anthracite coal region were not regarded as working in the mine within the meaning of the Pennsylvania law; and regular inspections of the breakers, with a view to the enforcement of the child labor law, were not being made by either department at the time this investigation was made.

Under the interpretation of the state law, followed by the state officials, children between fourteen and sixteen years of age were permitted to work on breakers, but they could not be legally so employed unless regularly issued work permits were on file and not then for more than fifty-one hours in any one week, or more than nine hours in any one day, or before 6 in the morning or after 8 in the evening.

In general the provisions of the Pennsylvania law with reference to the issuance of certificates of age were good. The law required certificates of all children between fourteen and sixteen years of age employed in any occupation except agriculture and domestic service. They were to be issued by the local school superintendent or someone authorized by him. The evidence of age required was: (a) transcript of birth certificate; (b) baptismal certificate; (c) passport showing age; (d) any other documentary record of age other than school record; (e) physician's certificate of evidence of age.

This system, devised for the protection of young children, did not always function in the Shenandoah district.

Some children reported that they began work with no certificate other than a "work paper" bought from the "Squire" for 50 cents. One child reported he had secured employment on a baptismal certificate when he was twelve. Another boy said that when he first applied for a "working paper," it was refused because he was under fourteen; but one was finally granted him for vacation work, and he started in a newspaper office. Here he learned to set type and liked his work. When school started, however, the newspaper refused to keep him as his employment certificate was for vacation only and he was not yet fourteen. He went to one of the mining companies, however, and was given work, though he still had no regular certificate. . . .

Seventy-two percent of the sixteen-year-old children, 58.9 percent of the fifteen-year-old, 31.6 percent of the fourteenyear-old, and 10.8 percent of the thirteen-year-old children had entered regular work. The total number of boys in the age groups studied was slightly less than the total number of girls; still, about twice as many boys as girls had entered regular work. Of the children who had entered regular employment, 896 (66.4 per-

cent) were boys and 453 (33.6 percent) were girls. . . .

The kind of work these children did was largely determined by the industrial character of the district. The life of the district revolves around the mines, and for the boys, more than for their fathers, their place of employment was the mines. The canvass made by the Children's Bureau showed that for the district as a whole, 90.4 percent of the boys doing full-time work were in mining, as compared with 78 percent of their fathers. A larger percent of the boys with native fathers (16.6) than of the boys with foreign-born fathers (6.8 percent) were able to find some place other than the mines in which to begin work.

The fact that the breakers offered opportunities for profitable employment of young boys is the explanation of the large number of boys employed in connection with the mining of anthracite coal. It also accounts for the poorer pay and the current opinion that the breakers should be reserved for the young boys or men who had long since passed their maximum working capacity. Of the 810 boys whose first regular work was in the mines, 723 (89 percent) began as breaker boys; 422 were in this classification at the time the investigation was made.

These breakers which tower above the town of Shenandoah to the east and the south and the west are great barnlike structures filled with chutes, sliding belts, and great crushing and sorting machines. Around these machines a scaffolding was built on which the workers stand or sit. The coal is raised from the mine to the top of the breaker and dumped down the chute into a crushing machine, which breaks it into somewhat smaller lumps. These are carried along a moving belt or gravity incline on each side of which men and boys stand or sit picking out pieces of slate and any coal which has slate mixed with it. The latter is carried into another crusher, where it is broken again and then carried down chutes to be sorted further by slate pickers or by sorting machines. After the coal has been broken and cleaned of slate or other alien materials, it is sorted by being shaken through a series of screens. . . .

Black coal dust is everywhere, covering the windows and filling the air and the lungs of the workers.

The slate is sharp so that the slate pickers often cut or bruise their hands; the coal is carried down the chute in water and this means sore and swollen hands for the pickers. The first few weeks after a boy begins work, his fingers bleed almost continuously and are called red tops by the other boys. Slate picking is not itself dangerous; the slate picker is, however, sometimes set at cleaning-up jobs, which require him to clean out shakers, the chute, or other machinery.

Sixty-three of the breaker boys included in this study were jig runners. In other words, they operated a jig machine, which has a series of sliding pans in which the coal is shaken up and down and back and forth in water so that the lighter slate is gradually shaken to the top and can be cleared from the pan so that only the coal will remain. It is a more dangerous job than slate picking and few boys are assigned to it as a first job. Usually the foreman promotes quick, bright slate pickers to be jig runners. However, four boys were included in this study who had begun at this work.

There were thirty-three boys employed as scraper line tenders and thirty-three as shaker watchers; none of the boys began at the former and only six at the latter occupation. The shaker watcher tends the sets of screens through which the coal is sorted, and the scraper line tender operates the scrapers which carry the coal from one process to another. Of the others who were at work in the breakers, thirteen were oilers; five were repair boys; eight, known as patchers, worked on the coal cars as coupler, switchman, etc.; twenty-eight were spraggers, a highly dangerous occupation, requiring them to thrust heavy wooden sticks in between the iron spokes of the wheels of the coal cars in order to stop them; twenty-four other boys were known as laborers and were assigned to do various kinds of unskilled work. There were six who worked above ground, although not in the breakers, driving mules where the work of excavating or stripping was being done as well as fifty-nine other boys who were outside workers.

Whatever the hazards and dangers of the breakers are, underground work is much more undesirable for young boys. In addition to isolation and darkness, much more intense than that which the coal dust makes in the breakers, the . . . miner sometimes works in mud and water, sometimes stripped to the waist because of the heat, sometimes in suffocating gas and smoke.

Young boys were working daily underground at the time this investigation was made. Of those employed underground, nine were spraggers, eighteen were patchers, thirty-four were drivers, forty-seven were trapper boys, one was a fan turner, three were oilers, and eighteen were laborers. . . .

Of the 163 boys who had been underground workers, 92 began as trapper boys, which means they sat or stood in darkness or semi-darkness by a door which led from one mine chamber to another and opened and closed the door to allow the coal cars as they came to pass through. Of the trapper boys, 17 were only thirteen and 3 were only twelve years old when they began to do regular, full-day duty at this work. An automatic contrivance which makes unnecessary the employment of either men or boys for this work is now available and has been introduced in many mines.

The boys who turned by hand the ventilating fans frequently worked on the dangerous robbing sections where the last remaining coal is being cut away from pillars and walls and where, in consequence, the roof sometimes falls in or the section is filled with a waste material known as slush. The men interviewed told of the nervous strain they experienced when they worked at robbing. Turning the fans for these workers was the first underground work for twelve boys included in this study; of that number one began when he was twelve years old, one at thirteen, four at fourteen, and six at fifteen years of age. A few other boys were employed underground as oilers and as laborers doing a variety of work.

It is unnecessary to point out the dangers of underground work. Where electric cars are operated, where dynamiting is done, where supports give way and cave-ins and squeezes occur, and rock and coal fall, serious accidents and sudden death, more terrible to endure because of the victim's isolation and consequent distance from relief of any kind, are incidents of the occupation. . . .

3. *One of the signs of change, and a leading influence on the way people would alter their ways of life, was the automobile. Confrontations between horses (which all Americans already knew) and automobiles (which only a few had seen or possessed) led to situations such as the following, which are quoted from Michael L. Berger,* The Social Impact of the Automobile on Rural America: 1893-1929, *by permission of the author.*

One of the worst problems that was to arise, and the least amenable to reasonable dialogue among the protagonists, was the dislike of the horse for the automobile. Various explanations were offered for why this was so. Some thought it was the appearance and/or shape of the vehicle which gave fright. Thus, Uriah Smith of Battle Creek, Michigan, offered the unique solution of mounting on the outer dashboard of his motor car the head and shoulders of a horse. Others blamed the antagonism on the sound and smell of the vehicle, particularly when it came in close proximity to the horse.

Whatever the reasons, L. E. French spoke for most early motorists when he offered these observations on his 1904 automobile tour of New Hampshire's White Mountain region:

Let me say right here that automobiles seem to exert a wonderfully rejuvenating influence upon White Mountain horses. Even the most ancient animals apparently go into a trance in which they have the most violent visions of their younger days. The occupants of the vehicles, who in most cases have been worrying for hours over the prospect of meeting an automobile, naturally catch the general excitement, and panic reigns. Under these circumstances we soon adopted the policy of stopping whenever a "hay motor" hove in sight, and remaining stationary until it was out of sight. It quite frequently happened that as we wended our way through some wooded lane, a horse-drawn vehicle rather unexpectedly appeared. The occupants almost invariably leaped as if shot, uttered sounds indicative of human agony, and waved their arms above their heads. The horses, startled by the unusual sounds and the appearance of the machine, promptly began vaudeville imitations of the Saint Vitus' dance, interspersed with touches of the Highland fling. About this time the ladies of the party generally forgot all conventionalities and began leaping from the vehicle like grasshoppers from a hot saucepan.

As a result of incidents such as this, there grew up an elaborate procedure, compounded of law and experience, to be followed whenever horse and automobile met. Hiram P. Maxim, one of the early pioneers of the automotive industry, had several such experiences during 1907 and 1908 while driving an experimental tricycle:

The horse's ears were sticking up very stiff and alert. I fancied I smelled trouble. I slowed away down, creeping along cautiously, prepared to dismount and make a dash for the horse's head the moment he indicated a tendency to turn sharp around, which was usually what did the damage. The horse was high-spirited and extremely nervous. When we had approached each other as closely as I considered safe, I pulled over on the grass at the roadside and stopped. This would have to be done anyway, since no horse would consent to pass close to the machine.

4.   *For the first time in American history, immigration began to be a source of concern during these years. In earlier times, jobs were more plentiful than workers and newcomers were especially welcomed. The shift in opinion can be observed in the following resolutions by the American Federation of Labor Convention in 1909, approving restrictions on immigration of people who could not read and write.*

Resolution 77, passed at the annual convention held at Toronto, Ontario, November, 1909:
WHEREAS, The illiteracy test is the most practical means for restricting the present stimulated influx of cheap labor, whose competition is so ruinous to the workers already here, whether native or foreign; and

WHEREAS, An increased head tax upon steamships is needed to provide better facilities, to more efficiently enforce our immigration laws, and to restrict immigration; and

WHEREAS, The requirement of some visible means of support would enable immigrants to find profitable employment; and

WHEREAS, The effect of the Federal Bureau of Distribution is to stimulate foreign immigration; therefore be it

Resolved, By the American Federation of Labor in Twenty-ninth Annual Convention assembled, that we demand the enactment of the illiteracy test, the money test, an increased head tax and the abolition of the Distribution Bureau; and, be it further

Resolved, That we favor heavily fining the foreign steamships for bringing debarable aliens where reasons for debarment could have been ascertained at the time of sale of ticket.

5.   *Educational reforms were also undertaken. The first of the documents which follow deals with the state of medical education and is quoted from the introduction to a 1910 report entitled* Medical Education in the United States and Canada. *This report resulted from a survey conducted by Dr. Abraham Flexner for the Carnegie Foundation.*

The second document is a selection from a 1918 report of a national commission set up by the National Education Association to study the operation of high schools and make recommendations for the reform of their aims and their programs.

Medical Education
The striking and signficant facts which are here brought out are of enormous consequence not only to the medical practitioner, but to every citizen of the United States and Canada; for it is a singular fact that the organization of medical education in this country has hitherto been such as not only to commercialize the process of education itself, but also to obscure in the minds of the public any discrimination between the well trained physician and the physician who has had no adequate training whatsoever. As a rule, Americans, when they avail themselves of the services of a physician, make only the slightest inquiry as to what his previous training and preparation have been. One of the problems of the future is to educate the public itself to appreciate the fact that very seldom, under existing conditions, does a patient receive the best aid which it is possible to give him in the present state of medicine, and that this is due mainly to the fact that a vast army of men is admitted to the practice of medicine who are untrained in sciences fundamental to the profession and quite without a sufficient experience with disease. A right

education of public opinion is one of the problems of future medical education.

The significant facts revealed by this study are these:

(1) For twenty-five years past there has been an enormous over-production of uneducated and ill trained medical practitioners. This has been in absolute disregard of the public welfare and without any serious thought of the interests of the public. Taking the United States as a whole, physicians are four or five times as numerous in proportion to population as in older countries like Germany.

(2) Over-production of ill trained men is due in the main to the existence of a very large number of commercial schools, sustained in many cases by advertising methods through which a mass of unprepared youth is drawn out of industrial occupations into the study of medicine.

(3) Until recently the conduct of a medical school was a profitable business, for the methods of instruction were mainly didactic. As the need for laboratories has become more keenly felt, the expenses of an efficient medical school have been greatly increased. The inadequacy of many of these schools may be judged from the fact that nearly half of all our medical schools have incomes below $10,000, and these incomes determine the quality of instruction that they can and do offer.

Colleges and universities have in large measure failed in the past twenty-five years to appreciate the great advance in medical education and the increased cost of teaching it along modern lines. Many universities desirous of apparent educational completeness have annexed medical schools without making themselves responsible either for the standards of the professional schools or for their support.

(4) The existence of many of these unnecessary and inadequate medical schools has been defended by the argument that a poor medical school is justified in the interest of the poor boy. It is clear that the poor boy has no right to go into any profession for which he is not willing to obtain adequate preparation; but the fact set forth in this report make it evident that this argument is insincere, and that the excuse which has hitherto been put forward in the name of the poor boy is in reality an argument in behalf of the poor medical school.

(5) A hospital under complete educational control is as necessary to a medical school as is a laboratory of chemistry or pathology. High grade teaching within a hospital introduces a most wholesome and beneficial influence into its routine. Trustees of hospitals, public and private, should therefore go to the limit of their authority in opening hospital wards to teaching, provided only that the universities secure sufficient funds on their side to employ as teachers men who are devoted to clinical science.

In view of these facts, progress for the future would seem to require a very much smaller number of medical schools, better equipped and better conducted than our schools now as a rule are; and the needs of the public would equally require that we have fewer physicians graduated each year, but that these should be better educated and better trained. With this idea accepted, it necessarily follows that the medical school will, if rightly conducted, articulate not only with the university, but with the general system of education. Just what form that articulation must take will vary in the immediate future in different parts of the country. Throughout the eastern and central states the movement under which the medical school articulates with the second year of the college has already gained such impetus that it can be regarded as practically accepted. In the southern states for the present it would seem that articulation with the four-year high school would be a reasonable starting-point for the future. In time the development of secondary education in the south and the growth of the colleges will make it possible for southern medical schools to accept the two-year college basis of preparation. With reasonable prophecy the time is not far distant when, with fair respect for the interests of the public and the need for physicians, the articulation of the medical school with the university may be the same throughout the entire country. For in the future the college or the university which accepts a medical school must make itself responsible for university standards in the medical school and for adequate support for the medical education. The day has gone by when any university can retain the respect of educated men, or when it can fulfill its duty to education, by retaining a low grade professional school for the sake of its own institutional completeness.

If these fundamental principles can be made clear to the people of the United States and of Canada, and to those who govern the colleges and the universities, we may confidently expect that the next ten years will see a very much smaller number of medical schools in this country, but a greatly increased efficiency in medical education, and that during the same period medical education will become rightly articulated with, and rightly related to, the general educational system of the whole country.

The development which is here suggested for medical education is conditioned largely upon three factors: first, upon the creation of a public opinion which shall discriminate between the ill trained and the rightly trained physician, and which will also insist upon the enactment of such laws as will require all practitioners of medicine, whether they belong to one sect or another, to ground themselves in the fundamentals upon which medical science rests; secondly, upon the universities and their attitude towards medical standards and medical support; finally, upon the attitude of the members of the medical profession towards the standards of their own practice and upon their sense of honor with respect to their own profession.

These last two factors are moral rather than educational. They call for an educational patriotism on the part of the institutions of learning and a medical patriotism on the part of the physician.

By educational patriotism I mean this: a university has a mission greater than the formation of a large student body or the attainment of institutional completeness, namely, the duty of loyalty to the standards of common honesty, of intellectual sincerity, of scientific accuracy. A university with educational patriotism will not take up the work of medical education unless it can discharge its duty by it; or if, in the days of ignorance once winked at, a university became entangled in a medical school alliance, it will frankly and courageously deal with a situation which is no longer tenable. It will either demand of its medical school university ideals and give it university support, or else it will drop the effort to do what it can only do badly.

By professional patriotism amongst medical men I mean that sort of regard for the honor of the profession and that sense of responsibility for its efficiency which will enable a member of that profession to rise above the consideration of personal or of professional gain. As Bacon truly wrote, "Every man owes a duty to his profession," and in no profession is this obligation more clear than in that of the modern physician. Perhaps in no other of the great professions does one find greater discrepancies between the ideals of those who represent it. No members of the social order are more self-sacrificing than the true physicians and surgeons, and of this fine group none deserve so much of society as those who have taken upon their shoulders the burden of medical education. On the other hand, the profession has been diluted by the presence of a great number of men who have come from weak schools with low ideals both of education and of professional honor. If the medical education of our country is in the immediate future to go upon a plane of efficiency and of credit, those who represent the higher ideals of the medical profession must make a stand for that form of medical education which is calculated to advance the true interests of the whole people and to better the ideals of medicine itself.

There is raised in the discussion of this question a far-reaching economic problem to which society has as yet given little attention; that is to say, What safeguards may society and the law throw about admission to a profession like that of law or of medicine in order that a sufficient number of men may be induced to enter it and yet the unfit and the undesirable may be excluded?

It is evident that in a society constituted as are our modern states, the interests of the social order will be served best when the number of men entering a given profession reaches and does not exceed a certain ratio. For example, in law and medicine one sees best in a small village the situation created by the over-production of inadequately trained men. In a town of two thousand people one will find in most of our states from five to eight physicians where two well trained men could do the work efficiently and make a competent livelihood. When, however, six or eight ill trained physicians undertake to gain a living in a town which can support only two, the whole plane of professional conduct is lowered in the struggle which ensues, each man becomes intent upon his own practice, public health and sanitation are neglected, and the ideals and standards of the profession tend to demoralization.

A similar state of affairs comes from the presence of too large a number of ill trained lawyers in a community. When six or eight men seek to gain their living from the practice of the law in a community in which, at the most, two good lawyers could do all the work, the demoralization to society becomes acute. Not only is the process of the law unduly lengthened, but the temptation is great to create business. No small proportion of the American lack of respect for the law grows out of the presence of this large number of ill trained men seeking to gain a livelihood from the business which ought in the nature of the case to support only a much smaller number. . . .

The point of view which keeps in mind the needs and qualifications of the medical student and the interests of the great public is quite a different one from that which the institution which conducts a medical department ordinarily occupies. The questions which look largest to the institutions are: Can we add a medical school to our other departments? and if so, where can we find the students? The questions which the other point of view suggest are: Is a medical school needed? Cannot those qualified to study medicine find opportunities in existing schools? If not, are the means and the facilities at hand for teaching medicine on a right basis?

While the aim of the Foundation has throughout been constructive, its attitude towards the difficulties and problems of the situation is distinctly sympathetic. The report indeed turns the light upon conditions which, instead of being fruitful and inspiring, are in many instances commonplace, in other places bad, and in still others, scandalous. It is nevertheless true that no one set of men or no one school of medicine is responsible for what still remains in the form of commercial medical education. Our hope is that this report will make plain once for all that the day of the commercial medical school has passed. It will be observed that, except for a brief historical introduction, intended to show how present conditions have come about, no account is given of the past of any institution. The situation is described as it exists today in the hope that out of it, quite regardless of the past, a new order may be speedily developed. There is no need now of recriminations over what has been, or of apologies by way of defending a régime practically obsolete. Let us address ourselves resolutely to the task of reconstructing the American medical school on the lines of the highest modern ideals of efficiency and in accordance with the finest conceptions of public service.

It is hoped that both the purpose of the Foundation and its point of view as thus stated may be remembered in any consideration of the report which follows, and that this publication may serve as a starting-point both for the intelligent citizen and for the medical practitioner in a new national effort to strengthen the medical profession and rightly to relate medical education to the general system of schools of our nation.

Report on Secondary Schools
I. The Need for Reorganization

Secondary education should be determined by the needs of the society to be served, the character of the individuals to be educated, and the knowledge of educational theory and practice available. These factors are by no means static. Society is always in process of development; the character of the secondary-school population undergoes modification; and the sciences on which educational theory and practice depend constantly furnish new information. Secondary education, however, like any other established agency of society, is conservative and tends to resist modification. Failure to make adjustments when the need arises leads to the necessity for extensive reorganization at irregular intervals. The evidence is strong that such a comprehensive reorganization of secondary education is imperative at the present time.

1. *Changes in society.*—Within the past few decades changes have taken place in American life profoundly affecting the activities of the individual. As a citizen, he must to a greater extent and in a more direct way cope with problems of community life, State and National Governments, and international relationships.

As a worker, he must adjust himself to a more complex economic order. As a relatively independent personality, he has more leisure. The problems arising from these three dominant phases of life are closely interrelated and call for a degree of intelligence and efficiency on the part of every citizen that can not be secured through elementary education alone, or even through secondary education unless the scope of that education is broadened.

The responsibility of the secondary school is still further increased because many social agencies other than the school afford less stimulus for education than heretofore. In many vocations there have come such significant changes as the substitution of the factory system for the domestic system of industry; the use of machinery in place of manual labor; and the breakdown of the apprentice system. In connection with home and family life have frequently come lessened responsibility on the part of the children; the withdrawal of the father and sometimes the mother from home occupations to the factory or store; and increased urbanization, resulting in less unified family life. Similarly, many important changes have taken place in community life, in the church, in the State, and in other institutions. These changes in American life call for extensive modifications in secondary education.

2. *Changes in the secondary-school population.*— In the past 25 years there have been marked changes in the secondary-school population of the United States. The number of pupils has increased, according to Federal returns, from one for every 210 of the total population in 1889-90, to one for every 121 in 1899-1900, to one for every 89 in 1909-10, and to one for every 73 of the estimated total population in 1914-15. The character of the secondary-school population has been modified by the entrance of large numbers of pupils of widely varying capacities, aptitudes, social heredity, and destinies in life. Further, the broadening of the scope of secondary education has brought to the school many pupils who do not complete the full course but leave at various stages of advancement. The needs of these pupils can not be neglected, nor can we expect in the near future that all pupils will be able to complete the secondary school as full-time students.

At present only about one-third of the pupils who enter the first year of the elementary school reach the four-year high school, and only about one in nine is graduated. Of those who enter the seventh school year, only one-half to two-thirds reach the first year of the four-year high school. Of those who enter the four-year high school about one-third leave before the beginning of the second year, about one-half are gone before the beginning of the third year, and fewer than one-third are graduated. These facts can no longer be safely ignored.

3. *Changes in educational theory.*—The sciences on which educational theory depends have within recent years made significant contributions. In particular, educational psychology emphasizes the following factors:

(a) *Individual differences in capacities and aptitudes among secondary-school pupils.* Already recognized to some extent, this factor merits fuller attention.

(b) *The reexamination and reinterpretation of subject values and the teaching methods with reference to "general discipline."*—While the final verdict of modern psychology has not as yet been rendered, it is clear that former conceptions of "general values" must be thoroughly revised.

(c) *Importance of applying knowledge.*—Subject values and teaching methods must be tested in terms of the laws of learning and the application of knowledge to the activities of life, rather than primarily in terms of the demands of any subject as a logically organized science.

(d) *Continuity in the development of children.*—It has long been held that psychological changes at certain stages are so pronounced as to overshadow the continuity of development. On this basis secondary education has been sharply separated from elementary education. Modern psychology goes to show that the development of the individual is in most respects a continuous process and that, therefore, any sudden or abrupt break between the elementary and the secondary school or between any two successive stages of education is undesirable.

The foregoing changes in society, in the character of the secondary-school population, and in educational theory, together with many other considerations, call for extensive modifications of secondary education. Such modifications have already begun in part. The present need is for the formulation of a comprehensive program of reorganization, and its adoption, with suitable adjustments, in all the secondary schools of the Nation. Hence, it is appropriate for a representative body like the National Education Association to outline such a program. This is the task entrusted by that association to the Commission on the Reorganization of Secondary Education.

II. The Goal of Education in a Democracy

Education in the United States should be guided by a clear conception of the meaning of democracy. It is the ideal of democracy that the individual and society may find fulfillment each in the other. Democracy sanctions neither the exploitation of the individual by society, nor the disregard of the interests of society by the individual. More explicitly—

The purpose of democracy is so to organize society that each member may develop his personality primarily through activities designed for the well-being of his fellow members and of society as a whole.

This idea demands that human activities be placed upon a high level of efficiency; that to this efficiency be added an appreciation of the significance of these activities and loyalty to the best ideals involved; and that the individual choose that vocation and those forms of social service in which his personality may develop and become most effective. For the achievement of these ends democracy must place chief reliance upon education.

Consequently, education in a democracy, both within and without the school, should develop in each individual the knowledge, interests, ideals, habits, and powers whereby he will find his place and use that place to shape both himself and society toward ever nobler ends.

III. The Main Objectives of Education

In order to determine the main objectives that should guide education in a democracy it is necessary to analyze the activities of the individual. Normally he is a member of a family, of a vocational group, and of various civic groups, and by virtue of these relationships he is called upon to engage in activities that enrich the family life, to render important vocational services to his fellows, and to promote the common welfare. It follows, therefore, that worthy home-membership, vocation, and citizenship, demand attention as three of the leading objectives.

Aside from the immediate discharge of these specific duties, every individual should have a margin of time for the cultivation of personal and social interests. This leisure, if worthily used, will re-create his powers and enlarge and enrich life, thereby making him better able to meet his responsibilities. The unworthy use of leisure impairs health, disrupts home life, lessens vocational efficiency and destroys civic-mindedness. The tendency in industrial life, aided by legislation, is to decrease the working hours of large groups of people. While shortened hours tend to lessen the harmful reactions that arise from prolonged strain, they increase, if possible, the importance of preparation for leisure. In view of these considerations, education for the worthy use of leisure is of increasing importance as an objective.

To discharge the duties of life and to benefit from leisure, one must have good health. The health of the individual is essential also to the vitality of the race and to the defense of the Nation. Health education is, therefore, fundamental.

There are various processes, such as reading, writing, arithmetical computations, and oral and written expression, that are needed as tools in the affairs of life. Consequently, command of these fundamental processes, while not an end in itself, is nevertheless an indispensable objective.

And finally, the realization of the objectives already named is dependent upon ethical character, that is, upon conduct founded upon right principles, clearly perceived and loyally adhered to. Good citizenship, vocational excellence, and the worthy use of leisure go hand in hand with ethical character; they are at once the fruits of sterling character and the channels through which such character is developed and made manifest. On the one hand, character is meaningless apart from the will to discharge the duties of life, and, on the other hand, there is no guarantee that these duties will be rightly discharged unless principles are substituted for impulses, however well-intentioned such impulses may be. Consequently ethical character is at once involved in all the other objectives and at the same time requires specific consideration in any program of national education.

This commission, therefore, regards the following as the main objectives of education: 1. Health. 2. Command of fundamental processes. 3. Worthy home-membership. 4. Vocation. 5. Citizenship. 6. Worthy use of leisure. 7. Ethical character.

The naming of the above objectives is not intended to imply that the process of education can be divided into separated fields. This can not be, since the pupil is indivisible. Nor is the analysis all-inclusive. Nevertheless, we believe that distinguishing and naming these objectives will aid in directing efforts; and we hold that they should constitute the principal aims in education.

VIII. Need for Explicit Values

The number of years that pupils continue in school beyond the compulsory school age depends in large measure upon the degree to which they and their parents realize that school work is worth while for them and that they are succeeding in it. Probably in most communities doubt regarding the value of the work offered causes more pupils to leave school than economic necessity. Consequently, it is important that the work of each pupil should be so presented as to convince him and his parents of its real value.

IX. Subordination of Deferred Values

Many subjects are now so organized as to be of little value unless the pupil studies them for several years. Since a large portion of pupils leave school in each of the successive years, each subject should be so organized that the first year of work will be of definite value to those who go no further; and this principle should be applied to the work of each year. Courses planned in accordance with this principle will deal with the simpler aspects, or those of more direct application, in the earlier years and will defer the refinements for later years when these can be better appreciated. The course as a whole will then be better adapted to the needs both of those who continue and of those who drop out of school.

6. *The period covered by this Resource Unit ends with the great economic depression which sorely tried all American institutions, including the system of business and government that had developed over the years since the Civil War. President Herbert Hoover, before he took office in March 1929, coined a phrase which described the way in which he and his supporters believed that men should behave in society. It was "rugged individualism". In the speech from which the following quotations are taken (made in October 1928, during the campaign for the presidential election), he summed up what he meant by the phrase.*

. . . During one hundred and fifty years we have built up a form of self-government and a social system which is peculiarly our own. It differs essentially from all others in the world. It is the American system. It is just as definite and positive a political and social system as has ever been developed on earth. It is founded upon a particular conception of self-government in which decentralized local responsibility is the very base. Further than this, it is founded upon the conception that only through ordered liberty, freedom, and equal opportunity to the individual will his initiative and enterprise spur on the march of progress. And in our insistence upon equality of opportunity has our system advanced beyond all the world.

During the war (*World War I*), we necessarily turned to the Government to solve every difficult economic problem. The Government having absorbed every energy of our people for war, there was no other solution. For the preservation of the State the Federal Government became a centralized despotism which undertook unprecedented responsibilities, assumed autocratic powers, and took over the business of citizens. To a large degree, we regimented our whole people temporarily into a socialistic State. However justified in time of war, if continued in peace-time it would destroy not only our American system but with it our progress and freedom as well.

When the war closed, the most vital of all issues both in our own country and throughout the world was whether governments should continue their war-time ownership and operation of many instrumentalities of production and distribution. We were challenged with a peace-time choice between the American system of rugged individualism and a European philosophy of diametrically opposed doctrines—doctrines of paternalism and State socialism. The acceptance of these ideas would have meant the destruction of self-government through centralization of government. It would have meant the undermining of the individual initiative and enterprise through which our people have grown to unparalleled greatness. . . .

There has been revived in this campaign, however, a series of proposals which, if adopted, would be a long step toward the abandonment of our American system and a surrender to the destructive operation of governmental conduct of commercial business. Because the country is faced with difficulty and doubt over certain national problems—that is, prohibition, farm relief, and electrical power—our opponents propose that we must thrust government a long way into the businesses which give rise to these problems. In effect, they abandon the tenets of their own party and turn to State socialism as a solution for the difficulties presented by all three. It is proposed that we shall change from prohibition to the State purchase and sale of liquor. If their agricultural relief program means anything, it means that the Government shall directly or indirectly buy and sell and fix prices of agricultural products. And we are to go into the hydro-electric power business. In other words, we are confronted with a huge program of government in business.

There is, therefore, submitted to the American people a question of fundamental principle. That is, shall we depart from the principles of our American political and economic system, upon which we have advanced beyond all the rest of the world, in order to adopt methods based on principles destructive of its very foundations? And I wish to emphasize the seriousness of these proposals. I wish to make my position clear; for this goes to the very roots of American life and progress.

I should like to state to you the effect that this projection of government in business would have upon our system of self-government and our economic system. That effect would reach to the daily life of every man and woman. It would impair the very basis of liberty and freedom not only for those left outside the fold of expanded bureaucracy but for those embraced within it. . . .

It is a false liberalism that interprets itself into the government operation of commercial business. Every step of bureaucratizing of the business of our country poisons the very roots of liberalism—that is, political equality, free speech, free assembly, free press, and equality of opportunity. It is the road not to more liberty, but to less liberty. Liberalism should be found not striving to spread bureaucracy, but striving to set bounds to it. True liberalism seeks all legitimate freedom first in the confident belief that without such freedom the pursuit of all other blessings and benefits is vain. That belief is the foundation of all American progress, political as well as economic.

Liberalism is a force truly of the spirit, a force proceeding from the deep realization that economic freedom cannot be sacrificed if political freedom is to be preserved. Even if governmental conduct of business could give us more efficiency instead of less efficiency, the fundamental objection to it would remain unaltered and unabated. It would destroy political equality. It would increase rather than decrease abuse and corruption. It would stifle initiative and invention. It would undermine the development of leadership. It would cramp and cripple the mental and spiritual energies of our people. It would extinguish equality and opportunity. It would dry up the spirit of liberty and progress. For these reasons primarily it must be resisted. For a hundred and fifty years liberalism has found its true spirit in the American system, not in the European systems.

I do not wish to be misunderstood in this statement. I am defining a general policy. It does not mean that our Government is to part with one iota of its national resources without complete protection to the public interest. I have already stated that where the Government is engaged in public works for purposes of flood control, of navigation, of irrigation, of scientific research or national defense, or in pioneering a new art, it will at times necessarily produce power or commodities as a by-product. But they must be a by-product of the major purpose, not the major purpose itself.

Nor do I wish to be misinterpreted as believing that the United States is a free-for-all and devil-take-the-hindmost. The very essence of equality of opportunity and of American individualism is that there shall be no domination by any group or combination in this republic, whether it be business or political. On the contrary, it demands economic justice as well as political and social justice. It is no system of *laissez-faire*.

I feel deeply on this subject, because during the war I had some practical experience with governmental operation and control. I have witnessed not only at home but abroad the many failures of government in business. I have seen its tyrannies, its injustices, its destructions of self-government, its undermining of the very instincts which carry our people forward to progress. I have witnessed the lack of advance, the lowered standards of living, the depressed spirits of people working under such a system. My objection is based not upon theory or upon a failure to recognize wrong or abuse, but I know the adoption of such methods would strike at the very roots of American life and would destroy the very basis of American progress. . . .

And what have been the results of the American system? Our country has become the land of opportunity to those born without inheritance, not merely because of the wealth of its resources and industry, but because of this freedom of initiative and enterprise. Russia has natural resources equal to ours. Her people are equally industrious, but she has not had the blessings of one hundred and fifty years of our form of government and our social system.

By adherence to the principles of decentralized self-government, ordered liberty, equal opportunity, and freedom to the individual, our American experiment in human welfare has yielded a degree of well-being unparalleled in all the world. It has come nearer to the abolition of poverty, to the abolition of fear of want, than humanity has ever reached before. Progress of the past seven years is the proof of it. This alone furnishes the answer to our opponents, who ask us to introduce destructive elements into the system by which this has been accomplished. . . .

I have endeavored to present to you that the greatness of America has grown out of a political and social system and a method of control of economic forces distinctly its own—our American system—which has carried this great experiment in human welfare further than ever before in all history. We are nearer to-day to the ideal of the abolition of poverty and fear from the lives of men and women than ever before in any land. . . .

CROSS REFERENCES

Refer to the following articles in the text volumes (Volumes 1 through 8) for background of the RESOURCE UNITS.

RESOURCE UNIT 7-A

AEROSPACE AND AIR TRANSPORT INDUSTRY
AIRMAIL
ALASKA
ARCTIC EXPLORATION
ARIZONA
BEAUMONT, TEXAS
BYRD, RICHARD E.
CALIFORNIA
COOK, FREDERICK
EXPLORATION AND DISCOVERY
FLORIDA
GARY, INDIANA
HAWAII
LINDBERGH, CHARLES A.
MIAMI, FLORIDA
NEW MEXICO
OKLAHOMA
PEARY, ROBERT
WRIGHT BROTHERS

RESOURCE UNIT 7-B

AGUINALDO, EMILIO
BAKER, NEWTON D.
BIG STICK
BLOCKADE
CANADA, RELATIONS WITH
DEWEY, GEORGE
DISARMAMENT
GOETHALS, GEORGE W.
GORGAS, WILLIAM C.
GREELY, ADOLPHUS W.
INTERNAL SECURITY AND ESPIONAGE
MACARTHUR, DOUGLAS
MAHAN, ALFRED T.
MEXICAN BORDER CAMPAIGN
MITCHELL, WILLIAM
NAVAL VESSELS
PERSHING, JOHN J.
PHILIPPINE INSURRECTION
PHILIPPINE ISLANDS
REED, WALTER
RESERVE FORCES
RICKENBACKER, EDWARD V.
ROUGH RIDERS
SAMPSON, WILLIAM T.
SCHLEY, WINFIELD S.
SELECTIVE SERVICE
SHIP BUILDING
SPANISH-AMERICAN WAR
UNITED STATES AIR FORCE
UNITED STATES ARMY
UNITED STATES COAST GUARD
UNITED STATES NAVY AND MARINE CORPS
UNKNOWN SOLDIER
VETERANS ADMINISTRATION
WORLD WAR I

RESOURCE UNIT 7-C

AGRICULTURE AND AGRICULTURAL TECHNOLOGY
ANTHONY, SUSAN B.

ANTITRUST ACTS

BANKS AND BANKING

COLLECTIVE BARGAINING

BEVERIDGE, ALBERT J.

BIMETALLISM

BLOCKADE

BONDS

BOULDER DAM

BOYCOTT

BRANDEIS, LOUIS D.

BRYAN, WIILLIAM JENNINGS

BULL MOOSE

BUSINESS CYCLE

CABINET, PRESIDENTIAL

CANNON, JOSEPH G.

CHEMICAL INDUSTRY

CITY MANAGER PLAN

CITY AND URBAN PLANNING

CIVIL SERVICE

COMMUNISM

CONTRABAND

CONSERVATION OF NATURAL RESOURCES

CONSTITUTION OF THE UNITED STATES

COOLIDGE, CALVIN

CORPORATIONS AND CORPORATION LAW

COX, JAMES M.

CUBA, RELATIONS WITH

DANIELS, JOSEPHUS

DAWES, CHARLES G.

DEBS, EUGENE V.

DEMOCRATIC PARTY

DOLLAR DIPLOMACY

DOLE, SANFORD B.

EXPORTS

FAIRBANKS, CHARLES WARREN

FARMERS' ORGANIZATIONS

FEDERAL RESERVE SYSTEM

FINANCE

FOREIGN POLICY OF THE UNITED STATES

FOURTEEN POINTS

FRANCE, RELATIONS WITH

GERMANY, RELATIONS WITH

GLASS, CARTER

GREAT BRITAIN, RELATIONS WITH

GUAM

HAITIAN INTERVENTION

HARDING, WARREN G.

HAY, JOHN

HOLMES, OLIVER WENDELL, JR.

HOOVER, HERBERT C.

HOUSE, EDWARD

HUGHES, CHARLES EVANS

IMPERIALISM

INCOME TAXATION

INFLATION

INITIATIVE

INJUNCTION

INSULAR CASES

INTERSTATE COMMERCE

ISOLATIONISM

JAPAN, RELATIONS WITH

JOHNSON, HIRAM W.

KLONDIKE

KNOX, PHILANDER

LA FOLLETTE, ROBERT M.

LANSING, ROBERT

LEAGUE OF NATIONS

LODGE, HENRY CABOT

MCADOO, WILLIAM G.

MCKINLEY, WILLIAM

MELLON, ANDREW W.

MONOPOLIES AND TRUSTS

MORGAN, J. P.

MUCKRAKERS

NEUTRALITY

NEW FREEDOM

NORTHERN SECURITIES CASE

OPEN DOOR POLICY

PAN-AMERICAN UNION

PANAMA CANAL

PARKER, ALTON B.

PHILIPPINE ISLANDS, RELATIONS WITH

PLATT AMENDMENT

PRESIDENTIAL ELECTIONS

PRIMARY ELECTIONS

PROGRESSIVE MOVEMENT

PUERTO RICO

PUJO REPORT

RECALL

RECOGNITION, DIPLOMATIC

RECONSTRUCTION FINANCE CORPORATION

RED CROSS

REFERENDUM

REPARATIONS

REPUBLICAN PARTY

ROOSEVELT, THEODORE

ROOSEVELT COROLLARY

ROOT, ELIHU

SEDITION

SILVER INDUSTRY, MINING AND MONEY

SMITH, ALFRED E.

SMUGGLING

SOCIALIST PARTY

SPAIN, RELATIONS WITH

SPANISH-AMERICAN WAR

STANDARD OIL COMPANY

STIMSON, HENRY L.

SUPREME COURT DECISIONS

TAFT, WILLIAM HOWARD

TARIFF POLICIES OF THE UNITED STATES

TAXATION IN THE UNITED STATES

TEAPOT DOME

TRADE, INTERNATIONAL
TRUSTS AND TRUSTEESHIP
VERSAILLES TREATY
VIRGIN ISLANDS
WAR DEBTS
WASHINGTON DISARMAMENT CONFERENCE
WILSON, WOODROW
WORLD COURT
YOUNG, OWEN D.
YOUNG PLAN

RESOURCE UNIT 7-D

ADVERTISING
ANTHRACITE COAL STRIKE
ANTI-SALOON LEAGUE
ARCHITECTURE, AMERICAN
ARMORY ART SHOW
ASSEMBLY LINE
AUTOMOBILE INDUSTRY
BONUS
BOOTLEGGING
BRAND NAMES AND TRADEMARKS
CAPITAL AND CAPITALISM
CHAIN STORES
CIVIL LIBERTIES AND CIVIL RIGHTS LEGISLATION
CLOSED SHOP
COMMUNICATIONS INDUSTRIES
CONSERVATION OF NATURAL RESOURCES
CONSERVATISM
DARROW, CLARENCE
DEPRESSIONS AND PANICS
DROUGHT
DUST BOWL
EDDY, MARY BAKER
EDISON, THOMAS A.
ELLIS ISLAND
FARMERS' ORGANIZATIONS
FITZGERALD, F. SCOTT
FORD, HENRY
GARVEY, MARCUS
GERSHWIN, GEORGE
GOMPERS, SAMUEL
HAYWOOD, WILLIAM D.
HEARST, WILLIAM R.
HERBERT, VICTOR
HUMANITARIANISM
IMMIGRATION POLICY
IMPERIALISM
INDIAN TERRITORY
INTERNAL SECURITY AND ESPIONAGE
ISOLATIONISM
LABOR ORGANIZATIONS
LANE, FRANKLIN K.
LIBERALISM
LITERATURE, AMERICAN
LOW, JULIETTE G.

MICHAEL, MOIRA
MICHELSON, ALBERT A.
MORTON, JULIUS S.
MUIR, JOHN
MUSIC, AMERICAN
NATURALIZATION
NOBEL PRIZES
NORRIS, GEORGE W.
O'NEILL, EUGENE
PAINTING AND SCULPTURE
PETROLEUM INDUSTRY
PHOTOGRAPHY
PROGRESSIVE MOVEMENT
PROHIBITION AND TEMPERANCE
PROPAGANDA
PUBLIC HEALTH SERVICE
PULITZER, JOSEPH
PULITZER PRIZES
PURE FOOD AND DRUG ACT
RACES AND PEOPLES OF THE UNITED STATES
RADIO AND TELEVISION
ROADS, HIGHWAYS AND TURNPIKES
ROGERS, WILL
SACCO-VANZETTI CASE
SALVATION ARMY
SCIENCE, PROGRESS OF, IN THE UNITED STATES
SCOPES TRIAL
SETTLEMENT HOUSE MOVEMENT
SOCIALISM
SOUSA, JOHN PHILIP
SPORTS
STRIKES
SULLIVAN, LOUIS
SYNTHETIC FIBERS AND FABRICS
TELEPHONE AND TELEGRAPH INDUSTRY
TRANSPORTATION IN THE UNITED STATES
UTILITIES, PUBLIC
VEBLEN, THORSTEIN
VOLSTEAD ACT
VOTING METHODS
WALD, LILLIAN
WHITE, WILLIAM ALLEN
WOMEN'S RIGHTS
YELLOW DOG CONTRACT
YELLOW JOURNALISM

BOOKS FOR FURTHER READING

Exploration and Settlement

P. K. Angell, *To the Top of the World*; W. T. Bonney,
The Heritage of Kitty Hawk; R. E. Byrd, *Little America*;
C. V. Glines, *The Wright Brothers*; W. H. Hobbs, *Peary*;
L. P. Kirwan, *History of Polar Exploration*; R. Knowles,
The Greatest Gamblers: The Epic of American Oil Ex-

ploration; C. A. Lindbergh, *The Spirit of St. Louis*; W. Lord, *Peary to the Pole*; M. McNeer, *Alaska Gold Rush*; K. Terzian, *Glenn Curtiss, Pioneer Pilot*; L. Tinkle, *The Story of Oklahoma*.

Military Developments

The Spanish-American War
J. B. Atkins, *The War in Cuba*; F. Freidel, *Splendid Little War*; W. Millis, *The Martial Spirit*; H. H. Sargent, *The Campaign of Santiago de Cuba*

World War I: Official Records
American Battle Monuments Commission, *American Armies and Battlefields in Europe*; Historical Division, Department of the Army, *United States Army in the World War, 1917–1919* and also *Papers Relating to the Foreign Relations of the United States, 1917*.

Books About World War I

American Heritage, *The American Heritage History of World War I*; R. Burlingame, *Victory Without Peace*; C. Falls, *The Great War, 1914–1918*; T. C. Frothingham, *The Naval History of the Great War*; W. Mitchell, *Our Air Force*; E. E. Morison, *Admiral Sims and the Modern American Navy*; J. J. Pershing, *My Experiences in the World War*; E. Upton, *The Military Policy of the United States*; I. Werstein, *The Lost Battalion*.

Politics—Progressivism, War and Isolationism

American Heritage, *Captains of Industry*; F. R. Dulles, *America's Rise to World Power: 1898-1954*; J-B. Duroselle, *From Wilson to Roosevelt*; E. F. Goldman, *Rendezvous with Destiny: A History of Modern American Reform*; J. D. Hicks, *Republican Ascendancy*; H. C. Hoover, *The Ordeal of Woodrow Wilson*; R. Hofstadter, *The Age of Reform: From Bryan to F.D.R.*; R. M. La Follette, *Autobiography*; A. S. Link, *Woodrow Wilson: A Brief Biography*; G. E. Mowry, *The Era of Theodore Roosevelt: 1900-1912*; A. R. Pinchot, *History of the Progressive Party, 1912-1916*; K. H. Porter and D. B. Johnson, *National Party Platforms, 1840-1964*; J. W. Pratt, *The Expansionists of 1898*; H. F. Pringle, *Theodore Roosevelt*; M. J. Pusey, *Charles Evans Hughes*; B. Severn, *William Howard Taft*; D. A. Shannon, *The Great Depression*; G. Smith, *When the Cheering Stopped*; D. M. Smith, *The Great Departure: The United States and World War I*; L. Steffens, *The Shame of the Cities*; D. Wecter, *The Age of the Great Depression*; A.

Weinberg, ed., *The Muckrakers;* W. A. White, *Puritan in Babylon;* W. Wilson, *The New Freedom;* H. Zink, *City Bosses in the United States.*

Social Developments

S. H. Adams, *Incredible Era;* F. L. Allen, *Only Yesterday;* J. P. Barry, *The Noble Experiment;* T. C. Cochran and W. Miller, *The Age of Enterprise: A Social History of Industrial America;* A. F. Davis, *Spearheads for Reform;* B. W. Epstein, *William Crawford Gorgas;* S. Gompers, *Seventy Years of Life and Labor;* O. Handlin, *Al Smith and His America;* H. Hapgood, *The Spirit of the Ghetto;* S. Holbrook, *Age of the Moguls;* H. Morrison, *Louis Sullivan, Prophet of Modern Architecture;* F. L. Mott, *American Journalism;* G. Myrdal, *An American Dilemma;* G. Osofsky, *Harlem: The Making of a Ghetto;* D. C. Seitz, *Joseph Pulitzer, His Life and Letters;* K. K. Shippen, *Andrew Carnegie and the Age of Steel;* P. W. Slosson, *The Great Crusade;* J. Spargo, *The Bitter Cry of the Children;* M. Sullivan, *Our Times;* P. Taft, *The American Federation of Labor;* I. M. Tarbell, *Life of Elbert H. Gray;* W. A. White, *Autobiography of William Allen White;* C. F. Wittke, *We Who Built America.*

Novels of the 20th Century

Upton Sinclair, *The Jungle*   Exposure of inhuman conditions in meat-packing plants at the turn of the century

Sinclair Lewis, *Main Street*   Struggle against the dull monotony of small town life

Betty Smith, *A Tree Grows in Brooklyn*   Tenement life in early years of the century

Thomas Wolfe, *Look Homeward, Angel*   Coming of age in North Carolina

Thomas Boyd, *Through the Wheat*   Americans in World War I

John W. Thomason, *Fix Bayonets*   Marines in World War I

F. Scott Fitzgerald, *The Great Gatsby*   Change in American life and aspirations after World War I

John Steinbeck, *Grapes of Wrath*   Plight of migrant farm family in the depression

Robert Penn Warren, *All the King's Men*   Rise and fall of a politician of the rural South

Edwin O'Connor, *The Last Hurrah*   The final campaign of a city political boss who has outlived his time

Allen Drury, *Advise and Consent*   How politicians work in Washington

7. EARLY TWENTIETH CENTURY: 1898-1933

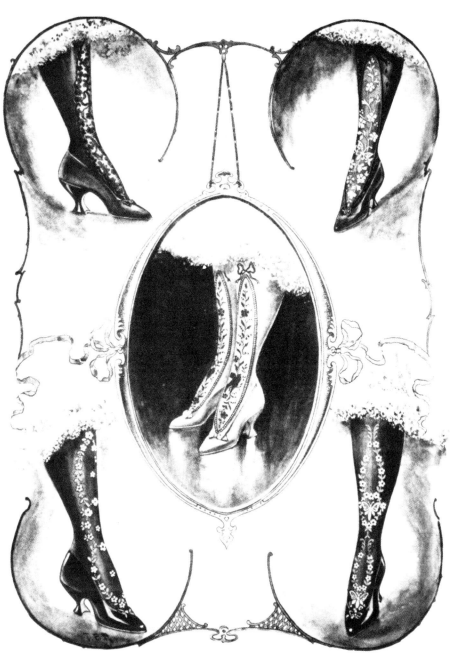

1. At the start of the 20th century women continued to emphasize their femininity with fashionable frilly petticoats, embroidered stockings and French heels. From *Town and Country*, Oct., 1902.

CLOTHING, 1898-1933

2. "The Wyndham Sisters," painted in 1900 by John Singer Sargent, typified the aristocratic pose of that time. *Courtesy,* The Metropolitan Museum of Art, Wolfe Fund 1927. 3. Maxine Elliott, well-known actress, was admired for her statuesque beauty. From *Town and Country,* October, 1903. 4. Stylish young men presented a clean-cut appearance in straw "boaters," stiff collars and well-tailored suits. *Courtesy,* "The Jayhawker," University of Kansas, Lawrence. 5. The shirtwaist was an immediate success early in the 1900's and continued on and on. From *Harper's Bazar,* January, 1901. 6. A bevy of shirtwaist wearers, 1911. *Courtesy,* Chicago Lawn Historical Society and Chicago Public Library, Illinois. 7. That long-stemmed look came from the steel-ribbed corset of 1909. *Courtesy,* N. W. Ayer & Son, Inc., Philadelphia, Pa. 8. At the Smith College Prom of 1914 the girls wore the new narrow draped skirt, and the men, high collars and white ties. *Courtesy,* Smith College Archives, Northampton, Mass.

5

6

7

8

9

10

9. Ladies' street wear, 1919. Note the slender silhouette and elaborate hats. *Courtesy,* Abraham and Straus, Brooklyn, New York. 10. By the mid-1920's women were active in sports. Here seen is Helen Wills, age sixteen, when she was National Women's Singles Champion. *Courtesy,* United Press International. 11. The Purdue Girls' Cross Country team of 1924. *Courtesy,* Purdue University, Lafayette, Indiana. 12. The raccoon coat especially, but other furs too were high style with the college crowd, ca. 1924. *Courtesy,* Wellesley College, Wellesley, Mass. 13. Actress Lenore Ulric typifies the razzle-dazzle of the Twenties with her "diamond" (rhinestone) necklace, bracelets and tiara. *Courtesy,* Picture Collection, The New York Public Library. 14. At the peak of the Jazz Age, evening dresses with fringe and floating panels caught the mood of restless movement. *Courtesy,* B. Altman Company. 15. The flapper, portrayed by John Held, Jr. From *Life,* 1926.

11

12

13

14

15

16

16. Girls in a Madison, Wisconsin, vocational High School dressed for their cooking lesson in 1927. *Courtesy,* State Historical Society of Wisconsin. 17. Fashionable friends admire the new automatic refrigerator. Note the cloche hat and dropped waistline of the late 1920's. *Courtesy,* Scribner Art File. 18. Men's clothing showed more fullness. Both the derby and the soft fedora were in demand. *Courtesy,* B. Kuppenheimer & Co., Chicago, Ill.

DEPEND ON KUPPENHEIMER VALUE

Kuppenheimer merchants are now showing suits of TIGERTWIST, TROJAN WEAVE and CASTILIANS-original in pattern and color-the ranking fabrics from the world's looms. Created to give you fine style and extra value-just as FAMOUS FIFTIES set the '50 standard.

18

17

INTERIORS AND HOUSE FURNISHINGS, 1898-1933

The opening of the 20th century brought lighter and more cheerful interiors and furnishings.   19. Here shown is an elegant version of that long-time favorite of the American home, the rocking chair. From *The Grand Rapids Furniture Record*, 1907.   20. Padded furniture gave an air of comfort to the parlor. From same source.   21. Here seen is a home library in the simple "Mission" style derived from California. From *The Grand Rapids Furniture Record*, 1908.

21

22. Imitations of ornate French taste lingered on. Seen here is a "Louis XV" parlor suite. From *The Grand Rapids Furniture Record*, 1908. 23. After World War I, the comfortable American living room such as this one included a piano, silk-shaded lamps and Oriental design rugs. *Courtesy,* The Smithsonian Institution.

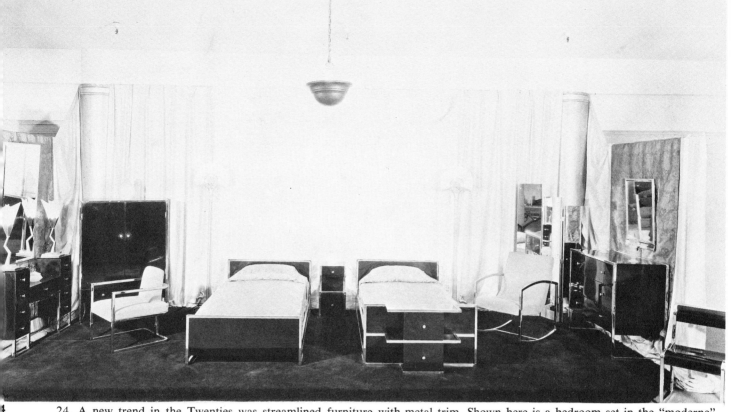

24. A new trend in the Twenties was streamlined furniture with metal trim. Shown here is a bedroom set in the "moderne" style. *Courtesy*, Scribner Art File.

LIFE IN AMERICA, 1898-1933

25. Many Spanish-American war soldiers were victims of Yellow Fever. Drawing by R. F. Zogbaum. From *Harper's Weekly*, 1898.
26. In 1904 the World's Fair in St. Louis marked the centennial of the Louisiana Purchase. Among other attractions, "wedding cake" architecture drew the crowds. *Courtesy*, Missouri Historical Society, St. Louis, Mo.

27

28

29

30

27. Imported from England, ping pong scored a great hit as a social pastime in the early 1900's. From *Harper's Weekly*, May, 1902.
28. At the Weber and Fields Music Hall, Lillian Russell was the star of the show. Photograph by Byron. From *Town & Country*, 1903. 29. An Italian immigrant family at Ellis Island, 1905, typical of tremendous numbers seeking a better life in the New World. Photograph by Lewis W. Hine. *Courtesy,* George Eastman House. 30. A Midwestern family sat for this picture before their vine-covered home, ca. 1907. *Courtesy,* Larchmont Historical Society. 31. Around the same time, the family seen here posed for the photographer in front of their homestead near Big Sandy, Montana. *Courtesy,* Great Northern Railway Company, St. Paul, Minn. 32. The cover of the new magazine shown here speaks for itself. *The Smart Set,* October, 1914.

32

31

33

33. Dancing at the popular "Cascades" ballroom of New York's Biltmore Hotel, around 1916. *Courtesy,* Brown Brothers. 34. By 1917 there were tearful good-byes as men went off to war, as this family scene shows. U. S. Army Signal Corps Photo. *Courtesy,* National Archives.

34

35

35. During World War I many housewives answered the call to "do their bit." Here shown are women at work in a munitions factory. U. S. Army Signal Corps Photo. *Courtesy,* National Archives. 36. Other women were making their contribution by serving in the Red Cross. *Courtesy,* American Red Cross. 37. A family get-together, early 1920's. Note the varied expressions of the individual members. *Courtesy,* State Historical Society Wisconsin. 38. An urban street scene of the 1920's. *Courtesy,* The Salvation Army.

36

37

38

39

39. The physical culture fad, one of many in the Twenties, prompted Bernarr MacFadden, publisher of health magazines, to hold a daily exercise period for his employees in 1923. *Courtesy,* United Press International.   40. Radio brought political speeches into the home for the first time, giving millions closer contact with the candidates. Here seen is Senator Robert La Follette Sr. and family, ca. 1924. *Courtesy,* State Historical Society Wisconsin.   41. Prohibition spawned gangsters who protected the bootlegger, who made his money by supplying illicit liquor. In the 1927 lineup seen here: Brooklyn's Ed Diamond, Jack "Legs" Diamond, Fatty Walsh and Charles Luciano. *Courtesy,* United Press International.

40

41

RESOURCE UNIT 8

Up to Now:
1933-1974

8-A EXPLORATION AND DISCOVERY

After more than four centuries of exploration, it seemed as if there could not possibly be any more strange, new places to discover or any more trails to blaze. And yet, during the years covered in this Resource Unit, several of the most sensational expeditions ever attempted by man were successfully completed. As new technology was introduced, new frontiers for exploration opened out.

PROBLEMS. *In what ways were human explorers and settlers occupied in exploration by the mid-20th century? In what ways has modern technology directed and influenced 20th-century discovery and communications?*

1. The newest area to be explored during the forty years of this period was Space itself. During the late 1950's, the first man-made satellites were put into orbit around earth by the Russians. A short time later, American satellites were also in orbit. Manned Space flight also began with Russian experiments, but U.S. astronauts soon were taking part in Space exploration. Colonel John Glenn became the first American astronaut to fly in full orbits around the earth. Unlike earlier explorations and trail-blazing efforts, Glenn's work was supported by a worldwide

complex of tracking stations, and radio and computer networks. These were to help insure his safety and success in orbit. In the following official history of the first American space flight, an entire new vocabulary is in use—new terms to describe new rockets, telemetry, and control systems. (The quotation is from This New Ocean: A History of Project Mercury, *by Loyd S. Swenson, James M. Grimwood and Charles C. Alexander. Washington: National Aeronautics and Space Administration, 1966.)*

AN AMERICAN IN ORBIT

Glenn was awakened once again at 2:20 a.m. on February 20. After showering, he sat down to a breakfast of steak, scrambled eggs, toast, orange juice, and coffee. At 3:05 the astronauts' flight surgeon, William Douglas, gave him a brief physical examination.

Douglas, Glenn, and his suit technician, Joe W. Schmitt, were only three of a multitude hard at work on the cloudy February morning. In the Mercury Control Center procedures log, the flight control team noted at 3:40 that they were "up and at it." The team immediately conducted a radar check, and although ionospheric conditions made the results poor the controllers believed the situation would improve soon. So they went on to check booster telemetry and the Control Center's voice intercom system, both of which were in good order. Shortly thereafter they found a faulty communication link that was supposed to be obtaining information about the capsule's oxygen system, but within minutes they had corrected the problem.

At 4:27 a.m. Christopher Kraft, sitting before his flight director's console, received word that the global tracking network had been checked out and was ready. In Hangar S, Douglas placed the biosensors on Glenn, and Joe Schmitt began helping the astronaut don his 20-pound pressure suit. At 5:01 the Mercury Control Center learned that the astronaut was in the van and on his way to the launch pad. The van moved slowly and arrived at 5:17, 20 minutes behind schedule. But the delay was of little consequence, for at 5:25 (T minus 120 minutes) trouble had cropped up in the booster's guidance system. Since this came during the built-in 90-minute hold part of the countdown for the astronaut insertion activity, the delay was not likely to halt the readying procedures for very long. The installation of a spare unit and an additional 45 minutes required for its checkout, however, made a total of 135 minutes lost.

Because of overcast weather and the guidance problem in the Atlas, Glenn relaxed comfortably in the van until 5:58, when the sky began to clear. The capsule and booster validation checks were progressing normally as he emerged from the van, saluted the onlookers, and boarded the gantry elevator. At 6:03, the operations team noted in its procedures log, the astronaut "put a foot into the spacecraft." Once inside *Friendship 7*, Glenn noticed that the respiration sensor—a thermistor attached to the astronaut's microphone in the air stream of his breath—had shifted from where it had been fixed during the simulated flight. Stanley C. White pointed out to Williams that a correction could only be made by opening the suit, a very tricky operation atop the gantry. So the two officials decided to disregard the slipped thermistor, even though faulty data would result. White advised the range to ignore all respiratory transmissions.

At last the technicians began to bolt the hatch onto the spacecraft, but at 7:10, with the countdown proceeding and most of the 70 bolts secured, a broken bolt was discovered. Although Grissom had flown in MR-4 with a broken hatch bolt, Williams, taking no chances this time, ordered removal and repair. Taking the hatch off and rebolting would require about 40 minutes, so the operations team took this opportunity to run still another check of the guidance system on Atlas 109–D. Glenn evidently maintained his composure during this hold, with his pulse ranging between 60 and 80 beats per minute. When a little more than half of the bolts had been secured, he peered through the periscope and remarked to Scott Carpenter and Alan Shepard

in the Control Center, "Looks like the weather is breaking up."

Minutes later, the hatch installation was completed and the cabin purge was started. A check of the cabin oxygen leakage rate indicated 500 cubic centimeters per minute, well within design specifications. At 8:05, T minus 60 minutes, the countdown continued, but after 15 minutes a hold was called to add about 10 gallons of propellant to the booster's tanks. Glenn had been busily going over his capsule systems checklist. As the holds continued, he occupied his time and relieved the pressure at various points on his cramped body by pulling on the bungee-cord exercising device in front of his head in the capsule. The countdown resumed while the liquid oxygen was being pumped aboard the Atlas, but at T minus 22 minutes, 8:58, a fuel pump outlet valve stuck, causing still another hold.

At that point in the countdown, Glenn, the blockhouse and Control Center crews, and workers scurrying around and climbing on the gantry were joined by some 100 million people watching television sets in about 40 million homes throughout the United States. Countless others huddled around radios in their homes or places of business and about 50,000 "bird watchers" stood on the beaches near Cape Canaveral, squinting toward the erect rocket gleaming in the distance. Some of the more hearty and sun-tanned spectators had been at the Cape since mid-January and had organized trailer towns, complete with "mayors." Mission announcer Powers, popularly known as "the voice of Mercury Control," who had been at his post in the Control Center since 5 o'clock that morning, went on the air to advise the waiting public of the status of the countdown and the cause for the present hold.

With the stuck valve cleared, the count picked up at 9:25, but another suspenseful moment came at 6½ minutes before launch time, when the Bermuda tracking station experienced an electrical power failure. Although the breakdown was brief, it took several more minutes to steady the Bermuda computer.

At 9:47, after two hours and 17 minutes of holds and three hours and 44 minutes after Glenn entered his "office," *Friendship 7* was launched on its orbital journey. The Atlas, supported by its tail of fire, lifted off its pad, and Powers made the announcement that this country had waited three long years to hear: "Glenn reports all spacecraft systems go! Mercury Control is go!" As Atlas 109–D lunged spaceward, Glenn's pulse rate climbed to 110, as expected. The Atlas and its control systems telemetered signals that they were functioning perfectly.

Half a minute after liftoff the General Electric-Burroughs guidance system locked onto a radio transponder in the booster to guide the vehicle until it was through the orbital insertion "window." The vibration at liftoff hardly bothered Glenn, but a hundred seconds later at max-q he reported, "It's a little bumpy about here." After the rocket plunged through the max-q region, the flight smoothed out; then two minutes and 14 seconds after launch, the outboard booster engines cut off and dropped away. Glenn saw a wisp of smoke and fleetingly thought the escape tower had jettisoned early, but that event occurred exactly on time 20 seconds later.

When the tower separated, the vehicle combination pitched over still further, giving Glenn his first view of the horizon, which he described as "a beautiful sight, looking eastward across the Atlantic." Vibration increased as the fuel supply spewed out the sustainer engine nozzle, then abruptly stopped when the sustainer shut down. The sustainer had accelerated the capsule to a velocity only seven feet per second below nominal and had put the Atlas into an orbital trajectory only .05 of a degree low. Joyously the operations team noted in the log, "9:52- - -We are through the gates." Glenn received word that he could make at least seven orbits with the orbital conditions MA–6 had achieved. To Goddard's computers in Maryland the orbital insertion conditions appeared good enough for almost 100 orbits.

Although the posigrade rockets ricked the capsule loose from the booster at the correct instant, the five-second rate-damping operation started two and a half seconds late. This brief lapse caused a substantial initial roll error just as the capsule began its turnaround. The attitude control system managed the deviation very well, but it was some 38 seconds before *Friendship 7* dropped into its proper orbital attitude. Turnaround spent 5.4 pounds of fuel from a total supply of 60.4 pounds (36 for automatic and 24.4 for manual control). Despite his slow automatic positioning maneuver, Glenn made his control checks with such ease that it seemed, he said, as if he were sitting in the procedures trainer. As Voas had asked him to do, the astronaut peered through the window at the tumbling Atlas tankage. It had come into view exactly as Ben F. McCreary of MSC had predicted it would. He could see the spent vehicle turning end over end, and he called out estimates of distances between the separating vehicles: "One hundred yards, two hundred yards." At one point Glenn's estimate matched the telemetry signal exactly. He visually tracked the sustainer intermittently for about eight minutes.

Glenn, noticing the onset of weightlessness, settled into orbital free flight with an inertial velocity of 17,544 miles per hour and reported that zero g was wholly pleasant. Although he could move well and see much through his trapezoidal window, he wanted to see even more. "I guess I'd like a glass capsule," he later quipped. Weightlessness also helped him as he used the hand-held camera. When his attention was drawn to a panel switch or readout, he simply left the "weightless" camera suspended and reached for the switch. Dutifully carrying out all of the head and body movements requested by Voas, he experienced none of the sensations reported by Gherman Titov. While any Glenn-Titov comparison might be ruled invalid since Titov reportedly became nauseated on his sixth orbit and Glenn flew only three orbits, MA–6 at least was to demonstrate to the American medical community that there were no discernible adverse physiological effects from over four hours of weightlessness.

The first orbit of *Friendship 7* began ticking off like clockwork with the Canary Islands reporting all capsule systems in perfect working order. Looking at the African coastline, and later the interior over Kano, Nigeria, Glenn told the tracking station team that he could see a dust storm. Kano flight communicators replied that the winds had been quite heavy for the past week.

Glenn, completing his spacecraft systems checks over the Canaries, had commented that he was getting a little behind in his schedule but that all systems still were "go." Then, over Kano, he had commenced his own first major yaw adjustment, involving a complete turnaround of the capsule until he was facing his flight path. Glenn noted that the attitude indicators disagreed with what he could see were true spacecraft attitudes. Despite the incorrect panel readouts, he was pleased to be facing the direction his spacecraft was going.

Over the Indian Ocean on his first orbit, Glenn became the first American to witness the sunset from above 100 miles. Awed but not poetically inclined, the astronaut described the moment of twilight simply as "beautiful." Space sky was very black, he said, with a thin band of blue along the horizon. He could see the cloud strata below, but the clouds in turn prevented his seeing a mortar flare fired by the Indian Ocean tracking ship. Glenn described the remarkable sunset: the sun went down fast but not quite as quickly as he expected; for five or six minutes there was a slow but continuous reduction in light intensity; and brilliant orange and blue layers spread out 45 to 60 degrees on either side of the sun, tapering gradually toward the horizon.

On the nightside of Earth, nearing the Australian coastline, Glenn made his planned star, weather, and landmark observations. He failed to see the dim light phenomenon of the heavens called the zodiacal light; he thought his eyes had not had sufficient time to adapt to the darkness. Within voice radio range of the Muchea, Australia, tracking station, Glenn and Gordon Cooper began a long space-to-Earth conversation. The astronaut reported that he felt fine, that he had no problems, and that he could see a very bright light and what appeared to be the outline of a city. Cooper answered that he probably saw the lights of Perth and Rockingham. Glenn also said that he could see stars as he looked down toward the "real" horizon—as distinguished from the haze layer he estimated to be about seven or eight degrees above the horizon on the nightside—and clouds reflecting the moonlight. "That sure was a short day," he excitedly told Cooper. "That was about the shortest day I've ever run into."

Moving onward above the Pacific over Canton Island, Glenn experienced an even shorter 45-minute night and prepared his periscope for viewing his first sunrise in orbit. As the day dawned over the island, he saw literally thousands of "little specks, brilliant specks, floating around outside the capsule." Glenn's first impression was that the spacecraft was tumbling or that he was looking into a star field, but a quick hard look out of the capsule window corrected this momentary illusion. He definitely thought the luminescent "fireflies," as he dubbed the specks, were streaming past his spacecraft from ahead. They seemed to flow leisurely but not to be originating from any part of the capsule. As *Friendship 7* sped over the Pacific expanse into brighter sunlight, the "fireflies" disappeared.

The global circuit was proceeding without any major problems, and Glenn still was enjoying his extended encounter with zero g. He ran into some bothersome interference on his broadband HF radio when he tried to talk with the Hawaiian site at Kauai. An aircraft from the Pacific Missile Range tried unsuccessfully to locate the noise source. Other than the mystery of the "fireflies" and the intermittent HF interference, the mission was going fine, with the capsule attitude control system performing perfectly.

Then the tracking station at Guaymas, Mexico, informed the control center in Florida that a yaw reaction jet was giving Glenn an attitude control problem that, as he later recalled, "was to stick with me for the rest of the flight." This was disheartening news for those in the operations team, who remembered that a sticking fuel valve discovered during the second orbital pass of the chimpanzee Enos had caused the early termination of MA–5. If Glenn could overcome this control problem he would furnish confirmation for Williams' and others' contention that man was an essential element in the loop. If the psychologists' failure task analyses were correct, the flexibility of man should now demonstrate the way to augment the reliability of the machine.

Glenn first noticed the control trouble when the automatic stabilization and control system allowed the spacecraft to drift about a degree and a half per second to the right, much like an automobile with its front wheels well out of alignment. This drift initiated a signal in the system that called for a one-pound yaw-left thrust, but there was no rate response. Glenn immediately switched to his manual-proportional control mode and eased *Friendship 7* back to orbital attitude. Then, switching from mode to mode, he sought to determine how to maintain the correct attitude position with the least cost in fuel. He reported that fly-by-wire seemed most effective and economical. Mercury Control Center recommended that he stay with his control system. After about 20 minutes the malfunctioning thruster mysteriously began working again, and with the exception of a few weak responses it seemed to be working well by the time Glenn was over Texas. After only about a minute of automated flight, however, the opposing yaw-right thruster ceased to function. When similar trials and waiting did not restore the yaw-right jet, Glenn realized that he would have to live with the problem and become a full-time pilot responsible for his own well-being.

To the operations team at the Cape and to the crews at the tracking sites, Glenn appeared to be coping with his attitude control problem well, even though he had to omit many of his observational assignments. But a still more serious problem bothered the Cape monitors as *Friendship 7* moved over them. An engineer at the telemetry control console, William Saunders, noted that "segment 51," an instrument providing data on the spacecraft landing system, was presenting a strange reading. According to the signal, the spacecraft heatshield and the compressed landing bag were no longer locked in position. If this was really the case, the all-important heatshield was being held on the capsule only by the straps of the retropackage. Almost immediately the Mercury Control Center ordered all tracking sites to monitor the instrumentation segment closely and, in their conversations with the pilot, to mention that the landing-bag deploy switch should be in the "off" position. Although Glenn was not immediately aware of his potential danger, he became suspicious when site after site consecutively asked him to make sure that the deploy switch was off. Meanwhile the operations team had to decide how to get the capsule and the astronaut back through the atmosphere with a loose heatshield. After huddling for several minutes, they decided that after retrofire the spent retropackage should be retained to keep the shield secure during re-entry. William M. Bland, Jr., in the control center, hurriedly telephoned Maxime A. Faget, the chief designer of the Mercury spacecraft, in Houston, to ask if there were any special considerations they needed to know or to watch. Faget replied that everything should be all right, providing all the retrorockets fired. If they did not, the retropack would have to be jettisoned because any unburned solid propellant would ignite during reentry. The operations team concluded that retaining the retropack was the only possible way of holding the shield in place and protecting Glenn during the early portion of his return to the dense atmosphere. The men in Mercury Control realized that the metallic retropack would burn away, but they felt that by the time it did, aerodynamic pressures would be strong enough to keep the shield in place. The decision once made, the members of the operations team fought off a gnawing uneasiness throughout the rest of the flight. This uneasiness was transmitted to the TV and radio audience before actual retrofire.

Meanwhile *Friendship 7* was vaulting the Atlantic on its second orbital pass, and Glenn was busy keeping his capsule's attitude correct and trying to accomplish as many of the flight plan tasks as possible. He had advised Virgil Grissom at Bermuda that the oculogyric test, involving visually following a light spot, had just been completed. Near the Canary Islands the sun, streaming through his window, made Glenn a little warm, but he refused to adjust the water coolant control on his suit circuit. This time around he observed that evidently the "fireflies" outside the spacecraft had no connection with the gas from the reaction control jets. Glenn skillfully positioned his ship to take some photographs of the cloud masses and Earth spinning past beneath him. As he mused over a small bolt floating around inside the capsule, the Kano and Zanzibar sites monitoring the capsule suddenly noted a 12 percent drop in the secondary oxygen supply.

Meanwhile the Indian Ocean tracking ship was preparing for the second-pass observation experiment. Battened down for heavy weather, the Mercury support crew decided that releasing balloons for Glenn to try to see was out of the question and instead they fired star-shell parachute flares. Glenn, however, was able to observe only lightning flashes in the storm clouds below.

Over the Indian Ocean, Glenn finally decided to adjust the water coolant flow in the suit circuit to improve on a condition he described as "comfortably warm." By the time he was over Woomera, Australia, the light signal warning of excess cabin water told him that the humidity level was rising. From then on throughout the rest of the flight he had to balance his suit cooling carefully against the cabin humidity, but the temperature inside his suit was never more than moderately uncomfortable. Another warning light appeared over Australia, indicating that the hydrogen peroxide fuel sup-

ply for the automatic system was down to 62 percent. Mercury Control Center recommended letting the capsule drift in orbit to conserve fuel. Glenn also complained that the roll horizon scanner did not seem to be working too well on the nightside of Earth and that it was difficult for him to obtain a visual reference to check the situation. To get a better view of Earth's horizon he pitched the spacecraft slightly downward, which helped some.

For the remainder of the second orbit and while going on into the third pass, *Friendship 7* encountered no new troubles. Glenn continued to control his attitude without allowing too much drift, and consequently consumed considerably more fuel than the automatic system would have used had the control system been working normally. He had used six pounds from the automatic tank and 11.8 pounds from the manual on the second orbit, or almost 30 percent of his supply. While he had to pay close attention to the control system to hold the expenditure as low as possible, he still had opportunities for photographing the constellation Orion, and executing a third 180-degree maneuver. . . .

Glenn and *Friendship 7* slowed down during their long reentry glide over the continental United States toward the hoped-for splashdown in the Atlantic. The Corpus Christi station told Glenn to retain the retropack until the g meter before him read 1.5. Busily involved with his control problems, Glenn reported over the Cape that he had been handling the capsule manually and would use the fly-by-wire control mode as a backup. Mercury Control then gave him the .05-g mark, and the pilot punched the override button, saying later that he seemed to be in the fringes of the g field before he pushed. Almost immediately Glenn heard noises that sounded like "small things brushing against the capsule." "That's a real fireball outside," he radioed the Cape, with a trace of anxiety perhaps evident in his tone. Then a strap from the retropackage swung around and fluttered over the window, and he saw smoke as the whole apparatus was consumed. Although his control system seemed to be holding well, his manual fuel supply was down to 15 percent, with the deceleration peak still to come. So he switched to fly-by-wire and the automatic tank supply.

Friendship 7 came now to the most fearful and fateful point of its voyage. The terrific frictional heat of reentry enveloped the capsule, and Glenn experienced his worst emotional stress of the flight. "I thought the retropack had jettisoned and saw chunks coming off and flying by the window," he said later. He feared that the chunks were pieces of his ablation protection, that the heatshield might be disintegrating, but he knew there was nothing to gain from stopping work.

Shortly after passing the peak g region, the spacecraft began oscillating so severely that Glenn could not control the ship manually. *Friendship 7* swung far past the "tolerable" 10 degrees on both sides of the zero-degree point. "I felt like a falling leaf," Glenn would recall. So he cut in the auxiliary damping system, which helped to stabilize the large yaw and roll rates to a more comfortable level. Fuel in the automatic tanks, however, was getting low. Obviously the heatshield had stayed in place; Glenn was still alive. But now he wondered whether his capsule would remain stable down to an altitude at which the drogue parachute could be deployed safely.

The pilot's fears proved real when both fuel supplies ran dry. Automatic fuel gave out at 111 seconds, and manual fuel depleted at 51 seconds, before the drogue deployment. The oscillations rapidly resumed, and at about 35,000 feet Glenn decided he had better try to deploy the drogue manually lest the spacecraft flip over into an antenna-downward instead of a heatshield-downward position. But just as he lifted his hand toward the switch, the drogue automatically shot out at 28,000 feet instead of the nominal 21,000. Suddenly the spacecraft straightened out and, as Glenn reported, "everything was in good shape."

2.   *The United States undertook to place men on the moon during the 1960's. A very complex program of space flights was established, in which astronauts approached the moon, circled it, and observed it carefully. Finally, in July, 1969, a three-man mission conducted a moon landing, to explore the surface features of the moon at close range. Neil Armstrong and Edwin E. Aldrin, Jr. conducted the actual lunar landing, while Michael Collins maintained their "command module" in orbit around the moon. One of the astronauts remarked before take-off that if the* Santa Maria *had followed such strict safety measures, she would never have left Spain. Engineering, space science, and astronomy were combined to insure the success of the first landing of men on the moon.*

The "Log" *of Apollo 11, of which a part is printed here was maintained in Houston, Texas, while the astronauts were on this mission.*

JULY 16

9:32 a.m. EDT—On schedule to within less than a second, Apollo 11 blasts off from Launch Pad 39A at Cape Kennedy, Florida to start what is looked upon as the greatest single step in human history—a trip to the Moon, a manned landing and return to Earth.

Watching is a world-wide television audience and an estimated million eyewitnesses. Standing three and one-half miles away on the sandflats or seated in grandstands are half the members of the United States Congress and more than 3,000 newsmen from 56 countries.

Strapped to their couches in the command module atop the 363-foot, 7.6-million-pound thrust space vehicle are three astronauts, each born in 1930, each weighing 165 pounds, all within an inch of the same height—five feet, 11 inches. They are Commander Neil A. Armstrong, civilian and ex-test pilot; Command Module Pilot Michael Collins, and Lunar Module Pilot Edwin E. (Buzz) Aldrin, Jr., the latter two, officers of the U. S. Air Force.

The launch comes after a 28-hour countdown. It takes place in highly suitable weather, with winds 10 knots from the southeast, temperature in the mid-80's, and clouds at 15,000 feet.

At 4:15 a.m., the astronauts had been awakened. After a breakfast of orange juice, steak, scrambled eggs, toast and coffee, they began suiting up at 5:35 a.m. At 6:27 a.m., they left in an air-conditioned van for the launch pad eight miles away. At 6:54 a.m., Armstrong entered the command module and took position on the left. He was followed five minutes later by Collins, on the right, and Aldrin, in the center.

Two minor problems that developed in the ground equipment, a leaky valve and a faulty signal light, were corrected while the astronauts were en route to the pad.

The Apollo access arm retracted at 9:27 a.m. Eight and nine-tenths seconds before launch time, the first of the Saturn V's first stage engines ignited. From the viewing stands, the flame appeared as a bright yellow-orange star on the horizon. Soon the other four engines fired and the light of the first engine became a huge fireball that lit the scene like a rising Sun. No sound was heard. For two seconds the vehicle built up thrust. The hold down clamps were released and the space vehicle began moving slowly upward from the pad, as near 9:32 a.m. as human effort could make it.

As it reached the top of the service tower, the hard-edged clattering thunder of the firing engines rolled over the scrubby Florida landscape and engulfed the viewers like a tidal wave. They witnessed the beginning of the fifth manned Apollo flight, the third to the vicinity of the Moon and the first lunar landing mission.

From Launch Control the last words were: "Good luck and Godspeed." Commander Armstrong replied, "Thank you very much. We know this will be a good flight."

9:35 a.m.—The spacecraft is 37 nautical miles high, downrange 61 nautical miles and traveling at 9,300 feet per second or about 6,340 miles per hour. Armstrong confirms the engine skirt and launch escape tower separations.

9:44 a.m.—With the three Saturn stages fired one after another and the first two jettisoned, Apollo 11 enters a 103 nautical mile-high Earth orbit, during which the vehicle is carefully checked by the astronauts and by the ground control crew.

12:22 p.m.—Another firing of the third-stage engine, still attached to the command service module, boosts Apollo 11 out of orbit midway in its second trip around the Earth and onto its lunar trajectory at an initial speed of 24,200 miles an hour.

12:49 p.m.—While the spacecraft moves farther and farther from Earth, the lunar landing craft, code-named Eagle, is unpacked from its compartment atop the launch rockets. The astronauts first fire some explosive bolts. These cause the main spaceship, given the name Columbia, to separate from the adapter and blow apart the four panels that make up its sides, exposing the lunar module (LM) tucked inside. They stop the spacecraft about 100 feet away—34 feet farther than they were supposed to—turn the ship around, facing the landing craft, and dock head-to-head with it. The docking complete, the LM's connections with the adapter are blown loose and the mated command/service and lunar modules separate from the rocket and continue alone toward the Moon.

2:38 p.m.—By dumping its leftover fuel the third rocket stage is fired into a long solar orbit to remove it from Apollo 11's path.

2:43 p.m.—With the flight on schedule and proceeding satisfactorily, the first scheduled midcourse correction is considered unnecessary.

2:54 p.m.—The space is reported 22,000 nautical miles from Earth and traveling at 12,914 feet per second. Crew members keep busy with housekeeping duties.

8:52 p.m.—Mission Control at Houston, Texas, says good night to the crew as they prepare to go to sleep two hours early.

10:59 p.m.—Because of the pull of Earth's gravity, the spacecraft has slowed to 7,279 feet per second at a distance of 63,880 nautical miles from Earth.

JULY 17

8:48 a.m.—Mission Control gives Apollo crew a brief review of the morning news, including sports developments. They are informed about the progress of the Russian space ship Lunar 15 and that Vice President Spiro T. Agnew, ranking government official at the Apollo 11 blastoff, has called for putting a man on Mars by the year 2000.

12:17 p.m.—Midcourse correction is made with a three-second burn, sharpening the course of the spacecraft and testing the engine that must get them in and out of lunar orbit.

7:31 p.m.—Astronauts begin first scheduled color telecast from spacecraft, showing view of the Earth from a distance of about 128,000 nautical miles. During the 36-minute transmission, views are also shown of the inside of the command module.

9:42 p.m.—Mission control bids the crew goodnight.

JULY 18

9:41 a.m.—Mission Control lets Astronauts sleep an hour later than scheduled on the third day of the outward journey. After breakfast, they begin housekeeping chores, such as charging batteries, dumping waste water, and checking fuel and oxygen reserves. Announcement is made to them that course corrections scheduled for afternoon will not be necessary.

2:57 p.m.—Astronauts are given report on day's news.

4:40 p.m.—One of the clearest television transmissions ever sent from space is begun, with the spacecraft 175,000 nautical miles from Earth and 48,000 from the Moon. It lasts an hour and 36 minutes. While in progress, the hatch to the LM is opened and Armstrong squeezes through the 30-inch-wide tunnel to inspect it. He is followed by Aldrin.

10:00 p.m.—Mission Control tells the crew goodnight.

11:12 p.m.—Velocity of spacecraft has slowed to 2,990 ft. per second just before entering the Moon's sphere of influence at a point 33,823 nautical miles away from it.

JULY 19

6:58 a.m.—Astronauts call Mission Control to inquire about scheduled course correction and are told it has been cancelled. They are also advised they may go back to sleep.

8:32 a.m.—Mission Control signals to arouse crew and to start them on breakfast and housekeeping chores.

10:01 a.m.—Astronauts are given review of day's news and are told of worldwide interest in Moon mission.

10:31 a.m.—Collins reports: "Houston, it's been a real change for us. Now we are able to see stars again and recognize constellations for the first time on the trip. The sky is full of stars, just like the nights on Earth. But all the way here we have just been able to see stars occasionally and perhaps through monoculars, but not recognize any star pattern."

10:42 a.m.—Armstrong announces: "The view of the Moon that we've been having recently is really spectacular. It fills about three-quarters of the hatch window and, of course, we can see the entire circumference, even though part of it is in complete shadow and part of it's in earth-shine. It's a view worth the price of the trip."

12:58 p.m.—The crew is informed by Mission Control: "We're 23 minutes away from the LOI (Lunar Orbit Insertion) burn. Flight Director Cliff Charlesworth is polling flight controllers for its status now." Then quickly, seconds later: "You are go for LOI." Aldrin replies: "Roger, go for LOI."

1:13 p.m.—Spacecraft passes completely behind the Moon and out of radio contact with the Earth for the first time.

1:28 p.m.—The spacecraft's main rocket, a 20,500-pound-thrust engine, is fired for about six minutes to slow the vehicle so that it can be captured by lunar gravity. It is still behind the Moon. The resulting orbit ranges from a low of 61.3 nautical miles to a high of 168.8 nautical miles.

1:55 p.m.—Armstrong tells Mission Control: "We're getting this first view of the landing approach. This time we are going over the Taruntius crater and the pictures and maps brought back by Apollos 8 and 10 give us a very good preview of what to look at here. It looks very much like the pictures, but like the difference between watching a real football game and watching it on TV—no substitute for actually being here."

About 15 minutes later he adds: "It gets to be a lighter gray, and as you get closer to the subsolar point, you can definitely see browns and tans on the ground."

And a few moments still later: "When a star sets up here, there's no doubt about it. One instant it's there and the next instant it's just completely gone."

3:56 p.m.—A 35-minute telecast of the Moon's surface begins. Passing westward along the eastern edge of the Moon's visible side, the camera is focused especially on the area chosen as a landing site.

5:44 p.m.—A second burn of the spacecraft's main engine, this one for 17 seconds, is employed while the spacecraft is on the back side of the Moon to stabilize the orbit at about 54 by 66 nautical miles.

6:57 p.m.—Armstrong and Aldrin crawl through the tunnel into the lunar module to give it another check. The spacecraft is orbiting the Moon every two hours.

JULY 20

9:27 a.m.—Aldrin crawls into the lunar module and starts to power-up the spacecraft. About an hour later, Armstrong enters the LM and together they continue to check the systems and deploy the landing legs.

1:46 p.m.—The landing craft is separated from the command module, in which Collins continues to orbit the Moon.

2:12 p.m.—Collins fires the command ship's rockets and moves about two miles away.

3:08 p.m.—Armstrong and Aldrin, flying feet first and face down, fire the landing craft's descent engine for the first time.

3:47 p.m.—Collins, flying the command ship from behind the Moon, reports to Earth that the landing craft is on its way down to the lunar surface. It is the first Mission Control has heard of the action. "Everything's going just swimmingly. Beautiful!" Collins reports.

4:05 p.m.—Armstrong throttles up the engine to slow the LM before dropping down on the lunar surface. The landing is not easy. The site they approach is four miles from the target point, on the southwestern edge of the Sea of Tranquility. Seeing that they are approaching a crater about the size of a football field and covered with large rocks, Armstrong takes over manual control and steers the craft to a smoother spot. His heartbeat has risen from a normal 77 to 156.

While Armstrong flies the landing craft, Aldrin gives him altitude readings: "Seven hundred and fifty feet, coming down at 23 degrees . . . 700 feet, 21 down . . . 400 feet, down at nine . . . Got the shadow out there . . . 75 feet, things looking good . . . Lights on . . . Picking up some dust . . . 30 feet, 2½ down . . . Faint shadow . . . Four forward. Four forward, drifting to the right a little . . . Contact light. Okay, engine stop."

When the 68-inch probes beneath three of the spacecraft's four footpads touch down, flashing a light on the instrument panel, Armstrong shuts off the ship's engine.

4:18 p.m.—The craft settles down with a jolt almost like that of a jet landing on a runway. It is at an angle of no more than four or five degrees on the right side of the Moon as seen from Earth. Armstrong immediately radios Mission Control: *"The Eagle has landed."*

Aldrin, looking out of the LM window, reports: "We'll get to the details around here, but it looks like a collection of just about every variety of shapes, angularities and granularities, every variety of rock you could find. The colors vary pretty much depending on how you're looking. . . . There doesn't appear to be much of a general color at all; however, it looks as though some of the rocks and boulders, of which there are quite a few in the near area . . . are going to have some interesting colors to them."

A few moments later he tells of seeing numbers of craters, some of them 100 feet across, but the largest number only one or two feet in diameter. He sees ridges 20 or 30 feet high, two-foot blocks with angular edges, and a hill half a mile to a mile away.

Finally, in describing the surface, Aldrin says: "It's

pretty much without color. It's gray and it's a very white, chalky gray, as you look into the zero phase line, and it's considerably darker gray, more like ashen gray as you look up 90 degrees to the Sun. Some of the surface rocks close in here that have been fractured or disturbed by the rocket engine are coated with this light gray on the outside, but when they've been broken they display a dark, very dark gray interior, and it looks like it could be country basalt."

The first task after landing is that of preparing the ship for launching, of seeing that all is in readiness to make the ascent back to a rendezvous with the command spacecraft orbiting above.

6:00 p.m.—With everything in order, Armstrong radios a recommendation that they plan to start the EVA (Extra Vehicular Activity), earlier than originally scheduled, at about 9:00 p.m. EDT. Mission Control replies: "We will support you anytime."

10:39 p.m.—Later than proposed at 6:00 p.m., but more than five hours ahead of the original schedule, Armstrong opens the LM hatch and squeezes through the opening. It is a slow process. Strapped to his shoulders is a portable life support and communications system weighing 84 pounds on Earth, 14 on the Moon, with provision for pressurization; oxygen requirements and removal of carbon dioxide.

Armstrong moves slowly down the 10-foot, nine-step ladder. On reaching the second step, he pulls a "D-ring," within easy reach, deploying a television camera, so arranged on the LM that it will depict him to Earth as he proceeds from that point.

Down the ladder he moves and halts on the last step. "I'm at the foot of the ladder," he reports. "The LM footpads are only depressed in the surface about one or two inches . . . the surface appears to be very, very finegrained, as you get close to it, it's almost like a powder."

10:56 p.m.—Armstrong puts his left foot to the Moon. It is the first time in history that man has ever stepped on anything that has not existed on or originated from the Earth.

"That's one small step for a man, one giant leap for mankind," Armstrong radios. Aldrin is taking photographs from inside the spacecraft.

3. Space exploration, and the possible uses of outer Space by men, became so much of a human problem that it was the subject of a special treaty. In December 1966, the United Nations developed a treaty draft, to insure that Space would be used for peaceful purposes. In the following statement, Pres-ident Lyndon Johnson announced the completion of the treaty draft. The treaty itself follows there-after.

The President's Statement

I am glad to confirm on the basis of Ambassador Goldberg's report to me this morning that agreement has been reached at the United Nations among members of the Outer Space Committee, including the United States, on a draft text of a treaty governing the exploration of outer space, including the moon and other celestial bodies.

In accordance with U.N. procedures, it is expected that a resolution endorsing the treaty will be submitted formally early next week with broad cosponsorship along with the agreed text of the Outer Space Treaty.

We look forward to early action by the Assembly on this matter.

Progress toward such a treaty commenced on May 7 of this year when I requested Ambassador Goldberg to initiate consultation for a treaty in the appropriate U.N. body.

After business-like negotiations within the U.N. Outer Space Committee in Geneva and at the U.N. in New York, this important step toward peace has been achieved.

It is the most important arms control development since the Limited Test Ban Treaty of 1963. It puts in treaty form the "no bombs in orbit" resolution of the U.N.

It guarantees access to all areas and installations of celestial bodies.

This openness taken with other provisions of the treaty should prevent war-like preparations on the moon and other celestial bodies.

This treaty has historical significance for the new age of space exploration.

I salute and commend all members of the U.N. who contributed to this significant agreement.

In the expectation that formal U.N. action will have been completed at an early date, I plan to present the treaty to the Senate for advice and consent at the next session of Congress and I hope that the United States will be one of the first countries to ratify it.

The Treaty

ARTICLE I

The exploration and use of outer space, including the moon and other celestial bodies, shall be carried out for the benefit and in the interests of all countries, irrespective of their degree of economic or scientific development, and shall be the province of all mankind.

Outer space, including the moon and other celestial bodies, shall be free for exploration and use by all States without discrimination of any kind, on a basis of equality and in accordance with international law, and there shall be free access to all areas of celestial bodies.

There shall be freedom of scientific investigation in outer space, including the moon and other celestial bodies, and States shall facilitate and encourage international co-operation in such investigation.

ARTICLE II

Outer space, including the moon and other celestial bodies, is not subject to national appropriation by claim of sovereignty, by means of use or occupation, or by any other means.

ARTICLE III

States Parties to the Treaty shall carry on activities in the exploration and use of outer space, including the moon and other celestial bodies, in accordance with international law, including the Charter of the United Nations, in the interest of maintaining international peace and security and promoting international co-operation and understanding.

ARTICLE IV

States Parties to the Treaty undertake not to place in orbit around the earth any objects carrying nuclear weapons or any other kinds of weapons of mass destruction, install such weapons on celestial bodies, or station such weapons in outer space in any other manner.

The moon and other celestial bodies shall be used by all States Parties to the Treaty exclusively for peaceful purposes. The establishment of military bases, installations and fortifications, the testing of any type of weapons and the conduct of military manoeuvres on celestial bodies shall be forbidden. The use of military personnel for scientific research or for any other peaceful purposes shall not be prohibited. The use of any equipment or facility necessary for peaceful exploration of the moon and other celestial bodies shall also not be prohibited.

ARTICLE V

States Parties to the Treaty shall regard astronauts as envoys of mankind in outer space and shall render to them all possible assistance in the event of accident, distress, or emergency landing on the territory of another State Party or on the high seas. When astronauts make such a landing, they shall be safely and promptly returned to the State of registry of their space vehicle.

In carrying on activities in outer space and on celestial bodies, the astronauts of one State Party shall render all possible assistance to the astronauts of other States Parties.

States Parties to the Treaty shall immediately inform the other States Parties to the treaty or the Secretary-General of the United Nations of any phenomena they discover in outer space, including the moon and other celestial bodies, which could constitute a danger to the life or health of astronauts.

ARTICLE VI

States Parties to the Treaty shall bear international responsibility for national activities in outer space, including the moon and other celestial bodies, whether such activities are carried on by governmental agencies or by non-governmental entities, and for assuring that national activities are carried out in conformity with the provisions set forth in the present Treaty. The activities of non-governmental entities in outer space, including the moon and other celestial bodies, shall require authorization and continuing supervision by the State concerned. When activities are carried on in outer space, including the moon and other celestial bodies, by an international organization, responsibility for compliance with this Treaty shall be borne both by the international organization and by the States Parties to the Treaty participating in such organization.

ARTICLE VII

Each State Party to the Treaty that launches or procures the launching of an object into outer space, including the moon and other celestial bodies, and each State Party from whose territory or facility an object is launched, is internationally liable for damage to another State Party to the Treaty or to its natural or juridical persons by such object or its component parts on the Earth, in air space or in outer space, including the moon and other celestial bodies.

ARTICLE VIII

A State Party to the Treaty on whose registry an object launched into outer space is carried shall retain jurisdiction and control over such object, and over any personnel thereof, while in outer space or on a celestial body. Ownership of objects launched into outer space, including objects landed or constructed on a celestial body, and of their component parts, is not affected by their presence in outer space or on a celestial body or by their return to the Earth. Such objects or component parts found beyond the limits of the State Party to the Treaty on whose registry they are carried shall be returned to that State, which shall, upon request, furnish identifying data prior to their return.

ARTICLE IX

In the exploration and use of outer space, including the moon and other celestial bodies, States Parties to the Treaty shall be guided by the principle of co-operation and mutual assistance and shall conduct all their activities in outer space, including the moon and other celestial bodies, with due regard to the corresponding interests of all other States Parties to the Treaty. States Parties to the Treaty shall pursue studies of outer space, including the moon and other celestial bodies, and conduct exploration of them so as to avoid their harmful contamination and also adverse changes in the environment of the Earth resulting from the introduction of extraterrestrial matter and, where necessary, shall adopt appropriate measures for this purpose. If a State Party to the Treaty has reason to believe that an activity or experiment planned by it or its nationals in outer space, including the moon and other celestial bodies, would cause potentially harmful interference with activities of other States Parties in the peaceful exploration and use of outer space, including the moon and other celestial bodies, it shall undertake appropriate international consultations before proceeding with any such activity or experiment. A State Party to the Treaty which has reason to believe that an activity or experiment planned by another State Party in outer space, including the moon and other celestial bodies, would cause potentially harmful interference with activities in the peaceful exploration and use of outer space, including the moon and other celestial bodies, may request consultation concerning the activity or experiment.

ARTICLE X

In order to promote international co-operation in the exploration and use of outer space, including the moon and other celestial bodies, in conformity with the purposes of this Treaty, the States Parties to the Treaty shall consider on a basis of equality any requests by other States Parties to the Treaty to be afforded an opportunity to observe the flight of space objects launched by those States.

The nature of such an opportunity for observation and the conditions under which it could be afforded shall be determined by agreement between the States concerned.

ARTICLE XI

In order to promote international co-operation in the peaceful exploration and use of outer space, States Parties to the Treaty conducting activities in outer space, including the moon and other celestial bodies, agree to inform the Secretary-General of the United Nations as well as the public and the international scientific community, to the greatest extent feasible and practicable, of the nature, conduct, locations and results of such activities. On receiving the said information, the Secretary-General of the United Nations should be prepared to disseminate it immediately and effectively.

ARTICLE XII

All stations, installations, equipment and space vehicles on the moon and other celestial bodies shall be open to representatives of other States Parties to the Treaty on a basis of reciprocity. Such representatives shall give reasonable advance notice of a projected visit, in order that appropriate consultations may be held and that maximum precautions may be taken to assure safety and to avoid interference with normal operations in the facility to be visited.

ARTICLE XIII

The provisions of this Treaty shall apply to the activities of States Parties to the Treaty in the exploration and use of outer space, including the moon and other celestial bodies, whether such activities are carried on by a single State Party to the Treaty or jointly with other States, including cases where they are carried on within the framework of international inter-governmental organizations.

Any practical questions arising in connexion with activities carried on by international inter-governmental organizations in the exploration and use of outer space, including the moon and other celestial bodies, shall be resolved by the States Parties to the Treaty either with the appropriate international organization or with one or more States members of that international organization, which are Parties to this Treaty.

ARTICLE XIV

1. This Treaty shall be open to all States for signature. Any State which does not sign this Treaty before its entry into force in accordance with paragraph 3 of this article may accede to it at any time.

2. This Treaty shall be subject to ratification by signatory States. Instruments of ratification and instruments of accession shall be deposited with the Governments of the Union of Soviet Socialist Republics, the United Kingdom of Great Britain and Northern Ireland and the United States of America, which are hereby designated the Depositary Governments.

3. This Treaty shall enter into force upon the de-

posit of instruments of ratification by five Governments including the Governments designated as Depositary Governments under this Treaty.

4. For States whose instruments of ratification or accession are deposited subsequent to the entry into force of this Treaty, it shall enter into force on the date of the deposit of their instruments of ratification or accession.

5. The Depositary Governments shall promptly inform all signatory and acceding States of the date of each signature, the date of deposit of each instrument of ratification of and accession to this Treaty, the date of its entry into force and other notices.

6. This Treaty shall be registered by the Depositary Governments pursuant to Article 102 of the Charter of the United Nations.

ARTICLE XV

Any State Party to the Treaty may propose amendments to this Treaty. Amendments shall enter into force for each State Party to the Treaty accepting the amendments upon their acceptance by a majority of the States Parties to the Treaty and thereafter for each remaining State Party to the Treaty on the date of acceptance by it.

ARTICLE XVI

Any State Party to the Treaty may give notice of its withdrawal from the Treaty one year after its entry into force by written notification to the Depositary Governments. Such withdrawal shall take effect one year from the date of receipt of this notification.

ARTICLE XVII

This Treaty, of which the Chinese, English, French, Russian and Spanish texts are equally authentic, shall be deposited in the archives of the Depositary Governments. Duly certified copies of this Treaty shall be transmitted by the Depositary Governments to the Governments of the signatory and acceding States.

4. Communications by means of space satellites began to be of practical advantage to the world during the 1960's. Satellites viewed weather conditions and televised pictures of the cloud formations around storms, so that forecasters could work more effectively. Other satellites were prepared to act as "mirrors" and relay messages from one part of the earth to another. Radio and television messages began to be transmitted in the early 1970's. Details of such communications work were included in the

COMSAT Report to the President and the Congress, issued in 1972. The following passage has been taken from that report:

Via Satellite: Expanding Global Services

Modern, high quality telecommunications have become so commonplace that the world tends to forget how recent are the technological achievements that make them possible.

For many centuries men dreamed vainly of instantaneous communication with other men in other lands on other continents. The progress of centuries was required to create the foundation on which modern telecommunications technology is built. Today, the existence of the global commercial communications satellite system, and the continuing expansion of this novel venture, is an historical fact.

As of August 1972 regular, full time commercial satellite services are being provided globally by four satellites of the INTELSAT IV series and by a network of 71 earth station antennas administered by 44 countries.

About 80 countries, territories, and possessions are being served directly and full time via the satellite system. For many of them, the global system provides the first direct access to economical, high quality telecommunications with the rest of the world.

Service is provided via over 200 communications paths through the network of earth stations and various satellites, a number which has grown rapidly with the addition of earth stations to the system.

In the present system it is possible for any earth station to communicate with any other earth station through a mutually visible satellite or through two satellites in a double-hop arrangement when appropriate. The multiple access capability of the satellites permits each of them to operate simultaneously with many earth stations, an advantage of flexibility and efficiency which cannot be matched by other telecommunications modes.

The system provides circuits for voice, data, teletype and facsimile as well as television channels, all of which meet or exceed international standards of quality. As Manager for INTELSAT, COMSAT is responsible for ensuring that these standards are maintained, as far as is practicable, at all times throughout the system of satellites and earth stations.

The swift expansion of the global system has required careful planning, and will continue to do so, to ensure that the system is capable of absorbing present and future traffic growth. To design a satellite (or an earth station), manufacture it, test it, and introduce it into service requires a significant expenditure of resources. Detailed planning for the employment of new facilities must be accomplished and coordinated many months in advance. Because delays may occur in placing major new facilities in service, alternate plans must be devised to provide interim service.

In addition to their great capacity, the INTELSAT IV satellites introduce new capabilities based on sophisticated techniques which permit more efficient use of satellite channels. The first of these satellites entered service in 1971, the second and third early in 1972, and the fourth in the summer of 1972.

5.   *While these complicated Space operations were going on, open land, owned by the government, was still available on which individuals could establish themselves as homesteaders or on which they could work as miners, ranchers, or lumbermen. In 1973, the Bureau of Land Management of the U.S. Department of the Interior released the following bulletin in question and answer form for prospective buyers of public land.*

How to Buy Public Lands

What is public land?

While there are all kinds of "public" land—Federal, State, county, municipal—this leaflet pertains to land owned by the Federal Government and administered by the U.S. Department of the Interior's Bureau of Land Management. For the most part, this is original public domain land which has never left Federal ownership. "Public land" as described in this leaflet does not mean National Forests or National Parks.

In what states is most public land for sale located?

Almost all of it is in the public land states of the West—Arizona, Montana, Wyoming, Colorado, New Mexico, Oregon, Nevada, Idaho, Utah, California, Washington. For information about public land in Alaska, write Bureau of Land Management, U.S. Department of the Interior, Washington, D.C. 20240 and ask for Information Bulletin No. 2.

What about public lands in the East and elsewhere?

Small amounts of public land still remain in Alabama, Arkansas, Florida, Louisiana, Michigan, Minnesota, Mississippi and Wisconsin, but land sales in these States are very rare. *There are no public lands in Delaware, Georgia, Hawaii, Illinois, Indiana, Iowa, Kentucky, Maine, Maryland, Massachusetts, Missouri, New Hampshire, New Jersey, New York, North Carolina, Ohio, Pennsylvania, Rhode Island, South Caro-* lina, Tennessee, Texas, Vermont, Virginia and West Virginia.

How is public land sold?

By public auction sale through sealed or oral bidding.

Where are the sales held?

In State Offices of the Bureau of Land Management as listed in this leaflet. No sales are held in Washington, D.C.

Is any of this land free or cheap?

Every parcel is appraised by the Government at fair market value. You cannot buy it for less than the appraised price. Don't be deceived by promoters who advertise "free" or "cheap" public land.

If I want to buy some public land what is the first thing I should do?

Get the very best information available. "Our Public Lands," a quarterly magazine published by the Bureau of Land Management, carries a listing of public lands to be sold in the near future. The magazine's "Public Sale Bulletin Board" gives a thumbnail description of these lands, including their general location, appraised price, and other information. If you live in the West, you may visit the nearest BLM Office and ask for information.

How do I subscribe to this magazine?

Send $2 to Superintendent of Documents, Government Printing Office, Washington, D.C. 20402 and ask for a year's subscription to "Our Public Lands." Be sure that your name and address, including zip code, are typed or printed clearly.

If a parcel listed in the magazine interests me, what is my next move?

When you have looked over the "Public Sale Bulletin Board" and found listed a parcel of public land that interests you, you should get additional information about the parcel. To do this, write the BLM State Office for the State in which the parcel is located.

What do I ask the State Office?

Ask for a prospectus describing in detail the tract you saw listed in "Our Public Lands." The prospectus will include date of sale, facts about preference rights for adjoining landowners, a more complete description of the parcel than given in the magazine, and other things you should know before buying. You can also ask for a bid form on which to make your bid.

If I decide I want to buy the parcel, what is the next thing I should do?

From the prospectus you obtain from the State

Office, you will be able to decide if you really want to bid. If you still aren't sure, you can write for additional details. If at all possible, inspect the property yourself or engage someone to do so for you.

Can land listed in "Our Public Lands" be taken off the market before sale?

Yes. For unexpected technical and legal reasons some tracts listed for sale must be taken off the market. Such action is unfortunate, but it happens from time to time. If this happens in your case, the BLM State Office can tell you why it was necessary.

Can I actually buy a parcel of public land by mail?

Yes, you can actually purchase Government land by mail. But, there is distinct advantage in being present for the sale or sending a representative. Bids sent in by mail cannot be raised unless the bidder, or his representative, is present at this sale.

8-B WAGING WARS AND SEEKING PEACE:
Military affairs, 1933-1973

The years from 1933 to 1973 were dominated by military problems, and by questions of war and peace, to a greater degree than any similar period in our country's history. At the start of the period, Americans had no more than a passing curiosity about the fighting that was going on between Japanese and Chinese troops in the Far East. At the end of the period, warfare anywhere in the world was seen as having an influence on American policies. At the start, the United States had no military alliances, and was outside the League of Nations by its own choice. By 1973, military alliances appeared to bind the United States to a majority of the powers of Europe and the Pacific Ocean areas, and the United States was a founding member of the United Nations. The period saw the United States participate in World War II, the costliest and bloodiest war in world history, and in indecisive wars in Korea and Vietnam.

PROBLEMS: *How and why did the United States become a participant in so many military actions? What steps have been taken to preserve, or to secure, a basis for peace among nations?*

1. At the start of this period in our history, most Americans could be called "isolationists". They wished no part in foreign wars, and saw little connection between events abroad and the well-being of the United States. When Civil War broke out in Spain in 1936, several European powers sent aid to one or another of the warring sides. Americans responded to the war threat by passing a strict new Neutrality Act in 1937. Important sections are quoted below. It was intended to eliminate the kind of problem that led the United States directly into World War I.

JOINT RESOLUTION.

To amend the joint resolution, approved 31 August 1935, as amended.

Resolved . . .

SEC. 1. (*a*) Whenever the President shall find that there exists a state of war between, or among, two or more foreign States, the President shall proclaim such fact, and it shall thereafter be unlawful to export, or attempt to export, or cause to be exported, arms, ammunition, or implements of war from any place in the United States to any belligerent State named in such proclamation, or to any neutral State for transshipment to, or for the use of, any such belligerent State.

(*b*) The President shall, from time to time, by proclamation, extend such embargo upon the export of arms, ammunition, or implements of war to other States as and when they may become involved in such war.

221

(*c*) Whenever the President shall find that a state of civil strife exists in a foreign State and that such civil strife is of a magnitude or is being conducted under such conditions that the export of arms, ammunition, or implements of war from the United States to such foreign State would threaten or endanger the peace of the United States, the President shall proclaim such fact, and it shall thereafter be unlawful to export, or attempt to export, or cause to be exported, arms, ammunition, or implements of war from any place in the United States to such foreign State, or to any neutral State for transshipment to, or for the use of, such foreign State.

(*d*) The President shall, from time to time by proclamation, definitely enumerate the arms, ammunition, and implements of war, the export of which is prohibited by this section.

SEC. 2. (*a*) Whenever the President shall have issued a proclamation under the authority of section 1 of this Act and he shall thereafter find that the placing of restrictions on the shipment of certain articles or materials in addition to arms, ammunition, and implements of war from the United States to belligerent States, or to a State wherein civil strife exists, is necessary to promote the security or preserve the peace of the United States or to protect the lives of citizens of the United States, he shall so proclaim, and it shall thereafter be unlawful, for any American vessel to carry such articles or materials to any belligerent State, or to a State wherein civil strife exists, named in such proclamation issued under the authority of section 1 of this Act, or to any neutral State for transshipment to, or for the use of, any such belligerent State or any such State wherein civil strife exists. The President shall by proclamation from time to time definitely enumerate the articles and materials which it shall be unlawful for American vessels to so transport. . . .

(*c*) The President shall from time to time by proclamation extend such restrictions as are imposed under the authority of this section to other States as and when they may be declared to become belligerent States under proclamations issued under the authority of section 1 of this Act. . . .

SEC. 3. (*a*) Whenever the President shall have issued a proclamation under the authority of section 1 of this Act, it shall thereafter be unlawful for any person within the United States to purchase, sell, or exchange bonds, securities, or other obligations of the government of any belligerent State, or of any State wherein civil strife exists, named in such proclamation, or of any political subdivision of any such State, or of any person acting for or on behalf of the government of any such

State, or of any faction or asserted government within any such State wherein civil strife exists, or of any person acting for or on behalf of any faction or asserted government within any such State wherein civil strife exists, issued after the date of such proclamation, or to make any loan or extend any credit to any such government, political subdivision, faction, asserted government, or person, or to solicit or receive any contribution for any such government, political subdivision, faction, asserted government, or person: *Provided,* That if the President shall find that such action will serve to protect the commercial or other interests of the United States or its citizens, he may, in his discretion, and to such extent and under such regulations as he may prescribe, except from the operation of this section ordinary commercial credits and short-time obligations in aid of legal transactions and of a character customarily used in normal peacetime commercial transactions. Nothing in this subsection shall be construed to prohibit the solicitation or collection of funds to be used for medical aid and assistance, or for food and clothing to relieve human suffering, when such solicitation or collection of funds is made on behalf of and for use by any person or organization which is not acting for or on behalf of any such government, political subdivision, faction, or asserted government, but all such solicitations and collections of funds shall be subject to the approval of the President and shall be made under such rules and regulations as he shall prescribe. . . .

SEC. 4. This Act shall not apply to an American republic or republics engaged in war against a non-American State or States, provided the American republic is not co-operating with a non-American State or States in such war.

SEC. 5. (*a*) There is hereby established a National Munitions Control Board (hereinafter referred to as the "Board") to carry out the provisions of this Act. The Board shall consist of the Secretary of State, who shall be chairman and executive officer of the Board, the Secretary of the Treasury, the Secretary of War, the Secretary of the Navy, and the Secretary of Commerce. Except as otherwise provided in this Act, or by other law, the administration of this Act is vested in the Department of State. The Secretary of State shall promulgate such rules and regulations with regard to the enforcement of this section as he may deem necessary to carry out its provisions. The Board shall be convened by the chairman and shall hold at least one meeting a year.

(*b*) Every person who engages in the business of manufacturing, exporting, or importing any of the arms, ammunition, or implements of war referred to in this Act, whether as an exporter, importer, manufacturer, or dealer, shall register with the Secretary of State his name, or business name, principal place of business, and places of business in the United States, and a list of the arms, ammunition, and implements of war which he manufactures, imports, or exports.

(*c*) Every person required to register under this section shall notify the Secretary of State of any change in the arms, ammunition, or implements of war which he exports, imports, or manufactures; . . .

(*d*) It shall be unlawful for any person to export, or attempt to export, from the United States to any other State, any of the arms, ammunition, or implements of war referred to in this Act, or to import, or attempt to import, to the United States from any other State, any of the arms, ammunition, or implements of war referred to in this Act, without first having obtained a license therefor. . . .

(*k*) The President is hereby authorized to proclaim upon recommendation of the Board from time to time a list of articles which shall be considered arms, ammunition, and implements of war for the purposes of this section.

SEC. 6. (*a*) Whenever the President shall have issued a proclamation under the authority of section 1 of this Act, it shall thereafter be unlawful, until such proclamation is revoked, for any American vessel to carry any arms, ammunition, or implements of war to any belligerent State, or to any State wherein civil strife exists, named in such proclamation, or to any neutral State for transshipment to, or for the use of, any such belligerent State or any such State wherein civil strife exists. . . .

SEC. 7. (*a*) Whenever, during any war in which the United States is neutral, the President, or any person thereunto authorized by him, shall have cause to believe that any vessel, domestic or foreign, whether requiring clearance or not, is about to carry out of a port of the United States, fuel, men, arms, ammunition, implements of war, or other supplies to any warship, tender, or supply ship of a belligerent State, but the evidence is not deemed sufficient to justify forbidding the departure of the vessel as provided for by section 1, title V, chapter 30, of the Act approved 15 June 1917, and if, in the President's judgment, such action will serve to maintain peace between the United States and foreign States, or to protect the commercial interests of the United States and its citizens, or to promote the security or neutrality of the United States, he shall have the power and it shall be his duty to require the owner, master, or person in command thereof, before departing from a port of the United States, to give a bond to the United States, with sufficient sureties, in such amount as he shall deem proper, conditioned that the vessel will not deliver the men, or any part of the cargo, to any warship, tender, or supply ship of a belligerent State.

(*b*) If the President, or any person thereunto authorized by him, shall find that a vessel, domestic or foreign, in a port of the United States, has previously cleared from a port of the United States during such war and delivered its cargo or any part thereof to a warship, tender, or supply ship of belligerent State, he may prohibit the departure of such vessel during the duration of the war.

SEC. 8. Whenever, during any war in which the United States is neutral, the President shall find that special restrictions placed on the use of the ports and territorial waters of the United States by the submarines or armed merchant vessels of a foreign State, will serve to maintain peace between the United States and foreign States, or to protect the commercial interests of the United States and its citizens, or to promote the security of the United States, and shall make proclamation therefore, it shall thereafter be unlawful for any such submarine or armed merchant vessel to enter a port or the territorial waters of the United States or to depart therefrom, except under such conditions and subject to such limitations as the President may prescribe. Whenever, in his judgment, the conditions which have caused him to issue his proclamation have ceased to exist, he shall revoke his proclamation, and the provisions of this section shall thereupon cease to apply.

SEC. 9. Whenever the President shall have issued a proclamation under the authority of section 1 of this Act it shall thereafter be unlawful for any citizen of the United States to travel on any vessel of the State or States named in such proclamation, except in accordance with such rules and regulations as the President shall prescribe: . . .

SEC. 10. Whenever the President shall have issued a proclamation under the authority of section 1, it shall thereafter be unlawful, until such proclamation is revoked, for any American vessel engaged in commerce with any belligerent State, or any State wherein civil strife exists, named in such proclamation, to be armed or to carry any armament, arms, ammunition, or implements of war, except small arms and ammunition therefor which the President may deem necessary and shall publicly designate for the preservation of discipline aboard such vessels. . . .

2. When World War II began, the United States was not directly involved. Some Americans had been sympathetic toward China in its fight against Japan; others saw no reason not to send war materials to Japan. There was much more sympathy in 1939 for Poland, France, Great Britain and the other allies who faced Nazi Germany. However, few Americans wished to become involved in the war.

The Neutrality Act was eventually modified, so that belligerents could buy supplies on a "cash-and-carry" basis in the United States. This meant that Allied ships could come to American ports and carry war materials to their home countries. Even this kind of passive help was opposed by many Americans who saw it as a step toward war.

In 1940, as the Nazi armies and air fleets appeared on the point of dominating Europe, a new plan for aid to the Allies was developed—"lend-lease". President Franklin D. Roosevelt believed that the defense of the United States depended on the success of the British and their allies in Europe, and he turned to radio as a means of convincing Americans that they should support his policies. One of President Roosevelt's "fireside chats", given on December 29, 1940, dealt with the proposed Lend-Lease program. The talk was also published as a State paper.

Never before since Jamestown and Plymouth Rock has our American civilization been in such danger as now.

For, on September 27, 1940, by an agreement signed in Berlin, three powerful nations, two in Europe and one in Asia, joined themselves together in the threat that if the United States interfered with or blocked the expansion program of these three nations—a program aimed at world control—they would unite in ultimate action against the United States.

The Nazi masters of Germany have made it clear that they intend not only to dominate all life and thought in their own country, but also to enslave the whole of Europe, and then to use the resources of Europe to dominate the rest of the world. . . .

In view of the nature of this undeniable threat, it can be asserted properly and categorically, that the United States has no right or reason to encourage talk of peace until the day shall come when there is a clear intention on the part of the aggressor nations to abandon all thought of dominating or conquering the world.

At this moment, the forces of the states that are leagued against all peoples who live in freedom are being held away from our shores. The Germans and Italians are being blocked on the other side of the Atlantic by the British, and by the Greeks, and by thousands of soldiers and sailors who were able to escape from subjugated countries. The Japanese are being engaged in Asia by the Chinese in another great defense.

In the Pacific is our fleet.

Some of our people like to believe that wars in Europe and in Asia are of no concern to us. But it is a matter of most vital concern to us that European and Asiatic war-makers should not gain control of the oceans which lead to this hemisphere.

One hundred and seventeen years ago the Monroe Doctrine was conceived by our Government as a measure of defense in the face of a threat against this hemisphere by an alliance in continental Europe. Thereafter, we stood on guard in the Atlantic, with the British as neighbors. There was no treaty. There was no "unwritten agreement."

Yet, there was the feeling, proven correct by history, that we as neighbors could settle any disputes in peaceful fashion. The fact is that during the whole of this time the Western Hemisphere has remained free from aggression from Europe or from Asia.

Does anyone seriously believe that we need to fear attack while a free Britain remains our most powerful naval neighbor in the Atlantic? Does any one seriously believe, on the other hand, that we could rest easy if the Axis powers were our neighbor there?

If Great Britain goes down, the Axis powers will control the continents of Europe, Asia, Africa, Australasia, and the high seas—and they will be in a position to bring enormous military and naval resources against this hemisphere. It is no exaggeration to say that all of us in the Americas would be living at the point of a gun—a gun loaded with explosive bullets, economic as well as military.

We should enter upon a new and terrible era in which the whole world, our hemisphere included, would be run by threats of brute force. To survive in such a world, we would have to convert ourselves permanently into a militaristic power on the basis of war economy.

Some of us like to believe that even if Great Britain falls, we are still safe, because of the broad expanse of the Atlantic and of the Pacific.

But the width of these oceans is not what it was in the days of clipper ships. At one point between Africa and Brazil the distance is less than from Washington to Denver—five hours for the latest type of bomber. And at the north of the Pacific Ocean, America and Asia almost touch each other.

Even today we have planes which could fly from the

British Isles to New England and back without refueling. And the range of the modern bomber is ever being increased. . . .

Frankly and definitely there is danger ahead—danger against which we must prepare. But we well know that we cannot escape danger, or the fear of it, by crawling into bed and pulling the covers over our heads.

Some nations of Europe were bound by solemn non-intervention pacts with Germany. Other nations were assured by Germany that they need never fear invasion. Non-intervention pact or not, the fact remains that they were attacked, overrun, and thrown into the modern form of slavery at an hour's notice or even without any notice at all. . . .

The experience of the past two years has proven beyond doubt that no nation can appease the Nazis. No man can tame a tiger into a kitten by stroking it. There can be no appeasement with ruthlessness. There can be no reasoning with an incendiary bomb. We know now that a nation can have peace with the Nazis only at the price of total surrender.

Even the people of Italy have been forced to become accomplices of the Nazis; but at this moment they do not know how soon they will be embraced to death by their allies.

The American appeasers ignore the warning to be found in the fate of Austria, Czechoslovakia, Poland, Norway, Belgium, the Netherlands, Denmark, and France. They tell you that the Axis powers are going to win anyway; that all this bloodshed in the world could be saved; and that the United States might just as well throw its influence into the scale of a dictated peace, and get the best out of it that we can.

They call it a "negotiated peace." Nonsense! Is it a negotiated peace if a gang of outlaws surrounds your community and on threat of extermination makes you pay tribute to save your own skins?

Such a dictated peace would be no peace at all. It would be only another armistice, leading to the most gigantic armament race and the most devastating trade wars in history. And in these contests the Americas would offer the only real resistance to the Axis powers.

With all their vaunted efficiency and parade of pious purpose in this war, there are still in their background the concentration camp and the servants of God in chains.

The history of recent years proves that shootings and chains and concentration camps are not simply the transient tools but the very altars of modern dictatorships. They may talk of a "new order" in the world, but what they have in mind is but a revival of the oldest and the worst tyranny. In that there is no liberty, no religion, no hope.

The proposed "new order" is the very opposite of a United States of Europe or a United States of Asia. It is not a government based upon the consent of the governed. It is not a union of ordinary, self-respecting men and women to protect themselves and their freedom and their dignity from oppression. It is an unholy alliance of power and pelf to dominate and enslave the human race.

The British people are conducting an active war against this unholy alliance. Our own future security is greatly dependent on the outcome of that fight. Our ability to "keep out of war" is going to be affected by that outcome.

Thinking in terms of today and tomorrow, I make the direct statement to the American people that there is far less chance of the United States getting into war if we do all we can now to support the nations defending themselves against attack by the Axis than if we acquiesce in their defeat, submit tamely to an Axis victory, and wait our turn to be the object of attack in another war later on.

If we are to be completely honest with ourselves, we must admit there is risk in *any* course we may take. But I deeply believe that the great majority of our people agree that the course that I advocate involves the least risk now and the greatest hope for world peace in the future.

The people of Europe who are defending themselves do not ask us to do their fighting. They ask us for the implements of war, the planes, the tanks, the guns, the freighters, which will enable them to fight for their liberty and our security. Emphatically we must get these weapons to them in sufficient volume and quickly enough, so that we and our children will be saved the agony and suffering of war which others have had to endure.

Let not defeatists tell us that it is too late. It will never be earlier. Tomorrow will be later than today.

Certain facts are self-evident.

In a military sense Great Britain and the British Empire are today the spearhead of resistance to world conquest. They are putting up a fight which will live forever in the story of human gallantry.

There is no demand for sending an American Expeditionary Force outside our own borders. There is no intention by any member of your Government to send such a force. You can, therefore, nail any talk about sending armies to Europe as deliberate untruth.

Our national policy is not directed toward war. Its sole purpose is to keep war away from our country and our people.

Democracy's fight against world conquest is being greatly aided, and must be more greatly aided, by the rearmament of the United States and by sending every ounce and every ton of munitions and supplies that we can possibly spare to help the defenders who are in the front lines. It is no more unneutral for us to do that than it is for Sweden, Russia, and other nations near Germany to send steel and ore and oil and other war materials into Germany every day.

We are planning our own defense with the utmost urgency; and in its vast scale we must integrate the war needs of Britain and the other free nations resisting aggression. . . .

As planes and ships and guns and shells are produced, your Government, with its defense experts, can then determine how best to use them to defend this hemisphere. The decision as to how much shall be sent abroad and how much shall remain at home must be made on the basis of our over-all military necessities.

We must be the great arsenal of democracy. For us this is an emergency as serious as war itself. We must apply ourselves to our task with the same resolution, the same sense of urgency, the same spirit of patriotism and sacrifice, as we would show were we at war.

3. A storm of protest arose from isolationist groups in the United States. One of the leaders of these groups was Senator Burton K. Wheeler of Montana. Wheeler, who had opposed many New Deal measures in the Senate, prophesied that Lend-Lease would lead to war. Note the shocking statement in the second paragraph of the speech that follows. Senator Wheeler made this speech on January 12, 1941, during debates on the Lend-Lease bill.

THE LEND-LEASE POLICY, translated into legislative form, stunned a Congress and a nation wholly sympathetic to the cause of Great Britain. The Kaiser's blank check to Austria-Hungary in the First World War was a piker compared to the Roosevelt blank check of World War II. It warranted my worst fears for the future of America, and it definitely stamps the President as war-minded.

The lend-lease-give program is the New Deal's triple-A foreign policy; it will plow under every fourth American boy.

Never before have the American people been asked or compelled to give so bounteously and so completely of their tax dollars to any foreign nation. Never before has the Congress of the United States been asked by any President to violate international law. Never before has this nation restored to duplicity in the conduct of its foreign affairs. Never before has the United States given to one man the power to strip this nation of its defenses. Never before has a Congress coldly and flatly been asked to abdicate.

If the American people want a dictatorship—if they want a totalitarian form of government and if they want war—this bill should be steam-rollered through Congress, as is the wont of President Roosevelt.

Approval of this legislation means war, open and complete warfare. I, therefore, ask the American people before they supinely accept it—Was the last World War worthwhile?

If it were, then we should lend and lease war materials. If it were, then we should lend and lease American boys. President Roosevelt has said we would be repaid by England. We will be. We will be repaid, just as England repaid her war debts of the First World War—repaid those dollars wrung from the sweat of labor and the toil of farmers with cries of "Uncle Shylock." Our boys will be returned—returned in caskets, maybe; returned with bodies maimed; returned with minds warped and twisted by sights of horrors and the scream and shriek of high-powered shells.

Considered on its merits and stripped of its emotional appeal to our sympathies, the lend-lease-give bill is both ruinous and ridiculous. Why should we Americans pay for war materials for Great Britain who still has $7 billion in credit or collateral in the United States? Thus far England has fully maintained rather than depleted her credits in the United States. The cost of the lend-lease-give program is high in terms of American tax dollars, but it is even higher in terms of our national defense. Now it gives to the President the unlimited power to completely strip our air force of its every bomber, of its every fighting plane.

It gives to one man—responsible to no one—the power to denude our shores of every warship. It gives to one individual the dictatorial power to strip the American Army of our every tank, cannon, rifle, or antiaircraft gun. No one would deny that the lend-lease-give bill contains provisions that would enable one man to render the United States defenseless, but they will tell you, "The President would never do it." To this I say, "Why does he ask the power if he does not intend to use it?" Why not I say, place some check on American donations to a foreign nation?

Is it possible that the farmers of America are willing to sell their birthright for a mess of pottage? Is it possible that American labor is to be sold down the river in return for a place upon the Defense Commission, or because your labor leaders are entertained at pink teas? Is it possible that the American people are so gullible that they will permit their representatives in Congress to sit supinely by while an American President demands totalitarian powers—in the name of saving democracy?

I say in the kind of language used by the President—shame on those who ask the powers—and shame on those who would grant them.

You people who oppose war and dictatorship, do not be dismayed because the warmongers and interventionists control most of the avenues of propaganda, including the motion-picture industry. Do not be dismayed because Mr. Willkie, of the Commonwealth & Southern, agrees with Mr. Roosevelt. This merely puts all the economic and foreign "royalists" on the side of war.

Remember, the interventionists control the money-bags, but you control the votes.

4.   The Lend-Lease plan of supplying the Allies was enacted, despite opposition from people who agreed with Wheeler. By midsummer 1941, President Roosevelt had moved very strongly to support the Allies, for he foresaw great danger to the United States in a victory for Germany. From August 9 through 12, a secret meeting took place between the American President and Prime Minister Winston S. Churchill of Great Britain. This meeting resulted in a joint statement of objectives; it is known as the Atlantic Charter.

The Atlantic Charter

. . . the President of the United States of America and the Prime Minister, Mr. Churchill, representing His Majesty's government in the United Kingdom, being met together, deem it right to make known certain common principles in the national policies of their respective countries on which they base their hopes for a better future for the world.

First, their countries seek no aggrandizement, territorial or other.

Second, they desire to see no territorial changes that do not accord with the freely expressed wishes of the peoples concerned.

Third, they respect the right of all peoples to choose the form of government under which they will live; and they wish to see sovereign rights and self-government restored to those who have been forcibly deprived of them.

Fourth, they will endeavor, with due respect for their existing obligations, to further the enjoyment by all states, great or small, victor or vanquished, of ac-

cess, on equal terms, to the trade and to the raw materials of the world which are needed for their economic prosperity.

Fifth, they desire to bring about the fullest collaboration between all nations in the economic field with the object of securing, for all, improved labor standards, economic advancement, and social security.

Sixth, after the final destruction of the Nazi tyranny, they hope to see established a peace which will afford to all nations the means of dwelling in safety within their own boundaries, and which will afford assurance that all the men in all the lands may live out their lives in freedom from fear and want.

Seventh, such a peace should enable all men to traverse the high seas and oceans without hindrance.

Eight, they believe that all of the nations of the world, for realistic as well as spiritual reasons, must come to the abandonment of the use of force. Since no future peace can be maintained if land, sea, or air armaments continue to be employed by nations which threaten, or may threaten, aggression outside of their frontiers, they believe, pending the establishment of a wider and permanent system of general security, that the disarmament of such nations is essential. They will likewise aid and encourage all other practicable measures which will lighten for peace-loving peoples the crushing burden of armaments.

5.   During the late months of 1941, the United States drifted closer to full-scale war. In the Atlantic, American destroyers escorted merchant ships past German submarines; in the Pacific, American and Japanese interests also clashed. The opening guns of actual war were fired over Hawaii, when a Japanese naval task force struck Pearl Harbor, December 7, 1941. This surprise attack, which was highly successful, led to a declaration of war. President Roosevelt's brief talk to Congress, requesting the declaration, follows.

Yesterday, December 7, 1941—a date which will live in infamy—the United States of America was suddenly and deliberately attacked by naval and air forces of the empire of Japan.

The United States was at peace with that nation and, at the solicitation of Japan, was still in conversation with its government and its emperor looking toward the maintenance of peace in the Pacific.

Indeed, one hour after Japanese air squadrons had commenced bombing in the American Island of Oahu the Japanese Ambassador to the United States and his colleague delivered to our Secretary of State a formal reply to a recent American message. And, while this reply stated that it seemed useless to continue the existing diplomatic negotiations, it contained no threat or hint of war or of armed attack.

It will be recorded that the distance of Hawaii from Japan makes it obvious that the attack was deliberately planned many days or even weeks ago. During the intervening time the Japanese Government has deliberately sought to deceive the United States by false statements and expressions of hope for continued peace.

The attack yesterday on the Hawaiian Islands has caused severe damage to American naval and military forces. I regret to tell you that very many American lives have been lost. In addition American ships have been reported torpedoed on the high seas between San Francisco and Honolulu.

Yesterday the Japanese Government also launched an attack against Malaya.

Last night Japanese forces attacked Hong Kong.

Last night Japanese forces attacked Guam.

Last night Japanese forces attacked the Philippine Islands.

Last night the Japanese attacked Wake Island.

And this morning the Japanese attacked Midway Island.

Japan has therefore undertaken a surprise offensive extending throughout the Pacific area. The facts of yesterday and today speak for themselves. The people of the United States have already formed their opinions and well understand the implications to the very life and safety of our nation.

As Commander in Chief of the Army and Navy I have directed that all measures be taken for our defense.

Always will our whole nation remember the character of the onslaught against us.

No matter how long it may take us to overcome this premeditated invasion, the American people, in their righteous might, will win through to absolute victory.

I believe that I interpret the will of the Congress and of the people when I assert that we will not only defend ourselves to the uttermost but will make it very certain that this form of treachery shall never again endanger us.

Hostilities exist. There is no blinking at the fact that our people, our territory and our interests are in grave danger.

With confidence in our armed forces, with the unbounding determination of our people, we will gain the inevitable triumph. So help us God.

I ask that the Congress declare that since the unprovoked and dastardly attack by Japan on Sunday, Dec. 7, 1941, a state of war has existed between the United States and the Japanese Empire.

6.   The military plans for World War II were developed in a series of conferences. President Roosevelt himself attended some, and many other conferences were conducted at lower levels of command. A major problem lay in the differences among the Allied powers, and conferences at the highest level ("Summit") were provided for to prevent such differences from blocking the war effort. A parallel problem was to find a way of preventing international differences from threatening peace after World War II would end. One of the key conferences was held at Yalta, in the Soviet Union. In the following selection, passages from the published Yalta agreements are provided.

I. WORLD ORGANIZATION

1. That a United Nations Conference on the proposed world organization should be summoned for Wednesday, 25 April, 1945, and should be held in the United States of America.

2. The nations to be invited to this conference should be:

(*a*) the United Nations as they existed on the 8 February, 1945, and

(*b*) such of the Associated Nations as have declared war on the common enemy by 1 March, 1945. (For this purpose by the term "Associated Nation" was meant the eight Associated Nations and Turkey.) When the Conference on World Organization is held, the delegates of the United Kingdom and United States of America will support a proposal to admit to original membership two Soviet Socialist republics, *i.e.*, the Ukraine and White Russia.

3. That the United States government on behalf of the Three Powers should consult the government of China and the French Provisional Government in regard to the decisions taken at the present conference concerning the proposed world organization.

4. That the text of the invitation to be issued to all the nations which would take part in the United Nations Conference should be as follows:

The government of the United States of America, on behalf of itself and of the governments of the United Kingdom, the Union of Soviet Socialist Republics, and the Republic of China and of the Provisional Government of the French Republic, invite the government of ———— to send representatives to a Conference of the United Nations to be held on 25 April, 1945, or soon thereafter, at San Francisco in the United States of America to prepare a charter for a general international organization for the maintenance of international peace and security.

The above-named governments suggest that the conference consider as affording a basis for such a charter the proposals for the establishment of a general international organization which were made public last October as a result of the Dumbarton Oaks Conference, and which have now been supplemented by the following provisions for Section C of Chapter VI:

1. Each member of the Security Council should have one vote.

2. Decisions of the Security Council on procedural matters should be made by an affirmative vote of seven members.

3. Decisions of the Security Council on all other matters should be made by an affirmative vote of seven members, including the concurring votes of the permanent members; provided that, in decisions under Chapter VIII, Section A, and under the second sentence of paragraph 1 of Chapter VIII, Section C, a party to a dispute should abstain from voting.

Further information as to arrangements will be transmitted subsequently.

In the event that the government of ———— desires in advance of the conference to present views or comments concerning the proposals, the government of the United States of America will be pleased to transmit such views and comments to the other participating governments.

It was agreed that the five nations which will have permanent seats on the Security Council should consult each other prior to the United Nations Conference on the question of territorial trusteeship.

The acceptance of this recommendation is subject to its being made clear that territorial trusteeship will only apply to (a) existing mandates of the League of Nations; (b) territories detached from the enemy as a result of the present war; (c) any other territory which might voluntarily be placed under trusteeship; and (d) no discussion of actual territories is contemplated at the forthcoming United Nations Conference or in the preliminary consultations, and it will be a matter for subsequent agreement which territories within the above categories will be placed under trusteeship.

II. Declaration on Liberated Europe

The following declaration has been approved:

The Premier of the Union of Soviet Socialist Republics, the Prime Minister of the United Kingdom, and the President of the United States of America have consulted with each other in the common interest of the peoples of their countries and those of liberated Europe. They jointly declare their mutual agreement to concert during the temporary period of instability in liberated Europe the policies of their three governments in assisting the peoples liberated from the domination of Nazi Germany and the peoples of the former Axis satellite states of Europe to solve by democratic means their pressing political and economic problems.

The establishment of order in Europe and the rebuilding of national economic life must be achieved by processes which will enable the liberated peoples to destroy the last vestiges of Nazism and Fascism and to create democratic institutions of their own choice. This is a principle of the Atlantic Charter—the right of all peoples to choose the form of government under which they will live—the restoration of sovereign rights and self-government to those peoples who have been forcibly deprived of them by the aggressor nations.

To foster the conditions in which the liberated peoples may exercise these rights, the three governments will jointly assist the people in any European liberated state or former Axis satellite state in Europe where in their judgment conditions require (a) to establish conditions of internal peace; (b) to carry out emergency measures for the relief of distressed peoples; (c) to form interim governmental authorities broadly representative of all democratic elements in the population and pledged to the earliest possible establishment through free elections of governments responsive to the will of the people; and (d) to facilitate where necessary the holding of such elections.

The three governments will consult the other United Nations and provisional authorities or other governments in Europe when matters of direct interest to them are under consideration.

When, in the opinion of the three governments, conditions in any European liberated state or any former Axis satellite state in Europe make such action necessary, they will immediately consult together on the measures necessary to discharge the joint responsibilities set forth in this declaration.

By this declaration we reaffirm our faith in the principles of the Atlantic Charter, our pledge in the Declaration by the United Nations, and our determination to build in cooperation with other peace-loving nations world order under law, dedicated to peace, security, freedom, and general well-being of all mankind.

In issuing this declaration, the Three Powers express the hope that the Provisional Government of the French Republic may be associated with them in the procedure suggested.

III. Dismemberment of Germany

It was agreed that Article 12 (*a*) of the Surrender Terms for Germany should be amended to read as follows:

> The United Kingdom, the United States of America, and the Union of Soviet Socialist Republics shall possess supreme authority with respect to Germany. In the exercise of such authority they will take such steps, including the complete disarmament, demilitarization, and the dismemberment of Germany as they deem requisite for future peace and security.

The study of the procedure for the dismemberment of Germany was referred to a committee consisting of Mr. Eden (chairman), Mr. Winant, and Mr. Gousev. This body would consider the desirability of associating with it a French representative.

IV. Zone of Occupation for the French and Control Council for Germany

It was agreed that a zone in Germany, to be occupied by the French forces, should be allocated to France. This zone would be formed out of the British and American zones and its extent would be settled by the British and Americans in consultation with the French Provisional Government.

It was also agreed that the French Provisional Government should be invited to become a member of the Allied Control Council for Germany.

V. Reparation

The following protocol has been approved:

1. Germany must pay in kind for the losses caused by her to the Allied Nations in the course of the war. Reparations are to be received in the first instance by those countries which have borne the main burden of the war; have suffered the heaviest losses, and have organized victory over the enemy.

2. Reparation in kind is to be exacted from Germany in the three following forms.

(*a*) Removals within two years from the surrender of Germany or the cessation of organized resistance from the national wealth of Germany located on the territory of Germany herself, as well as outside her territory (equipment, machine tools, ships, rolling stock, German investments abroad, shares of industrial transport, and other enterprises in Germany, etc.), these removals to be carried out chiefly for purpose of destroying the war potential of Germany.

(*b*) Annual deliveries of goods from current production for a period to be fixed.

(*c*) Use of German labor.

3. For the working out on the above principles of a detailed plan for exaction of reparation from Germany, an Allied Reparation Commission will be set up in Moscow. It will consist of three representatives—one from the Union of Soviet Socialist Republics, one from the United Kingdom, and one from the United States of America.

4. With regard to the fixing of the total sum of the reparation as well as the distribution of it among the countries which suffered from the German aggression, the Soviet and American delegations agreed as follows:

> The Moscow Reparation Commission should take in its initial studies as a basis for discussion the suggestion of the Soviet government that the total sum of the reparation in accordance with the points (*a*) and (*b*) of the paragraph 2 should be $20 billion and that 50 percent of it should go to the Union of Soviet Socialist Republics.

The British delegation was of the opinion that pending consideration of the reparation question by the Moscow Reparation Commission no figures of reparation should be mentioned.

The above Soviet-American proposal has been passed to the Moscow Reparation Commission as one of the proposals to be considered by the Commission.

VI. Major War Criminals

The Conference agreed that the question of the major war criminals should be the subject of inquiry by the three foreign secretaries for report in due course after the close of the conference.

VII. Poland

The following Declaration on Poland was agreed by the conference:

A new situation has been created in Poland as a result of her complete liberation by the Red Army. This calls for the establishment of a Polish Provisional Government which can be more broadly based than was possible before the recent liberation of the western part of Poland. The Provisional Government which is now functioning in Poland should therefore be reorganized on a broader democratic basis with the inclusion of democratic leaders from Poland itself and from Poles abroad. This new government should then be called the Polish Provisional Government of National Unity.

M. Molotov, Mr. Harriman, and Sir A. Clark Kerr are authorized as a commission to consult in the first instance in Moscow with members of the present Provisional Government and with other Polish democratic leaders from within Poland and from abroad, with a view to the reorganization of the present government along the above lines. This Polish Provisional Government of National Unity shall be pledged to the holding of free and unfettered elections as soon as possible on the basis of universal suffrage and secret ballot. In these elections all democratic and anti-Nazi parties shall have the right to take part and to put forward candidates.

When a Polish Provisional Government of National Unity has been properly formed in conformity with the above, the government of the U.S.S.R., which now maintains diplomatic relations with the present Provisional Government of Poland, and the government of the United Kingdom and the government of the U.S.A. will establish diplomatic relations with the new Polish Provisional Government of National Unity, and will exchange ambassadors by whose reports the respective governments will be kept informed about the situation in Poland.

The three heads of government consider that the eastern frontier of Poland should follow the Curzon Line, with digressions from it in some regions of five to eight kilometers in favor of Poland. They recognize that Poland must receive substantial accessions of territory in the north and west. They feel that the opinion of the new Polish Provisional Government of National Unity should be sought in due course on the extent of these accessions and that the final delimitation of the western frontier of Poland should thereafter await the Peace Conference.

VIII. YUGOSLAVIA

It was agreed to recommend to Marshal Tito and to Dr. Subasic:

1. That the Tito-Subasic Agreement should immediately be put into effect and a new government formed on the basis of the agreement.

2. That as soon as the new government has been formed it should declare:

(a) that the Anti-Fascist Assembly of National Liberation (AUNOJ) will be extended to include members of the last Yugoslav Skupstina who have not compromised themselves by collaboration with the enemy, thus forming a body to be known as a temporary parliament and

(b) that legislative acts passed by the Anti-Fascist Assembly of National Liberation (AUNOJ) will be subject to subsequent ratification by a constituent assembly. And that this statement should be published in the communique of the conference.

IX. ITALO-YUGOSLAVIA FRONTIER; ITALO-AUSTRIA FRONTIER

Notes on these subjects were put in by the British delegation and the American and Soviet delegations agreed to consider them and give their views later.

X. YUGOSLAV-BULGARIAN RELATIONS

There was an exchange of views between the foreign secretaries on the question of the desirability of a Yugoslav-Bulgarian pact of alliance. The question at issue was whether a state still under an armistice regime could be allowed to enter into a treaty with another state. Mr. Eden suggested that the Bulgarian and Yugoslav governments should be informed that this could not be approved. Mr. Stettinius suggested that the British and American ambassadors should discuss the matter further with M. Molotov in Moscow. M. Molotov agreed with the proposal of Mr. Stettinius.

XI. SOUTHEASTERN EUROPE

The British delegation put in notes for the consideration of their colleagues on the following subjects:

(a) the Control Commission in Bulgaria

(b) Greek claims upon Bulgaria, more particularly with reference to reparations.

(c) Oil equipment in Rumania.

XII. IRAN

Mr. Eden, Mr. Stettinius, and M. Molotov exchanged views on the situation in Iran. It was agreed that this matter should be pursued through the diplomatic channel.

XIII. MEETINGS OF THE THREE FOREIGN SECRETARIES

The conference agreed that the permanent machinery should be set up for consultation between the three foreign secretaries, they should meet as often as necessary, probably about every three or four months. These meetings will be held in rotation in the three capitals, the first meeting being held in London.

XIV. THE MONTREUX CONVENTION AND THE STRAITS

It was agreed that at the next meeting of the three foreign secretaries to be held in London they should consider proposals which it was understood the Soviet government would put forward in relation to the Montreux Convention and report to their governments. The Turkish government should be informed at the appropriate moment.

7. World War II made many military people famous in its course. General Dwight D. Eisenhower, who commanded the Allied forces on the western front in Europe, eventually became President of the United States. The commanding general in the campaigns against Japan was Douglas MacArthur. MacArthur presided at the ceremony when Japan surrendered to the United States and its allies, and he delivered the following "end of war" address:

TODAY THE GUNS ARE SILENT. A great tragedy has ended. A great victory has been won. The skies no longer rain death—the seas bear only commerce—men everywhere walk upright in the sunlight. The entire world lies quietly at peace. The holy mission has been completed. And in reporting this to you, the people, I speak for the thousands of silent lips, forever stilled among the jungles and the beaches and in the deep waters of the Pacific which marked the way. I speak for the unnamed brave millions homeward bound to take up the challenge of that future which they did so much to salvage from the brink of disaster.

As I look back on the long, tortuous trail from those grim days of Bataan and Corregidor, when an entire world lived in fear, when democracy was on the defensive everywhere, when modern civilization trembled in the balance, I thank a merciful God that He has given us the faith, the courage, and the power from which to mold victory. We have known the bitterness of defeat and the exultation of triumph, and from both we have learned there can be no turning back. We must go forward to preserve in peace what we won in war.

A new era is upon us. Even the lesson of victory itself brings with it profound concern, both for our future security and the survival of civilization. The destructiveness of the war potential, through progressive advances in scientific discovery, has in fact now reached a point which revises the traditional concept of war.

Men since the beginning of time have sought peace. Various methods through the ages have been attempted to devise an international process to prevent or settle disputes between nations. From the very start workable methods were found insofar as individual citizens were concerned, but the mechanics of an instrumentality of larger international scope have never been successful. Military alliances, balance of power, Leagues of Nations all in turn failed, leaving the only path to be by way of the crucible of war. The utter destructiveness of war now blots out this alternative. We have had our last chance. If we do not devise some greater and more equitable system, Armageddon will be at our door. The problem basically is theological and involves a spiritual recrudescence and improvement of human character that will synchronize with our almost matchless advance in science, art, literature, and all material and cultural developments of the past 2,000 years. It must be of the spirit if we are to save the flesh.

We stand in Tokyo today reminiscent of our countryman Commodore Perry ninety-two years ago. His purpose was to bring to Japan an era of enlightenment and progress by lifting the veil of isolation to the friendship, trade, and commerce of the world. But, alas, the knowledge thereby gained of Western science was forged into an instrument of oppression and human enslavement. Freedom of expression, freedom of action, even freedom of thought were denied through suppression of liberal education, through appeal to superstition, and through the application of force. We are committed by the Potsdam Declaration of Principles to see that the Japanese people are liberated from this condition of slavery. It is my purpose to implement this commitment just as rapidly as the armed forces are demobilized and other essential steps taken to neutralize the war potential. The energy of the Japanese race, if properly directed, will enable expansion vertically rather than horizontally. If the talents of the race are turned into constructive channels, the country can lift itself from its present deplorable state into a position of dignity.

To the Pacific basin has come the vista of a new emancipated world. Today, freedom is on the offensive, democracy is on the march. Today, in Asia as well as in Europe, unshackled peoples are tasting the full sweetness of liberty, the relief from fear.

In the Philippines, America has evolved a model for this new free world of Asia. In the Philippines, America has demonstrated that peoples of the East and peoples of the West may walk side by side in mutual respect and with mutual benefit. The history of our sovereignty there has now the full confidence of the East.

And so, my fellow countrymen, today I report to you that your sons and daughters have served you well and faithfully with the calm, deliberate, determined fighting spirit of the American soldier and sailor based upon a tradition of historical truth, as against the fanaticism of an enemy supported only by mythological fiction. Their spiritual strength and power has brought us through to victory. They are homeward bound—take care of them.

8. *The United Nations Organization, begun during the fighting, became a permanent, international, peace-keeping agency with the writing and adoption of its Charter in 1945. Americans reacted to the United Nations far more favorably than they had to the League of Nations a quarter-century earlier. In fact, by the end of World War II, most Americans seemed convinced that the surest way to maintain peace was through some international organization. The United Nations Charter (of which important Chapters are quoted below) was speedily adopted by the United States Senate.*

We, The Peoples Of The United Nations, Determined to save succeeding generations from the scourge of war, which twice in our lifetime has brought untold sorrow to mankind, and to reaffirm faith in fundamental human rights, in the dignity and worth of the human person, in the equal rights of men and women and of nations large and small, and to establish conditions under which justice and respect for the obligations arising from treaties and other sources of international law can be maintained, and to promote social progress and better standards of life in larger freedom.

And For These Ends

to practice tolerance and live together in peace with one another as good neighbors, and to unite our strength to maintain international peace and security, and to ensure, by the acceptance of principles and the institution of methods, that armed force shall not be used, save in the common interest, and to employ international machinery for the promotion of the economic and social advancement of all peoples,

Have Resolved To Combine Our Efforts To Accomplish These Aims.

Accordingly, our respective Governments, through representatives assembled in the city of San Francisco, who have exhibited their full powers found to be in good and due form, have agreed to the present Charter of the United Nations and do hereby establish an international organization to be known as the United Nations.

Chapter 1
PURPOSES AND PRINCIPLES
ARTICLE 1

The Purposes of the United Nations are:

1. To maintain international peace and security, and to that end to take effective collective measures for the prevention and removal of threats to the peace, and for the suppression of acts of aggression or other breaches of the peace, and to bring about by peaceful means, and in conformity with the principles of justice and international law, adjustment or settlement of international disputes or situations which might lead to a breach of the peace;

2. To develop friendly relations among nations based on respect for the principle of equal rights and self-determination of peoples, and to take other appropriate measures to strengthen universal peace;

3. To achieve international cooperation in solving international problems of an economic, social, cultural, or humanitarian character, and in promoting and encouraging respect for human rights and for fundamental freedoms for all without distinction as to race, sex, language, or religion; and

4. To be a center for harmonizing the actions of nations in the attainment of these common ends.

ARTICLE 2

The Organization and its Members, in pursuit of the Purposes stated in Article 1, shall act in accordance with the following Principles.

1. The Organization is based on the principles of the sovereign equality of all its Members.

2. All Members, in order to ensure to all of them the rights and benefits resulting from membership, shall fulfill in good faith the obligations assumed by them in accordance with the present Charter.

3. All Members shall settle their international disputes by peaceful means in such a manner that international peace and security, and justice, are not endangered.

4. All Members shall refrain in their international relations from the threat or use of force against the territorial integrity or political independence of any state, or in any other manner inconsistent with the Purposes of the United Nations.

5. All Members shall give the United Nations every assistance in any action it takes in accordance with the present Charter, and shall refrain from giving assistance to any state against which the United Nations is taking preventive or enforcement action.

6. The Organization shall ensure that states which are not Members of the United Nations act in accordance with these Principles so far as may be necessary for the maintenance of international peace and security.

7. Nothing contained in the present Charter shall authorize the United Nations to intervene in matters which are essentially within the domestic jurisdiction of any state or shall require the Members to submit such matters to settlement under the present Charter; but this principle shall not prejudice the application of enforcement measure under Chapter VII.

Chapter II
MEMBERSHIP
ARTICLE 3

The original Members of the United Nations shall be the states which, having participated in the United Nations Conference on International Organization at San Francisco, or having previously signed the Declaration by United Nations of January 1, 1942, sign the present Charter and ratify it in accordance with Article 110.

ARTICLE 4

1. Membership in the United Nations is open to all other peace-loving states which accept the obligations contained in the present Charter and, in the judgment of the Organization, are able and willing to carry out these obligations.

2. The admission of any such state to membership in the United Nations will be effected by a decision of the General Assembly upon the recommendation of the Security Council.

ARTICLE 5

A Member of the United Nations against which preventive or enforcement action has been taken by the Security Council may be suspended from the exercise of the rights and privileges of membership by the General Assembly upon the recommendation of the Security Council. The exercise of these rights and privileges may be restored by the Security Council.

ARTICLE 6

A Member of the United Nations which has persistently violated the Principles contained in the present Charter may be expelled from the Organization by the General Assembly upon the recommendation of the Security Council.

Chapter III
ORGANS
ARTICLE 7

1. There are established as the principal organs of the United Nations a General Assembly, a Security Council, a Trusteeship Council, an International Court of Justice, and a Secretariat.

2. Such subsidiary organs as may be found necessary may be established in accordance with the present Charter.

ARTICLE 8

The United Nations shall place no restrictions on the eligibility of men and women to participate in any capacity and under conditions of equality in its principal and subsidiary organs.

Chapter IV
THE GENERAL ASSEMBLY

Composition

ARTICLE 9

1. The General Assembly shall consist of all the Members of the United Nations.

2. Each Member shall have not more than five representatives in the General Assembly.

Functions and Powers

ARTICLE 10

The General Assembly may discuss any questions or any matters within the scope of the present Charter or relating to the powers and functions of any organs provided for in the present Charter, and, except as provided in Article 12, may make recommendations to the Members of the United Nations or to the Security Council or to both on any such questions or matters.

ARTICLE 11

1. The General Assembly may consider the general principles of cooperation in the maintenance of international peace and security, including the principles governing disarmament and the regulation of armaments, and may make recommendations with regard to such principles to the Members or to the Security Council or to both.

2. The General Assembly may discuss any questions relating to the maintenance of international peace and security brought before it by any Member of the United Nations, or by the Security Council, or by a state which is not a Member of the United Nations in accordance with Article 35, paragraph 2, and, except as provided in Article 12, may make recommendations with regard to any such question to the state or states concerned or to the Security Council or to both. Any such question on which action is necessary shall be referred to the Security Council by the General Assembly either before or after discussion.

3. The General Assembly may call the attention of the Security Council to situations which are likely to endanger international peace and security. . . .

Voting

ARTICLE 18

1. Each member of the General Assembly shall have one vote.

2. Decisions of the General Assembly on important questions shall be made by a two-thirds majority of the members present and voting. These questions shall include: recommendations with respect to the maintenance of international peace and security, the election of the non-permanent members of the Security Council, the election of the members of the Economic and Social Council, the election of members of the Trusteeship Council in accordance with paragraph 1(c) of Article 86, the admission of new Members to the United Nations, the suspension of the rights and privileges of membership, the expulsion of Members, questions relating to the operation of the trusteeship system, and budgetary questions.

3. Decisions on other questions, including the deter-

mination of additional categories of questions to be decided by a two-thirds majority, shall be made by a majority of the members present and voting.

ARTICLE 19

A Member of the United Nations which is in arrears in the payment of its financial contributions to the Organization shall have no vote in the General Assembly if the amount of its arrears equals or exceeds the amount of the contributions due from it for the preceding two full years. The General Assembly may, nevertheless, permit such a Member to vote if it is satisfied that the failure to pay is due to conditions beyond the control of the Member. . . .

Chapter V
THE SECURITY COUNCIL

Composition

ARTICLE 23

1. The Security Council shall consist of eleven Members of the United Nations. The Republic of China, France, the Union of Soviet Socialist Republics, the United Kingdom of Great Britain and Northern Ireland, and the United States of America shall be permanent members of the Security Council. The General Assembly shall elect six other Members of the United Nations to be non-permanent members of the Security Council, due regard being specially paid, in the first instance to the contribution of Members of the United Nations to the maintenance of international peace and security and to the other purposes of the Organization, and also to equitable geographical distribution.

2. The non-permanent members of the Security Council shall be elected for a term of two years. In the first election of the non-permanent members, however, three shall be chosen for a term of one year. A retiring member shall not be eligible for immediate re-election.

3. Each member of the Security Council shall have one representative.

Functions and Powers

ARTICLE 24

1. In order to ensure prompt and effective action by the United Nations, its Members confer on the Security Council primary responsibility for the maintenance of international peace and security, and agree that in carrying out its duties under this responsibility the Security Council acts on their behalf.

2. In discharging these duties the Security Council shall act in accordance with the Purposes and Principles of the United Nations. The specific powers granted to the Security Council for the discharge of these duties are laid down in Chapters VI, VII, VIII, and XII.

3. The Security Council shall submit annual and, when necessary, special reports to the General Assembly for its consideration.

ARTICLE 25

The Members of the United Nations agree to accept and carry out the decisions of the Security Council in accordance with the present Charter.

ARTICLE 26

In order to promote the establishment and maintenance of international peace and security with the least diversion for armaments of the world's human and economic resources, the Security Council shall be responsible for formulating, with the assistance of the Military Staff Committee referred to in Article 47, plans to be submitted to the Members of the United Nations for the establishment of a system for the regulation of armaments.

Voting

ARTICLE 27

1. Each member of the Security Council shall have one vote.

2. Decisions of the Security Council on procedural matters shall be made by an affirmative vote of seven members.

3. Decisions of the Security Council on all other matters shall be made by an affirmative vote of seven members including the concurring votes of the permanent members; provided that, in decisions under Chapter VI, and under paragraph 3 of Article 52, a party to a dispute shall abstain from voting. . . .

Chapter VI
PACIFIC SETTLEMENT OF
DISPUTES
ARTICLE 33

1. The parties to any dispute, the continuance of which is likely to endanger the maintenance of international peace and security, shall, first of all, seek a solution by negotiation, enquiry, mediation, conciliation, arbitration, judicial settlement, resort to regional agencies or arrangements, or other peaceful means of their own choice.

2. The Security Councils hall, when it deems necessary, call upon the parties to settle their dispute by such means.

ARTICLE 34

The Security Council may investigate any dispute, or

any situation which might lead to international friction or give rise to a dispute, in order to determine whether the continuance of the dispute or situation is likely to endanger the maintenance of international peace and security.

ARTICLE 35

1. Any Member of the United Nations may bring any dispute, or any situation of the nature referred to in Article 34, to the attention of the Security Council or of the General Assembly.

2. A state which is not a Member of the United Nations may bring to the attention of the Security Council or of the General Assembly any dispute to which it is a party if it accepts in advance, for the purposes of the dispute, the obligations of pacific settlement provided in the present Charter. . . .

Chapter VII
ACTION WITH RESPECT TO THREATS TO THE PEACE, ETC.
ARTICLE 39

The Security Council shall determine the existence of any threat to the peace, breach of the peace, or act of aggression and shall make recommendations, or decide what measures shall be taken in accordance with Articles 41 and 42, to maintain or restore international peace and security.

ARTICLE 40

In order to prevent an aggravation of the situation, the Security Council may, before making the recommendations or deciding upon the measures provided for in Article 39, call upon the parties concerned to comply with such provisional measures as it deems necessary or desirable. Such provisional measures shall be without prejudice to the rights, claims, or position of the parties concerned. The Security Council shall duly take account of failure to comply with such provisional measures.

ARTICLE 41

The Security Council may decide what measures not involving the use of armed force are to be employed to give effect to its decisions, and it may call upon the Members of the United Nations to apply such measures. These may include complete or partial interruption of economic relations and of rail, sea, air, postal, telegraphic, radio, and other means of communication, and the severance of diplomatic relations.

ARTICLE 42

Should the Security Council consider that measures provided for in Article 41 would be inadequate or have proved to be inadequate, it may take such action by air, sea, or land forces as may be necessary to maintain or restore international peace and security. Such action may include demonstrations, blockade, and other operations by air, sea, or land forces of Members of the United Nations.

ARTICLE 43

1. All Members of the United Nations, in order to contribute to the maintenance of international peace and security, undertake to make available to the Security Council, on its call and in accordance with a special agreement or agreements, armed forces, assistance, and facilities, including rights of passage, necessary for the purpose of maintaining international peace and security. . . .

ARTICLE 51

Nothing in the present Charter shall impair the inherent right of individual or collective self-defense if an armed attack occurs against a Member of the United Nations, until the Security Council has taken measures necessary to maintain international peace and security. Measures taken by Members in the exercise of this right of self-defense shall be immediately reported to the Security Council and shall not in any way affect the authority and responsibility of the Security Council under the present Charter to take at any time such action as it deems necessary in order to maintain or restore international peace and security.

Chapter VIII
REGIONAL ARRANGEMENTS
ARTICLE 52

1. Nothing in the present Charter precludes the existence of regional arrangements or agencies for dealing with such matters relating to the maintenance of international peace and security as are appropriate for regional action, provided that such arrangements or agencies and their activities are consistent with the Purposes and Principles of the United Nations.

2. The Members of the United Nations entering into such arrangements or constituting such agencies shall make every effort to achieve pacific settlement of local disputes through such regional arrangements or by such regional agencies before referring them to the Security Council. . . .

ARTICLE 54

The Security Council shall at all times be kept fully

informed of activities undertaken or in contemplation under regional arrangements or by regional agencies for the maintenance of international peace and security.

Chapter IX
INTERNATIONAL ECONOMIC AND SOCIAL COOPERATION
ARTICLE 55

With a view to the creation of conditions of stability and well-being which are necessary for peaceful and friendly relations among nations based on respect for the principle of equal rights and self-determination of peoples, the United Nations shall promote:

a. higher standards of living, full employment, and conditions of economic and social progress and development;

b. solutions of international economic, social, health, and related problems; and international cultural and educational cooperation; and

c. universal respect for, and observance of, human rights and fundamental freedoms for all without distinction. . . .

Chapter XI
DECLARATION REGARDING NON-SELF-GOVERNING TERRITORIES
ARTICLE 73

Members of the United Nations which have or assume responsibilities for the administration of territories whose peoples have not yet attained a full measure of self-government recognize the principle that the interests of the inhabitants of these territories are paramount, and accept as a sacred trust the obligation to promote to the utmost, within the system of international peace and security established by the present Charter, the well-being of the inhabitants of these territories, and, to this end:

a. to ensure, with due respect for the culture of the peoples concerned, their political, economic, social, and educational advancement, their just treatment, and their protection against abuses;

b. to develop self-government, to take due account of the political aspirations of the peoples, and to assist them in the progressive development of their free political institutions, according to the particular circumstances of each territory and its peoples and their varying stages of advancement;

c. to further international peace and security;

d. to promote constructive measures of development, to encourage research, and to cooperate with one another and, when and where appropriate, with special-

ized international bodies with a view to the practical achievement of the social, economic, and scientific purposes set forth in this Article; and

e. to transmit regularly to the Secretary-General for information purposes, subject to such limitation as security and constitutional considerations may require, statistical and other information of a technical nature relating to economic, social, and educational conditions in the territories for which they are respectively responsible other than those territories to which Chapters XII and XIII apply.

ARTICLE 74

Members of the United Nations also agree that their policy in respect of the territories to which this Chapter applies, no less than in respect of their metropolitan areas, must be based on the general principle of good-neighborliness, due account being taken of the interests and well-being of the rest of the world, in social, economic, and commercial matters.

Chapter XII
INTERNATIONAL TRUSTEESHIP SYSTEM
ARTICLE 75

The United Nations shall establish under its authority an international trusteeship system for the administration and supervision of such territories as may be placed thereunder by subsequent individual agreements. These territories are hereinafter referred to as trust territories.

ARTICLE 76

The basic objectives of the trusteeship system, in accordance with the Purposes of the United Nations laid down in Article I of the present Charter, shall be:

a. to further international peace and security;

b. to promote the political, economic, social, and educational advancement of the inhabitants of the trust territories, and their progressive development towards self-government or independence as may be appropriate to the particular circumstances of each territory and its peoples and the freely expressed wishes of the peoples concerned, and as may be provided by the terms of each trusteeship agreement;

c. to encourage respect for human rights and for fundamental freedoms for all without distinction as to race, sex, language, or religion, and to encourage recognition of the interdependence of the peoples of the world; and

d. to ensure equal treatment in social, economic, and commercial matters for all Members of the United Nations and their nationals, and also equal treatment for the latter in the administration of justice, without prejudice to the attainment of the foregoing objectives and, subject to the provisions of Article 80.

ARTICLE 77

1. The trusteeship system shall apply to such territories in the following categories as may be placed thereunder by means of trusteeship agreements:

a. territories now held under mandate;

b. territories which may be detached from enemy states as a result of the Second World War; and

c. territories voluntarily placed under the system by states responsible for their administration.

2. It will be a matter for subsequent agreement as to which territories in the foregoing categories will be brought under the trusteeship system and upon what terms. . . .

Chapter XIV
THE INTERNATIONAL COURT OF JUSTICE
ARTICLE 92

The International Court of Justice shall be the principal judicial organ of the United Nations. It shall function in accordance with the annexed Statute, which is based upon the Statute of the Permanent Court of International Justice and forms an integral part of the present Charter.

ARTICLE 93

1. All Members of the United Nations are *ipso facto* parties to the Statute of the International Court of Justice.

2. A state which is not a Member of the United Nations may become a party to the Statute of the International Court of Justice on condition to be determined in each case by the General Assembly upon the recommendation of the Security Council.

ARTICLE 94

1. Each Member of the United Nations undertakes to comply with the decision of the International Court of Justice in any case to which it is a party.

2. If any party to a case fails to perform the obligations incumbent upon it under a judgment rendered by the Court, the other party may have recourse to the Security Council, which may, if it deems necessary, make recommendations. . . .

Chapter XV
THE SECRETARIAT
ARTICLE 97

The Secretariat shall comprise a Secretary-General and such staff as the Organization may require. The Secretary-General shall be appointed by the General Assembly upon the recommendation of the Security Council. He shall be the chief administrative officer of the Organization.

ARTICLE 98

The Secretary-General shall act in that capacity in all meetings of the General Assembly, of the Security Council, of the Economic and Social Council, and of the Trusteeship Council, and shall perform such other functions as are entrusted to him by these organs. The Secretary-General shall make an annual report to the General Assembly on the work of the Organization.

ARTICLE 99

The Secretary-General may bring to the attention of the Security Council any matter which in his opinion may threaten the maintenance of international peace. . . .

ARTICLE 100

1. In the performance of their duties the Secretary-General and the staff shall not seek to receive instruction from any government or from any other authority external to the Organization. They shall refrain from any action which might reflect on their position as international officials responsible only to the Organization.

2. Each Member of the United Nations undertakes to respect the exclusively international character of the responsibilities of the Secretary-General and the staff. . . .

Chapter XVII
TRANSITIONAL SECURITY ARRANGEMENTS
ARTICLE 106

Pending the coming into force of such special agreements referred to in Article 43 as in the opinion of the Security Council enable it to begin the exercise of its responsibilities under Article 42, the parties to the Four-Nation Declaration, signed at Moscow, October 30, 1943, and France, shall, in accordance with the provisions of paragraph 5 of that Declaration, consult with one another and as occasion requires with other Members of the United Nations with a view to such joint action on behalf of the Organization as may be necessary for the purpose of maintaining international peace and security. . . .

9. The shift in American policy from the neutrality of the early 1930's was dramatized after World War II ended. The United States undertook to help other countries rebuild their cities and industries, as a means of encouraging them to live peacefully. President Harry S. Truman announced his "Truman Doctrine"—that American military aid would go to countries trying to maintain themselves free from Communist control. In the spring of 1947, American military equipment was shipped to Greece and Turkey. A few months later, that same year, Secretary of State George C. Marshall announced a plan to provide supplies for civilan rebuilding of war damage in Europe, open to both eastern and western countries. Significant parts of the Truman Doctrine (as stated in the President's message to Congress) and of the Marshall Plan are quoted below.

The Truman Doctrine

The gravity of the situation which confronts the world today necessitates my appearance before a joint session of the Congress. The foreign policy and the national security of the country are involved.

One aspect of the present situation, which I wish to present to you at this time for your consideration and decision, concerns Greece and Turkey.

The United States has received from the Greek Government an urgent appeal for financial and economic assistance. Preliminary reports from the American Economic Mission now in Greece and reports from the American Ambassador in Greece corroborate the statement of the Greek Government that assistance is imperative if Greece is to survive as a free nation. . . .

The very existence of the Greek state is today threatened by the terrorist activities of several thousand armed men, led by Communists, who defy the Government's authority at a number of points, particularly along the northern boundaries. A commission appointed by the United Nations Security Council is at present investigating disturbed conditions in Northern Greece and alleged border violations along the frontier between Greece on the one hand and Albania, Bulgaria and Yugoslavia on the other.

Meanwhile, the Greek Government is unable to cope with the situation. The Greek Army is small and poorly equipped. It needs supplies and equipment if it is to restore the authority to the Government throughout Greek territory.

Greece must have assistance if it is to become a self-supporting and self-respecting democracy. The United States must supply this assistance. We have already extended to Greece certain type of relief and economic aid but these are inadequate. There is no other country to which democratic Greece can turn. No other nation is willing and able to provide the necessary support for a democratic Greek Government.

The British Government, which has been helping Greece, can give no further financial or economic aid after March 31. Great Britain finds itself under the necessity of reducing or liquidating its commitments in several parts of the world, including Greece.

We have considered how the United Nations might assist in this crisis. But the situation is an urgent one requiring immediate action, and the United Nations and its related organzations are not in a position to extend help of the kind that is required. . . .

Greece's neighbor, Tunrkey, also deserves our attention. The future of Turkey as an independent and economically sound state is clearly no less important to the freedom-loving peoples of the world than the future of Greece. The circumstances in which Turkey finds itself today are considerably different from those of Greece. Turkey has been spared the disasters that have beset Greece. And during the war, the United States and Great Britain furnished Turkey with material aid.

Nevertheless, Turkey now needs our support.

Since the war Turkey has sought financial assistance from Great Britain and the United States for the purpose of effecting that modernization necessary for the maintenance of its national integrity.

That integrity is essential to the preservation of order in the Middle East.

The British Government has informed us that, owing to its own difficulties, it can no longer extend financial or economic aid to Turkey. As in the case of Greece, if Turkey is to have the assistance it needs, the United States must supply it. We are the only country able to provide that help.

I am fully aware of the broad implications involved if the United States extends assistance to Greece and Turkey, and I shall discuss these implications with you at this time.

One of the primary objectives of the foreign policy of the United States is the creation of conditions in which we and other nations will be able to work out a way of life free from coercion. . . .

The peoples of a number of countries of the world have recently had totalitarian regimes forced upon them against their will. The Government of the United States has made frequent protests against coercion and intimidation, in violation of the Yalta Agreement, in Poland, Rumania, and Bulgaria. I must also state that in a number of other countries there have been similar developments.

At the present moment in world history nearly every nation must choose between alternative ways of life. The choice is too often not a free one.

The Marshall Plan

. . . In considering the requirements for the rehabilitation of Europe, the physical loss of life, the visible destruction of cities, factories, mines, and railroads was correctly estimated, but it has become obvious during recent months that this visible destruction was probably less serious than the dislocation of the entire fabric of European economy. For the past 10 years conditions have been highly abnormal. The feverish preparation for war and the more feverish maintenance of the war effort engulfed all aspects of national economies. Machinery has fallen into disrepair or is entirely obsolete. Under the arbitrary and destructive Nazi rule, virtually every possible enterprise was geared into the German war machine. Long-standing commercial ties, private institutions, banks, insurance companies, and shipping companies disappeared, through loss of capital, absorption through nationalization, or by simple destruction. In many countries, confidence in the local currency has been severely shaken. The breakdown of the business structure of Europe during the war was complete. Recovery has been seriously retarded by the fact that two years after the close of hostilities a peace settlement with Germany and Austria has not been agreed upon. But even given a more prompt solution of these difficult problems, the rehabilitation of the economic structure of Europe quite evidently will require a much longer time and greater effort than had been foreseen.

There is a phase of this matter which is both interesting and serious. The farmer has always produced the foodstuffs to exchange with the city dweller for the other necessities of life. This division of labor is the basis of modern civilization. At the present time it is threatened with breakdown. The town and city industries are not producing adequate goods to exchange with the food-producing farmer. Raw materials and fuel are in short supply. Machinery is lacking or worn out. The farmer or the peasant cannot find the goods for sale which he desires to purchase. So the sale of his farm produce for money which he cannot use seems to him an unprofitable transaction. He, therefore, has withdrawn many fields from crop cultivation and is using them for grazing. He feeds more grain to stock and finds for himself and his family an ample supply of food, however short he may be on clothing and the other ordinary gadgets of civilization. Meanwhile people in the cities are short of food and fuel. So the governments are forced to use their foreign money and credits to procure these necessities abroad. This process exhausts funds which are urgently needed for reconstruction. Thus a very serious situation is rapidly developing which bodes no good for the world. The modern system of the division of labor upon which the exchange of products is based is in danger of breaking down.

The truth of the matter is that Europe's requirements for the next three or four years of foreign food and other essential products—principally from America—are so much greater than her present ability to pay that she must have substantial additional help or face economic, social, and political deterioration of a very grave character.

The remedy lies in breaking the vicious circle and restoring the confidence of the European people in the economic future of their own countries and of Europe as a whole. The manufacturer and the farmer throughout wide areas must be able and willing to exchange their products for currencies the continuing value of which is not open to question.

Aside from the demoralizing effect on the world at large and the possibilities of disturbances arising as a result of the desperation of the people concerned, the consequences to the economy of the United States should be apparent to all. It is logical that the United States should do whatever it is able to do to assist in the return of normal economic health in the world, without which there can be no political stability and no assured peace. Our policy is directed not against any country or doctrine but against hunger, poverty, desperation, and chaos. Its purpose should be the revival of a working economy in the world so as to permit the emergence of political and social conditions in which free institutions can exist. Such assistance, I am convinced, must not be on a piecemeal basis as various crises develop. Any assistance that this Government may render in the future should provide a cure rather than a mere palliative. Any government that is willing to assist in the task of recovery will find full cooperation, I am sure, on the part of the United States Government. Any government which maneuvers to block the recovery of other countries cannot expect help from us. Furthermore, governments, political parties, or groups which seek to perpetuate human misery in order to profit therefrom politically or otherwise will encounter the opposition of the United States.

It is already evident that, before the United States Government can proceed much further in its efforts to alleviate the situation and help start the European world on its way to recovery, there must be some agreement among the countries of Europe as to the requirements of the situation and the part those countries themselves will take in order to give proper effect to whatever action might be undertaken by this Government. It would be neither fitting nor efficacious for this Government to undertake to draw up unilaterally a program designed to place Europe on its feet economically. This is the business of the Europeans. The initiative, I think, must come from Europe. The role of this country should consist of friendly aid in the drafting of a European program and of later support of such a program so far as it may be practical for us to do so. The program should be a joint one, agreed to by a number, if not all, European nations. . . .

10.   The years immediately following World War II were marked by the start of the so-called Cold War—a series of rivalries between the United States and its allies on one side, and the Soviet Union and its Communist-managed states on the other. After it became clear that the Cold War would continue for some time, the western European countries and the United States signed a treaty of alliance in 1949. The treaty established the North Atlantic Treaty Organization.

PREAMBLE. The parties to this treaty reaffirm their faith in the purposes and principles of the Charter of the United Nations and their desire to live in peace with all peoples and all governments.

They are determined to safeguard the freedom, common heritage and civilization of their peoples, founded on the principles of democracy, individual liberty and the rule of law.

They seek to promote stability and well-being in the North Atlantic Area.

They are resolved to unite their efforts for collective defense and for the preservation of peace and security.

They therefore agree to this North Atlantic Treaty:

ARTICLE 1. The parties undertake, as set forth in the Charter of the United Nations, to settle any international disputes in which they may be involved by peaceful means in such a manner that international peace and security, and justice, are not endangered, and to refrain in their international relations from the threat or use of force in any manner inconsistent with the purposes of the United Nations.

ARTICLE 2. The parties will continue toward the further development of peaceful and friendly international relations by strengthening their free institutions, by bringing about a better understanding of the principles upon which these institutions are founded, and by promoting conditions of stability and well-being. They will seek to eliminate conflict in their international economic policies and will encourage economic collaboration between any or all of them.

ARTICLE 3. In order more effectively to achieve the objectives of this treaty, the parties, separately and jointly, by means of continuous and effective self-help and mutual aid, will maintain and develop their individual and collective capacity to resist armed attack.

ARTICLE 4. The parties will consult together whenever, in the opinion of any of them, the territorial integrity, political independence or security of any of the parties is threatened.

ARTICLE 5. The parties agree that an armed attack against one or more of them in Europe or North America shall be considered an attack against them all; and consequently they agree that, if such an armed attack occurs, each of them, in exercise of the right of individual or collective self-defense recognized by Article 51 of the Charter of the United Nations, will assist the party or parties so attacked by taking forthwith, individually and in concert with the other parties, such action as it deems necessary including the use of armed force, to restore and maintain the security of the North Atlantic Area.

Any such armed attack and all measures taken as a result thereof shall immediately be reported to the Security Council. Such measures shall be terminated when the Security Council has taken the measures necessary to restore and maintain international peace and security.

ARTICLE 6. For the purpose of Article 5 an armed attack on one or more of the parties is deemed to include an armed attack on the territory of any of the parties in Europe or North America, on the Algerian Departments of France, on the occupation forces of any party in Europe, on the islands under the jurisdiction of any party in the North Atlantic Area north of the Tropic of Cancer or on the vessels or aircraft in this area of any of the parties.

ARTICLE 7. This treaty does not affect, and shall not be interpreted as affecting, in any way the rights and obligations under the Charter of the parties which are members of the United Nations, or the primary responsibility of the Security Council for the maintenance of international peace and security.

ARTICLE 8. Each party declares that none of the international engagements now in force between it and any other of the parties or any third state is in conflict with the provisions of this treaty, and undertakes not to enter into any international engagement in conflict with this treaty.

ARTICLE 9. The parties hereby establish a Council, on which each of them shall be represented, to consider matters concerning the implementation of this treaty. The Council shall be so organized as to be able to meet promptly at any time. The Council shall set up such subsidiary bodies as may be necessary; in particular it shall establish immediately a Defense Committee which shall recommend measures for the implementation of Articles 3 and 5.

ARTICLE 10. The parties may, by unanimous agreement, invite any other European state in a position to further the principles of this treaty and to contribute to the security of the North Atlantic Area to accede to this treaty. Any state so invited may become a party to the treaty by depositing its instrument of accession with the Government of the United States of America. The Government of the United States of America will inform each of the parties of the deposit of each such instrument of accession.

ARTICLE 11. This treaty shall be ratified and its provisions carried out by the parties in accordance with their respective constitutional processes. The instruments of ratification shall be deposited as soon as possible with the Government of the United States of America, which will notify all the other signatories of each deposit. The treaty shall enter into force between the states which have ratified it as soon as the ratifications of Belgium, Canada, France, Luxemburg, the Netherlands, the United Kingdom and the United States, have been deposited and shall come into effect with respect to other states on the date of the deposit of their ratification.

ARTICLE 12. After the treaty has been in force for ten years, or at any time thereafter, the parties shall, if any of them so requests, consult together for the purpose of reviewing the treaty, having regard for the factors then affecting peace and security in the North Atlantic Area, including the development of universal as well as regional arrangements under the Charter of the United Nations for the maintenance of international peace and security.

ARTICLE 13. After the treaty has been in force for twenty years, any party may cease to be a party one year after its notice of denunciation has been given to the Government of the United States of America, which will inform the governments of the other parties of the deposit of each notice of denunciation.

ARTICLE 14. This treaty, of which the English and French texts are equally authentic, shall be deposited in the archives of the Government of the United States of America. Duly certified copies thereof will be transmitted by that government to the government of the other signatories.

In witness whereof, the undersigned plenipotentiaries have signed this treaty.

11. In 1950, large-scale fighting broke out in Korea. An American-supported government in South Korea was attacked by North Korean troops, under the orders of a Communist government. President Harry S. Truman ordered that troops and supplies be furnished to aid South Korea in this situation. Troops were sent first from Japan, where they were on duty as an army of occupation. President Truman appealed to the United Nations for approval of his acts to repel aggression in Korea, and he received this approval. The following statements were released to the public by President Truman:

Statement of June 26, 1950

I CONFERRED Sunday evening with the Secretaries of State and Defense, their senior advisers, and the Joint Chiefs of Staff about the situation in the Far East created by unprovoked aggression againt the Republic of Korea.

The Government of the United States is pleased with the speed and determination with which the United Nations Security Council acted to order a withdrawal of the invading forces to position north of the 38th parallel. In accordance with the resolution of the Security Council, the United States will vigorously support the effort of the Council to terminate this serious breach of the peace.

Our concern over the lawless action taken by the forces from North Korea, and our sympathy and support for the people of Korea in this situation, are being demonstrated by the cooperative action of American personnel in Korea, as well as by steps taken to expedite and augment assistance of the type being furnished under the Mutual Defense Assistance Program.

Those responsible for this act of aggression must realize how seriously the Government of the United States views such threats to the peace of the world. Willful disregard of the obligation to keep the peace cannot be tolerated by nations that support the United Nations Charter.

Statement of June 27, 1950

IN KOREA the Government forces, which were armed to prevent border raids and to preserve internal security, were attacked by invading forces from North Korea. The Security Council of the United Nations called upon the invading troops to cease hostilities and to withdraw to the 38th parallel. This they have not done, but on the contrary have pressed the attack. The Security Council called upon all members of the United Nations to render every assistance to the United Nations in the execution of this resolution. In these circumstances I have ordered United States air and sea forces to give the Korean Government troops cover and support.

The attack upon Korea makes it plain beyond all doubt that communism has passed beyond the use of subversion to conquer independent nations and will now use armed invasion and war. It has defied the orders of the Security Council of the United Nations issued to preserve international peace and security. In these circumstances the occupation of Formosa by Communist forces would be a direct threat to the security of the Pacific area and to United States forces performing their lawful and necessary functions in that area.

Accordingly I have ordered the 7th Fleet to prevent any attack on Formosa. As a corollary of this action I am calling upon the Chinese Government on Formosa to cease all air and sea operations against the mainland. The 7th Fleet will see that this is done. The determination of the future status of Formosa must await the restoration of security in the Pacific, a peace settlement with Japan, or consideration by the United Nations.

I have also directed that United States Forces in the Philippines be strengthened and that military assistance to the Philippine Government be accelerated.

I have similarly directed acceleration in the furnishing of military assistance to the forces of France and the Associated States in Indochina and the dispatch of a military mission to provide close working relations with those forces.

I know that all members of the United Nations will consider carefully the consequences of this latest aggression in Korea in defiance of the Charter of the United Nations. A return to the rule of force in international affairs would have far-reaching effects. The United States will continue to uphold the rule of law.

I have instructed Ambassador Austin, as the representative of the United States to the Security Council, to report these steps to the Council.

12. The overall command in Korea was held by General Douglas MacArthur. As the war went on, MacArthur and President Truman differed with each other on strategy and worldwide plans. MacArthur apparently wished to attack supply centers of the North Koreans which were located in China. Truman ordered that the fighting be restricted to Korea alone. After the two leaders had met, and continued to differ, President Truman dismissed MacArthur and relieved him of military command. The incident led to sharp debates in the United States over the proper relationship between professional military men and their civilian superiors. MacArthur, returning to the United States for the first time since World War II, received a warm welcome. Invited to address Congress, he spoke (in part) as follows on April 19, 1951.

While I was not consulted prior to the President's decision to intervene in support of the Republic of Korea, that decision, from a military standpoint, proved a sound one. As I say, it proved a sound one, as we hurled back the invader and decimated his forces. Our victory was complete, and our objectives within reach, when Red China intervened with numerically superior ground forces.

This created a new war and an entirely new situation, a situation not contemplated when our forces were committed against the North Korean invaders; a situation which called for new decisions in the diplomatic sphere to permit the realistic adjustment of military strategy. Such decisions have not been forthcoming.

While no man in his right mind would advocate sending our ground forces into continental China, and such was never given a thought, the new situation did urgently demand a drastic revision of strategic planning if our political aim was to defeat this new enemy as we had defeated the old.

Apart from the military need, as I saw it, to neutralize sanctuary protection given the enemy north of the Yalu, I felt that military necessity in the conduct of the war made necessary—

1. The intensification of our economic blockade against China.

2. The imposition of a naval blockade against the China coast.

3. Removal of restriction on air reconnaissance of China's coastal areas and of Manchuria.

4. Removal of restrictions on the forces of the Republic of China on Formosa, with logistical support to contribute to their effective operations against the Chinese mainland.

For entertaining these views, all professionally designed to support our forces committed to Korea and bring hostilities to an end with the least possible delay and at a saving of countless American and Allied lives, I have been severely criticized in lay circles, principally abroad, despite any understanding that from a military standpoint the above views have been fully shared in the past by practically every military leader concerned with the Korean campaign, including our own Joint Chiefs of Staff.

I called for reinforcements, but was informed that reinforcements were not available. I made clear that if not permitted to destroy the enemy built-up bases north of the Yalu, if not permitted to utilize the friendly Chinese force of some 600,000 men on Formosa, if not permitted to blockade the China coast to prevent the Chinese Reds from getting succor from without, and if there were to be no hope of major reinforcements, the position of the command from the military stand-point forbade victory.

We could hold in Korea by constant maneuver and at an approximate area where our supply line advantages were in balance with the supply line disadvantages of the enemy, but we could hope at best for only an indecisive campaign with its terrible and constant attrition upon our forces if the enemy utilized his full military potential.

I have constantly called for the new political decisions essential to a solution.

Efforts have been made to distort my position. It has been said in effect that I was a warmonger. Nothing could be further from the truth.

I know war as few other men now living know it, and nothing to me is more revolting. I have long advocated its complete abolition, as its very destructiveness on both friend and foe has rendered it useless as a means of settling international disputes. . . .

But once forced upon us, there is no other alternative than to apply every available means to bring it to a swift end. War's very object is victory, not prolonged indecision. In war there can be no substitute for victory.

There are some who for varying reasons would appease Red China. They are blind to history's clear lesson, for history teaches with unmistakable emphasis that appeasement but begets new and bloodier war. It points to no single instance where the end has justified that means, where appeasement has led to more than a sham peace. Like blackmail, it lays the basis for new and successively greater demands until, as in blackmail, violence becomes the only other alternative. Why, my soldiers asked of me, surrender military advantages to an enemy in the field? I could not answer.

Some may say to avoid spread of the conflict into an all-out war with China. Others, to avoid Soviet intervention. Neither explanation seems valid, for China is already engaging with the maximum power it can commit, and the Soviet will not necessarily mesh its actions with our moves. Like a cobra, any new enemy will more likely strike whenever it feels that the relativity in military or other potential is in its favor on a world-wide basis.

The tragedy of Korea is further heightened by the fact that its military action is confined to its territorial limits. It condemns that nation, which it is our purpose to save, to suffer the devastating impact of full naval and air bombardment while the enemy's sanctuaries are fully protected from such attack and devastation.

Of the nations of the world, Korea alone, up to now, is the sole one which has risked its all against communism. The magnificence of the courage and fortitude of the Korean people defies description. They have chosen to risk death rather than slavery. Their last words to me were: "Don't scuttle the Pacific.". . .

13.   Other critical situations developed during the period. None appeared to be a greater threat to world peace than the "Missile Crisis" in Cuba in 1962. Soviet-made missiles were observed to be emplaced in Cuba. Additional weapons were expected to be sent there, and, since the United States and the Castro government of Cuba were on hostile terms, these weapons seemed to be a threat to the United States. It appeared that the Soviet Union was supporting Cuba (if not acting directly itself) in the crisis. President John F. Kennedy issued the following proclamation on October 23, as a statement of United States policy for the area. The "quarantine" plan worked, and a shooting war was avoided.

By the President of the United States of America:
A Proclamation

WHEREAS the peace of the world and the security of the United States and of all American states are endangered by reason of the establishment by the Sino-Soviet powers of an offensive military capability in Cuba, including bases for ballistic missiles with a potential range covering most of North and South America:

WHEREAS by a joint resolution passed by the Congress of the United States and approved on Oct. 3, 1962, it was declared that the United States is determined to prevent by whatever means be necessary, including the use of arms, the Marxist-Leninist regime in Cuba from extending, by force or the threat of force, its aggressive or subversive activities to any part of this hemisphere, and to prevent in Cuba the creation or use of an externally supported military capability endangering the security of the United States; and

WHEREAS the Organ of Consultation of the American republics meeting in Washington on Oct. 23, 1962, recommended that the member states, in accordance with Articles 6 and 8 of the Inter-American Treaty of Reciprocal Assistance, take all measures, individually and collectively, including the use of armed force, which they may deem necessary to insure that the Government of Cuba cannot continue to receive from the Sino-Soviet powers military material and related supplies which may threaten the peace and security of the continent and to prevent the missiles in Cuba with offensive capability from ever becoming an active threat to the peace and security of the continent:

Now, THEREFORE, I, John F. Kennedy, President of

the United States of America, acting under and by virtue of the authority conferred upon me by the Constitution and statutes of the United States, in accordance with the aforementioned resolutions of the United States Congress and of the Organ of Consultation of the American Republics, and to defend the security of the United States, do hereby proclaim that the forces under my command are ordered, beginning at 2:00 P.M. Greenwich time Oct. 24, 1962, to interdict, subject to the instructions herein contained, the delivery of offensive weapons and associated material to Cuba.

For the purposes of this proclamation, the following are declared to be prohibited material:

Surface-to-surface missiles; bomber aircraft; bombs; air-to-surface rockets and guided missiles; warheads for any of the above weapons; mechanical or electronic equipment to support or operate the above items; and any other classes of material hereafter designated by the Secretary of Defense for the purpose of effectuating this proclamation.

To enforce this order, the Secretary of Defense shall take appropriate measures to prevent the delivery of prohibited material to Cuba, employing the land, sea and air forces of the United States in cooperation with any forces that may be made available by other American states.

The Secretary of Defense may make such regulations and issue such directives as he deems necessary to ensure the effectiveness of this order, including the designation, within a reasonable distance of Cuba, of prohibited or restricted zones and of prescribed routes.

Any vessel or craft which may be proceeding toward Cuba may be intercepted and may be directed to identify itself, its cargo, equipment and stores and its ports of call, to stop, to lie to, to submit to visit and search, or to proceed as directed. Any vessel or craft which fails or refuses to respond to or comply with directions shall be subjected to being taken into custody. Any vessel or craft which is believed en route to Cuba and may be carrying prohibited material or may itself constitute such material shall, wherever possible, be directed to proceed to another destination of its own choice and shall be taken into custody if it fails or refuses to obey such directions. All vessels or craft taken into custody shall be sent into a port of the United States for appropriate disposition.

In carrying out this order, force shall not be used except in case of failure or refusal to comply with directions, or with regulations or directives of the Secretary of Defense issued hereunder, after reasonable efforts have been made to communicate them to the vessel or craft, or in case of self-defense. In any case, force shall be used only to the extent necessary.

IN WITNESS WHEREOF, I have hereunto set my hand and caused the seal of the United States of America to be affixed.

Done in the city of Washington this 23d day of October in the year of Our Lord, 1962, and of the independence of the United States of America the 187th.

JOHN F. KENNEDY

By the President
DEAN RUSK
    Secretary of State

14.   The foreign war in which the forces of the United States were engaged for the longest period of time was the war in Vietnam. American participation in the war in Southeast Asia began with the sending of specialists to help the South Vietnamese troops with advice. Covert air raids and other actions were undertaken during early 1964 in support of the efforts of the South Vietnamese to defend themselves (this was revealed by the unauthorized publication of the so-called Pentagon Papers in 1971). After a reported attack by the North Vietnamese on U.S. Navy vessels in the Gulf of Tonkin, and the presentation of this information to Congress by President Lyndon Johnson on August 5, 1964, Congress responded with a joint resolution (called the "Gulf of Tonkin" resolution) which pledged the fullest support to the President in his declared policy. In part, President Johnson said:

Last night I announced to the American people that the North Vietnamese regime had conducted further deliberate attacks against U.S. naval vessels operating in international waters, and that I had therefore directed air action against gunboats and supporting facilities used in these hostile operations. This air action has now been carried out with substantial damage to the boats and facilities. Two U.S. aircraft were lost in the action.

After consultation with the leaders of both parties in the Congress, I further announced a decision to ask the Congress for a resolution expressing the unity and determination of the United States in supporting freedom and in protecting peace in southeast Asia.

These latest actions of the North Vietnamese regime have given a new and grave turn to the already serious situation in southeast Asia. Our commitments in that area are well known to the Congress. They were first made in 1954 by President Eisenhower. They were further defined in the Southeast Asia Collective Defense Treaty approved by the Senate in February 1955.

This treaty with its accompanying protocol obligates the United States and other members to act in accordance with their constitutional processes to meet Communist aggression against any of the parties or protocol states.

Our policy in southeast Asia has been consistent and unchanged since 1954. I summarized it on June 2 in four simple propositions :

1. *America keeps her word.* Here as elsewhere, we must and shall honor our commitments.

2. *The issue is the future of southeast Asia as a whole.* A threat to any nation in that region is a threat to all, and a threat to us.

3. *Our purpose is peace.* We have no military, political, or territorial ambition in the area.

4. *This is not just a jungle war, but a struggle for freedom on every front of human activity.* Our military and economic assistance to South Vietnam and Laos in particular has the purpose of helping these countries to repel aggression and strengthen their independence.

The threat to the free nations of southeast Asia has long been clear. The North Vietnamese regime has constantly sought to take over South Vietnam and Laos. This Communist regime has violated the Geneva accords for Vietnam. It has systematically conducted a campaign of subversion, which includes the direction, training, and supply of personnel and arms for the conduct of guerrilla warfare in South Vietnamese territory. In Laos, the North Vietnamese regime has maintained military forces, used Laotian territory for infiltration into South Vietnam, and most recently carried out combat operations—all in direct violation of the Geneva agreements of 1962.

In recent months, the actions of the North Vietnamese regime have become steadily more threatening. . . .

As President of the United States I have concluded that I should now ask the Congress, on its part, to join in affirming the national determination that all such attacks will be met, and that the United States will continue in its basic policy of assisting the free nations of the area to defend their freedom.

As I have repeatedly made clear, the United States intends no rashness, and seeks no wider war. We must make it clear to all that the United States is united in its determination to bring about the end of Communist subversion and aggression in the area.

15.   Years went by in negotiation and discussion, while U.S. servicemen were involved in greater and greater numbers in Vietnam. At last, in January 1973, a truce was arranged. President Richard M. Nixon announced the news in an address to the nation on January 23. The President's address is the first of the documents which follow; the text of the Vietnam Agreement is the second. Both are quoted from the U.S. Department of State Bulletin.

President Nixon's Address

Good evening. I have asked for this radio and television time tonight for the purpose of announcing that we today have concluded an agreement to end the war and bring peace with honor in Viet-Nam and in Southeast Asia.

The following statement is being issued at this moment in Washington and Hanoi:

"At 12:30 Paris time today, January 23, 1973, the Agreement on Ending the War and Restoring Peace in Vietnam was initiated by Dr. Henry Kissinger on behalf of the United States, and Special Advisor Le Duc Tho on behalf of the Democratic Republic of Vietnam.

"The agreement will be formally signed by the parties participating in the Paris Conference on Vietnam on January 27, 1973, at the International Conference Center in Paris.

"The cease-fire will take effect at 2400 Greenwich Mean Time, January 27, 1973. The United States and the Democratic Republic of Vietnam express the hope that this agreement will insure stable peace in Vietnam and contribute to the preservation of lasting peace in Indochina and Southeast Asia."

That concludes the formal statement.

Throughout the years of negotiations, we have insisted on peace with honor. In my addresses to the Nation from this room of January 25 and May 8, I set forth the goals that we considered essential for peace with honor.

In the settlement that has now been agreed to, all the conditions that I laid down then have been met. A cease-fire, internationally supervised, will begin at 7 p.m. this Saturday, January 27, Washington time. Within 60 days from this Saturday, all Americans held prisoners of war throughout Indochina will be released. There will be the fullest possible accounting for all of those who are missing in action.

During the same 60-day period, all American forces will be withdrawn from South Viet-Nam.

The people of South Viet-Nam have been guaranteed the right to determine their own future without outside interference.

By joint agreement, the full text of the agreement and the protocols to carry it out will be issued tomorrow.

Throughout these negotiations we have been in the closest consultation with President Thieu and other representatives of the Republic of Viet-Nam. This settlement meets the goals and has the full support of President Thieu and the Government of the Republic of Viet-Nam, as well as that of our other allies who are affected.

The United States will continue to recognize the Government of the Republic of Viet-Nam as the sole legitimate government of South Viet-Nam.

We shall continue to aid South Viet-Nam within the terms of the agreement, and we shall support efforts by the people of South Viet-Nam to settle their problems peacefully among themselves.

We must recognize that ending the war is only the first step toward building the peace. All parties must now see to it that this is a peace that lasts, and also a peace that heals, and a peace that not only ends the war in Southeast Asia but contributes to the prospects of peace in the whole world.

This will mean that the terms of the agreement must be scrupulously adhered to. We shall do everything the agreement requires of us, and we shall expect the other parties to do everything it requires of them. We shall also expect other interested nations to help insure that the agreement is carried out and peace is maintained.

As this long and very difficult war ends, I would like to address a few special words to each of those who have been parties in the conflict.

First, to the people and Government of South Viet-Nam: By your courage, by your sacrifice, you have won the precious right to determine your own future, and you have developed the strength to defend that right. We look forward to working with you in the future, friends in peace as we have been allies in war.

To the leaders of North Viet-Nam: As we have ended the war through negotiations, let us now build a peace of reconciliation. For our part, we are prepared to make a major effort to help achieve that goal; but just as reciprocity was needed to end the war, so, too, will it be needed to build and strengthen the peace.

To the other major powers that have been involved, even indirectly: Now is the time for mutual restraint so that the peace we have achieved can last.

And finally, to all of you who are listening, the American people: Your steadfastness in supporting our insistence on peace with honor has made peace with honor possible. I know that you would not have wanted that peace jeopardized. With our secret negotiations at the sensitive stage they were in during this recent period, for me to have discussed publicly our efforts to secure peace would not only have violated our understanding with North Viet-Nam; it would have

seriously harmed and possibly destroyed the chances for peace. Therefore, I know that you now can understand why during these past several weeks I have not made any public statements about those efforts.

The important thing was not to talk about peace, but to get peace and to get the right kind of peace. This we have done.

Now that we have achieved an honorable agreement, let us be proud that America did not settle for a peace that would have betrayed our allies, that would have abandoned our prisoners of war, or that would have ended the war for us but would have continued the war for the 50 million people of Indochina. Let us be proud of the 2½ million young Americans who served in Viet-Nam, who served with honor and distinction in one of the most selfless enterprises in the history of nations. And let us be proud of those who sacrificed, who gave their lives so that the people of South Viet-Nam might live in freedom and so that the world might live in peace.

In particular, I would like to say a word to some of the bravest people I have ever met—the wives, the children, the families, of our prisoners of war and the missing in action. When others called on us to settle on any terms, you had the courage to stand for the right kind of peace so that those who died and those who suffered would not have died and suffered in vain and so that where this generation knew war the next generation would know peace. Nothing means more to me at this moment than the fact that your long vigil is coming to an end.

Just yesterday, a great American who once occupied this office died. In his life President Johnson endured the vilification of those who sought to portray him as a man of war. But there was nothing he cared about more deeply than achieving a lasting peace in the world.

I remember the last time I talked with him. It was just the day after New Year's. He spoke then of his concern with bringing peace, with making it the right kind of peace, and I was grateful that he once again expressed his support for my efforts to gain such a peace. No one would have welcomed this peace more than he.

And I know he would join me in asking for those who died and for those who live: Let us consecrate this moment by resolving together to make the peace we have achieved a peace that will last.

Thank you and good evening.

Texts of Agreement and Protocols

The Parties participating in the Paris Conference on Vietnam,

With a view to ending the war and restoring peace

in Vietnam on the basis of respect for the Vietnamese people's fundamental national rights and the South Vietnamese people's right to self-determination, and to contributing to the consolidation of peace in Asia and the world,

Have agreed on the following provisions and undertake to respect and to implement them:

Chapter I
The Vietnamese People's Fundamental National Rights
Article 1

The United States and all other countries respect the independence, sovereignty, unity, and territorial integrity of Vietnam as recognized by the 1954 Geneva Agreements on Vietnam.

Chapter II
Cessation of Hostilities—Withdrawal of Troops
Article 2

A cease-fire shall be observed throughout South Vietnam as of 2400 hours G.M.T., on January 27, 1973.

At the same hour, the United States will stop all its military activities against the territory of the Democratic Republic of Vietnam by ground, air and naval forces, wherever they may be based, and end the mining of the territorial waters, ports, harbors, and waterways of the Democratic Republic of Vietnam. The United States will remove, permanently deactivate or destroy all the mines in the territorial waters, ports, harbors, and waterways of North Vietnam as soon as this Agreement goes into effect.

The complete cessation of hostilities mentioned in this Article shall be durable and without limit of time.

Article 3

The parties undertake to maintain the cease-fire and to ensure a lasting and stable peace.

As soon as the cease-fire goes into effect:

(a) The United States forces and those of the other foreign countries allied with the United States and the Republic of Vietnam shall remain in-place pending the implementation of the plan of troop withdrawal. The Four-Party Joint Military Commission described in Article 16 shall determine the modalities.

(b) The armed forces of the two South Vietnamese parties shall remain in-place. The Two-Party Joint Military Commission described in Article 17 shall determine the areas controlled by each party and the modalities of stationing.

(c) The regular forces of all services and arms and the irregular forces of the parties in South Vietnam shall stop all offensive activities against each other and shall strictly abide by the following stipulations:

—All acts of force on the ground, in the air, and on the sea shall be prohibited;

—All hostile acts, terrorism and reprisals by both sides will be banned.

Article 4

The United States will not continue its military involvement or intervene in the general affairs of South Vietnam.

Article 5

Within sixty days of the signing of this Agreement, there will be a total withdrawal from South Vietnam of troops, military advisers, and military personnel, including technical military personnel and military personnel associated with the pacification program, armaments, munitions, and war material of the United States and those of the other foreign countries mentioned in Article 3 (a). Advisers from the above-mentioned countries to all paramilitary organizations and the police force will also be withdrawn within the same period of time.

Article 6

The dismantlement of all military bases in South Vietnam of the United States and of the other foreign countries mentioned in Article 3 (a) shall be completed within sixty days of the signing of this Agreement.

Article 7

From the enforcement of the cease-fire to the formation of the government provided for in Articles 9 (b) and 14 of this Agreement, the two South Vietnamese parties shall not accept the introduction of troops, military advisers, and military personnel including technical military personnel, armaments, munitions, and war material into South Vietnam.

The two South Vietnamese parties shall be permitted to make periodic replacement of armaments, munitions and war material which have been destroyed, damaged, worn out or used up after the cease-fire, on the basis of piece-for-piece, of the same characteristics and properties, under the supervision of the International Commission of Control and Supervision.

Chapter III
The Return of Captured Military Personnel and Foreign Civilians, and Captured and Detained Vietnamese Civilian Personnel
Article 8

(a) The return of captured military personnel and foreign civilians of the parties shall be carried out simultaneously with and completed not later than the same day as the troop withdrawal mentioned in Article 5. The parties shall exchange complete lists of the above-mentioned captured miiltary personnel and foreign civilians on the day of the signing of this Agreement.

(b) The parties shall help each other to get information about those military personnel and foreign civilians of the parties missing in action, to determine the location and take care of the graves of the dead so as to facilitate the exhumation and repatriation of the remains, and to take any such other measures as may be required to get information about those still considered missing in action.

(c) The question of the return of Vietnamese civilian personnel captured and detained in South Vietnam will be resolved by the two South Vietnamese parties on the basis of the principles of Article 21 (b) of the Agreement on the Cessation of Hostilities in Vietnam of July 20, 1954. The two South Vietnamese parties will do so in a spirit of national reconciliation and concord, with a view to ending hatred and enmity, in order to ease suffering and to reunite families. The two South Vietnamese parties will do their utmost to resolve this question within ninety days after the cease-fire comes into effect.

Chapter IV
The Exercise of the South Vietnamese People's Right to Self-Determination
Article 9

The Government of the United States of America and the Government of the Democratic Republic of Vietnam undertake to respect the following principles for the exercise of the South Vietnamese people's right to self-determination:

(a) The South Vietnamese people's right to self-determination is sacred, inalienable, and shall be respected by all countries.

(b) The South Vietnamese people shall decide themselves the political future of South Vietnam through genuinely free and democratic general elections under international supervision.

(c) Foreign countries shall not impose any political tendency or personality on the South Vietnamese people.

Article 10

The two South Vietnamese parties undertake to respect the cease-fire and maintain peace in South Vietnam, settle all matters of contention through negotiations, and avoid all armed conflict.

Article 11

Immediately after the cease-fire, the two Vietnamese parties will:

—achieve national reconciliation and concord, end hatred and enmity, prohibit all acts of reprisal and discrimination against individuals or organizations that have collaborated with one side or the other;

—ensure the democratic liberties of the people: personal freedom, freedom of speech, freedom of the press, freedom of meeting, freedom of organization, freedom of political activities, freedom of belief, freedom of movement, freedom of residence, freedom of work, right to property ownership, and right to free enterprise.

Article 12

(a) Immediately after the cease-fire, the two South Vietnamese parties shall hold consultation in a spirit of national reconciliation and concord, mutual respect, and mutual non-elimination to set up a National Council of National Reconciliation and Concord of three equal segments. The Council shall operate on the principle of unanimity. After the National Council of National Reconciliation and Concord has assumed its functions, the two South Vietnamese parties will consult about the formation of councils at lower levels. The two South Vietnamese parties shall sign an agreement on the internal matters of South Vietnam as soon as possible and do their utmost to accomplish this within ninety days after the cease-fire comes into effect, in keeping with the South Vietnamese people's aspirations for peace, independence and democracy.

(b) The National Council of National Reconciliation and Concord shall have the task of promoting the two South Vietnamese parties' implementation of this Agreement, achievement of national reconciliation and concord and ensurance of democratic liberties. The National Council of National Reconciliation and Concord will organize the free and democratic general elections provided for in Article 9 (b) and decide the procedures and modalities of these general elections. The institutions for which the general elections are to be held will be agreed upon through consultations between the two South Vietnamese parties. The National Council of National Reconciliation and Concord will also decide the procedures and modalities of such local elections as the two South Vietnamese parties agree upon.

Article 13

The question of Vietnamese armed forces in South Vietnam shall be settled by the two South Vietnamese parties in a spirit of national reconciliation and concord, equality and mutual respect, without foreign interference, in accordance with the postwar situation. Among the questions to be discussed by the two South Vietnamese parties are steps to reduce their military effectiveness and to demobilize the troops being reduced. The two South Vietnamese parties will accomplish this as soon as possible.

Article 14

South Vietnam will pursue a foreign policy of peace and independence. It will be prepared to establish relations with all countries irrespective of their political and social systems on the basis of mutual respect for independence and sovereignty and accept economic and technical aid from any country with no political conditions attached. The acceptance of military aid by South Vietnam in the future shall come under the authority of the government set up after the general elections in South Vietnam provided for in Article 9 (b).

Chapter V
The Reunification of Vietnam and the Relationship Between North and South Vietnam
Article 15

The reunification of Vietnam shall be carried out step by step through peaceful means on the basis of discussions and agreements between North and South Vietnam, without coercion or annexation by either party, and without foreign interference. The time for reunification will be agreed upon by North and South Vietnam.

Pending reunification:

(a) The military demarcation line between the two zones at the 17th parallel is only provisional and not a political or territorial boundary, as provided for in paragraph 6 of the Final Declaration of the 1954 Geneva Conference.

(b) North and South Vietnam shall respect the Demilitarized Zone on either side of the Provisional Military Demarcation Line.

(c) North and South Vietnam shall promptly start negotiations with a view to reestablishing normal relations in various fields. Among the questions to be negotiated are the modalities of civilian movement across the Provisional Military Demarcation Line.

(d) North and South Vietnam shall not join any military alliance or military bloc and shall not allow foreign powers to maintain military bases, troops, military advisers, and military personnel on their respective territories, as stipulated in the 1954 Geneva Agreements on Vietnam.

Chapter VI
The Joint Military Commissions, the International Commission of Control and Supervision, the International Conference
Article 16

(a) The Parties participating in the Paris Conference on Vietnam shall immediately designate representatives to form a Four-Party Joint Military Commission with the task of ensuring joint action by the parties in implementing the following provisions of this Agreement:

—The first paragraph of Article 2, regarding the enforcement of the cease-fire throughout South Vietnam;

—Article 3 (a), regarding the cease-fire by U.S. forces and those of the other foreign countries referred to in that Article;

—Article 3 (c), regarding the cease-fire between all parties in South Vietnam;

—Article 5, regarding the withdrawal from South Vietnam of U.S. troops and those of the other foreign countries mentioned in Article 3 (a);

—Article 6, regarding the dismantlement of military bases in South Vietnam of the United States and those of the other foreign countries mentioned in Article 3 (a);

—Article 8 (a), regarding the return of captured military personnel and foreign civilians of the parties;

—Article 8 (b), regarding the mutual assistance of the parties in getting information about those military personnel and foreign civilians of the parties missing in action.

(b) The Four-Party Joint Military Commission shall begin operating immediately after the signing of this Agreement and end its activities in sixty days, after the completion of the withdrawal of U.S. troops and those of the other foreign countries mentioned in Article 3 (a) and the completion of the return of captured military personnel and foreign civilians of the parties.

(d) The four parties shall agree immediately on the organization, the working procedure, means of activity, and expenditures of the Four-Party Joint Military Commission.

Article 17

(a) The two South Vietnamese parties shall immediately designate representatives to form a Two-Party Joint Military Commission with the task of ensuring joint action by the two South Vietnamese parties in implementing the following provisions of this Agreement:

—The first paragraph of Article 2, regarding the enforcement of the cease-fire throughout South Vietnam, when the Four-Party Joint Military Commission has ended its activities;

—Article 3 (b), regarding the cease-fire between the two South Vietnamese parties;

—Article 3 (c), regarding the cease-fire between all parties in South Vietnam, when the Four-Party Joint Military Commission has ended its activities;

—Article 7, regarding the prohibition of the introduction of troops into South Vietnam and all other provisions of this article;

—Article 8 (c), regarding the question of the return of Vietnamese civilian personnel captured and detained in South Vietnam;

—Article 13, regarding the reduction of the military effectives of the two South Vietnamese parties and the demobilization of the troops being reduced.

(b) Disagreements shall be referred to the International Commission of Control and Supervision.

(c) After the signing of this Agreement, the Two-Party Joint Military Commission shall agree immediately on the measures and organization aimed at enforcing the cease-fire and preserving peace in South Vietnam.

Article 18

(a) After the signing of this Agreement, an International Commission of Control and Supervision shall be established immediately.

(b) Until the International Conference provided for in Article 19 makes definitive arrangements, the International Commission of Control and Supervision will report to the four parties on matters concerning the control and supervision of the implementation of the following provisions of this Agreement:

—The first paragraph of Article 2, regarding the enforcement of the cease-fire throughout South Vietnam;

—Article 3 (a), regarding the cease-fire by U.S. forces and those of the other foreign countries referred to in that Article;

—Article 3 (c), regarding the cease-fire between all the parties in South Vietnam;

—Article 5, regarding the withdrawal from Vietnam of U.S. troops and those of the other foreign countries mentioned in Article 3 (a);

—Article 6, regarding the dismantlement of military bases in South Vietnam of the United States and those of the other foreign countries mentioned in Article 3 (a);

—Article 8 (a), regarding the return of captured military personnel and foreign civilians of the parties.

The International Commission of Control and Supervision shall form control teams for carrying out its tasks. The four parties shall agree immediately on the location and operation of these teams. The parties will facilitate their operation.

(c) Until the International Conference makes definitive arrangements, the International Commission of Control and Supervision will report to the two South Vietnamese parties on matters concerning the control and supervision of the implementation of the following provisions of this Agreement:

—The first paragraph of Article 2, regarding the enforcement of the cease-fire throughout South Vietnam, when the Four-Party Joint Military Commission has ended its activities;

—Article 3 (b), regarding the cease-fire between the two South Vietnamese parties;

—Article 3 (c), regarding the cease-fire between all parties in South Vietnam, when the Four-Party Joint Military Commission has ended its activities;

—Article 7, regarding the prohibition of the introduction of troops into South Vietnam and all other provisions of this Article;

—Article 8 (c), regarding the question of the return of Vietnamese civilian personnel captured and detained in South Vietnam;

—Article 9 (b), regarding the free and democratic general elections in South Vietnam;

—Article 13, regarding the reduction of the military effectives of the two South Vietnamese parties and the demobilization of the troops being reduced.

The International Commission of Control and Supervision shall form control teams for carrying out its tasks. The two South Vietnamese parties shall agree immediately on the location and operation of these teams. The two South Vietnamese parties will facilitate their operation.

(d) The International Commission of Control and Supervision shall be composed of representatives of four countries: Canada, Hungary, Indonesia and Poland. The chairmanship of this Commission will rotate among the members for specific periods to be determined by the Commission.

(e) The International Commission of Control and Supervision shall carry out its tasks in accordance with the principle of respect for the sovereignty of South Vietnam.

(f) The International Commission of Control and Supervision shall operate in accordance with the principle of consultations and unanimity.

(g) The International Commission of Control and Supervision shall begin operating when a cease-fire comes into force in Vietnam. As regards the provisions in Article 18 (b) concerning the four parties, the International Commission of Control and Supervision shall end its activities when the Commission's tasks of control and supervision regarding these provisions have been fulfilled. As regards the provisions in Article 18 (c) concerning the two South Vietnamese parties, the International Commission of Control and Supervision shall end its activities on the request of the government formed after the general elections in South Vietnam provided for in Article 9 (b).

(h) The four parties shall agree immediately on the organization, means of activity, and expenditures of the International Commission of Control and Supervision. The relationship between the International Commission and the International Conference will be agreed upon by the International Commission and the International Conference.

Article 19

The parties agree on the convening of an International Conference within thirty days of the signing of this Agreement to acknowledge the signed agreements; to guarantee the ending of the war, the maintenance of peace in Vietnam, the respect of the Vietnamese people's fundamental national rights, and the South Vietnamese people's right to self-determination; and to contribute to and guarantee peace in Indochina.

The United States and the Democratic Republic of Vietnam, on behalf of the parties participating in the Paris Conference on Vietnam, will propose to the following parties that they participate in this International Conference: the People's Republic of China, the Republic of France, the Union of Soviet Socialist Republics, the United Kingdom, the four countries of the International Commission of Control and Supervision, and the Secretary General of the United Nations, together with the parties participating in the Paris Conference on Vietnam.

Chapter VII
Regarding Cambodia and Laos
Article 20

(a) The parties participating in the Paris Conference on Vietnam shall strictly respect the 1954 Geneva Agreements on Cambodia and the 1962 Geneva Agreements on Laos, which recognized the Cambodian and the Lao peoples' fundamental national rights, i.e., the independence, sovereignty, unity, and territorial integrity of these countries. The parties shall respect the neutrality of Cambodia and Laos.

The parties participating in the Paris Conference on Vietnam undertake to refrain from using the territory of Cambodia and the territory of Laos to encroach on the sovereignty and security of one another and of other countries.

(b) Foreign countries shall put an end to all military activities in Cambodia and Laos, totally withdraw from and refrain from reintroducing into these two countries troops, military advisers and military personnel, armaments, munitions and war material.

(c) The internal affairs of Cambodia and Laos shall be settled by the people of each of these countries without foreign interference.

(d) The problems existing between the Indochinese countries shall be settled by the Indochinese parties on the basis of respect for each other's independence, sovereignty, and territorial integrity, and non-interference in each other's internal affairs.

Chapter VIII
The Relationship Between the United States and the Democratic Republic of Vietnam
Article 21

The United States anticipates that this Agreement will usher in an era of reconciliation with the Democratic Republic of Vietnam as with all the peoples of Indochina. In pursuance of its traditional policy, the United States will contribute to healing the wounds of war and to postwar reconstruction of the Democratic Republic of Vietnam and throughout Indochina.

Article 22

The ending of the war, the restoration of peace in Vietnam, and the strict implementation of this Agreement will create conditions for establishing a new, equal and mutually beneficial relationship between the United States and the Democratic Republic of Vietnam on the basis of respect for each other's independence and sovereignty, and non-interference in each other's internal affairs. At the same time this will ensure stable peace in Vietnam and contribute to the preservation of lasting peace in Indochina and Southeast Asia.

Chapter IX
Other Provisions
Article 23

This Agreement shall enter into force upon signature by plenipotentiary representatives of the parties participating in the Paris Conference on Vietnam. All the parties concerned shall strictly implement this Agreement and its Protocols.

Done in Paris this twenty-seventh day of January, One Thousand Nine Hundred and Seventy-Three in Vietnamese and English. The Vietnamese and English texts are official and equally authentic.

For the Government of the United States of America	For the Government of the Republic of Vietnam
William P. Rogers *Secretary of State*	Tran Van Lam *Minister for Foreign Affairs*
For the Government of the Democratic Republic of Vietnam	For the Provisional Revolutionary Government of the Republic of South Vietnam
Nguyen Duy Trinh *Minister for Foreign Affairs*	Nguyen Thi Binh *Minister for Foreign Affairs*

Agreement on Ending the War and Restoring
Peace in Vietnam

The Government of the United States of America,
with the concurrence of the Government of the Republic of Vietnam,

The Government of the Democratic Republic of Vietnam, with the concurrence of the Provisional Revolutionary Government of the Republic of South Vietnam,

With a view to ending the war and restoring peace in Vietnam on the basis of respect for the Vietnamese people's fundamental national rights and the South Vietnamese people's right to self-determination, and to contributing to the consolidation of peace in Asia and the world,

Have agreed on the following provisions and undertake to respect and to implement them:

[Text of Agreement Chapter I–VIII Same as Above]

Chapter IX
Other Provisions
Article 23

The Paris Agreement on Ending the War and Restoring Peace in Vietnam shall enter into force upon signature of this document by the Secretary of State of the Government of the United States of America and the Minister for Foreign Affairs of the Government of the Democratic Republic of Vietnam, and upon signature of a document in the same terms by the Secretary of State of the Government of the United States of America, the Minister for Foreign Affairs of the Government of the Republic of Vietnam, the Minister for Foreign Affairs of the Government of the Democratic Republic of Vietnam, and the Minister for Foreign Affairs of the Provisional Revolutionary Government of the Republic of South Vietnam. The Agreement and the protocols to it shall be strictly implemented by all the parties concerned.

Done in Paris this twenty-seventh day of January, One Thousand Nine Hundred and Seventy-Three in Vietnamese and English. The Vietnamese and English texts are official and equally authentic.

For the Government of the United States of America

William P. Rogers
Secretary of State

For the Government of the Democratic Republic of Vietnam

Nguyen Duy Trinh
Minister for Foreign Affairs

(*There then follows a very long series of "Protocols," or precise agreements on specific points.*)

8-C POLITICAL DEVELOPMENTS

In the second and third quarters of this century, several unusual developments took place in American government. More and more power seemed to concentrate in the Federal government. Government began to play an active part in labor relations, welfare programs, health and school affairs. The government enjoyed far more power at the start of 1973 than had been imagined at the start of 1933. This growth of government power came about partly as the result of the great depression of the 1930's, partly as the result of World War II and the Cold War.

PROBLEMS: *What are some of the most important changes in the powers and activities of the Federal government during the years from 1933 to 1973? How were these changes brought about? What influence did each of the branches of government—the legislative (Congress), the judiciary, and the executive (presidency)—have in causing change?*

1. *The country was deep in economic depression at the start of 1933. The Democrats had won a smashing victory in the 1932 elections, electing President Franklin D. Roosevelt, and a large majority in both the House of Representatives and the Senate. The depression was practically at its worst in March 1933 when the new President was sworn into office. Roosevelt's first inaugural address (which follows) sounded the keynote for his program of change and reform—the New Deal.*

This is a day of national consecration, and I am certain that my fellow-Americans expect that on my induction into the Presidency I will address them with a candor and a decision which the present situation of our nation impels.

This is pre-eminently the time to speak the truth, the whole truth, frankly and boldly. Nor need we shrink from honestly facing conditions in our country today. This great nation will endure as it has endured, will revive and will prosper.

So first of all let me assert my firm belief that the only thing we have to fear is fear itself—nameless, unreasoning, unjustified terror which paralyzes needed efforts to convert retreat into advance.

In every dark hour of our national life a leadership of frankness and vigor has met with that understanding and support of the people themselves which is essential to victory. I am convinced that you will again give that support to leadership in these critical days.

In such a spirit on my part and on yours we face our common difficulties. They concern, thank God, only material things. Values have shrunken to fantastic levels; taxes have risen; our ability to pay has fallen, government of all kinds is faced by serious curtailment of income; the means of exchange are frozen in the currents of trade; the withered leaves of industrial enterprise lie on every side; farmers find no markets for their produce; the savings of many years in thousands of families are gone.

More important, a host of unemployed citizens face the grim problem of existence, and an equally great number toil with little return. Only a foolish optimist can deny the dark realities of the moment.

Yet our distress comes from no failure of substance. We are stricken by no plague of locusts. Compared with the perils which our forefathers conquered because they believed and were not afraid, we have still much to be thankful for. Nature still offers her bounty and human efforts have multiplied it. Plenty is at our doorstep, but a generous use of it languishes in the very sight of the supply.

Primarily, this is because the rulers of the exchange of mankind's goods have failed through their own stubbornness and their own incompetence, have admitted that failure and abdicated. Practices of the unscrupulous money changers stand indicted in the court of public opinion, rejected by the hearts and minds of men.

True, they have tried, but their efforts have been cast in the pattern of an unknown tradition. Faced by failure of credit, they have proposed only the lending of more money.

Stripped of the lure of profit by which to induce our people to follow their false leadership, they have resorted to exhortations, pleading tearfully for restored confidence. They know only the rules of a generation of self-seekers.

They have no vision, and when there is no vision the people perish.

The money changers have fled from their high seats in the temple of our civilization. We may now restore that temple to the ancient truths.

The measure of the restoration lies in the extent to which we apply social values more noble than mere monetary profit.

Happiness lies not in the mere possession of money; it lies in the joy of achievement; in the thrill of creative effort.

The joy and moral stimulation of work no longer must be forgotten in the mad chase of evanescent profits. These dark days will be worth all they cost us if they teach us that our true destiny is not to be ministered unto but to minister to ourselves and to our fellow-men.

Recognition of the falsity of material wealth as the standard of success goes hand in hand with the abandonment of the false belief that public office and high political position are to be valued only by the standards of pride of place and personal profit; and there must be an end to a conduct in banking and in business which too often has given to a sacred trust the likeness of callous and selfish wrong-doing.

Small wonder that confidence languishes, for it thrives only on honesty, on honor, on the sacredness of obligations, on faithful protection, on unselfish performance. Without them it cannot live.

Restoration calls, however, not for changes in ethics alone. This nation asks for action, and action now.

Our greatest primary task is to put people to work. This is no unsolvable problem, if we face it wisely and courageously.

It can be accomplished in part by direct recruiting by the government itself, treating the task as we would treat the emergency of a war, but at the same time, through this employment, accomplishing greatly needed projects to stimulate the use of our natural resources.

Hand in hand with this, we must frankly recognize the overbalance of population in our industrial centers and, by engaging on a national scale in the redistribution, endeavor to provide a better use of the land for those best fitted for the land.

The task can be helped by definite efforts to raise the values of agricultural products and with this the power to purchase the output of our cities.

It can be helped by preventing realistically the tragedy of the growing loss, through foreclosure, of our small homes and our farms.

It can be helped by insistence that the Federal, State and local governments act forthwith on the demand that their cost be drastically reduced.

It can be helped by the unifying of relief activities which today are often scattered, uneconomical and unequal. It can be helped by national planning for and supervision of all forms of transportation and of communications and other utilities which have a definitely public character.

There are many ways in which it can be helped, but it can never be helped merely by talking about it. We must act, and act quickly.

Finally, in our progress toward a resumption of work we require two safeguards against a return to the evils of the old order; there must be a strict supervision of all banking and credits and investments; there must be an end to speculation with other people's money, and there must be provision for an adequate but sound currency.

These are the lines of attack. I shall presently urge upon a new Congress in special session detailed measures for their fulfillment, and I shall seek the immediate assistance of the several States.

Through this program of action we address ourselves to putting our own national house in order and making income balance outgo.

Our international trade relations, though vastly important, are, in point of time and necessity, secondary to the establishment of a sound national economy.

I favor as a practical policy the putting of first things first. I shall spare no effort to restore world trade by international economic readjustment, but the emergency at home cannot wait on that accomplishment.

The basic thought that guides these specific means of national recovery is not narrowly nationalistic.

It is the insistence, as a first consideration, upon the interdependence of the various elements in, and parts of, the United States—a recognition of the old and permanently important manifestation of the American spirit of the pioneer.

It is the way to recovery. It is the immediate way. It is the strongest assurance that the recovery will endure.

In the field of world policy I would dedicate this nation to the policy of the good neighbor—the neighbor who resolutely respects himself and, because he does so, respects the rights of others—the neighbor who respects his obligations and respects the sanctity of his agreements in and with a world of neighbors.

If I read the temper of our people correctly, we now realize as we have never before, our interdependence on each other; that we cannot merely take, but we must give as well; that if we are to go forward we must move as a trained and loyal army willing to sacrifice for the good of a common discipline, because, without such discipline, no progress is made, no leadership becomes effective.

We are, I know, ready and willing to submit our lives and property to such discipline because it makes possible a leadership which aims at a larger good.

This I propose to offer, pledging that the larger purposes will bind upon us all as a sacred obligation with a unity of duty hitherto evoked only in time of armed strife.

With this pledge taken, I assume unhesitatingly the leadership of this great army of our people, dedicated to a disciplined attack upon our common problems.

Action in this image and to this end is feasible under the form of government which we have inherited from our ancestors.

Our Constitution is so simple and practical that it is possible always to meet extraordinary needs by changes in emphasis and arrangement without loss of essential form.

That is why our constitutional system has proved it-

self the most superbly enduring political mechanism the modern world has produced. It has met every stress of vast expansion of territory, of foreign wars, of bitter internal strife, of world relations.

It is to be hoped that the normal balance of executive and legislative authority may be wholly adequate to meet the unprecedented task before us. But it may be that an unprecedented demand and need for undelayed action may call for temporary departure from that normal balance of public procedure.

I am prepared under my constitutional duty to recommend the measures that a stricken nation in the midst of a stricken world may require.

These measures, or such other measures as the Congress may build out of its experience and wisdom, I shall seek, within my constitutional authority, to bring to speedy adoption.

But in the event that the Congress shall fail to take one of these two courses, and in the event that the national emergency is still critical, I shall not evade the clear course of duty that will then confront me.

I shall ask the Congress for the one remaining instrument to meet the crisis—broad executive power to wage a war against the emergency as great as the power that would be given me if we were in fact invaded by a foreign foe.

For the trust reposed in me I will return the courage and the devotion that befit the time. I can do no less.

We face the arduous days that lie before us in the warm courage of national unity; with the clear consciousness of seeking old and precious moral values; with the clean satisfaction that comes from the stern performance of duty by old and young alike.

We aim at the assurance of a rounded and permanent national life.

We do not distrust the future of essential democracy. The people of the United States have not failed. In their need they have registered a mandate that they want direct, vigorous action.

They have asked for discipline and direction under leadership. They have made me the present instrument of their wishes. In the spirit of the gift I take it.

In this dedication of a nation we humbly ask the blessing of God. May He protect each and every one of us! May He guide me in the days to come!

2. At the start of the New Deal, many new laws were passed. Unlike earlier laws, they dealt with new problems—with labor-management relations, control of farm output, unemployment insurance and retirement allowances for workers, and a regional approach to agriculture, industry, conserva-

tion, and electric power. The laws which follow are samples of the "first New Deal" legislation. They were very long documents because they detailed many new arrangements to be followed, so the text has been cut in places.

The National Industrial Recovery Act (June 1933)

An Act to encourage national industrial recovery, to foster fair competition, and to provide for the construction of certain useful public works, and for other purposes.

Title I.
Industrial Recovery.
Declaration of Policy.

SEC. 1. A national emergency productive of widespread unemployment and disorganization of industry, which burdens interstate and foreign commerce, affects the public welfare, and undermines the standards of living of the American people, is hereby declared to exist. It is hereby declared to be the policy of Congress to remove obstructions to the free flow of interstate and foreign commerce which tend to diminish the amount thereof; and to provide for the general welfare by promoting the organization of industry for the purpose of co-operative action among trade groups, to induce and maintain united action of labor and management under adequate governmental sanctions and supervision, to eliminate unfair competitive practices, to promote the fullest possible utilization of the present productive capacity of industries, to avoid undue restriction of production (except as may be temporarily required), to increase the consumption of industrial and agricultural products by increasing purchasing power, to reduce and release unemployment, to improve standards of labor, and otherwise to rehabilitate industry and to conserve natural resources.

Administrative Agencies.

SEC. 2. (*a*) To effectuate the policy of this title, the President is hereby authorized to establish such agencies, to accept and utilize such voluntary and uncompensated services, to appoint, without regard to the provisions of the civil service laws, such officers and employees, and to utilize such Federal officers and employees, and, with the consent of the State, such State and local officers and employees, as he may find necessary, to prescribe their authorities, duties, responsibilities, and tenure, and, without regard to the Classification Act of 1923, as amended, to fix the compensation of any officers and employees so appointed.

(*b*) The President may delegate any of his functions and powers under this title to such officers, agents, and employees as he may designate or appoint, and may establish an industrial planning and research agency to aid in carrying out his functions under this title.

(*c*) This title shall cease to be in effect and any agencies established hereunder shall cease to exist at the expiration of two years after the date of enactment of this Act, or sooner if the President shall by proclamation or the Congress shall by joint resolution declare that the emergency recognized by section 1 has ended.

Codes of Fair Competition.

SEC. 3. (*a*) Upon the application to the President by one or more trade or industrial associations or groups, the President may approve a code or codes of fair competition for the trade or industry or subdivision thereof, represented by the applicant or applicants, if the President finds (1) that such associations or groups impose no inequitable restriction on admission to membership therein and are truly representative of such trades or industries or subdivisions thereof, and (2) that such code or codes are not designed to promote monopolies or to eliminate or oppress small enterprises and will not operate to discriminate against them, and will tend to effectuate the policy of this title: *Provided*, That such code or codes shall not permit monopolies or monopolistic practices: *Provided further*, That where such code or codes affect the services and welfare of persons engaged in other steps of the economic process, nothing in this section shall deprive such persons of the right to be heard prior to approval by the President of such code or codes. The President may, as a condition of his approval of any such code, impose such conditions (including requirements for the making of reports and the keeping of accounts) for the protection of consumers, competitors, employees, and others, and in furtherance of the public interest, and may provide such exceptions to and exemptions from the provisions of such code, as the President in his discretion deems necessary to effectuate the policy herein declared.

(*b*) After the President shall have approved any such code, the provisions of such code shall be the standards of fair competition for such trade or industry or subdivision thereof. Any violation of such standards in any transaction in or affecting interstate or foreign commerce shall be deemed an unfair method of competition in commerce within the meaning of the Federal Trade Commission Act, as amended; but nothing in this title shall be construed to impair the powers of the Federal Trade Commission under such Act, as amended.

(*c*) The several district courts of the United States are hereby invested with jurisdiction to prevent and restrain violations of any code of fair competition approved under this title; and it shall be the duty of the several district attorneys of the United States, in their respective districts, under the direction of the Attorney-General, to institute proceedings in equity to prevent and restrain such violations.

(*d*) Upon his motion, or if complaint is made to the President that abuses inimical to the public interest and contrary to the policy herein declared are prevalent in any trade or industry or subdivision thereof, and if no code of fair competition therefor has theretofore been approved by the President, the President, after such public notice and hearing as he shall specify, may prescribe and approve a code of fair competition for such trade or industry or subdivision thereof. . . .

Agreements and Licences.

SEC. 4. (*a*) The President is authorized to enter into agreements with, and to approve voluntary agreements between and among, persons engaged in a trade or industry, labor organizations, and trade or industrial organizations, associations, or groups, relating to any trade or industry, if in his judgment such agreements will aid in effectuating the policy of this title with respect to transactions in or affecting interstate or foreign commerce, and will be consistent with the requirements of clause (2) of subsection (*a*) of section 3 for a code of fair competition.

(*b*) Whenever the President shall find that destructive wage or price cutting or other activities contrary to the policy of this title are being practised in any trade or industry or any subdivision thereof, and, after such public notice and hearing as he shall specify, shall find it essential to license business enterprises in order to make effective a code of fair competition or an agreement under this title or otherwise to effectuate the policy of this title, and shall publicly so announce, no person shall, after a date fixed in such announcement, engage in or carry on any business, in or affecting interstate or foreign commerce, specified in such announcement, unless he shall have first obtained a license issued pursuant to such regulations as the President shall prescribe. The President may suspend or revoke any such license, after due notice and opportunity for hearing, for violation of the terms or conditions thereof. . . .

SEC. 5. While this title is in effect . . . and for sixty days thereafter, any code, agreement, or license approved, prescribed, or issued and in effect under this title, and any action complying with the provisions thereof taken during such period, shall be exempt from the provisions of the anti-trust laws of the United States.

Nothing in this Act, and no regulation thereunder, shall prevent an individual from pursuing the vocation of manual labor and selling or trading the products thereof; nor shall anything in this Act, or regulation thereunder, prevent anyone from marketing or trading the produce of his farm.

Limitations upon Application of Title.

SEC. 6. (*a*) No trade or industrial association or group shall be eligible to receive the benefit of the provisions of this title until it files with the President a statement containing such information relating to the activities of the association or group as the President shall by regulation prescribe. . . .

SEC. 7. (*a*) Every code of fair competition, agreement, and license approved, prescribed, or issued under this title shall contain the following conditions: (1) That employees shall have the right to organize and bargain collectively through representatives of their own choosing, and shall be free from the interference, restraint, or coercion of employers of labor, or their agents, in the designation of such representatives or in self-organization or in other concerted activities for the purpose of collective bargaining or other mutual aid or protection; (2) that no employee and no one seeking employment shall be required as a condition of employment to join any company union or to refrain from joining, organizing, or assisting a labor organization of his own choosing; and (3) that employers shall comply with the maximum hours of labor, minimum rates of pay, and other conditions of employment, approved or prescribed by the President.

(*b*) The President shall, so far as practicable, afford every opportunity to employers and employees in any trade or industry or subdivision thereof with respect to which the conditions referred to in clauses (1) and (2) of subsection (*a*) prevail, to establish by mutual agreement, the standards as to the maximum hours of labor, minimum rates of pay, and such other conditions of employment as may be necessary, in such trade or industry or subdivision thereof to effectuate the policy of this title; and the standards established in such agreements, when approved by the President, shall have the same effect as a code of fair competition approved by the President under subsection (*a*) of section 3.

(*c*) Where no such mutual agreement has been approved by the President he may investigate the labor practices, policies, wages, hours of labor, and conditions of employment in such trade or industry or subdivision thereof; and upon the basis of such investigations, and after such hearings as the President finds advisable, he is authorized to prescribe a limited code of fair competition fixing such maximum hours of labor, minimum rates of pay, and other conditions of employment in the trade or industry or subdivision thereof investigated as he finds to be necessary to effectuate the policy of this title, which shall have the same effect as a code of fair competition approved by the President under subsection (*a*) of section 3. The President may differentiate according to experience and skill of the employees affected and according to the locality of employment; but no attempt shall be made to introduce any classification according to the nature of the work involved which might tend to set a maximum as well as a minimum wage. . . .

Title II.
Public Works and Construction Projects.
Federal Emergency Administration of Public Works.

SEC. 201. (*a*) To effectuate the purposes of this title the President is hereby authorized to create a Federal Emergency Administration of Public Works, all the powers of which shall be exercised by a Federal Emergency Administrator of Public Works (hereafter referred to as the "Administrator"), and to establish such agencies, to accept and utilize such voluntary and uncompensated services, to appoint, without regard to the civil service laws, such officers and employees, and to utilize such Federal officers and employers, and, with the consent of the State, such State and local officers and employees as he may find necessary, to prescribe their authorities, duties, responsibilities, and tenure, and, without regard to the Classification Act of 1923, as amended, to fix the compensation of any officers and employees so appointed. The President may delegate any of his functions and powers under this title to such officers, agents, and employees as he may designate or appoint.

(*b*) The Administrator may, without regard to the civil service laws or the Classification Act of 1923, as amended, appoint and fix the compensation of such experts and such other officers and employees as are necessary to carry out the provisions of this title; and may make such expenditures (including expenditures for personal services and rent at the seat of government and elsewhere, for law books and books of reference, and for paper, printing, and binding) as are necesary to carry out the provisions of this title.

(*c*) All such compensation, expenses, and allowances shall be paid out of funds made available by this Act.

(*d*) After the expiration of two years after the date of the enactment of this Act, or sooner if the President shall by proclamation or the Congress shall by joint resolution declare that the emergency recognized by section 1 has ended, the President shall not make any further loans or grants or enter upon any new construction under this title, and any agencies estab-

lished hereunder shall cease to exist and any of their remaining functions shall be transferred to such departments of the Government as the President shall designate. . . .

SEC. 202. The Administrator, under the direction of the President, shall prepare a comprehensive program of public works, which shall include among other things the following: (*a*) Construction, repair, and improvement of public highways and park ways, public buildings, and any publicly owned instrumentalities and facilities; (*b*) conservation and development of natural resources, including control, utilization, and purification of waters, prevention of soil or coastal erosion, development of water power, transmission of electrical energy, and construction of river and harbour improvements and flood control and also the construction of any river or drainage improvement required to perform or satisfy any obligation incurred by the United States through a treaty with a foreign Government heretofore ratified and to restore or develop for the use of any State or its citizens water taken from or denied to them by performance on the part of the United States of treaty obligations heretofore assumed: *Provided,* That no river or harbor improvements shall be carried out unless they shall have heretofore or hereafter been adopted by the Congress or are recommended by the Chief of Engineers of the United States Army; (*c*) any projects of the character heretofore constructed or carried on either directly by public authority or with public aid to serve the interests of the general public; (*d*) construction, reconstruction, alteration, or repair under public regulation or control of low-cost housing and slum-clearance projects; (*e*) any project (other than those included in the foregoing classes) of any character heretofore eligible for loans under subsection (*a*) of section 201 of the Emergency Relief and Construction Act of 1932, as amended, and paragraph (3) of such subsection (*a*) shall for such purposes be held to include loans for the construction or completion of hospitals the operation of which is partly financed from public funds, and of reservoirs and pumping plants and for the construction of dry docks; and if in the opinion of the President it seems desirable, the construction of naval vessels within the terms and or limits established by the London Naval Treaty of 1930 and of aircraft required therefor and construction of heavier-than-air aircraft and technical construction for the Army Air Corps and such Army housing projects as the President may approve, and provision of original equipment for the mechanization or motorization of such Army tactical units as he may designate: *Provided, however,* That in the event of an international agreement for the further limitation of armament, to which the United States is signatory, the President is hereby authorized and empowered to suspend, in whole or in part, any such naval or military construction or mechanization and motorization of Army units. . . .

SEC. 203. (a) With a view to increasing employment quickly (while reasonably securing any loans made by the United States) the President is authorized and empowered, through the Administrator or through such other agencies as he may designate or create, (1) to construct, finance, or aid in the construction or financing of any public-works project included in the program prepared pursuant to section 202; (2) upon such terms as the President shall prescribe, to make grants to States, municipalities, or other public bodies for the construction, repair, or improvement of any such project, but no such grant shall be in excess of 30 per centum of the cost of labor and materials employed upon such project; (3) to acquire by purchase, or by exercise of the power of eminent domain, any real or personal property in connection with the construction of any such project, and to sell any security acquired or any property so constructed or acquired or to leave any such property with or without the privilege of purchase: *Provided,* That all moneys received from any such sale or lease or the repayment of any loan shall be used to retire obligations issued pursuant to section 209 of this Act, in addition to any other moneys required to be used for such purpose; (4) to aid in the financing of such railroad maintenance and equipment as may be approved by the Interstate Commerce Commission as desirable for the improvement of transportation facilities; . . .

(d) The President, in his discretion, and under such terms as he may prescribe, may extend any of the benefits of this title to any State, county, or municipality notwithstanding any constitutional or legal restriction or limitation on the right or power of such State, county, or municipality to borrow money or incur indebtedness.

SEC. 204. (a) For the purpose of providing for emergency construction of public highways and related projects, the President is authorized to make grants to the highway departments of the several States in an amount not less than $400,000,000, to be expended by such departments in accordance with the provisions of the Federal Highway Act, approved 9 November 1921, as amended and supplemented. . . .

SEC. 205. (a) Not less than $50,000,000 of the amount made available by this Act shall be allotted for (A) national forest highways, (B) national forest roads, trails, bridges, and related projects, (C) national park roads and trails in national parks owned or authorized, (D) roads on Indian reservations, and (E) roads through public lands. . . .

SEC. 206. All contracts let for construction projects and all loans and grants pursuant to this title shall contain such provisions as are necessary to insure (1) that no convict labor shall be employed on any such project; (2) that (except in executive, administrative, and supervisory positions), so far as practicable and feasible, no individual directly employed on any such project shall be permitted to work more than thirty hours in any one week; (3) that all employees shall be paid just and reasonable wages which shall be compensation sufficient to provide, for the hours of labor as limited, a standard of living in decency and comfort; (4) that in the employment of labor in connection with any such project, preference shall be given, where they are qualified, to ex-service men with dependents, and then in the following order: (A) To citizens of the United States and aliens who have declared their intention of becoming citizens, who are bona fide residents of the political subdivision and/or county in which the work is to be performed, and (B) to citizens of the United States and aliens who have declared their intention of becoming citizens, who are bona fide residents of the State, Territory, or district in which the work is to be performed: *Provided,* That these preferences shall apply only where such labor is available and qualified to perform the work to which the employment relates; and (5) that the maximum of human labor shall be used in lieu of machinery wherever practicable and consistent with sound economy and public advantage. . . .

Subsistence Homesteads.

SEC. 208. To provide for aiding the redistribution of the overbalance of population in industrial centres $25,000,000 is hereby made available to the President, to be used by him through such agencies as he may establish and under such regulations as he may make, for making loans for and otherwise aiding in the purchase of subsistence homesteads. . . .

The Agricultural Adjustment Act (May 1933)

An Act to relieve the existing national economic emergency by increasing agricultural purchasing power.

Title I.—Agricultural Adjustment.
Declaration of Emergency.

That the present acute economic emergency being in part the consequence of a severe and increasing disparity between the prices of agricultural and other commodities, which disparity has largely destroyed the purchasing power of farmers for industrial products, has broken down the orderly exchange of commodities, and has seriously impaired the agricultural assets supporting the national credit structure, it is hereby declared that these conditions in the basic industry of agriculture have affected transactions in agricultural commodities with a national public interest, have burdened and obstructed the normal currents of commerce in such commodities, and render imperative the immediate enactment of Title I of this Act.

Declaration of Policy.

SEC. 2. It is hereby declared to be the policy of Congress—

(1) To establish and maintain such balance between the production and consumption of agricultural commodities, and such marketing conditions therefor, as will re-establish prices to farmers at a level that will give agricultural commodities a purchasing power with respect to articles that farmers buy, equivalent to the purchasing power of agricultural commodities in the base period. The base period in the case of all agricultural commodities except tobacco shall be the pre-war period, August 1909–July 1914. In the case of tobacco, the base period shall be the post-war period, August 1919–July 1929.

(2) To approach such equality of purchasing power by gradual correction of the present inequalities therein at as rapid a rate as is deemed feasible in view of the current consumptive demand in domestic and foreign markets.

(3) To protect the consumers' interest by readjusting farm production at such level as will not increase the percentage of the consumers' retail expenditures for agricultural commodities, or products derived therefrom, which is returned to the farmer, above the percentage which was returned to the farmer in the pre-war period, August 1909–July 1914. . . .

SEC. 6. (a) The Secretary of Agriculture is hereby authorized to enter into option contracts with the producers of cotton to sell to any such producer an amount of cotton to be agreed upon not in excess of the amount of reduction in production of cotton by such producer below the amount produced by him in the preceding crop year, in all cases where such producer agrees in writing to reduce the amount of cotton produced by him in 1933, below his production in the previous year, by not less than 30 per centum, without increase in commercial fertilization per acre.

(b) To any such producer so agreeing to reduce production the Secretary of Agriculture shall deliver a nontransferable-option contract agreeing to sell to said producer an amount, equivalent to the amount of his agreed reduction, of the cotton in the possession and control of the Secretary.

(c) The producer is to have the option to buy said cotton at the average price paid by the Secretary for the cotton procured under section 3, and is to have the right at any time up to 1 January 1934 to exercise his option, upon proof that he has complied with his contract and with all the rules and regulations of the Secretary of Agriculture with respect thereto, by taking said cotton upon payment by him of his option price and all actual carrying charges on such cotton; or the Secretary may sell such cotton for the account of such producer, paying him the excess of the market price at the date of sale over the average price above referred to after deducting all actual and necessary carrying charges: *Provided*, That in no event shall the producer be held responsible or liable for financial loss incurred in the holding of such cotton or on account of the carrying charges therein: *Provided further*, That such agreement to curtail cotton production shall contain a further provision that such cotton producer shall not use the land taken out of cotton production for the production for sale, directly or indirectly, of any other nationally produced agricultural commodity. . . .

Part 2.—Commodity Benefits.
General Powers.

SEC. 8. In order to effectuate the declared policy, the Secretary of Agriculture shall have power—

(1) To provide for reduction in the acreage or reduction in the production for market, or both, of any basic agricultural commodity, through agreements with producers or by other voluntary methods, and to provide for rental or benefit payments in connection therewith or upon that part of the production of any basic agricultural commodity required for domestic consumption, in such amounts as the Secretary deems fair and reasonable. . . .

(2) To enter into marketing agreements with processors, associations of producers, and others engaged in the handling, in the current of interstate or foreign commerce of any agricultural commodity or project thereof, after due notice and opportunity for hearing to interested parties. The making of any such agreement shall not be held to be in violation of any of the antitrust laws of the United States. . .

Processing Tax.

SEC. 9. (a) To obtain revenue for extraordinary expenses incurred by reason of the national economic emergency, there shall be levied processing taxes as hereinafter provided. When the Secretary of Agriculture determines that rental or benefit payments are to be made with respect to any basic agricultural commodity, he shall proclaim such determination, and a processing tax shall be in effect with respect to such commodity from the beginning of the marketing year therefor next following the date of such proclamation. The processing tax shall be levied, assessed, and collected upon the first domestic processing of the commodity, whether of domestic production or imported, and shall be paid by the processor. . . .

(*b*) The processing tax shall be at such rate as equals the difference between the current average farm price for the commodity and the fair exchange value of the commodity; except that if the Secretary has reason to believe that the tax at such rate will cause such reduction in the quantity of the commodity or products thereof domestically consumed as to result in the accumulation of surplus stocks of the commodity or products thereof or in the depression of the farm price of the commodity, then he shall cause an appropriate investigation to be made and afford due notice and opportunity for hearing to interested parties. If thereupon the Secretary finds that such result will occur, then the processing tax shall be at such rate as will prevent such accumulation of surplus stocks and depression of the farm price of the commodity. . . .

Tennessee Valley Act (May 1933)
An Act to improve the navigability and to provide for the flood control of the Tennessee River; to provide for reforestation and the proper use of marginal lands in the Tennessee Valley; to provide for the agricultural and industrial development of said valley; to provide for the national defense by the creation of a corporation for the operation of Government properties at and near Muscle Shoals, in the State of Alabama, etc.

Be it enacted, That for the purpose of maintaining and operating the properties now owned by the United States in the vicinity of Muscle Shoals, Alabama, . . . there is hereby created a body corporate by the name of the "Tennessee Valley Authority."
(*Sections 1, 2, and 3 omitted.*)
SEC. 4. Except as otherwise specifically provided in this Act, the Corporation . . .

Shall have power in the name of the United States of America to exercise the right of eminent domain, and in the purchase of any real estate or the acquisition of real estate by condemnation proceedings, the title to such real estate shall be taken in the name of the United States of America.

Shall have power to acquire real estate for the construction of dams, reservoirs, transmission lines, power houses, and other structures, and navigation projects at any point along the Tennessee River, or any of its tributaries.

Shall have power to construct dams, reservoirs, power houses, power structures, transmission lines, navigation projects, and incidental works in the Tennessee River and its tributaries, and to unite the various power installations into one or more systems by transmission lines.

SEC. 5. The board is hereby authorized—

To arrange with farmers and farm organizations for large-scale practical use of the new forms of fertilizers under conditions permitting an accurate measure of the economic return they produce.

To co-operate with National, State, district, or county experimental stations or demonstration farms, for the use of new forms of fertilizer or fertilizer practices during the initial or experimental period of their introduction.

The board in order to improve and cheapen the production of fertilizer is authorized to manufacture and sell fixed nitrogen, fertilizer, and fertilizer ingredients at Muscle Shoals by the employment of existing facilities, by modernizing existing plants, or by any other process or processes that in its judgment shall appear wise and profitable for the fixation of atmospheric nitrogen or the cheapening of the production of fertilizer.

Under the authority of this Act the board may make donations or sales of the product of the plant or plants operated by it to be fairly and equitably distributed through the agency of county demonstration agents, agricultural colleges, or otherwise as the board may direct, for experimentation, education, and introduction of the use of such products in co-operation with practical farmers so as to obtain information as to the value, effort, and best methods of their use.

The board is authorized to make alterations, modifications, or improvements in existing plants and facilities, and to construct new plants.

In the event it is not used for the fixation of nitrogen for agricultural purposes or leased, then the board shall maintain in stand-by condition nitrate plant numbered 2, or its equivalent, for the fixation of atmospheric nitrogen, for the production of explosives in the event of war or a national emergency, until the Congress shall by joint resolution release the board from this obligation, and if any part thereof be used by the board for the manufacture of phosphoric acid or potash, the balance of nitrate plant numbered 2 shall be kept in stand-by condition.

To establish, maintain, and operate laboratories and experimental plants, and to undertake experiments for the purpose of enabling the Corporation to furnish nitrogen products for military purposes, and nitrogen and other fertilizer products for agricultural purposes in the most economical manner and at the highest standard of efficiency.

(*Several provisions are omitted.*)

To produce, distribute, and sell electric power, as herein particularly specified.

No products of the Corporation shall be sold for use outside of the United States, its Territories and possessions, except to the United States Government for the use of its Army and Navy, or to its allies in case of war.

(*The intervening sections are omitted.*)

SEC. 10. The board is hereby empowered and authorized to sell the surplus power not used in its operations, and for operation of locks and other works generated by it, to States, counties, municipalities, corporations, partnerships, or individuals, according to the policies hereinafter set forth; and to carry out said authority, the board is authorized to enter into contracts for such sale for a term not exceeding twenty years, and in the sale of such current by the board it shall give preference to States, counties, municipalities, and co-operative organizations of citizens or farmers, not organized or doing business for profit, but primarily for the purpose of supplying electricity to its own citizens or members: . . . In order to promote and encourage the fullest possible use of electric light and power on farms within reasonable distance of any of its transmission lines the board in its discretion shall have power to construct transmission lines to farms and small villages that are not otherwise supplied with electricity at reasonable rates, and to make such rules and regulations governing such sale and distribution of such electric power as in its judgment may be just and equitable. . . .

SEC. 11. It is hereby declared to be the policy of the Government, so far as practical, to distribute and sell the surplus power generated at Muscle Shoals equitably among the States, counties, and municipalities within transmission distance. This policy is further declared to be that the projects herein provided for shall be considered primarily as for the benefit of the people of the section as a whole and particularly the domestic and rural consumers to whom the power can economically be made available, and accordingly that sale to and use by industry shall be a secondary purpose, to be utilized principally to secure a sufficiently high load factor and revenue returns which will permit domestic and rural use at the lowest possible rates and in such manner as to encourage increased domestic and rural use of electricity. It is further hereby declared to be the policy of the Government to utilize the Muscle Shoals properties so far as may be necessary to improve, in-

crease, and cheapen the production of fertilizer and fertilizer ingredients by carrying out the provision of this Act. . . .

3. The New Deal legislative program represented such a sharp break with earlier systems that some opposition was to be expected. One group of anti-New Deal leaders organized the American Liberty League. Its platform as announced in 1934 included the following declarations.

1. To preserve American institutions which safeguard, to citizens in all walks of life, the right to liberty and the pursuit of happiness. Therefore to uphold American principles which oppose the tendency shown in many countries to restrict freedom of speech, freedom of the press, religious liberty, the right to peaceable assembly and the right to petition the government; and to combat the growth of bureaucracy, the spread of monopoly, the socialization of industry and the regimentation of American life.

2. To maintain the right of an equal opportunity for all to work, earn, save and acquire property in order that every man may enjoy the fruit of his own ability and labor, and thus have, in his declining years, the peace of mind that comes from a sense of security for himself and for his wife and children who may survive him.

3. To uphold the principle that the levying of taxes, the appropriation of public funds and the designation of the purposes for which they are to be expended are exclusively the functions of the Congress and should not be exercised by administrative officials.

4. To advocate economy in government by abolishing useless commissions and offices, consolidating departments and bureaus and eliminating extravagance; to advocate a sound fiscal policy and the maintenance of a sound and stable currency to be preserved at all hazards.

5. To further the restoration of employment and the rehabilitation of agriculture, business and industry, and to oppose all unnecessary interference and competition by government with legitimate industry.

6. To oppose all measures that may threaten the security of the invested savings of the millions of savings bank depositors, holders of insurance policies and other investors. Also to support governmental policies that will protect invested funds that go to the maintenance of churches, colleges, hospitals and all institutions that care for the aged, the poor, the orphans and the afflicted.

7. To support government in the obligation to provide for those who, because of involuntary unemployment or disability, cannot provide for themselves.

8. To uphold the American principle that laws be made only by the direct representatives of the people in the Congress, and that the laws be interpreted only by the Courts, and to oppose the delegation of either of these functions to executive departments, commissions or bureau heads.

9. To provide for the rank and file of the American people, who are unorganized and too often have no voice in legislation that affects their welfare, an opportunity, through united effort and a service of public information, to offset the influence of any and all groups working for selfish purposes.

10. Finally, to preserve for succeeding generations the principles of the Declaration of Independence, the safeguards of personal liberty and the opportunity for initiative and enterprise provided under the Constitution. These are the foundation stones upon which America has built the most successful governmental structure thus far devised.

4.   Far more important than the views of the Liberty League were those of the U.S. Supreme Court. Several key New Deal laws were declared unconstitutional when cases concerning them reached the Court. The President believed that his policies had been approved by the people in the 1936 election which he had won by a landslide. He undertook, therefore, to change the makeup of the Supreme Court. This attempt to "pack" the Court was his one major political failure. In the radio address of which a part follows (March 9, 1937). President Roosevelt gave his reasons for his action against the Court.

I want to talk with you very simply about the need for present action in this crisis—the need to meet the unanswered challenge of one-third of a nation ill-nourished, ill-clad, ill-housed.

Last Thursday I described the American form of government as a three-horse team provided by the Constitution to the American people so that their field might be plowed. The three horses are, of course, the three branches of government—the Congress, the Executive and the Courts. Two of the horses are pulling in unison today, the third is not. Those who have intimated that the President of the United States is trying to drive that team overlook the simple fact that the President, as Chief Executive, is, himself, one of the three horses.

It is the American people themselves who are in the driver's seat.

It is the American people themselves who want the furrow plowed.

It is the American people themselves who expect the third horse to pull in unison with the other two. . . .

Since the rise of the modern movement for social and economic progress through legislation, the Court has more and more often and more and more boldly asserted a power to veto laws passed by the Congress and State Legislatures in complete disregard of this original limitation. (*By the U.S. Constitution.*)

In the last four years the sound rule of giving statutes the benefit of all reasonable doubt has been cast aside. The Court has been acting not as a judicial body but as a policy-making body.

When the Congress has sought to stabilize national agriculture, to improve the conditions of labor, to safeguard business against unfair competition, to protect our national resources, and in many other ways to serve our clearly national needs, the majority of the Court has been assuming the power to pass on the wisdom of these acts of the Congress—and to approve or disapprove the public policy written into these laws.

That is not only my accusation. It is the accusation of most distinguished justices of the present Supreme Court. I have not the time to quote to you all the language used by dissenting justices in many of these cases. But in the case holding the Railroad Retirement Act unconstitutional, for instance, Chief Justice Hughes said in a dissenting opinion that the majority opinion was a "departure from sound principles" and placed "an unwarranted limitation upon the commerce clause." And three other justices agreed with him.

In the case holding the AAA unconstitutional, Justice Stone said of the majority opinion that it was a "tortured construction of the Constitution." And two other justices agreed with him.

In the case holding the New York Minimum Wage Law unconstitutional, Justice Stone said that the majority were actually reading into the Constitution their own "personal economic predilections" and that if the legislative power is not left free to choose the methods of solving the problems of poverty, subsistence and health of large numbers in the community, then "government is to be rendered impotent." And two other justices agreed with him.

In the face of these dissenting opinions, there is no basis for the claim made by some members of the Court that something in the Constitution has compelled them regretfully to thwart the will of the people.

In the face of such dissenting opinions, it is perfectly clear, that as Chief Justice Hughes has said: "We are under a Constitution but the Constitution is what the judges say it is."

The Court in addition to the proper use of its judicial functions has improperly set itself up as a third house of the Congress—a super-legislature, as one of the justices has called it—reading into the Constitution words and implications which are not there, and which were never intended to be there.

We have, therefore, reached the point as a nation where we must take action to save the Constitution from the Court and the Court from itself. We must find a way to take an appeal from the Supreme Court to the Constitution itself. We want a Supreme Court which will do justice under the Constitution—not over it. In our courts we want a government of laws and not of men.

I want—as all Americans want—an independent judiciary as proposed by the framers of the Constitution. That means a Supreme Court that will enforce the Constitution as written—that will refuse to amend the Constitution by the arbitrary exercise of judicial power—amendment by judicial say-so. It does not mean a judiciary so independent that it can deny the existence of facts universally recognized.

How then could we proceed to perform the mandate given us? It was said in last year's Democratic platform "If these problems cannot be effectively solved within the Constitution, we shall seek such clarifying amendment as will assure the power to enact those laws, adequately to regulate commerce, protect public health and safety and safeguard economic security." In other words, we said we would seek an amendment only if every other possible means by legislation were to fail.

When I commenced to review the situation with the problem squarely before me, I came by a process of elimination to the conclusion that short of amendments the only method which was clearly constitutional, and would at the same time carry out other much-needed reforms, was to infuse new blood into all our courts. We must have men worthy and equipped to carry out impartial justice. But, at the same time, we must have judges who will bring to the courts a present-day sense of the Constitution—judges who will retain in the courts the judicial functions of a court and reject the legislative powers which the courts have today assumed. . . .

During the past half century the balance of power between the three great branches of the Federal Government has been tipped out of balance by the courts in direct contradiction of the high purposes of the framers of the Constitution. It is my purpose to restore that balance. You who know me will accept my solemn assurance that in a world in which democracy is under attack I seek to make American democracy succeed.

5. One of the most significant changes in American business and labor relations came about with the Wagner-Connery Act. The National Labor Relations Board was established by that law. (Like many other New Deal innovations, the N.L.R.B. has been retained through later periods, even when Republican party majorities existed in Congress.) Significant sections of the Wagner-Connery Act follow.

The Wagner-Connery Act (July 1935)
An Act to diminish the causes of labor disputes burdening or obstructing interstate and foreign commerce, to create a National Labor Relations Board, and for other purposes.

Findings and Policy.

SEC. 1. The denial by employers of the right of employees to organize and the refusal by employers to accept the procedure of collective bargaining lead to strikes and other forms of industrial strife or unrest, which have the intent or the necessary effect of burdening or obstructing commerce by (*a*) impairing the efficiency, safety, or operation of the instrumentalities of commerce; (*b*) occurring in the current of commerce; (*c*) materially affecting, restraining, or controlling the flow of raw materials or manufactured or processed goods from or into the channels of commerce, or the prices of such materials or goods in commerce; or (*d*) causing diminution of employment and wages in such volume as substantially to impair or disrupt the market for goods flowing from or into the channels of commerce.

The inequality of bargaining power between employers who do not possess full freedom of association or actual liberty of contract, and employers who are organized in the corporate or other forms of ownership association, substantially burdens and affects the flow of commerce, and tends to aggravate recurrent business depressions, by depressing wage rates and the purchasing power of wage earners in industry and by preventing the stabilization of competitive wage rates and working conditions within and between industries.

Experience has proved that protection by law of the right of employees to organize and bargain collectively safeguards commerce from injury, impairment, or interruption, and promotes the flow of commerce by removing certain recognized sources of industrial strife and unrest, by encouraging practices fundamental to the friendly adjustment of industrial disputes arising out of differences as to wages, hours, or other working conditions, and by restoring equality of bargaining power between employers and employees.

It is hereby declared to be the policy of the United States to eliminate the causes of certain substantial obstructions to the free flow of commerce and to mitigate and eliminate these obstructions when they have occurred by encouraging the practice and procedure of collective bargaining and by protecting the exercise by workers of full freedom of association, self-organization, and designation of representatives of their own choosing, for the purpose of negotiating the terms and conditions of their employment or other mutual aid or protection.

SEC. 2. When used in this Act—

(1) The term "person" includes one or more individuals, partnerships, associations, corporations, legal representatives, trustees, trustees in bankruptcy, or receivers.

(2) The term "employer" includes any person acting in the interest of an employer, directly or indirectly, but shall not include the United States, or any State or political subdivision thereof, or any person subject to the Railway Labor Act, as amended from time to time, or any labor organization (other than when acting as an employer), or anyone acting in the capacity of officer or agent of such labor organization.

(3) The term "employee" shall include any employee, and shall not be limited to the employees of a particular employer, unless the Act explicitly states otherwise, and shall include any individual whose work has ceased as a consequence of, or in connection with, any current labor dispute or because of any unfair labor practice, and who has not obtained any other regular and substantially equivalent employment, but shall not include any individual employed as an agricultural laborer, or in the domestic service of any family or person at his home, or any individual employed by his parent or spouse. . . .

(5) The term "labor organization" means any organization of any kind, or any agency or employee representation committee or plan, in which employees participate and which exists for the purpose, in whole or in part, of dealing with employers concerning grievances, labor disputes, wages, rates of pay, hours of employment, or conditions of work.

(6) The term "commerce" means trade, traffic, commerce, transportation, or communication among the several States. . . .

(7) The term "affecting commerce" means in commerce, or burdening or obstructing commerce or the free flow of commerce, or having led or tending to lead to a labor dispute burdening or obstructing commerce. . . .

(9) The term "labor dispute" includes any controversy concerning terms, tenure, or conditions of employment, or concerning the association or representation of persons in negotiating, fixing, maintaining, changing, or seeking to arrange terms or conditions of employment, regardless of whether the disputants stand in the proximate relation of employer and employee. . . .

National Labor Relations Board.

SEC. 3. (a) There is hereby created a board, to be known as the "National Labor Relations Board," which shall be composed of three members, who shall be appointed by the President, by and with the advice and consent of the Senate. One of the original members shall be appointed for a term of one year, one for a term of three years, and one for a term of five years, but their successors shall be appointed for terms of five years each, except that any individual chosen to fill a vacancy shall be appointed only for the unexpired term of the member whom he shall succeed. The President shall designate one member to serve as chairman of the Board. Any member of the Board may be removed by the President, upon notice and hearing, for neglect of duty or malfeasance in office, but for no other cause. . . .

Rights of Employees.

SEC. 7. Employees shall have the right of self-organization, to form, join, or assist labor organizations, to bargain collectively through representatives of their own choosing, and to engage in concerted activities, for the purpose of collective bargaining or other mutual aid or protection.

SEC. 8. It shall be an unfair labor practice for an employer—

(1) To interfere with, restrain, or coerce employees in the exercise of the rights guaranteed in section 7.

(2) To dominate or interfere with the formation or administration of any labor organization or contribute financial or other support to it: *Provided,* That subject to rules and regulations made and published by the Board pursuant to section 6 (*a*), an employer shall not be prohibited from permitting employees to confer with him during working hours without loss of time or pay.

(3) By discrimination in regard to hire or tenure of employment or any term or condition of employment to encourage or discourage membership in any labor organization: *Provided,* That nothing in this Act, or in the National Industrial Recovery Act, as amended from time to time, or in any code or agreement approved or prescribed thereunder, or in any other statute of the United States, shall preclude an employer from making an agreement with a labor organization (not estab-

lished, maintained, or assisted by any action defined in this Act as an unfair labor practice) to require as a condition of employment membership therein, if such labor organization is the representative of the employees as provided in section 9 (a), in the appropriate collective bargaining unit covered by such agreement when made.

(4) To discharge or otherwise discriminate against an employee because he has filed charges or given testimony under this Act.

(5) To refuse to bargain collectively with the representatives of his employees, subject to the provisions of section 9 (a).

Representatives and Elections.

SEC. 9. (a) Representatives designated or selected for the purposes of collective bargaining by the majority of the employees in a unit appropriate for such purposes, shall be the exclusive representatives of all the employees in such unit for the purposes of collective bargaining in respect to rates of pay, wages, hours of employment, or other conditions of employment: *Provided*, That any individual employee or a group of employees shall have the right at any time to present grievances to their employer.

(b) The Board shall decide in each case whether, in order to insure to employees the full benefit of their right to self-organization and to collective bargaining, and otherwise to effectuate the policies of this Act, the unit appropriate for the purposes of collective bargaining shall be the employer unit, craft unit, plant unit, or subdivision thereof.

(c) Whenever a question affecting commerce arises concerning the representation of employees, the Board may investigate such controversy and certify to the parties, in writing, the name or names of the representatives that have been designated or selected. In any such investigation, the Board shall provide for an appropriate hearing upon due notice, either in conjunction with a proceeding under section 10 or otherwise, and may take a secret ballot of employees, or utilize any other suitable method to ascertain such representatives.

(d) Whenever an order of the Board made pursuant to section 10 (c) is based in whole or in part upon facts certified following an investigation pursuant to subsection (c) of this section, and there is a petition for the enforcement or review of such order, such certification and the record of such investigation shall be included in the transcript of the entire record required to be filed under subsection 10 (e) or 10 (f), and thereupon the decree of the court enforcing, modifying, or setting aside in whole or in part the order of the Board shall be made and entered upon the pleadings, testimony, and proceedings set forth in such transcript.

Prevention of Unfair Labor Practices.

SEC. 10. (a) The Board is empowered, as hereinafter provided, to prevent any person from engaging in any unfair labor practice (listed in section 8) affecting commerce. This power shall be exclusive, and shall not be affected by any other means of adjustment or prevention that has been or may be established by agreement, code, law, or otherwise.

(b) Whenever it is charged that any person has engaged in or is engaging in any such unfair labor practice, the Board, or any agent or agency designated by the Board for such purposes, shall have power to issue and cause to be served upon such person a complaint stating the charges in that report, and continuing a notice of hearing before the Board or a member thereof, or before a designated agent or agency, at a place therein fixed, not less than five days after the serving of said complaint. Any such complaint may be amended by the member, agent, or agency conducting the hearing, or the Board in its discretion at any time prior to the issuance of an order based thereon. The person so complained of shall have the right to file an answer to the original or amended complaint and to appear in person or otherwise and give testimony at the place and time fixed in the complaint. In the discretion of the member, agent, or agency conducting the hearing or the Board, any other person may be allowed to intervene in the said proceeding and to present testimony. In any such proceeding the rules of evidence prevailing in courts of law or equity shall not be controlling.

(c) The testimony taken by such member, agent or agency, or the Board shall be reduced to writing and filed with the Board. Thereafter, in its discretion, the Board upon notice may take further testimony or hear argument. If upon all the testimony taken, the Board shall be of the opinion that any person named in the complaint has engaged in or is engaging in any such unfair labor practice, then the Board shall state its findings of fact and shall issue and cause to be served on such person an order requiring such person to cease and desist from such unfair labor practice, and to take such affirmative action, including reinstatement of employees with or without back pay, as will effectuate the policies of this Act. Such order may further require such person to make reports from time to time showing the extent to which it has complied with the order. If upon all the testimony taken, the Board shall be of the opinion that no person named in the complaint has engaged in or is engaging in any such unfair labor practice, then the Board shall state its findings of fact and shall issue an order dismissing the said complaint. . . .

(e) The Board shall have power to petition any circuit court of appeals of the United States, or if all the circuit courts of appeals to which application may be made are in vacation, any district court of the United States, within any circuit or district, respectively, wherein the unfair labor practice in question occurred or wherein such person resides or transacts business, for the enforcement of such order and for appropriate temporary relief or restraining order, and shall certify and file in the court a transcript of the entire record in the proceeding, including the pleadings and testimony upon which such order was entered and the findings and order of the Board. Upon such filing, the court shall cause notice thereof to be served upon such person, and thereupon shall have jurisdiction of the proceeding and of the question determined therein, and shall have power to grant such temporary relief or restraining order as it deems just and proper, and to make and enter upon the pleadings, testimony, and proceedings set forth in such transcript a decree enforcing, modifying, and enforcing as so modified, or setting aside in whole or in part the order of the Board. No objection that has not been urged before the Board, its member, agent, or agency, shall be considered by the court, unless the failure or neglect to urge such objection shall be excused because of extraordinary circumstances. The findings of the Board as to the facts, if supported by evidence, shall be conclusive. . . . The jurisdiction of the court shall be exclusive and its judgment and decree shall be final, except that the same shall be subject to review by the appropriate circuit court of appeals if application was made to the district court as hereinabove provided, and by the Supreme Court of the United States upon writ of certiorari or certification. . . .

(f) Any person aggrieved by a final order of the Board granting or denying in whole or in part the relief sought may obtain a review of such order in any circuit court of appeals of the United States in the circuit wherein the unfair labor practice in question was alleged to have been engaged in or wherein such person resides or transacts business. . . .

Investigatory Powers.

SEC. 11. For the purpose of all hearings and investigations, . . .

(1) The Board, or its duly authorized agents or agencies, shall at all reasonable times have access to, for the purpose of examination, and the right to copy any evidence of any person being investigated or proceeded against that relates to any matter under investigation or in question. Any member of the Board shall have power to issue subpenas requiring the attendance and testimony of witnesses and the production of any evidence that relates to any matter under investigation or in question, before the Board, its member, agent, or agency conducting the hearing or investigation. . . .

Limitations.

SEC. 13. Nothing in this Act shall be construed so as to interfere with or impede or diminish in any way the right to strike. . . .

6. *During World War II, President Roosevelt led his Democratic Party to two further consecutive presidential victories. The third- and fourth-term victories established Roosevelt as the only man in American history to hold office as President for more than eight years. In one of his 1944 campaign speeches, Republican candidate Thomas E. Dewey mounted a vigorous attack on Roosevelt's record in domestic affairs, although supporting the war effort.*

At the very outset (*said Dewey*) I want to make one thing clear. This is not merely a campaign against an individual or a political party. It is not merely a campaign to displace a tired, exhausted, quarreling and bickering administration with a fresh and vigorous administration. It is a campaign against an administration which was conceived in defeatism, which failed for eight straight years to restore our domestic economy, which has been the most wasteful, extravagant and incompetent administration in the history of the Nation. . . .

When this administration took office the depression was already over three years old. Then what happened? In 1934, when the depression was then 5 years old— longer than any other in a century, we still had 12,000,-000 unemployed. By 1940 the depression was almost 11 years old. This administration had been in power for 7 straight years and there were still 10,000,000 Americans unemployed.

It took a world war to get jobs for the American people.

Let's get one thing clear and settled. Who was President during the depression that lasted from 1933 until some time in 1940, when war orders from all over the world began to bring us full employment again? The New Deal kept this country in a continuous state of depression for 7 straight years. It made a 3-year depression last 11 years—over twice as long as any other depression in a whole century.

Now, Washington is getting all set for another depression. They intend to keep the young men in the Army. The New Deal spokesmen are daily announcing that reconversion will be difficult, if not impossible. They say that relief rolls will be enormous. They drearily promise us that we shall need to prepare for an army of unemployed bigger than the armies we have put in the field against the Germans and the Japanese. That's what's wrong with the New Deal. That's why it's time for a change.

The reason for this long-continued failure is twofold. First, because there never was a worse job done of running our Government. When one agency fails, the New Deal just piles another on and we pay for both.

The other reason for this long continued failure— the reason why they are now dismally preparing for another depression—is because this administration has so little faith in the United States. They believe in the defeatest philosophy that our industrial plant is built, that our task is not to produce more goods but to fight among ourselves over what we have. I believe that we have not even begun to build our industrial plant. We have not exhausted our inventive genius. We have not exhausted our capacity to produce more goods for our people. No living man has yet dreamed of the limit to which we can go if we have a Government which believes in the American economic system and in the American people. . . . The war has proved that despite the New Deal, America can mightily increase its frontiers of production. With competent government America can produce mightily for peace.

We know from long experience that we shall not provide jobs and restore small business by the methods of the New Deal. We cannot keep our freedom and at the same time continue experimentation with a new policy every day by the National Government. We cannot succeed with a controlled and regulated society under a Government which destroys incentive, chokes production, fosters disunity and discourages men with vision and imagination from creating employment and opportunity.

The New Deal really believes that unemployment is bound to be with us permanently. It says so. They will change this 12-year-old tune between now and election. They have done it every time. But they've always come back to it after election. The New Deal really believes that we cannot have good social legislation and also good jobs for all. I believe with all my heart and soul that we can have both.

Of course we need security regulation. Of course we need bank deposit insurance. Of course we need price support for agriculture. Of course the farmers of this country cannot be left to the hazards of a world price

while they buy their goods at an American price. Of course we need unemployment insurance and old-age pensions and also relief whenever there are not enough jobs. Of course the rights of labor to organize and bargain collectively are fundamental. My party blazed the trail in that field by passage of the Railway Labor Act in 1926.

But we must also have a Government which believes in enterprise and Government policies which encourage enterprise. We must see to it that a man who wants to start a business is encouraged to start it, that the man who wants to expand a going business is encouraged to expand it. We must see to it that the job-producing enterprises of America are stimulated to produce more jobs. We must see to it that the man who wants to produce more jobs is not throttled by the Government— but knows that he has a Government as eager for him to succeed as he is himself. . . .

7.   Following World War II, the major parties in the United States began to experience great changes in voting patterns. There were "landslide" victories (although very narrow electoral results) in the presidential elections, while an apparent Democratic majority controlled Congress most of the time. The Democratic majority was only apparent because the old "Solid South" had been split by Republicans, and southern congressmen often voted with northern Republicans against northern Democrats.

Foreign aid became a major issue in domestic policy, because any such assistance required a change in the American budget. President Harry S. Truman became the first President to make widespread foreign assistance a key part of his program in peacetime. He announced it as "Point Four" in his inaugural address in 1949 (below).

Fourth, we must embark on a bold new program for making the benefits of our scientific advances and industrial progress available for the improvement and growth of underdeveloped areas.

More than half the people of the world are living in conditions approaching misery. Their food is inadequate. They are victims of disease. Their economic life is primitive and stagnant. Their poverty is a handicap and a threat both to them and to more prosperous areas.

For the first time in history, humanity possesses the knowledge and skill to relieve the suffering of these people.

The United States is pre-eminent among nations in

the development of industrial and scientific techniques. The material resources which we can afford to use for assistance of other peoples are limited. But our imponderable resources in technical knowledge are constantly growing and are inexhaustible.

I believe that we should make available to peace-loving peoples the benefits of our store of technical knowledge in order to help them realize their aspirations for a better life. And, in cooperation with other nations, we should foster capital investment in areas needing development.

Our aim should be to help the free peoples of the world, through their own efforts, to produce more food, more clothing, more materials for housing, and more mechanical power to lighten their burdens.

We invite other countries to pool their technological resources in this undertaking. Their contributions will be warmly welcomed. This should be a cooperative enterprise in which all nations work together through the United Nations and its specialized agencies whenever practicable. It must be a worldwide effort for the achievement of peace, plenty, and freedom.

With the cooperation of business, private capital, agriculture, and labor in this country, this program can greatly increase the industrial activity in other nations and can raise substantially their standards of living.

Such new economic developments must be devised and controlled to the benefit of the peoples of the areas in which they are established. Guarantees to the investor must be balanced by guarantees in the interest of the people whose resources and whose labor go into these developments.

The old imperialism—exploitation for foreign profit—has no place in our plans. What we envisage is a program of development based on the concepts of democratic fair-dealing.

All countries, including our own, will greatly benefit from a constructive program for the better use of the world's human and natural resources. Experience shows that our commerce with other countries expands as they progress industrially and economically.

Greater production is the key to prosperity and peace. And the key to greater production is a wider and more vigorous application of modern scientific and technical knowledge.

Only by helping the least fortunate of its members to help themselves can the human family achieve the decent, satisfying life that is the right of all people.

Democracy alone can supply the vitalizing force to stir the peoples of the world into triumphant action, not only against their human oppressors, but also against their ancient enemies—hunger, misery, and despair.

On the basis of these four major courses of action we hope to help create the conditions that will lead eventually to personal freedom and happiness for all mankind.

If we are to be successful in carrying out these policies, it is clear that we must have continued prosperity in this country and we must keep ourselves strong.

Slowly but surely we are weaving a world fabric of international security and growing prosperity.

We are aided by all who wish to live in freedom from fear—even by those who live today in fear under their own governments.

We are aided by all who want relief from lies and propaganda—those who desire truth and sincerity.

We are aided by all who desire self-government and a voice in deciding their own affairs.

We are aided by all who long for economic security —for the security and abundance that men in free societies can enjoy.

We are aided by all who desire freedom of speech, freedom of religion, and freedom to live their own lives for useful ends.

Our allies are the millions who hunger and thirst after righteousness.

In due time, as our stability becomes manifest, as more and more nations come to know the benefits of democracy and to participate in growing abundance, I believe that those countries which now oppose us will abandon their delusions and join with the free nations of the world in a just settlement of international differences.

Events have brought out American democracy to new influence and new responsibilities. They will test our courage, our devotion to duty, and our concept of liberty.

But I say to all men, what we have achieved in liberty, we will surpass in greater liberty.

Steadfast in our faith in the Almighty, we will advance toward a world where man's freedom is secure. . . .

8. Just before leaving office as President (in January 1961) Dwight D. Eisenhower delivered the following "farewell address" to the American people. In it, he attempted to draw Americans to his view of the country's character. He included a strong warning against a threat that he noticed—that a combination of military power and of industrial power associated with military production might grow overstrong within the government.

. . . This evening, I come to you with a message of leave-taking and farewell, and to share a few final thoughts with you, my countrymen.

Like every other citizen, I wish the new President, and all who will labor with him, Godspeed. I pray that the coming years will be blessed with peace and prosperity to all.

Our people expect their President and the Congress to find essential agreement on issues of great moment, the wise resolution of which will better shape the future of the Nation.

My own relations with the Congress, which began on a remote and tenuous basis when, long ago, a member of the Senate appointed me to West Point, have since ranged to the intimate during the war and immediate post-war period, and, finally, to the mutually interdependent during these past eight years.

In this final relationship, the Congress and the Administration have, on most vital issues, cooperated well, to serve the national good rather than mere partisanship, and so have assured that the business of the Nation should go forward. So, my official relationship with the Congress ends in a feeling, on my part, of gratitude that we have been able to do so much together.

We now stand ten years past the midpoint of a century that has witnessed four major wars among great nations. Three of these involved our own country. Despite these holocausts America is today the strongest, the most influential and most productive nation in the world. Understandably proud of this pre-eminence, we yet realize that America's leadership and prestige depend, not merely upon our unmatched material progress, riches and military strength, but on how we use our power in the interests of world peace and human betterment.

Throughout America's adventure in free government, our basic purposes have been to keep the peace; to foster progress in human achievement and to enhance liberty, dignity and integrity among people and among nations. To strive for less would be unworthy of a free and religious people. Any failure traceable to arrogance, or our lack of comprehension or readiness to sacrifice would inflict upon us grievous hurt both at home and abroad.

Progress toward these noble goals is persistently threatened by the conflict now engulfing the world. It commands our whole attention, absorbs our very beings. We face a hostile ideology—global in scope, atheistic in character, ruthless in purpose, and insidious in method. Unhappily the danger it poses promises to be of indefinite duration. To meet it successfully, there is called for, not so much the emotional and transitory sacrifices of crisis, but rather those which enable us to carry forward steadily, surely, and without complaint the burdens of a prolonged and complex struggle—with liberty the stake. Only thus shall we remain, despite every provocation, on our charted course toward permanent peace and human betterment.

Crises there will continue to be. In meeting them, whether foreign or domestic, great or small, there is a recurring temptation to feel that some spectacular and costly action could become the miraculous solution to all current difficulties. A huge increase in newer elements of our defense; development of unrealistic programs to cure every ill in agriculture; a dramatic expansion in basic and applied research—these and many other possibilities, each possibly promising in itself, may be suggested as the only way to the road we wish to travel.

But each proposal must be weighed in the light of a broader consideration: the need to maintain balance in and among national programs—balance between the private and the public economy, balance between cost and hoped for advantage—balance between the clearly necessary and the comfortably desirable; balance between our essential requirements as a nation and the duties imposed by the nation upon the individual; balance between actions of the moment and the national welfare of the future. Good judgment seeks balance and progress; lack of it eventually finds imbalance and frustration.

The record of many decades stands as proof that our people and their government have, in the main, understood these truths and have responded to them well, in the face of stress and threat. But threats, new in kind or degree, constantly arise. I mention two only.

A vital element in keeping the peace is our military establishment. Our arms must be mighty, ready for instant action, so that no potential aggressor may be tempted to risk his own destruction.

Our military organization today bears little relation to that known by any of my predecessors in peacetime, or indeed by the fighting men of World War II or Korea.

Until the latest of our world conflicts, the United States had no armaments industry. American makers of plowshares could, with time and as required, make swords as well. But now we can no longer risk emergency improvisation of national defense; we have been compelled to create a permanent armaments industry of vast proportions. Added to this, three and a half million men and women are directly engaged in the defense establishment. We annually spend on military security more than the net income of all United States corporations.

This conjunction of an immense military establishment and a large arms industry is new in the American experience. The total influence—economic, political, even spiritual—is felt in every city, every State house, every office of the Federal government. We recognize the imperative need for this development. Yet we must not fail to comprehend its grave implications. Our toil, resources and livelihood are all involved; so is the very structure of our society.

In the councils of government, we must guard against the acquisition of unwarranted influence, whether sought or unsought, by the military-industrial complex. The potential for the disastrous rise of misplaced power exists and will persist.

We must never let the weight of this combination endanger our liberties or democratic processes. We should take nothing for granted. Only an alert and knowledgeable citizenry can compel the proper meshing of the huge industrial and military machinery of defense with our peaceful methods and goals, so that security and liberty may prosper together.

Akin to, and largely responsible for the sweeping changes in our industrial-military posture, has been the technological revolution during recent decades.

In this revolution, research has become central; it also becomes more formalized, complex, and costly. A steadily increasing share is conducted for, by, or at the direction of, the Federal government.

Today, the solitary inventor, tinkering in his shop, has been overshadowed by task forces of scientists in laboratories and testing fields. In the same fashion, the free university, historically the fountainhead of free ideas and scientific discovery, has experienced a revolution in the conduct of research. Partly because of the huge costs involved, a government contract becomes virtually a substitute for intellectual curiosity. For every old blackboard there are now hundreds of new electronic computers.

The prospect of domination of the nation's scholars by Federal employment, project allocations, and the power of money is ever present—and is gravely to be regarded.

Yet, in holding scientific research and discovery in respect, as we should, we must also be alert to the equal and opposite danger that public policy could itself become the captive of a scientific-technological elite.

It is the task of statesmanship to mold, to balance, and to integrate these and other forces, new and old, within the principles of our democratic system—ever aiming toward the supreme goals of our free society.

Another factor in maintaining balance involves the element of time. As we peer into society's future, we—you and I, and our government—must avoid the impulse to live only for today, plundering, for our own ease and convenience, the precious resources of tomorrow. We cannot mortgage the material assets of our grandchildren without risking the loss also of their political and spiritual heritage. We want democracy to survive for all generations to come, not to become the insolvent phantom of tomorrow.

Down the long lane of the history yet to be written America knows that this world of ours, ever growing smaller, must avoid becoming a community of dreadful fear and hate, and be, instead, a proud confederation of mutual trust and respect.

Such a confederation must be one of equals. The weakest must come to the conference table with the same confidence as do we, protected as we are by our moral, economic, and military strength. That table, though scarred by many past frustrations, cannot be abandoned for the certain agony of the battlefield.

Disarmament, with mutual honor and confidence, is a continuing imperative. Together we must learn how to compose differences, not with arms, but with intellect and decent purpose. . . .

9. On his Inauguration day, early in 1961, President John F. Kennedy delivered the following address in which he called for a reassertion of the nation's traditional ideals and emphasized the need for his fellow-citizens to serve, not themselves alone, but their country and all mankind.

Vice President Johnson, Mr. Speaker, Mr. Chief Justice, President Eisenhower, Vice President Nixon, President Truman, Reverend Clergy, Fellow Citizens: WE OBSERVE today not a victory of a party but a celebration of freedom—symbolizing an end as well as a beginning—signifying renewal as well as change. For I have sworn before you and Almighty God the same solemn oath our forebears prescribed nearly a century and three quarters ago.

The world is very different now. For man holds in his mortal hands the power to abolish all forms of human poverty and all forms of human life. And yet the same revolutionary beliefs for which our forebears fought are still at issue around the globe—the belief that the rights of man come not from the generosity of the state but from the hand of God.

We dare not forget today that we are the heirs of that first revolution. Let the word go forth from this time and place, to friend and foe alike, that the torch has been passed to a new generation of Americans—born in this century, tempered by war, disciplined by a hard and bitter peace, proud of our ancient heritage—and unwilling to witness or permit the slow undoing of those human rights to which this Nation has always been committed, and to which we are committed today at home and around the world.

Let every nation know, whether it wishes us well or ill, that we shall pay any price, bear any burden, meet any hardship, support any friend, oppose any foe to assure the survival and success of liberty.

This much we pledge—and more.

To those old allies whose cultural and spiritual origins we share, we pledge the loyalty of faithful friends. United there is little we cannot do in a host of cooperative ventures. Divided, there is little we can do—for we dare not meet a powerful challenge at odds and split asunder.

To those new states whom we welcome to the ranks of the free, we pledge our word that one form of colonial control shall not have passed away merely to be replaced by a far more iron tyranny. We shall not always expect to find them supporting our view. But we shall always hope to find them strongly supporting their own freedom—and to remember that, in the past, those who foolishly sought power by riding the back of the tiger ended up inside.

To those peoples in the huts and villages of half the globe struggling to break the bonds of mass slavery, we pledge our best efforts to help them help themselves, for whatever period is required—not because the Communists may be doing it, not because we seek their votes, but because it is right. If a free society cannot help the many who are poor, it cannot save the few who are rich.

To our sister republics south of our border, we offer a special pledge—to convert our good words into good deeds—in a new alliance for progress—to assist free men and free governments in casting off the chains of poverty. But this peaceful revolution of hope cannot become the prey of hostile powers. Let all our neighbors know that we shall join with them to oppose aggression or subversion anywhere in the Americas. And let every other power know that this hemisphere intends to remain the master of its own house.

To that world assembly of sovereign states, the United Nations, our last best hope in an age where the instruments of war have far outpaced the instruments of peace, we renew our pledge of support—to prevent it from becoming merely a forum for invective—to strengthen its shield of the new and the weak—and to enlarge the area in which its writ may run.

Finally, to those nations who would make themselves our adversary, we offer not a pledge but a request: that both sides begin anew the quest for peace, before the dark powers of destruction unleashed by science engulf all humanity in planned or successful self-destruction.

We dare not tempt them with weakness. For only when our arms are sufficient beyond doubt can we be certain beyond doubt that they will never be employed.

But neither can two great and powerful groups of nations take comfort from our present course—both sides overburdened by the cost of modern weapons, both rightly alarmed by the steady spread of the deadly atom, yet both racing to alter that uncertain balance of terror that stays the hand of mankind's final war.

So let us begin anew—remembering on both sides that civility is not a sign of weakness, and sincerity is always subject to proof. Let us never negotiate out of fear. But let us never fear to negotiate.

Let both sides explore what problems unite us instead of belaboring those problems which divide us. Let both sides, for the first time, formulate serious and precise proposals for the inspection and control of arms—and bring the absolute power to destroy other nations under the absolute control of all nations.

Let both sides seek to invoke the wonders of science instead of its terrors. Together let us explore the stars, conquer the deserts, eradicate disease, tap the ocean depths and encourage the arts and commerce.

Let both sides unite to heed in all corners of the earth the command of Isaiah—to "undo the heavy burdens and to let the oppressed go free."

And if a beach-head of cooperation may push back the jungle of suspicion, let both sides join in a new endeavor; not a new balance of power, but a new world of law, where the strong are just and the weak secure and the peace preserved.

All this will not be finished in the first one hundred days. Nor will it be finished in the first one thousand days, nor in the life of this Administration, nor even perhaps in our lifetime on this planet. But let us begin.

In your hands, my fellow citizens, more than mine, will rest the final success or failure of our course. Since this country was founded, each generation of Americans has been summoned to give testimony to its national loyalty. The graves of young Americans who answered the call to service surround the globe.

Now the trumpet summons us again—not as a call to bear arms, though arms we need—not as a call to battle, though embattled we are—but a call to bear the burden of a long twilight struggle, year in and year out, "rejoicing in hope, patient in tribulation"—a struggle against the common enemies of man: tyranny, poverty, disease and war itself.

Can we forge against these enemies a grand and global alliance, North and South, East and West, that can assure a more fruitful life for all mankind? Will you join in that historic effort?

In the long history of the world, only a few generations have been granted the role of defending freedom in its hour of maximum danger. I do not shrink from this responsibility—I welcome it. I do not believe that any of us would exchange places with any other people or any other generation. The energy, the faith, the devotion which we bring to this endeavor will light our country and all who serve it—and the glow from that fire can truly light the world.

And so, my fellow Americans: Ask not what your country can do for you—ask what you can do for your country.

My fellow citizens of the world: Ask not what America will do for you, but what together we can do for the freedom of man.

Finally, whether you are citizens of America or citizens of the world, ask of us here the same high standards of strength and sacrifice which we ask of you. With a good conscience our only sure reward, with history the final judge of our deeds, let us go forth to lead the land we love, asking His blessing and His help, but knowing that here on earth God's work must truly be our own.

10. President Richard M. Nixon resigned his office on August 9, 1974. His resignation was the climax of a long political crisis and took place before the House of Representatives acted on Articles of Impeachment which the Judiciary Committee of the House had recommended to it.

Each of the three Articles below was accompanied by a listing of particular instances which were cited to support the charges in the Articles.

Article I. In his conduct of the office of President of the United States, Richard M. Nixon, in violation of his constitutional oath faithfully to execute the office of President of the United States and, to the best of his ability, preserve, protect, and defend the Constitution of the United States, and in violation of his constitutional duty to take care that the laws be faithfully executed, has prevented, obstructed, and impeded the administration of justice, in that:

On June 17, 1972, and prior thereto, agents of the Committee for the Re-election of the President committed unlawful entry of the headquarters of the Democratic National Committee in Washington, District of Columbia, for the purpose of securing political intelligence. Subsequent thereto, Richard M. Nixon, using the powers of his high office, engaged personally and through his close subordinates and agents, in a course

of conduct or plan designed to delay, impede, and obstruct the investigation of such unlawful entry; to cover up, conceal and protect those responsible; and to conceal the existence and scope of other unlawful covert activities.

Article II. Using the powers of the office of President of the United States, Richard M. Nixon, in violation of his constitutional oath faithfully to execute the office of President of the United States, and to the best of his ability preserve, protect and defend the Constitution of the United States, and in disregard of his constitutional duty to take care that the laws be faithfully executed, has repeatedly engaged in conduct violating the constitutional rights of citizens, impairing the due and proper administration of justice in the conduct of lawful inquiries, and contravening the law governing agencies of the executive branch and the purposes of these agencies.

Article III. In his conduct of the office of President of the United States, Richard M. Nixon . . . has failed without lawful cause or excuse to produce papers and things, as directed by duly authorized subpoenas issued by the Committee on the Judiciary of the House of Representatives on April 11, 1974, May 15, 1974, May 30, 1974 and June 24, 1974 and willfully disobeyed such subpoenas.

The subpoenaed papers and things were deemed necessary by the Committee in order to resolve by direct evidence fundamental factual questions relating to Presidential direction, knowledge or approval of actions demonstrated by other evidence to be substantial grounds for impeachment of the President.

In refusing to produce these papers and things, Richard M. Nixon, substituting his judgment as to what materials were necessary for the inquiry, interposed the powers of the Presidency against the lawful subpoenas of the House of Representatives, thereby assuming for himself functions and judgments necessary to the exercise of the sole power of impeachment vested by the Constitution in the House of Representatives.

In all of this, Richard M. Nixon has acted in a manner contrary to his trust as President and subversive of constitutional government, to the great prejudice of the cause of law and justice, and to the manifest injury of the people of the United States.

Wherefore, Richard M. Nixon, by such conduct, warrants impeachment and trial and removal from office.

8-D DEVELOPMENTS IN AMERICAN SOCIETY

The middle years of the 20th century witnessed many major changes in American life. The period had begun in a depression, with about a third of all American workers unemployed, and with very weak union organizations. By 1973, Americans became extremely concerned if unemployment reached six percent of the work force, and unions had reached a place of prestige, power, and respectability in American society. The proper treatment of racial, religious, or national minorities, meanwhile, had become a critical national question.

PROBLEMS: *What were some of the important changes in American society brought about during this period? What influences led to these changes? In what ways was American society more democratic, or less democratic, in the 1970's than it had been in earlier periods?*

1. The first area in which major changes took place in the 1930's was in the field of labor relations. John L. Lewis, longtime head of the United Mine Workers, was a spokesman in favor of setting up "industrial" unions instead of purely "craft" unions of skilled workers. His speech below was made at the 1935 Convention of the A.F. of L.

Mr. Chairman and delegates of the convention—I rise to support the minority report as presented to this convention by Delegate Howard. I do not speak without some background and some knowledge on this subject acquired in the field of actual experience. I have not gained that knowledge through delving into academic treatises or in sitting in a swivel chair pondering upon the manner in which those upon the firing line should meet their daily problems. I have had perhaps as much experience in organizing workers in the various industries as any member of the Executive Council of the American Federation of Labor or any officer thereof. I served an apprenticeship of five and one-half years as a general organizer for the American Federation of Labor before I became an officer of the United Mine Workers of America. During that period of time I worked in the steel industry, the rubber industry, the glass industry, the lumber industry, the copper industry and other industries in most of the states of this Union.

Then, as now, the American Federation of Labor offered to the workers in these industries a plan of organization into Federal labor unions or local trade unions with the understanding that when organized they would be segregated into the various organizations of their respective crafts. Then, as now, practically every attempt to organize those workers broke upon the same rock that it breaks upon today—the rock of utter futility, the lack of reasonableness in a policy that failed to take into consideration the dreams and requirements of the workers themselves, and failing to take into consideration the recognized power of the adversaries of labor to destroy these feeble organizations in the great modern industries set up in the form of Federal labor unions or craft organizations functioning in a limited sphere.

For twenty-five years or more the American Federation of Labor has been following this precise policy, and surely in the absence of any other understanding of the question, a record of twenty-five years of constant unbroken failure should be convincing to those who actually have a desire to increase the prestige of our great labor movement by expanding its membership to permit it to occupy its natural place in the sun.

What is the record? Delegate Howard expressed it when he said that we laid claim to a membership of approximately three and a half million, out of an organizable number of approximately thirty-nine million. There is the answer. . . .

Those of us who have had experience in these mass production industries are ready to state our professional judgment for what it may be worth and say that it is an absolute fact that America's great modern industries cannot be successfully organized and those organizations maintained against the power of the adversaries of labor in this country under the policy which has been followed for the last quarter of a century in dealing with that subject.

There has been a change in industry, a constant daily change in its processes, a constant change in its employment conditions, a great concentration of opposition to the extension and the logical expansion of the trade union movement. Great combinations of capital have assembled great industrial plants, and they are strung across the borders of our several states from the north to the south and from the east to the west in such a manner that they have assembled to themselves tremendous power and influence, and they are almost 100 per cent effective in opposing organization of the workers under the policies of the American Federation of Labor.

What are we going to do about it? There are some of us who say, let us take council, one with the other, let us put into effect a policy in these certain specified mass production industries that will enable the workers to stand together as a unit against these great commercial units that are exploiting industry at the present time. And the great voice of the workers in those industries, as articulate as their own circumstances will permit, comes to the American Federation of Labor in the form of messages and communications and resolutions to this convention and articles in the press, and in the liberal press, encouraging attention to that

subject. Why do we hesitate? We hesitate, perhaps, because there are men here representing great organizations that have rendered a splendid service to their membership formed, on craft lines, who fear that such a policy would jeopardize the interests of their members and jeopardize the interests of their own positions. Their unions are already jeopardized and their membership is already jeopardized because unless the American Federation of Labor may be successful on organizing these unorganized workers, it is extremely doubtful whether many of these organizations now so perfect, now so efficient, will long be permitted to endure and to function in a manner that is conducive to the well-being of their membership.

There are great influences abroad in the land, and the minds of men in all walks of life are disturbed. We are all disturbed by reason of the changes and the hazards in our economic situation and as regards our own political security. There are forces at work in this country that would wipe out, if they could, the labor movement of America, just as it was wiped out in Germany or just as it was wiped out in Italy.

There are those of us who believe that the best security against that menace and against that trend and against that tendency is a more comprehensive and more powerful labor movement. We believe that the way should be paved so that those millions of workers who are clamoring for admission into our councils might be made welcome upon a basis that they understand and that they believe is suited to their requirements. And in consequence of that we are assembled in this convention with the eyes of these millions of workers upon the convention to decide this momentous question. Methinks that upon this decision of this convention may rest the future of the American Federation of Labor, because, upon this decision will rest the question of whether the American Federation of Labor may be forged into an instrumentality that will render service to all of the workers or whether the American Federation of Labor and its leaders will rest content in that comfortable situation that has prevailed through the years, where they are only required to render service to a paltry three or four or five million of the forty odd million wage workers of this country who, after all, want to be union men. . . .

2. *By the start of the 1940's, labor had become well enough recognized for major leaders to appear as spokesmen before Congress. The whole idea of "collective bargaining" was still in doubt, however, when Philip Murray appeared before a Senate committee to present this argument.*

I WELCOME THE OPPORTUNITY to appear before the honorable committee on behalf of the Steel Workers Organizing Committee, as its chairman, to present the point of view of my organization on the proposed amendments to the National Labor Relations Act, which are now pending before the Congress.

In presenting this point of view I do not propose to deal with the conflicting legal and technical points involved in this controversy. Instead I wish to take the honorable members of this committee, in the course of my discussion, behind the stage of collective bargaining in the great iron and steel industry. I want to show you the inside workings of collective bargaining in the industry. As a participant in the development of employee-employer relations on a democratic basis during the past few crucial years, I have a human story to relate about the steel industry. It is the story of management and workers adjusting themselves to new kinds of relationships, orienting themselves in their everyday economic activities to the democratic ways of our political life, and resolving their differences around the conference table.

My story is a personal one, a human drama. It has been the good fortune of living generations to witness the start of a new cycle in worker-management relations in the basic steel-producing industry. From the historic, and bloody, Homestead, Pa., strike of 1892 until the equally historic, but peaceful, signing of the March 1937 collective-bargaining contract between the Steel Workers Organizing Committee (SWOC) and the United States Steel Corporation and subsidiaries, a period of forty-five years, one single policy governed the relations between steelworkers and their employers. That policy was, as steel employers put it: "We will deal with our employees as individuals only, and refuse to recognize or deal with them as an organized group or trade union."

That policy was undemocratic, inhuman, and contravened the fundamental tenets of the federal Constitution. It was undemocratic because it denied the steelworkers their rights of free association for their mutual protection. It was inhuman because it pitted the overpowering corporate wealth of giant industrialists against the puny strength of a single, individual workingman. It violated the federal Constitution because it forbade the individual worker to join hands with his fellow workers so that together, as an organized trade union, their power might begin to equal that of the huge corporation which gave them employment. That policy was enforced by coal and iron police, labor spies, tear and sickening gas, and other reprehensible means that mark the history of the 1901 and 1909 strikes against United States Steel, the 1910 strike against

Bethlehem Steel, the 1917 strike against Youngstown Steel, the 1919 strike against the entire industry, and the 1933 strike against the Weirton Steel Co.

The cycle of industrial relations, which ran from 1892 to 1937, was marked by recurrent warfare between steel employers and their workers, who periodically strove to end the cycle. They strove, at great sacrifice and the loss of many lives, to start a new cycle of industrial relations. Not until 1937 were the steelworkers successful in their trying efforts. In the spring of that year the basic steel-producing industry embarked upon a new cycle of industrial relations which was based on the fundamental democratic principles, as stated by Mr. Myron C. Taylor, then chairman of the board of the United States Steel Corporation, to wit:

> The company recognizes the right of its employees to bargain collectively through representatives freely chosen by them. . . . It will negotiate and contract with the representatives of any group of its employees so chosen and with any organization as the representatives of its members. . . .

Three-fourths of the steel industry followed the lead of United States Steel. My story is concerned primarily with the peaceful development of collective bargaining during the past two years, which represent the first two years of a new cycle of industrial relations for the steel industry, except for a minority segment of the industry which has tried, in vain, to prolong the cycle of industrial relations which started in 1892 and ended in 1937.

This new cycle of industrial relations, based on the fundamental principles of a political democracy, has been encouraged and guided by the industrial-relations policy of the federal government. This policy has been to encourage industry to operate its plants on the same democratic basis that our federal, state, and local governments operate, namely, that:

(a) Workers may associate themselves together into a group or trade union for their mutual protection.

(b) Workers may select representatives of their own choosing to advance their mutual interests; and

(c) Workers may enjoy these rights without interference from their employers, and the federal government, as it protects the other rights of its citizens, will protect these rights of the workers with its power.

This policy of the federal government has been administered by the National Labor Relations Board since July 5, 1935, although the administration of this policy was delayed and impeded by the gratuitous opinions of self-appointed kangaroo courts, until the Supreme Court of the United States validated the National Labor Relations Act on April 12, 1937, twenty-one months later.

The major experience of the SWOC with the National Labor Relations Board has been either as an alternative to the stoppage of work or as a means to facilitate the settlement of an industrial dispute already in progress. One of the chief functions of the board is to administer in industry the democratic principle of majority rule. Prior to the creation of the board, workers were forced to engage in a strike through their trade union to prove to their employer that a majority of his workers belonged to the union. There was no other way of establishing their majority claims. There were no elections, since no impartial board existed to conduct them. The union's majority could not be established by comparing its membership cards with the company's payroll because the union justly feared its members would be fired and blacklisted if their names were divulged to the company. Under these conditions, in pre-board days, the only way left open to establish its majority for a group of workers, who had managed to organize into a trade union despite the belligerent opposition of their employer, was to go on strike. When the employer challenged the majority claims of a union, its leaders could only say: "If you doubt our majority, then we will have to show you it on the picket line." The consequence, as a rule, was costly warfare, bloodshed, the loss of lives, and other irreparable losses.

To illustrate how the National Labor Relations Board has actually rendered invaluable public service when the question of majority rule has been the chief point of controversy. I shall recite our experiences with the Jones & Laughlin Steel Corporation. I want to take the honorable members of this committee in my discussion to a point twenty miles below Pittsburgh on the Ohio River to the steel town of Aliquippa, Pa. Approximately 13,000 steelworkers are employed in the huge works of Jones & Laughlin, which stretch for more than four miles along the Ohio River in Aliquippa. When the Aliquippa steelworkers attempted to organize a trade union in 1933, ten of their leaders were discharged. It was their case which was settled by the United States Supreme Court in April of 1937. A long history of antiunionism is the story of Aliquippa prior to 1937. I shall not take the time of this committee to tell this story, although it has a vital bearing on the problems this committee is considering, but I am appending a brief history of Aliquippa to my statement, and I commend it to the honorable members of this committee for their careful study. My present purpose is to tell the story of Aliquippa since 1937.

By May 1937 a distinct majority of Aliquippa's steelworkers had become members of the SWOC. In addition, a majority of the Jones & Laughlin Steel Corporation's 12,000-odd employees in its Pittsburgh Works had also become members of the SWOC. On behalf of these members the SWOC requested a conference with the corporation's officials early in May. The United States Steel Corporation had already recognized SWOC and signed a collective-bargaining contract with it. The same form of recognition was requested from Jones & Laughlin, which rushed plans to convert its company union, or employee representative plan, into a so-called independent union to compete with the SWOC. This brought negotiations to a head, and in self-defense the Jones & Laughlin workers went on strike.

The strike, at once, was successful; in fact, it was 100 percent. When the Jones & Laughlin officials saw their works completely closed down for the first time in their history, they reentered negotiations with the SWOC. The corporation officials told me and my associates that they would sign a contract similar to the one between the SWOC and U.S. Steel, provided we could show that a majority of Jones & Laughlin's workers were SWOC members. Unlike the case of Judge Elbert Gary in 1919, these Jones & Laughlin officials were sincere. The real question in dispute was not the right of the union to exist, as was the case in 1919, but merely whether the union actually represented a majority of the workers.

Happily for the workers and the corporation, the National Labor Relations Board was in existence. Because of the existence of the board, the Jones & Laughlin strike was one of the shortest on record, involving approximately 25,000 workers. It lasted just thirty-six hours.

In the past there would have been no other way out than a long-draw-out battle, but here under the Wagner Act there was a definite, sane, constitutional, and democratic way of settling our differences. The company said we did not really represent its men. SWOC insisted that it did. The obvious way to settle it, therefore, was to hold an election.

The National Labor Relations Board provided the machinery for this, and the strike was settled with an agreement that the terms of the U.S. Steel contract would be in effect until an election was held by the National Labor Relations Board within ten days to determine whether or not the Steel Workers Organizing Committee represented a majority of the Jones & Laughlin employees. The result was a smashing victory —17,208 for the union and 7,207 against the union.

The Jones & Laughlin Steel Corporation thereupon signed a collective-bargaining contract with the SWOC, recognizing it as the sole bargaining agency for all of its production and maintenance workers. This contract was the beginning of the extension of democratic principles and procedures into the operation of the Jones & Laughlin works. Twenty-five thousand workers who had been governed for years by the dictatorial rules that management arbitrarily promulgated elected their own representatives. These representatives sat around the conference table with management and negotiated fair, democratic rules to govern the operations of the Jones & Laughlin mills. Here was an overt experiment in democratic ways. I am happy to report to this committee, as a firm believer in democratic principles, that this experiment in industrial democracy has been altogether successful. . . .

Today, employers no longer publicly state that they will only deal with their workers as individuals. All employers, from enlightened ones down to Tom Girdler, publicly proclaim their belief in collective bargaining and the free right of their workers to organize into unions of their own choosing. The actual practices of some employers, however, have been much at variance with these public statements. While, on the one hand, they publicly recognize the right of their workers to organize freely, on the other hand, they secretly strove to control the organization of their workers by creating company unions. Beginning with the NIRA in 1933 and continuing through 1936, American industry saw the mushroom growth of company unions. They seemed to grow up from almost nowhere, although with just enough exceptions to prove the rule they were hatched in the offices of corporation attorneys. . . .

Meanwhile, the Steel Workers Organizing Committee had grown in industry-wide proportions. It was obvious that a majority of the steel workers in the United States had joined the union and that they wished to be represented by it. On March 2, 1937, Carnegie-Illinois Steel Corporation, largest subsidiary of the United States Steel Corporation, signed a preliminary recognition contract with the Steel Workers Organizing Committee. Two weeks later this contract was expanded into a formal contract embodying definite terms and conditions of employment for a specific period of time.

This Carnegie-Illinois-U.S. Steel contract served as a standard for the entire industry. It provided for recognition of the Steel Workers Organizing Committee as bargaining agent for its members; it raised wages 10 cents an hour over and above a 10 percent wage raise of five months previous and established an eight-hour day, forty-hour week with time and one-half for overtime; it granted vacations with pay; it introduced seniority rights in layoffs and recall; it set up a democratic machinery for the adjustment of grievances, with arbitration as the final step; it outlawed strikes and lockouts during the term of the contract; it reaffirmed the basic rights of ownership to management; it made

safety and health a matter of joint company-union concern; it enumerated holidays; it set a date at which joint conferences for renewal were to take place; and, lastly, defined the terms of the contract.

Shortly thereafter the other U.S. Steel units signed identical contracts with the Steel Workers Organizing Committee. This is the first time United States Steel Corporation was under contract for all its producing subsidiaries at the same time and with the same union. Various steel plants of the company had had labor contracts before but those had been inherited and were discarded as soon as possible.

On April 26, 1937, the Carnegie-Illinois Steel Corporation, through its counsel, appeared before the National Labor Relations Board and made a statement for the record with reference to the proceedings based on charges of company violation of the Wagner Act. The corporation stated that it would not interfere with the employees' rights under the act; that it would not dominate or interfere with the formation or administration of any labor organization, or contribute financial or other support to it; that it would not contribute any support to or participate in and would withdraw all recognition from and would completely disestablish its relations with the existing plans of employee representation; and that a copy of the statement would be posted on all bulletin boards of its plants. On the same day President B. F. Fairless of the Carnegie-Illinois Steel Corporation announced the corporation's new policy to its employees. It should be noted that this company-dominated employee representative plan was inaugurated in 1933, two years before the passage of the Wagner Act. Thus ended U.S. Steel's venture into organizing unions. It washed its hands of company unions and adopted a policy of bargaining collectively with a bona fide trade union democratically controlled by U.S. Steel workers. . . .

This collective-bargaining development is unparalleled in American industrial and labor history. A great change has taken place in management's attitude toward its workers. In view of the fact that the character of industrial relations, by and large, is determined by the attitude of management, this new and changed attitude is a healthy sign. It is a bulwark to our democratic form of government. I am happy to report that not a single company that embarked upon contractual relations with the SWOC beginning in 1937 has severed relations with SWOC. Every single firm has renewed its collective-bargaining contract with SWOC, and others have since signed SWOC contracts. The part the industrial-relations policy of the federal government, as administered by the National Labor Relations Board, played in this development, and continues to play in it, is indeterminable. But to the credit and glory of our political democracy, it has been substantial, and rightly so.

Up to the present date, three-fourths of the steel industry has followed the lead of U.S. Steel and embarked upon a new cycle of industrial relations. Unfortunately, a minority of the basic steel industry took a different course in 1937. The so-called Little Steel firms attempted, in vain, to prolong the cycle of industrial relations which began with the bloody Homestead strike of 1892. In their futile attempt to stop the development of collective bargaining in the steel industry which has since taken place, the Little Steel firms designed and provoked a bloody strike more murderous than the Homestead strike in 1892.

The strike took place in the summer of 1937. Its leader was Tom Girdler. In contrast to the Jones & Laughlin Steel Corporation situation, the National Labor Relations Board was powerless to render any service. The question in dispute was not whether SWOC represented a majority of the workers involved, as in the Jones & Laughlin case. Instead the issue was the same as in the 1919 steel strike, namely, does the union, in this instance the SWOC, have a right to exist. Tom Girdler provoked the Little Steel strike for the sole purpose of maintaining his unfair advantage over his workers. Backed by huge financial and industrial interests, Tom Girdler was able to beat down any single individual worker his management employed. Tom Girdler opposed the organization of his workers because he knew that as an organized trade union his workers could meet him on equal grounds. . . .

The number of companies under contract with us has now reached 638. . . . These contracts are for the most part patterned after the standard U.S. Steel agreement. Variations and allowances are made for peculiar industrial and special local conditions. Quite frequently, certification by the NLRB is embodied in the recognition clause which has accordingly been expanded from limitation for members only to sole bargaining rights. Generally, one contract covers all the production and maintenance workers at all the plants of a particular company. However, there are some instances where separate agreements are entered into for each plant.

The members of the Steel Workers Organizing Committee are organized into 1,100 lodges, or local unions, on the basis of 1 for each plant. Thus there may be a number of local unions for a single company. These lodges have elected over 10,000 officers and grievance committeemen, each of whom is an employee of the respective company or plant, and therefore a fellow worker of the persons who elected him. Here is industrial democracy patterned after our old New En-

gland town meetings, for the general body of workers convene regularly, usually once a month, to discuss and decide upon the policies their officers are to pursue.

Steelworkers are now more than employees. They are citizens of the steel industry. They have just as strong an interest in its welfare as management. And through the Steel Workers Organizing Committee they are taking part in its development and improvement. They are making a real contribution. In 1938 the SWOC issued a handbook, a copy of which I should like inserted in the record, entitled *Production Problems*. This handbook sets forth a joint program for management and men to improve productive efficiency and thereby enlarge their participation in the national income.

I want to bring the first part of my discussion to a close by observing that a new cycle of industrial relations is now in its fourth year for a majority of the basic steel-producing industry. Despite the ill-advised and futile efforts of Tom Girdler and the misguided steep employers that followed his lead, a majority of the steelworkers and steel employers of this country now determine their relationships by democratic means. Whether this economic and industrial development of democracy shall continue in the steel industry, or whether the industry shall revert to the chaotic and barbarous ways Tom Girdler is trying to perpetuate will be determined, in large measure, by the action of the federal Congress. The SWOC is doing its part to bolster democracy in America, and most certainly the Congress should not do anything to frustrate this development or encourage the decaying seeds of the old autocracy now represented by Tom Girdler.

3. The years of World War II revolutionized the working force of the country in several respects. For example, many workers learned that it was convenient and reasonable to move long distances from their original homes to seek and hold jobs. For another, the laboring force was greatly expanded by the introduction of large numbers of woman workers. The following comments are from a report in the Bulletin of the Women's Bureau (Washington, 1944).

Recent and Unprecedented Employment of Women

Just a little over two years ago the subject and purpose of this bulletin would have been considered as fanciful as a tale from the Arabian Nights. That American women should take active part in the man's job of building and repairing ships was almost inconceivable. As recently as July 1941 an outstanding periodical made sport of the extreme anti-feminine attitude of what is now one of the most publicized woman-employing ship building and repair corporations in the country. At that time, nearly 2 years after war began in Europe and but 5 months before Pearl Harbor, women were not accepted by the firm even as office secretaries and the lone women telephone operators were, as it was facetiously reported, "kept under lock and key."

Times have changed with lightning speed. By late 1943, thousands of women along both coasts and on the Gulf, Great Lakes, and inland waterways were actively engaged in almost every phase of ship building and repair work, and it is anticipated that it will be necessary to recruit thousands more before the war is over. Though the introduction of women into the shipyards did not begin in earnest until the fall of 1942, by January 1943 as many as 4 per cent of all the production wage earners in the industry were women. The proportion had risen to a little over 5 per cent by March, and by September to 9.5 per cent. In January 1944 it was 10 per cent. These figures include the 8 navy yards engaged in ship construction and repair, in which women have made extensive gains and comprised in September nearly one-fourth of the women wage earners in the industry.

Many Adjustments Required in an Expanding Industry

The unprecedented influx of women into the shipyards has been the inevitable accompaniment of this country's tremendous war shipbuilding program, for which it has been necessary to recruit hundreds of thousands of additional workers since Pearl Harbor. The first 17 months of wartime production witnessed an increase of 189 per cent in shipyard personnel. Old-established yards employing from 3,000 to 10,000 workers in 1939 and 1940 had 5 to nearly 8 times that many late in 1943, and there are some shipyards for which ground had not even been broken in 1940 that employed 20,000 to 40,000 workers in the spring of 1943 when the peak had not yet been reached. Expansion on so gigantic a scale in competition with other war industries and Selective Service brought shipbuilders face to face with the necessity of employing women to help to produce the enormous tonnage so urgently needed.

Such rapid development alone carries with it innumerable problems of administration and plant adjustment, but coupled with the necessity for drawing on a labor element never before tried in the industry, the problems became extremely numerous and complex. Organized training programs had to be set up within the shipyards to provide instruction for the thousands of workers, men as well as women, who had never held tools before, much less seen a ship under construction. Special training was necessary for the supervisors who had never had so many workers under them, many having themselves only recently been promoted from the ranks. Rapid upgrading of men into the skilled and leadership jobs became a practical necessity for the most economical utilization of labor. As the nucleus of skilled and experienced workers has become dispersed and proportionately smaller, the training structure has grown in size and importance. In many yards now the training director helps to control the rate of accession and allocation of the labor force.

Personnel, medical, and safety programs have had to be enlarged and modified to accommodate the mass hiring, placement, and protection of inexperienced workers. Effective selection of thousands of employees in short periods of time has required careful study of procedures and change in methods and policies. Alarming turn-over and labor scarcity have resulted in the introduction in many places of transfer bureaus and exit interviewing.

If the administrative offices have been affected by the magnitude of the war shipbuilding program, those planning and supervising the actual work have had to make even more fundamental and drastic adjustments. Under normal circumstances, ship construction is custom work; each vessel, whether a "sister ship" or one of a kind, differs from every other in detail if not design and requires a complete set of templates of its own. Now, however, hundreds of ships of the same kind, particularly cargo vessels, are being made with standardized materials according to a single pattern. Consequently, mass-production techniques involving assembly-line and prefabrication methods have been sought and developed. Even in the case of the many ships that still are built to individual plan, the work has been broken down to meet the dearth of all-round craftsmen, thus allowing introduction and training of specialists to perform one part of a process, operate one machine, or concern themselves with but one section of the ship. Making all this more possible, the speedier and easier assembly technique of welding has almost replaced riveting wherever feasible and hand welding and burning are giving way to machine methods in some yards and on larger jobs. Automatic assembly fasteners are being used here and there instead of track welding.

Such examples of the effect on the industry of the tremendously accelerated shipbuilding program could be multiplied. In their broader aspects most of the changes are similar to those made in other industries under like pressure. Many have eased the way for the employment of women, especially those changes developed to meet the need for training and employing inexperienced men in great numbers and for building many ships of the same design. Others, however, have been required only because women were employed.

Lack of Preparation for Women's Employment

But the need to draw from the woman labor force often was not realized and accepted till the very last moment, leaving little time for study and planning. In many cases the management plunged headlong even before essential and obvious provision had been made to accommodate the newcomers. This was not surprising in view of acute manpower shortages in shipbuilding areas, yet it was nothing less than daring in an industry so bound in the tradition of dirt, sweat, and rough and tumble, so thoroughly male that any woman who ventured into a yard was greeted with hooting and whistling. The physical and administrative adaptations that should be introduced to insure women's efficient performance and necessary comfort on the job frequently are as nothing compared with the mental hurdles that must be overcome. Problems that are brought to the attention of those interested in women's success often stem as much from attitudes toward women workers in the man's world of shipbuilding as from the actual situation. Yet women frequently were taken on before the human or psychological adaptations necessary to avoid confusion, discontent, and waste, much less the physical and sometimes administrative changes necessary, had been attempted.

When field representatives of the Women's Bureau made visits to 41 shipyards between the beginning and the early fall of 1943, few yards had employed women for as long as a year; many had begun hiring women to do production work only a few months before; 6 had not yet hired any women for production work. Though the yards with women workers still were feeling their way, over half already were employing hundreds of women, some of them thousands, and in many cases expecting to hire hundreds or thousands more. While building more ships than ever before and servicing the Fleet, not a few were functioning under inadequate arrangements, hoping gradually to arrive at a satisfactory solution of their personnel problems with women. To be sure, some had already made excellent progress. Most had forged ahead in at least some phases, such as securing good safety observance, satisfactory rest- and wash-room facilities, and productively efficient distribution of the women on jobs; others were struggling with these aspects of the situation but had mastered other aspects. Many, aware of

inadequacies, sought advice. Women's Bureau field representatives were asked in several of the yards visited to submit formal recommendations based on analysis and study of individual yard conditions and problems.

It is clear, then, that the shipyards are charting new seas in the utilization of the woman labor force, and the mistakes or successes that result many have a profound effect not only on the production and repair of ships, but on the cost and efficiency of such production and the health, work, and life histories of thousands of women. It is important to take stock now. Misconceptions should be dispelled, well-founded facts pooled, and the fund of information available from industries with longer histories in the employment of women disseminated. It is with these objects in view that the present report is submitted. It is the aim of the Women's Buerau through the recommendations and suggestions made here to promote conditions for the woman shipyard worker conducive to her most efficient and productive employment and her well-being as a member of society and the labor force. . . .

1. Secure the cooperation of men supervisors and workers.
2. Select and place women carefully.
3. Employ women only in jobs found to be suitable.
4. Pay women and upgrade them on the same basis as men.
5. Schedule an 8-hour day and a 48-hour 6-day week; allow a lunch period of at least 30 minutes, and rest periods of 10 to 15 minutes in each work spell of as much as 4 hours. Rotate shifts no more frequently than every two months.
6. Set up an effective woman employee counselor system.
7. Give new women workers preliminary induction into the work and environment of the shipyard before putting them on the job.
8. Provide personal-service, food, and medical facilities that meet approved standards of adequacy and quality.
9. Study and expand the safety program to adapt it to women workers, and instruct women thoroughly in safe work practice.

4.   In the years following World War II, a number of employment problems faced American industry and labor. Competition with foreign countries forced some industries to shift their product lines completely, and encouraged others to "automate". Automation, with its possibilities for greatly increased production, carried with it a threat of reduced job opportunities. Walter Reuther, another major American labor leader, presented these ideas to Congress in 1955.

We have been told so often that automation is going to bring on the second industrial revolution that there is, perhaps, a danger we may dismiss the warning as a catch-phrase, and lose sight of the fact that, not only the technique, but the philosophy of automation is revolutionary, in the truest sense of the word. Automation does not only produce changes in the methods of manufacturing, distribution, many clerical operations, and in the structure of business organization, but the impact of those changes on our economy and our whole society bids fair to prove quite as revolutionary as were those of the first industrial revolution.

Through the application of mechanical power to machinery, and the development of new machinery to use this power, the first industrial revolution made possible a vast increase in the volume of goods produced for each man-hour of work. Succeeding technological improvements—such as the development of interchangeable parts and the creation of the assembly line which were essential to the growth of mass production industries—have led to continuous increases in labor productivity. But however much these machines were improved, they still required workers to operate and control them. In some operations, the worker's function was little more than to feed the material in, set the machine in operation and remove the finished product. In others, proper control of the machine required the exercise of the highest conceivable skills. But whether the required skill was little or great, the presence of a human being, using human judgment, was essential to the operation of the machine.

The revolutionary change produced by automation is its tendency to displace the worker entirely from the direct operation of the machine, through the use of automatic control devices. No one, as far as I know, has yet produced a fully satisfactory definition of automation, but I think John Diebold came close to expressing its essential quality when he described automation as "the integration of machines with each other into fully automatic, and, in some cases, self-regulating systems. . . ."

The revolutionary implications of this new technology can best be understood by looking at a few examples of what is actually being done through automation today, in scattered parts of the economy.

The application of automation ranges all the way from individual automatic machines to virtually automatic factories.

An example of the first is an automatic lathe, produced by the Sundstrand Machine Tool Co., described in *American Machinist*, March 14, 1955, page 117, which gages each part as it is produced and automatically resets the cutting tools to compensate for tool wear. In addition, when the cutting tools have been worn down to a certain predetermined limit, the machine automatically replaces them with sharp tools. The parts are automatically loaded onto the machine and are automatically unloaded as they are finished. These lathes can be operated for 5 to 8 hours without attention, except for an occasional check to make sure that parts are being delivered to the loading mechanism.

A completely automatic plant is now producing mixed and ready-to-use concrete for the Cleveland Builders Supply Co. (*Business Week*, Apr. 16, 1955, p. 80). Operated from an electronic control panel, the plant can produce and load into ready-mix trucks any one of some 1,500 different mixing formulas that may be demanded. This plant uses no manual labor at any point in the process.

By a combination of teletype and radio, the control operator is informed as to the particular formula to be loaded into each truck as it arrives. He gets out a punched card, coded for that formula, and the automatic mechanisms take over. Specified amounts of the required materials are delivered by conveyors, in precisely the right quantities, to a mixing bin where they are automatically mixed and then loaded into the waiting truck. The control mechanisms even measure and compensate for any deficiency or excess of water in the aggregate (sand, coarse rock, slag, etc.) which goes into the mixer, and if the order calls for a dry mix, the materials are automatically routed through a dry spout.

This automatic plant has a capacity of 200 cubic yards of concrete per hour, as against 100 cubic yards per hour in the company's conventional plants. . . .

One of the factors which has been responsible for the steadily increasing rate of productivity since World War II has been the enormous increase in research expenditures both by industry and by Government. Alfred North Whitehead, the British philosopher, once said, "The greatest invention of the 19th century was the invention of the art of inventing." We might add that one of the great developments of the 20th century has been to change inventing from an art to a standard business procedure. The research department is now a fixture in every important corporation, while the needs of government, especially in national defense, have added to the numbers of research workers, many of whose discoveries are readily applied to industry.

As a result, the flow of what may be considered routine technological innovations—new production methods, new materials and machines applicable only to specific processes or industries, and improvements in work flow—has been greatly accelerated. Harlow Curtice, president of General Motors, noted recently that "new products, new processes are coming off the drawing boards of the engineers and out of the laboratories of the scientists at ever faster pace."

This great expansion of industrial research, and the flood of routine technological innovations it produces, have been sufficient, alone, in recent years, to boost the rate of rising productivity to the extent that past notions of what were normal productivity increases are already obsolete. Technological improvements of this sort, and on an increasing scale, can be expected to continue. By themselves, they would pose serious problems of adjusting our economy so as to provide sufficient purchasing power to absorb the steadily accelerating flow of goods which can be produced with every man-hour of labor. . . .

What is the attitude of the trade-union movement, and specifically of the CIO, to this new technology of automation?

First of all, we fully realize that the potential benefits of automation are great, if properly handled. If only a fraction of what technologists promise for the future is true, within a very few years automation can and should make possible a 4-day workweek, longer vacation periods, opportunities for earlier retirement, as well as a vast increase in our material standards of living.

At the same time, automation can bring freedom from the monotonous drudgery of many jobs in which the worker today is no more than a servant of the machine. It can free workers from routine, repetitious tasks which the new machines can be taught to do, and can give to the workers who toil at those tasks the opportunity of developing higher skills.

But in looking ahead to the many benefits which automation can produce, we must not overlook or minimize the many problems which will inevitably arise in making the adjustment to the new technology— problems for individual workers and individual companies, problems for entire communities and regions, problems for the economy as a whole.

What should be done to help the worker who will be displaced from his job, or the worker who will find that his highly specialized skill has been taken over by a machine? What about the businessman who lacks sufficient capital to automate his plant, yet has to face the competition of firms whose resources enable them to build whole new automatic factories? Will automation mean the creation of whole new communities in some areas, while others are turned into ghost towns? How can we increase the market for goods and services sufficiently, and quickly enough, to match greatly accelerated increases in productivity?

Finding the answers to these questions, and many others like them, will not be an easy process, and certainly not an automatic one. Even if the greatest care is taken to foresee and meet these problems, adjustments for many people will prove difficult and even painful. If there is no care and no foresight, if we subscribe to the laissez-faire belief that "these things will work themselves out," untold harm can be done to millions of innocent people and to the whole structure of our economy and our free society.

The CIO insists that we must recognize these problems and face up to them. But our recognition that there will be problems, and serious problems, to be solved, does not mean that we are opposed to automation. We are not. We fully recognize the desirability, as well as the inevitability of technological progress. But we oppose those who would introduce automation blindly and irresponsibly, with no concern for any result except the achievement of the largest possible quick profit for themselves.

5. The question of equal access to public facilities remained an open one until the middle 1950's. Then a series of law cases reached the United States Supreme Court; in these cases, the question was raised whether it was constitutional to bar Americans from public schools, parks, or other facilities on the basis of race. Earlier Supreme Court decisions, since the Plessy v. Ferguson *case of 1896, had permitted such action if other "separate but equal" facilities were available. The first key case in the civil rights cases of the 1950's was* Brown v. Board of Education of Topeka.

As in many other Supreme Court hearings, Brown v. Topeka *was combined with several similar cases in other states; the Supreme Court reviewed and decided the group of cases at one time.*

THESE cases come to us from the States of Kansas, South Carolina, Virginia, and Delaware. They are premised on different facts and different local conditions, but a common legal question justifies their consideration together in this consolidated opinion.

In each of the cases, minors of the Negro race, through their legal representatives, seek the aid of the courts in obtaining admission to the public schools of their community on a nonsegregated basis. In each instance, they had been denied admission to schools attended by white children under laws requiring or permitting segregation according to race. This segregation was alleged to deprive the plaintiffs of the equal protection of the laws under the Fourteenth Amendment. In each of the cases other than the Delaware case, a three-judge federal district court denied relief to the plaintiffs on the so-called "separate but equal" doctrine announced by this Court in *Plessy* v. *Ferguson*, 163 U.S. 537. 16 S. Ct. 1138, 41 L. Ed. 256. Under that doctrine, equality of treatment is accorded when the races are provided substantially equal facilities, even though these facilities be separate. In the Delaware case, the Supreme Court of Delaware adhered to that doctrine, but ordered that the plaintiffs be admitted to the white schools because of their superiority to the Negro schools.

The plaintiffs contend that segregated public schools are not "equal" and cannot be made "equal," and that hence they are deprived of the equal protection of the laws. Because of the obvious importance of the question presented, the Court took jurisdiction. Argument was heard in the 1952 Term, and reargument was heard this Term on certain questions propounded by the Court.

Reargument was largely devoted to the circumstances surrounding the adoption of the Fourteenth Amendment in 1868. It covered exhaustively consideration of the Amendment in Congress, ratification by the states, then existing practices in racial segregation, and the views of proponents and opponents of the Amendment. This discussion and our own investigation convince us that, although these sources cast some light, it is not enough to resolve the problem with which we are faced. At best, they are inconclusive. The most avid proponents of the post-War Amendments undoubtedly intended them to remove all legal distinctions among "all persons born or naturalized in the United States." Their opponents, just as certainly, were antagonistic to both the letter and the spirit of the Amendments and wished them to have the most limited effect. What others in Congress and the state legislatures had in mind cannot be determined with any degree of certainty.

An additional reason for the inconclusive nature of the Amendment's history, with respect to segregated schools, is the status of public education at that time. In the South, the movement toward free common schools, supported by general taxation, had not yet taken hold. Education of white children was largely in the hands of private groups. Education of Negroes was almost non-existent, and practically all of the race were illiterate. In fact, any education of Negroes was forbidden by law in some states. Today, in contrast, many Negroes have achieved outstanding success in the arts and sciences as well as in the business and professional world. It is true that public school education at the time of the Amendment had advanced further in the North, but the effect of the Amendment on Northern States was generally ignored in the con-

gressional debates. Even in the North, the conditions of public education did not approximate those existing today. The curriculum was usually rudimentary; ungraded schools were common in rural areas; the school term was but three months a year in many states; and compulsory school attendance was virtually unknown. As a consequence, it is not surprising that there should be so little in the history of the Fourteenth Amendment relating to its intended effect on public education.

In the first cases in this Court construing the Fourteenth Amendment, decided shortly after its adoption, the Court interpreted it as proscribing all state-imposed discriminations against the Negro race. The doctrine of "separate but equal" did not make its appearance in this Court until 1896 in the case of *Plessy* v. *Ferguson supra*, involving not education but transportation. American courts have since labored with the doctrine for over half a century. In this Court, there have been six cases involving the "separate but equal" doctrine in the field of public education. In *Cumming* v. *Board of Education of Richmond County*, 175 U.S. 528, and *Gong Lum* v. *Rice*, 275 U.S. 78, the validity of the doctrine itself was not challenged. In more recent cases, all on the graduate school level, inequality was found in that specific benefits enjoyed by white students were denied to Negro students of the same educational qualifications. *Missouri ex rel. Gaines* v. *Canada*, 305 U.S. 337; *Sipuel* v. *Board of Regents of University of Oklahoma*, 332 U.S. 631; *Sweatt* v. *Painter*, 339 U.S. 629; *McLaurin* v. *Oklahoma State Regents*, 339 U.S. 637. In none of these cases was it necessary to re-examine the doctrine to grant relief to the Negro plaintiff. And in *Sweatt* v. *Painter, supra*, the Court expressly reserved decision on the question whether *Plessy* v. *Ferguson* should be held inapplicable to public education.

In the instant cases, that question is directly presented. Here, unlike *Sweatt* v. *Painter*, there are findings below that the Negro and white schools involved have been equalized, or are being equalized, with respect to buildings, curricula, qualifications and salaries of teachers, and other "tangible" factors. Our decision, therefore, cannot turn on merely a comparison of these tangible factors in the Negro and white schools involved in each of the cases. We must look instead to the effect of segregation itself on public education.

In approaching this problem, we cannot turn the clock back to 1868 when the Amendment was adopted, or even to 1896 when *Plessy* v. *Ferguson* was written. We must consider public education in the light of its full development and its present place in American life throughout the Nation. Only in this way can it be determined if segregation in public schools deprives these plaintiffs of the equal protection of the laws.

Today, education is perhaps the most important function of state and local governments. Compulsory school attendance laws and the great expenditures for education both demonstrate our recognition of the importance of education to our democratic society. It is required in the performance of our most basic public responsibilities, even service in the armed forces. It is the very foundation of good citizenship. Today it is a principal instrument in awakening the child to cultural values, in preparing him for later professional training and in helping him to adjust normally to his environment. In these days, it is doubtful that any child may reasonably be expected to succeed in life if he is denied the opportunity of an education. Such an opportunity, where the state has undertaken to provide it, is a right which must be made available to all on equal terms.

We come then to the question presented: Does segregation of children in public schools solely on the basis of race, even though the physical facilities and other "tangible" factors may be equal, deprive the children of the minority group of equal educational opportunities? We believe that it does.

In *Sweatt* v. *Painter, supra,* in finding that a segregated law school for Negroes could not provide them equal educational opportunities, this Court relied in large part on "those qualities which are incapable of objective measurement but which make for greatness in a law school." In *McLaurin* v. *Oklahoma State Regents, supra,* the Court, in requiring that a Negro admitted to a white graduate school be treated like all other students, again resorted to intangible considerations: ". . . his ability to study, to engage in discussions and exchange views with other students, and, in general, to learn his profession." Such considerations apply with added force to children in grade and high schools. To separate them from others of similar age and qualifications solely because of their race generates a feeling of inferiority as to their status in the community that may affect their hearts and minds in a way unlikely ever to be undone. The effect of this separation on their educational opportunities was well stated by a finding in the Kansas case by a court which nevertheless felt compelled to rule against the Negro plantiffs:

> Segregation of white and colored children in public schools has a detrimental effect upon the colored children. The impact is greater when it has the sanction of the law; for the policy of separating the races is usually interpreted as denoting the inferiority of the negro group. A sense of inferiority affects the motivation of a child to learn. Segregation with the sanction of law, therefore, has a tendency to [retard] the educational and mental development of negro children and to deprive them of some of the benefits they would receive in a racial[ly] integrated school system.

Whatever may have been the extent of psychological knowledge at the time of *Plessy* v. *Ferguson,* this finding is amply supported by modern authority. Any language in *Plessy* v. *Ferguson* contrary to this finding is rejected.

We conclude that in the field of public education the doctrine of "separate but equal" has no place. Separate educational facilities are inherently unequal. Therefore, we hold that the plaintiffs and others similarly situated for whom the actions have been brought are, by reason of the segregation complained of, deprived of the equal protection of the laws guaranteed by the Fourteenth Amendment. This disposition makes unnecessary any discussion whether such segregation also violates the Due Process Clause of the Fourteenth Amendment.

Because these are class actions, because of the wide applicability of this decision, and because of the great variety of local conditions, the formulation of decree in these cases presents problems of considerable complexity. On reargument, the consideration of appropriate relief was necessarily subordinated to the primary question—the constitutionality of segregation in public education. We have now announced that such segregation is a denial of the equal protection of the laws. In order that we may have the full assistance of the parties in formulating decrees, the cases will be restored to the docket, and the parties are requested to present further argument on Questions 4 and 5 previously propounded by the Court for the reargument this Term. The Attorney General of the United States is again invited to participate. The Attorneys General of the states requiring or permitting segregation in public education will also be permitted to appear as *amici curiae* upon request to do so by September 5, 1954, and submission of briefs by October 1, 1954.

6.   *The Civil Rights Act of 1964 passed only after a three-month-long filibuster, and after President Johnson exercised extreme pressure to insure that Congress would approve the Act. Special features of the Act dealt with voting rights, education, and prohibitions against racial discrimination in public facilities. When the Act became law with President Johnson's signature, he broadcast a special talk to the country. The transcript of his talk follows:*

Civil Rights Bill. July 2, 1964
My Fellow Americans:

I am about to sign into law the Civil Rights Act of 1964. I want to take this occasion to talk to you about what that law means to every American.

One hundred and eighty-eight years ago this week a small band of valiant men began a long struggle for freedom. They pledged their lives, their fortunes, and their sacred honor not only to found a nation, but to forge an ideal of freedom—not only for political independence, but for personal liberty—not only to eliminate foreign rule, but to establish the rule of justice in the affairs of men.

That struggle was a turning point in our history. Today in far corners of distant continents, the ideals of those American patriots still shape the struggle of men who hunger for freedom.

This is a proud triumph. Yet those who founded our country knew that freedom would be secure only if each generation fought to renew and enlarge its meaning. From the minutemen at Concord to the soldiers in Viet-Nam, each generation has been equal to that trust.

Americans of every race and color have died in battle to protect our freedom. Americans of every race and color have worked to build a nation of widening opportunities. Now our generation of Americans has been called on to continue the unending search for justice within our own borders.

We believe that all men are created equal. Yet many are denied equal treatment.

We believe that all men have certain unalienable rights. Yet many Americans do not enjoy those rights.

We believe that all men are entitled to the blessings of liberty. Yet millions are being deprived of those blessings—not because of their own failures, but because of the color of their skin.

The reasons are deeply imbedded in history and tradition and the nature of man. We can understand—without rancor or hatred—how this all happened.

But it cannot continue. Our Constitution, the foundation of our Republic, forbids it. The principles of our freedom forbid it. Morality forbids it. And the law I will sign tonight forbids it.

That law is the product of months of the most careful debate and discussion. It was proposed more than one year ago by our late and beloved President John F. Kennedy. It received the bipartisan support of more than two-thirds of the Members of both the House and the Senate. An overwhelming majority of Republicans as well as Democrats voted for it.

It has received the thoughtful support of tens of thousands of civic and religious leaders in all parts of this Nation. And it is supported by the great majority of the American people.

The purpose of the law is simple.

It does not restrict the freedom of any American, so long as he respects the rights of others.

It does not give special treatment to any citizen.

It does say the only limit to a man's hope for happiness, and for the future of his children, shall be his own ability.

It does say that there are those who are equal before God shall now also be equal in the polling booths, in the classrooms, in the factories, and in hotels, restaurants, movie theaters, and other places that provide service to the public.

I am taking steps to implement the law under my constitutional obligation to "take care that the laws are faithfully executed."

First, I will send to the Senate my nomination of LeRoy Collins to be Director of the Community Relations Service. Governor Collins will bring the experience of a long career of distinguished public service to the task of helping communities solve problems of human relations through reason and commonsense.

Second, I shall appoint an advisory committee of distinguished Americans to assist Governor Collins in his assignment.

Third, I am sending Congress a request for supplemental appropriations to pay for necessary costs of implementing the law, and asking for immediate action.

Fourth, already today in a meeting of my Cabinet this afternoon I directed the agencies of this Government to fully discharge the new responsibilities imposed upon them by the law and to do it without delay, and to keep me personally informed of their progress.

Fifth, I am asking appropriate officials to meet with representative groups to promote greater understanding of the law and to achieve a spirit of compliance.

We must not approach the observance and enforcement of this law in a vengeful spirit. Its purpose is not to punish. Its purpose is not to divide, but to end divisions—divisions which have all lasted too long. Its purpose is national, not regional.

Its purpose is to promote a more abiding commitment to freedom, a more constant pursuit of justice, and a deeper respect for human dignity.

We will achieve these goals because most Americans are law-abiding citizens who want to do what is right.

This is why the Civil Rights Act relies first on voluntary compliance, then on the efforts of local communities and States to secure the rights of citizens. It provides for the national authority to step in only when others cannot or will not do the job.

This Civil Rights Act is a challenge to all of us to go to work in our communities and our States, in our homes and in our hearts, to eliminate the last vestiges of injustice in our beloved country.

So tonight I urge every public official, every religious leader, every business and professional man, every workingman, every housewife—I urge every American—to join in this effort to bring justice and hope to all our people—and to bring peace to our land.

My fellow citizens, we have come now to a time of testing. We must not fail.

Let us close the springs of racial poison. Let us pray for wise and understanding hearts. Let us lay aside irrelevant differences and make our Nation whole. Let us hasten that day when our unmeasured strength and our unbounded spirit will be free to do the great works ordained for this Nation by the just and wise God who is the Father of us all.

Thank you and good night.

7. *The country experienced a series of violent riots in 1967, especially centered in the black ghettoes of large cities. President Lyndon B. Johnson appointed a special commission to investigate the causes of these disorders, and to recommend changes. This "Kerner Commission" (named after its chairman) provided an extensive report; some of the Commission's recommendations are excerpted below:*

Recommendations for National Action

The Commission has already addressed itself to the need for immediate action at the local level. Because the city is the focus of racial disorder, the immediate responsibility rests on community leaders and local institutions. Without responsive and representative local government, without effective processes of interracial communication within the city, and without alert, well-trained and adequately supported local police, national action—no matter how great its scale—cannot be expected to provide a solution.

Yet the disorders are not simply a problem of the racial ghetto or the city. As we have seen, they are symptoms of social ills that have become endemic in our society and now affect every American—black or white, businessman or factory worker, suburban commuter or slum dweller.

None of us can escape the consequences of the continuing economic and social decay of the central city and the closely related problem of rural poverty. The convergence of these conditions in the racial ghetto and the resulting discontent and disruption threaten democratic values fundamental to our progress as a free society.

The essential fact is that neither existing conditions nor the garrison state offer acceptable alternatives for the future of this country. Only a greatly enlarged commitment to national action—compassionate, massive and sustained, backed by the will and resources of the most powerful and the richest nation on this earth—can shape a future that is compatible with the historic ideals of American society.

It is this conviction that leads us, as a commission on civil disorders, to comment on the shape and dimensions of the action that must be taken at the national level.

In this effort we have taken account of the work of scholars and experts on race relations, the urban condition and poverty. We have studied the reports and work of other commissions, of congressional committees and of many special task forces and groups both within the government and within the private sector.

Financing the Cost

The Commission has also examined the question of financing; although there are grave difficulties, we do not regard them as insoluble. The nation has substantial financial resources—not enough to do everything some might wish, but enough to make an important start on reducing our critical "social deficit," in spite of a war and in spite of current budget requirements.

The key factors having a hearing on our ability to pay for the cost are the great productivity of the American economy, and a Federal revenue system which is highly responsive to economic growth. In combination, these produce truly astounding automatic increases in Federal budget receipts, provided only that the national economy is kept functioning at capacity, so that actual national income expands in line with potential.

These automatic increases—the "fiscal dividend"—from the Federal revenue system range from $11 billion to $14 billion under conditions of steady economic growth.

The tax surcharge requested by the President, including continuation of excise taxes, would add about $16 billion to a fiscal dividend of about $28.5 billion over a two-year period.

While competing demands are certain to grow with every increase in federal revenues, so that hard choices are inevitable, these figures demonstrate the dimension of resources—apart from changes in tax rates—which this country can generate.

Federal Program Coordination

The spectacle of Detroit and New Haven engulfed in civil turmoil despite a multitude of federally-aided programs raised basic questions as to whether existing "delivery system" is adequate to the bold new purposes of national policy. Many who voiced these concerns overlooked the disparity between the size of the problems at which the programs are aimed and the level of funding provided by the federal government.

Yet there is little doubt that the system through which

federal programs are translated into services to people is a major problem in itself. There are now over 400 grant programs operated by a broad range of federal agencies and channeled through a much larger array of semi-autonomous state and local government entities. Reflective of this complex scheme, federal programs often seem self-defeating and contradictory: and officials unable to make decisions on their own programs and unaware of related efforts; agencies unable or unwilling to work together; programs conceived and administered to achieve different and sometimes conflicting purposes.

The new social development legislation has put great strain upon obsolescent machinery and administrative practices at all levels of government. It has loaded new work on federal departments. It has required a level of skill, a sense of urgency, and a capacity for judgment never planned for or encouraged in departmental field offices. It has required planning and administrative capacity rarely seen in statehouses, county courthouses and city halls.

Deficiencies in all of these areas have frustrated accomplishment of many of the important goals set by the President and the Congress.

In recent years serious efforts have been made to improve program coordination. During the 1961-1965 period, almost 20 executive orders were issued for the coordination of federal programs involving intergovernmental administration. Some two dozen interagency committees have been established to coordinate two or more federal aid programs. Departments have been given responsibility to lead others in areas within their particular competence—OEO, in the poverty field, HUD in Model Cities. Yet, despite these and other efforts, the Federal Government has not yet been able to join talent, funds and programs for concentrated impact in the field. Few agencies are able to put together a comprehensive package of related programs to meet priority needs.

There is a clear and compelling requirement for better coordination of federally funded programs, particularly those designed to benefit the residents of the inner city. If essential programs are to be preserved and expanded, this need must be met.

The Commission's Recommendations

We do not claim competence to chart the details of programs within such complex and interrelated fields as employment, welfare, education and housing. We do believe it is essential to set forth goals and to recommend strategies to reach these goals.

That is the aim of the pages that follow. They contain our sense of the critical priorities. We discuss and recommend programs not to commit each of us to specific parts of such programs but to illustrate the type and dimension of action needed.

Much has been accomplished in recent years to formulate new directions for national policy and new channels for national energy. Resources devoted to social programs have been greatly increased in many areas. Hence, few of our program suggestions are entirely novel. In some form, many are already in effect.

All this serves to underscore our basic conclusion: the need is not so much for the government to design new programs as it is for the nation to generate new will. Private enterprise, labor unions, the churches, the foundations, the universities—all our urban institutions —must deepen their involvement in the life of the city and their commitment to its revival and welfare.

Objectives for National Action

Just as Lincoln, a century ago, put preservation of the Union above all else, so should we put creation of a true union—a single society and a single American identity—as our major goal. Toward that goal, we propose the following objectives for national action:

- Opening up all opportunities to those who are restricted by racial segregation and discrimination, and eliminating all barriers to their choice of jobs, education and housing.
- Removing the frustration of powerlessness among the disadvantaged by providing the means for them to deal with the problems that affect their own lives, and by increasing the capacity of our public and private institutions to respond to these problems.
- Increasing communication across racial lines to destroy stereotypes, to halt polarization, to end distrust and hostility, and to create common ground for efforts toward common goals of public order and social justice.

There are those who oppose these aims as "rewarding the rioters." They are wrong. A great nation is not so easily intimidated. We propose these aims to fulfill our pledge of equality and to meet the fundamental needs of a democratic, civilized society—domestic peace, social justice, and urban centers that are citadels of the human spirit.

There are others who say that violence is necessary—that fear alone can prod the nation to act decisively on behalf of racial minorities. They too are wrong. Violence and disorder compound injustice; they must be ended and they will be ended.

Our strategy is neither blind repression nor capitulation to lawlessness. Rather it is the affirmation of common possibilities, for all, within a single society.

8-E TWO CONSTITUTIONS

1. THE CONSTITUTION OF THE UNITED STATES

WE THE PEOPLE OF THE UNITED STATES, in Order to form a more perfect Union, establish Justice, insure domestic Tranquility, provide for the common defence, promote the general Welfare, and secure the Blessings of Liberty to ourselves and our Posterity, do ordain and establish this Constitution for the United States of America.

ARTICLE I.

Section 1. All legislative Powers herein granted shall be vested in a Congress of the United States, which shall consist of a Senate and House of Representatives.

Section 2. The House of Representatives shall be composed of Members chosen every second Year by the People of the several States, and the Electors in each State shall have the Qualifications requisite for Electors of the most numerous Branch of the State Legislature.

No Person shall be a Representative who shall not have attained to the age of twenty five Years, and been seven Years a Citizen of the United States, and who shall not, when elected, be an Inhabitant of that State in which he shall be chosen.

Representatives and direct Taxes shall be apportioned among the several States which may be included within this Union, according to their respective Numbers, which shall be determined by adding to the whole Number of free Persons, including those bound to Service for a Term of Years, and excluding Indians not taxed, three fifths of all other Persons. The actual Enumeration shall be made within three Years after the first Meeting of the Congress of the United States, and within every subsequent Term of ten Years, in such Manner as they shall by Law direct. The Number of Representatives shall not exceed one for every thirty Thousand, but each State shall have at Least one Representative; and until such enumeration shall be made, the State of New Hampshire shall be entitled to chuse three, Massachusetts eight, Rhode-Island and Providence Plantations one, Connecticut five, New-York six, New Jersey four, Pennsylvania eight, Delaware one, Maryland six, Virginia ten, North Carolina five, South Carolina five, and Georgia three.

When vacancies happen in the Representation from any State, the Executive Authority thereof shall issue Writs of Election to fill such Vacancies.

The House of Representatives shall chuse their Speaker and other Officers; and shall have the sole Power of Impeachment.

Section 3. The Senate of the United States shall be composed of two Senators from each State, chosen by the Legislature thereof, for six Years; and each Senator shall have one Vote.

Immediately after they shall be assembled in Consequence of the first Election, they shall be divided as equally as may be into three Classes. The Seats of the Senators of the first Class shall be vacated at the Expiration of the second Year, of the second Class at the

Expiration of the fourth Year, and of the third Class at the Expiration of the sixth Year, so that one third may be chosen every second Year, and if Vacancies happen by Resignation, or otherwise, during the Recess of the Legislature of any State, the Executive thereof may make temporary Appointments until the next Meeting of the Legislature, which shall then fill such Vacancies.

No Person shall be a Senator who shall not have attained to the Age of thirty Years, and been nine Years a Citizen of the United States, and who shall not, when elected, be an Inhabitant of that State for which he shall be chosen.

The Vice President of the United States shall be President of the Senate, but shall have no Vote, unless they be equally divided.

The Senate shall chuse their other Officers, and also a President pro tempore, in the Absence of the Vice President, or when he shall exercise the Office of President of the United States.

The Senate shall have the sole Power to try all Impeachments. When sitting for that Purpose, they shall be on Oath or Affirmation. When the President of the United States is tried, the Chief Justice shall preside: And no Person shall be convicted without the Concurrence of two thirds of the Members present.

Judgment in Cases of Impeachment shall not extend further than to removal from Office, and disqualification to hold and enjoy any Office of honor, Trust or Profit under the United States: but the Party convicted shall nevertheless be liable and subject to Indictment, Trial, Judgment and Punishment, according to Law.

Section 4. The Times, Places and Manner of holding Elections for Senators and Representatives, shall be prescribed in each State by the Legislature thereof; but the Congress may at any time by Law make or alter such Regulations, except as to the Places of chusing Senators.

The Congress shall assemble at least once in every Year, and such Meeting shall be on the first Monday in December, unless they shall by Law appoint a different Day.

Section 5. Each House shall be the Judge of the Elections, Returns and Qualifications of its own Members, and a Majority of each shall constitute a Quorum to do Business; but a smaller Number may adjourn from day to day, and may be authorized to compel the Attendance of absent Members, in such Manner, and under such Penalties as each House may provide.

Each House may determine the Rules of its Proceedings, punish its Members for disorderly Behaviour, and, with the Concurrence of two thirds, expel a Member.

Each House shall keep a Journal of its Proceedings, and from time to time publish the same, excepting such Parts as may in their Judgment require Secrecy; and the Yeas and Nays of the Members of either House on any question shall, at the Desire of one fifth of those Present, be entered on the Journal.

Neither House, during the Session of Congress, shall, without the Consent of the other, adjourn for more than three days, nor to any other Place than that in which the two Houses shall be sitting.

Section 6. The Senators and Representatives shall receive a Compensation for their Services, to be ascertained by Law, and paid out of the Treasury of the United States. They shall in all Cases, except Treason, Felony and Breach of the Peace, be privileged from Arrest during their Attendance at the Session of their respective Houses, and in going to and returning from the same: and for any Speech or Debate in either House, they shall not be questioned in any other Place.

No Senator or Representative shall, during the Time for which he was elected, be appointed to any civil Office under the Authority of the United States, which shall have been created, or the Emoluments whereof shall have been encreased during such time; and no Person holding any Office under the United States, shall be a Member of either House during his Continuance in Office.

Section 7. All Bills for raising Revenue shall originate in the House of Representatives; but the Senate may propose or concur with Amendments as on other Bills.

Every Bill which shall have passed the House of Representatives and the Senate, shall, before it become a Law, be presented to the President of the United States; If he approve he shall sign it, but if not he shall return it, with his Objections to that House in which it shall have originated, who shall enter the Objections at large on their Journal, and proceed to reconsider it. If after such Reconsideration two thirds of that House shall agree to pass the Bill, it shall be sent, together with the Objections, to the other House, by which it shall likewise be reconsidered, and if approved by two thirds of that House, it shall become a Law. But in all such Cases the Votes of both Houses shall be determined by yeas and Nays, and the Names of the Persons voting for and against the Bill shall be entered on the Journal of each House respectively. If any Bill shall not be returned by the President within ten Days (Sundays excepted) after it shall have been presented to him, the Same shall be a Law, in like Manner as if he had signed it, unless the Congress by their Adjournment prevent its Return, in which Case it shall not be a law.

Every Order, Resolution, or Vote to which the

Concurrence of the Senate and House of Representatives may be necessary (except on a question of Adjournment) shall be presented to the President of the United States; and before the Same shall take Effect, shall be approved by him, or being disapproved by him, shall be repassed by two thirds of the Senate and House of Representatives, according to the Rules and Limitations prescribed in the Case of a Bill.

Section 8. The Congress shall have Power To lay and collect Taxes, Duties, Imposts and Excises, to pay the Debts and provide for the common Defence and general Welfare of the United States; but all Duties, Imposts and Excise shall be uniform throughout the United States;

To borrow Money on the credit of the United States;

To regulate Commerce with foreign Nations, and among the several States, and with the Indian Tribes;

To establish an uniform Rule of Naturalization, and uniform Laws on the subject of Bankruptcies throughout the United States;

To coin Money, regulate the Value thereof, and of foreign Coin, and fix the Standard of Weights and Measures;

To provide for the Punishment of counterfeiting the Securities and current Coin of the United States;

To establish Post Offices and post Roads;

To promote the Progress of Science and useful Arts, by securing for limited Times to Authors and Inventors the exclusive Right to their respective Writings and Discoveries;

To constitute Tribunals inferior to the supreme Court;

To define and punish Piracies and Felonies committed on the high Seas, and Offences against the Law of Nations;

To declare War, grant Letters of Marque and Reprisal, and make Rules concerning Captures on Land and Water;

To raise and support Armies, but no Appropriation of Money to that Use shall be for a longer Term than two Years;

To provide and maintain a Navy;

To make Rules for the Government and Regulation of the land and naval Forces;

To provide for calling forth the Militia to execute the Laws of the Union, suppress Insurrections and repel Invasions;

To provide for organizing, arming, and disciplining, the Militia, and for governing such Part of them as may be employed in the Service of the United States, reserving to the States respectively, the Appointment of the Officers, and the Authority of training the Militia according to the discipline prescribed by Congress;

To exercise exclusive Legislation in all Cases whatsoever, over such District (not exceeding ten Miles square) as may, by Cession of particular States, and the Acceptance of Congress, become the Seat of the Government of the United States, and to exercise like Authority over all Places purchased by the Consent of the Legislature of the State in which the Same shall be, for the Erection of Forts, Magazines, Arsenals, dock-Yards, and other needful Buildings;—And

To make all Laws which shall be necessary and proper for carrying into Execution the foregoing Powers, and all other Powers vested by this Constitution in the Government of the United States, or in any Department or Officer thereof.

Section 9. The Migration or Importation of such Persons as any of the States now existing shall think proper to admit, shall not be prohibited by the Congress prior to the Year one thousand eight hundred and eight, but a Tax or duty may be imposed on such Importation, not exceeding ten dollars for each Person.

The Privilege of the Writ of Habeas Corpus shall not be suspended, unless when in Cases of Rebellion or Invasion the public Safety may require it.

No Bill of Attainder or ex post facto Law shall be passed.

No Capitation, or other direct, Tax shall be laid, unless in Proportion to the Census or Enumeration herein before directed to be taken.

No Tax or Duty shall be laid on Articles exported from any State.

No Preference shall be given by any Regulation of Commerce or Revenue to the Ports of one State over those of another: nor shall Vessels bound to, or from, one State, be obliged to enter, clear or pay Duties in another.

No Money shall be drawn from the Treasury, but in Consequence of Appropriations made by Law; and a regular Statement and Account of the Receipts and Expenditures of all public Money shall be published from time to time.

No Title of Nobility shall be granted by the United States: And no Person holding any Office of Profit or Trust under them, shall, without the Consent of the Congress, accept of any present, Emolument, Office, or Title, of any kind whatever, from any King, Prince, or foreign State.

Section 10. No State shall enter into any Treaty, Alliance, or Confederation; grant Letters of Marque and Reprisal; coin Money; emit Bills of Credit; make any Thing but gold and silver Coin a Tender in Payment of Debts; pass any Bill of Attainder, ex post facto Law, or Law impairing the Obligation of Contracts, or grant any Title of Nobility.

No State shall, without the Consent of the Congress, lay any Imposts or Duties on Imports or Exports, except what may be absolutely necessary for executing its inspection Laws: and the net Produce of all Duties and Imposts, laid by any State on Imports or Exports, shall be subject to the Revision and Controul of the Congress.

No State shall, without the Consent of Congress, lay any Duty of Tonnage, keep Troops, or Ships of War in time of Peace, enter into any Agreement or Compact with another State, or with a foreign Power, or engage in War, unless actually invaded, or in such imminent Danger as will not admit of delay.

ARTICLE II.

Section 1. The executive Power shall be vested in a President of the United States of America. He shall hold his Office during the Term of four Years, and, together with the Vice President, chosen for the same Term, be elected, as follows

Each State shall appoint, in such Manner as the Legislature thereof may direct, a Number of Electors, equal to the whole Number of Senators and Representatives to which the State may be entitled in the Congress: but no Senator or Representative, or Person holding an Office of Trust or Profit under the United States, shall be appointed an Elector.

The Electors shall meet in their respective States, and vote by Ballot for two Persons, of whom one at least shall not be an Inhabitant of the same State with themselves. And they shall make a List of all the Persons voted for, and of the Number of Votes for each; which List they shall sign and certify, and transmit sealed to the Seat of the Government of the United States, directed to the President of the Senate. The President of the Senate shall, in the Presence of the Senate and House of Representatives, open all the Certificates, and the Votes shall then be counted. The Person having the greatest Number of Votes shall be the President, if such Number be a Majority of the whole Number of Electors appointed; and if there be more than one who have such Majority, and have an equal Number of Votes, then the House of Representatives shall immediately chuse by Ballot one of them for President; and if no Person have a Majority, then from the five highest on the List the said House shall in like Manner chuse the President. But in chusing the President, the Votes shall be taken by States, the Representation from each State having one Vote; A quorum for this Purpose shall consist of a Member or Members from two thirds of the States, and a Majority of all the States shall be necessary to a Choice. In every Case, after the Choice of the President, the Person having the greatest Number of Votes of the Electors shall be the Vice President. But if there should remain two or more who have equal Votes, the Senate shall chuse from them by Ballot the Vice President.

The Congress may determine the Time of chusing the Electors, and the Day on which they shall give their Votes; which Day shall be the same throughout the United States.

No Person except a natural born Citizen, or a Citizen of the United States, at the time of the Adoption of this Constitution, shall be eligible to the Office of President; neither shall any Person be eligible to that Office who shall not have attained to the Age of thirty five Years, and been fourteen Years a Resident within the United States.

In Case of the Removal of the President from Office, or of his Death, Resignation, or Inability to discharge the Powers and Duties of the said Office, the Same shall devolve on the Vice President, and the Congress may by Law provide for the Case of Removal, Death, Resignation or Inability, both of the President and Vice President, declaring what Officer shall then act as President, and such Officer shall act accordingly, until the Disability be removed, or a President shall be elected.

The President shall, at stated Times, receive for his Services, a Compensation, which shall neither be encreased nor diminished during the Period for which he shall have been elected, and he shall not receive within that Period any other Emolument from the United States, or any of them.

Before he enter on the Execution of his Office, he shall take the following Oath or Affirmation:—"I do solemnly swear (or affirm) that I will faithfully execute the Office of President of the United States, and will to the best of my ability, preserve, protect and defend the Constitution of the United States."

Section 2. The President shall be Commander in Chief of the Army and Navy of the United States, and of the Militia of the several States, when called into the actual Service of the United States; he may require the Opinion, in writing, of the principal Officer in each of the executive Departments, upon any Subject relating to the Duties of their respective Offices, and he shall have Power to grant Reprieves and Pardons for Offences against the United States, except in Cases of Impeachment.

He shall have Power, by and with the Advice and Consent of the Senate to make Treaties, provided two thirds of the Senators present concur; and he shall nominate, and by and with the Advice and Consent of the Senate, shall appoint Ambassadors, other public Ministers and Consuls, Judges of the supreme Court, and all other Officers of the United States, whose Appointments are not herein otherwise provided for, and which shall be established by Law: but the Congress may by Law vest the Appointment of such inferior Officers, as they think proper, in the President alone, in the Courts of Law, or in the Heads of Departments.

The President shall have Power to fill up all Vacancies that may happen during the Recess of the Senate, by granting Commissions which shall expire at the End of their next Session.

Section 3. He shall from time to time give to the Congress Information of the State of the Union, and recommend to their Consideration such Measures as he shall judge necessary and expedient; he may, on extraordinary Occasions, convene both Houses, or either of them, and in Case of Disagreement between them, with Respect to the Time of Adjournment, he may adjourn them to such Time as he shall think proper; he shall receive Ambassadors and other public Ministers; he shall take Care that the Laws be faithfully executed, and shall Commission all the Officers of the United States.

Section 4. The President, Vice President and all civil Officers of the United States, shall be removed from Office on Impeachment for, and Conviction of, Treason, Bribery, or other high Crimes and Misdemeanors.

ARTICLE III.

Section 1. The judicial Power of the United States, shall be vested in one supreme Court, and in such inferior Courts as the Congress may from time to time ordain and establish. The Judges, both of the supreme and inferior Courts, shall hold their Offices during good Behaviour, and shall, at stated Times, receive for their Services, a Compensation, which shall not be diminished during their Continuance in Office.

Section 2. The judicial Power shall extend to all Cases, in Law and Equity, arising under this Constitution, the Laws of the United States, and Treaties made, or which shall be made, under their Authority;—to all Cases affecting Ambassadors, other public Ministers and Consuls;—to all Cases of admiralty and maritime Jurisdiction;—to Controversies to which the United States shall be a Party;—to Controversies between two or more States;—between a State and Citizens of another State;—between Citizens of different States;—between Citizens of the same State claiming Lands under Grants of different States, and between a State, or the Citizens thereof, and foreign States, Citizens or Subjects.

In all Cases affecting Ambassadors, other public Ministers and Consuls, and those in which a State shall be Party, the supreme Court shall have original jurisdiction. In all the other Cases before mentioned, the supreme Court shall have appellate Jurisdiction, both as to Law and Fact, with such Exceptions, and under such Regulations as the Congress shall make.

The Trial of all Crimes, except in Cases of Impeachment, shall be by Jury, and such Trial shall be held in the State where the said Crimes shall have been committed; but when not committed within any State, the Trial shall be at such Place or Place as the Congress may by Law have directed.

Section 3. Treason against the United States, shall consist only in levying War against them, or in adhering to their Enemies, giving them Aid and Comfort. No Person shall be convicted of Treason unless on the Testimony of two Witnesses to the same overt Act, or on Confession in open Court.

The Congress shall have Power to declare the Punishment of Treason, but no Attainder of Treason shall work Corruption of Blood, or Forfeiture except during the Life of the Person attained.

ARTICLE IV.

Section 1. Full Faith and Credit shall be given in each State to the public Acts, Records, and judicial Proceedings of every other State. And the Congress may by general Laws prescribe the Manner in which such Acts, Records and Proceedings shall be proved, and the Effect thereof.

Section 2. The Citizens of each State shall be entitled to all Privileges and Immunities of Citizens in the several States.

A Person charged in any State with Treason, Felony, or other Crime, who shall flee from Justice, and be found in another State, shall on Demand of the executive Authority of the State from which he fled, be delivered up, to be removed to the State having Jurisdiction of the Crime.

No Person held to Service or Labour in one State, under the Laws thereof, escaping into another, shall, in Consequence of any Law or Regulation therein, be discharged from such Service or Labour, but shall be delivered up on Claim of the Party to whom such Service or Labour may be due.

Section 3. New States may be admitted by the Congress into this Union; but no new States shall be formed or erected within the Jurisdiction of any other State; nor any State be formed by the Junction of two or more States, or Parts of States, without the Consent of the Legislatures of the State concerned as well as of the Congress.

The Congress shall have Power to dispose of and make all needful Rules and Regulations respecting the Territory or other Property belonging to the United States; and nothing in this Constitution shall be so construed as to Prejudice any Claims of the United States, or of any particular State.

Section 4. The United States shall guarantee to every State in this Union a Republican Form of Government, and shall protect each of them against Invasion; and on Application of the Legislature, or of the Executive (when the Legislature cannot be convened) against domestic Violence.

ARTICLE V.

The Congress, whenever two thirds of both Houses shall deem it necessary, shall propose Amendments to this Constitution, or, on the Application of the Legislatures of two thirds of the several States, shall call a Convention for proposing Amendments, which, in either Case shall be valid to all Intents and Purposes, as Part of this Constitution, when ratified by the Legislatures of three fourths of the several States, or by Conventions in three fourths thereof, as the one or the other Mode of Ratification may be proposed by the Congress; Provided that no Amendment which may be made prior to the Year One thousand eight hundred and eight shall in any Manner affect the first and fourth Clauses in the Ninth Section of the first Article; and that no State, without its Consent, shall be deprived of its equal Suffrage in the Senate.

ARTICLE VI.

All Debts contracted and Engagements entered into, before the Adoption of this Constitution, shall be as valid against the United States under this Constitution, as under the Confederation.

This Constitution, and the Laws of the United States which shall be made in Pursuance thereof; and all Treaties made, or which shall be made, under the Authority of the United States, shall be the supreme Law of the Land; and the Judges in every State shall be bound thereby, any Thing in the Constitution or Laws of any State to the Contrary notwithstanding.

The Senators and Representatives before mentioned, and the Members of the several State Legislatures, and all executive and judicial Officers, both of the United States and of the several States, shall be bound by Oath or Affirmation, to support this Constitution; but no religious Test shall ever be required as a Qualification to any Office or public Trust under the United States.

ARTICLE VII.

The Ratification of the Conventions of nine States, shall be sufficient for the Establishment of this Constitution between the States so ratifying the Same.

done in Convention by the Unanimous Consent of the States present the Seventeenth Day of September in the Year of our Lord one thousand seven hundred and Eighty seven and of the Independence of the United States of America the Twelfth. In witness whereof We have hereunto subscribed our Names,

G° Washington—Presid[t]
and deputy from Virginia

New Hampshire	John Langdon
	Nicholas Gilman
Massachusetts	Nathaniel Gorham
	Rufus King
Connecticut	W[m] Sam[l] Johnson
	Roger Sherman
New York	Alexander Hamilton
New Jersey	Wil: Livingston
	David Brearley.
	W[m] Paterson
	Jona: Dayton
Pennsylvania	B Franklin
	Thomas Mifflin
	Rob[t] Morris
	Geo. Clymer
	Tho.[s] FitzSimons
	Jared Ingersoll
	James Wilson
	Gouv Morris
Delaware	Geo: Read
	Gunning Bedford jun
	John Dickinson
	Richard Bassett
	Jaco: Broom
Maryland	James M[c]Henry
	Dan of S[t] Tho.[s] Jenifer
	Dan[l] Carroll

Virginia	{	John Blair—
		James Madison Jr.
North Carolina	{	Wm Blount
		Richd Dobbs Spaight
		Hu Williamson
South Carolina	{	J. Rutledge
		Charles Cotesworth Pinckney
		Charles Pinckney
		Pierce Butler.
Georgia	{	William Few
		Abr Baldwin

The Amendments to the Constitution follow. (The first ten Amendments are known as the Bill of Rights.) Each Amendment is the subject of a separate article in the text volumes (1 through 8) of the RECORD OF AMERICA.

AMENDMENT I

Congress shall make no law respecting an establishment of religion, or prohibiting the free exercise thereof; or abridging the freedom of speech, or of the press; or the right of the people peaceably to assemble, and to petition the Government for a redress of grievances.

AMENDMENT II

A well regulated Militia, being necessary to the security of a free State, the right of the people to keep and bear Arms, shall not be infringed.

AMENDMENT III

No Soldier shall, in time of peace be quartered in any house, without the consent of the Owner, nor in time of war, but in a manner to be prescribed by law.

AMENDMENT IV

The right of the people to be secure in their persons, houses, papers, and effects, against unreasonable searches and seizures, shall not be violated, and no Warrants shall issue, but upon probable cause, supported by Oath or affirmation, and particularly describing the place to be searched, and the persons or things to be seized.

AMENDMENT V

No person shall be held to answer for a capital, or otherwise infamous crime, unless on a presentment or indictment of a Grand Jury, except in cases arising in the land or naval forces, or in the Militia, when in actual service in time of War or public danger; nor shall any person be subject for the same offence to be twice put in jeopardy of life or limb; nor shall be compelled in any criminal case to be a witness against himself, nor be deprived of life, liberty, or property, without due process of law; nor shall private property be taken for public use, without just compensation.

AMENDMENT VI

In all criminal prosecutions, the accused shall enjoy the right to a speedy and public trial, by an impartial jury of the State and district wherein the crime shall have been committed, which district shall have been previously ascertained by law, and to be informed of the nature and cause of the accusation; to be confronted with the witnesses against him; to have compulsory process for obtaining witnesses in his favor, and to have the Assistance of Counsel for his defence.

AMENDMENT VII

In Suits at common law, where the value in controversy shall exceed twenty dollars, the right of trial by jury shall be preserved, and no fact tried by a jury, shall be otherwise re-examined in any Court of the United States, than according to the rules of the common law.

AMENDMENT VIII

Excessive bail shall not be required, nor excessive fines imposed, nor cruel and unusual punishments inflicted.

AMENDMENT IX

The enumeration in the Constitution, of certain rights, shall not be construed to deny or disparage others retained by the people.

AMENDMENT X

The powers not delegated to the United States by the Constitution, nor prohibited by it to the States, are reserved to the States respectively, or to the people.

AMENDMENT XI

The Judicial power of the United States shall not be construed to extend to any suit in law or equity, commenced or prosecuted against one of the United States by Citizens of another State, or by Citizens or Subjects of any Foreign State.

AMENDMENT XII

The Electors shall meet in their respective states, and vote by ballot for President and Vice-President, one of whom, at least, shall not be an inhabitant of the same state with themselves; they shall name in their ballots the person voted for as President, and in distinct ballots the person voted for as Vice-President, and they shall make distinct lists of all persons voted for as President, and of all persons voted for as Vice-President, and of the number of votes for each, which lists they shall sign and certify, and transmit sealed to the seat of the government of the United States, directed to the President of the Senate;—The President of the

Senate shall, in the presence of the Senate and House of Representatives, open all the certificates and the votes shall then be counted;—The person having the greatest number of votes for President, shall be the President, if such number be a majority of the whole number of Electors appointed; and if no person have such majority, then from the persons having the highest numbers not exceeding three on the list of those voted for as President, the House of Representatives shall choose immediately, by ballot, the President. But in choosing the President, the votes shall be taken by states, the representation from each state having one vote; a quorum for this purpose shall consist of a member or members from two-thirds of the states, and a majority of all the states shall be necessary to a choice. And if the House of Representatives shall not choose a President whenever the right of choice shall devolve upon them, before the fourth day of March next following, then the Vice-President shall act as President, as in the case of the death or other constitutional disability of the President. The person having the greatest number of votes as Vice-President, shall be the Vice-President, if such number be a majority of the whole number of Electors appointed, and if no person have a majority, then from the two highest numbers on the list, the Senate shall choose the Vice-President; a quorum for the purpose shall consist of two-thirds of the whole number of Senators, and a majority of the whole number shall be necessary to a choice. But no person constitutionally ineligible to the office of President shall be eligible to that of Vice-President of the United States.

AMENDMENT XIII

Section 1. Neither slavery nor involuntary servitude, except as a punishment for crime whereof the party shall have been duly convicted, shall exist within the United States, or any place subject to their jurisdiction.

Section 2. Congress shall have power to enforce this article by appropriate legislation.

AMENDMENT XIV

Section 1. All persons born or naturalized in the United States, and subject to the jurisdiction thereof, are citizens of the United States and of the State wherein they reside. No State shall make or enforce any law which shall abridge the privileges or immunities of citizens of the United States; nor shall any State deprive any person of life, liberty, or property, without due process of law; nor deny to any person within its jurisdiction the equal protection of the laws.

Section 2. Representatives shall be apportioned among the several States according to their respective numbers, counting the whole number of persons in each State, excluding Indians not taxed. But when the right to vote at any election for the choice of electors for President and Vice President of the United States, Representatives in Congress, the Executive and Judicial officers of a State, or the members of the Legislature thereof, is denied to any of the male inhabitants of such State, being twenty-one years of age, and citizens of the United States, or in any way abridged, except for participation in rebellion, or other crime, the basis of representation therein shall be reduced in the proportion which the number of such male citizens shall bear to the whole number of male citizens twenty-one years of age in such State.

Section 3. No person shall be a Senator or Representative in Congress, or elector of President and Vice President, or hold any office, civil or military, under the United States, or under any State, who, having previously taken an oath, as a member of Congress, or as an officer of the United States, or as a member of any State legislature, or as an executive or judicial officer of any State, to support the Constitution of the United States, shall have engaged in insurrection or rebellion against the same, or given aid or comfort to the enemies thereof. But Congress may by a vote of two-thirds of each House, remove such disability.

Section 4. The validity of the public debt of the United States, authorized by law, including debts incurred for payment of pensions and bounties for services in suppressing insurrection or rebellion, shall not be questioned. But neither the United States nor any State shall assume or pay any debt or obligation incurred in aid of insurrection or rebellion against the United States, or any claim for the loss or emancipation of any slave; but all such debts, obligations and claims shall be held illegal and void.

Section 5. The Congress shall have power to enforce, by appropriate legislation, the provisions of this article.

AMENDMENT XV

Section 1. The right of citizens of the United States to vote shall not be denied or abridged by the United States or by any State on account of race, color, or previous condition of servitude.

Section 2. The Congress shall have power to enforce this article by appropriate legislation.

AMENDMENT XVI

The Congress shall have power to lay and collect taxes on incomes, from whatever source derived, without apportionment among the several States, and without regard to any census or enumeration.

AMENDMENT XVII

The Senate of the United States shall be composed

of two Senators from each State, elected by the people thereof, for six years; and each Senator shall have one vote. The electors in each State shall have the qualifications requisite for electors of the most numerous branch of the State legislatures.

When vacancies happen in the representation of any State in the Senate, the executive authority of such State shall issue writs of election to fill such vacancies: *Provided*, That the legislature of any State may empower the executive thereof to make temporary appointments until the people fill the vacancies by election as the legislature may direct.

This amendment shall not be so construed as to affect the election or term of any Senator chosen before it becomes valid as part of the Constitution.

AMENDMENT XVIII

[Section 1. After one year from the ratification of this article the manufacture, sale, or transportation of intoxicating liquors within, the importation thereof into, or the exportation thereof from the United States and all territory subject to the jurisdiction thereof for beverage purposes is hereby prohibited.

[Sec. 2. The Congress and the several States shall have concurrent power to enforce this article by appropriate legislation.

[Sec. 3. This article shall be inoperative unless it shall have been ratified as an amendment to the Constitution by the legislatures of the several States, as provided in the Constitution, within seven years from the date of the submission hereof to the States by the Congress.]

AMENDMENT XIX

The right of citizens of the United States to vote shall not be denied or abridged by the United States or by any State on account of sex.

Congress shall have power to enforce this article by appropriate legislation.

AMENDMENT XX

Section 1. The terms of the President and Vice President shall end at noon on the 20th day of January, and the terms of Senators and Representatives at noon on the 3d day of January, of the years in which such terms would have ended if this article had not been ratified; and the terms of their successors shall then begin.

Sec. 2. The Congress shall assemble at least once in every year, and such meeting shall begin at noon on the 3d day of January, unless they shall by law appoint a different day.

Sec. 3. If, at the time fixed for the beginning of the term of the President, the President elect shall have died, the Vice President elect shall become President.

If a President shall not have been chosen before the time fixed for the beginning of his term, or if the President elect shall have failed to qualify, then the Vice President elect shall act as President until a President shall have qualified; and the Congress may by law provide for the case wherein neither a President elect nor a Vice President elect shall have qualified, declaring who shall then act as President, or the manner in which one who is to act shall be selected, and such person shall act accordingly until a President or Vice President shall have qualified.

Sec. 4. The Congress may by law provide for the case of the death of any of the persons from whom the House of Representatives may choose a President whenever the right of choice shall have devolved upon them, and for the case of the death of any of the persons from whom the Senate may choose a Vice President whenever the right of choice shall have devolved upon them.

Sec. 5. Sections 1 and 2 shall take effect on the 15th day of October following the ratification of this article.

Sec. 6. This article shall be inoperative unless it shall have been ratified as an amendment to the Constitution by the legislatures of three-fourths of the several States within seven years from the date of its submission.

AMENDMENT XXI

Section 1. The eighteenth article of amendment to the Constitution of the United States is hereby repealed.

Sec. 2. The transportation or importation into any State, Territory, or possession of the United States for delivery or use therein of intoxicating liquors, in violation of the laws thereof, is hereby prohibited.

Sec. 3. This article shall be inoperative unless it shall have been ratified as an amendment to the Constitution by conventions in the several States, as provided in the Constitution, within seven years from the date of the submission hereof to the States by Congress.

AMENDMENT XXII

Section 1. No person shall be elected to the office of the President more than twice, and no person who has held the office of President, or acted as President, for more than two years of a term to which some other person was elected President shall be elected to the office of the President more than once. But this Article shall not apply to any person holding the office of President when this Article was proposed by the Congress, and shall not prevent any person who may be holding the office of President, or acting as President, during the term within which this Article becomes operative from holding the office of President or acting as President during the remainder of such term.

Sec. 2. This article shall be inoperative unless it shall have been ratified as an amendment to the Constitution by the legislatures of three-fourths of the several States within seven years from the date of its submission to the States by the Congress.

AMENDMENT XXIII

Section 1. The District constituting the seat of Government of the United States shall appoint in such manner as the Congress may direct:

A number of electors of President and Vice President equal to the whole number of Senators and Representatives in Congress to which the District would be entitled if it were a State, but in no event more than the least populous State; they shall be in addition to those appointed by the States, but they shall be considered, for the purposes of the election of President and Vice President, to be electors appointed by a State; and they shall meet in the District and perform such duties as provided by the twelfth article of amendment.

Section 2. The Congress shall have power to enforce this article by appropriate legislation.

AMENDMENT XXIV

Section 1. The right of citizens of the United States to vote in any primary or other election for President or Vice President, for electors for President or Vice President, or for Senator or Representative in Congress, shall not be denied or abridged by the United States or any State by reason of failure to pay any poll tax or other tax.

Section 2. The Congress shall have power to enforce this article by appropriate legislation.

AMENDMENT XXV

Section 1. In case of removal of the President from office or of his death or resignation, the Vice President shall become President.

Sec. 2. Whenever there is a vacancy in the office of the Vice President, the President shall nominate a Vice President who shall take office upon confirmation by a majority vote of both Houses of Congress.

Sec. 3. Whenever the President transmits to the President pro tempore of the Senate and the Speaker of the House of Representatives his written declaration that he is unable to discharge the powers and duties of his office, and until he transmits to them a written declaration to the contrary, such powers and duties shall be discharged by the Vice President as Acting President.

Sec. 4. Whenever the Vice President and a majority of either the principal officers of the executive departments or of such other body as Congress may by law provide, transmit to the President pro tempore of the Senate and the Speaker of the House of Representatives their written declaration that the President is unable to discharge the powers and duties of his office, the Vice President shall immediately assume the powers and duties of the office as Acting President.

Thereafter, when the President transmits to the President pro tempore of the Senate and the Speaker of the House of Representatives his written declaration that no inability exists, he shall resume the powers and duties of his office unless the Vice President and a majority of either the principal officers of the executive department or of such other body as Congress may by law provide, transmit within four days to the President pro tempore of the Senate and the Speaker of the House of Representatives their written declaration that the President is unable to discharge the powers and duties of his office. Thereupon Congress shall decide the issue, assembling within forty-eight hours for that purpose if not in session. If the Congress, within twenty-one days after receipt of the latter written declaration, or, if Congress is not in session, within twenty-one days after Congress is required to assemble, determines by two-thirds vote of both Houses that the President is unable to discharge the powers and duties of his office, the Vice President shall continue to discharge the same as Acting President; otherwise, the President shall resume the powers and duties of his office.

AMENDMENT XXVI

Section 1. The right of citizens of the United States, who are eighteen years of age or older, to vote shall not be denied or abridged by the United States or by any State on account of age.

Sec. 2. The Congress shall have power to enforce this article by appropriate legislation.

2.   THE CONSTITUTION OF CONNECTICUT

Each State of the Union has its own Constitution. These documents are the basic laws of the States. They define the shape of each State's government, and the powers which it may exercise. Some are so specific that they run into dozens of Amendments and numerous sub-sections which explain or add details; others are more compact and concern themselves with the general powers granted their respective State governments.

The Constitution of the State of Connecticut which follows is an example of a relatively compact, modern Constitution. It was adopted in 1965, and has been modified by Amendments in 1970 and 1972. The student will find it useful for comparison with the U.S. Constitution, and with the provisions in the Constitutions of other States.

PREAMBLE.

The People of Connecticut acknowledging with gratitude, the good providence of God, in having permitted them to enjoy a free government; do, in order more effectually to define, secure, and perpetuate the liberties, rights and privileges which they have derived from their ancestors; hereby, after a careful consideration and revision, ordain and establish the following constitution and form of civil government.

ARTICLE FIRST.
DECLARATION OF RIGHTS.

That the great and essential principles of liberty and free government may be recognized and established.

WE DECLARE:

SEC. 1. All men when they form a social compact, are equal in rights; and no man or set of men are entitled to exclusive public emoluments or privileges from the community.

SEC. 2. All political power is inherent in the people, and all free governments are founded on their authority, and instituted for their benefit; and they have at all times an undeniable and indefeasible right to alter their form of government in such manner as they may think expedient.

SEC. 3. The exercise and enjoyment of religious profession and worship, without discrimination, shall forever be free to all persons in the state; provided, that the right hereby declared and established, shall not be so construed as to excuse acts of licentiousness, or to justify practices inconsistent with the peace and safety of the state.

SEC. 4. Every citizen may freely speak, write and publish his sentiments on all subjects, being responsible for the abuse of that liberty.

SEC. 5. No law shall ever be passed to curtail or restrain the liberty of speech or of the press.

SEC. 6. In all prosecutions or indictments for libels, the truth may be given in evidence, and the jury shall have the right to determine the law and the facts, under the direction of the court.

SEC. 7. The people shall be secure in their persons, houses, papers and possessions from unreasonable searches or seizures; and no warrant to search any place, or to seize any person or things, shall issue with-out describing them as nearly as may be, nor without probable cause supported by oath or affirmation.

SEC. 8. In all criminal prosecutions, the accused shall have a right to be heard by himself and by counsel; to be informed of the nature and cause of the accusation; to be confronted by the witness against him; to have compulsory process to obtain witnesses in his behalf; to be released on bail upon sufficient security, except in capital offenses, where the proof is evident or the presumption great; and in all prosecutions by indictment or information, to a speedy, public trial by an impartial jury. No person shall be compelled to give evidence against himself, nor be deprived of life, liberty or property without due process of law, nor shall excessive bail be required nor excessive fines imposed. No persons shall be held to answer for any crime, punishable by death or life imprisonment, unless on a presentment or an indictment of a grand jury, except in the armed forces, or in the militia when in actual service in time of war or public danger.

SEC. 9. No person shall be arrested, detained or punished, except in cases clearly warranted by law.

SEC. 10. All courts shall be open, and every person, for an injury done to him in his person, property or reputation, shall have remedy by due course of law, and right and justice administered without sale, denial or delay.

SEC. 11. The property of no person shall be taken for public use, without just compensation therefor.

SEC. 12. The privileges of the writ of habeas corpus shall not be suspended, unless, when in case of rebellion or invasion, the public safety may require it; nor in any case, but by the legislature.

SEC. 13. No person shall be attainted for treason or felony, by the legislature.

SEC. 14. The citizens have a right, in a peaceable manner, to assemble for their common good, and to apply to those invested with the powers of government, for redress of grievances, or other proper purposes, by petition, address or remonstrance.

SEC. 15. Every citizen has a right to bear arms in defense of himself and the state.

SEC. 16. The military shall, in all cases, and at all times, be in strict subordination to the civil power.

SEC. 17. No soldier shall, in time of peace, be quartered in any house, without the consent of the owner; nor in time of war, but in a manner to be prescribed by law.

SEC. 18. No hereditary emoluments, privileges or honors, shall ever be granted, or conferred in this state.

SEC. 19. The right of trial by jury shall remain inviolate.

SEC. 20. No person shall be denied the equal protection of the law nor be subjected to segregation or discrimination in the exercise or enjoyment of his civil or political rights because of religion, race, color, ancestry or national origin.

ARTICLE SECOND.
OF THE DISTRIBUTION OF POWERS.

The powers of government shall be divided into three distinct departments, and each of them confided to a separate magistracy, to wit, those which are legislative, to one; those which are executive, to another; and those which are judicial, to another.

ARTICLE THIRD.
OF THE LEGISLATIVE DEPARTMENT.

SEC. 1.   The legislative power of the state shall be vested in two distinct houses or branches; the one to be styled the senate, the other the house of representatives, and both together the general assembly. The style of their laws shall be: Be it enacted by the Senate and the House of Representatives in General Assembly convened.

SEC. 2.   There shall be a regular session of the general assembly to commence on the Wednesday following the first Monday of the January next succeeding the election of its members, and at such other times as the general assembly shall judge necessary; but the person administering the office of governor may, on special emergencies, convene the general assembly at any other time. All regular and special sessions of the general assembly shall be held at Hartford, but the person administering the office of governor may, in case of special emergency, convene the assembly at any other place in the state. The general assembly shall adjourn each regular session not later than the first Wednesday after the first Monday in June following its organization and shall adjourn each special session upon completion of its business. If any bill passed by any regular or special session or any appropriation item described in Section 16 of Article Fourth has been disapproved by the governor prior to its adjournment, and has not been reconsidered by the assembly, or is so disapproved after such adjournment, the secretary of the state shall reconvene the general assembly on the second Monday after the last day on which the governor is authorized to transmit or has transmitted every bill to the secretary with his objections pursuant to Section 15 of Article Fourth of this constitution, whichever occurs first; provided if such Monday falls on a legal holiday the general assembly shall be reconvened on the next following day. The reconvened session shall be for the sole purpose of reconsidering

and, if the assembly so desires, repassing such bills. The general assembly shall adjourn sine die not later than three days following its reconvening.

SEC. 3.   The senate shall consist of not less than thirty and not more than fifty members, each of whom shall be an elector residing in the senatorial district from which he is elected. Each senatorial district shall be contiguous as to territory and shall elect no more than one senator.

SEC. 4.   The house of representatives shall consist of not less than one hundred twenty-five and not more than two hundred twenty-five members, each of whom shall be an elector residing in the assembly district from which he is elected. Each assembly district shall be contiguous as to territory and shall elect no more than one representative. For the purpose of forming assembly districts no town shall be divided except for the purpose of forming assembly districts wholly within the town.

SEC. 5.   The establishment of districts in the general assembly shall be consistent with federal constitutional standards.

SEC. 6.   a.   The assembly and senatorial districts as now established by law shall continue until the regular session of the general assembly next after the completion of the next census of the United States. Such general assembly shall, upon roll call, by a yea vote of at least two-thirds of the membership of each house, enact such plan of districting as is necessary to preserve a proper apportionment of representation in accordance with the principles recited in this article. Thereafter the general assembly shall decennially at its next regular session following the completion of the census of the United States, upon roll call, by a yea vote of at least two-thirds of the membership of each house, enact such plan of districting as is necessary in accordance with the provisions of this article.

b.   If the general assembly fails to enact a plan of districting by the first day of the April next following the completion of the decennial census of the United States, the governor shall forthwith appoint a commission consisting of the eight members designated by the president pro tempore of the senate, the speaker of the house of representatives, the minority leader of the senate and the minority leader of the house of representatives, each of whom shall designate two members of the commission, provided that there are members of no more than two political parties in either the senate or the house of representatives. In the event that there are members of more than two political parties in a house of the general assembly, all members of that house belonging to the parties other than that of the president pro tempore of the senate or the speaker of the house of representatives, as the case may be, shall select one of their number, who shall designate two members of the commission in lieu of the designation by the minority leader of that house.

c. The commission shall proceed to consider the alteration of districts in accordance with the principles recited in this article and it shall submit a plan of districting to the secretary of the state by the first day of the July next succeeding the appointment of its members. No plan shall be submitted to the secretary unless it is certified by at least six members of the commission. Upon receiving such plan the secretary shall publish the same forthwith, and, upon publication, such plan of districting shall have the full force of law.

d. If by the first day of the July next succeeding the appointment of its members the commission fails to submit a plan of districting, a board of three persons shall forthwith be empaneled. The speaker of the house of representatives and the minority leader of the house of representatives shall each designate, as one member of the board, a judge of the superior court of the state, provided that there are members of no more than two political parties in the house of representatives. In the event that there are members of more than two political parties in the house of representatives, all members belonging to the parties other than that of the speaker shall select one of their number, who shall then designate, as one member of the board, a judge of the superior court of the state, in lieu of the designation by the minority leader of the house of representatives. The two members of the board so designated shall select an elector of the state as the third member.

e. The board shall proceed to consider the alteration of districts in accordance with the principles recited in this article and shall, by the first day of the October next succeeding its selection, submit a plan of districting to the secretary. No plan shall be submitted to the secretary unless it is certified by at least two members of the board. Upon receiving such plan, the secretary shall publish the same forthwith, and, upon publication, such plan of districting shall have the full force of law.

SEC. 7. The treasurer, secretary of the state, and comptroller shall canvass publicly the votes for senators and representatives. The person in each senatorial district having the greatest number of votes for senator shall be declared to be duly elected for such district, and the person in each assembly district having the greatest number of votes for representative shall be declared to be duly elected for such district. The general assembly shall provide by law the manner in which an equal and the greatest number of votes for

two or more persons so voted for for senator or representative shall be resolved. The return of votes, and the result of the canvass, shall be submitted to the house of representatives, and to the senate on the first day of the session of the general assembly. Each house shall be the final judge of the election returns and qualifications of its own members.

SEC. 8. A general election for members of the general assembly shall be held on the Tuesday after the first Monday of November, biennially, in the even-numbered years. The general assembly shall have the power to enact laws regulating and prescribing the order and manner of voting for such members, for filling vacancies in either the house of representatives or the senate, and providing for the election of representatives or senators at some time subsequent to the Tuesday after the first Monday of November in all cases when it shall so happen that the electors in any district shall fail on that day to elect a representative or senator.

SEC. 9. At all elections for members of the general assembly the presiding officers in the several towns shall receive the votes of the electors, and count and declare them in open meeting. The presiding officers shall make and certify duplicate lists of the persons voted for, and of the number of votes for each. One list shall be delivered within three days to the town clerk, and within ten days after such meeting, the other shall be delivered under seal to the secretary of the state.

SEC. 10. The members of the general assembly shall hold their offices from the Wednesday following the first Monday of the January next succeeding their election until the Wednesday after the first Monday of the third January next succeeding their election, and until their successors are duly qualified.

SEC. 11. No member of the general assembly shall, during the term for which he is elected, hold or accept any appointive position or office in the judicial or executive department of the state government, or in the courts of the political subdivisions of the state, or in the government of any county. No member of congress, no person holding any office under the authority of the United States and no person holding any office in the judicial or executive department of the state government or in the government of any county shall be a member of the general assembly during his continuance in such office.

SEC. 12. The house of representatives, when assembled, shall choose a speaker, clerk and other officers. The senate shall choose a president pro tempore, clerk and other officers, except the president. A majority of each house shall constitute a quorum to do business; but a smaller number may adjourn from day to day, and compel the attendance of absent members in such manner and under such penalties as each house may prescribe.

SEC. 13.   Each house shall determine the rules of its own proceedings, and punish members for disorderly conduct, and, with the consent of two-thirds, expel a member, but not a second time for the same cause; and shall have all other powers necessary for a branch of the legislature of a free and independent state.

SEC. 14.   Each house shall keep a journal of its proceedings, and publish the same when required by one-fifth of its members, except such parts as in the judgment of a majority require secrecy. The yeas and nays of the members of either house shall, at the desire of one-fifth of those present, be entered on the journals.

SEC. 15.   The senators and representatives shall, in all cases of civil process, be privileged from arrest, during any session of the general assembly, and for four days before the commencement and after the termination of any session thereof. And for any speech or debate in either house, they shall not be questioned in any other place.

SEC. 16.   The debates of each house shall be public, except on such occasions as in the opinion of the house may require secrecy.

SEC. 17.   The salary of the members of the general assembly and the transportation expenses of its members in the performance of their legislative duties shall be determined by law.

ARTICLE FOURTH.
OF THE EXECUTIVE DEPARTMENT.

SEC. 1.   A general election for governor, lieutenant-governor, secretary of the state, treasurer and comptroller shall be held on the Tuesday after the first Monday of November, 1966, and quadrennially thereafter.

SEC. 2.   Such officers shall hold their respective offices from the Wednesday following the first Monday of the January next succeeding their election until the Wednesday following the first Monday of the fifth January succeeding their election and until their successors are duly qualified.

SEC. 3.   In the election of governor and lieutenant-governor, voting for such offices shall be as a unit. The name of no candidate for either office, nominated by a political party or by petition, shall appear on the voting machine ballot labels except in conjunction with the name of the candidate for the other office.

SEC. 4.   At the meetings of the electors in the re-

spective towns held quadrennially as herein provided for the election of state officers, the presiding officers shall receive the votes and shall count and declare the same in the presence of the electors. The presiding officers shall make and certify duplicate lists of the persons voted for, and of the number of votes for each. One list shall be delivered within three days to the town clerk, and within ten days after such meeting, the other shall be delivered under seal to the secretary of the state. The votes so delivered shall be counted, canvassed and declared by the treasurer, secretary, and comptroller, within the month of November. The vote for treasurer shall be counted, canvassed and declared by the secretary and comptroller only; the vote for secretary shall be counted, canvassed and declared by the treasurer and comptroller only; and the vote for comptroller shall be counted, canvassed and declared by the treasurer and secretary only. A fair list of the persons and number of votes given for each, together with the returns of the presiding officers, shall be, by the treasurer, secretary and comptroller, made and laid before the general assembly, then next to be held, on the first day of the session thereof. In the election of governor, lieutenant-governor, secretary, treasurer, comptroller and attorney general, the person found upon the count by the treasurer, secretary and comptroller and in the manner herein provided, to be made and announced before December fifteenth of the year of the election, to have received the greatest number of votes of such offices, respectively, shall be elected thereto; provided, if the election of any of them shall be contested as provided by statute, and if such a contest shall proceed to final judgment, the person found by the court to have received the greatest number of votes shall be elected. If two or more persons shall be found upon the count of the treasurer, secretary and comptroller to have received an equal and the greatest number of votes for any of said offices, and the election is not contested, the general assembly on the second day of its session shall hold a joint convention of both houses, at which, without debate, a ballot shall be taken to choose such officer from those persons who received such a vote; and the balloting shall continue on that or subsequent days until one of such persons is chosen by a majority vote of those present and voting. The general assembly shall have power to enact laws regulating and prescribing the order and manner of voting for such officers. The general assembly shall by law prescribe the manner in which all questions concerning the election of a governor or lieutenant-governor shall be determined.

SEC. 5.   The supreme executive power of the state shall be vested in the governor. No person who is not an elector of the state, and who has not arrived at the age of thirty years, shall be eligible.

SEC. 6. The lieutenant-governor shall possess the same qualifications as are herein prescribed for the governor.

SEC. 7. The compensations of the governor and lieutenant-governor shall be established by law, and shall not be varied so as to take effect until after an election, which shall next succeed the passage of the law establishing such compensations.

SEC. 8. The governor shall be captain general of the militia of the state, except when called into the service of the United States.

SEC. 9. He may require information in writing from the officers in the executive department, on any subject relating to the duties of their respective offices.

SEC. 10. The governor, in case of a disagreement between the two houses of the general assembly, respecting the time of adjournment, may adjourn them to such time as he shall think proper, not beyond the day of the next stated session.

SEC. 11. He shall, from time to time, give to the general assembly, information of the state of the government, and recommend to their consideration such measures as he shall deem expedient.

SEC. 12. He shall take care that the laws be faithfully executed.

SEC. 13. The governor shall have power to grant reprieves after conviction, in all cases except those of impeachment, until the end of the next session of the general assembly, and no longer.

SEC. 14. All commissions shall be in the name and by authority of the state of Connecticut; shall be sealed with the state seal, signed by the governor, and attested by the secretary of the state.

SEC. 15. Each bill which shall have passed both houses of the general assembly shall be presented to the governor. Bills may be presented to the governor after the adjournment of the general assembly, and the general assembly may prescribe the time and method of performing all ministerial acts necessary or incidental to the administration of this section. If the governor shall approve a bill, he shall sign and transmit it to the secretary of the state, but if he shall disapprove, he shall transmit it to the secretary with his objections, and the secretary shall thereupon return the bill with the governor's objections to the house in which it originated. After the objections shall have been entered on its journal, such house shall proceed to reconsider the bill. If, after such reconsideration, that house shall again pass it, but by the approval of at least two-thirds of its members, it shall be sent with the objections to the other house, which shall

also reconsider it. If approved by at least two-thirds of the members of the second house, it shall be a law and be transmitted to the secretary; but in such case the votes of each house shall be determined by yeas and nays and the names of the members voting for and against the bill shall be entered on the journal of each house respectively. In case the governor shall not transmit the bill to the secretary, either with his approval or with his objections, within five calendar days, Sundays and legal holidays excepted, after the same shall have been presented to him, it shall be a law at the expiration of that period; except that, if the general assembly shall then have adjourned any regular or special session, the bill shall be a law unless the governor shall, within fifteen calendar days after the same has been presented to him, transmit it to the secretary with his objections, in which case it shall not be a law unless such bill is reconsidered and re-passed by the general assembly by at least a two-thirds vote of the members of each house of the general assembly at the time of its reconvening.

SEC. 16. The governor shall have power to disapprove of any item or items of any bill making appropriations of money embracing distinct items while at the same time approving the remainder of the bill, and the part or parts of the bill so approved shall become effective and the item or items of appropriations so disapproved shall not take effect unless the same are separately reconsidered and repassed in accordance with the rules and limitations prescribed for the passage of bills over the executive veto. In all cases in which the governor shall exercise the right of disapproval hereby conferred he shall append to the bill at the time of signing it a statement of the item or items disapproved, together with his reasons for such disapproval, and transmit the bill and such appended statement to the secretary of the state. If the general assembly be then in session he shall forthwith cause a copy of such statement to be delivered to the house in which the bill originated for reconsideration of the disapproved items in conformity with the rules prescribed for legislative action in respect to bills which have received executive disapproval.

SEC. 17. The lieutenant-governor shall by virtue of his office, be president of the senate, and have, when in committee of the whole, a right to debate, and when the senate is equally divided, to give the casting vote.

SEC. 18. In case of the death, resignation, refusal to serve or removal from office of the governor, the lieutenant-governor shall, upon taking the oath of office of governor, be governor of the state until another is chosen at the next regular election for governor and is duly qualified. In case of the inability of the governor to exercise the powers and perform the duties of his office, or in case of his impeachment or of his absence from the state, the lieutenant-governor shall exercise the powers and authority and perform the duties appertaining to the office of governor until the disability is removed or, if the governor has been impeached, he is acquitted or, if absent, he has returned.

SEC. 19.   If the lieutenant-governor succeeds to the office of governor, or if the lieutenant-governor dies, resigns, refuses to serve or is removed from office, the president pro tempore of the senate shall, upon taking the oath of office of lieutenant-governor, be lieutenant-governor of the state until another is chosen at the next regular election for lieutenant-governor and is duly qualified. Within fifteen days of the administration of such oath the senate, if the general assembly is in session, shall elect one of its members president pro tempore. In case of the inability of the lieutenant-governor to exercise the powers and perform the duties of his office or in case of his impeachment or absence from the state, the president pro tempore of the senate shall exercise the powers and authority and perform the duties appertaining to the office of lieutenant-governor until the disability is removed or, if the lieutenant-governor has been impeached, he is acquitted or, if absent, he has returned.

SEC. 20.   If, while the general assembly is not in session, there is a vacancy in the office of president pro tempore of the senate, the secretary of the state shall within fifteen days convene the senate for the purpose of electing one of its members president pro tempore.

SEC. 21.   If, at the time fixed for the beginning of the term of the governor, the governor-elect shall have died or shall have failed to qualify, the lieutenant-governor-elect, after taking the oath of office of lieutenant-governor, may qualify as governor, and, upon so qualifying, shall become governor. The general assembly may by law provide for the case in which neither the governor-elect nor the lieutenant-governor-elect shall have qualified, by declaring who shall, in such event, act as governor or the manner in which the person who is so to act shall be selected, and such person shall act accordingly until a governor or a lieutenant-governor shall have qualified.

SEC. 22.   The treasurer shall receive all monies belonging to the state, and disburse the same only as he may be directed by law. He shall pay no warrant, or order for the disbursement of public money, until the same has been registered in the office of the comptroller.

SEC. 23.   The secretary of the state shall have the safe keeping and custody of the public records and documents, and particularly of the acts, resolutions and orders of the general assembly, and record the same; and perform all such duties as shall be prescribed by law. He shall be the keeper of the seal of the state, which shall not be altered.

SEC. 24.   The comptroller shall adjust and settle all public accounts and demands, except grants and orders of the general assembly. He shall prescribe the mode of keeping and rendering all public accounts. He shall, ex officio, be one of the auditors of the accounts of the treasurer. The general assembly may assign to him other duties in relation to his office, and to that of the treasurer, and shall prescribe the manner in which his duties shall be performed.

SEC. 25.   Sheriffs shall be elected in the several counties, on the Tuesday after the first Monday of November, 1966, and quadrennially thereafter, for the term of four years, commencing on the first day of June following their election. They shall become bound with sufficient sureties to the treasurer of the state, for the faithful discharge of the duties of their office. They shall be removable by the general assembly. In case the sheriff of any county shall die or resign, or shall be removed from office by the general assembly, the governor may fill the vacancy occasioned thereby, until the same shall be filled by the general assembly.

SEC. 26.   A statement of all receipts, payments, funds, and debts of the state, shall be published from time to time, in such manner and at such periods, as shall be prescribed by law.

ARTICLE FIFTH.
OF THE JUDICIAL DEPARTMENT.

SEC. 1.   The judicial power of the state shall be vested in a supreme court, a superior court, and such lower courts as the general assembly shall, from time to time, ordain and establish. The powers and jurisdiction of these courts shall be defined by law.

SEC. 2.   The judges of the supreme court and of the superior court shall, upon nomination by the governor, be appointed by the general assembly in such manner as shall by law be prescribed. They shall hold their offices for the term of eight years, but may be removed by impeachment. The governor shall also remove them on the address of two-thirds of each house of the general assembly.

SEC. 3.   Judges of the lower courts shall, upon nomination by the governor, be appointed by the general assembly in such manner as shall by law be prescribed, for terms of four years.

SEC. 4.   Judges of probate shall be elected by the electors residing in their respective districts on the

Tuesday after the first Monday of November, 1966, and quadrennially thereafter, and shall hold office for four years from and after the Wednesday after the first Monday of the next succeeding January.

SEC. 5. Justices of the peace for the several towns in the state shall be elected by the electors in such towns; and the time and manner of their election, the number for each town, the period for which they shall hold their offices and their jurisdiction shall be prescribed by law.

SEC. 6. No judge or justice of the peace shall be eligible to hold his office after he shall arrive at the age of seventy years, except that a chief justice or judge of the supreme court, a judge of the superior court, or a judge of the court of common pleas, who has attained the age of seventy years and has become a state referee may exercise, as shall be prescribed by law, the powers of the superior court or court of common pleas on matters referred to him as a state referee.

ARTICLE SIXTH.
OF THE QUALIFICATIONS OF ELECTORS.

SEC. 1. Every citizen of the United States who has attained the age of twenty-one years, who has resided in the town in which he offers himself to be admitted to the privileges of an elector at least six months next preceding the time he so offers himself, who is able to read in the English language any article of the constitution or any section of the statutes of the state, and who sustains a good moral character, shall, on his taking such oath as may be prescribed by law, be an elector.

SEC. 2. The qualifications of electors as set forth in Section 1 of this article shall be decided at such times and in such manner as may be prescribed by law.

SEC. 3. The general assembly shall by law prescribe the offenses on conviction of which the privileges of an elector shall be forfeited and the conditions on which and methods by which such rights may be restored.

SEC. 4. Laws shall be made to support the privilege of free suffrage, prescribing the manner of regulating and conducting meetings of the electors, and prohibiting, under adequate penalties, all undue influence therein . . .

SEC. 5. In all elections of officers of the state, or members of the general assembly, the votes of the electors shall be by ballot, either written or printed, except that voting machines or other mechanical devices for voting may be used in all elections in the state, under such regulations as may be prescribed by law. The right of secret voting shall be preserved.

At every election where candidates are listed by party designation and where voting machines or other mechanical devices are used, each elector shall be able at his option to vote for candidates for office under a single party designation by operating a straight ticket device, or to vote for candidates individually after first operating a straight ticket device, or to vote for candidates individually without first operating a straight ticket device.

SEC. 6. At all elections of officers of the state, or members of the general assembly, the electors shall be privileged from arrest during their attendance upon, and going to, and returning from the same, on any civil process.

SEC. 7. The general assembly may provide by law for voting in the choice of any officer to be elected or upon any question to be voted on at an election by qualified voters of the state who are unable to appear at the polling place on the day of election because of absence from the city or town of which they are inhabitants or because of sickness or physical disability or because the tenets of their religion forbid secular activity.

SEC. 8. The general assembly may provide by law for the admission as electors in absentia of members of the armed forces, the United States merchant marine, members of religious or welfare groups or agencies attached to and serving with the armed forces and civilian employees of the United States, and the spouses and dependents of such persons.

SEC. 9. Any person admitted as an elector in any town shall, if he removes to another town, have the privileges of an elector in such other town after residing therein for six months. The general assembly shall prescribe by law the manner in which evidence of the admission of an elector and of the duration of his current residence shall be furnished to the town to which he removes.

SEC. 10. Every elector shall be eligible to any office in the state, except in cases provided for in this constitution.

ARTICLE SEVENTH.
OF RELIGION.

It being the right of all men to worship the Supreme Being, the Great Creator and Preserver of the Universe, and to render that worship in a mode consistent with the dictates of their consciences, no person shall by law be compelled to join or support, nor be classed or associated with, any congregation, church or religious association. No preference shall be given by law to any religious society or denomination in the state. Each shall have and enjoy the same and equal powers, rights and privileges, and may support and maintain the ministers or teachers of its society or denomination, and may build and repair houses for public worship.

ARTICLE EIGHTH.
OF EDUCATION.

SEC. 1. There shall always be free public elementary and secondary schools in the state. The general assembly shall implement this principle by appropriate legislation.

SEC. 2. The state shall maintain a system of higher education, including The University of Connecticut, which shall be dedicated to excellence in higher education. The general assembly shall determine the size, number, terms and method of appointment of the governing boards of The University of Connecticut and of such constituent units or coordinating bodies in the system as from time to time may be established.

SEC. 3. The charter of Yale College, as modified by agreement with the corporation thereof, in pursuance of an act of the general assembly, passed in May, 1792, is hereby confirmed.

SEC. 4. The fund, called the SCHOOL FUND, shall remain a perpetual fund, the interest of which shall be inviolably appropriated to the support and encouragement of the public schools throughout the state, and for the equal benefit of all the people thereof. The value and amount of said fund shall be ascertained in such manner as the general assembly may prescribe, published, and recorded in the comptroller's office; and no law shall ever be made, authorizing such fund to be diverted to any other use than the encouragement and support of public schools, among the several school societies, as justice and equity shall require.

ARTICLE NINTH.
OF IMPEACHMENTS.

SEC. 1. The house of representatives shall have the sole power of impeaching.

SEC. 2. All impeachments shall be tried by the senate. When sitting for that purpose, they shall be on oath or affirmation. No person shall be convicted without the concurrence of at least two-thirds of the members present. When the governor is impeached, the chief justice shall preside.

SEC. 3. The governor, and all other executive and judicial officers, shall be liable to impeachment; but judgments in such cases shall not extend further than to removal from office, and disqualification to hold any office of honor, trust or profit under the state. The party convicted, shall, nevertheless, be liable and sub-

ject to indictment, trial and punishment according to law.

SEC. 4. Treason against the state shall consist only in levying war against it, or adhering to its enemies, giving them aid and comfort. No person shall be convicted of treason, unless on the testimony of at least two witnesses to the same overt act, or on confession in open court. No conviction of treason, or attainder, shall work corruption of blood, or forfeiture.

ARTICLE TENTH.
OF HOME RULE.

SEC. 1. The general assembly shall by general law delegate such legislative authority as from time to time it deems appropriate to towns, cities and boroughs relative to the powers, organization, and form of government of such political subdivisions. The general assembly shall from time to time by general law determine the maximum terms of office of the various town, city and borough elective offices. After July 1, 1969, the general assembly shall enact no special legislation relative to the powers, organization, terms of elective offices or form of government of any single town, city or borough, except as to (a) borrowing power, (b) validating acts, and (c) formation, consolidation or dissolution of any town, city or borough, unless in the delegation of legislative authority by general law the general assembly shall have failed to prescribe the powers necessary to effect the purpose of such special legislation.

SEC. 2. The general assembly may prescribe the methods by which towns, cities and boroughs may establish regional governments and the methods by which towns, cities, boroughs and regional governments may enter into compacts. The general assembly shall prescribe the powers, organization, form, and method of dissolution of any government so established.

ARTICLE ELEVENTH.
GENERAL PROVISIONS.

SEC. 1. Members of the general assembly, and all officers, executive and judicial, shall, before they enter on the duties of their respective offices, take the following oath or affirmation to wit:

You do solemnly swear (or affirm, as the case may be) that you will support the constitution of the United States, and the constitution of the state of Connecticut, so long as you continue a citizen thereof; and that you will faithfully discharge, according to law, the duties of the office of . . . .
. . . . to the best of your abilities. So help you God.

SEC. 2. Neither the general assembly nor any county, city, borough, town or school district shall have power to pay or grant any extra compensation to any public officer, employee, agent or servant, or increase the compensation of any public officer or employee, to take effect during the continuance in office of any person whose salary might be increased thereby, or increase the pay or compensation of any public contractor above the amount specified in the contract.

SEC. 3. In order to insure continuity in operation of state and local governments in a period of emergency resulting from disaster caused by enemy attack, the general assembly shall provide by law for the prompt and temporary succession to the powers and duties of all public offices, the incumbents of which may become unavailable for carrying on their powers and duties.

SEC. 4. Claims against the state shall be resolved in such manner as may be provided by law.

SEC. 5. The rights and duties of all corporations shall remain as if this constitution had not been adopted; with the exception of such regulations and restrictions as are contained in this constitution. All laws not contrary to, or inconsistent with, the provisions of this constitution shall remain in force, until they shall expire by their own limitation, or shall be altered or repealed by the general assembly, in pursuance of this constitution. The validity of all bonds, debts, contracts, as well of individuals as of bodies corporate, or the state, of all suits, actions, or rights of action, both in law and equity, shall continue as if no change had taken place. All officers filling any office by election or appointment shall continue to exercise the duties thereof, according to their respective commissions or appointments, until their offices shall have been abolished or their successors selected and qualified in accordance with this constitution or the laws enacted pursuant thereto.

ARTICLE TWELFTH.
OF AMENDMENTS TO THE CONSTITUTION.

Amendments to this constitution may be proposed by any member of the senate or house of representatives. An amendment so proposed, approved upon roll call by a yea vote of at least a majority, but by less than three-fourths, of the total membership of each house, shall be published with the laws which may have been passed at the same session and be continued to the regular session of the general assembly elected at the general election to be held on the Tuesday after the first Monday of November in the next even-

numbered year. An amendment so proposed, approved upon roll call by a yea vote of at least three-fourths of the total membership of each house, or any amendment which, having been continued from the previous general assembly, is again approved upon roll call by a yea vote of at least a majority of the total membership of each house, shall, by the secretary of the state, be transmitted to the town clerk in each town in the state, whose duty it shall be to present the same to the electors thereof for their consideration at the general election to be held on the Tuesday after the first Monday of November in the next even-numbered year. If it shall appear, in a manner to be provided by law, that a majority of the electors present and voting on such amendment at such election shall have approved such amendment, the same shall be valid, to all intents and purposes, as a part of this constitution. Electors voting by absentee ballot under the provisions of the statutes shall be considered to be present and voting.

ARTICLE THIRTEENTH.
OF CONSTITUTIONAL CONVENTIONS.

SEC. 1. The general assembly may, upon roll call, by a yea vote of at least two-thirds of the total membership of each house, provide for the convening of a constitutional convention to amend or revise the constitution of the state not earlier than ten years from the date of convening any prior convention.

SEC. 2. The question "Shall there be a Constitutional Convention to amend or revise the Constitution of the State?" shall be submitted to all the electors of the state at the general election held on the Tuesday after the first Monday in November in the even-numbered year next succeeding the expiration of a period of twenty years from the date of convening of the last convention called to revise or amend the constitution of the state, including the Constitutional Convention of 1965, or next succeeding the expiration of a period of twenty years from the date of submission of such a question to all electors of the state, whichever date shall last occur. If a majority of the electors voting on the question shall signify "yes", the general assembly shall provide for such convention as provided in Section 3 of this article.

SEC. 3. In providing for the convening of a constitutional convention to amend or revise the constitution of the state the general assembly shall upon roll call, by a yea vote of at least two-thirds of the total membership of each house, prescribe by law the manner of selection of the membership of such convention, the date of convening of such convention, which shall be not later than one year from the date of the roll call vote under Section 1 of this article or one year from the date of the election under Section 2 of this article, as the case may be, and the date for final adjournment of such convention.

SEC. 4. Proposals of any constitutional convention to amend or revise the constitution of the state shall be submitted to all the electors of the state not later than two months after final adjournment of the convention, either as a whole or in such parts and with such alternatives as the convention may determine. Any proposal of the convention to amend or revise the constitution of the state submitted to such electors in accordance with this section and approved by a majority of such electors voting on the question shall be valid, to all intents and purposes, as a part of this constitution. Such proposals when so approved shall take effect thirty days after the date of the vote thereon unless otherwise provided in the proposal.

ARTICLE FOURTEENTH.
OF THE EFFECTIVE DATE OF THIS CONSTITUTION.

This proposed constitution, submitted by the Constitutional Convention of 1965, shall become the constitution of the state of Connecticut upon approval by the people and proclamation by the governor as provided by law.

Amendments to the Constitution of the State of Connecticut

ARTICLE I.

Section 1 of article fourth of the constitution is amended to read as follows: A general election for governor, lieutenant-governor, secretary of the state, treasurer, comptroller and attorney general shall be held on the Tuesday after the first Monday of November, 1974, and quadrennially thereafter.

ARTICLE II.

SEC. 1. Section 3 of article third of the constitution is amended to read as follows: The senate shall consist of not less than thirty and not more than fifty members, each of whom shall have attained the age of twenty-one years and be an elector residing in the senatorial district from which he is elected. Each senatorial district shall be contiguous as to territory and shall elect no more than one senator.

SEC. 2. Section 4 of said article third is amended to read as follows: The house of representatives shall consist of not less than one hundred twenty-five and not more than two hundred twenty-five members, each of whom shall have attained the age of twenty-one years and be an elector residing in the assembly district from which he is elected. Each assembly district shall be contiguous as to territory and shall elect no more than one representative. For the purpose of forming assembly districts no town shall be divided except for the purpose of forming assembly districts wholly within the town.

SEC. 3. Section 10 of article sixth of the constitution is amended to read as follows: Every elector who has attained the age of twenty-one years shall be eligible to any office in the state, but no person who has not attained the age of twenty-one shall be eligible therefor, except in cases provided for in this constitution.

ARTICLE III.

Section 2 of article third of the constitution is amended to read as follows: There shall be a regular session of the general assembly on the Wednesday following the first Monday of January in the odd-numbered years and on the Wednesday following the first Monday of February in the even-numbered years, and at such other times as the general assembly shall judge necessary; but the person administering the office of governor may, on special emergencies, convene the general assembly at any other time. All regular and special sessions of the general assembly shall be held at Hartford, but the person administering the office of governor may, in case of special emergency, convene the assembly at any other place in the state. The general assembly shall adjourn each regular session in the odd-numbered years not later than the first Wednesday after the first Monday in June and in the even-numbered years not later than the first Wednesday after the first Monday in May and shall adjourn each special session upon completion of its business. If any bill passed by any regular or special session or any appropriation item described in Section 16 of Article Fourth has been disapproved by the governor prior to its adjournment, and has not been reconsidered by the assembly, or is so disapproved after such adjournment, the secretary of the state shall reconvene the general assembly on the second Monday after the last day on which the governor is authorized to transmit or has transmitted every bill to the secretary with his objections pursuant to Section 15 of Article Fourth of this constitution, whichever occurs first; provided if such Monday falls on a legal holiday the general assembly shall be reconvened on the next following day. The reconvened session shall be for the sole purpose of reconsidering and, if the assembly so desires, repassing such bills. The general assembly shall adjourn sine die not later than three days following its reconvening. In the even year session the general assembly shall consider no business other than budgetary, revenue and financial matters, bills and resolutions raised by committees of the general assembly and those matters certified in writing by the speaker of the house of representatives and president pro tempore of the senate to be of an emergency nature.

ARTICLE IV.

Section 19 of article first of the constitution is amended to read as follows: The right of trial by jury shall remain inviolate, the number of such jurors, which shall not be less than six, to be established by law; but no person shall, for a capital offense, be tried by a jury of less than twelve jurors without his consent. In all civil and criminal actions tried by a jury, the parties shall have the right to challenge jurors peremptorily, the number of such challenges to be established by law. The right to question each juror individually by counsel shall be inviolate.

CROSS REFERENCES

Refer to the following articles in the text volumes (Volumes 1 through 8) for background of the RESOURCE UNITS.

RESOURCE UNIT 8-A

AEROSPACE AND AIR TRANSPORT INDUSTRY
ALASKA
ASTRONAUTS
ATOMIC ENERGY
BARTLETT, ROBERT A.
BYRD, RICHARD EVELYN
CALIFORNIA
CITY AND URBAN PLANNING
COMMUNICATIONS INDUSTRY
EARHART, AMELIA
ECHO I
EINSTEIN, ALBERT
ELLSWORTH, LINCOLN
FUELS
GODDARD, ROBERT
LINDBERGH, CHARLES A.
LITTLE AMERICA
MCMAHON ACT
NATIONAL AERONAUTICS AND SPACE ADMINISTRATION
NAVIGATION
SATELLITES
TELSTAR

RESOURCE UNIT 8-B

AEROSPACE AND AIR TRANSPORT INDUSTRY
ALLIANCES
ARMS MANUFACTURING
ATOMIC ENERGY
BERLIN BLOCKADE AND AIRLIFT
BRADLEY, OMAR
CORAL SEA, BATTLE OF
EISENHOWER, DWIGHT D.
HIROSHIMA
HOBBY, OVETA CULP
HYDROGEN BOMB
KING, ERNEST J.
KNOX, FRANK
KOREAN WAR
MACARTHUR, DOUGLAS
MANHATTAN PROJECT
MARSHALL, GEORGE C.
MIDWAY ISLAND
MILITIA
NATIONAL GUARD
NATIONAL SECURITY COUNCIL
NAVAL VESSELS
NORTH ATLANTIC TREATY ORGANIZATION (N.A.T.O.)
PATTON, GEORGE S.
RESERVE FORCES
RESERVE OFFICERS TRAINING CORPS (R.O.T.C.)
SOUTHEAST ASIA TREATY ORGANIZATION (S.E.A.T.O.)
SPACE EXPLORATION
STIMSON, HENRY L.
STRATEGIC MATERIALS
U.S. AIR FORCE
U.S. ARMY
U.S. COAST GUARD
U.S. NAVY AND MARINE CORPS
UNITED STATES IN WORLD WAR II
WORLD WAR II CONFERENCES
VETERANS ADMINISTRATION
VIETNAM WAR

RESOURCE UNIT 8-C

ACHESON, DEAN G.
ADMINISTRATIVE JUSTICE
AGNEW, SPIRO T.
ALLIANCES
AMERICA FIRST COMMITTEE
APPORTIONMENT
ARMS EMBARGO
ATLANTIC CHARTER
BALANCE OF PAYMENTS
BALANCE OF TRADE
BANKS AND BANKING
BARKLEY, A. W.
BONUS
BOYCOTT
BRAIN TRUST
BRETTON WOODS CONFERENCE

UNITED NATIONS
UNITED STATES INFORMATION SERVICE (U.S.I.A.)
VANDENBERG, ARTHUR
VINSON, FRED
VOICE OF AMERICA
WAGNER, ROBERT F.
WALLACE, HENRY A.
WARREN, EARL
WELLES, SUMNER
WILLKIE, WENDELL
WORKS PROGRESS ADMINISTRATION (W.P.A.)
WORLD COURT
WORLD WAR II CONFERENCES
YALTA CONFERENCE

RESOURCE UNIT 8-D

ADVERTISING
AGRICULTURE AND AGRICULTURAL TECHNOLOGY
AMERICAN CIVIL LIBERTIES UNION
AMNESTY
ARCHITECTURE, AMERICAN
AUTOMATION
AUTOMOBILE INDUSTRY
BASEBALL
BASKETBALL
BOYCOTT
BROWN V. TOPEKA
CENSUS
CIVIL LIBERTIES AND CIVIL RIGHTS LEGISLATION
CLOSED SHOP
COLLECTIVE BARGAINING
CONSERVATION OF NATURAL RESOURCES
DISPLACED PERSONS
EDUCATION IN THE UNITED STATES
EXPORT-IMPORT BANK
FAIR EMPLOYMENT PRACTICES COMMISSION (F.E.P.C.)
FARMERS' ORGANIZATIONS
FAULKNER, WILLIAM
FOOTBALL
GREAT SOCIETY
HEMINGWAY, ERNEST
HILLMAN, SIDNEY
HOBBY, OVETA CULP
HOSPITALS
HOUSING
IMMIGRATION POLICIES
IRON AND STEEL INDUSTRY
JOURNALISM
KING, MARTIN LUTHER, JR.
LABOR ORGANIZATIONS
LEWIS, JOHN L.
LIBRARIES
LUCE, HENRY A.
MAYO BROTHERS
MEDICARE
MEDICINE AND SURGERY
MOST-FAVORED NATION

MOTION PICTURE INDUSTRY
MUSIC IN THE UNITED STATES
N.A.A.C.P. (NATIONAL ASSOCIATION FOR THE ADVANCE-
MENT OF COLORED PEOPLE)
N.C.C.J. (NATIONAL CONFERENCE OF CHRISTIANS AND
JEWS)
N.C.C.C. (NATIONAL COUNCIL OF CHURCHES OF CHRIST)
NATIONAL PARKS SERVICE
NATIONAL SCIENCE FOUNDATION
NATURAL RIGHTS
NOBEL PRIZES
NUREMBURG TRIALS
PETROLEUM INDUSTRY
OLYMPIC GAMES
PAINTING AND SCULPTURE
PEACE CORPS
PENSIONS
PLASTICS INDUSTRY
POLICE POWERS OF THE STATES
POST OFFICE AND POSTAL SERVICE
PRISONS
PRICE CONTROLS
PUERTO RICO
PULITZER PRIZES
RACES AND PEOPLES OF THE UNITED STATES
RADIO AND TELEVISION
RAILROADS
RED CROSS
REFUGEE
RELIGION IN AMERICAN LIFE
RESERVATIONS
"RIGHT TO WORK" LAWS
ST. LAWRENCE SEAWAY
SEPARATION OF CHURCH AND STATE
SHARECROPPING
SHIPBUILDING
SIT-DOWN STRIKE
SLUMS AND SLUM CLEARANCE
SOCIAL SECURITY SYSTEM
SPORTS
STANDARD OF LIVING
STATES' RIGHTS
SUFFRAGE
SWEATSHOP
TAFT-HARTLEY ACT
TELEPHONE AND TELEGRAPH INDUSTRY
THEATER IN AMERICA
TRADE, INTERNATIONAL
TRANSPORTATION
UNION SHOP
VOTING METHODS
WAGE AND PRICE CONTROLS
WAR ON POVERTY
WATER CONSERVATION
WELFARE SERVICES
WOMEN'S RIGHTS
WRIGHT, FRANK LLOYD

BOOKS FOR FURTHER READING

Exploration and Discovery

National Aeronautics and Space Administration, *Semi-Annual Report to the Congress* (as issued); W. O. Anderson, *Nautilus 90 North*; S. Chapman, *I.G.Y.: Year of Discovery*; M. Caidin, *Astronauts: The Story of Project Mercury*; A. C. Clarke, *Into Space*; G. F. Dufek, *Operation Deepfreeze*; L. Fermi, *Atoms in the Family: My Life with Enrico Fermi*; R. S. Lewis, *Appointment on the Moon*.

Military Developments

Office of the Chief of Military History, *The United States Army in World War II*; Office of Air Force History, *The Army Air Force in World War II*; Historical Branch, Headquarters U.S. Marine Corps, *History of the U.S. Marine Corps Operations in World War II*; S. E. Morison, *History of United States Naval Operations in World War II*.

H. Baldwin, *Battles Lost and Won*; A. R. Buchanan, *The United States and World War II*; C. L. Castillo, *Flat-tops*; K. S. Davis, *Experience of War: the United States in World War II*; F. Donovan, *Medal: The Story of the Medal of Honor*; D. D. Eisenhower, *Crusade in Europe*; H. Faber, *Soldier and Statesman: General George C. Marshall*; L. Farrago, *Patton: Ordeal and Triumph*; T. R. Fehrenbach, *This Kind of War* (Korea); J. Hersey, *Hiroshima*; E. J. King and W. M. Whitehill, *Fleet Admiral King: A Naval Record*; R. Leckie, *The War in Korea, 1950-1953*; B. H. Liddell-Hart, *History of the Second World War*; D. MacArthur, *Reminiscenses*; W. H. Mauldin, *Up Front*; R. F. Meyer, *The Stars and Stripes Story of World War II*; S. E. Morison, *The Two-Ocean War*; E. T. Pyle, *Brave Men*; C. Ryan, *The Longest Day: June 6, 1944*; J. Toland, *The Last Hundred Days*.

Political Developments

The Public Papers of the President of the United States. Issued annually, this publication includes the public papers of Presidents since Harry S. Truman. *The Public Papers of President Franklin D. Roosevelt* (edited by S. Rosenman) are also available.

D. W. Brogan, *Era of Franklin D. Roosevelt*; J. McG. Burns, *Roosevelt: The Lion and the Fox*; M. L. Coit, *Mr. Baruch*; F. Cook, *The Army-McCarthy Hearings*; J. A. Farley, *Behind the Ballots*; T. R. Fehrenbach, *The United Nations in War and Peace*; H. Feis, *Churchill-Roosevelt-Stalin: The War They Waged and the Peace They Sought*; E. F. Goldman, *The Crucial Decade and After: America, 1945-1960*; E. F. Goldman, *The Tragedy of Lyndon Johnson*; S. H. Johnson, *Blue Eagle, from Egg to Earth*; G. F. Kennan, *American Diplomacy, 1900-1950*; G. F. Kennan, *Memoirs*; R. F. Kennedy, *Thirteen Days*; H. Kissinger, *American Foreign Policy*; I. Leighton, ed., *The Aspirin Age, 1919-1941*; W. E. Leuchtenburg, *Franklin D. Roosevelt and the New Deal: 1932-1940*; W. E. Leuchtenburg, ed., *The New Deal: A Documentary History*; S. Lubell, *The Future of American Politics*; B. Mitchell, *Depression Decade*; D. Perkins, *The New Age of Franklin Roosevelt*; E. O. Reischauer, *Beyond Vietnam: The United States and Asia*; E. O. Reischauer, *The United States and Japan*; A. M. Schlesinger, Jr., *The Age of Roosevelt*; A. M. Schlesinger, Jr., *A Thousand Days*; R. E. Sherwood, *Roosevelt and Hopkins: An Intimate History*; H. S. Truman, *Memoirs*; T. H. White, *The Making of the President, 1960*; *—1964*; *—1968*; *—1972*.

Social Developments

The Economic Report of the President, which has appeared each year since 1947, contains the President's official views on the economic needs of the country, and an explanation of his proposed measures to meet those needs. The close linkage of economic policy and social policy is evidenced by these annual Economic Reports, which deal with unemployment, education, welfare services and other social problems.

F. L. Allen, *Since Yesterday*; F. Cormier, *Reuther*; S. Davis, Jr., *Yes, I Can: The Story of Sammy Davis, Jr.*; W. O. Douglas, *A Wilderness Bill of Rights*; A. J. Goldberg, *Equal Justice: The Warren Era of the Supreme Court*; E. Goodman, *The Rights of the People*; H. Golden, *Only in America*; M. Harrington, *The Other America: Poverty in the United States*; W. A. Heaps, *Riots, U.S.A.: 1765-1970*; S. C. Hirsch, *Guardians of Tomorrow*; B. Jaffe, *Men of Science in America*; M. L. King, Jr., *I Have a Dream*; M. L. King, Jr., *Stride Toward Freedom*; R. McGill, *The South and the Southerner*; M. Pupin, *From Immigrant to Inventor*; L. C. Rosten, *Hollywood: The Movie Colony, The Movie Makers*; C. Sims, *Labor Unions in the United States*; N. K. Smith, *Frank Lloyd Wright*.

8. UP TO NOW: 1933-1974

1. Ever since the stock market crash of 1929, the country had been in the throes of the Depression. As stocks sank lower, so did skirts, a phenomenon that nobody could explain. Here shown are the longer styles that replaced above-the-knee lengths of the late Twenties. *Courtesy,* Bonwit Teller, New York City.

CLOTHING, 1933-1974

2. Though it was only a "coke" date, the college crowd of 1934 still dressed for a special occasion. *Courtesy,* Purdue University, Lafayette, Indiana.   3. On campus the sweater and skirt, or simple dress was popular. *Courtesy,* Wellesley College, Wellesley, Mass.   4. In the lean days of the Thirties, consumers learned how to get the best value for their money at such sessions as this one. *Courtesy,* State Historical Society of Wisconsin.

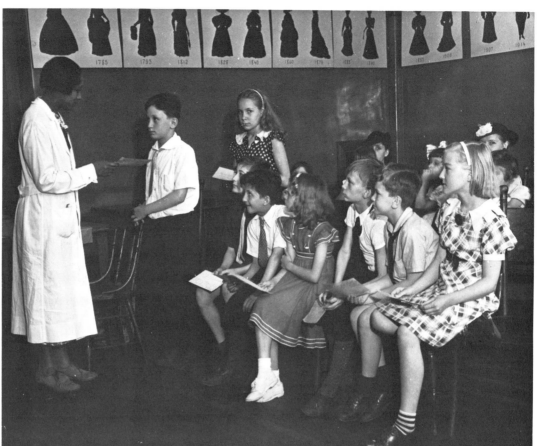

5. At school, girls wore pretty frocks and boys, white blouses and ties. *Courtesy*, National Archives, W.P.A. Federal Art Project, Photo Section. 6. By 1941 blue jeans made their appearance for sportswear as seen here in this group at the Crow Indian Fair in Montana. *Courtesy*, Collections of the Library of Congress. Photograph by Marion P. Wolcott. 7. After World War II, hats disappeared, and the page-boy hairdo and mid-calf skirts became fashionable.

8

8. By the late 1950's synthetic fabrics cut the cost of care of clothing, helping the consumer's purse. *Courtesy,* Du Pont Public Relations Department. 9. The clothes "revolution" of the 1960's, initiated in part by the Beat Generation of the decade before, brought the dress-as-you-please principle to wearing apparel. However, these young people shown here in San Francisco in 1967 kept pretty close to the rules of long hair, well-worn jeans, boots and the ubiquitous guitar. *Courtesy,* United Press International.

9

10

LIFE IN AMERICA, 1933-1974

11

10. In 1932 teachers were still in firm control of pupils. Here shown are contestants in the New York Statewide spelling bee held in Syracuse.   11. Plane travel was becoming more usual as the airlines publicized the speed and comfort of flying. Here seen is the interior of a luxury passenger plane about 1935. *Courtesy*, T.W.A.   12. Advertisements, such as this one for furniture, appealed to the buyer who had to watch his pennies during the Depression. *Courtesy*, Picture Collection, The New York Public Library.

COLONIAL FURNITURE

featuring the pioneer virtue of thrift

13.

14

13. Migrants, mainly farmers from the Dust Bowl, took to the road in the Thirties in broken-down cars, heading West with their families in search of jobs and homes. *Courtesy,* Collections of Library of Congress. Farm Security Administration Photo. 14. In the cities, neighborhoods decayed as unemployment prevailed. Seen here, a corner in St. Louis, Mo., 1936. *Courtesy,* Collections of Library of Congress. Resettlement Administration Photo by Arthur Rothstein. 15. A farmer, who stayed on the farm, and his family in front of their home in North Dakota, ca. 1938. *Courtesy,* Collections of Library of Congress. Photograph by Russell Lee.

16

15

17

18

16. Radio comedians brought inexpensive cheer to the public during the hard times. Here is Ed Wynn, "The Fire Chief," entertaining a live audience in New York. *Courtesy,* National Broadcasting Corporation. 17. Square dancing, reminiscent of pioneer days, is shown here in a group at a May Day Festival at Ashwood Plantations, S.C. in 1939. *Courtesy,* Collections of Library of Congress. Farm Security Administration Photo by Marion P. Wolcott. 18. Singer and band leader Cab Calloway was a top entertainer in the Thirties and continued his success in later years. *Courtesy,* Picture Collection, The New York Public Library. 19. Once an expensive winter sport, skiing came to be enjoyed by a wider range of enthusiasts when Sun Valley Lodge in Idaho opened its trails in 1937. *Courtesy,* Union Pacific Railroad.

19

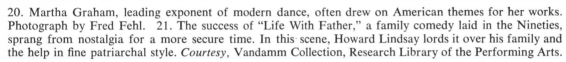

20. Martha Graham, leading exponent of modern dance, often drew on American themes for her works. Photograph by Fred Fehl. 21. The success of "Life With Father," a family comedy laid in the Nineties, sprang from nostalgia for a more secure time. In this scene, Howard Lindsay lords it over his family and the help in fine patriarchal style. *Courtesy,* Vandamm Collection, Research Library of the Performing Arts.

21

22. Smalltown life in America continued its leisurely pace as war broke out in Europe. Here is Main Street, Lexington, Mississippi, October, 1939. *Courtesy,* Collection of Library of Congress. Farm Security Administration Photo by Marion P. Wolcott. 23. The "jalopy," a do-it-yourself car, was all the rage with young men, many of whom were waiting to be drafted. *Courtesy,* Collections of Library of Congress.

23

24. By 1942 urgent calls went out for war workers, such as the people in this view of Springfield, Mass. *Courtesy,* Standard Oil Company (N.J.). 25. A Servicemen's dance in Lincoln, Nebraska, during World War II. *Courtesy,* Nebraska State Historical Society.

25

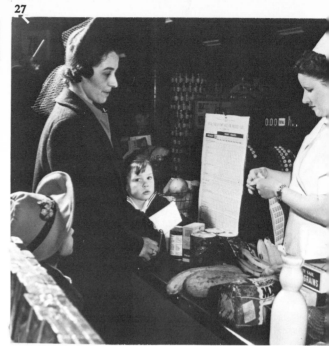

26. Garment factories converted to war work, such as making parachutes. Photograph by Harry Rubenstein. *Courtesy,* International Ladies' Garment Workers Union.   27. To assure equal shares for all, the government rationed food and other commodities. Here the shopper waits while the clerk tears out the requisite ration stamps. *Courtesy,* National Archives.   28. After the war, war brides from Europe streamed into the United States. U. S. Army Photo.   29. By 1950 television was supplanting radio as home entertainment. Seen here is the very popular children's favorite, "Howdy Doody," center, and his friends, "Mr. Bluster" and "Dilly Dally." *Courtesy,* National Broadcasting Corporation.

30

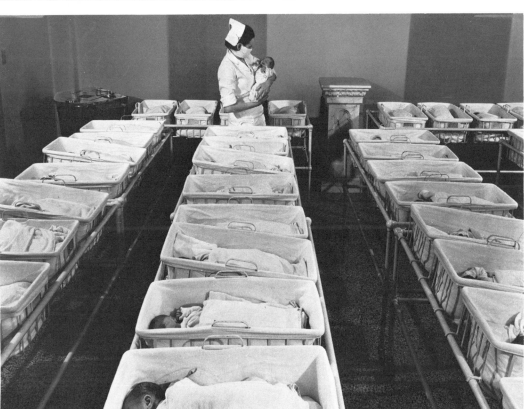

30. While the country was enjoying the postwar mood of peace, conflict broke out in Korea. Here shown is a veteran, returning from Korea on a rotation plan, being greeted by his family in Seattle, 1951. U. S. Army Photo.   31. The "baby boom" of the 1950's. *Courtesy,* Monkmeyer Press Photo Service.

32

33

34

32. After the war, many women continued to go to work along with tending to their domestic duties. Shown here in 1960 are operators in a bicycle factory. *Courtesy,* American Machine and Foundry.   33. Their added income could furnish such family pleasures as boating. *Courtesy,* Evinrude Motors, Milwaukee, Wis.   34. The earlier exodus to the suburbs in the 1950's went on, bringing a whole new informal life style to American families. *Courtesy,* Monkmeyer/Paul Conklin.   35. Youth took up causes—one was the fight against pollution of natural resources. Here shown is a demonstration on Earth Day (April, 1970)—paddling on the Milwaukee River in strange boats. *Courtesy,* United Press International.   36. Ecology, the science of conservation, inspired the young people seen here to eat without waste. *Courtesy,* Monkmeyer/Sam Falk.

37

38

37. The demand for less rigid educational methods led to new school architecture. Here seen is a New York City ungraded elementary school with several classes at work in adjoining areas. *Courtesy,* Monkmeyer/ Zimbel.   38. In colleges, student rebellion against the academic establishment exploded with uncontrolled fury, for example, the riot at Columbia University in 1968. *Courtesy,* Wide World Photos.

39

39. Many older people, called "Senior Citizens" maintained active lives in retirement communities. Here shown is such a group on wheels in St. Petersburg, Fla. *Courtesy,* Florida News Bureau. 40. The day care center for children such as this one in Manchester, N. H., permitted mothers to leave their pre-schoolers under responsible supervision during working hours. *Courtesy,* Monkmeyer/Strickler.

40

41. Speedy mobility, now in the guise of the motorcycle, continued to attract young Americans. *Courtesy,* Monkmeyer / Hugh Rogers. 42. But the quiet family hour, as shown here, still kept its importance in the 1970's. *Courtesy,* Monkmeyer / Sybil Shelton.

42

SUPPLEMENTARY STATISTICAL TABLES

The statistics of national population change, just as the population does. These tables give the latest population figures for the States (*Table I*) and for the Standard Metropolitan Areas (*Table II*) which were made available by the Census Bureau in 1974 as this book was about to be printed. Since the statistical data on popu-

lation in Volumes 1 through 8 was taken from the preliminary figures reported for the Census of 1970, the student should refer to these tables to see if the Census Bureau has altered its preliminary estimate for any given State or city.

The tables are reprinted from *Current Population Reports: Population Estimates and Projections, Series P-25, No. 505* (September 1973).

TABLE I

ESTIMATES OF THE POPULATION OF STATES: JULY 1, 1972 AND 1973

(Population in thousands. Resident population includes estimated Armed Forces personnel residing in each State)

Region, division, and State	July 1, 1973 (provisional)	July 1, 1972	April 1, 1970 (census)	Change, 1970 to 1973 Number	Change, 1970 to 1973 Percent
United States	209,851	208,230	203,235	6,616	3.3
REGIONS					
Northeast	49,678	49,726	49,051	628	1.3
North Central	57,601	57,410	56,577	1,024	1.8
South	66,005	65,059	62,798	3,206	5.1
West	36,567	36,036	34,809	1,758	5.0
NORTHEAST:					
New England	12,151	12,105	11,847	303	2.6
Middle Atlantic	37,528	37,621	37,203	325	0.9
NORTH CENTRAL:					
East North Central	40,897	40,793	40,253	645	1.6
West North Central	16,704	16,617	16,324	379	2.3
SOUTH:					
South Atlantic	32,459	31,921	30,671	1,787	5.8
East South Central	13,289	13,156	12,805	484	3.8
West South Central	20,257	19,982	19,322	935	4.8
WEST:					
Mountain	9,149	8,880	8,284	866	10.5
Pacific	27,417	27,156	26,526	892	3.4
NEW ENGLAND:					
Maine	1,028	1,026	994	35	3.5
New Hampshire	791	774	738	53	7.2
Vermont	464	460	445	19	4.4
Massachusetts	5,818	5,796	5,689	129	2.3
Rhode Island	973	969	950	23	2.5
Connecticut	3,076	3,080	3,032	44	1.4
MIDDLE ATLANTIC:					
New York	18,265	18,367	18,241	24	0.1
New Jersey	7,361	7,349	7,168	193	2.7
Pennsylvania	11,902	11,905	11,794	108	0.9
EAST NORTH CENTRAL:					
Ohio	10,731	10,722	10,652	79	0.7
Indiana	5,316	5,286	5,194	123	2.4
Illinois	11,236	11,244	11,114	122	1.1
Michigan	9,044	9,013	8,875	169	1.9
Wisconsin	4,569	4,526	4,418	152	3.4

TABLE I

ESTIMATES OF THE POPULATION OF STATES: JULY 1, 1972 AND 1973—Continued

Region, division, and State	Resident population				
	July 1, 1973 (provisional)	July 1, 1972	April 1, 1970 (census)	Change, 1970 to 1973	
				Number	Percent
WEST NORTH CENTRAL:					
Minnesota	3,897	3,877	3,805	92	2.4
Iowa	2,904	2,884	2,825	79	2.8
Missouri	4,757	4,747	4,677	79	1.7
North Dakota	640	634	618	22	3.5
South Dakota	685	680	666	18	2.7
Nebraska	1,542	1,528	1,484	59	4.0
Kansas	2,279	2,268	2,249	30	1.4
SOUTH ATLANTIC:					
Delaware	576	571	548	27	5.0
Maryland	4,070	4,048	3,922	147	3.8
District of Columbia	746	752	757	−11	−1.4
Virginia	4,811	4,765	4,648	162	3.5
West Virginia	1,794	1,795	1,744	50	2.9
North Carolina	5,273	5,221	5,082	191	3.8
South Carolina	2,726	2,688	2,591	135	5.2
Georgia	4,786	4,733	4,590	196	4.3
Florida	7,678	7,347	6,789	888	13.1
EAST SOUTH CENTRAL:					
Kentucky	3,342	3,306	3,219	123	3.8
Tennessee	4,126	4,072	3,924	202	5.2
Alabama	3,539	3,521	3,444	95	2.8
Mississippi	2,281	2,256	2,217	64	2.9
WEST SOUTH CENTRAL:					
Arkansas	2,037	2,008	1,923	113	5.9
Louisiana	3,764	3,738	3,643	121	3.3
Oklahoma	2,663	2,633	2,559	103	4.0
Texas	11,794	11,604	11,197	597	5.3
MOUNTAIN:					
Montana	721	716	694	26	3.8
Idaho	770	755	713	57	7.9
Wyoming	353	346	332	21	6.3
Colorado	2,437	2,364	2,207	230	10.4
New Mexico	1,106	1,076	1,016	90	8.9
Arizona	2,058	1,963	1,772	285	16.1
Utah	1,157	1,127	1,059	98	9.2
Nevada	548	533	489	59	12.1
PACIFIC:					
Washington	3,429	3,418	3,409	20	0.6
Oregon	2,225	2,185	2,091	134	6.4
California	20,601	20,411	19,953	648	3.2
Alaska	330	325	302	28	9.3
Hawaii	832	816	770	62	8.1

TABLE II

METROPOLITAN AREAS BY POPULATION RANK SIZE, 1970

(Corrected 1970 populations. SMSA's as currently defined. Nearest county or metropolitan SEA equivalent in New England)

Rank, 1970	Standard metropolitan statistical area	Population July 1, 1972 (provisional estimate)	Population April 1, 1970 (census)	Rank, 1970	Standard metropolitan statistical area	Population July 1, 1972 (provisional estimate)	Population April 1, 1970 (census)
1	New York, N.Y.-N.J.	9,943,800	9,973,716	61	Fort Lauderdale-Hollywood, Fla. ...	684,900	620,100
2	Los Angeles-Long Beach, Calif. ...	6,999,600	7,041,980	62	Jersey City, N.J.	610,600	607,839
3	Chicago, Ill.	7,084,700	6,977,611	63	Allentown-Bethlehem-Easton, Pa.-N.J.	607,900	594,382
4	Philadelphia, Pa.-N.J.	4,877,500	4,824,110	64	New Brunswick-Perth Amboy-Sayreville, N.J. ...	595,600	583,813
5	Detroit, Mich.	4,488,900	4,435,051	65	Springfield-Chicopee-Holyoke, Mass.-Conn.[1] ...	591,100	583,031
6	Boston, Mass.[1]	3,417,000	3,376,328	66	Charlotte-Gastonia, N.C.	569,200	557,785
7	San Francisco-Oakland, Calif	3,131,800	3,108,782	67	Tulsa, Okla.	559,600	549,154
8	Washington, D.C.-Md.-Va.	2,998,900	2,909,355	68	Omaha, Nebr.-Iowa	568,800	542,646
9	Nassau-Suffolk, N.Y.	2,597,300	2,555,868	69	Richmond, Va.	552,600	542,242
10	St. Louis, Mo.-Ill.	2,399,800	2,410,492	70	Grand Rapids, Mich.	548,500	539,225
11	Pittsburgh, Pa.	2,395,900	2,401,362	71	Youngstown-Warren, Ohio	544,100	537,124
12	Dallas-Fort Worth, Tex.	(2)	2,378,353	72	Flint, Mich	521,200	508,664
13	Baltimore, Md.	2,125,000	2,071,016	73	Wilmington, Del.-N.J.-Md.	512,400	499,493
14	Cleveland, Ohio	2,045,500	2,063,729	74	Greenville-Spartanburg, S.C.	497,100	473,454
15	Newark, N.J.	2,082,000	2,057,468	75	Long Branch-Asbury Park, N.J. ...	478,600	461,849
16	Houston, Tex.	(2)	1,999,316	76	Paterson-Clifton-Passaic, N.J.	464,300	460,782
17	Minneapolis-St. Paul, Minn.-Wis. ..	1,995,800	1,965,391	77	Orlando, Fla.	506,200	453,270
18	Atlanta, Ga.	1,683,600	1,595,517	78	Fall River, Mass.-R.I.[1]	457,200	444,301
19	Seattle-Everett, Wash.	1,399,600	1,424,605	79	Lansing-East Lansing, Mich.	436,900	424,271
20	Anaheim-Santa Ana-Garden Grove, Calif.	1,527,300	1,421,233	80	Raleigh-Durham, N.C.	438,700	419,394
21	Milwaukee, Wis.	1,423,200	1,403,884	81	Fresno, Calif.	430,500	413,329
22	Cincinnati, Ohio-Ky.-Ind.	1,391,400	1,385,103	82	Tacoma, Wash.	405,300	412,344
23	San Diego, Calif.	1,443,100	1,357,854	83	Harrisburg, Pa.	422,100	410,505
24	Buffalo, N.Y.	1,353,100	1,349,211	84	Knoxville, Tenn.	420,800	409,409
25	Kansas City, Mo.-Kans.	1,303,600	1,273,926	85	Canton, Ohio	398,600	393,789
26	Miami, Fla.	1,331,100	1,267,792	86	Wichita, Kans.	375,600	389,352
27	Denver-Boulder, Colo.	1,309,200	1,231,070	87	Oxnard-Simi Valley-Ventura, Calif.	404,700	378,497
28	Riverside-San Bernardino-Ontario, Calif.	1,178,500	1,141,307	88	Mobile, Ala.	386,300	376,690
29	Indianapolis, Ind.	1,128,000	1,111,352	89	Baton Rouge, La.	386,100	375,628
30	Tampa-St. Petersburg, Fla.	1,189,000	1,088,549	90	Chattanooga, Tenn.-Ga.	380,600	370,857
31	San Jose, Calif.	1,126,700	1,065,313	91	Davenport-Rock Island-Moline, Iowa-Ill.	361,300	362,638
32	New Orleans, La.	1,076,600	1,046,470	92	Fort Wayne, Ind.	372,400	361,984
33	Columbus, Ohio	1,057,700	1,017,847	93	El Paso, Tex.	373,900	359,291
34	Portland, Oreg.-Wash.	1,036,300	1,007,130	94	Tucson, Ariz.	387,000	351,667
35	Phoenix, Ariz.	1,053,000	969,425	95	West Palm Beach-Boca Raton, Fla.	378,000	348,993
36	Rochester, N.Y.	968,600	961,516	96	Beaumont-Port Arthur-Orange, Tex.	(2)	347,568
37	San Antonio, Tex.	(2)	888,179	97	Peoria, Ill.	352,500	341,979
38	Louisville, Ky.-Ind.	887,700	867,330	98	Utica-Rome, N.Y.	343,500	340,670
39	Dayton, Ohio	857,300	852,531	99	Charleston, S.C.	342,200	336,125
40	Memphis, Tenn.-Ark.-Miss.	847,100	834,103	100	Shreveport, La.	340,000	333,826
41	Hartford, Conn.[1]	833,800	816,737	101	Brockton, Mass.[1]	350,200	333,314
42	Sacramento, Calif.	851,300	803,793	102	Albuquerque, N. Mex.	(2)	333,266
43	Bridgeport, Conn.[1]	793,900	792,814	103	Newport News-Hampton, Va.	338,700	333,140
44	Albany-Schenectady-Troy, N.Y. ...	792,900	777,977	104	Bakersfield, Calif.	336,000	330,234
45	Providence-Warwick-Pawtucket, R.I.-Mass.[1]	782,600	769,789	105	York, Pa.	338,500	329,540
46	Birmingham, Ala.	778,500	767,230	106	Little Rock-North Little Rock, Ark.	336,400	323,296
47	Toledo, Ohio-Mich.	780,600	762,658	107	Austin, Tex.	(2)	323,158
48	New Haven-West Haven, Conn.[1] ..	760,800	744,948	108	Columbia, S.C.	335,800	322,880
49	Greensboro—Winston-Salem—High Point, N.C.	745,100	724,129	109	Lancaster, Pa.	329,900	320,079
50	Salt Lake City-Ogden, Utah	744,300	705,458	110	Des Moines, Iowa	324,500	313,562
51	Nashville-Davidson, Tenn.	715,700	699,271	111	Trenton, N.J.	315,300	304,116
52	Oklahoma City, Okla.	735,800	699,092	112	Binghamton, N.Y.-Pa.	305,700	302,672
53	Norfolk-Virginia Beach-Portsmouth, Va.-N.C.	683,000	687,576	113	Reading, Pa.	301,400	296,382
54	Akron, Ohio	682,200	679,239	114	Stockton, Calif.	297,200	291,073
55	Worcester, Mass.[1]	644,700	637,037	115	Madison, Wis.	300,200	290,040
56	Syracuse, N.Y.	643,400	636,596	116	Spokane, Wash.	301,800	287,487
57	Gary-Hammond-East Chicago, Ind.	644,100	633,367	117	Huntington-Ashland, W. Va.-Ky.-Ohio	292,600	286,935
58	Honolulu, Hawaii	660,100	630,528	118	Evansville, Ind.-Ky.	288,800	284,959
59	Northeast Pennsylvania	631,500	621,882	119	Corpus Christi, Tex.	298,300	284,832
60	Jacksonville, Fla.	635,500	621,827	120	Huntsville, Ala.	286,000	232,450

See footnotes at end of table.

TABLE II

METROPOLITAN AREAS BY POPULATION RANK SIZE, 1970—Continued

(Corrected 1970 populations. SMSA's as currently defined. Nearest county or metropolitan SEA equivalent in New England)

Rank, 1970	Standard metropolitan statistical area	Population July 1, 1972 (provisional estimate)	Population April 1, 1970 (census)	1970 Rank,	Standard metropolitan statistical area	Population July 1, 1972 (provisional estimate)	Population April 1, 1970 (census)
121	South Bend, Ind.	281,600	280,031	186	Lake Charles, La.	148,200	145,415
122	Appleton-Oshkosh, Wis.	282,900	276,943	187	Yakima, Wash.	148,900	145,212
123	Augusta, Ga.-S.C.	272,400	275,787	188	Amarillo, Tex.	149,100	144,396
124	Las Vegas, Nev.	295,800	273,288	189	Jackson, Mich.	144,100	143,274
125	Rockford, Ill.	268,000	272,063	190	Brownsville-Harlingen-San Benito, Tex.	151,900	140,368
126	Lexington, Ky.	272,700	266,701				
127	Duluth-Superior, Minn.-Wis.	267,000	265,350	191	Anderson, Ind.	141,100	138,522
128	Santa Barbara-Santa Maria-Lompoc, Calif.	271,800	264,324	192	Provo-Orem, Utah	149,700	137,776
129	Erie, Pa.	271,800	264,324	193	Altoona, Pa.	137,600	135,356
130	Johnstown, Pa.	267,400	262,822	194	St. Cloud, Minn.	141,600	134,585
				195	Lynchburg, Va.	140,200	133,258
131	Jackson, Miss.	267,200	258,906				
132	Kalamazoo-Portage, Mich.	263,400	257,723	196	Waterloo-Cedar Falls, Iowa	134,500	132,916
133	Charleston, W. Va.	258,800	257,140	197	Alexandria, La.	134,500	131,749
134	Lorain-Elyria, Ohio	261,100	256,843	198	Mansfield, Ohio	128,600	129,997
135	Vallejo-Fairfield-Napa, Calif.	264,500	251,129	199	Muncie, Ind.	131,500	129,219
				200	Petersburg-Colonial Heights-Hopewell, Va.	127,600	128,809
136	Salinas-Seaside-Monterey, Calif.	254,400	247,450				
137	Pensacola, Fla.	252,400	243,075	201	Wichita Falls, Tex.	(2)	128,642
138	Kingsport-Bristol, Tenn.-Va.	248,000	241,154	202	Fayetteville-Springdale, Ark.	135,300	127,846
139	Colorado Springs, Colo.	262,500	239,288	203	Anchorage, Alaska	(NA)	126,385
140	Columbus, Ga.-Ala.	226,500	238,584	204	Decatur, Ill.	122,700	125,010
				205	Santa Cruz, Calif.	135,700	123,790
141	Ann Arbor, Mich.	240,600	234,103				
142	New London-Norwich, Conn.-R.I.[3]	237,100	230,654	206	Abilene, Tex.	(2)	122,164
143	Melbourne-Titusville-Cocoa, Fla.	227,400	230,006	207	Vineland-Millville-Bridgeton, N.J.	129,300	121,374
144	Lakeland-Winter Haven, Fla.	238,300	228,515	208	Reno, Nev.	130,500	121,068
145	Macon, Ga.	229,900	226,782	209	Sarasota, Fla.	135,900	120,413
				210	Fargo-Moorhead, N. Dak.-Minn.	125,600	120,261
146	Hamilton-Middletown, Ohio	232,900	226,207				
147	Montgomery, Ala.	236,200	225,911	211	Pueblo, Colo.	120,700	118,238
148	Manchester, N.H.[1]	237,500	223,941	212	Kenosha, Wis.	119,600	117,917
149	Poughkeepsie, N.Y.	228,500	222,295	213	Florence, Ala.	119,900	117,743
150	Saginaw, Mich.	226,600	219,743	214	Bay City, Mich.	119,300	117,339
				215	Sioux City, Iowa-Nebr.	119,600	116,189
151	Eugene-Springfield, Oreg.	224,600	215,401				
152	Fayetteville, N.C.	214,600	212,042	216	Tuscaloosa, Ala.	121,400	116,029
153	Lima, Ohio	210,700	210,074	217	Monroe, La.	120,000	115,387
154	Savannah, Ga.	202,700	207,987	218	Texarkana, Tex.-Texarkana, Ark.	112,400	113,488
155	Santa Rosa, Calif.	219,200	204,885	219	Williamsport, Pa.	114,800	113,296
				220	Boise City, Idaho	120,200	112,230
156	Roanoke, Va.	207,300	203,153				
157	Modesto, Calif.	201,300	194,506	221	Lafayette, La.	116,400	111,643
158	Portland, Maine[1]	197,500	192,528	222	Lafayette-West Lafayette, Ind.	111,800	109,378
159	Springfield, Ohio	189,700	187,606	223	Tallahassee, Fla.	119,100	109,355
160	Salem, Oreg.	195,800	186,658	224	Lawton, Okla.	101,700	108,144
				225	Wilmington, N.C.	115,700	107,219
161	Wheeling, W. Va.-Ohio	184,600	182,712				
162	McAllen-Pharr-Edinburg, Tex.	199,500	181,535	226	Fort Myers, Fla.	120,900	105,216
163	Topeka, Kans.	184,400	180,619	227	Gainesville, Fla.	108,500	104,764
164	Battle Creek, Mich.	181,400	180,129	228	Bloomington-Normal, Ill.	110,100	104,389
165	Lubbock, Tex.	189,900	179,295	229	Elmira, N.Y.	101,800	101,537
				230	St. Joseph, Mo.	100,400	98,828
166	Muskegon-Muskegon Hgts., Mich.	179,100	175,410				
167	Terre Haute, Ind.	178,300	175,143	231	Tyler, Tex.	100,800	97,096
168	Atlantic City, N.J.	186,600	175,043	232	Albany, Ga.	102,200	96,683
169	Springfield, Ill.	174,600	171,020	233	Burlington, N.C.	99,800	96,362
170	Racine, Wis.	173,900	170,838	234	Sioux Falls, S. Dak.	96,700	95,209
				235	Gadsden, Ala.	95,100	94,144
171	Galveston-Texas City, Tex.	177,800	169,812				
172	Daytona Beach, Fla.	178,000	169,487	236	Richland-Kennewick, Wash.	96,000	93,356
173	Springfield, Mo.	177,600	168,053	237	Odessa, Tex.	93,600	92,660
174	Lincoln, Nebr.	177,100	167,972	238	Lewiston-Auburn, Maine[4]	92,600	91,279
175	Steubenville-Weirton, Ohio-W. Va.	167,500	165,627	239	Dubuque, Iowa	95,300	90,609
				240	Billings, Mont.	92,200	87,367
176	Champaign-Urbana-Rantoul, Ill.	160,600	163,281				
177	Cedar Rapids, Iowa	167,500	163,213	241	Pine Bluff, Ark.	83,000	85,329
178	Asheville, N.C.	162,800	161,059	242	Rochester, Minn.	87,100	84,104
179	Fort Smith, Ark.-Okla.	167,400	160,421	243	Sherman-Denison, Tex.	75,800	83,225
180	Biloxi-Gulfport, Miss.	167,500	160,070	244	Great Falls, Mont.	84,900	81,804
				245	Columbia, Mo.	85,000	80,935
181	Killeen-Temple, Tex.	180,300	159,794				
182	Green Bay, Wis.	163,400	158,244				
183	Pittsfield, Mass.[1]	150,900	149,402				
184	Parkersburg-Marietta, W. Va.-Ohio	147,100	148,132				
185	Waco, Tex.	150,400	147,553				

TABLE II

METROPOLITAN AREAS BY POPULATION RANK SIZE, 1970—Continued

(Corrected 1970 populations. SMSA's as currently defined. Nearest county or metropolitan SEA equivalent in New England)

Rank, 1970	Standard metropolitan statistical area	Population		1970 Rank,	Standard metropolitan statistical area	Population	
		July 1, 1972 (provisional estimate)	April 1, 1970 (census)			July 1, 1972 (provisional estimate)	April 1, 1970 (census)
246	LaCrosse, Wis.	83,000	80,468				
247	Owensboro, Ky.	79,300	79,486				
248	Laredo, Tex.	79,100	72,859				
249	San Angelo, Tex.	71,900	71,047				
250	Midland, Tex.	65,000	65,433				
251	Bryan-College Station, Tex.	61,700	57,978				

NA Not available.
[1]Metropolitan State economic area. See table 1 for detail.
[2]Estimates not available for all counties in SMSA. For those counties available, the population is as follows:

Rank	SMSA	1972 estimate	1970 census	Rank	SMSA	1972 estimate	1970 census
12	Dallas-Fort Worth, Tex.	2,383,800	2,318,410	102	Albuquerque, N. Mex.	337,500	315,774
16	Houston, Tex.	2,105,600	1,985,031	107	Austin, Tex.	318,400	295,516
37	San Antonio, Tex.	909,700	864,014	201	Wichita Falls, Tex.	117,900	120,563
96	Beaumont-Port Arthur-Orange, Tex.	319,700	317,572	206	Abilene, Tex.	119,000	113,959

[3]New London County, Conn.
[4]Androscoggin County, Maine.

GENERAL BIBLIOGRAPHY

This list is a very brief introduction to works of a *general* nature which can serve the student of history. Many excellent works of this kind have been issued as single volumes in a series. In the list that follows, several of these series have been cited as such and the names of the series editors given, but the titles of the individual volumes contained in the series have not been given. An asterisk (*) precedes the general title of each series. Books which discuss *specific* periods or incidents in American History will be found by reference to the short notes at the end of the articles in Volumes 1 through 8, which deal with the required period or incident, and in the special bibliographies at the end of the appropriate Resource Units in Volume 9 or 10. Much more detailed information about books which have been written on almost every topic in our history is available in *Harvard Guide to American History*, edited by O. Handlin and five other eminent historians, and in *A Guide to the Study of the United States of America*, prepared by R. P. Basler, D. H. Mugridge, and B. P. McCrum for the Library of Congress.

Among the many valuable periodicals which are devoted to American History, the *American Historical Review* and the *Journal of American History* will be found useful for the authoritative reviews of new books which they contain. For the evidence of current research in special areas, the publications of State and regional historical societies are of value; also, the publications of societies devoted to the history of special topics such as education, business and economics, religion and religious groups, philosophy and ideas.

1. Collections of Source Materials

Angle, P. M., ed., *The American Reader*
*(Encyclopedia Britannica, publ.) *Annals of America*
Bailey, T. A., ed., *The American Spirit*
Commager, H. S., ed., *Documents of American History*
Hart, A. B., ed., *American History Told by Contemporaries*
Hofstadter, R., *Great Issues in American History*
*Jameson, J. F., general ed., *Original Narratives of Early American History*
Meltzer, M., ed., *In Their Own Words: A History of the American Negro*

2. U.S. Government Publications

U.S. Department of Commerce, *Historical Statistics of the United States: Colonial Times to 1957*
U.S. Department of Commerce, *Statistical Abstract of the United States* (issued annually)
Congressional Record
U.S. Department of Agriculture, *Yearbook* (issued annually)
U.S. Office of Management and Budget, *The Budget of the United States Government* (issued annually)
Economic Reports of the President (issued annually)
Public Papers of the President (issued annually)
U.S. Department of State, *Bulletin* (issued weekly)

3. Atlases and Historical Atlases

Adams, J. T., ed., *Atlas of American History*

Esposito, V. J., ed., *The West Point Atlas of American Wars*

Lord, C. and E. H., *Historical Atlas of the United States*

U.S. Geological Survey, *National Atlas of the United States*

4. Pictorial Sources

Adams, J. T., ed., *Album of American History*

Butterfield, R., *The American Past*

Davidson, M., *Life in America*

*Gabriel, R. H., ed., *The Pageant of America*

5. Other Readings

Bemis, S. F., *A Diplomatic History of the United States*

*Boorstin, D. J., ed., *The Chicago History of American Civilization*

Clark, T. D., *Frontier America: The Story of the Westward Movement*

Clark, T. D., *Three Paths to the Modern South: Education, Agriculture, and Conservation*

*Commager, H. S. and R. B. Morris, eds., *The New American Nation Series*

David, H., ed., *The Economic History of the United States*

De Conde, Alexander, *A History of American Foreign Policy*

Faulkner, H. U., *American Economic History*

Ferrell, R. H., *American Diplomacy*

Franklin, J. H., *From Slavery to Freedom: A History of Negro Americans*

Garraty, J. A., *The American Nation*

Hicks, J., G. E. Mowry and R. E. Burke, *The Federal Union* and *The American Nation*

Hopkins, J. G. E., ed., *Concise Dictionary of American Biography*

Jaffe, Bernard, *Men of Science in America*

*Johnson, A. and D. Malone, eds., *Dictionary of American Biography*

Kelly, A. H. and W. A. Harbison, *The American Constitution: Its Origins and Development*

Kohn, H., *American Nationalism*

Link, A. S. and W. B. Caton, *American Epoch: A History of the United States Since the 1890's*

May, E. R., *The American Foreign Policy*

Morison, S. E., *Oxford History of the American People*

Mott, F. L., *American Journalism* and *A History of American Magazines*

Porter, K. H. and D. B. Johnson, *National Party Platforms*

Spiller, R. E., and others, eds., *Literary History of the United States*

*Stephenson, W. H. and E. M. Coulter, eds., *A History of the South*

Wish, H., *Society and Thought in America*

CHRONOLOGICAL TABLES

1492	• Columbus' first voyage
	• Spaniards end Moorish rule in Granada, unify Spain
1493	• Columbus' second voyage; discovers Puerto Rico
1494	• Treaty of Tordesillas
1495	
1496	
1497	• John Cabot reaches North America
1498	• Vasco da Gama completes voyage, Portugal to India and return
1499	• Amerigo Vespucci sails on South American exploration
1500	• Pedro Cabral discovers Brazil
1501	• Corte-Real brothers explore Greenland and Newfoundland
1502	• Portuguese and English explore Newfoundland (to 1504)
1503	
1504	• Spain takes over rule of Naples in Italy
1505	
1506	
1507	• New World named "America" by mapmaker Waldseemuller
1508	• Spanish conquer Puerto Rican Indian tribes
1509	• Henry VIII becomes King of England
1510	
1511	
1512	
1513	• Balboa discovers Pacific Ocean
	• Ponce de Leon's expedition to Florida
1514	
1515	
1516	
1517	• Martin Luther publishes 95 Theses; Protestant Reformation begins
1518	
1519	• Cortez begins conquest of Mexico
	• Magellan starts circumnavigation of world
	• King of Spain becomes Holy Roman Emperor (as Charles V)
1520	
1521	• San Juan (Puerto Rico) founded
	• Magellan killed in Philippine Islands
1522	• War between England and France (to 1525)
1523	• Verrazzano's voyage to Atlantic coast of North America
1524	• Exploration of Atlantic Coast of Estevan Gomez (Spanish) and Verrazzano (French)
1525	
1526	
1527	• German and Spanish troops seize Rome
1528	• War between England and the Empire (to 1529)
	• Narvaez expedition to Florida and Gulf Coast
1529	• Cabeza de Vaca and survivors of Narvaez explore American Southwest (to 1535)
1530	• English seamen trade in Brazil
1531	
1532	• Pizarro begins conquest of Peru for Spain
1533	
1534	• Michelangelo begins work on Sistine Chapel ceiling ("Last Judgment")
	• Jacques Cartier's first exploration (Labrador)
1535	• Cartier's second exploration (St. Lawrence River; winters in Canada)
	• Spaniards found Lima and Buenos Aires
1536	• War by France, Turkey and Portugal against Charles V (to 1539)
	• John Calvin begins rule in Geneva
1537	
1538	
1539	• De Soto begins exploration of American Southeast
	• Ulloa explores Gulf of California, Colorado River
1540	• Coronado expedition begins
1541	• Cartier's third exploration
1542	• Cabrillo explores California coast
1543	• Cartier's fourth exploration of Canada
	• Copernicus publishes astronomical work
1544	• War between England and Charles V against France (to 1546)
1545	• Council of Trent begins (Catholic Counter-Reformation)

1546
1547 • Henry VIII dies. Edward VI becomes King of England
1548
1549
1550
1551
1552
1553 • Edward VI dies. Mary Tudor becomes Queen of England
1554
1555
1556 • Charles V abdicates. Philip II becomes King of Spain
         • Mercator publishes world map in Netherlands
1557
1558 • Mary Tudor dies. Elizabeth I becomes Queen of England
1559 • Treaty of Cateau-Cambrésis ends series of wars between France and Empire
1560
1561
1562 • Religious wars begin in France (Catholics vs. Huguenots)
         • Huguenots attempt to colonize Florida
         • John Hawkins begins English slave trade, Africa to America
1563
1564 • Undeclared sea war begins between England and Spain
1565 • Spanish troops wipe out French Florida colony. St. Augustine founded
1566
1567 • Mary Queen of Scots forced to abdicate
1568
1569
1570
1571 • Battle of Lepanto ends Turkish naval threat in Mediterranean
1572 • Drake begins raids on Spanish ports in America
         • Dutch war for independence from Spain begins
1573
1574
1575 • Humphrey Gilbert proposes English colonies in America
1576 • Martin Frobisher makes first voyage seeking Northwest Passage
1577 • Drake begins voyage around world
1578
1579 • Drake on California coast, claims it for England
1580 • Spain and Portugal united under Philip II
1581
1582 • Gregorian Calendar reform in effect
1583 • Gilbert founds first English colony in Newfoundland
1584
1585 • First Virginia colony attempted (Roanoke; ended 1586)
         • John Davis explores for Northwest Passage
1586
1587 • Second Roanoke colony established (disappeared)
         • Mary Queen of Scots beheaded
1588 • Spanish Armada defeated by English
1589
1590
1591 • Shakespeare begins to produce plays (to 1616)
1592
1593 • French King Henry IV becomes Catholic
1594
1595 • Henry IV declares war on Spain
         • Hawkins dies in Caribbean campaign against Spain
1595-1596   • Spanish missions established in Georgia and South Carolina
1596 • England, Dutch and French fight Spain
         • Drake dies in Caribbean fighting
1597
1598 • French war against Spain ends
         • Philip II of Spain dies. Philip III becomes King
         • Edict of Nantes ends French religious wars; Huguenots granted toleration
         • Juan de Onate exploring Southwestern area (Colorado to California)
1599

	1600	1601	1602	1603	1604
EXPLORATION & SETTLEMENT	• East India Company chartered in England			• Champlain explores St. Lawrence to Lachine	• Champlain's second voyage: Nova Scotia, Cape Cod, Martha's Vineyard (to 1606) • French settlement in Acadia
COLONIAL EVENTS	• East India Company chartered in England			• Queen Elizabeth dies; James VI of Scotland becomes King James I of England	
ABOLITION & SLAVERY					
FOREIGN EVENTS				• Galileo conducting research on gravity	

1605	1606	1607	1608	1609
• George Weymouth explores Nantucket and Maine coasts for English	• Charters granted to Virginia Company of London and Virginia Company of Plymouth • John Popham explores Maine for Plymouth Company	• Jamestown founded • Gorges attempts settlement in Maine		• Henry Hudson explores Atlantic Coast, Delaware Bay and Hudson River • Santa Fe, New Mexico, founded by Spaniards • Champlain builds fort at Quebec, discovers Lake Champlain
			• Captain John Smith forces Virginia settlers to work	• Second charter to Virginia Company • "Starving time" begins in Virginia (winter of 1609–1610) • Church of England established in Virginia
• *Don Quixote* published in Spain			• Telescope developed in Netherlands	• Spain and Netherlands agree to truce; Dutch independence established

	1610	1611	1612	1613	1614
EXPLORATION & SETTLEMENT	• Hudson explores for Northwest Passage; dies in Hudson Bay			• Champlain explores Ottawa River, Canada • Adrian Block explores New York and Long Island Sound for Dutch	• John Smith explores New England coast
COLONIAL EVENTS	• Lord De La Warr becomes Governor of Virginia		• "Dale Code" of severe laws for Virginia (to 1619) • Tobacco production begun by John Rolfe • Third charter for Virginia	• Individual land grants available to Virginia farmers	
ABOLITION & SLAVERY					
FOREIGN EVENTS		• Dutch open trade in Japan			• Civil war begins in France

1615	1616	1617	1618	1619
• Champlain explores Lake Ontario, Finger Lakes region, Susquehanna River; reaches Delaware Bay		• Dutch trading fort located at site of Albany, N.Y.		
				• Revised government in Virginia: Gov. George Yeardley and House of Burgesses
				• Negro "servants" sold in Jamestown (first slaves)
			• Thirty Years War begins in Europe	• Batavia, Java, founded by Dutch

	1620	1621	1622	1623	1624
EXPLORATION & SETTLEMENT	• Plymouth founded by Pilgrims	• Dutch West India Company founded		• Biddeford, Maine, founded	• First Dutch settlers at Ft. Nassau (Albany) and Gloucester (N.J.)
COLONIAL EVENTS	• Mayflower Compact among Pilgrims	• William Bradford becomes Governor of Plymouth • Congregational Church established in Plymouth	• Indian attack on Virginia settlements; widespread disease in Virginia • Council for New England grants Maine to Gorges and Mason	• Virginia Company bankrupt • Each Plymouth family receives private land title	• Virginia charter revoked; royal colony established
ABOLITION & SLAVERY					
FOREIGN EVENTS					• Cardinal Richelieu dominates French government (to 1642) • English take Barbados in West Indies

1625	1626	1627	1628	1629
	• Salem, Mass., founded • Dutch establish settlement at New Amsterdam (New York City)		• Dutch settlement on site of Jersey City, N.J.	• Champlain captured as Quebec is taken by British
• King James I dies; Charles I becomes King of England	• Plymouth settlers buy out European owners of Company		• New England Company secures right to plant colony in Massachusetts area	• House of Burgesses called by royal governor to act as Virginia legislature • New England Company merges with Massachusetts Bay Company • Puritans dominate Massachusetts Bay Company
		• Japan excludes all foreigners	• Harvey publishes study on circulation of the blood	

	1630	1631	1632	1633	1634
EXPLORATION & SETTLEMENT	• Massachusetts Bay towns founded: Boston, Charlestown, Dorchester			• Dutch establish Ft. Good Hope (near Hartford, Ct., site)	• First Maryland settlement at St. Mary's
COLONIAL EVENTS	• Massachusetts Bay holds General Court; John Winthrop is governor	• Only some church members and landowners permitted to vote in Massachusetts	• Charter for Maryland issued to Calverts		• Commission for Foreign Plantations (part of Privy Council) in charge of colonial affairs • Indian attack on some Dutch settlements
ABOLITION & SLAVERY					
FOREIGN EVENTS	• Buccaneers establish control of Tortuga Island in Caribbean			• First English trading post in Madras, India	

1635	1636	1637	1638	1639
• Hartford, Wethersfield and Windsor, Ct., founded	• Providence, R.I., founded	• New Haven, Ct., established (as Quinnipiac)	• Swedish colony begun at Ft. Christina (Wilmington, Del.) • Exeter, N.H., established	
• Roger Williams banished from Massachusetts • Maryland-Virginia dispute over Kent Island in Chesapeake Bay • Council in Virginia deposes royal governor; he regains post • Massachusetts settlers agree to move to Connecticut	• Pequot War begins in New England (to 1637) • Anne Hutchinson tried in Massachusetts • Harvard College and Boston Latin Grammar School authorized		• English Privy Council demands Massachusetts Bay charter; ignored by Governor Winthrop	• Baptist Church organized in Rhode Island
• French occupy Martinique and Guadaloupe in Caribbean		• English trading post at Canton, China		

	1640	1641	1642	1643	1644
EXPLORATION & SETTLEMENT		• Dutch settle on Staten Island in New York harbor • Settlers from New England move to Long Island			
COLONIAL EVENTS	• *Bay Psalm Book* published	• Indian attacks on Dutch in New Netherland (to 1644)	• English Civil War begins (to 1649) • William Berkeley becomes Governor of Virginia	• Colony of New Haven formed	• Freedom of worship established in Rhode Island • Massachusetts opens missions to "Praying Indians"
ABOLITION & SLAVERY		• First colonial law (Massachusetts) recognizing black and Indian slaves			
FOREIGN EVENTS	• Portugal becomes independent of Spain		• Dutch discover Tasmania and New Zealand	• Louis XIV becomes King of France	• First Manchu Emperor of China

1645	1646	1647	1648	1649
	• Breukelen (Brooklyn) established by Dutch • Yonkers settled by Dutch			
		• Newport, Providence and Portsmouth form Rhode Island colony		• Maryland passes Toleration Act • King Charles I beheaded in England; Oliver Cromwell controls England

	1650	1651	1652	1653	1654
EXPLORATION & SETTLEMENT				• Permanent settlement in Albemarle Sound, North Carolina	
COLONIAL EVENTS	• Treaty of Hartford between Dutch and New England colonies	• Indian Bible appears in Massachusetts (completed in 1663) • First Navigation Act governing colonial commerce • Baptists and Quakers persecuted in Massachusetts	• Virginia Governor Berkeley forced out of office for supporting King • First Anglo-Dutch War (to 1654)		• Toleration Act repealed in Maryland; Puritans control colonial legislature
ABOLITION & SLAVERY			• Dutch permit import of slaves into New Netherland		
FOREIGN EVENTS			• Cape Town (South Africa) founded by Dutch		

1655	1656	1657	1658	1659
• French begin systematic exploration of Great Lakes region (to 1735)				• El Paso settled as Spanish outpost
• New Sweden taken over by Dutch			• Cromwell dies; his son and a military group rule England	
• English acquire Jamaica in West Indies				

	1660	1661	1662	1663	1664
EXPLORATION & SETTLEMENT					
COLONIAL EVENTS	• Military rule ends in England; King Charles II restored to throne • Navigation Act • Committee for Trade and Plantations manages colonial affairs in England • Berkeley resumes governorship of Virginia		• Connecticut receives royal charter, absorbs New Haven colony	• Charter granted to Rhode Island • Navigation Act encourages shipbuilding • Royal charter to Proprietors of Carolina	• Royal charter to Berkeley and Carteret as Proprietors of the Jerseys • Second Anglo-Dutch War (1664–1667) begins • New Netherland surrenders to English fleet; becomes New York, proprietary colony under Duke of York
ABOLITION & SLAVERY				• First organized black slave conspiracy in Gloucester County, Va.	• Maryland law mandates lifelong slavery for Negro slaves, even if they become Christian (later laws on same topic in New York, New Jersey, North Carolina, South Carolina, Virginia) • Interracial marriages prohibited (Maryland)
FOREIGN EVENTS	• Royal African Company founded				

1665	1666	1667	1668	1669
	• Newark (N.J.) established		• French found Sault Ste. Marie	• La Salle expedition to Ohio River
	•			
• Separate government for Maine	• Royal commission in Massachusetts Bay ignored by General Court		• Maine joined to Massachusetts Bay	
• Plague in London	• Great Fire in London		• East India Company takes over Bombay	

	1670	1671	1672	1673	1674
EXPLORATION & SETTLEMENT	• Charles Town, South Carolina, established			• Marquette and Jolliet explore upper Mississippi River	
COLONIAL EVENTS	• Fundamental Constitutions of Carolinas (frame of government)		• Third Anglo-Dutch War begins (to 1674)	• New York retaken by Dutch; held briefly • Navigation Act sets duties on certain goods, appoints collectors	• Quakers buy control of East Jersey proprietary
ABOLITION & SLAVERY					
FOREIGN EVENTS		• Panama City destroyed by pirates	• Russian Czar proclaimed as protector of Greek Orthodox Christians • French establish posts in India as trade rivals of British		• Leibniz develops differential calculus in mathematics

1675	1676	1677	1678	1679
				• La Salle, with Hennepin, explores Great Lakes area, Niagara Falls; founds Ft. Crèvecoeur (Illinois) in 1680
• King Philip's War (to 1676)	• Bacon's Rebellion in Virginia • Brief rebellion in Maryland	Culpeper's rebellion in Carolina (to 1680) • Berkeley replaced as Governor of Virginia; House of Burgesses opposes royal governor's financial plans		
	• Indian survivors of King Philip's War sold into slavery			

	1680	1681	1682	1683	1684
EXPLORATION & SETTLEMENT		• La Salle explores Mississippi River to its mouth (continues in 1682)	• Philadelphia, Pa., founded • Norfolk, Va., founded	• Germantown, Pa., founded	• Dominguez and Lopez explorations in Texas (Spanish)
COLONIAL EVENTS	• New Hampshire separated from Massachusetts Bay	• William Penn gets charter as Proprietor of Pennsylvania	• Penn's Frame of Government published	• First representative assembly meets in New York • Assembly in New Jersey claims power to elect governor	• Charter of Massachusetts Bay annulled by King
ABOLITION & SLAVERY					
FOREIGN EVENTS				• Chinese conquer Formosa (Taiwan)	

1685	1686	1687	1688	1689
• French Fort St. Louis attempted in Texas (La Salle) • Eusebio Kino begins mapping and mission work in Arizona	• New York City charter received from King James II		• Alonso de Leon expedition to East Texas locates abandoned French fort; explores region (to 1690)	
• King Charles II dies; James II becomes King of England	• New York becomes royal colony • Dominion of New England established (includes New Jersey, New York and all New England)		• "Glorious" Revolution in England; James II flees	• William and Mary become British sovereigns • Bill of Rights in England • King William's War begins (to 1697) • Leisler's Rebellion in New York
			• First formal opposition to slavery (Germantown, Pa., Quaker Meeting)	
• Edict of Nantes revoked in France				

	1690	1691	1692	1693	1694
EXPLORATION & SETTLEMENT	• Temporary Spanish forts in east Texas		• Spanish missions and presidios begun in Texas		
COLONIAL EVENTS	• French raid Schenectady, N.Y., and outposts in Massachusetts	• Charter for Massachusetts establishes a royal colony, absorbing Plymouth	• Salem witchcraft trials • Church of England established in Maryland	• William and Mary College founded in Virginia	• Queen Mary II dies; King William III continues to rule
ABOLITION & SLAVERY					
FOREIGN EVENTS					

1695	1696	1697	1698	1699
				• Biloxi, Miss., founded by French
• Maryland capital moved to Annapolis	• Board of Trade established in London to manage colonial affairs • Navigation Act establishes Vice-Admiralty Courts in Colonies			• Parliament passes Wool Act (colonies prohibited from exporting wool to England)
	• New England merchants permitted to enter African slave trade			
		• Peter the Great of Russia visits western Europe		

	1700	1701	1702	1703	1704
EXPLORATION & SETTLEMENT		• Detroit, Mich., founded (French)	• Mobile, Ala., founded (French)	• Kaskaskia, Ill., founded (French)	
COLONIAL EVENTS		• New Jersey becomes royal colony • Pennsylvania Charter of Privileges • Delaware secures right to a separate legislature	King William III dies; Queen Anne succeeds to throne • Queen Anne's War begins (to 1713) • Carolinians attack Spaniards in Florida • Massachusetts General Court refuses to pay governor's salary on permanent appropriation		
ABOLITION & SLAVERY	• First abolitionist writing (Samuel Sewell, *Selling of Joseph*)				• Indian allies of Spain, captured, are sold as slaves
FOREIGN EVENTS	• Philip, grandson of Louis XIV of France, becomes King of Spain	• War of the Spanish Succession in Europe			• British capture Gibraltar; defeat French at Battle of Blenheim

1705	1706	1707	1708	1709
	• Albuquerque, New Mexico, founded (Spanish)			
• First subsidy voted in England for colonial production of naval stores and indigo • Virginia law requires that poor children be taught to read				
	• Russian forces control Kamchatka Peninsula, facing Pacific Ocean	• Kingdoms of England and Scotland combined as United Kingdom		

	1710	1711	1712	1713	1714
EXPLORATION & SETTLEMENT					• Natchitoches, La., founded (French)
COLONIAL EVENTS	• Germans ("Pennsylvania Dutch") begin migration to Pennsylvania • New England forces help British capture Port Royal (Nova Scotia)				• Queen Anne dies; George I becomes King of England
ABOLITION & SLAVERY			• Slave revolt in New York City		
FOREIGN EVENTS	• English South Sea Company founded				• Mercury thermometer constructed by Fahrenheit

1715	1716	1717	1718	1719
			• San Antonio, Texas, founded (Spanish) • New Orleans, La., founded (French)	
• Yamassee Indian war in Carolinas (to 1716)				
	• First slaves imported into Louisiana			
• Louis XIV of France dies; great-grandson Louis XV succeeds			• "Quadruple Alliance" (Britain, France, Netherlands, German Empire) against Spain	

	1720	1721	1722	1723	1724
EXPLORATION & SETTLEMENT					• Fort Dummer, Vermont, founded by Massachusetts as military outpost
COLONIAL EVENTS		• South Carolina taken over as royal colony • Inoculation against smallpox introduced in Boston			
ABOLITION & SLAVERY					
FOREIGN EVENTS	• "South Sea Bubble" financial panic in England		• Johann Sebastian Bach active (to 1750)		

1725	1726	1727	1728	1729
				• Baltimore, Md., founded
	• "Great Awakening" begins	• King George I dies; George II, King of England		• North Carolina taken over as royal colony

	1730	1731	1732	1733	1734
EXPLORATION & SETTLEMENT				• Savannah, Ga., founded • Richmond, Va., founded	• Augusta, Ga., founded
COLONIAL EVENTS	• Massachusetts General Court blocked by royal governor from issuing paper money		• Proprietary charter issued for Georgia • *Poor Richard's Almanac* appears • Hat Act passed by Parliament restricts export of colonial hats	• Molasses Act passed by Parliament imposes taxes on rum and molasses in West Indies and America	• John Peter Zenger tried for libel in New York
ABOLITION & SLAVERY	• Slave conspiracy detected in Virginia		• Georgia charter prohibits slavery		
FOREIGN EVENTS		• Navigation improved by introduction of quadrant		• "Family Compact" of Bourbon Kings of France and Spain	

1735	1736	1737	1738	1739
				• Forts built along Georgia-Florida border • Treaty between Oglethorpe (Georgia) and Creek Indians
				• War of Jenkins' Ear (Britain v. Spain) begins over slave-smuggling by Jenkins

	1740	1741	1742	1743	1744
EXPLORATION & SETTLEMENT	• Spanish fort on site of Jacksonville, Fla.	• Vitus Bering explores Alaskan coast and northern Pacific for Russia (to 1743)	• La Vérendrye expedition explores northern Great Plains		
COLONIAL EVENTS	Oglethorpe attacks Florida, checked at St. Augustine				• King George's War begins (to 1748) • Iroquois cede land north of Ohio River to Virginia, Maryland and Pennsylvania
ABOLITION & SLAVERY		• "New York Conspiracy"; Negro and white participants executed		• John Woolman, Quaker, preaches on slavery as an evil	
FOREIGN EVENTS	• Frederick I ("the Great") becomes King of Prussia • Maria Theresa inherits Austrian throne • War of Austrian Succession begins (to 1748)				

1745	1746	1747	1748	1749
			• Cumberland Gap discovered by Thomas Walker	
• Colonial troops under Pepperrell capture Louisbourg from French • Saratoga captured and burned by French		• Franklin's experiments with electricity announced		• French build Fort Niagara, move troops into Ohio River valley
			• Slavery permitted in colony of Georgia	
		• Montesquieu's *Spirit of the Laws* is published in France		

	1750	1751	1752	1753	1754
EXPLORATION & SETTLEMENT	• George Croghan and Conrad Weiser explore Ohio for Pennsylvania • Christopher Gist explores Ohio River valley for Ohio Company		• Erie, Pa., founded as Ft. Presque Isle (French)		
COLONIAL EVENTS	• Iron Act passed by Parliament; encourages colonial pig iron production, but prohibits fabrication of iron in colonies	• Money Act passed by Parliament prohibits colonies from issuing paper money as legal tender • Franklin's Academy founded	• Georgia becomes royal colony • "New Style" (Gregorian Calendar) dates adopted in Britain and British colonies		• French and Indian War begins • Albany Congress
ABOLITION & SLAVERY					
FOREIGN EVENTS	• War in India between English and French Companies	• *Encyclopedia* begun in France (completed 1772)			

1755	1756	1757	1758	1759
		• Fort Pitt and Pittsburgh founded on site of French Ft. Duquesne		
• Braddock's defeat • Acadians expelled from Nova Scotia	• Strict Quakers withdraw from Pennsylvania Assembly over military appropriations		• Ft. Louisbourg (French) taken and destroyed • Ft. Duquesne destroyed and evacuated by French	• British victories at Ft. Niagara, Ft. Ticonderoga, Quebec
	• Seven Years War begins in Europe	• Clive dominates India for (English) East India Company		

	1760	1761	1762	1763	1764
EXPLORATION & SETTLEMENT					• St. Louis, Missouri, founded
COLONIAL EVENTS	• Montreal surrenders to British. French power ended in North America • King George II dies; George III, King of England	• James Otis opposes "writs of assistance"	• France turns Louisiana over to Spain	• Peace treaty in Paris ends (European) Seven Years War • Proclamation of 1763 • East and West Florida become British possessions • Parson's Cause case in Virginia • Pontiac's Conspiracy (Indian War) to 1764	• Sugar Act and Currency Act applied by Parliament to all British colonies • British Customs Service in colonies restructured
ABOLITION & SLAVERY					
FOREIGN EVENTS			• Catherine the Great becomes Czarina of Russia (to 1796)		

1765	1766	1767	1768	1769
				• Spanish exploration of California coast resumes • San Diego, Cal., founded as mission by Serra
• Stamp Act passed by Parliament • Sons of Liberty organized in colonies • Stamp Act Congress	• Stamp Act repealed; Declaratory Act passed by Parliament • Crisis in New York over quartering troops at colony's expense	• Parliament passes Townshend Revenue Acts • Non-Importation agreements in colonies	• Massachusetts Circular Letter to other colonies	• Virginia Resolves, and Association for Non-Importation
			• France purchases Corsica	

	1770	1771	1772	1773	1774
EXPLORATION & SETTLEMENT	• Pacific coast exploration directed by Galvez (Spanish)				
POLITICAL EVENTS	• Parliament limits Townshend Acts to raise revenue on tea • Boston Massacre		• Committees of Correspondence organized in colonies	• Tea Act passed in Parliament • Boston Tea Party • Tea shipments resisted in other colonies	• Coercion Acts and Intolerable Acts passed by Parliament • Franklin denounced in Privy Council • First Continental Congress meets
ABOLITION & SLAVERY				• Petition for freedom by Massachusetts slaves	• Association slows importing of slaves from British merchants
FOREIGN EVENTS	• Capt. James Cook explores coast of Australia		• First "partition" of Poland among Austria, Prussia, Russia		• King Louis XV of France dies; Louis XVI becomes King, Marie Antoinette is Queen • Russia makes peace with Turkey: wins Crimea and river mouth on Black Sea

1775

REVOLUTIONARY WAR (*Note*: *British victories are in italics*)

1775   *Apr. 19*: Lexington and Concord;
                 Siege of Boston begins
        May 10: Fort Ticonderoga captured
        June 15: Washington named army commander
        June 17: Battle of Bunker Hill
        September: Two expeditions against Quebec (Montgomery & B. Arnold)
        Nov. 13: Montgomery takes Montreal, Canada
        December: Esek Hopkins named commodore of naval forces;
                 Royal Governor (Dunmore) forced out of Virginia
        Dec. 31: *Quebec garrison turns back Arnold attack*

• Second Continental
Congress meets
• Continental Army
established by
Congress

1776   *Feb. 27*: Loyalists beaten at Moore's Creek Bridge, N.C.
        March 17: British leave Boston
        March: American ships capture Nassau, Bahamas, in raid
        May: Americans retreat from Canada to Lake Champlain
        June: British attack on Charleston, S.C., turned back
        August: British attack New York. *Battle of Long Island* (Brooklyn) Aug. 27-28
        September: *British capture New York City* (Sept. 15, 16);
                 Major fire in New York blamed on patriots (Sept. 21);
                 Nathan Hale executed as spy (Sept. 22)
        Oct. 11: British lake squadron defeated at Valcour Bay, Lake Champlain
        Oct. 28: *Battle of White Plains*
        Nov. 16-18: *British take Ft. Washington and Ft. Lee in New York area*
        Dec. 26: Hessian troops defeated at Trenton

1777   *Jan. 3*: Battle of Princeton
        June 14: United States flag authorized
        July-September: British attack Philadelphia: *Battle of Brandywine* (Sept. 11);
                 British capture Philadelphia (Sept. 26)
        June-October: British drive in New York State:
                 Battle of Oriskany (Aug. 6);
                 Battle of Bennington (Aug. 16);
                 St. Leger turns back from Ft. Stanwix (Aug. 22);
                 Battle at Freeman's Farm (Sept. 19) near Saratoga;
                 British drive from N.Y. City turned back (Oct. 16);
                 Battle of Saratoga (Bemis Heights, Oct. 7-8);
                 Burgoyne surrenders (Oct. 17)
        December: Washington leads army to Valley Forge for winter

1778   *April*: John Paul Jones raids Scottish coast
        June: British move out of Philadelphia
        June 28: Battle of Monmouth
        July 4: George Rogers Clark captures Kaskaskia (Illinois)
        August: *British hold Newport, R.I., against attack*
        Dec. 29: *British capture Savannah, Georgia*

1779   *July 15*: Wayne captures fort at Stony Point, N.Y.
        August: Loyalists and Iroquois defeated in upper New York State
        Sept. 23: *Bonhomme Richard* (Jones) defeats *H. M. S. Serapis*
        September-October: *British hold Savannah against American and French attack*
        October: British evacuate Newport, R.I.

1780   *May 12*: *British capture Charleston, S.C., with over 5,000 prisoners*
        July: French Army lands, headquarters at Newport, R.I.
        Aug. 16: *Major victory for British at Camden, S.C.*
        Sept. 23: Major John André captured by New York militia
        Sept. 25: Benedict Arnold flees to British
        Sept. 30: André executed as spy
        Oct. 7: American militia victory at King's Mountain

1781   *January-May*: Mutinies in Continental Army
        Jan. 17: Battle of Cowpens, S.C.
        April-September: American victories won by Greene in Carolinas
        June-August: Cornwallis campaigns in Virginia
        August-October: American and French campaign against Yorktown
        Oct. 19: Cornwallis surrenders at Yorktown
        November: American siege of New York resumes

1782   *April-November*: Peace negotiations in Paris
                 Treaty prepared (Nov. 30, 1782)

1783   *Jan. 20*: Peace officially in effect
        Nov. 25: British forces leave New York City
        December: Washington resigns his commission to Congress

	1776	1777	1778	1779	1780
EXPLORATION & SETTLEMENT	• San Francisco, Cal., founded • Tucson, Ariz., founded by Father Kino	• San Jose, Cal., founded	• Louisville, Kentucky, founded • Captain James Cook (British) discovers Hawaii; calls area the Sandwich Islands	• Nashville, Tenn., founded	
POLITICAL EVENTS	• *Common Sense* published • Declaration of Independence • Congress conducts a united government for United States • American flag adopted • Foreign representatives sent to and from Congress • New State constitutions drawn up in most States				
ABOLITION & SLAVERY	• British enlist regiment of ex-slaves in Virginia; promise freedom to those who join British forces	• Vermont laws prohibit slavery	• Rhode Island permits slaves to enlist in State regiments		• Slavery abolished in Massachusetts by State constitution • Pennsylvania law provides that all newborn Negroes shall be free
FOREIGN EVENTS				• Spain declares war on England (to 1783)	• "Armed Neutrality" in American Revolution proclaimed by Russia; Netherlands joins Russia in this policy • Galvani announces discoveries in electricity

1781	1782	1783	1784	1785
• Los Angeles, Cal., founded			• Russians settle at Three Saints Bay (now Kodiak), Alaska	
• Robert Morris heads finance office for Congress • Virginia cedes western lands to the United States • Articles of Confederation go into effect		• Washington prevents military action against Congress • Webster's "Blue-Backed Speller" published		• Mount Vernon Conference • Charter issued for University of Georgia (first State University charter) • Land Ordinance passed to govern western public lands
	• Virginia permits owners to emancipate slaves by wills or other legal orders	• Slave trade outlawed in Maryland	• Slavery abolished in New Hampshire; gradual abolition approved in Connecticut and Rhode Island	• Gradual abolition adopted in New York
• Prussia joins Russia and Netherlands in Armed Neutrality		• Sicily joins Armed Neutrality • Peace is made by Great Britain, France, Spain and the United States • Montgolfier brothers fly a hot-air balloon in France		

	1786	1787	1788	1789		
EXPLORATION & SETTLEMENT				• Capt. Robert Gray begins exploration of Columbia River, Oregon and Washington coast.	**EXPLORATION & SETTLEMENT**	
POLITICAL EVENTS	• Widespread depression; trade reduced; governments (U.S. and States) in debt; Shays' Rebellion in Massachusetts	• Ordinance of 1787 passed to govern Northwest Territory • Congress approves call for Convention to revise Articles of Confederation			**PRESIDENCY**	
					LAW & THE COURTS	
					POLITICAL EVENTS	
ABOLITION & SLAVERY	• Gradual abolition adopted in New Jersey	• Slavery barred from Northwest Territory • Free African Society formed in Philadelphia • Slavery issues at Constitutional Convention: *a*) Representation of slave population; *b*) Protection of slave trade; *c*) Fugitive slave provisions			**ABOLITION & SLAVERY**	
FOREIGN EVENTS	• Frederick the Great of Prussia dies • Cornwallis made Governor-General of India				**FOREIGN POLICY**	
					FOREIGN EVENTS	

[1787]	[1788]	[1789]	1790	1791
			• U.S. population (census) is 3.9 million • Site for Washington, D.C., determined	• Vermont becomes State
	• George Washington elected first President	• Washington inaugurated, April 30 • Executive Departments (Justice, Post Office, State, Treasury, War) established		
• Constitutional Convention. U.S. Constitution ratified by Del., Pa., N.J.	• U.S. Constitution ratified by Ga., Conn., Mass., Md., S.C., N.H., Va., N.Y.; officially in force on June 21	• U.S. Constitution ratified by N.C. • John Jay, Chief Justice	• U.S. Constitution ratified by R.I.	• Constitutional Amendments I–X ratified (Bill of Rights)
	• Majority of elected U.S. Congress members are supporters of new Constitution (Federalists)	• First U.S. Congress meets in New York City; first Speaker of House is F. A. Muhlenberg • First Tariff law passed gives moderate protection for some businesses	• Assumption Bill passes (Hamilton's plan); Congress sets permanent capital city site on Potomac River	• Second U.S. Congress meets (Federalist majority, minority of Democratic-Republicans). Jonathan Trumbull is Speaker • First Bank of the United States chartered • Whiskey Tax and other excises imposed
			• First abolition petition to Congress (Quaker movement) • First U.S. Census reports 697,000 slaves	
	• Sydney, Australia, established as British penal colony	• Revolution begins in France		• "Upper" and "Lower" Canada separated

	1792	1793	1794	1795	1796
EXPLORATION & SETTLEMENT	• Kentucky becomes State	• Syracuse, N.Y., founded		• Cincinnati (Ft. Washington), O., founded	• Tennessee becomes State • Cleveland and Dayton, O., founded
PRESIDENCY	• George Washington reelected without opposition	• George Washington's second inaugural			• Washington's Farewell Address • John Adams (Federalist) elected over Thomas Jefferson (Democratic-Republican)
LAW & THE COURTS		• *Chisholm v. Georgia*		• John Jay resigns as Chief Justice • John Rutledge named Chief Justice by President Washington; not confirmed by Senate	• Oliver Ellsworth, Chief Justice
POLITICAL EVENTS		• Federalist majority in Third Congress. Muhlenberg is Speaker	• Whiskey Rebellion in Pennsylvania	• Fourth Congress has small Federalist majority. Jonathan Dayton is Speaker • Naturalization Act requires 5 years residence before becoming citizen	
ABOLITION & SLAVERY		• First Fugitive Slave Law			
FOREIGN POLICY		• Neutrality Proclamation • Genet Affair	• Neutrality Act • Jay's Treaty with Great Britain	• Pinckney's Treaty with Spain	
FOREIGN EVENTS	• France declares war on Austria • French army conquers Belgian area (Austrian Netherlands) • French Republic proclaimed	• "First Coalition" fights France • King Louis XVI and Queen Marie Antoinette beheaded • Second partition of Poland	• Slavery ended in French colonies • Kosciusko leads rebellion of Poles	• Final partition of Poland	• 1796–1797 Napoleon wins victories over Austrians in Italy

1797	1798	1799	1800	1801
• Columbus, O., founded			• U.S. population (census) is 5.3 million	
• John Adams inaugurated	• Navy Department organized		• Thomas Jefferson (Democratic-Republican) and Aaron Burr defeat John Adams in presidential election	• Jefferson chosen President by House of Representatives after tie with Burr in Electoral College. Jefferson inaugurated.
	• Constitutional Amendment XI ratified	• Oliver Ellsworth resigns as Chief Justice		• John Marshall, Chief Justice
• Fifth Congress has increased Federalist majority. Dayton is Speaker • Authorization for privateers; new warships built	• Alien and Sedition Acts passed • Kentucky and Virginia Resolutions published	• Sixth Congress has Federalist majority. Theodore Sedgwick is Speaker	• Congress meets for first time in Washington, D.C.	• Congress passes Judiciary Act; "midnight judges" appointed • Seventh Congress has Democratic-Republican majority in both houses. Nathaniel Macon is Speaker
			• Second U.S. Census reports 894,000 slaves • Virginia legislature recommends recolonizing Negroes in Africa	• Gabriel slave revolt fails in Virginia
• X.Y.Z. Affair	• 1798–1800 Undeclared Naval War with France		• Convention of 1800 (Treaty of Morfontaine)	
	• Napoleon in Egypt; Nelson destroys French fleet at Battle of Nile	• Napoleon takes control of French government	• Ireland merged into United Kingdom	

	1802	1803	1804	1805	1806
EXPLORATION & SETTLEMENT		• Ohio becomes State • Buffalo, N.Y., founded	• Lewis and Clark expedition (to 1806)	• Zebulon Pike explores upper Mississippi River valley (to 1806)	• Pike explores Colorado-New Mexico region (to 1807)
PRESIDENCY			• Jefferson reelected (George Clinton, Vice President)	• Jefferson's second inaugural	
LAW & THE COURTS		• *Marbury v. Madison*	• Constitutional Amendment XII ratified		
POLITICAL EVENTS	• Judiciary Act of 1801 repealed; six Supreme Court Justices authorized • U.S. Military Academy established by law	• Eighth Congress has Democratic-Republican majority. Macon is Speaker • Hamilton-Burr duel		• Ninth Congress has large Democratic-Republican majority. Macon is Speaker	• First Non-Importation Act passed
ABOLITION & SLAVERY					
FOREIGN POLICY	• 1801–1805 Naval war (undeclared) with Tripoli	• Louisiana Purchase			
FOREIGN EVENTS	• Peace of Amiens (between France and Britain)		• Napoleon crowned Emperor of the French	• Third Coalition war against France; great French land victories. Nelson destroys combined French and Spanish fleets at Trafalgar	

1807	1808	1809	1810	1811
		• Russians establish Fort Ross in California	• U.S. population (census) is 7.2 million • Rochester, N.Y., founded	• Astoria (Oregon) and Ft. Okanagon (Washington) established
• Former Vice President Aaron Burr tried for treason, acquitted	• James Madison (Democratic-Republican) elected President, defeating Charles C. Pinckney (Federalist)	• James Madison inaugurated		
			• *Fletcher v. Peck*	
• Tenth Congress has large Democratic-Republican majority. Joseph Varnum is Speaker • Embargo Act passed		• 11th Congress has large Democratic-Republican majority. Varnum is Speaker	• Macon's Bill No. 2	• First Bank of the United States ends business • 12th Congress has large Democratic-Republican majority. Henry Clay is Speaker
• Importing of slaves (foreign slave trade) prohibited by law	• Legal importing of slaves ends (Jan. 1)		• Third U.S. Census reports 1,191,000 slaves	
• *Chesapeake v. Leopard* • Embargo Act applies to commerce with Europe		• Non-Intercourse Act	• West Florida annexed to the United States	• U.S. frigate *President* defeats British *Little Belt*
• British Orders in Council • Napoleon's Milan Decree and Continental System	• Peninsular War in Spain (until 1814)		• Mexico declares independence	

	1812	1813	1814	1815	1816
EXPLORATION & SETTLEMENT	• Louisiana becomes State				• Indiana becomes State
PRESIDENCY	• Madison reelected, defeating De Witt Clinton (Federalist)	• Madison's second inaugural			• James Monroe (Democratic-Republican) elected, defeating Rufus King (Federalist)
LAW & THE COURTS					• *Martin v. Hunter's Lessee*
POLITICAL EVENTS	• Congress passes strict embargo against British trade • Declaration of War against England	• 13th Congress has Democratic-Republican majority. Speakers are Clay (1813) and Langdon Cheves (1814) • Wartime embargo imposed on foreign trade (ended 1814)	• Hartford Convention	• 14th Congress has Democratic-Republican majority. Clay is Speaker	• Second Bank of the United States chartered • Tariff of 1816, a protective measure
ABOLITION & SLAVERY					
FOREIGN POLICY	• War declared on Great Britain; Czar of Russia offers to mediate		• Peace negotiations with British; Treaty of Ghent (Dec. 24)	• Naval war against Algiers; treaty ends Algerian piracy • Treaties and agreements with Tunis and Tripoli • Commercial treaty with Great Britain	
FOREIGN EVENTS	• Napoleon invades Russia; retreats from Moscow in winter	• Battle of Leipzig. Allies defeat Napoleon, invade France • Colombia becomes independent of Spain	• Napoleon abdicates, Bourbon King returns to France	• Napoleon returns for the "Hundred Days"; is defeated and captured; Waterloo • Napoleon exiled to St. Helena • Congress of Vienna redraws map of Europe	• Chile declares independence of Spain

WAR OF 1812

	LAND	SEA
1812	*July-August*: Gen. Hull invades Canada; retreats; surrenders Detroit (Aug. 16) *November*: British victories on Niagara River	*Aug. 19*: *Constitution* defeats *Guerriere* *Oct. 25*: *United States* defeats *Macedonian* British blockade in effect
1813	*Apr. 27*: American raid takes and burns York (Toronto) *October*: Battle of the Thames *July*: British turn back drive on Montreal *December*: British capture Ft. Niagara	*Sept. 10*: Battle of Lake Erie British blockade in effect

1814	Summer invasion of Canada:
	   July 5: Chippewa Creek
	   July 25: Lundy's Lane
	Aug. 24-25: British take and burn Wash., D.C.
	Sept 14: British turned back from Baltimore
		Sept. 11: Battle of Lake Champlain

1815	*Jan. 8*: Battle of New Orleans	

LIFE IN THE UNITED STATES

	ECONOMICS	CULTURAL	RACES & PEOPLES
1790	• First powered textile factory in U.S.	• Copyright and patent Acts passed	
1791	• Philadelphia Stock Exchange	• Opera house in New Orleans	• First Bank of the United States
1792	• New York Stock Exchange opens		
1793	• Whitney devises cotton gin	• Yellow fever epidemic in Philadelphia	
1794		• C. W. Peale opens Museum • University of North Carolina begins classes	
1795	• Wilderness Road opens		
1796			• Indian mission societies set up in New York and Connecticut
1797	• Cast-iron plow devised		
1799	• First major strike by Philadelphia cordwainers		
1800		• Library of Congress established	
1802	• Bowditch publishes *New American Practical Navigator*	• Ohio grants lands to support public schools	
1804			• First "Black Code" on free blacks passed in Ohio
1805		• Pennsylvania Academy of Fine Arts established	
1806	• Court finds Philadelphia Cordwainers strike a conspiracy		
1807	• Robert Fulton's *Clermont* steams up Hudson River		
1810		• Congregational Church begins foreign mission work	
1811	• Battle of Tippecanoe		
1812			• "Gerrymandering" in Mass.
1814			• Creek and Cherokee Indians defeated at Horseshoe Bend
1816			• First Seminole Indian War (to 1818)
1818	• Trans-Atlantic Packet Lines from New York-England		• Congregational Church disestablished in Connecticut
1819	• Financial panic and depression	• William Ellery Channing becomes chief Unitarian spokesman • Washington Irving publishes *The Sketch Book* (1819–1820)	• Congregational Church disestablished in New Hampshire
1821		• Sequoyah devises Cherokee alphabet • First High School in Boston • Troy Female Seminary established	• Kentucky abolishes debtors' jails
1822	• Textile mills begun at Lowell, Massachusetts • Banking crisis in U.S.		
1824			• Prison at Auburn N.Y. introduces group labor by prisoners • August 2: Emancipation Day for slaves still living in Illinois

	1817	1818	1819	1820	1821
EXPLORATION & SETTLEMENT	• Mississippi becomes State • Henry R. Schoolcraft explores Arkansas and Missouri area • Toledo, O., founded	• Memphis, Tenn., founded • Illinois becomes State	• Flint, Mich., founded • Stephen Long's exploration of eastern Rocky Mountains • Alabama becomes State	• U.S. population (census) is 9.6 million • Tampa, Fla., founded • Cass explores upper Mississippi River • Indianapolis, Ind., founded • Maine becomes State	• Missouri becomes State • Kansas City, Mo., founded • Austin permitted to bring colonists into Texas
PRESIDENCY	• James Monroe inaugurated			• James Monroe reelected with no opposition • "Era of Good Feeling"	• Monroe's second inaugural
LAW & THE COURTS			• *McCulloch v. Maryland* • *Trustees of Dartmouth College v. Woodward*		• *Cohens v. Virginia*
POLITICAL EVENTS	• 15th Congress has large Democratic-Republican majority. Clay is Speaker	• Andrew Jackson leads troops into Spanish-held Florida	• 16th Congress has increased Democratic-Republican majority. Clay is Speaker	• Missouri Compromise. John W. Taylor becomes Speaker of House • Foreign slave trade declared to be piracy • "Era of Good Feeling"	• 17th Congress, dominated by Democratic-Republicans. Federalists disappearing. Philip P. Barbour is Speaker
ABOLITION & SLAVERY	• American Colonization Society founded			• Fourth U.S. Census reports 1,538,000 slaves • Missouri Compromise • First shipload of Negroes sails to Sierra Leone, Africa	• Abolitionist journal, *Genius of Universal Emancipation*
FOREIGN POLICY	• Rush-Bagot Agreement (disarms Great Lakes border with Canada)	• Convention of 1818 covering Canadian border, Oregon and fishing rights	• Adams-Oñis Treaty; Florida cession to U.S.		
FOREIGN EVENTS			• Singapore founded as British outpost in Asia	• Revolution in Spain, Naples, Portugal against strict monarchies	• Peru declares independence; Mexico wins its war for independence • Greece begins war for independence from Turkey (to 1829)

1822	1823	1824	1825
	• Stephen Long explores Minnesota River, Canadian border, Lake Superior	• Jim Bridger discovers Great Salt Lake	
		• Four candidates for President divide electoral votes: Andrew Jackson, John Quincy Adams, William Crawford, Henry Clay	
		• *Gibbons v. Ogden*	
	• 18th Congress—Democratic-Republicans rule. Clay is Speaker	• New tariff law with increased protection • Clay describes "American System"	• 19th Congress. No formal party lines. Taylor is Speaker
• Denmark Vesey slave revolt crushed in South Carolina			
	• Monroe Doctrine announced	• Agreement with Russia sets Alaska's southern border at 54°40'	
• Brazil separates from Portugal as Empire of Brazil	• French invade Spain to assist Spanish King regain his power	• Last Spanish army in South America stops fighting	

	[1825]	1826	1827	1828	1829
EXPLORATION & SETTLEMENT	• Akron, O., founded	• Jedediah Smith explores routes to California and Northwest (to 1830)			• Society for the settlement of Oregon established
PRESIDENCY	• John Quincy Adams elected President by House of Representatives			• Andrew Jackson (Democrat) defeats John Quincy Adams (National Republican)	• Andrew Jackson inaugurated
LAW & COURTS			• *Martin v. Mott*		
POLITICAL EVENTS			• 20th Congress; majority favor Andrew Jackson. Andrew Stevenson, Speaker • High tariff bill rejected in Senate	• Tariff of Abominations becomes law; Georgia, Mississippi, South Carolina and Virginia protest • South Carolina Exposition and Protest issued	• 21st Congress; Democratic majority. Stevenson is Speaker • "Spoils System" extended by Jackson
ABOLITION & SLAVERY					
FOREIGN POLICY	• First U.S. diplomatic mission to Mexico				
FOREIGN EVENTS					• Greek independence recognized by Turkey • 1828–1829 War between Russia and Turkey

1830	1831	1832	1833	1834
• U.S. population (census), 12.9 million	• Henry R. Schoolcraft explores for source of Mississippi River (Lake Itasca) (to 1832)			• Jason Lee begins mission in Willamette Valley, Oregon
		• Jackson reelected, defeating Henry Clay (Whig)	• Jackson's second inaugural	
		• *Worcester v. Georgia*		
• Webster-Hayne debate	• 22nd Congress; Democratic majority. Stevenson is Speaker • Vice President Calhoun opposes President Jackson's policies • Anti-Masonic Party organized	• Ordinance of Nullification passed in South Carolina • Jackson vetoes bill to re-charter Second Bank of the United States	• 23rd Congress; Democratic majority in House; Senate divided. Speaker is Stevenson • Tariff of 1833 lowers duties • Whig Party develops around opposition to Jackson	
• Fifth U.S. Census records 2,009,000 slaves	• William Lloyd Garrison publishes *The Liberator* • Nat Turner slave revolt crushed in Virginia	• "Underground Railroad" operating to help fugitives escape	• American Anti-Slavery Society founded	
• July Revolution in France; King Charles X removed, Louis Philippe becomes King			• Zollverein (Customs Union) of German states created	• Slavery abolished in British Empire • Melbourne, Australia, established

• 1830–32 Revolution in Poland put down by Russian troops

• 1830–33 Revolution by Belgians against Dutch rule succeeds

	1835	1836	1837	1838	1839
EXPLORATION & SETTLEMENT	• Milwaukee, Wisc., founded	• Houston, Tex., founded • Marcus Whitman establishes mission at Walla Walla, Washington • Arkansas becomes State	• Terminus, Ga., founded (now Atlanta) • Chicago incorporated as a city • Michigan becomes State	• Wilkes expedition to South Sea (Pacific) and Antarctica (to 1840)	• Sacramento, Calif., founded
PRESIDENCY		• Martin Van Buren (Democrat) defeats William Henry Harrison (Whig)	• Vice-presidential election settled in Senate; Richard M. Johnson elected • Van Buren inaugurated		
LAW & COURTS	• John Marshall dies (July 6)	• Roger Brooke Taney, Chief Justice	• Charles River Bridge Case		
POLITICAL EVENTS	• 24th Congress; small Democratic majority. James K. Polk is Speaker	• Jackson issues Specie Circular	• 25th Congress; Democratic plurality. Polk is Speaker • House of Representatives refuses to receive Abolitionist petitions		• 26th Congress; small Democratic majority. Robert Hunter is Speaker • Liberty Party organized
ABOLITION & SLAVERY	• Abolitionist publications seized from Charleston post office and burned		• Elijah Lovejoy killed in Alton, Ill.	• Frederick Douglass escapes from slavery	
FOREIGN POLICY	• France pays "spoliation claims" over losses from Napoleonic wars	• U.S. recognizes Republic of Texas		• Aroostook War on Maine-New Brunswick border	
FOREIGN EVENTS		• Texas becomes independent from Mexico	• Victoria becomes Queen of England • Rebellions in Upper and Lower Canada	• Chartist movement in England • Canadian rebellions end	• Opium War, Great Britain against China. British take Hong Kong

1840	1841	1842	1843	1844
• U.S. population (census), 17.1 million • Portland, Ore., founded • St. Paul, Minn., founded		• Fort Worth, Tex., founded • Frémont first expedition	• Frémont second expedition	
• William Henry Harrison (Whig) defeats incumbent Van Buren (Democrat)	• William Henry Harrison inaugurated (March 4) • William Henry Harrison dies (April 4) • John Tyler succeeds as President			• James K. Polk (Democrat) defeats Henry Clay (Whig)
		• *Prigg v. Pennsylvania*		
• Independent Treasury system established	• 27th Congress; Whig majority. John White is Speaker • Independent Treasury system repealed by Whig majority • President Tyler vetoes Whig banking bills		• 28th Congress; Whig majority in Senate; Democratic majority in House. John W. Jones is Speaker	
• Sixth U.S. Census records 2,487,000 slaves	• Slave-ship *Creole* seized by slaves, sailed to Bahamas; slaves freed by British authorities			• Expansion of slavery issue blocks annexation of Texas • "Gag" rule in House of Representatives removed • Van Buren leads abolitionist group in Democratic party
		• Webster-Ashburton Treaty		• Dispute over Oregon Territory with Great Britain • Dispute with Mexico over U.S. relations with Texas
• Union of Upper Canada and Lower Canada				

	1845	1846	1847	1848	1849
EXPLORATION & SETTLEMENT	• Florida becomes State • Texas becomes State	• Iowa becomes State • Dallas, Tex., founded	• Salt Lake City, Utah, founded	• Wisconsin becomes State	• Minneapolis, Minn., founded
PRESIDENCY	• Polk inaugurated			• Zachary Taylor (Whig) defeats Lewis Cass (Democrat) and Martin Van Buren (Free Soil)	• Taylor inaugurated • Department of Interior established in Cabinet
LAW & COURTS					
POLITICAL EVENTS	• Native American Party organized • 29th Congress: Democratic majority. John W. Davis is Speaker	• Independent Treasury system reestablished • Wilmot Proviso • Walker Tariff law	• 30th Congress: Democratic majority. Robert C. Winthrop is Speaker	• Free Soil Party organized	• 31st Congress; Democratic majority in Senate; Democratic plurality in House. Howell Cobb is Speaker
ABOLITION & SLAVERY					• Slaveholding in Territories threatens to split Union
FOREIGN POLICY	• Texas annexation treaty approved by Congress	• Treaty with Great Britain settles Oregon Territory boundary • War declared on Mexico (May 13, 1846)		• Treaty of Guadalupe Hidalgo; Mexican Cession	
FOREIGN EVENTS	• Start of potato blight in Ireland	• Corn Laws repealed in England • Famine in Ireland and Germany	• Liberia becomes independent republic	• Widespread revolutions in Europe. France becomes republic; revolts in Sicily, Venice, Rome, Milan, Berlin, Vienna • *Communist Manifesto* published	

MEXICAN WAR

1846	*May 8*: Battle of Palo Alto
	May 9: Battle of Resaca de la Palma
	June: Naval blockade of Mexico begins
	July: Naval force lands at San Francisco
	Aug. 18: Santa Fe, N.M. occupied by U.S.
	September: Californian revolt against U.S. occupation
	Sept. 25: Taylor's Army takes Monterey
1847	*Feb. 23*: Taylor defeats Santa Anna at Monterey
	March 29: Scott takes Vera Cruz after siege
	April 18: Battle of Cerro Gordo
	Aug. 20: Battle of Churubusco
	Sept. 13: Chapultepec is taken
	Sept. 14: Mexico City captured and occupied
1848	*Feb. 2*: Treaty of Guadalupe Hidalgo signed

LIFE IN THE UNITED STATES

1850

	ECONOMICS	CULTURAL	RACES & PEOPLES	
				• U.S. population (census), 23.3 million • California becomes State • Oakland, Calif., founded
1825	• "Suffolk System" of banking introduced in Massachusetts • Erie Canal opened		• Indian Removal Policy begins (to 1840)	
1826		• *Last of the Mohicans* by James Fenimore Cooper		
1827		• Audubon's *Birds of America* begins to appear in parts • Joseph Henry begins studies of electricity		
1828	• Railroad construction begins in South Carolina and Maryland	• Noah Webster's *Dictionary*		• President Taylor dies (July 9); Vice President Millard Fillmore succeeds as President
1830	• Peter Cooper builds first locomotive	• Mormon Church organized	• Underground railroad begins work with fugitive slaves	
1832			• Black Hawk War	
1833		• Congregational Church disestablished in Massachusetts	• Oberlin College admits women as students	
1834			• "Indian Country" established by Congress	
1835	• Colt patents revolver		• North Carolina removes last legal restrictions on Catholics • Second Seminole Indian War (to 1842)	
1837	• John Deere develops steel plow • Business panic	• Horace Mann directs school reform in Massachusetts • Ralph Waldo Emerson's *American Scholar* lecture		
1838	• Steamboats introduced to North Atlantic trade • Banking failures			• Compromise of 1850 • Nashville Convention of slave States discusses secession
1839	• Charles Goodyear develops vulcanization process	• First State training school for teachers (Massachusetts)		
1840			• Civilized Tribes established in Oklahoma	
1843	• Low point of depression			
1844	• S. F. B. Morse introduces telegraph		• Mormons persecuted in Illinois; Joseph Smith lynched	
1845		• Edgar Allen Poe's *The Raven and Other Poems*		
1846	• Elias Howe patents sewing machine	• Smithsonian Institution established		• Seventh U.S. Census records 3,204,000 slaves • Compromise of 1850
1847	• Rotary printing press introduced • Steam engines used to run textile machinery			
1848	• Gold found in California		• Woman's Rights Convention, Seneca Falls, N.Y. • German "48'ers" begin to move to United States • "Know Nothing" nativist movement	
1849	• Gold Rush to California			
1850		• Hawthorne's *The Scarlet Letter*		
1851	• Illinois Central R.R. (first "Land-Grant" railroad)	• Melville publishes *Moby Dick* • Y.M.C.A. established in Boston		• Clayton-Bulwer Treaty
1852	• Elisha Otis patents passenger elevator		• Harriet Beecher Stowe's *Uncle Tom's Cabin*	
1854	• Clipper *Flying Cloud* sets speed record, Boston-San Francisco	• Thoreau publishes *Walden*		
1855		• Longfellow's *Song of Hiawatha*		
1856	• Gail Borden patents method for condensing milk			
1857	• Financial panic in country, banks in crisis (except in New Orleans)			
1858		• Y.W.C.A. organized		
1859	• Edwin Drake brings in oil from Pennsylvania well			

	1851	1852	1853	1854	1855
EXPLORATION & SETTLEMENT	• Seattle, Wash., founded • Des Moines, Ia., founded		• Pacific Railroad Surveys conducted by U.S. Army Topographical Engineers (to 1860)	• Omaha, Neb., founded	
PRESIDENCY		• Franklin Pierce (Democrat) defeats Winfield Scott (Whig) and John P. Hale (Free Soil)	• Pierce inaugurated		
LAW & COURTS					
POLITICAL EVENTS	• 32nd Congress: Democratic majority. Linn Boyd is Speaker		• 33rd Congress: Democratic majority. Boyd is Speaker	• Kansas-Nebraska Act passed • New England Emigrant Aid Company sends free-soil settlers to Kansas • Republican Party organized • Ostend Manifesto	• 34th Congress: Democratic majority. Nathaniel Banks is Speaker • Two rival constitutions and governments in Kansas
ABOLITION & SLAVERY	• Extensive "Personal Liberty" laws in northern States	• *Uncle Tom's Cabin* published			
FOREIGN POLICY			• Gadsden Purchase from Mexico	• Perry opens Japanese ports to American trade	
FOREIGN EVENTS	• Louis Napoleon takes control of France	• Most 1848 liberal constitutions end; Louis Napoleon becomes Napoleon III • Count Cavour becomes Premier of Kingdom of Sardinia (*Risorgimento* of Italy)	• 1853–1856 Crimean War. Britain, France, Sardinia, Turkey against Russia		

1856	1857	1858	1859	1860
	• Denver, Colo., founded	• Minnesota becomes State	• Oregon becomes State	
• James Buchanan (Democrat) defeats John C. Frémont (Republican) and Millard Fillmore (American)	• Buchanan inaugurated			
	• Dred Scott Decision			
• Civil war in Kansas ("Bleeding Kansas") • Sumner-Brooks battle in U.S. Senate	• Kansas "Lecompton" Constitution • 35th Congress: small Democratic majority. James L. Orr is Speaker	• Kansas voters reject Lecompton Constitution; fighting continues • Lincoln-Douglas debates in Illinois	• 36th Congress: Democratic majority in Senate; Republican majority in House. William Pennington is Speaker • John Brown's raid on Harper's Ferry	
	• Dred Scott Case involves legal status of slave		• John Brown's raid on Harper's Ferry	
• Louis Pasteur becomes professor in France		• Czar Alexander II begins to emancipate serfs in Russia	• Rebellions against Austrian rule in several states of Italy • Suez Canal construction begins • Charles Darwin publishes *Origin of Species*	

	[1860]	**1861**	**1862**	**1863**
EXP. & SET.	• U.S. population (census), 31.5 million	• Kansas becomes State		• West Virginia becomes State
PRESIDENCY	• James Buchanan, President • Abraham Lincoln (Republican) defeats Stephen A. Douglas (Democrat)	• Lincoln's first inaugural		
LAW & THE COURTS		• *ex parte Merryman*		

LIFE IN THE UNITED STATES

	ECONOMICS	RACES & PEOPLES
1860	• Winchester repeating rifle devised • Pony Express begins (April 3)	
1861	• Gold found in Idaho	• Confederate treaties with Indians • *Habeas corpus* suspended
1862	• Jay Cooke sells war bonds for Union fund raising	• Indian brigade organized in Union Army
1863	• National Banking System • Gold rush to Montana	• Draft riots (anti- Negro)
1864	• Bessemer and Kelly processes for steel making in operation	• Cheyenne- Arapaho War; Chivington Massacre
1865		• First Sioux War begins (to 1867)

	[1860]	**1861**	**1862**	**1863**
POLITICAL EVENTS	• Jefferson Davis offers Senate resolutions supporting slavery; splits Senate Democrats and moderates. • Southern Democrats withdraw from party's nominating convention • South Carolina Convention passes ordinance of secession (Dec. 20) • Crittenden Compromise resolutions offered in Senate	• Secession announced by Mississippi (Jan. 9); Florida (Jan. 10); Alabama (Jan. 11); Georgia (Jan. 19); Louisiana (Jan 26); Texas (Feb. 1) • Confederate constitutional convention and provisional government (Feb. 8) • Jefferson Davis named President, Alexander Stephens, Vice President, of Confederate States of America • Lincoln calls for Union Army volunteers (April 15) • Secession announced by Virginia (April | 17); Arkansas (May 6); Tennessee (May 7); North Carolina (May 20) • 37th (U.S.) Congress; Republican majority in both houses. Galusha Grow is Speaker • Congress establishes Joint Committee on Conduct of the War (Dec. 20) • Congress imposes income tax and direct tax on States • Morrill Tariff Act raises duties as protective measure • Confederate States authorize issuance of paper money (treasury notes)	• Confederate Constitution established as permanent • First conscription act passed by Confederate congress (April) • U.S. Congress passes Homestead Act; Morrill Land-Grant College Act; Pacific Railway Act • Union government authorizes use of paper money ("Greenbacks")	• U.S. Congress passes conscription act (March 3) • National Bank System established by Congress • 38th (U.S.) Congress; Republican majority. Schuyler Colfax is Speaker • Confederate congress imposes high tax rates; Confederate State banknotes drop in value • West Virginia recognized as a separate State within the Union
ABOLITION & SLAVERY	• Eighth U.S. Census records 3,954,000 slaves • Jefferson Davis presents resolutions to protect slavery in future	• President Lincoln rescinds Frémont's order emancipating slaves in Missouri		• Captured slaves regarded as "contraband of war" • Slavery abolished in District of Columbia and Federal Territories	• Definitive Emancipation Proclamation issued
FOREIGN POLICY		• President Lincoln proclaims blockade of Confederate ports • *Trent* affair		• Confederate commerce raiders *Alabama* and *Florida* sail from British ports	• After Gettysburg, British and French governments stop sale of ships to Confederate Navy
FOREIGN EVENTS	• Garibaldi victorious in Sicily and Naples; leads small Italian states to unite with Kingdom of Sardinia and Piedmont	• Kingdom of Italy proclaimed (except for Rome and Venice) • Serfs emancipated in Russia		• Bismarck becomes premier of Prussia • French establish control in Indochina • French troops land in Mexico	

	1864	**1865**
	• Nevada becomes State • Wichita, Kansas, founded	
	• Lincoln renominated; defeats George B. McClellan (Democrat)	• Lincoln's second inaugural • Lincoln assassinated (April 14) • Andrew Johnson succeeds as President
	• *ex parte Vallandigham* • Roger Brooke Taney dies (Oct. 12) • Salmon P. Chase, Chief Justice	
	• President Lincoln pocket-vetoes Wade-Davis Bill • Immigration Act authorizes admission of "contract laborers" • Confederate President Davis authorizes arming slaves willing to serve in Confederate forces • Arkansas and Louisiana meet Lincoln's terms for recognition as State governments	• Congress refuses to permit Arkansas and Louisiana legislators to take seats
		• Confederates permit arming of slaves, for Army • 13th Amendment ends slavery in the United States
	• Maximilian (Habsburg Archduke) becomes Emperor of Mexico, with French support • Austria and Prussia defeat Denmark in brief war	

THE CIVIL WAR (*Confederate victories italicized*)

WEST	EAST	SEA
1861 *Aug. 10: Wilson's Creek, Mo.*	*Apr. 13: Ft. Sumter surrenders* *July 21: First Battle of Bull Run* July 26: George B. McClellan, commanding Union forces	Apr. 19: Blockade announced by Lincoln
1862 Jan. 20: Mill Springs, Ky. Feb. 6 and 15: Fts. Henry & Donelson surrender to Gen. U. S. Grant March 8: Pea Ridge, Ark. April 7: Shiloh	March-July: McClellan's Peninsular Campaign June 1: Robert E. Lee commands Confederate forces *Seven Pines or Fair Oaks* *Aug. 30: Second Battle of Bull Run* Sept. 17: Antietam *Dec. 13: Fredericksburg*	*March 9: Monitor* v. *Merrimac* April 26: New Orleans taken by Union fleet & army
1863 Jan. 2: Murfreesboro, Tenn. March-July 4: Siege of Vicksburg Sept. 19: Battle of Chickamauga, Ga. *Sept. 20: Texans under Dick Dowling hold Sabine Pass* Nov. 23-25: Battle of Chattanooga, Tenn.	*May 2-4: Chancellorsville* July 1-3: Gettysburg	*Jan. 1: Texans recapture Galveston* Confederate blockade runners and commerce raiders
1864 *April: Red River campaign by Union Army checked* May-Sept.: Sherman, commanding, Union drive to Atlanta Sept 2: Atlanta, Ga., captured by Union Nov.-Dec. 22: March to the Sea Dec. 16: Union victory at Nashville, Tenn. Dec. 22: Sherman takes Savannah	March: Grant commands Union forces May 5-6: Battle of the Wilderness *June 1-3: Cold Harbor* June 15-18: Petersburg	June 19: Confederate raider *Alabama* sunk by *Kearsarge* August: Union fleet takes Mobile, Alabama Oct. 20: Confederate raider *Florida* captured off Brazil
1865 Feb.-April: Sherman drive through both Carolinas Apr. 18: Johnston surrenders to Sherman May 16: Western Confederate army surrenders	April 2: Grant takes Richmond April 9: Lee surrenders at Appomattox May 10: Jefferson Davis captured	Confederate raider *Shenandoah* destroys New England whaling fleet in Bering Sea

	[1865]	1866	1867	1868
EXP. & SET.			• Neb. becomes State • Phoenix, Ariz., founded • C. King's exploration and survey of 40th Parallel (to 1878) • Hayden's survey of Nebraska and Wyoming (to 18	
PRESIDENCY	• Andrew Johnson, President			• President Johnson impeached by House (Feb. 24) • President Johnson acquitted by Senate (May 16) • Ulysses S. Grant (Republican) defeats Horatio Seymour (Democrat)
LAW & COURTS	• 13th Amendment ratified (Dec. 18)	• *ex parte Milligan*		• 14th Amendment ratified (July 28)
POLITICAL EVENTS	• 39th Congress; Republican majority. Schuyler Colfax is Speaker • Freedmen's Bureau established • President Johnson extends amnesty to most Confederates; recognizes "reconstructed" governments in all Confederate States but Texas • Congress refuses to seat all legislators sent by former Confederate States	• Congress establishes Joint Committee on Reconstruction of the South	• First Civil Rights Act passed over Johnson's veto • Congress reduces size of Supreme Court to seven Justices • Ku Klux Klan organized in South	• 40th Congress; Republican majority. Schuyler Colfax is Speaker • Tenure of Office Act and First Reconstruction Act passed over Johnson's veto	• Congress limits jurisdiction of Supreme Court, blocking *habeas corpus* cases • Congress recognizes Alabama, Arkansas, Florida, Louisiana, North Carolina and South Carolina as readmitted to Union • Johnson removes Secretary of War Edwin M. Stanton from office • Johnson issues amnesty to all former Confederates
FOREIGN POLICY		• U.S. Army moves to Mexican border	• French withdraw from Mexico • Alaska purchased from Russia • U.S. Navy occupies Midway Island	• Burlingame Treaty with China
FOREIGN EVENTS	• Argentina, Brazil and Uruguay war against Paraguay (to 1870)	• Seven Weeks War in Europe (Prussia crushes Austria; Italy takes Venice)	• Confederation in Canada (four original provinces: Nova Scotia, New Brunswick, Quebec and Ontario) • Maximilian tried and shot by Mexicans • British reform law permits workmen to vote for Parliament members	

1869	1870	1871	1872	1873
• First Colorado River exploration by John Wesley Powell	• U.S. population (census), 39.9 million		• Spokane, Wash., founded • Wheeler survey of 100th Meridian (to 1879)	
• Grant inaugurated			• Grant reelected, defeating Horace Greeley (Liberal Republican and Democrat)	• Grant's second inaugural
• *Texas v. White*	• 15th Amendment ratified (March 30)			• Slaughterhouse Cases • Salmon P. Chase dies (May 7)
• 41st Congress; Republican majority. James G. Blaine is Speaker	• Ku Klux Klan Act; Congress recognizes Georgia, Mississippi, Texas and Virginia as "Reconstructed" States	• 42nd Congress; Republican majority. Blaine is Speaker • Tweed Ring exposed and ousted in New York	• Crédit Mobilier scandal • Liberal Republicans split from Radicals over Reconstruction and corruption	• 43rd Congress; Republican majority. Blaine is Speaker • Coinage Act stops coinage of silver ("Crime of '73")
		• Treaty of Washington with Great Britain	• *Alabama* Claims settled by international arbitration	
• Suez Canal opens	• Franco-Prussian War: Napoleon III captured; French Republic proclaimed • Italian army takes Rome	• Wilhelm I of Prussia proclaimed German Emperor • Alsace and Lorraine ceded to Germany by France • Trade unions become legal in England	• Civil wars (Carlist Wars) in Spain	

	1874	1875	1876	1877	1878
EXP. & SET.		• Powell's fourth exploration of Colorado basin	• Colorado becomes State		
PRESIDENCY			• Disputed election between Rutherford B. Hayes (Republican) and Samuel J. Tilden (Democrat)	• Electoral Commission awards disputed votes to Hayes • Hayes inaugurated	
LAW & COURTS	• Morrison R. Waite, Chief Justice			• *Munn v. Illinois* ("Granger Cases")	
POLITICAL EVENTS		• 44th Congress; Republican majority in Senate, Democratic majority in House. Speakers: Michael C. Kerr (1875) and Samuel J. Randall (1876) • Whiskey Ring investigated • Civil Rights Act passed	• Greenback Party organized and offers candidates	• Federal troops withdrawn from southern civil duty • 45th Congress; Republican Senate, Democratic House. Randall is Speaker	• Bland-Allison Act passes over President Hayes' veto; silver mining increases
FOREIGN POLICY					• Treaty with Samoan chiefs grants U.S. a naval base at Pago Pago
FOREIGN EVENTS		• Universal Postal Union established		• Queen Victoria of England proclaimed Empress of India	• Romania and Serbia recognized as independent

1879	1880	1881	1882	1883
• U.S. Geological Survey established	• U.S. population (census), 50.3 million • Long Beach, Calif., founded		• Tulsa, Okla., founded	
	• James A. Garfield (Republican) defeats Winfield Scott Hancock (Democrat)	• Garfield inaugurated • Garfield shot (July 2) and dies (Sept. 19) • Vice President Chester A. Arthur succeeds as President		
				• Civil Rights Cases
• 46th Congress; Democratic majority. Randall is Speaker • Government resumes paying gold for "greenbacks"		• 47th Congress; Republican majority. J. Warren Kiefer is Speaker		• 48th Congress; Republican Senate, Democratic House. John G. Carlisle is Speaker • Pendleton Act for Civil Service reform • Minor reductions in rates on Tariff of 1883
	• Treaty with China permits U.S. to limit Chinese laborers' entry to U.S.		• Treaty with Korea recognizes Korean independence, sets trade relations	
	•Bolivia and Peru war against Chile (to 1883) • Transvaal (Dutch) wars against South African Republic (British-controlled)	• Russian laws limit areas of Jewish residence	• Triple Alliance formed (German Empire Austrian Empire, and Italy)	

	1884	1885	1886	1887	1888
EXP. & SET.					
PRESIDENCY	• Grover Cleveland (Democrat) defeats James G. Blaine (Republican)	• Cleveland inaugurated			• Benjamin Harrison (Republican) defeats Grover Cleveland
LAW & COURTS	• Ku Klux Klan Cases		• *San Mateo County v. Southern Pacific R.R.* • *Wabash, St. Louis & Pacific R.R. v. Illinois* ("Granger Cases")		• Morrison R. Waite dies (March 23) • Melville W. Fuller, Chief Justice
POLITICAL EVENTS		• 49th Congress; Republican Senate, Democratic House. Carlisle is Speaker	• Presidential Succession Act lists Cabinet officers to succeed a deceased or removed Vice President	• Interstate Commerce Act • 50th Congress; Republican Senate, Democratic House. Carlisle is Speaker • President Cleveland vetoes Dependant Pension Act	
FOREIGN POLICY				• Treaty with Hawaiian kingdom grants naval base at Pearl Harbor to U.S.	
FOREIGN EVENTS		• Congo Free State established under King Leopold II of Belgium • First Canadian transcontinental railroad completed (Canadian Pacific)			• Emperor of Brazil proclaims end of slavery • Wilhelm II becomes German Emperor

1889	1890	1891	1892	1893
• North Dakota, South Dakota, Montana, Washington become States	• U.S. population (census), 63.1 million • Idaho becomes State • Wyoming becomes State			
• Harrison inaugurated, • Department of Agriculture established in Cabinet			• Grover Cleveland (Democrat) defeats Benjamin Harrison (Republican) and James B. Weaver (Populist)	• Cleveland's second inaugural
• 51st Congress; Republican majority. Thomas B. Reed is Speaker	• Dependant Pension Act passed • Sherman Silver Purchase Act • McKinley Tariff imposes high rates • Sherman Anti-Trust Act	• 52nd Congress; Republican Senate, Democratic House. Charles Crisp is Speaker	• Populist Party organized; presidential candidate polls over a million votes	• 53rd Congress; Democratic majority. Crisp is Speaker • Gold reserves in Treasury drop to record low level
• Crisis with Germany over Samoa, settled by negotiation • First International American Conference at Washington (1889–1890)	• First International American Conference ends (Pan-American Union)	• Crisis with Chile	• Pelagic Sealing Dispute in Bering Sea (to 1898)	• U.S. Marines land in Hawaii during revolution
• Emperor Pedro II of Brazil abdicates; republic established	• First Japanese Diet (legislature) opens meetings • Chancellor Bismarck dismissed by Wilhelm II			• France and Russia make military agreements and commercial treaty

	1894	1895	1896	1897	1898
EXP. & SET.			• Utah becomes State • Miami, Fla., founded		
PRESIDENCY			• William McKinley (Republican) defeats William Jennings Bryan (Democrat and Populist)	• McKinley inaugurated	
LAW & COURTS		• *Pollack v. Farmers' Loan and Trust Co.* • *U.S. v. E. C. Knight Co.*	• *Plessy v. Ferguson*		
POLITICAL EVENTS	• Coxey's Army marches on Washington • Wilson-Gorman Tariff lowers rates; includes income tax provision	• 54th Congress; Republican majority. Thomas B. Reed is Speaker • Gold reserves increased by loan from bankers (J. P. Morgan group)		• 55th Congress; Republican majority. Reed is Speaker • Dingley Tariff (highest rates to date in U.S. history)	
FOREIGN POLICY	• U.S. recognizes independence of Republic of Hawaii	• President Cleveland intervenes in border dispute between Venezuela and Great Britain	• Congress recognizes belligerent status of Cuban rebels, offers to help end Cuban revolution against Spain		• U.S.S. *Maine* blows up in Havana harbor • War declared against Spain (April 25) • Hawaii annexed to United States (July 7) • Treaty of Paris (Dec. 10) ends war with Spain
FOREIGN EVENTS	• Massacres of Armenians in Turkey begin (through 1896) • Japan wars on China • First Dreyfus court-martial in France	• X-rays discovered (Roentgen); Marconi wireless developed • Cuban revolution against Spain (to 1898) • Japan receives Formosa after peace with China		• Greek-Turkish war	

SPANISH-AMERICAN WAR

1898 *May 1*: Naval battle of Manila Bay
Blockade of Cuba
July 1: Battles of El Caney and San Juan Hill
July 3: Naval Battle of Santiago
July 25: U.S. troops occupy Puerto Rico
Aug. 13: U.S. troops occupy Manila
Oct. 1: Peace conference begins in Paris
Dec. 10: Treaty of Paris

LIFE IN THE UNITED STATES

	ECONOMICS	CULTURAL	RACES & PEOPLES
1865			• Sioux War begins (to 1867)
1866			• Ku Klux Klan organized
1867	• Sholes develops first practical typewriter		
1868	• Westinghouse develops first railroad air brake	• Louisa May Alcott's *Little Women*	• Indian rising under Black Kettle against railroaders and cattlemen (to 1874)
1869	• Knight of Labor organized • "Black Friday" gold crisis		• National Women's Suffrage Association formed
1870	• Standard Oil Co. (Ohio) founded		
1871			• Congress ceases to negotiate treaties with Indian tribes • Apache War begins (to 1886)
1872	• Crédit Mobilier scandal		
1873	• Jay Cooke failure leads to business panic and depression	• U.S. funds appropriated for Indian schools • Cable cars built in San Francisco	
1874	• Depression deepens (to 1878) • Barbed wire patented by Glidden	• Chautauqua Assembly organized	• Women's Christian Temperance Union founded
1875	• Black Hills (Dakota) Gold Rush		• Sioux War begins, under Sitting Bull and Crazy Horse
1876	• A. G. Bell patents telephone	• Mark Twain's *Tom Sawyer* • Johns Hopkins University founded	• Custer's Last Stand • Sioux defeated, forced on reservations
1877		• Henry James's *The American*	• Military government ends in southern states (Reconstruction ends) • Nez Percé War begins (to 1878)
1878	• First city telephone exchange (New Haven, Ct.) • Edison phonograph developed		
1879	• Edison incandescent light developed	• Mary Baker Eddy organizes First Church of Christ Scientist • Henry George publishes *Progress and Poverty*	
1880	• Eastman patents roll film	• Salvation Army unit established in U.S.	
1881		• First Carnegie Public Library opened	
1882	• Central generator for electricity operating in New York City		
1884	• "Boomers" attempt to enter Oklahoma; are turned back 1885	• First skyscraper built in Chicago, Ill.	
1885		• Leland Stanford University founded • Mark Twain's *Huckleberry Finn*	
1886	• American Federation of Labor organized	• Neighborhood Guild, first Settlement House in New York City	• Fort Apache incident; Geronimo captured • Haymarket Riot in Chicago
1887		• Electric trolley cars operating in Richmond, Va.	• Individual Indians permitted to own land (outside tribal ownership)
1888			• Secret (Australian) ballot introduced in Kentucky
1889		• Hull House established in Chicago	
1890			• Ghost Dance War ends at Wounded Knee, S.D.
1892	• Phone connections between N.Y. and Chicago • Standard Oil Co. of N.J. founded		• Homestead Strike
1893		• Chicago World's Fair	
1895	• First U.S. automobile manufactured for sale	• Stephen Crane's *The Red Badge of Courage*	• Anti-Saloon League founded
1896	• Klondike gold veins found	• First Junior High School established	

	[1898]	[1899]	1900	1901	1902
EXP. & SET.			• U.S. population (census), 76.1 million	• Discovery of Spindletop well (Texas) sets off "oil rush"	
PRESIDENCY	• William McKinley, President		• McKinley (Republican) defeats William Jennings Bryan (Democrat and Populist)	• McKinley's second inaugural • McKinley shot by assassin (Sept. 6; died Sept. 14) • Vice President Theodore Roosevelt succeeds as President	
LAW & COURTS				• Insular Cases: *De Lima v. Bidwell; Dooley v. U.S.; Downes v. Bidwell*	
POLITICAL EVENTS		• 56th Congress; Republican majority David B. Henderson is Speaker	• Socialist Party (U.S.) organized • Currency Act placed U.S. on gold standard	• "Progressive Era" begins on national scale • 57th Congress; Republican majority. Henderson is Speaker	• President Roosevelt calls for action against trusts; the "Square Deal" • Initiative and referendum introduced in Oregon State government • National Reclamation Act (Newlands Act)
FOREIGN POLICY			• Boxer Rebellion in China	• Platt Amendment • Hay-Pauncefote Treaty (gives U.S. right to build isthmian canal)	
		• 1899–1900 "Open Door" Policy on China announced			
FOREIGN EVENTS		• Boer War in Africa (Britain against Orange Free State and Transvaal Republic)	• Boxer Rebellion in China		• Boer War ends

1903	1904	1905	1906	1907
		• Gary, Ind., founded as model industrial city		• Oklahoma becomes State
• Department of Commerce and Labor established in Cabinet	• Theodore Roosevelt (Republican) defeats Alton B. Parker (Democrat) and Eugene V. Debs (Socialist)	• Theodore Roosevelt's second inaugural		
	• *Northern Securities Co. v. U.S.*	• *Swift & Co. v. U.S.* • *Lochner v. New York*		
• 58th Congress; Republican majority. Joseph G. Cannon is Speaker • Elkins Act		• 59th Congress; Republican majority. Cannon is Speaker	• Hepburn Act • Pure Food and Drug Act	• 60th Congress; Republican majority. Cannon is Speaker
• Panama's independence recognized by U.S. • Canal Zone leased by U.S. • Alaska boundary question with Canada	• Roosevelt Corollary to Monroe Doctrine announced	• President Roosevelt mediates Russo-Japanese War	• "Gentlemen's Agreement" with Japan	
	• Trans-Siberian Railroad completed • Entente Cordiale between Britain and France • Russo-Japanese War (to 1905) • 1904–1905 Anti-Semitic pogroms in Russia	• Norway becomes separate Kingdom from Sweden		• Triple Entente (Britain, France, Russia)

	1908	1909	1910	1911	1912
EXP. & SET.	• Robert Peary's polar expedition (to 1909)		• U.S. population (census), 92.4 million		• Arizona becomes State • New Mexico becomes State
PRESIDENCY	• William Howard Taft (Republican) defeats William Jennings Bryan (Democrat) and Eugene V. Debs (Socialist)	• Taft's inaugural			• Woodrow Wilson (Democrat) defeats William Howard Taft (Republican), Theodore Roosevelt (Progressive) and Eugene V. Debs (Socialist)
LAW & COURTS	• *Adair v. United States* • *Danbury Hatters Case* (*Loewe v. Lawlor*) • *Muller v. Oregon*		• Melville W. Fuller dies (July 4) • Edward D. White, Chief Justice	• *Standard Oil Co. v. U.S.* • *U.S. v. American Tobacco Co.*	
POLITICAL EVENTS	• White House Conference on Conservation • Federal Bureau of Investigation established	• 61st Congress; Republican majority. Cannon is Speaker	• House rules changed; Speaker's power reduced • Gifford Pinchot fired as head of Forest Service • Postal Savings Bank established • Mann-Elkins Act	• U.S. Steel Corp. sued under antitrust laws • 62nd Congress; Progressive Republican and Democratic majority. Champ Clark is Speaker • Reciprocal tariff agreement with Canada	• First State minimum wage law (Massachusetts) • Theodore Roosevelt announces new Progressive Party ("Bull Moose") • Democratic convention casts 46 ballots before nominating Wilson
FOREIGN POLICY		• 1909–1912 "Dollar Diplomacy"		• Pelagic Sealing controversy ended by treaty	• Agreement between U.S. and Great Britain on Atlantic fishing rights • U.S. Marines occupy customs posts in Nicaragua
FOREIGN EVENTS	• Congo now "Belgian Congo"	• Japan takes control of Korea	• Union of South Africa established as Dominion		• Balkan Wars begin (three in 1912–1913) • Chinese Empire ends; republic established

1913	1914	1915	1916	1917
		• Kingsport, Tenn., establishes plan for new industrial city		
• Woodrow Wilson's inaugural • Department of Commerce established in Cabinet • Department of Labor established in Cabinet			• Wilson (Democrat) defeats Charles Evans Hughes (Republican)	• Wilson's second inaugural
• 16th Amendment ratified (Feb. 25) • 17th Amendment ratified (May 31)				• *Wilson v. New*
• 63rd Congress; Democratic majority. Clark is Speaker • "New Freedom" announced by Wilson • Pujo Committee report • Federal Reserve Act • Underwood Tariff Act; reduced duties, imposed 1% income tax rates	• Clayton Antitrust Act • Federal Trade Commission established	• 64th Congress; Democratic majority. Clark is Speaker • Seamen's Act for Merchant Marine sailors	• President Wilson and ex-President Roosevelt argue for "Preparedness" • National Defense Act • Farm Loan Act	• Immigration Act requires literacy test; passed over Wilson's veto • 65th Congress; Democratic majority. Clark is Speaker • Wartime acts: Liberty Loan drives; Selective Service; Espionage Act • Income tax increased; corporation profits taxes imposed; excise taxes increased
• Arbitration treaties to settle disputes signed with 30 nations	• U.S. Navy bombards Vera Cruz, Mexico; ABC powers mediate dispute • Neutrality proclamation by President Wilson • Disputes with British over neutral-owned shipping in blockade zones	• Dispute with Germans over neutral rights in war zones and *Lusitania* • U.S. Marines intervene in Haiti	• Pancho Villa pursued by U.S. troops in Mexico • U.S. troops intervene in Dominican Republic • Bryan-Chamorro Treaty with Nicaragua • *Sussex* crisis with Germany • President Wilson invites World War rivals to state war aims	• Virgin Islands purchased from Denmark • German submarine warfare leads to break in diplomatic relations (Feb. 3) • War declared on Germany (April 6)
	• Austrian Archduke Franz Ferdinand assassinated • World War I begins; deadlock after Battle of Marne on western front	• Anglo-French attack on Dardanelles fails • Russian and Balkan victories for Austrians and Germans	• Verdun held by French against German drive	• Russian Revolution follows defeats in land war • British troops take Jerusalem from Turks

<table>
<tr><td>EXP. & SET.</td></tr>
<tr><td>PRESIDENCY</td></tr>
<tr><td>LAW & COURTS</td></tr>
<tr><td>POLITICAL EVENTS</td></tr>
<tr><td>FOREIGN POLICY</td></tr>
<tr><td>FOREIGN EVENTS</td></tr>
</table>

UNITED STATES IN WORLD WAR I

1918

1917	*April 7*: Declaration of War
	May 4: U.S. Navy destroyers join British and French fleets in North Sea
	Convoy system developed
	May 18: Selective Service Act passed
	June 13: Gen. John J. Pershing arrives in France
	Oct. 21: U.S. 1st Division takes position in battle lines
1918	*April 18*: French General Foch becomes Supreme Commander of Allies
	June: Chateau-Thierry and Belleau Wood actions
	July: U.S. forces with French in Aisne-Marne offensive
	August: U.S. forces land in Murmansk-Archangel and in Vladivostok regions of Russia
	September: U.S. Army eliminates St. Mihiel Salient
	U.S. begins Meuse-Argonne offensive
	November 6: U.S. troops take Sedan
	9: German Kaiser abdicates
	11: Armistice

LIFE IN THE UNITED STATES

	ECONOMICS	CULTURAL	RACES & PEOPLES	
1899			• Voting machines introduced (Rochester)	• Finance Corporation established to lend to war industries
			• Philippine Insurrection (to 1902)	• Sedition Act
1900		• Walter Reed research on yellow fever		
1901	• U.S. Steel Corporation formed		• Indians in Civilized Tribes (Okla.) granted citizenship	
1902	• Rayon patented	• First Junior College opens	• Anthracite Coal Strike	
1903	• Wright Brothers first flight	• Jack London's *Call of the Wild*		
1905	•.Industrial Workers of the World organized	• Muckrakers flourish	• Niagara Movement starts under W.E.B. Du Bois	
1906	• Lee De Forest develops the vacuum tube			
1907	• Business depression (to 1908)	• United Press founded		
1909			• N.A.A.C.P. founded	
1911	• Gyroscope developed			
1912		• Zane Gray's *Riders of the Purple Sage*		
1915		• Edgar Lee Masters' *Spoon River Anthology*	• Ku Klux Klan reorganized	• Wilson's Fourteen Points announced
1919	• Radio Corporation of America organized	• Atomic model developed by Irving Langmuir	• Race riots (white-black) in Chicago, Washington, and other cities	• Armistice reached with Germany (Nov. 11)
			• Approximately half-million blacks moved from South to North during decade	
1920	• Business depression (to 1921)	• Eugene O'Neill's *Beyond the Horizon* produced	• "Red scare" in cities	
1921	• Farm depression: low prices and growing costs, through decade			
1924			• All Indians in U.S. become citizens	
1925		• F. Scott FitzGerald's *The Great Gatsby*	• Scopes Trial	
1926	• Florida real estate boom collapses	• First sound motion picture		
1927	• Mechanical cotton picker developed	• Thornton Wilder's *Bridge of San Luis Rey*		• Treaty of Brest-Litovsk removes Russia from war
1928			• National Council of Christians and Jews organized	• Armistice ends fighting on all fronts (Nov.)
			• Anti-Catholic activities during election	
1929	• High prosperity (1.6 million unemployed) before stock market crash	• Ernest Hemingway's *Farewell To Arms*		
1930	• Depression; 8.7% of labor force unemployed			
1931	• Empire State Building completed			
1932	• Depression deepens; 23.6% of labor force unemployed			

1919	1920	1921	1922	1923
	• U.S. population (census), 106.5 million	• Coral Gables, Fla., designed as model residential city		
	• Woodrow Wilson, President • Warren G. Harding (Republican) defeats James M. Cox (Democrat) and Eugene V. Debs (Socialist)	• Harding's inaugural		• President Harding dies (Aug. 2) • Vice President Calvin Coolidge succeeds as President
• *Schenck v. U.S.* • *Abrams v. U.S.* • 18th Amendment ratified (Jan. 13)	• 19th Amendment ratified (Aug. 26)	• Edward D. White dies (May 19) • William Howard Taft, Chief Justice		
• 66th Congress; Republican majority. Federick Gillett is Speaker • Republican Senators oppose League of Nations • Communist Party (U.S.) organized • Raids against anarchists and communists (through May 1920)	• Bipartisan action in Senate defeats Versailles Treaty • Democratic Party endorses League of Nations in national platform •Federal Power Commission established • Railroad Labor Board established (Esch-Cummins Act)	• 67th Congress; large Republican majority. Frederick Gillett is Speaker • Veterans Bureau established • Revenue Act reduces tax rates • Budget Bureau established • Immigration limited on basis of nation of origin		• 68th Congress; narrower Republican majority. Gillett is Speaker
• Peace Conference in Paris • Versailles Treaty rejected in U.S. Senate	• League of Nations a key campaign issue	• Washington Disarmament Conference (and 1922)		
• Peace Conference in Paris • German republic established; communists rule briefly in Hungary, Berlin, Bavaria • Civil war in Russia	• League of Nations organized • Polish army defeats Russian (Red) Army at Warsaw • Two "parliaments" established in Ireland • British and French occupy former Turkish-held Arab lands	• First parliament meets in India	• Irish Free State established • Mussolini takes control of Italian government	• Union of Soviet Socialist Republics established by Constitution • Hitler fails in "Beer Hall Putsch"

	1924	1925	1926	1927	1928
EXP. & SET.			• Byrd's North Polar flight	• Lindbergh's transatlantic flight	
PRESIDENCY	• Coolidge (Republican) defeats John W. Davis (Democrat) and Robert M. La Follette (Progressive)	• Coolidge's second inaugural			• Herbert Hoover (Republican) defeats Alfred E. Smith (Democrat) and Norman Thomas (Socialist)
LAW & COURTS		• *Gitlow v. New York*			
POLITICAL EVENTS	• Teapot Dome scandal uncovered • Federal Bureau of Investigation reorganized • Indians in U.S. recognized as citizens • Robert M. La Follette organizes Progressive Party • Democratic national convention goes to 103 ballots to nominate J. W. Davis	• 69th Congress; large Republican majority. Nicholas Longworth is Speaker • Court-martial of William Mitchell		• 70th Congress; narrower Republican majority. Longworth is Speaker	• Jones-White Act *re* Merchant Marine
FOREIGN POLICY	• Dawes Plan			• Agreement between U.S. and Mexico on U.S. investments and oil exploration in Mexico	
FOREIGN EVENTS		• Locarno Pacts (Germany agrees to final borders with France and Belgium)	• Germany admitted to League of Nations	• Chiang Kai-shek controls Chinese government	• First Russian "Five-Year Plan" to industrialize U.S.S.R.

1929	1930	1931	1932	1933
• Byrd's South Polar flight	• U.S. population (census), 123.2 million			
• Hoover's inaugural			• Franklin D. Roosevelt (Democrat) defeats Herbert Hoover (Republican) and Norman Thomas (Socialist)	
	• William Howard Taft dies (March 8) • Charles Evans Hughes, Chief Justice	• *Near v. Minnesota*		
• 71st Congress; large Republican majority. Longworth is Speaker • Federal Farm Board created by Agricultural Marketing Act	• Hawley-Smoot Tariff Act; very high rates	• 72nd Congress; Republican Senate, Democratic House. John N. Garner is Speaker • Proposed public project at Muscle Shoals vetoed by Hoover • High dam on Colorado River begun (Hoover or Boulder Dam)	• Reconstruction Finance Corporation (R.F.C.) • Federal Home Loan Act • Veterans stage "Bonus March" on Washington	
• Young Plan	• London Naval Conference	• President Hoover proposes moratorium on war debts	• Stimson Doctrine announced	
• Italy and Pope agree on establishing Vatican City (Lateran Treaty)	• Civil disobedience campaign begins in India • Statute of Westminster establishes status of Dominions in British Empire	• Kingdom of Spain overturned; Republic established • Japanese invade Manchuria	• Colombia wars on Peru; Bolivia on Paraguay	

	[1933]	1934	1935	1936	1937
EXP. & SET.					
PRESIDENCY	• Franklin D. Roosevelt inaugural (March 4)			• Franklin D. Roosevelt (Democrat) defeats Alf M. Landon (Republican) and William Lemke (Union)	• Franklin D. Roosevelt's second inaugural (Jan. 20) • President Roosevelt attempts to "pack" Supreme Court
LAW & COURTS	• 20th Amendment ratified (Feb. 6) • 21st Amendment ratified (Dec. 5)		• *U.S. v. Banker's Trust Company* • *Schechter v. U.S.*	• *U.S. v. Butler* • *Ashwander v. T.V.A.*	• Minimum Wage Law; National Labor Relations Act; Social Security Act upheld as constitutional:
POLITICAL EVENTS	• 73rd Congress; large Dem. majority. Henry Rainey is Speaker • Bank Holiday proclaimed by President Roosevelt • Unemployment Relief Act and Federal Emergency Relief Act • Agricultural Adjustment Act • Tennessee Valley Authority Act • National Industrial Recovery Act • Gold clause canceled in all contracts • Dollar devalued	• Securities Exchange Act • Reciprocal Trade Agreements Act authorizes tariff reductions • Home Owners Loan Act • Federal Housing Administration established	• 74th Congress; larger Democratic majority. Speakers: Joseph W. Byrns, and in 1936, William Bankhead • Huey P. Long assassinated • Works Progress Administration • Soil Conservation Act • Rural Electrification Administration • National Labor Relations Act • Social Security Act • Tax rates increased on higher incomes • Estate and gift taxes increased	• U.S. Maritime Commission established	• 75th Congress; largest Democratic majority. Bankhead is Speaker • Farm Security Administration established • U.S. Housing Authority established
FOREIGN POLICY	• Good Neighbor Policy announced (Latin America) • U.S. recognizes Soviet Union	• U.S. troops withdrawn from Haiti	• Constitution for Philippine Islands approved; independence to be in effect on July 4, 1946 • Neutrality Act	• Neutrality Act revised	• Neutrality Act of 1937 • *Panay* incident with Japan • President Roosevelt calls for international "quarantine" of aggressor nations
FOREIGN EVENTS	• Adolf Hitler becomes German Chancellor; Nazi regime begins • Japan leaves League of Nations (March) • Germany leaves League of Nations (October)	• U.S.S.R. joins League of Nations • Socialist and Nazi revolutions curbed in Austria	• Saarland votes to rejoin Germany • Nazi Germany strips Jews of citizenship • Italy invades Abyssinia	• Military revolution in Japan establishes pro-military government • Japan and German agree on anti-Communist statement • Spanish Civil War begins (to 1939); General Franco leads insurgents	• Purges of Russian Army officers and anti-Stalin civilians in U.S.S.R. • Japanese army invades China

1938	1939	1940	1941
		• U.S. population (census), 132.1 million	
		• Franklin D. Roosevelt (Democrat) defeats Wendell Willkie (Republican) and Norman Thomas (Socialist)	• Franklin D. Roosevelt's third inaugural
	• *Graves v. New York ex rel O'Keefe*		• *Edwards v. California* • Charles Evans Hughes resigns • Harlan Fiske Stone, Chief Justice
• Second Agricultural Administration Act • Naval Expansion Act • "Purge" of anti-New Deal Democrats by President fails at election	• 76th Congress; reduced Democratic majority. Bankhead is Speaker • Hatch Act	• America First Committee formed • First peacetime Selective Service draft • Republicans enter Roosevelt's Cabinet (Stimson, Secretary of War; Knox, Secretary of the Navy) • Political controversy over third term for President Roosevelt • Alien Registration Act	• 77th Congress; Democratic majority. Sam Rayburn is Speaker • Lend-Lease Act
	• President Roosevelt proclaims U.S. neutrality in European war • Inter-American Conference proclaims safety areas in western hemisphere • Neutrality Act of 1939	• U.S. military supplies released for British use • Destroyer deal secures naval and air bases • Pan-American Union "Act of Havana" (American republics may take over European | possessions under attack) • Notice to Japan that a move on French Indochina would bring U.S. reaction • Embargo on steel and scrap iron exports, except to Great Britain	• Lend-Lease plan for aid to British and allies • U.S. troops garrison Iceland • Atlantic Charter announced
• Munich conference (Germany, Italy, Britain and France) on Czechoslovakia • Austria merged into Germany (*Anschluss*)	• Germany seizes control of Czechoslovakia and port of Memel in Lithuania • German-Soviet pact • Germans invade Poland; World War II starts in Europe • First Russo-Finnish War (to 1940)		• 1941-5 Nazi policy of mass murder of Jews and European resistance groups

1942

EXP. & SET.	
PRESIDENCY	
LAW & COURTS	
POLITICAL EVENTS	• Board of Economic Warfare established • Japanese-Americans forced to relocate from Pacific Coast • Office of Price Administration • Office of Civilian Defense • War Manpower Commission
FOREIGN POLICY	• United Nations Declaration • World War II Conferences (to 1945)
FOREIGN EVENTS	

UNITED STATES IN WORLD WAR II (*Enemy victories italicized*)

PACIFIC	ATLANTIC-EUROPE-AFRICA
1941 *Dec. 8: Pearl Harbor* *Dec. 22: Wake Island*	Naval patrol and convoy services against submarines
1942 *May: Philippine campaign* *March 1: Battle of Java Sea* April 18: First air raid on Tokyo (Doolittle raid) *May 6: Corregidor surrendered* May 7-8: Battle of Coral Sea June 3-6: Battle of Midway Aug. 7: American landings on Guadalcanal *Aug. 9: Naval battle of Savo Island;* Guadalcanal campaign to Feb. 1943	Naval convoys and patrols; Army and Air Force units convoyed to Great Britain Aug. 17: First U.S.A.A.F. heavy bomber raid on Germany Nov. 8: Landings in Africa (Algeria and Morocco); African campaign continues to May 13, 1943
1943 *January-April*: Campaign in New Guinea March 2-4: Battle of Bismarck Sea August: Aleutian islands (Attu and Kiska) reoccupied Nov. 21-24: Central Pacific drive starts at Tarawa and Makin Islands December: Americans in Burma join offensive to open route to China	*February 14: German victory at Kasserin Pass* May 7: Americans capture Bizerte May 13: German and Italian African army surrenders to British and Americans July-August: Anglo-American invasion of Sicily; 8th U.S. Air Force conducting regular day raids on German targets Sept. 9: U.S. 5th Army lands in Italy
1944 *February*: Central Pacific islands campaign. Kwajalein; Eniwetok; Saipan (June); Guam (July-August) June 16: First B-29 (Superfortress) raid on Japan June 19-December: Philippine Campaign June 19-20: Battle of Philippine Sea Oct. 23-25: Battle of Leyte Gulf	Jan. 22: Landing at Anzio, Italy June 4: Rome occupied by 5th Army June 6: Anglo-American invasion of Normandy June 27: U.S. troops take Cherbourg July 25: U.S. armor breaks through German lines at St. Lô Aug. 15: U.S. 7th Army lands in southern France Aug. 25: U.S. troops enter Paris Oct. 21: U.S. troop take Aachen, Germany Dec. 16-26: Battle of Bulge (Bastogne relieved, Dec. 26)
1945 Jan. 9: U.S. troops land on Luzon (Philippines) Feb. 19-March 17: U.S. Marines take Iwo Jima Feb. 24: U.S. and Philippine troops enter Manila April 1: U.S. landings on Okinawa; Japanese *kamikaze* attacks on ships June 21: Okinawa campaign ends; airbases used to bomb Japan July-August: Intense B-29 raids and naval bombardment of Japan Aug. 6: Atomic bomb strikes Hiroshima Aug. 9: Atomic bomb strikes Nagasaki Aug. 10: Japanese surrender announced Sept. 2: Formal surrender signed aboard *U.S.S. Missouri* in Tokyo Bay	*January 21: Original line before Battle of Bulge restored by Anglo-American armies* *February 22*: U.S. forces cross Saar River *March 7*: U.S. forces capture Remagen Bridge across Rhine *March-April*: U.S. forces surround German army in Ruhr, capture area April 25: U.S. troops and Russian drive from the east join at Torgau *May 1*: Hitler's death announced by Germans *May 8*: Formal surrender of German forces to Allies June: American Army of Occupation takes over zone in Germany

1943	1944	1945	1946	1947
• Oak Ridge, Tenn., founded			• Levittown, N.Y., founded	
	• Franklin D. Roosevelt (Democrat) defeats Thomas E. Dewey (Republican)	• Franklin D. Roosevelt's fourth inaugural • Franklin D. Roosevelt dies (April 12) • Vice President Harry S. Truman succeeds as President		• Department of Defense established in Cabinet, combining former War and Navy Departments. It includes subordinate Departments of Air Force, Army and Navy
	• *Korematsu v. U.S.* • *Smith v. Allwright*		• Harlan Fiske Stone dies (April 22) • Fred M. Vinson, Chief Justice	• *Friedman v. Schwellenbach*
• 78th Congress; smaller Democratic majority. Rayburn is Speaker • War Labor Disputes Act passed over Roosevelt's veto • Bipartisan Senate move to establish international organization after war		• 79th Congress; Democratic majority. Rayburn is Speaker • Demobilization begins	• Wartime price and wage controls end • Atomic Energy Commission established	• 80th Congress; Republican majority. Joseph W. Martin is Speaker • President Truman issues order to investigate loyalty of Federal employees • Taft-Hartley Act passed
		• Act of Chapultepec (defense agreement among American republics) • U.N. Charter written; U.S. ratifies it • War Crimes Trials in Germany and in Japan (to 1948)	• U.S. efforts to mediate civil war in China (to 1947)	• Marshall Plan announced • Truman Doctrine; aid to Greece and Turkey
			• British Labor government nationalizes Bank of England	• India and Pakistan separated; Burma leaves British Commonwealth • Civil war in China (Communists against Nationalists) • Indonesia becomes independent

	1948	1949	1950
EXP. & SET.			• 1950 population (census), 151.7 million
PRESIDENCY	• Harry S. Truman (Dem.)defeats Thomas E. Dewey (Rep.), J. Strom Thurmond (States Rights) and Henry A. Wallace (Progressive)	• Harry S. Truman's second inaugural	
LAW & COURTS	• "McCollum Decision"		
POLITICAL EVENTS	• Displaced Persons Act admits refugee immigrants • President Truman calls for civil rights, health and housing laws; uses 80th Congress as issue in presidential campaign • Extreme wings of Democratic party separate: States Rights Party (Thurmond) and Progressive Party (Wallace) in presidential campaign	• 81st Congress; Democratic majority. Sam Rayburn is Speaker • Government Reorganization Act based on Hoover Commission report	• Subversive Activities Control Board established • National Science Foundation • Kefauver Senate committee investigates organized crime
FOREIGN POLICY	• U.S. recognizes independent State of Israel • Organization of American States forms collective security system • Berlin Blockade and Berlin Airlift (June 24, 1948–May 12, 1949)	• North Atlantic Treaty Organization	• U.S. forces in unified UN command in Korea
FOREIGN EVENTS	• Israel declares independence; war against Arabs (to 1949) • Communist government in Czechoslovakia • Separate North and South Korean governments established	• Separate East and West German republics established • Chinese Communists control mainland, Nationalists control Taiwan (Formosa)	• Alliance announced between U.S.S.R. and China (Communist) • India becomes republic

---

KOREAN WAR

1950
June 25: North Koreans begin invasion of South Korea;
U.N. Security Council demands cease-fire, calls for military aid to South Korea
June 27: U.S. air and naval forces intervene in Korea
June 28: Soeul captured by North Koreans
July 8: Gen. Douglas MacArthur placed in command of U.N. forces in Korea
August: Greatest North Korean penetration: South Korean-U.N. forces in southeastern corner of peninsula ("Pusan Beachhead")
Sept. 15: Amphibious landings at Inchon
Sept. 26: Soeul recaptured
Oct. 1: U.N. troops cross 38th parallel, push into North Korea
Nov. 24: Offensive by U.N. forces aimed at Yalu River border of Korea-China
Nov. 26: Chinese army enters war, launches counter-offensive

1951
January: Battle lines stabilize around 38th parallel
March: MacArthur publicly differs with President Truman on war policy
April 11: Truman removes MacArthur from command of U.N. forces
July 10: Truce negotiations begin at Panmunjom, but are indecisive; limited battles continue to end of truce talks

1953
July 27: Armistice reached. Demilitarized zone established between forces

1951	1952	1953	1954	1955
	• Columbia, Md., planned			
	• Dwight D. Eisenhower (Republican) defeats Adlai E. Stevenson (Democrat)	• Dwight D. Eisenhower's inaugural • Department of Health, Education and Welfare established in Cabinet		
• 22nd Amendment ratified (Feb. 26) • *Dennis v. U.S.*	• *Zorach v. Clausen* • *Sawyer v. Youngstown Sheet and Tube Co.*	• Fred M. Vinson dies (Sept. 8) • Earl Warren, Chief Justice	• *Brown v. Board of Education of Topeka*	
• Internal Security Act passed over Truman's veto • Corruption exposed in Truman administration • MacArthur removed from Korean command; addresses Congress • 82nd Congress; Democratic majority. Rayburn is Speaker	• Regular Republican organization split in convention; Dwight D. Eisenhower nominated	• 83rd Congress; Republican majority. Joseph W. Martin is Speaker • Bricker Amendment blocked in Senate by one vote • Senator Joseph McCarthy's investigation of internal security (to 1954)	• Atomic Energy Act permits nuclear power plants	• 84th Congress; Democratic majority. Sam Rayburn is Speaker • Soil Bank established • Interstate Highway System established
• Peace treaty with Japan • Truce negotiations in Korea (to 1953)		• Korean armistice (June 26)	• U.S. and Nationalist China sign treaty for defense of Taiwan • Southeast Asia Treaty Organization formed • Geneva Conference on Indochina armistice and partition of Vietnam	• U.S. military advisers supplied to South Vietnamese
• U.S.S.R. explodes atomic bomb	• Britain explodes atomic bomb	• Josef Stalin dies	• Algerian revolution against French rule begins • Armistice agreement in Indochina; French forces end fighting	• Warsaw Pact signed

	1956	1957	1958	1959	1960
EXP. & SET.	• International exploration of Antarctica (through 1959)			• Alaska becomes State • Hawaii becomes State	• U.S. population (census), 180.7 million
PRESIDENCY	• Dwight D. Eisenhower (Republican) defeats Adlai E. Stevenson (Democrat)	• Dwight D. Eisenhower's second inaugural			• John F. Kennedy (Democrat) defeats Richard M. Nixon (Republican)
LAW & COURTS		• *Yates v. U.S.*		• *Abbate v. U.S.*	
POLITICAL EVENTS		•85th Congress; Democratic majority. Rayburn is Speaker • Civil Rights Act	• National Defense Education Act	• 86th Congress; large Democratic majority. Rayburn is Speaker • St. Lawrence Seaway opened	• Televised debates by presidential candidates Kennedy and Nixon
FOREIGN POLICY		• Eisenhower Doctrine (U.S. aid promised Middle Eastern countries resisting Communist takeovers)	• U.S. forces land in Lebanon for short period	• U.S. opposes Cuban moves to take over U.S. property on island; cuts quota for Cuban sugar imports	• Treaty of mutual assistance with Japan • U-2 photo plane shot down over Soviet Union; summit meeting of Eisenhower and Khrushchev canceled
FOREIGN EVENTS	• Khrushchev, Russian leader, speaks against Stalin policies • Revolution in Hungary put down by Russian forces • Israel-Egyptian war; British and French occupy Suez • Japan admitted to United Nations	• Russian satellites (Sputnik I and II) orbit earth	• Gen. Charles de Gaulle becomes President of France	• Fidel Castro takes control of Cuban government	• Ghana and Nigeria become independent; fighting in Congo, newly independent • France explodes atomic bomb

1961	1962	1963	1964	1965
	• First U.S. astronaut orbits earth (John Glenn)			• Aerial mapping from satellites begins
• John F. Kennedy's inaugural		• John F. Kennedy assassinated (Nov. 22) • Vice President Lyndon B. Johnson succeeds as President	• Lyndon B. Johnson (Democrat) defeats Barry Goldwater (Republican)	• Lyndon B. Johnson's second inaugural
• 23rd Amendment ratified (March 29) • *Mapp v. Ohio*	• *Baker v. Carr*	• *School District of Abington Township v. Schempp*	• 24th Amendment ratified (Jan. 23) • *Westberry v. Sanders* • *Escobeda v. Illinois*	
• 87th Congress; large Democratic majority. Sam Rayburn is Speaker • President Kennedy describes "New Frontier" • Committee on Equal Employment Opportunity established • Peace Corps established	• Trade Expansion Act permits President to negotiate tariffs • John W. McCormack is Speaker of the House • President Kennedy forces steel price rollback	• President intervenes in racial dispute in Birmingham, Ala. • 88th Congress; large Democratic majority. John W. McCormack is Speaker	• President Johnson calls for "War on Poverty" • Office of Economic Opportunity established; Job Corps • Civil Rights Act • Warren Commission reports on Kennedy assassination	• 89th Congress; larger Democratic majority. McCormack is Speaker • President Johnson calls for "Great Society" • Medicare established • Immigration Act sets national needs of U.S. as bases for immigration
• Kennedy and Khrushchev meet; Berlin Wall built; no agreement over German peace treaty • Bay of Pigs invasion of Cuba • Both U.S. and U.S.S.R. resume testing nuclear weapons	• Additional U.S. troops enter Vietnam as advisers • Cuban crisis over Soviet missiles • Kennedy announces blockade of Cuba (Oct. 22); Kennedy-Khrushchev agreement ends war threat (Oct. 28)	• Nuclear Test-Ban Treaty signed by U.S., U.S.S.R. and Great Britain • Increased number of U.S. troops in Vietnam	• Tonkin Gulf incident; Vietnam War formally involves U.S. troops • Crisis with Panama over Canal Zone	
• Union of South Africa leaves British Commonwealth • Division between Russian and Chinese Communists	• Algeria recognized as independent • Vatican Council II of Catholic Church		• China explodes atomic bomb	• Indonesian army crushes Communist attempt at takeover

	1966	1967	1968	1969	1970
EXP. & SET.				• First U.S. astronaut lands on moon	• U.S. population (census), 204.8 million
PRESIDENCY	• Department of Housing and Urban Development established in Cabinet • Department of Transportation established in Cabinet		• Richard M. Nixon (Republican) defeats Hubert H. Humphrey (Democrat) and George C. Wallace (American Independent)	• Richard M. Nixon's inaugural	
LAW & COURTS	• *Miranda v. Arizona*	• 25th Amendment ratified (Feb. 10)		• *O'Callahan v. Parker* • *Shapiro v. Thompson* • Earl Warren retires • Warren E. Burger, Chief Justice	
POLITICAL EVENTS	• Tax reductions voted, with record Federal spending • Peace activists oppose Vietnam War	• Riots in several cities (Detroit, New York, Birmingham) • 90th Congress; reduced Democratic majority. McCormack is Speaker	• President Johnson withdraws name from presidential primaries after strong opposition showing of Sen. Eugene McCarthy in New Hampshire • Senator Robert Kennedy and Rev. Martin Luther King, Jr. assassinated • Civil Rights Act passed • Riots mark Democratic National Convention in Chicago • American Independent Party organized	• 91st Congress; reduced Democratic majority. McCormack is Speaker	• Organized Crime Control Act • Drug Abuse Prevention and Control Act • Emergency Housing Act • Uniform rules for voting in Federal elections: age, 18 years
FOREIGN POLICY	• Manila Conference (President Johnson and representatives of six Pacific countries pledge to continue Vietnam War until a "just peace" is reached)	• Agreement by U.S., U.S.S.R. and Great Britain to bar nuclear weapons in space	• U.S.S. *Pueblo* seized by North Korean government; U.S. appeals to U.N. • Truce talks on Vietnam begin in Paris	• President Nixon calls for greater self-help by other nations, and "Vietnamization" of war in southeast Asia. Reduction in U.S. troops in Vietnam begins • SALT talks begin in Helsinki, Finland	• U.S. offers plan for cease-fire in Arab-Israeli fighting
FOREIGN EVENTS	• French troops withdrawn from N.A.T.O.	• "Six Day War" between Israel and Arab States • Biafra rebels against Nigerian rule (rebellion ended 1970)	• Czech rebellion against Communist regime crushed by Russian army		• Rhodesia becomes independent republic

LIFE IN THE UNITED STATES

	ECONOMICS	CULTURAL	RACES & PEOPLES
1933	• Banking crisis; 24.9% of labor force unemployed		
1934			• Indian Reorganization Act
1935	• C.I.O. organized	• W.P.A. organized; operates writers, actors, artists projects (to 1942)	
1936	• C.I.O. splits from AFL		
1937	• Sit-down strikes in auto industry; 14.3% unemployed	• John Steinbeck's *Of Mice and Men*	
1938	• Recession; 19% unemployed		• Negroes ordered admitted to law school at University of Missouri
1939	• Slow economic recovery. 17.2% unemployed • FM radio introduced		
1941	• War demands bring fuller employment. Fair Employment practices imposed in war industries		• Four Freedoms speech by President Roosevelt
1942	• Wage and price controls; rationing of foods, gasoline, scarce products		• Japanese-Americans forced from homes on Pacific coast
1944		• G.I. Bill of Rights	
1946	• War-to-peace conversion of industries; agriculture continues very large demands		• United Mineworkers Strike (President seizes mines, ends strike)
1948	• Transistor invented		• Civil Rights a presidential campaign issue
1949			• Over 1.3 million American blacks moved to North from South during 1940's
1950		• National Council of Churches of Christ organized	• Puerto Rican Nationalists attempt to assassinate President Truman
1953	• Recession in business		
1954	• Many States pass "Right to Work" laws		
1955	• Labor unions seek guaranteed annual wage in union contracts • A.F.L. and C.I.O. merge	• Salk vaccine introduced	• Boycott of segregated buses in Montgomery, Alabama, led by Rev. Martin Luther King, Jr.
1957	• Business recession (to 1958) • "Compact" cars become popular		• Commission on Civil Rights • Little Rock (Ark.) school crisis • Southern Christian Leadership Conference founded
1958	• Increased defense and space age industries	• National Defense Education Act	
1960	• Business recession		
1961		• Robert Frost, poet, reads at President Kennedy inauguration	• Justice Department intervenes to secure voting rights for southern Negroes
1963			• Civil rights march to Washington
1964			• Equal Employment Opportunities Commission in operation • Riots in New York, Philadelphia, Chicago
1965		• Elementary and Secondary Education Act	• Malcolm X assassinated • Civil rights march, Selma-Montgomery, Alabama • "Black Power" advocated by some American blacks
1967	• Value of dollar attacked in international financial crisis (to 1968)	• Major strikes by public school teachers (N.Y.C.)	• Riots in Detroit, New York, Birmingham
1968			• Widespread resistance against Vietnam War
1969	• Government follows anti-inflation program; inflation continues		
1970	• Decreasing business activity; inflation and unemployment rising		
1974	• Sharp increase in cost of living and rate of inflation		

	1971	1972	1973	1974
EXP. & SET.	• Mariner 9, unmanned spacecraft, explores Mars	• Pioneer 10, unmanned spacecraft, explores vicinity of Jupiter	• Skylab orbiting, observation and laboratories (continue to 1974)	
PRESIDENCY	• Post Office Department ceases to exist as executive agency, Postmaster General leaves Cabinet	• Richard M. Nixon (Republican) defeats George McGovern (Democrat)	• Richard M. Nixon's second inaugural • Vice President Spiro T. Agnew resigns office (Oct. 10) • Gerald Ford nominated for Vice President	• Richard M. Nixon resigns; Vice President Ford succeeds as President (Aug. 9) • Nelson Rockefeller nominated (Aug. 20) to become Vice President
LAW & COURTS	• 26th Amendment ratified (March 28) • *The New York Times v. U.S.* (Pentagon Papers Case)	• *Furman v. Georgia*		
POLITICAL EVENTS	• 92nd Congress; Democratic majority. Carl B. Albert is Speaker • Congress rejects project for Supersonic Transport (SST)	• Gov. George Wallace (Alabama) shot while campaigning for Democratic presidential nomination • Democratic Party headquarters at Watergate burglarized by agents of committee to reelect President Nixon • Revenue-sharing by Federal and State governments approved • American Indians begin campaign to improve their condition	• 93rd Congress; increased Democratic majority. Albert is Speaker • Disputes between President and Congress on "impounding" funds • Alaska pipeline construction approved • President Nixon directs price, wage and fiscal controls to attack inflation and unemployment • Senate appoints committee to investigate Watergate break-in	• Widened Congressional investigation of President Nixon's conduct in office and in 1972 political campaign • House of Representatives committee recommends impeachment of President
FOREIGN POLICY	• Henry Kissinger visits Communist China and U.S.S.R.	• President Nixon visits China (Feb. 17–28), reopening national contacts • President Nixon visits U.S.S.R., signs Strategic Arms Limitation Talks (SALT) agreement	• Cease-fire agreement signed for Vietnam War (Jan. 27)	• Kissinger, as U.S. Secretary of State, arranges disengagement of Arab and Israeli forces in Middle East • Nixon visits Middle East countries (June)
FOREIGN EVENTS	• Rebellion in West Pakistan put down by Pakistani army • India-Pakistan War; Bengal becomes independent as Bangladesh • British adopt decimal system for currency	• British assume direct rule in Northern Ireland • Japan and China end state of war	• Revolt in Chile by military removes President Allende • "Yom Kippur" war in Middle East; Arab States against Israel (Oct.)	• India explodes atomic bomb